Range Rover
Service and Repair Manual

P Methuen and I M Coomber

Models covered

(606-336-1AG8)

Range Rover models with V8 petrol engines, including special/limited editions
3528cc and 3947cc

Does not cover Diesel engine models, specialist conversions or 4.2 litre models introduced in October 1992

© J H Haynes & Co. Ltd. 2003

A book in the **Haynes Service and Repair Manual Series**

ISBN **978 0 85733 599 9**

British Library Cataloguing in Publication Data
A catalogue record for this book is available from the British Library.

J H Haynes & Co. Ltd.
Haynes North America, Inc

www.haynes.com

Contents

LIVING WITH YOUR RANGE ROVER

Roadside Repairs

Routine Maintenance

Recommended Lubricants and Fluids

Contents

Introduction to the Range Rover

The Range Rover was first introduced in 1970 and has not looked back since, as it has been a remarkable success both at home and abroad. Production has never been able to keep up with demand even though output has been considerably increased. The introduction of the Range Rover was not intended to eclipse the success story of the more basic Land-Rover but to complement it and widen the scope of Land-Rover capability.

Powered by the well proven all alloy Rover 3 1/2 litre V8 engine and with permanent 4-wheel drive, the Range Rover set totally new standards in the field of both on and off-road performance and comfort. The engine is fitted with low compression cylinder heads to enable it to work happily on 2-star (91 octane rating) petrol. This may be some compensation for its thirst (around 12 to 14 mpg on average).

Transmission is by an all-synchromesh four-speed gearbox and transfer box to both front and rear axles simultaneously, but this is a different gearbox to the Land-Rover itself.

Not only can the Range Rover perform as a rugged workhorse in much the same way as the Land-Rover, but it also has an amazing main road performance, when it is considered that the top speed is around 95 mph. Also the luggage area is cavernous, and it is good as a towing vehicle.

Like the Land-Rover it features a rigid box section chassis and most of the body panels are aluminium, although the tailgate is not, and this rusts very quickly. In really tough going the differential unit in the transfer gearbox can be locked up to provide maximum traction at all four wheels. Unlike the Land-Rover however braking is by disc brakes on all four wheels.

Throughout the years of Range Rover production there have been many additions and modifications, but the basic vehicle has remained the same. The 1980 model has been given a facelift externally and internally to bring it up to modern motoring standards.

Not only has the Range Rover been a huge success as a vehicle in its own right, but it has also become a status symbol both here and in Europe.

Acknowledgements

Certain illustrations are the copyright of Land Rover Ltd., and are used with their permission. Thanks are also due to Draper Tools Limited, who supplied some of the workshop tools, and to all the staff at Sparkford who assisted in the production of this manual.

We take great pride in the accuracy of information given in this manual, but vehicle manufacturers make alterations and design changes during the production run of a particular vehicle of which they do not inform us. No liability can be accepted by the authors or publishers for loss, damage or injury caused by any errors in, or omissions from, the information given.

1980 Range Rover in use

1980 Range Rover in unusually clean condition

Working on your car can be dangerous. This page shows just some of the potential risks and hazards, with the aim of creating a safety-conscious attitude.

General hazards

Scalding

• Don't remove the radiator or expansion tank cap while the engine is hot.
• Engine oil, automatic transmission fluid or power steering fluid may also be dangerously hot if the engine has recently been running.

Burning

• Beware of burns from the exhaust system and from any part of the engine. Brake discs and drums can also be extremely hot immediately after use.

Crushing

• When working under or near a raised vehicle, always supplement the jack with axle stands, or use drive-on ramps. **Never venture under a car which is only supported by a jack.**
• Take care if loosening or tightening high-torque nuts when the vehicle is on stands. Initial loosening and final tightening should be done with the wheels on the ground.

Fire

• Fuel is highly flammable; fuel vapour is explosive.
• Don't let fuel spill onto a hot engine.
• Do not smoke or allow naked lights (including pilot lights) anywhere near a vehicle being worked on. Also beware of creating sparks (electrically or by use of tools).
• Fuel vapour is heavier than air, so don't work on the fuel system with the vehicle over an inspection pit.
• Another cause of fire is an electrical overload or short-circuit. Take care when repairing or modifying the vehicle wiring.
• Keep a fire extinguisher handy, of a type suitable for use on fuel and electrical fires.

Electric shock

• Ignition HT voltage can be dangerous, especially to people with heart problems or a pacemaker. Don't work on or near the ignition system with the engine running or the ignition switched on.

• Mains voltage is also dangerous. Make sure that any mains-operated equipment is correctly earthed. Mains power points should be protected by a residual current device (RCD) circuit breaker.

Fume or gas intoxication

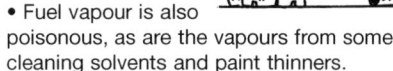

• Exhaust fumes are poisonous; they often contain carbon monoxide, which is rapidly fatal if inhaled. Never run the engine in a confined space such as a garage with the doors shut.
• Fuel vapour is also poisonous, as are the vapours from some cleaning solvents and paint thinners.

Poisonous or irritant substances

• Avoid skin contact with battery acid and with any fuel, fluid or lubricant, especially antifreeze, brake hydraulic fluid and Diesel fuel. Don't syphon them by mouth. If such a substance is swallowed or gets into the eyes, seek medical advice.
• Prolonged contact with used engine oil can cause skin cancer. Wear gloves or use a barrier cream if necessary. Change out of oil-soaked clothes and do not keep oily rags in your pocket.
• Air conditioning refrigerant forms a poisonous gas if exposed to a naked flame (including a cigarette). It can also cause skin burns on contact.

Asbestos

• Asbestos dust can cause cancer if inhaled or swallowed. Asbestos may be found in gaskets and in brake and clutch linings. When dealing with such components it is safest to assume that they contain asbestos.

Special hazards

Hydrofluoric acid

• This extremely corrosive acid is formed when certain types of synthetic rubber, found in some O-rings, oil seals, fuel hoses etc, are exposed to temperatures above 400°C. The rubber changes into a charred or sticky substance containing the acid. *Once formed, the acid remains dangerous for years. If it gets onto the skin, it may be necessary to amputate the limb concerned.*
• When dealing with a vehicle which has suffered a fire, or with components salvaged from such a vehicle, wear protective gloves and discard them after use.

The battery

• Batteries contain sulphuric acid, which attacks clothing, eyes and skin. Take care when topping-up or carrying the battery.
• The hydrogen gas given off by the battery is highly explosive. Never cause a spark or allow a naked light nearby. Be careful when connecting and disconnecting battery chargers or jump leads.

Air bags

• Air bags can cause injury if they go off accidentally. Take care when removing the steering wheel and/or facia. Special storage instructions may apply.

Diesel injection equipment

• Diesel injection pumps supply fuel at very high pressure. Take care when working on the fuel injectors and fuel pipes.

⚠️ *Warning: Never expose the hands, face or any other part of the body to injector spray; the fuel can penetrate the skin with potentially fatal results.*

Remember...

DO

• Do use eye protection when using power tools, and when working under the vehicle.

• Do wear gloves or use barrier cream to protect your hands when necessary.

• Do get someone to check periodically that all is well when working alone on the vehicle.

• Do keep loose clothing and long hair well out of the way of moving mechanical parts.

• Do remove rings, wristwatch etc, before working on the vehicle – especially the electrical system.

• Do ensure that any lifting or jacking equipment has a safe working load rating adequate for the job.

DON'T

• Don't attempt to lift a heavy component which may be beyond your capability – get assistance.

• Don't rush to finish a job, or take unverified short cuts.

• Don't use ill-fitting tools which may slip and cause injury.

• Don't leave tools or parts lying around where someone can trip over them. Mop up oil and fuel spills at once.

• Don't allow children or pets to play in or near a vehicle being worked on.

For modifications, and information applicable to later models, see Supplement at end of manual

Dimensions

	m	in
Overall length	4.470	176
Overall width	1.780	70
Overall height (maximum)	1.800	71
Wheelbase	2.540	100
Track – front and rear	1.490	58.5
Ground clearance:		
Under differential	0.190	7.5
Under centre of vehicle	0.317	12.5
Turning circle	11.280	444
Tailgate opening – width	1.400	55.25
Loading platform height	0.660	26

Weights

	kg	lb
Kerb weight (includes oil, water and 5 gallons fuel)	1723	3800
Maximum vehicle weight (GVW):		
Front axle	998	2200
Rear axle	1506	3320
Total GVW	2504	5520
Maximum payload	780	1720

Note: *Included in these figures are 100 kg (220 lb) for fitting auxiliaries (eg winches) which must only be fitted to the front of the vehicle*

Towing capacities

	kg	lb
4-wheel road trailer with power braking:		
Trailer weight	4000	8816
Trailer and vehicle weight (GTW)	6504	14 336
'Off-road' trailer:		
Trailer weight	1000	2204
Trailer and vehicle weight (GTW)	3504	7724
Emergency use *only* – maximum road speed 18 mph (30 km/h):		
Trailer weight	6000	13 224
Trailer and vehicle weight (GTW)	8504	18 744
Roof rack load – maximum	50	112

Capacities

	litres	pints
Engine oil:		
Sump	5.1	9
Oil filter	0.56	1
Main gearbox	2.6	4.5
Transfer gearbox	3.1	5.5
Front differential:		
Early models	2.5	4.5
Later models	1.7	3.0
Rear differential	1.7	3.0
Swivel housing	0.26	0.5
Steering box (not power-assisted)	0.40	0.75

Fuel tank:	litres	gallons
Early models	86	19
Later models	81.5	18
Cooling system	11.3	2.5

HAYNES HiNT *Jump starting will get you out of trouble, but you must correct whatever made the battery go flat in the first place. There are three possibilities:*

1 *The battery has been drained by repeated attempts to start, or by leaving the lights on.*

2 *The charging system is not working properly (alternator drivebelt slack or broken, alternator wiring fault or alternator itself faulty).*

3 *The battery itself is at fault (electrolyte low, or battery worn out).*

When jump-starting a car using a booster battery, observe the following precautions:

✔ Before connecting the booster battery, make sure that the ignition is switched off.

✔ Ensure that all electrical equipment (lights, heater, wipers, etc) is switched off.

✔ Take note of any special precautions printed on the battery case.

Jump starting

✔ Make sure that the booster battery is the same voltage as the discharged one in the vehicle.

✔ If the battery is being jump-started from the battery in another vehicle, the two vehicles MUST NOT TOUCH each other.

✔ Make sure that the transmission is in neutral (or PARK, in the case of automatic transmission).

1 Connect one end of the red jump lead to the positive (+) terminal of the flat battery

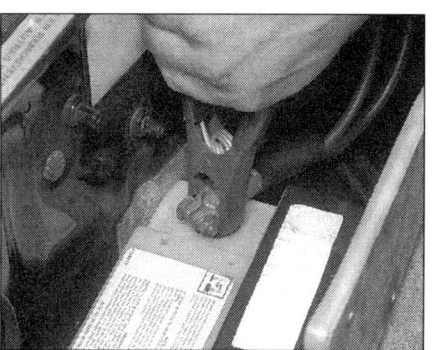

2 Connect the other end of the red lead to the positive (+) terminal of the booster battery.

3 Connect one end of the black jump lead to the negative (-) terminal of the booster battery

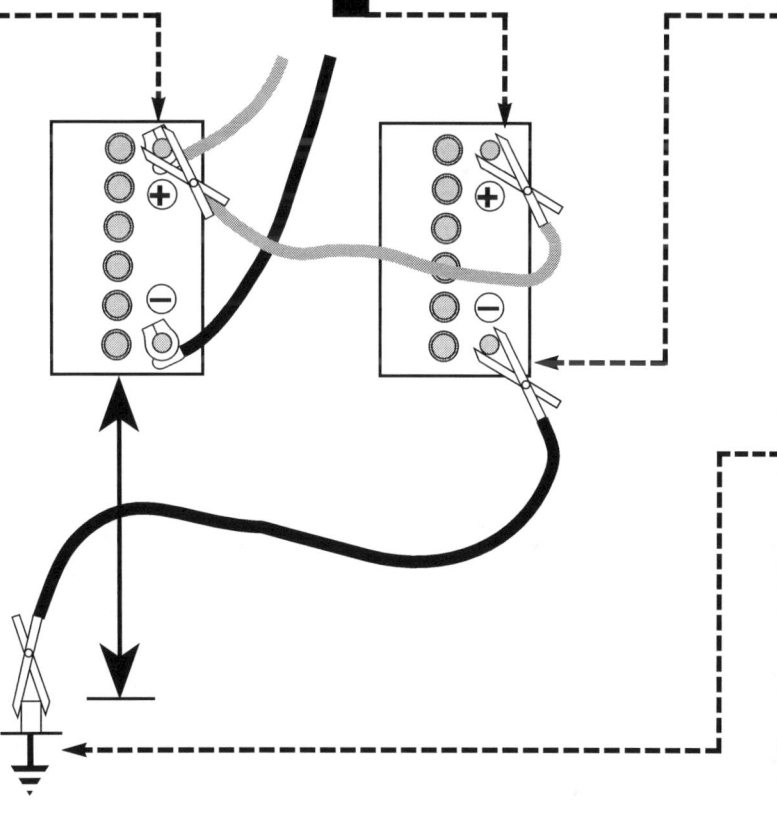

4 Connect the other end of the black jump lead to a bolt or bracket on the engine block, well away from the battery, on the vehicle to be started.

5 Make sure that the jump leads will not come into contact with the fan, drivebelts or other moving parts of the engine.

6 Start the engine using the booster battery and run it at idle speed. Switch on the lights, rear window demister and heater blower motor, then disconnect the jump leads in the reverse order of connection. Turn off the lights etc.

Identifying leaks

Puddles on the garage floor or drive, or obvious wetness under the bonnet or underneath the car, suggest a leak that needs investigating. It can sometimes be difficult to decide where the leak is coming from, especially if the engine bay is very dirty already. Leaking oil or fluid can also be blown rearwards by the passage of air under the car, giving a false impression of where the problem lies.

⚠️ *Warning: Most automotive oils and fluids are poisonous. Wash them off skin, and change out of contaminated clothing, without delay.*

> **HAYNES HiNT** *The smell of a fluid leaking from the car may provide a clue to what's leaking. Some fluids are distinctively coloured. It may help to clean the car carefully and to park it over some clean paper overnight as an aid to locating the source of the leak.*
>
> *Remember that some leaks may only occur while the engine is running.*

Sump oil

Engine oil may leak from the drain plug...

Oil from filter

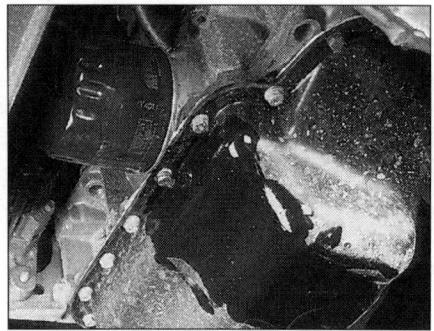

...or from the base of the oil filter.

Gearbox oil

Gearbox oil can leak from the seals at the inboard ends of the driveshafts.

Antifreeze

Leaking antifreeze often leaves a crystalline deposit like this.

Brake fluid

A leak occurring at a wheel is almost certainly brake fluid.

Power steering fluid

Power steering fluid may leak from the pipe connectors on the steering rack.

Jacking and towing

Jacking

It is vital that the correct procedure is always followed when changing a roadwheel, or the results could hazard the operator and damage the vehicle. Because the Range Rover is fitted with a transmission-mounted handbrake it is imperative that the main gearbox is engaged in bottom gear (1st) and that the gearbox differential lock is engaged before the vehicle is jacked up. It is also better if low range is selected in the transfer box. *The handbrake alone will not be effective if one or both of the rear wheels are jacked up while either the main or transfer gearbox is in the neutral position, without the differential lock being engaged.* Also, because of the amount of backlash in the transmission, and therefore potential fore-and-aft movement when the vehicle is jacked up, especially on sloping ground, the wheels, except the one to be removed, must always be chocked.

If the vehicle has been standing for some time (eg overnight) and has a flat tyre that needs to be changed, it will be necessary first to start the engine to build up a vacuum in order to operate the gearbox differential lock. This is engaged only when the warning light in the top of the switch (early models) or on the dashboard (later models) is illuminated when the ignition is switched on. Once engaged, the engine can then be switched off.

Here is a summary of the jacking procedure:

(a) *Engage bottom gear and low transfer gear*
(b) *Engage the differential lock and switch off engine*
(c) *Apply the handbrake*
(d) *Chock the roadwheels*
(e) *Position the jack under the appropriate axle*
(f) *Loosen the wheel nuts*
(g) *Raise the jack*
(h) *Change the roadwheel*
(j) *Lower the jack*
(k) *Tighten the wheel nuts*

Remember to disengage the differential lock and low transfer gear after completing the wheel change and before continuing on the road.

Jack positioning – the jack must be placed under the axle casing adjacent to the wheel to be removed and directly below the coil spring. On the front axle it should be located between the flange on the outer end of the axle casing and the suspension arm mounting bracket. On the rear axle it should be located as near the shock absorber mounting brackets as possible.

When working under the vehicle never rely solely on the vehicle jack. Always use axle stands or blocks to adequately support the vehicle before attempting to work underneath it.

Towing

When towing a trailer or another vehicle, the specified maximum weights must not be exceeded. Remember also that it is the driver's responsibility to ensure that all current regulations with regard to towing are complied with.

In the event of the Range Rover being on the receiving end of a tow-rope, towing eyes are provided on the front bumper mountings (photo)

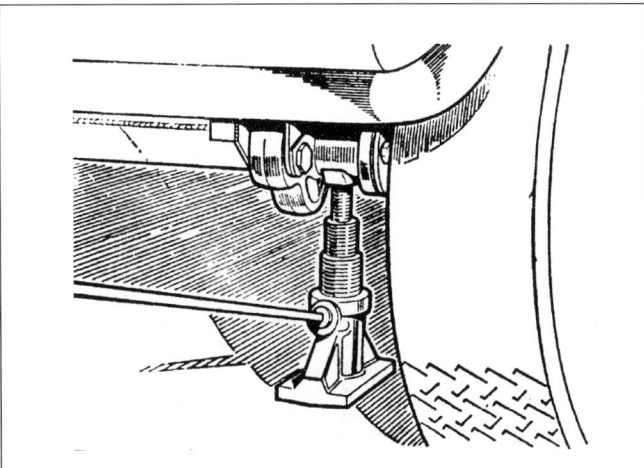

Correct position for jack at the front of the vehicle

Front towing eye

The maintenance schedules listed in this Section are based on those recommended by the makers and apply to a Range Rover that is being used in the conventional manner, ie, normal roadwork, trailer towing and light cross-country duties.

If the vehicle is used in rough terrain and is constantly working in mud and dust, the oil should be changed more frequently and the air cleaner should be checked more frequently than would be usual. In exceptionally harsh conditions or if the vehicle is used for deep wading, the engine oil should also be checked daily, as should the gearbox and transfer box oils.

The gearbox, transfer box, differential and swivel pin oils should also be changed more frequently if the vehicle is being used in the conditions described in the previous paragraph. In particular the propeller shaft sliding joints should be lubricated frequently if driving through sand. The main gearbox and transfer box oils should be changed at least monthly under deep wading conditions.

When the vehicle is being used for very muddy work or where any form of wading is involved, the flywheel housing can be completely sealed by means of a plug, which is located in the bellhousing flange during normal use. This plug must be removed after the job has been completed and before roadwork is resumed. If constant wading is being undertaken, or if severe conditions prevail, then the plug must be removed periodically to allow any accumulated oil to drain out, before it is refitted.

Every 250 miles (400 km), weekly, or before a long journey

- ☐ Check the engine oil level and top up if necessary (photos)
- ☐ Check the coolant level in the expansion tank and top up if necessary (photo)
- ☐ Check the brake fluid level and top up if necessary (photo)
- ☐ Check and top up the windscreen and tailgate washer reservoirs using a screen wash (photo)
- ☐ Check that all the lights work correctly
- ☐ Check the battery electrolyte level and top up if necessary
- ☐ Check the horn operation
- ☐ Check the washer and wiper operation
- ☐ Check the tyre pressures including the spare

Every 6000 miles (10 000 km) or 6 months, whichever occurs first

- ☐ Check for oil, fuel or coolant leaks
- ☐ Check the crankcase breathing hoses for condition and security
- ☐ Drain the engine oil when hot (photo) and refill with fresh oil
- ☐ Renew the oil filter
- ☐ Remove flywheel housing drain plug if in use, and allow to drain (photo)
- ☐ Check and adjust the fan belt tension
- ☐ Check the heater and coolant hoses for condition
- ☐ Check and if necessary adjust the carburettor or fuel injection idle speed and mixture settings
- ☐ Check the exhaust system for tightness and leaks
- ☐ Check the fuel pipes for chafing and leaks

Checking the engine oil level on the dipstick

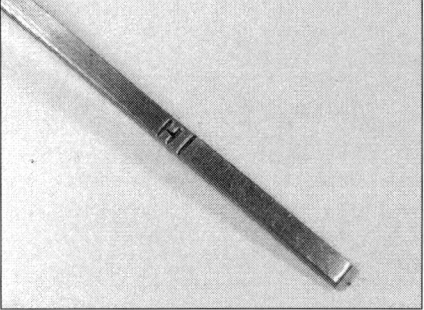

Typical dipstick markings. Oil level should be kept up to mark

Topping up the engine oil

Brake fluid reservoir must be kept full

Topping up the coolant

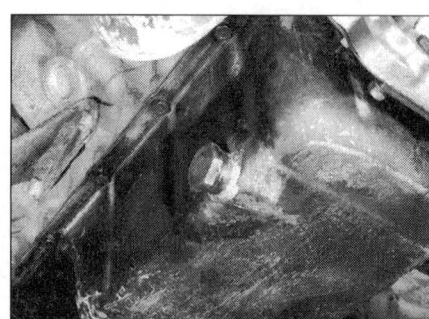

Engine sump drain plug

- ☐ Lubricate the accelerator linkage and check its operation
- ☐ Lubricate the accelerator pedal pivot
- ☐ Top up the carburettor piston dampers (photo)
- ☐ Check the ignition timing and reset if necessary
- ☐ Clean and adjust the ignition contact breaker points
- ☐ Clean and adjust the spark plugs
- ☐ Lubricate the distributor
- ☐ Check the hydraulic pipes for leaks and corrosion
- ☐ Check the clutch fluid reservoir level (photo)
- ☐ Check the automatic transmission fluid level
- ☐ Check the oil level in the main gearbox (photos)
- ☐ Check and top up the transfer box oil (photo)
- ☐ Check the automatic transmission parking pawl engagement
- ☐ Check the propeller shaft flange coupling bolts and nuts for tightness
- ☐ Lubricate the propeller shaft internal joints (photo)
- ☐ Check and top up the front axle differential oil
- ☐ Check and top up the front axle swivel pin housings with oil (photo)
- ☐ Check and top up the rear axle differential oil (photo)
- ☐ Check the brake servo hose for condition and tightness
- ☐ Check the condition and wear of the brake pads
- ☐ Check the condition of the brake discs
- ☐ Check the footbrake for correct operation
- ☐ Check the handbrake operation and adjust as necessary

- ☐ Check the transmission handbrake and adjust if necessary
- ☐ Lubricate the handbrake linkage
- ☐ Check the correct functioning of all electrical equipment
- ☐ Check the headlamp alignment
- ☐ Check the wiper blades and renew if necessary
- ☐ Clean the battery terminals and smear them with petroleum jelly
- ☐ Check the condition of steering joints and gaiters
- ☐ Check the front wheel alignment and adjust as necessary
- ☐ Check the power steering fluid reservoir (where fitted) and top up as necessary
- ☐ Check the power steering system for leaks
- ☐ Check the self-levelling unit for fluid leaks
- ☐ Check the shock absorbers for fluid leaks
- ☐ Check the steering wheel for play
- ☐ Check the tightness of the roadwheel nuts
- ☐ Check the tyres for tread depth, cuts, lumps or bulges (don't forget the spare)
- ☐ Check that all the doors open and close correctly (including the tailgate)
- ☐ Check that all the windows work correctly
- ☐ Check that the bonnet lock operates correctly
- ☐ Check the rear view mirrors for condition
- ☐ Check the safety belts for condition and the mountings for security
- ☐ Lubricate all locks and hinges (except the steering lock)

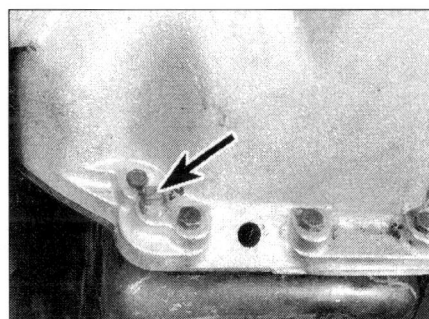

Flywheel housing plug (arrowed) can be screwed into hole at right to prevent entry of water or mud

Topping up a carburettor damper

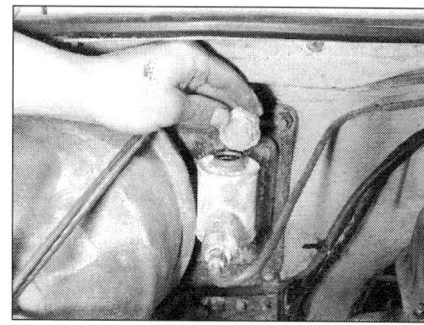

Clutch hydraulic reservoir

Main gearbox oil dipstick. Some models have level plug instead

Main gearbox oil filler hole

Transfer box oil filler plug. Level plug is on rear face of gearbox, below mainshaft rear cover

Every 12 000 miles (20 000 km) or every 12 months, whichever occurs first

In addition to the servicing operations listed under the 6000 mile (10 000 km) headings

☐ Renew the engine breather filter on rear of crankcase
☐ Renew the engine flame traps
☐ Check the air intake flap valve for correct operation (if fitted)
☐ Renew the air cleaner elements
☐ Renew the main fuel filter element and in-line filter (if fitted)
☐ Check the condition of the HT leads
☐ Clean and examine the distributor cap and rotor arm
☐ Renew the distributor contact breaker points
☐ Renew the spark plugs
☐ Renew the main gearbox oil
☐ Renew the transfer box oil
☐ Check propeller shaft bolts for tightness
☐ Clean the alternator moulded cover and slip ring end bracket
☐ Check all the suspension mountings for security
☐ Check and if necessary adjust the steering box
☐ Check the manual steering box and top up as necessary

Every 18 000 miles (30 000 km) or 18 months, whichever occurs first

In addition to the items listed previously

☐ Renew the hydraulic fluid in the braking system

Every 24 000 miles (40 000 km) or 24 months, whichever occurs first

In addition to those items listed previously

☐ Drain, flush and refill the cooling system
☐ Adjust the automatic transmission brake bands (Chrysler 3-speed transmission)
☐ Drain and refill the automatic transmission fluid, and renew the filter screen
☐ Renew the front axle oil
☐ Renew the front axle swivel pin housings oil
☐ Renew the rear axle oil
☐ Renew power steering reservoir filter (if applicable)

Every 36 000 miles (60 000 km) or 36 months, whichever occurs first

In addition to those items listed previously

☐ Renew all the rubber seals in the braking system

Every 48 000 miles (80 000 km) or 4 years, whichever occurs first

In addition to all the items listed previously

☐ Renew the crankcase ventilation PCV valve (1990-on models)*
☐ Renew all the cooling and heater hoses
☐ Check the fuel evaporative emission control system for leaks (1990-on models)
☐ Clean the filter in the electric fuel pump (later models)
☐ Renew the charcoal canister (1990-on models)*
☐ Renew the fuel filter on fuel injected engines
☐ Renew the Lambda oxygen sensors (1990-on models)*
☐ Clean the distributor

The maintenance work marked with an asterisk is not mandatory at the present time but is recommended only. Refer to your Rover dealer for current emission regulations and recommendations as these are updated frequently.

Every 96 000 miles (160 000 km) or 8 years, whichever occurs first

☐ Renew catalytic converters (1990-on models)*

The maintenance work marked with an asterisk is not mandatory at the present time but is recommended only. Refer to your Rover dealer for current emission regulations and recommendations as these are updated frequently.

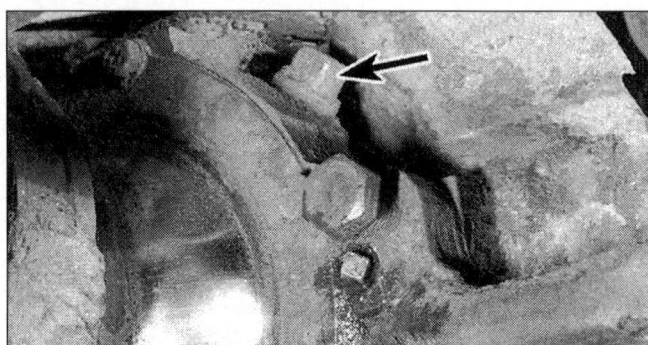

Swivel pin filler plug (arrowed, top) and level plug (arrowed, bottom)

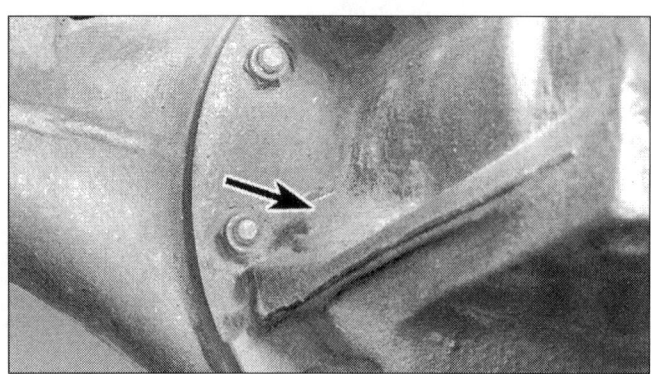

Rear differential filler/level plug (arrowed)

View of the engine compartment - 1987 fuel injection model with conventional braking system

1 Battery
2 Cooling system expansion tank
3 Air conditioning compressor
4 Brake master cylinder reservoir
5 Engine flame trap
6 Automatic transmission dipstick/filler tube
7 Cold start injector
8 Plenum chamber
9 Extra air valve
10 Distributor
11 Power steering pump
12 Alternator
13 Oil filler cap
14 Idle speed adjustment screw
15 Idle mixture adjustment screw
16 Washer reservoir
17 Ignition coil
18 Air cleaner
19 Power steering reservoir

View of the engine compartment - 1990 fuel injection model with ABS

1 ABS hydraulic booster unit
2 Brake fluid reservoir
3 Air conditioning receiver/dryer
4 Automatic transmission fluid level dipstick
5 Plenum chamber
6 Throttle potentiometer
7 Engine oil level dipstick
8 Windscreen washer fluid reservoir
9 Airflow meter
10 Ignition coil
11 Air cleaner assembly
12 Alternator
13 Power steering fluid reservoir
14 Cooling system top hose
15 Power steering pump
16 Distributor
17 Water pump
18 Drivebelt
19 Air conditioning compressor
20 Radiator
21 Battery
22 Cooling system expansion tank
23 Fuel evaporative charcoal canister
24 Hydraulic pump

View of the front underbody - 1990 fuel injection model with ABS

1 Engine sump
2 Front radius arm
3 Left-hand catalyst
4 Automatic transmission
5 Transfer gearbox
6 Right-hand catalyst
7 Front propeller shaft
8 Front axle
9 Panhard rod
10 Damper
11 Steering drag link
12 Steering track rod

View of the rear underbody - 1990 fuel injection model with ABS

1 Fuel filler neck
2 Fuel tank
3 Rear axle
4 Rear radius arm
5 Rear propeller shaft
6 Self-levelling unit
7 Intermediate exhaust silencer
8 A-frame pivot
9 Rear shock absorber
10 Rear exhaust silencer

Tyre conditon and pressure

It is very important that tyres are in good condition, and at the correct pressure - having a tyre failure at any speed is highly dangerous. Tyre wear is influenced by driving style - harsh braking and acceleration, or fast cornering, will all produce more rapid tyre wear. As a general rule, the front tyres wear out faster than the rears. Interchanging the tyres from front to rear ("rotating" the tyres) may result in more even wear. However, if this is completely effective, you may have the expense of replacing all four tyres at once! Remove any nails or stones embedded in the tread before they penetrate the tyre to cause deflation. If removal of a nail does reveal that

the tyre has been punctured, refit the nail so that its point of penetration is marked. Then immediately change the wheel, and have the tyre repaired by a tyre dealer.

Regularly check the tyres for damage in the form of cuts or bulges, especially in the sidewalls. Periodically remove the wheels, and clean any dirt or mud from the inside and outside surfaces. Examine the wheel rims for signs of rusting, corrosion or other damage. Light alloy wheels are easily damaged by "kerbing" whilst parking; steel wheels may also become dented or buckled. A new wheel is very often the only way to overcome severe damage.

New tyres should be balanced when they are fitted, but it may become necessary to re-balance them as they wear, or if the balance weights fitted to the wheel rim should fall off. Unbalanced tyres will wear more quickly, as will the steering and suspension components. Wheel imbalance is normally signified by vibration, particularly at a certain speed (typically around 50 mph). If this vibration is felt only through the steering, then it is likely that just the front wheels need balancing. If, however, the vibration is felt through the whole car, the rear wheels could be out of balance. Wheel balancing should be carried out by a tyre dealer or garage.

1 Tread Depth - visual check
The original tyres have tread wear safety bands (B), which will appear when the tread depth reaches approximately 1.6 mm. The band positions are indicated by a triangular mark on the tyre sidewall (A).

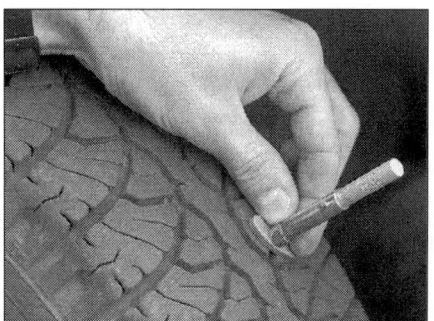

2 Tread Depth - manual check
Alternatively, tread wear can be monitored with a simple, inexpensive device known as a tread depth indicator gauge.

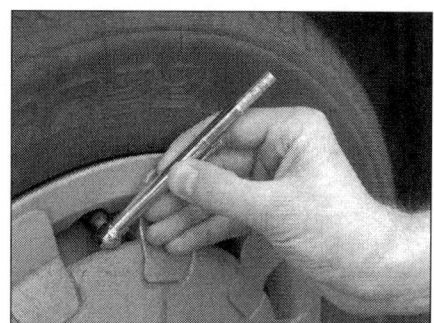

3 Tyre Pressure Check
Check the tyre pressures regularly with the tyres cold. Do not adjust the tyre pressures immediately after the vehicle has been used, or an inaccurate setting will result.

Choosing your engine oil

Engines need oil, not only to lubricate moving parts and minimise wear, but also to maximise power output and to improve fuel economy. By introducing a simplified and improved range of engine oils, Duckhams has taken away the confusion and made it easier for you to choose the right oil for your engine.

HOW ENGINE OIL WORKS

• Beating friction

Without oil, the moving surfaces inside your engine will rub together, heat up and melt, quickly causing the engine to seize. Engine oil creates a film which separates these moving parts, preventing wear and heat build-up.

• Cooling hot-spots

Temperatures inside the engine can exceed 1000° C. The engine oil circulates and acts as a coolant, transferring heat from the hot-spots to the sump.

• Cleaning the engine internally

Good quality engine oils clean the inside of your engine, collecting and dispersing combustion deposits and controlling them until they are trapped by the oil filter or flushed out at oil change.

OIL CARE - FOLLOW THE CODE

To handle and dispose of used engine oil safely, always:

OIL CARE
FOLLOW THE CODE
OIL BANK LINE
0800 66 33 66
www.oilbankline.org.uk

• *Avoid skin contact with used engine oil. Repeated or prolonged contact can be harmful.*
• *Dispose of used oil and empty packs in a responsible manner in an authorised disposal site. Call 0800 663366 to find the one nearest to you. Never tip oil down drains or onto the ground.*

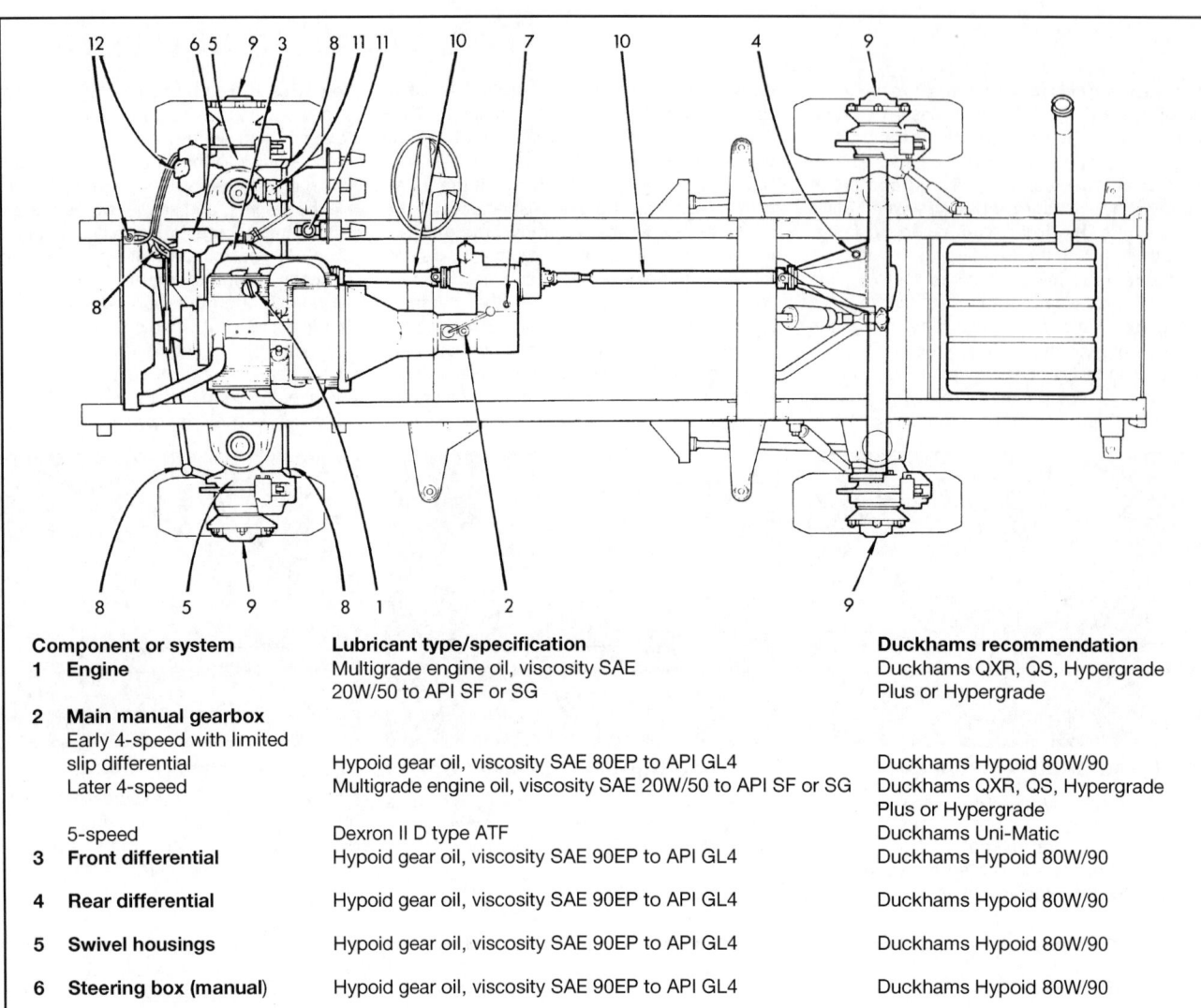

Component or system	Lubricant type/specification	Duckhams recommendation
1 **Engine**	Multigrade engine oil, viscosity SAE 20W/50 to API SF or SG	Duckhams QXR, QS, Hypergrade Plus or Hypergrade
2 **Main manual gearbox**		
Early 4-speed with limited slip differential	Hypoid gear oil, viscosity SAE 80EP to API GL4	Duckhams Hypoid 80W/90
Later 4-speed	Multigrade engine oil, viscosity SAE 20W/50 to API SF or SG	Duckhams QXR, QS, Hypergrade Plus or Hypergrade
5-speed	Dexron II D type ATF	Duckhams Uni-Matic
3 **Front differential**	Hypoid gear oil, viscosity SAE 90EP to API GL4	Duckhams Hypoid 80W/90
4 **Rear differential**	Hypoid gear oil, viscosity SAE 90EP to API GL4	Duckhams Hypoid 80W/90
5 **Swivel housings**	Hypoid gear oil, viscosity SAE 90EP to API GL4	Duckhams Hypoid 80W/90
6 **Steering box (manual)**	Hypoid gear oil, viscosity SAE 90EP to API GL4	Duckhams Hypoid 80W/90
6 **Power steering (if fitted)**	Dexron IID type ATF	Duckhams Uni-Matic
7 **Transfer box**		
Early 4-speed manual transmission with limited slip differential	Hypoid gear oil, viscosity SAE 90EP to API GL4	Duckhams Hypoid 80W/90
Later 4-speed manual transmission	Multigrade engine oil, viscosity SAE 20W/50 to API SF or SG	Duckhams QXR, QS, Hypergrade Plus or Hypergrade
5-speed manual transmission	Hypoid gear oil, viscosity SAE 90EP to API GL4	Duckhams Hypoid 80W/90
Automatic transmission	Hypoid gear oil, viscosity SAE 90EP to API GL4	Duckhams Hypoid 80W/90
8 **Balljoints**	Multi-purpose lithium based grease to NLGI 2	Duckhams LB 10
9 **Front and rear hubs**	Multi-purpose lithium based grease to NLGI 2	Duckhams LB 10
10 **Propeller shafts**	Multi-purpose lithium based grease to NLGI 2	Duckhams LB 10
11 **Brake and clutch hydraulic reservoirs**	Hydraulic fluid to SAE J1703	Duckhams Universal Brake and Clutch Fluid
12 **Cooling system**	Ethylene glycol based antifreeze to BS 3150, 3151, or 6580	Duckhams Antifreeze and Summer Coolant
Automatic transmission	Dexron II D type ATF	Duckhams Uni-Matic

Chapter 1 Engine

For modifications, and information applicable to later models, see Supplement at end of manual

Contents

Degrees of difficulty

Easy, suitable for novice with little experience	**Fairly easy,** suitable for beginner with some experience	**Fairly difficult,** suitable for competent DIY mechanic 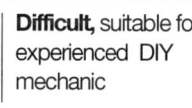	**Difficult,** suitable for experienced DIY mechanic	**Very difficult,** suitable for expert DIY or professional

Specifications

General

Engine type	V8, 4-stroke, water-cooled, ohv
Cubic capacity	3528 cc (215 cu in)
Bore	88.90 mm (3.50 in)
Stroke	71.12 mm (2.80 in)
Compression ratio:	
Pre-1974 models	8.5 : 1
1974 to 1979	8.25 : 1
1979 onwards	8.13 : 1
Certain export models	7.1 : 1
Power output (DIN):	
Up to 1979	130 BHP (98 kW) at 5000 rpm
1979 onwards	156 BHP (116 kW) at 5000 rpm
Maximum torque (DIN):	
Up to 1979	25.6 kgf m (185 lbf ft) at 2500 rpm
1979 onwards	28.3 kgf m (205 lbf ft) at 3000 rpm
Firing order	1 - 8 - 4 - 3 - 6 - 5 - 7 - 2
Cylinder numbering (front to rear):	
Left-hand bank	1 - 3 - 5 - 7
Right-hand bank	2 - 4 - 6 - 8
Compression pressure at cranking speed	9.5 kgf/cm² (135 lbf/in²) minimum

Cylinder block

Material	Aluminium alloy
Cylinder liner type	Dry, cast integrally with block
Liner material	Cast Iron

Cylinder heads

Material	Aluminium alloy
Type	Two separate heads, in-line valves, separate inlet manifold
Valve seat material	Piston ring iron
Valve seat angle	46° ± 1/4°
Oversize inserts available	+ 0.25 and 0.50 mm (0.010 and 0.020 in)
Inlet valve seat diameter:	
Early models	35.25 mm (1.388 in)
Later models	37.03 mm (1.458 in)
Exhaust valve seat diameter:	
Early models	30.48 mm (1.200 in)
Later models	31.50 mm (1.240 in)

Valves

Overall length	116.58 to 117.34 mm (4.590 to 4.620 in)	
Angle of face	45°	
Stem height above spring seat when fitted	47.63 mm (1.875 in) maximum	
Valve lift	9.9 mm (0.39 in)	
Valve clearance	Not adjustable (hydraulic self-adjusting tappets)	
Valve head diameter:	**Inlet**	**Exhaust**
Early models	37.97 to 38.22 mm (1.495 to 1.505 in)	33.215 to 33.466 mm (1.3075 to 1.3175 in)
Later models	39.75 to 40.00 mm (1.565 to 1.575 in)	34.341 to 34.595 mm (1.3475 to 1.3575 in)
Valve stem diameter:		
At valve head	8.640 to 8.666 mm (0.3402 to 0.3412 in)	8.628 to 8.654 mm (0.3397 to 0.3407 in)
Increasing to	8.653 to 8.679 mm (0.3407 to 0.3417 in)	8.640 to 8.666 mm (0.3402 to 0.3412 in)
Stem-to-guide clearance:		
Top	0.02 to 0.07 mm (0.001 to 0.003 in)	0.038 to 0.088 mm (0.0015 to 0.0035 in)
Bottom	0.013 to 0.063 mm (0.0005 to 0.0025 in)	0.05 to 0.10 mm (0.002 to 0.004 in)

Valve springs

Number per valve	2 on early engines, 1 on later engines
Spring length under given load:	
Early models, outer	40.6 mm (1.60 in)/17.6 to 20.4 kgf (39 to 45 lbf)
Early models, inner	41.2 mm (1.63 in)/9.7 to 12.0 kgf (21.5 to 26.5 lbf)
Later models (single spring)	40.0 mm (1.577 in)/30 to 33 kgf (66.5 to 73.5 lbf)

Valve gear

Type	Overhead, alloy rockers operated by pushrods
Tappets (cam followers)	Self-adjusting hydraulic

Valve timing

	Inlet	Exhaust
Valve opens	30° BTDC	68° BBDC
Valve closes	75° ABDC	37° ATDC
Duration	285°	285°
Peak opening	112° 30' ATDC	105° 30' BTDC

Camshaft

Material	Cast iron
Location	Central, in vee of cylinder block
Drive	Inverted tooth chain (54 links)
Bearings:	
Number	5
Type	Steel-backed, babbit lined

Crankshaft and bearings

Material	Iron, spheroidal graphite
Number of main bearings	5
Main bearing journal diameter (standard)	58.400 to 58.413 mm (2.2992 to 2.2997 in)
Main bearing clearance	0.023 to 0.061 mm (0.0009 to 0.0024 in)
Undersizes available	0.25, 0.50, 0.76 and 1.02 mm (0.010, 0.020, 0.030 and 0.040 in)
Big-end bearing journal diameter (standard)	50.800 to 50.812 mm (2.0000 to 2.0005 in)
Big-end bearing clearance	0.015 to 0.055 mm (0.0006 to 0.0022 in)
Undersizes available	As for main bearings
Journal ovality	0.04 mm (0.0015 in) maximum
Crankshaft endthrust	Taken on centre (No 3) main bearing shell flanges
Crankshaft endfloat	0.10 to 0.20 mm (0.004 to 0.008 in)

Connecting rods

Type	Horizontally split big-end, solid small-end
Length between centres	143.71 to 143.81 mm (5.658 to 5.662 in)
Endfloat on crankpin	0.15 to 0.37 mm (0.006 to 0.014 in)

Gudgeon pins

Length	72.67 to 72.79 mm (2.861 to 2.866 in)
Diameter	22.215 to 22.220 mm (0.8746 to 0.8749 in)
Fit in connecting rod	Press fit
Fit in piston	Sliding fit
Clearance in piston	0.002 to 0.007 mm (0.0001 to 0.0003 in)

Pistons

Type	Aluminium alloy, with flat or concave crown depending on year of manufacture. The two types are not interchangeable
Clearance in bore:	
Top land	0.647 to 0.812 mm (0.0255 to 0.0320 in)
Skirt top	0.0178 to 0.0330 mm (0.0007 to 0.0013 in)
Skirt bottom	0.008 to 0.043 mm (0.0003 to 0.0017 in)
Ring groove depth	4.930 to 5.118 mm (0.1940 to 0.2015 in)
Piston grades:	
Standard (Grade Z)	Nominal size to + 0.0075 mm (0.0003 in)
Grade A	+ 0.0075 to 0.0150 mm (0.0003 to 0.0006 in)
Grade B	+ 0.0150 to 0.0225 mm (0.0006 to 0.0009 in)
Grade C	+ 0.0225 to 0.0300 mm (0.0009 to 0.0012 in)
Grade D	+ 0.0300 to 0.0375 mm (0.0012 to 0.0015 in)
Grade letter location	Piston crown and cylinder block face
Oversize pistons available after rebore (ungraded)	+ 0.25 and 0.50 mm (0.010 and 0.020 in)

Piston rings

Number of compression rings	2
Number of oil rings	1
Number one compression ring	Chrome faced
Number two compression ring	Stepped, L-shaped and marked TOP or T
Compression ring end gap in bore	0.44 to 0.57 mm (0.017 to 0.022 in)
Compression ring clearance in groove	0.05 to 0.10 mm (0.002 to 0.004 in)
Oil control ring type	Expander ring with top and bottom rails
Oil control ring gap in bore	0.38 to 1.40 mm (0.015 to 0.055 in)

Flywheel

Ring gear thickness:	
Early models	9.52 to 9.65 mm (0.375 to 0.380 in)
Later models	10.97 to 11.22 mm (0.432 to 0.442 in)
Minimum flywheel overall thickness for refacing:	
Early models	38.35 mm (1.510 in)
Later models	39.93 mm (1.572 in)

Lubrication system

Oil type/specification	Multigrade engine oil, viscosity SAE 20W/50 to API SF or SG
Oil pump type	Gear
Oil pump drive	From bottom end of distributor driveshaft, off camshaft gear
Clearance between pump gears and front cover	0.05 mm (0.0018 in)
Bypass valve seat location (early models only)	0.5 to 1.0 mm (0.020 to 0.040 in) below surface of casing
Oil pressure at 2400 rpm (50 mph in top gear) with engine warm	2.11 to 2.81 kgf/cm^2 (30 to 40 lbf/in^2)

Torque wrench settings

	lbf ft	kgf m
Main bearing cap bolts (1 to 4)	50 to 55	7.0 to 7.6
Rear (No 5) main bearing cap bolts	65 to 70	9.0 to 9.6
Connecting rod cap nuts	30 to 35	4.0 to 4.9
Flywheel bolts	50 to 60	7.0 to 8.5
Oil pump cover bolts	10 to 15	1.4 to 2.0
Oil pressure relief valve	30 to 35	4.0 to 4.9
Cylinder head bolts:		
Inner and centre rows (nos 1 to 10)	65 to 70	9.0 to 9.6
Outer row (nos 11 to 14)	40 to 45	5.5 to 6.2
Cylinder head bolts	65 to 70	9.0 to 9.6
Rocker shaft bolts	25 to 30	3.5 to 4.0
Timing chain cover bolts	20 to 25	2.8 to 3.5
Crankshaft pulley/starter dog bolt	140 to 160	19.3 to 22.3
Water pump retaining bolts:		
1/4 inch	7 to 10	0.9 to 1.4
5/16 inch	16 to 20	2.2 to 2.7
Distributor drivegear-to-camshaft front end bolt	40 to 45	5.5 to 6.2
Engine mounting rubbers - nuts	13 to 16	1.8 to 2.2
Inlet manifold bolts	25 to 30	3.5 to 4.0
Inlet manifold gasket clamp bolts	10 to 15	1.4 to 2.0
Exhaust manifold bolts	10 to 15	1.4 to 2.0
Clutch cover bolts	35 to 38	4.9 to 5.2

1 General description

The engine is an overhead valve high performance V8. The cylinder block and cylinder heads are aluminium alloy castings and the two banks of four cylinders are set at 90° to each other. The cylinder liners are of cast iron and are integral with the block so they can be rebored within certain tolerances. The valve guides and seats are also of iron and can be renewed. A large one-piece aluminium alloy inlet manifold is mounted between the cylinder heads and is fitted with two Stromberg carburettors. Separate cast iron exhaust manifolds are fitted to the outside of each bank of cylinders. The camshaft is mounted centrally at the bottom of the Vee of the engine and is driven by a chain from the crankshaft. There is no chain tensioner.

The valves are operated by pushrods and hydraulic tappets which are self-adjusting to ensure quiet engine operation. The pistons are made in special lightweight alloy and are of full skirt design. Depending upon the model year they will have either a flat crown or a crown with a shallow circular depression. This is because of the changes that have occurred in the compression ratio since 1970.

The crankshaft runs in five main bearings and is fitted with a torsional vibration damper. The thrust of the crankshaft is taken on the centre main bearing.

Lubrication is by a gear-driven oil pump at the front of the engine, which delivers oil under pressure to all the main, big-end and camshaft bearings, the valve gear, distributor driveshaft and cylinder bores. A full flow cartridge type of disposable oil filter is fitted at the front of the engine.

IMPORTANT: Because the engine is of aluminium construction, it is vital when tightening bolts related to the engine, that the correct torque settings specified should be strictly observed. It is also of equal importance that bolt lengths are noted and bolts refitted in the same location from which they were removed. Where specified, always use thread lubricant and sealer.

Because of the weight and bulk of this unit it is essential that substantial lifting tackle is

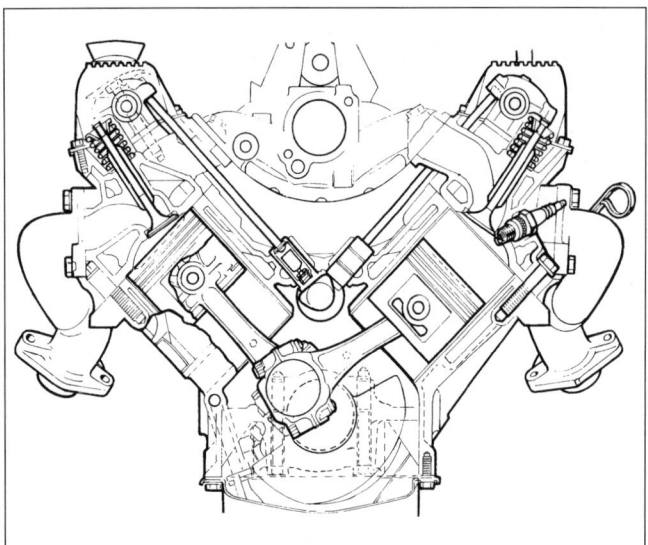

Fig. 1.1 Sectional view of the engine from the front (Sec 1)

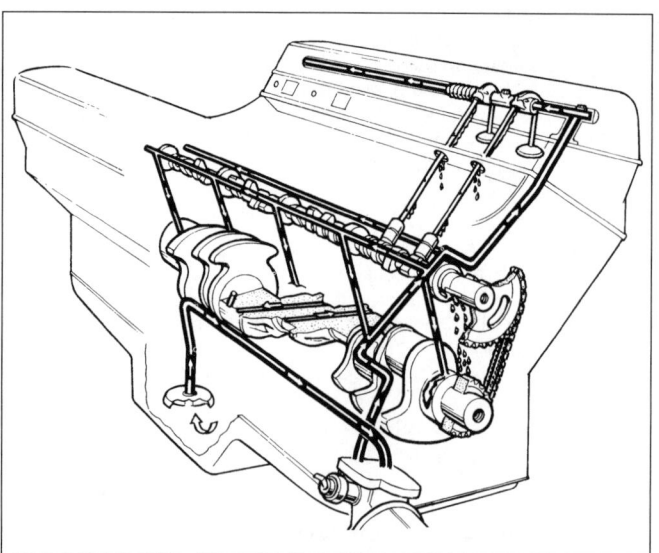

Fig. 1.2 Lubrication system (Sec 1)

available, otherwise the removal of the engine is undesirable and impractical for the average home mechanic. It is fully realised that any major overhaul tasks could be greatly facilitated if the unit were out of the frame and supported on an engine stand or strong workbench. For those who are determined, or find it really necessary to remove the unit, the procedure is outlined in the following text. In the following section all the items that can be tackled with the engine in position are progressively listed, and the owner must fully assess the amount of work entailed before starting the task.

2 Major operations which can be performed with the engine in the car

It is possible to remove the following components for inspection and/or overhaul without having to lift the engine out of the vehicle:
(a) *Radiator and cooling fan*
(b) *Water pump*
(c) *Carburettors*
(d) *Inlet manifold*
(e) *Distributor*
(f) *Alternator*
(g) *Starter motor*
(h) *Cylinder heads and valve assembly*
(j) *Hydraulic tappets*
(k) *Camshaft*
(l) *Timing chain and gearwheels*
(m) *Sump*
(n) *Big-end bearings*
(p) *Pistons and connecting rods*
(q) *Oil pump*
(r) *Timing chain cover*
(s) *Gearbox*

3 Operations which require removal of the engine from the car

Any internal engine work (other than listed previously) such as refitting of crankshaft and main bearings, will require removal of the engine from the car.

4 Engine removal - general

The engine of the Range Rover must be removed separately from the gearbox. Because of the size of the vehicle the task is not very difficult, as there is generally enough space within the engine compartment to reach most of the retaining bolts. The exceptions are the upper bellhousing bolts and the right-hand exhaust pipe-to-manifold joint.

The vehicle is quite high off the ground, therefore ensure that the lifting tackle is

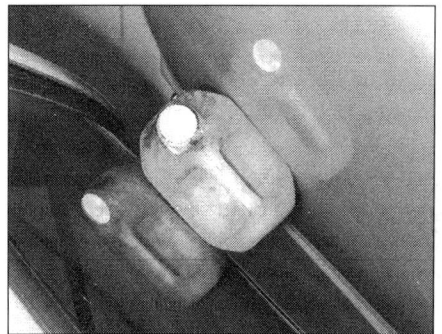

5.2 The bonnet can be propped open like this

adequate so that the engine can be lifted up far enough to clear the bodywork when it is removed. A standard 1/2 ton garage crane (hired from the local tool and equipment hire centre) is perfectly adequate for this task.

This operation is a two-man task. Remember that at no time during the lifting operation should either person be directly beneath the suspended weight of the engine.

5 Engine - removal

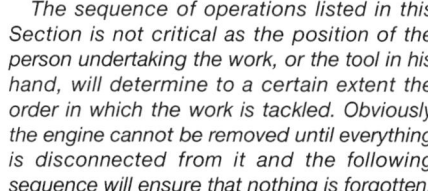

The sequence of operations listed in this Section is not critical as the position of the person undertaking the work, or the tool in his hand, will determine to a certain extent the order in which the work is tackled. Obviously the engine cannot be removed until everything is disconnected from it and the following sequence will ensure that nothing is forgotten.

Assemble a collection of containers for the small parts, nuts and bolts, etc, that are removed and keep them in convenient groups.
1 Because of the height of the vehicle off the ground it is advisable to protect the wings when leaning over into the engine compartment.
2 Open the bonnet and, with the help of your assistant, place a thick pad against the upper part of the windscreen in the centre. The bonnet can then be lifted up until it rests against the pad. We found that an empty one

5.10 Disconnecting the throttle cable

5.8 Disconnecting the fuel supply to the fuel pump (early models)

gallon plastic container was the ideal size for this purpose. The bonnet is very heavy and this saves a lot of time and effort that would otherwise be spent in removing it. Unless the task is being carried out in conditions with very low headroom, this should normally be quite practical (photo).
3 Disconnect the battery leads, undo the battery clamp and remove the battery from the vehicle. Put it in a safe place. It is probably a good idea to put it on charge for a while.
4 Drain the cooling system as described in Chapter 2.
5 Remove the air cleaner assembly as described in Chapter 3.
6 Remove the radiator, fan cowl, fan and drivebelt(s) as described in Chapter 2.
7 Disconnect the HT and LT leads from the coil to the distributor.
8 On models with a mechanical fuel pump, disconnect and plug the fuel line from the tank to the pump (photo).
9 On models with an electric fuel pump, disconnect and plug the fuel line at the in-line filter.
10 On all models, disconnect the throttle and choke cables (as applicable) from the left-hand carburettor (photo). Refer to Chapter 3 if necessary.
11 Disconnect the fuel return pipe from the right-hand carburettor, and tuck it out of the way (photo).
12 Disconnect the brake servo vacuum pipe from the inlet manifold and tuck it out of the way.

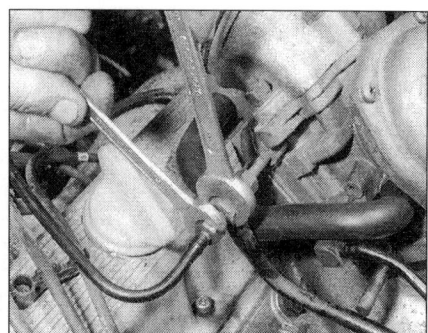

5.11 Disconnecting the fuel return pipe

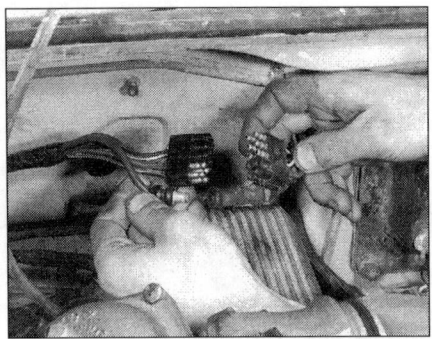

5.15 Disconnecting the wiring loom and electrical supply

5.20 Disconnecting the earthing strap

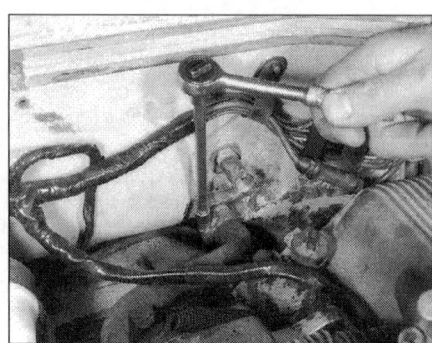

5.21 Disconnecting the heater hoses

13 Similarly disconnect the differential lock actuator vacuum pipe.

14 The electrical connections may be tackled in two ways. Either remove all the connections first and leave the loom in the vehicle, or unplug the wiring loom for the engine from the main loom and remove it with the engine. The second method is easier in many ways and it means that there are fewer loose ends to snag the engine assembly as it is lifted out. The procedure below covers the second way.

15 Disconnect the engine wiring loom from the main loom and also the main electrical supply connectors at the rear of the left-hand rocker cover (photo).

16 Disconnect the engine wiring loom from the wiring clips of the engine compartment rear bulkhead.

17 Disconnect the handbrake warning light switch cable from the loom.

18 Disconnect the oil pressure warning light switch cable.

19 Disconnect the power cable from the starter solenoid; that is, the heavy black cable.

20 Disconnect the engine earthing strap from the starter to the right-hand side of the body (photo).

21 Undo the hose clips and disconnect the heater flow and return hoses from the inlet manifold (photo).

22 Working underneath the car undo the two exhaust pipe-to-exhaust manifold connections. There are three brass nuts per side. Because of the heat shield on the right-hand side, the nuts

are some of the most difficult to undo in the whole engine removal operation (photo).

23 Undo the upper and lower nuts on both engine mountings (photo).

24 Undo the bellhousing lower cover plate and stiffening plate nuts and bolts and remove the plates (photo).

25 Undo the bellhousing to engine retaining bolts. Some are accessible from under the car, the others from inside the engine compartment. However it must be said that the latter are very difficult to reach and this is probably the worst part of the operation.

26 The engine is now ready to be lifted out, if an overhead lifting system is being employed. However, if an ordinary floor crane is being used then the front grille and top panel will have to be removed to allow the necessary space and reduce the lifting height.

27 To remove the grille, undo the four self-tapping screws in the top and the two in the lower edge, outer corners.

28 The top panel is secured by four bolts on each side, and the two bolts in the centre which retain the locking plate also retain the two bracing bars. With all the bolts removed, release the wiring loom from the clips on the underside of the panel and the panel can be lifted away and placed on the inner left-hand wing with the locking cable still attached to it. Note that the two horizontal bolts on each side retain the horn mounting brackets. Disconnect the wiring to the horns and place them to one side (photos).

5.22 Undoing the left-hand exhaust pipe-to-manifold connection

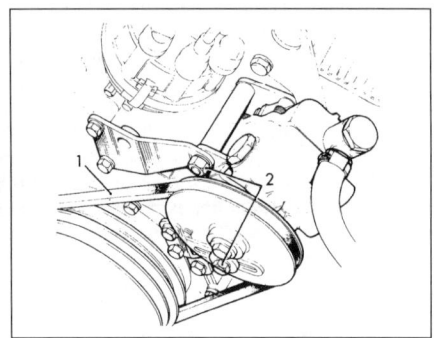

Fig. 1.3 Power steering pump arrangement (if fitted) (Sec 5)

1 Drivebelt
2 Adjuster and mounting bolts

5.23 Undoing the left-hand engine mounting lower nut

5.24 Withdrawing the bellhousing lower cover plate

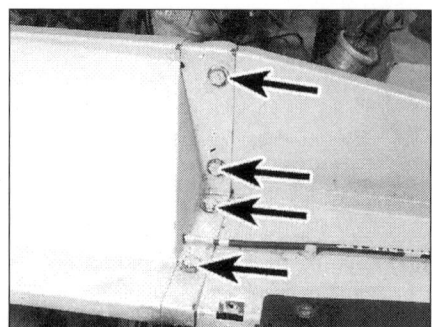

5.28a Undo the four bolts (arrowed) on each side to remove the panel

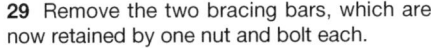

5.28b The diagonal bracing bars can be removed when the panel is out of the way. (Note the horns on either side)

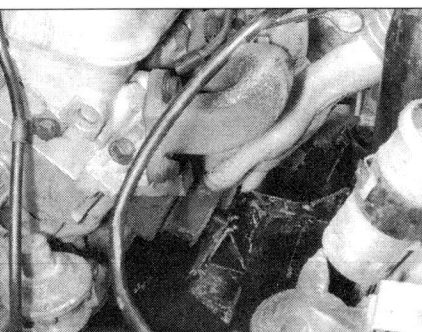

5.34 Removing the engine left-hand mounting rubber

5.36 Lifting the engine out

29 Remove the two bracing bars, which are now retained by one nut and bolt each.

30 On models with power steering, undo the power steering pump mounting bolts and free the pump from its mounting. Remove the belt from the pulleys.

31 Tie the pump up so that the fluid lines are not stretched.

32 Release the wiring loom from the clips on the outer front panels behind the wings. Push the wiring down so that it rests on the chassis front crossmember out of the way.

33 Attach lifting chains or slings to the engine lifting eyes. Ensure that they are securely attached before attempting to remove the engine.

34 Take the weight of the engine and lift it just enough to remove the engine mounting rubbers (photo).

35 Pull the engine forward to disengage the bellhousing dowels, and the input shaft from the clutch. Do not allow the weight of the engine to rest on the input shaft.

36 Lift the engine upwards and forwards in stages. Ensure that all cables, pipes and wires have been disconnected and removed from retaining clips. As the engine is removed check carefully that no wires, pipes, etc, become snagged (photo).

37 Lift the engine high enough to clear the front body panel, then pull it clear of the vehicle.

6 Engine dismantling - general

1 It is best to mount the engine on a dismantling stand but if one is not available, then stand the engine on a strong bench so it is at a comfortable working height. Failing this, the engine can be stripped down on the floor.

2 During the dismantling process the greatest care should be taken to keep the exposed parts free from dirt. As an aid to achieving this, if is sound advice to thoroughly clean the outside of the engine, removing all traces of oil and congealed dirt.

3 Use paraffin or a good grease solvent. The latter will make the job much easier, after the solvent has been applied and allowed to stand for a time, a vigorous jet of water will wash off the solvent and all the grease and filth. If the dirt is thick and deeply embedded, work the solvent into it with a wire brush.

4 Finally wipe down the exterior of the engine with a rag and only then, when it is quite clean, should the dismantling process begin. As the engine is stripped, clean each part in a bath of paraffin or petrol.

5 Never immerse parts with oilways in paraffin, eg, the crankshaft, but to clean, wipe down carefully with a petrol-dampened rag. Oilways can be cleaned out with wire.

> **HAYNES HiNT**
> *If an air line is present, all parts can be blown dry and the oilways blown through as an added precaution.*

6 Re-use of old engine gaskets is false economy and can give rise to oil and water leaks, if nothing worse. To avoid the possibility of trouble after the engine has been reassembled, **always** use new gaskets throughout.

7 Do not throw away old gaskets as it sometimes happens that an immediate replacement cannot be found and the old gasket is then very useful as a template. Hang up the old gaskets as they are removed on a suitable hook or nail.

8 To strip the engine it is best to work from the top down. The sump provides a firm base on which the engine can be supported in an upright position. When the stage is reached where the sump must be removed, the engine can be turned on its side and all other work carried out with it in this position.

9 Wherever possible, refit nuts, bolts and washers fingertight from wherever they were removed. This helps avoid later loss and muddle. If they cannot be refitted then lay them out in such a fashion that it is clear from where they came.

7 Ancillary components - removal prior to engine overhaul

1 With the engine out of the vehicle and thoroughly cleaned, the externally mounted components should now be removed as follows:

(a) *Alternator - as described in Chapter 10*

(b) *Distributor cap and plug leads: Unclip the distributor cap spring clips, disconnect the plug leads from the plugs and remove the cap and leads complete*

(c) *Wiring loom. Disconnect the temperature gauge transmitter wire, the inlet manifold transmitter wire and the oil transmitter wires (photos)*

(d) *Wiring loom retaining brackets*

(e) *Distributor - as described in Chapter 4*

7.1a The plug leads are all numbered

7.1b The coolant temperature transmitter wire is at the front

7.1c The inlet manifold transmitter is on top

(f)   Starter motor - as described in Chapter 10
(g)   Fuel pump (mechanical) - as described in Chapter 3 (early models only)
(h)   Clutch assembly - as described in Chapter 5
(j)   Oil filter- as described in Section 19
(k)   Spark plugs
(l)   Exhaust manifolds - as described in Chapter 3
(m)   Retaining plate for oil dipstick tube. This is secured to the left-hand cylinder head by one bolt (photo)

8   Ancillary components - removal (engine in situ)

1   If the inlet manifold, cylinder heads, rocker assembly, valves, pistons, timing chain, etc, are to be removed with the engine in the vehicle, a different procedure is called for.
2   Begin by draining the radiator and cylinder block, as described in Chapter 2, and remove the top hose.
3   Disconnect the battery negative terminal.
4   Remove the air cleaner assembly as described in Chapter 3.
5   Disconnect the HT lead to the coil, unclip the distributor cap spring clips, pull off the plug leads from the plugs, unclip the leads from the rocker cover brackets and remove them as one assembly.
6   Disconnect the throttle and choke cables (as applicable) from the left-hand carburettor as described in Chapter 3.

9.2a A single screw retains the crankcase breather filter

7.1d The oil dipstick tube is retained by a plate and bolt

7   Disconnect and remove the fuel feed pipe between the left-hand carburettor and the fuel pump. On later models the fuel pipe to the in-line fuel filter attached to the engine lifting eye needs to be detached.
8   Disconnect the fuel return pipe from the right-hand carburettor.
9   Disconnect and remove the engine breather hoses between the carburettors and rocker covers.
10   Disconnect the brake servo and differential lock actuator vacuum hoses from the inlet manifold.
11   Detach the distributor advance/retard vacuum pipe from the left-hand carburettor.
12   Disconnect the wiring to the transmitters on the inlet manifold, noting which wires fit where.
13   Disconnect the water inlet hoses to the front of the manifold and the two heater hoses from the rear of the inlet manifold.
14   If the overhaul involves removal of the timing cover (ie camshaft removal or timing gear/chain renewal) then the radiator bottom hose, bypass hose, cooling fan (Chapter 2) and the alternator (Chapter 10) will also have to be removed. In addition, remove the power steering pump (if fitted), where applicable the mechanical fuel pump (Chapter 3) and the oil filter.
15   If the cylinder heads are to be removed, the exhaust manifolds (Chapter 3), the alternator (Chapter 10) and the oil dipstick tube retaining plate and bolt must first be removed.

9.2b Disconnect the bypass and heater hoses from the water pump

9   Inlet manifold - removal

1   With the ancillary components removed it is now possible to remove the inlet manifold. For engine overhaul purposes, the carburettors need not be disturbed.
2   Disconnect the following items first if they have not already been removed:
(a)   Distributor advance/retard vacuum pipe. This can be disconnected from the left-hand carburettor and its retaining bracket from the inlet manifold, or from the distributor
(b)   The differential lock actuator vacuum pipe from the inlet manifold union
(c)   The engine breather hoses and flame traps from between the carburettors and rocker covers
(d)   The crankcase breather filter retaining bracket from the rear of the inlet manifold (photo)
(e)   The various transmitter leads, and the EGR valve connections where fitted (see Chapter 3)
(f)   The bypass hoses from the front of the inlet manifold to the water pump and the heater hoses (photo)
3   There are twelve bolts securing the inlet manifold to the cylinder heads. These should be eased off progressively and then removed. The bolts are of differing length so take note of their exact locations.
   Note: Any bolts removed from the cylinder heads or block should have their threads cleaned with a wire brush dipped in paraffin or clean petrol.
   If this cleaning cannot be carried out immediately, it is vital that they are stored in petrol or paraffin as the sealant used when the bolts were originally fitted will tend to harden on exposure to the air making its removal difficult.
4   Move aside the heater hoses and the hose from the water pump, and ease the manifold away from the cylinder head (photo).
5   Before removing the gasket clamps ensure that there is no coolant lying on top of the gasket. Remove the clamps and lift away the

9.4 Lifting the inlet manifold off

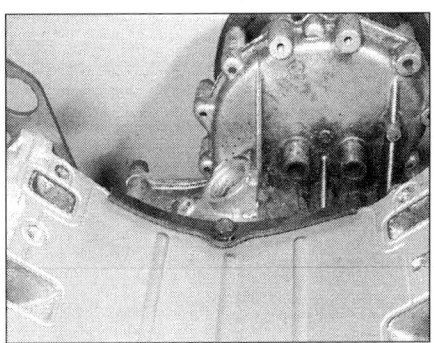

9.5a There is one clamp at each end of the engine

9.5b Removing the rear seal

10.2 Each rocker cover is retained by four cross-head screws

gasket followed by the rubber gasket seals (photos). Although tempting, do not think that you can re-use the gasket, as it is certain to leak.

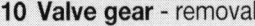
10 Valve gear - removal
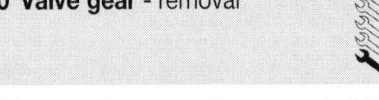

1 This operation covers the removal of the rocker arms and shaft assembly, the pushrods and hydraulic tappets for one cylinder head. Repeat the procedure, if necessary, for the other one. First drain the cooling system, remove the air cleaner and the inlet manifold as already described.
2 Remove the rocker cover, which is retained by four cross-head screws (photo).
3 Undo the four rocker shaft assembly retaining bolts in stages so that the assembly rises evenly on the pressure of the valve springs (photo).
4 Lift out the assembly complete with bolts and place it to one side. Note that the baffle plate will be at the rear of the assembly on the right-hand side and at the front on the left-hand side.
5 Make up a piece of card with 8 numbered holes punched in it. Then remove the pushrods and place them in order through the holes in the card (photo).
6 Take a box and section it into eight compartments. An alternative container is a section of an old egg-tray. Number the sections 1 to 8.

7 Carefully withdraw each tappet and place it in the appropriate section in the container. This operation can be performed in conjunction with the pushrod removal sequence provided the card for the pushrods and the container for the tappets are to hand, as the tappets will usually lift up as the pushrod is carefully pulled upwards and can then be removed more easily (photo).
8 If a tappet is difficult to remove, and the engine is being completely stripped, leave it until the camshaft has been withdrawn and then push it downwards to remove it.

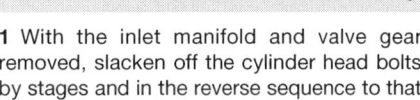
11 Cylinder heads - removal

1 With the inlet manifold and valve gear removed, slacken off the cylinder head bolts by stages and in the reverse sequence to that used for tightening down (see Fig. 1.25).
2 Remove the cylinder head bolts, noting where the three different length bolts fit.
3 Lift the cylinder head straight off and place it to one side. Remove and discard the gasket.
4 Repeat the operation for the other cylinder head if that is also to be removed. If the alternator mounting bracket is left attached to the righthand head, there is no danger of mixing up the two cylinder heads when both are removed for a complete overhaul.

10.3 Each rocker shaft is retained by four bolts (arrowed)

12 Valves - removal

1 Before starting to remove the valves from the cylinder head, take a piece of cardboard and pierce 8 numbered holes in it. If both cylinder heads are being done together then make two such cards and mark one LEFT and the other RIGHT.
2 The procedure for each cylinder head is the same. Start at the front of the head and arrange a valve spring compressor tool over the first valve.
3 Clamp the tool and remove the two split collets, then release the tool (photo).
4 Remove the upper cup, valve springs (or

10.5 Removing a pushrod

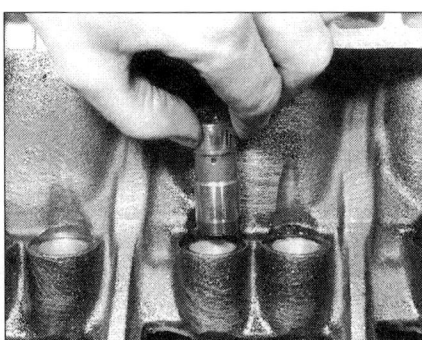

10.7 Removing a tappet

12.3 Clamp the compressor and remove the collets

12.4a Remove the upper cup . . .

12.4b . . . and the valve springs . . .

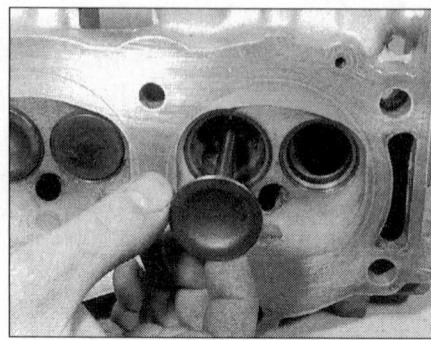

12.4c . . . followed by the valve

spring in later models which only have single valve springs) and valve from the cylinder head (photos).

5 Place the valve in the No 1 hole in the card and the spring(s), collets and upper cup in a suitable container.

6 Remove the rest of the valves in turn in each cylinder head, making sure that they are put into the correct holes in the card for their particular head.

13 Timing cover, chain and gears - removal

1 Having removed all the ancillary components as described in Sections 7 and 8, do not forget to remove the wires from the oil pressure switch if the job is being done with the engine in situ.

2 Begin by removing the starter dog and crankshaft pulley retaining bolt. This requires a deep 1 5/16 inch socket or box spanner. If the engine is in the vehicle, engage bottom low range gear to stop the engine rotating whilst the bolt is undone. If the job is being tackled on the workbench, a plate will have to be made up to lock the flywheel to stop the crankshaft rotating (photo).

3 If the task is being done with the engine in the car without removing the cylinder heads, set the engine so that No 1 piston (front of

left-hand bank) is at TDC on the firing stroke. Rotate the engine and observe the rotor arm of the distributor. When it points to the No 1 cylinder HT lead position the engine is firing on No 1 cylinder. This can be verified by the timing pointer (bracket) which should be in line with the TDC mark on the crankshaft pulley.

4 If the vehicle is fitted with power steering, slacken the power steering pump adjuster bolt, release the tension on the drivebelt and remove it. Remove the power steering pump from its mounting bracket and support it securely within the engine compartment. There is no need to disconnect the hoses from the pump.

5 Pull off the crankshaft pulley. This may require a three-legged puller, but should slide off quite easily by hand (photo).

6 Mark the relationship of the distributor to the timing gear cover, undo the clamp bolt and remove the clamp and the distributor.

7 Undo and remove the two sump bolts which locate in the bottom of the timing cover.

8 Undo and remove the nine bolts which retain the timing cover and remove the complete assembly which includes the water and oil pumps. Be careful not to damage the oil sump gasket. Place the power steering pump mounting brackets to one side, noting where they fit.

9 Remove the old timing cover gasket.

10 Check that the timing marks on the two timing gears are in line.

11 Undo the retaining bolt for the distributor drivegear and remove it and the washer, gear and fuel pump cam (or spacer in later models) from the front end of the camshaft. Make sure that the camshaft does not turn when the bolt is undone (photo).

12 The chain and both chainwheels can now be slid off together from their respective shafts.

13 If the rocker assemblies are to remain in place, **do not** on any account allow the crankshaft or camshaft to be rotated, otherwise damage will be caused by the pistons and valves coming into contact with each other.

14 Camshaft - removal

1 To remove the camshaft first remove the following engine sub-assemblies as already described:

(a) Ancillary components (Section 7 or 8)
(b) Inlet manifold (Section 9)
(c) Valve gear (Section 10)
(d) Timing cover, chain and gears (Section 13)

2 Withdraw the camshaft from the cylinder block. Take care when doing so that the

13.2 Removing the starter dog and crankshaft pulley bolt

13.5 Removing the crankshaft pulley. Note alignment of timing marks

13.11 The distributor drivegear and mechanical fuel pump cam are retained by the bolt and washer to the front of the camshaft

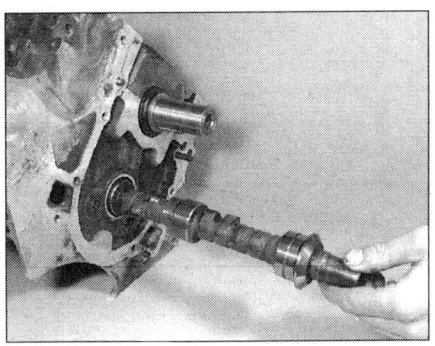

14.2 Withdrawing the camshaft

16.2 Removing the oil pick-up and strainer

16.6 Withdrawing No 1 cylinder connecting rod cap

bearings are not damaged (photo). The bearings cannot be renewed; if they are damaged, a new block will be required.

15 Sump - removal

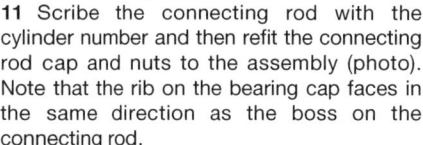

1 Drain the engine oil into a suitable container, having first raised the front of the vehicle if this task is being done with the engine in the vehicle. Make sure that it is adequately supported.
2 Undo the sump retaining bolts either from beneath the car, or tilt the engine onto first one side of the block and then the other to reach all the bolts (engine on the bench).
3 Prise off the sump, but do not use excessive force.
4 Place the sump to one side.
5 Remove the two bolts and withdraw the oil pick-up pipe and strainer if necessary.

16 Pistons and connecting rods - removal

1 To remove the piston and connecting rod assemblies first remove the ancillary components, inlet manifold, valve gear, cylinder heads and sump as already described.
2 Remove the oil pick-up pipe and strainer with the engine lying on one side if the engine is out of the vehicle. Alternatively this operation can be performed from underneath with the engine still in the vehicle (photo).
3 Before the removal operation commences note that the cylinders are numbered from front to rear, even numbers on the right-hand bank and odd numbers on the left-hand bank. The big-end caps for the odd numbered assemblies are on the front of the shared crankshaft journals and the even numbered assemblies fit on the rear of the journals. The big-end caps and con-rods are not marked, so great care must be taken and each connecting rod and cap must be scribed with its appropriate number as it is removed. So

that no confusion can arise, make up two boxes big enough to each take four piston and connecting rod assemblies. Mark one box 2-4-6-8 and the other one 1-3-5-7. Place each assembly in order in its correct box as it is removed.
4 If the operation is being carried out with the engine in the vehicle, the assemblies can be removed from front to rear, starting at No 1 and working through to No 8, since it is easy to withdraw the pistons through the tops of both banks of cylinders with the engine upright.
5 With the engine on the workbench it is easier to work down one side, removing the odd or even numbered assemblies first, and then to turn the cylinder block over onto the other side and repeat the operation for the other cylinder bank. Because of the design of the block it is easier to do one side at a time.
6 Rotate the crankshaft so that the connecting rod cap nuts for No 1 cylinder are easily accessible. Undo and remove the nuts and withdraw the cap (photo).
7 Mark the cap with the appropriate cylinder number.
8 Cut two short lengths of plastic tubing and fit them over the connecting rod bolts so that when the assembly is withdrawn the bolt threads do not damage the journals or cylinder walls (photo).
9 Push the connecting rod and piston assembly up the bore: if necessary tap the end of the connecting rod bolts with the wooden handle of a hammer.

16.8 Protect the connecting rod bolts to damage to the bores

10 Withdraw the piston and connecting rod through the top of the bore, and remove the protective tubing from the bolts.
11 Scribe the connecting rod with the cylinder number and then refit the connecting rod cap and nuts to the assembly (photo). Note that the rib on the bearing cap faces in the same direction as the boss on the connecting rod.
12 Place the assembly in the appropriate box in its correct place.
13 Rotate the crankshaft to reach the next pair of connecting rod cap nuts and repeat the operation as already described for all the other piston and connecting rod assemblies.

17 Flywheel - removal and refitting

1 The flywheel can only be removed with the engine out of the vehicle.
2 If a major engine overhaul is being undertaken, leave the flywheel in position as long as possible as it can be used for stopping the engine rotating whilst the crankshaft pulley bolt is removed, and for rotating the crankshaft to remove the piston and connecting rod assemblies. However, before the starter dog is undone, slightly slacken the flywheel retaining bolts.
3 If the main task, having removed the engine, is to remove the flywheel, then first

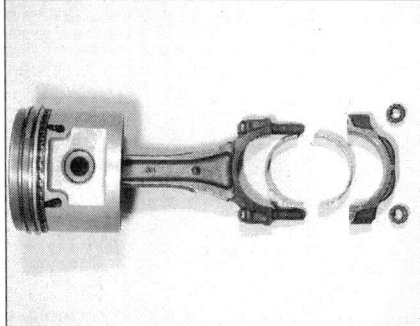

16.11 One complete assembly should contain all these parts

17.4 The flywheel is secured by six bolts

17.7 Insert a wedge (arrowed) to stop the flywheel rotating

18.4 Removing the centre main bearing with special flanged bearing shell

remove the clutch assembly as described in Chapter 5.

4 Undo and remove the 6 retaining bolts and then remove the flywheel (photo). Be careful, it is heavy!

5 When refitting the flywheel it will be found that the bolt holes are offset so that it cannot be fitted incorrectly.

6 Offer the flywheel to the spigot end of the crankshaft with the starter ring gear towards the engine and align the holes.

7 Fit all the 6 bolts and screw them in. Before finally tightening them to the specified torque, take up any clearance by rotating the flywheel against the direction of rotation of the engine. Make up a wedge or bracket to stop the assembly rotating when the bolts are tightened (photo).

18.6 Lift the crankshaft straight out

18 Crankshaft - removal

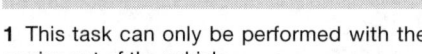

1 This task can only be performed with the engine out of the vehicle.

2 Strip the engine completely as described in the previous Sections so that only the crankshaft remains in the cylinder block.

3 Undo the main bearing cap retaining bolts.

4 Remove the bearing caps and bolts together with the lower bearing shells. Note that the first four caps are numbered from the front 1-2-3-4. The rear one, which is larger and easily identified, is not marked. The caps also have arrows on them which point to the front of the engine (photo).

5 The rear cap will have to be eased out as it also forms part of the rear oil seal construction.

6 Hold the crankshaft at both ends and lift it out carefully. The later lip type rear oil seal will come out with it (photo).

7 Remove the upper bearing shells from the bearing seats. Note that the centre bearing (No 3) has a flanged shell as this bearing takes the endthrust of the crankshaft (photo). Identify the shells if they are to be re-used.

8 Remove the lower bearing shells from the bearing caps only if they are to be renewed (photo).

19 Oil pump and oil filter - removal and refitting

1 In the course of a major engine overhaul the oil pump will be removed as part of the timing cover assembly and can then be removed and overhauled on the bench. This procedure covers the removal and refitting of the oil filter and oil pump independently during servicing or overhaul.

Oil filter

2 Two types of oil filter are fitted. The early type has a hexagonal nut on the end and the later one is plain, but it also has an internal relief valve. The two types are not interchangeable.

3 Unscrew the oil filter. The early type with the nut can be undone by a spanner, whereas the later type will require a filter wrench.

4 Take care when removing the filter as it will be full of oil.

5 Remove the sealing ring and discard it.

6 Do not delay in fitting a new filter, as the oil may drain out of the pump which will then have to be removed and primed as described below.

7 Fit a new sealing ring to the new oil filter and screw it on by hand until the filter and sealing ring touch the oil pump mating face. Screw it on another half turn **only** by hand. It is extremely important not to overtighten the

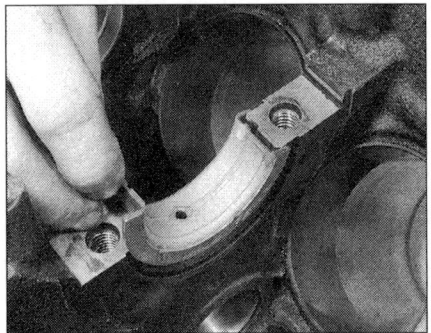

18.7 Removing the centre main bearing upper shell

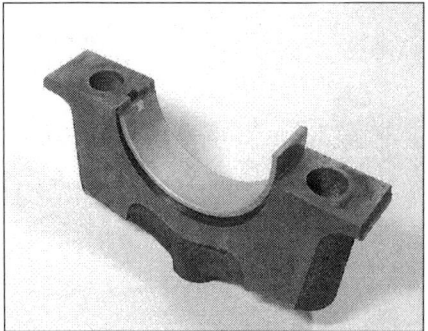

18.8 Lower main bearing shell freed from its cap

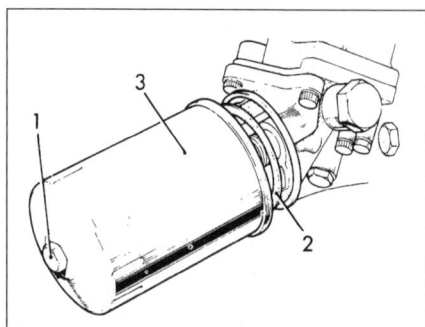

Fig. 1.4 Oil filter – early type (Sec 19)

1 Hexagonal nut   2 Sealing ring   3 Filter

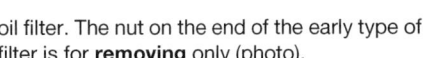

19.7 Fitting a new oil filter (later type)

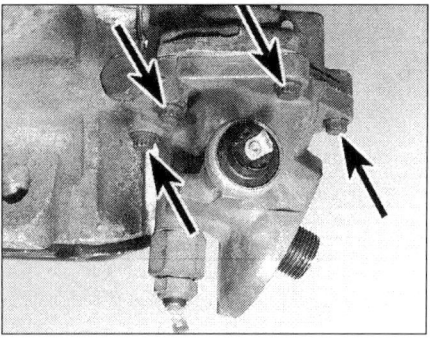

19.11 The oil pump cover is retained by 6 special bolts (4 of them arrowed here)

19.13 Sliding out the pump gears

oil filter. The nut on the end of the early type of filter is for **removing** only (photo).

8 If the oil in the sump has not been changed, then check the level on the dipstick after the engine is next run and top up as necessary.

Oil pump

9 Remove the oil filter as described above. If the same filter is to be re-used, do not allow it to drain.

10 Disconnect the electrical connector from the pressure switch.

11 Release the special bolts securing the pump cover. Place an oil tray underneath. Remove the bolts and cover (photo).

12 Remove and discard the old cover gasket.

13 Slide out the pump gears (photo).

14 When refitting use a new gasket, placing it on the pump cover.

15 Pack the pump housing with petroleum jelly (no other type of grease will do).

16 Locate the pump gears into their correct positions, ensuring that the petroleum jelly is filling every visible cavity. If the pump is not completely packed with jelly then the pump may not prime itself when the engine is restarted (photo).

17 Offer up the pump cover to the body and locate it in position. Have the special fixing bolts handy, refit them and finger tighten.

18 Finally tighten all the securing bolts evenly, working in alternate sequence to a final torque figure as given in the Specifications.

19 Check the oil level in the sump and top up as necessary.

20 Engine components - examination for wear

When the engine has been stripped down and all parts properly cleaned, decisions have to be made as to what needs renewal and the following sections tell the examiner what to look for. In any borderline case it is always best to decide in favour of a new part. Even if a part may be serviceable its life will have been reduced by wear and the degree of trouble needed to replace it in the future must be taken into consideration. However, these things are relative and it depends on whether a quick 'survival' job is being done or whether the vehicle as a whole is being regarded as having many thousands of miles of useful and economical life remaining.

The Sections which follow consider the examination and renovation of the various components.

21 Rocker shaft assemblies - inspection and overhaul

1 With the rocker shaft assemblies removed from the vehicle the first job is to inspect the rockers and shafts for wear, in order to determine whether the assemblies need to be stripped and overhauled.

2 Take one assembly at a time and do not mix up left and right-hand assemblies. The shafts are handed and can only fit one way.

3 First examine the rockers. The rockers themselves are alloy but they have hardened inserts at each end. The pads bear on the ends of the valve stems and the cups fit over the upper ends of the pushrods. With high mileage or hard wear the hardened cup inserts tend to crack up and wear badly. If bad wear is evident in a cup then the pushrod will be badly worn as well. Similarly the pads will wear and if this is noticeable the rockers need renewing (photo).

4 Check the amount of lateral movement of the rockers on the shafts. If play is evident then look further. Slide the rockers along the shaft against their springs and examine the rocker shaft itself. If this is done from above only, the wear pattern on the rocker shaft may be missed as the wear occurs on the underside of the shaft: the rockers cut into the shaft under pressure from the valves and pushrods below. With high mileage engines or those which have been used for hard work, or where there has been a lack of oil being fed to the top of the engine, the amount of wear can be quite severe (photo).

5 Remove the pedestal bolts and slide the pedestals along the shaft. Check for wear in the pedestal/shaft contact areas.

19.16 Packing the pump housing with petroleum jelly

21.3 New rocker (left) compared with old one (right). Note damage to cup

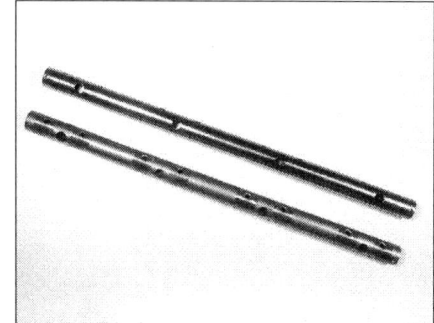

21.4 Worn (bottom) and new (top) rocker shafts being compared

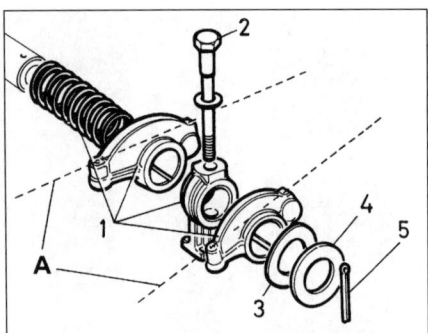

Fig. 1.5 Dotted lines (A) indicating slope of rocker arms away from the pedestals (Sec 21)

1 Pedestal, rocker   3 Wave washer
  arms and spring   4 Plain washer
2 Bolt   5 Split pin

6 To overhaul the rocker shaft assembly proceed as follows. Remove the split pin from one end of the rocker shaft and slide off the components carefully retaining them in the correct order of sequence for reassembly, as follows: split pin, plain washer, wave washer, rocker arm, pedestal, rocker and spring (photos).

7 If new rocker arms are being fitted ensure that the protective coating material used in storage is removed from the oil holes, and the new rocker given a smearing of clean oil before fitting to the shaft.

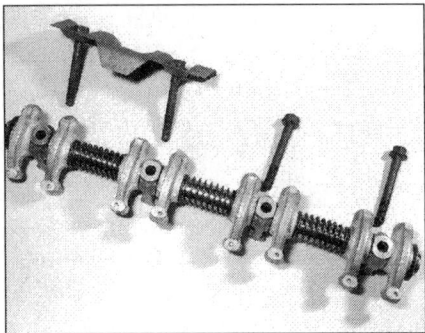

21.9 Rocker shaft assembly laid out prior to refitting to engine

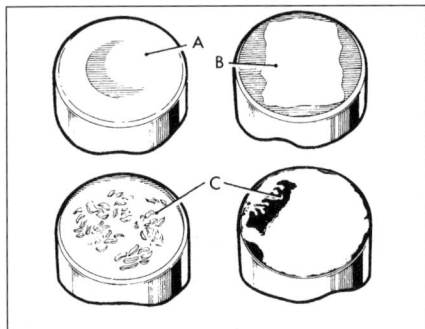

Fig. 1.6 Tappet wear patterns (Sec 22)

A Correct rotating wear pattern
B Wear pattern for non-rotating tappet
C Typical examples of excessive wear

21.6a Refit split pin, plain washer and wave washer – notch uppermost

Note: *The rocker arms are handed each side of the pedestals, and must be fitted correctly so that the metal pads locate over the valve stems. The valve ends of the rocker arms should slope away from the pedestals as shown by the dotted lines in Fig. 1.5.*

8 The rocker shafts are notched at one end to ensure that the oil feed holes are positioned correctly facing upwards. The notches must be located uppermost. On the right-hand bank (viewed from the driver's seat) the notch must be facing towards the front of the engine, and on the left-hand bank it must be facing towards the rear of the engine. Always use new split pins.

9 Refit the baffle plate and pedestal bolts to the shaft. Note that the plate fits at the opposite end of the shaft to the notch (photo).

10 The rocker shaft assembly is now ready for refitting. Carry out the same inspection and overhaul procedure for the other assembly.

22 Tappets and pushrods - inspection

1 If an hydraulic tappet has to be removed downwards then there is a good chance that the lower end has become belled or rimmed. Inspect and renew if wear is bad.

2 If there is a prominent wear pattern just above the lower end of the body, this should

22.5 Check the pushrod seat in the top of the tappet

only merit renewal of the tappet if it is badly grooved or scored. This condition is caused by the side thrust of the cam against the body whilst the tappet moves vertically in its guide.

3 Inspect the tappet inner and outer surfaces for blow holes and scoring. Renew the tappet if the body is roughly grooved or scored, or has a blow hole extending through the wall.

4 Inspect the tappet/camshaft lobe contact area. Fit a new tappet if the surface is badly worn or damaged. The tappet must rotate as it moves up and down and should produce an even circular wear pattern.

If the tappet has not been rotating the wear pattern will be square with a dip in the centre. Non-rotating tappets must be renewed. Check the wear on the camshaft lobe if there is a non-rotating tappet. When renewing a tappet check that it moves freely in the guide in the cylinder block.

5 Check the pushrod contact end of the tappet for roughness or damage. If either sorts of wear are apparent then the tappet must be renewed (photo).

6 Check the pushrods. Firstly ensure that they are all straight. If any one is bent or distorted, renew it.

7 Check the ends of each pushrod. If the ball end or seat is rough, damaged or badly worn, it must be renewed. If one pushrod is discovered that is badly worn and you have not rejected either the rocker or tappet for that rod, then check the tappet and/or rocker again (photo).

21.6b Then refit two rockers with pedestal between – note relationship of valve bearing faces away from pedestal

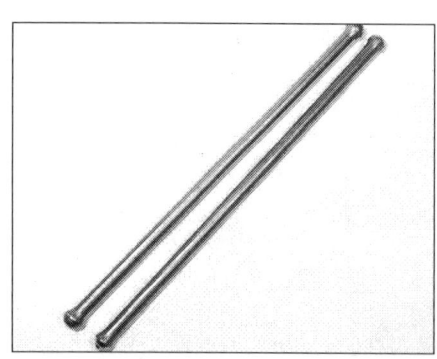

22.7 Comparing the badly worn end of the old pushrod (right) with a new one

23 Camshaft - inspection

1 Thoroughly clean the camshaft and dry off, handling with care.
2 Examine all the bearing surfaces for obvious defects, wear, score marks, etc.
3 Similarly inspect the cam lobes for excessive wear.
4 Ensure that the key or keyway is not damaged or burred and that the key is a tight fit in its keyway.
5 If in doubt seek professional advice and/or replace with a new component.
6 The camshaft bearings in the cylinder block are not renewable. If they are badly worn or damaged, a new block will be required.

24 Cylinder heads - inspection and overhaul

1 This section covers the cleaning/decarbonising of the cylinder heads and valves, the examination and recutting of valve seats, and valve seat insert renewal. Tackle one cylinder head at a time.

Cylinder head

2 Thoroughly clean the cylinder heads using paraffin, or a mixture of paraffin and petrol, and dry off.
3 Clean the combustion chambers and ports using a brass wire brush. Draw clean rag through each valve guide bore.
4 Wash or, using a tyre pump, blow away all loose carbon particles.
5 Check the fit of the valves in their guides. If appreciable lateral movement of the valve in the guide is possible, new valves and/or

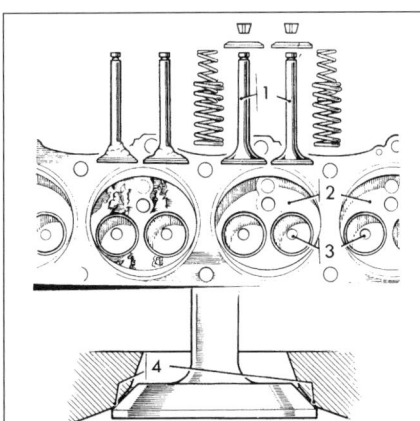

Fig. 1.7 Cylinder heads and valves – inspection and cleaning (Sec 24)

1 Valves
2 Combustion chambers
3 Valve guide bores
4 Valve and seat should meet at the outer edge

guides are required. (New valves can be fitted without renewing the guides, but not vice versa). The fitting of new valve guides should be left to your Rover dealer.

Valve seats - recutting and valve seat insert fitting

6 Having examined the valves and valve seats and discovered that the seats are badly worn or pitted then the seats will have to be recut. If, however, the valve seats are so worn that they cannot be recut then it will be necessary to fit new valve seat inserts. These latter two jobs should be entrusted to the local Rover agent. In practice it is seldom that the seats are so badly worn that they require renewal. Normally, it is the exhaust valve that is too badly worn, and the owner can easily purchase a new set of valves and match them to the seats by valve grinding.

Valve cleaning

7 Clean the valves. Remove all the hard carbon deposit from the tops and underside using a blunt knife blade. Care should be taken not to mark or score the valve seating faces. Finish off the valve cleaning with a soft wire brush, again exercising care not to touch the seat face or valve stems.

25 Valves - examination and grinding-in

Examination

1 Examine the heads of the valves for pitting and burning especially the heads of the exhaust valves. The valve seating should be examined at the same time. If the pitting on valve and seat is very slight, the marks can be removed by grinding the seats and valves together with coarse, and then fine grading paste. Where bad pitting has occurred to the valve seats it will be necessary to recut them and fit new valves as described in the last Section. If however the valves and valve seats require grinding-in to remove pitting or slight wear, or if new valves are being fitted to the original seats, then follow the instructions below.

Grinding-in

2 Support the head on wooden blocks and start with No 1 valve.

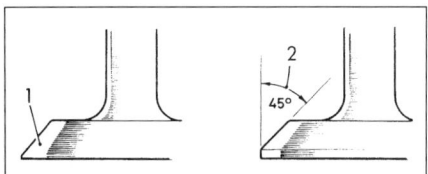

Fig. 1.8 Valve grinding and valve faces (Sec 25)

1 If a valve has to be reground like this – renew It
2 Valve face correct angle

3 Smear a trace of coarse or medium carborundum paste on the seat face and apply a suction grinder tool to the valve head. With a semi-rotary motion, grind the valve head to its seat, lifting the valve occasionally to redistribute the grinding paste. When a dull matt even surface finish is produced on both the valve seat and the valve, then wipe off the paste and repeat the process with fine carborundum paste, lifting and turning the valve to redistribute the paste as before.

> **HAYNES HiNT** *A light spring placed under the valve head will greatly ease the grinding-in operation.*

4 When a smooth unbroken ring of light grey matt finish is produced, on both valve and valve seat faces, the grinding operation is completed. Carefully clean away every trace of grinding compound, taking great care to leave none in the ports or in the valve guides. Clean the valves and valve seats with a paraffin soaked rag then with a clean rag. If an air line is available, blow the valves, valve guides and valve parts clean.
5 Finally give the cylinder head a rinse in clean paraffin to remove any remaining traces of valve grinding paste. Discard this paraffin, and dry the head with a clean non-fluffy rag.
6 Draw clean rag through each guide bore.

26 Timing cover oil seal - renewal

1 The timing cover casing need not be removed in order to remove and insert the oil seal of the later 'lip' type. For the earlier type the timing cover must be removed first. Refer to Section 42 for details of renewing the earlier type of seal.
2 If the later type seal is to be renewed with the cover in situ, then take care to prevent damaging the cover when extracting the old seal.
3 Follow the instructions given in Section 13 for removal of the crankshaft pulley. Then undo the ring of self-tapping screws and withdraw the mud shield from the front of the cover (photo).

26.3 Undo the screws and remove the mud shield

26.7 Offer up a new seal

26.8 Using a suitable piece of tube to drive the seal into position

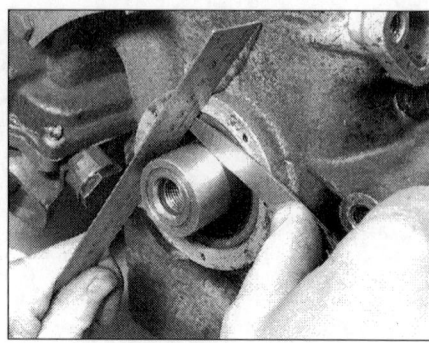

26.9 Checking the seating depth of the oil seal

4 Drill two small holes on opposite sides of the front face of the seal and screw in two self-tapping screws, leaving enough of each screw sticking out so that it can be gripped with a pair of pliers. The seal can then be worked out of the front cover.

5 Where the timing cover has to be removed then drive the seal out from the cover squarely, having removed the mud shield.

6 After extracting the old seal, clean the housing and remove any burrs on the front edge.

7 Lubricate the new seal and fit it squarely with the lip face leading (photo).

8 Drive the seal carefully into position with a suitable drift. A flat block of wood and a hammer are ideal if the cover has been removed. Otherwise a large socket or similar object can be used (photo).

9 Check that the seal is seated to the correct depth and is square with the casing using a straight-edge as a guide. It should be 1.5 mm (0.062 in) below the front edge of the cover (photo).

10 Refit the mud shield and secure it with the ring of self-tapping screws.

27 Timing gears and chain - inspection

1 Examine the teeth on the camshaft and crankshaft gearwheels. If they are worn they should be renewed.

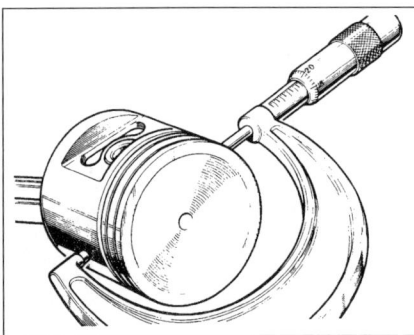

Fig. 1.9 Checking the piston diameter using a micrometer (Sec 28)

2 Inspect the camshaft wheel for signs of cracking.

3 Inspect the chain for wear, and the links for slackness. There should be no undue slackness in the chain. When the timing cover is removed during the overhaul procedure the chain should not have any 'sag' in it. There are no chain tensioners, and a slack chain could jump off the gearwheels. Renew the chain if necessary.

28 Pistons and connecting rods - inspection and overhaul

1 The condition of the pistons, rings, and the big-end bearings and small end bushes will be governed by many factors, but principally:
(a) The total mileage covered by the vehicle
(b) The maintenance of oil level and regular oil and filter changes and usage to which the vehicle has been subjected

2 The home mechanic is advised that to assess the true condition of these components, he must be in possession of, or have access to, certain professional equipment and tools. For instance, the gudgeon pin has to be removed by means of an hydraulic press or ram that will exert a pressure of not less than 8 tons (8128 kg). A micrometer especially constructed for measurement of cylinder bore wear and ovality and a normal micrometer capable of encircling a piston to assess the degree of piston wear will also be required.

3 'Standard' size pistons are available in five grades (see Specifications). The grade originally fitted is marked by matching letters stamped on the piston crown and cylinder block face.

4 If fitting new pistons to a standard size bore, select the appropriate grade of piston to give the specified piston-to-bore clearance. Note that the wear ridge at the top of the bore must be removed, or the top piston ring must be stepped, in order to avoid the top piston ring hitting the wear ridge and breaking.

5 Where the same pistons are to be refitted, then they must be marked to correspond with their respective connecting rods, and cylinder bore positions.

6 If new rings are to be fitted, this can be achieved without removing the pistons from their connecting rods.

7 Carefully remove the piston rings and retain in sequence.

8 Clean all the carbon deposits from the piston head. Clean out the ring grooves using a piece of a broken piston ring as a scraper. Protect your fingers - piston rings are sharp! Take care not to scratch the piston during this operation.

9 Examine the piston carefully for any scoring of the bearing surfaces, cracking or chipping particularly at the skirt. Examine the crown for dents or marks caused by foreign objects in the combustion chamber or broken rings, plug electrodes, etc. Rings that have been broken in the bore during running will have caused damage to the grooves in the piston, making the rings sloppy through having excessive clearance in the grooves. Damaged or faulty pistons of this nature should be renewed. It is also possible that broken rings will have scratched the cylinder wall - in bad cases this will necessitate a rebore. Refer to Section 32.

10 If the engine has been rebored then oversize pistons of 0.010 in (0.25 mm) and 0.020 in (0.50 mm) are available.

11 Examine the connecting rods carefully. They are not subject to wear, but in extreme cases such as partial engine seizure they could be distorted. Such conditions may be visually apparent, but if doubt exists they should be changed or checked for alignment by engine reconditioning specialists.

29 Piston rings - fitting

Note: *If fitting new piston rings in worn bores, either the top ring must be stepped or the wear ridge at the top of the cylinder bore must be removed. If one of these conditions is not met the new ring may hit the wear ridge and break.*

1 When fitting new rings it is advisable to remove the glaze from the cylinder bores. It is strongly advised that the deglazed bore

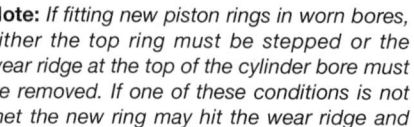

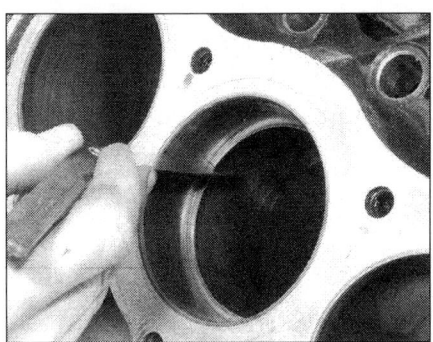

29.5 Checking the piston ring gap in the cylinder bore

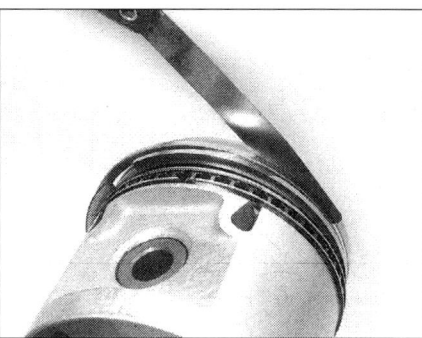

29.6 Checking the piston ring gap in the groove

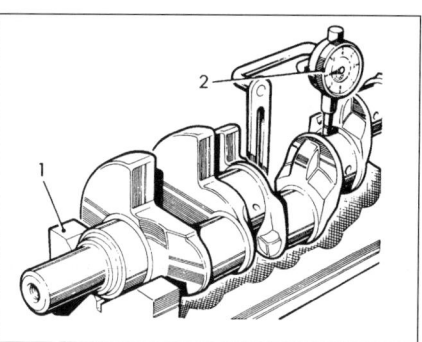

Fig. 1.10 Checking the crankshaft for straightness (Sec 30)

1 Vee block   2 Dial gauge

should have a cross hatch finish (diamond pattern) and should be carried out in such a way as not to increase the bore size in any way. This cross hatch finish provides the cylinder walls with good oil retention properties.

2 The top compression ring on early models must be fitted with the *T* or *Top* marking facing uppermost (inner bevel downwards). Later models have a plain top compression ring which is unmarked and can be fitted either way up. The second compression ring is of the stepped type and must only be fitted from the top of the piston. The second compression ring is marked *T* or *Top* and it is this side of the ring which must face uppermost.

3 The special oil control ring needs no gapping, but care must be taken to ensure that the ends of the expander, (fitted first), do not overlap but just abut each other. Fit the rails, one at a time, making sure that they locate snugly within the piston groove.

4 Fit the rings by holding them open, using both hands, thumbs at the gaps with fingers around the outer edges, easing them open enough to slip over the piston top and straight to the groove in which they belong. Use feeler gauges or strips of tin as guides to prevent the rings dropping into the wrong groove. Do not twist the rings whilst doing this or they will snap.

5 Before fitting however, a word on gapping. Push a compression ring down the cylinder bore using a piston to position it squarely at about 1 in (25 mm) below the top of the block and measure the piston ring gap with a feeler gauge (photo). The gap should be within the limits given in the Specifications. If required, file the gap using a flat fine cut file. Exercise care and judgement not to overdo it. Refit the ring, square off with the piston as before and re-measure. Repeat the process until correct. If the gap is too big initially then a new ring will be required.

6 Once the rings have been fitted to the piston, then the vertical clearance in the groove should be checked (photo). The correct clearance is given in the Specifications.

7 Fit the compression rings so that the gap in

each ring is diametrically opposite, and the oil control ring so that its gap appears on the same side between gudgeon pin and the piston thrust face but staggered. Locate the rail ring gaps approximately 1 in (25 mm) either side of the expander join. This will ensure good compression.

30 Crankshaft - inspection

1 With the crankshaft suitably mounted on V blocks at No 1 and 5 main bearing journals, give a thorough visual check for scoring of, or white metal sticking to, the journals. Heavy scoring indicates that the crankshaft should be reground.

2 Check using a dial test indicator (Fig. 1.10) as follows:

(a) The run-out at main journals 2, 3 and 4
(b) Note the relative eccentricity of each journal to the others
(c) The maximum indication should come at nearly the same angular location on all journals

3 With an engineer's micrometer check, each journal for ovality. If this proves to be in excess of the specified maximum, the crankshaft must be reground.

4 Undersize bearings are available in four sizes as listed in the Specifications.

31 Crankshaft main and big-end bearing clearances

Crankshaft bearings (big-end and main) should only be re-used if they are known to have done a very low mileage only (less than 15 000 miles). As replacement bearings are relatively cheap it is false economy to refit the old ones. Where the condition of the bearings and journals was so bad that the crankshaft has to be reground, new bearings of the correct undersize will be provided by the firm which carried out the regrinding.

If new bearings of standard size are being fitted, or if for some reason you do not know

which undersize bearings should be used the following paragraphs detail a method of establishing bearing clearance, and therefore correct bearing size.

1 Use Plastigage to measure the bearing clearances.

2 Before using Plastigage, all the parts to be measured must be clean, dry and free from oil.

3 With a piece of the Plastigage laid on the top of each main bearing journal, (Fig. 1.11), refit the bearing caps as though reassembling. The inner bearing shells must be in position as well.

4 The crankshaft rear oil seals should not be fitted during this operation.

5 Tighten all bolts to the correct torque as listed in the Specifications. **Do not** rotate the crankshaft.

6 Remove the main bearing caps - the Plastigage will be found sticking to either the journal or the shell face. *Do not remove it.*

7 With the scale provided, measure the compressed piece of Plastigage on each bearing at its widest point.

8 The graduation number that most closely corresponds to this width indicates the bearing clearance in thousandths of an inch.

9 The clearance of a new main bearing is given in the Specifications.

10 Wipe off the Plastigage with an oily rag. **Do not** scrape it off.

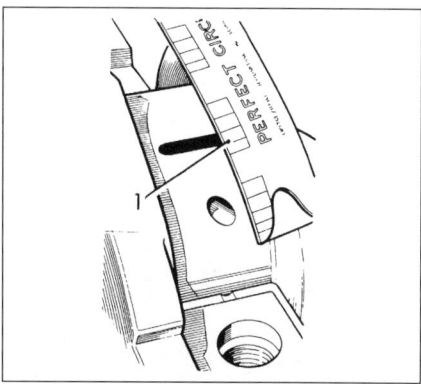

Fig. 1.11 Use Plastigage (1) to check the bearing clearances (Sec 31)

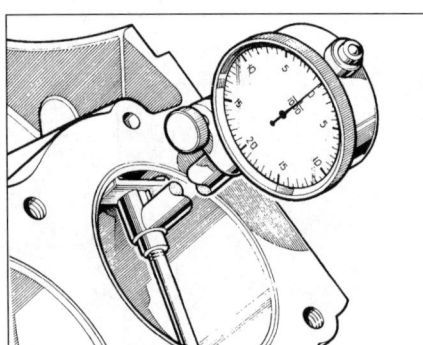

Fig. 1.12 Measuring the cylinder bore with a micrometer (Sec 32)

11 To check the big-end bearing clearances, refit the connecting rod and inner shell to the appropriate crankshaft journal. Ensure it is the right way round.

12 Place a piece of Plastigage over the centre of the exposed half of the journal.

13 Refit the bearing cap, outer shell and nuts. Tighten them to the specified torque. **Do not** rotate the crankshaft.

14 Remove the bearing cap and shell and measure the Plastigage as described above.

15 The correct clearance for a new big-end bearing is given in the Specifications. If the bearings being checked are the ones that were removed earlier, they must be renewed if the clearance is greater than 0.003 in (0.08 mm).

16 Wipe off the Plastigage using an oily rag. It must not be scraped off.

32 Cylinder block and crankcase - inspection

1 The cylinder bores must be examined for taper, ovality, scoring and scratches. Start by carefully examining the top of the cylinder bores. If they are at all worn a very slight ridge will be found on the thrust side. This marks the top of the piston ring travel. The owner will have a good indication of the bore wear prior to dismantling the engine, or removing the cylinder head. Excessive oil consumption accompanied by blue smoke from the exhaust is a sure sign of worn cylinder bores and piston rings.

2 Measure the bore diameter just under the ridge with a bore micrometer, at right-angles to the gudgeon pin and about 1 1/2 to 2 in (40 to 50 mm) below the top of the block face.

3 Measure the dimension of the piston, also at right-angles to the gudgeon pin, at the top of the skirt.

4 The piston must be smaller than the bore diameter by the amount given in the Specifications for piston skirt clearance in the bore.

5 If the bores are slightly worn but not so badly worn as to justify reboring them, then special oil control rings and pistons can be fitted which will restore compression and stop the engine burning oil. Several different types are available and the manufacturer's instructions concerning their fitting must be followed closely.

6 Deglaze the bores with a hone or abrasive paper if reboring is not being carried out. See Section 29 for details.

7 If the engine is rebored, the crankshaft main bearing caps must be in position and tightened to the specified torque during the reboring process.

8 Examine the crankcase for cracks and leaking core plugs. To renew a core plug, drill a hole in its centre and tap a thread in it. Screw in a bolt and using a distance piece, tighten the bolt and extract the core plug. When fitting the new plug, smear its outer edge with gasket cement.

9 Probe oil galleries and waterways with a piece of wire to make sure that they are quite clear.

33 Sump - overhaul

1 Thoroughly clean the exterior, removing all traces of encrusted road dirt.

2 Wash the sump interior with paraffin, brushing out any sludge which may be there.

3 With the sump now perfectly clean, carefully scrape off the remains of the sump gasket.

4 Similarly clean the mating surface of the crankcase, paying particular attention to the joints between the timing cover and cylinder block.

5 Renew the sump if it is cracked or badly dented.

34 Oil pump - inspection and overhaul

If the car has covered a high mileage then be prepared to renew all the working parts contained in the oil pump.

1 First clean all the components as they are dismantled.

2 Visually check the gears for obvious scoring or chipping of the teeth. Renew if they are in poor condition (photo).

3 Now work on the components contained within the cover.

4 Dismantle the pressure relief valve and inspect it for excessive wear and/or scoring (photo).

5 Pay special attention to the pressure relief valve spring. Note whether it shows signs of wear on its sides or whether it is on the point of collapse, if not collapsed.

6 Thoroughly clean the gauze filter housed within the relief valve bore.

7 Test the valve in its bore in the cover; it should have no more clearance than to make it an easy sliding fit. If any side movement is obviously apparent, then the valve and/or cover will have to be renewed.

8 With earlier engines, inspect the oil filter bypass valve located in the pump cover. Prise out the seat and withdraw the valve and spring. Check the valve for cracks, nicks or scoring.

9 Wash the stripped casting in clean paraffin or petrol. Dry with a clean rag. Smear parts with clean engine oil before reassembly.

10 With the gears refitted in the pump housing, check the pump gear endfloat (photo). Lay a straight-edge across the two gear wheels and with a feeler gauge, measure the clearance between the straight-edge and the surface of the front cover. The clearance should be within the specified limits. If the

34.2 Visually check the condition of the gears

34.4 Inspect the pressure relief valve assembly

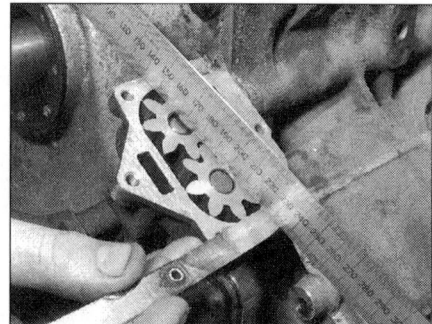

34.10 Checking the pump gear endfloat

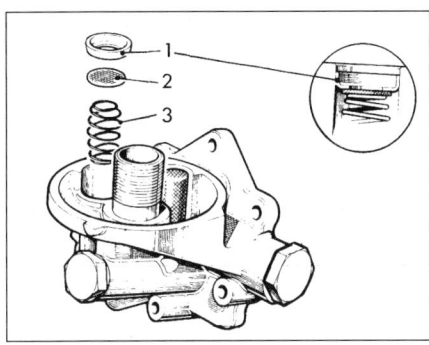

Fig. 1.13 Oil filter bypass valve (early engines) (Sec 34)

1 Seat   2 Valve   3 Spring

measurement is less than the minimum specified, inspect the front cover recess for signs of wear.

11 Reassemble the relief valve components, and the bypass valve assembly on earlier models.

12 Lubricate the relief valve and fit it into its bore, then insert the relief valve spring. Fit the washer to the plug and screw it home. Tighten it to the specified torque.

13 Insert the bypass spring into its bore, place the valve on the spring and press in the valve seat with its concave face outwards. The outer rim should be located 0.020 to 0.040 in (0.5 to 1.0 mm) below the surface of the bore.

35 Flywheel - inspection and refacing

1 Remove the flywheel as described in Section 17.

2 Two different types of flywheel are fitted to the Range Rover. They are identified by the thickness of the starter ring gear - see Specifications.

3 Examine the surface of the flywheel which mates with the clutch driven plate. If this is scored or shows signs of many small cracks then it must be refaced or renewed.

4 To determine whether the flywheel can be

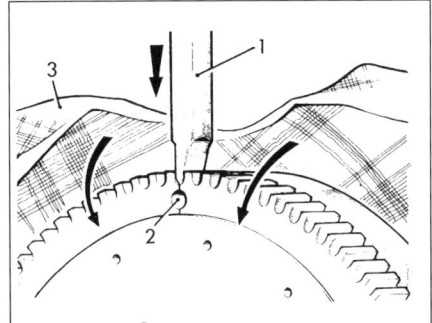

Fig. 1.15 Starter ring gear renewal (Sec 36)

1 Cold chisel   3 Protective cloth
2 Drilled hole

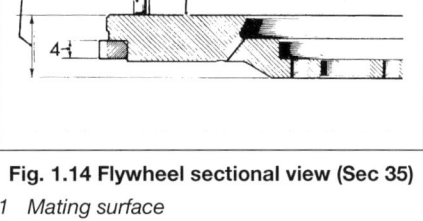

Fig. 1.14 Flywheel sectional view (Sec 35)

1 Mating surface
2 Dowel
3 Overall flywheel thickness
4 Starter ring gear thickness

refaced, check its overall thickness. If it is less than the minimum specified, it is not possible to reface it.

5 If the flywheel is thicker than the above dimensions then it can be refaced. The dowels must be removed and it must be refaced over the complete surface.

6 When the refacing has been carried out, check the flywheel thickness once more. If the refacing has taken the overall thickness below the minimum specified, then it must be renewed.

36 Starter ring gear - renewal

1 With the flywheel removed from the engine, drill a small hole approximately 0.375 in (10 mm) laterally across the starter ring gear. Take care not to allow the drill to enter or score the flywheel or flange. The hole should be made between the root of any gear teeth. This will weaken the ring gear and facilitate removal by breaking with a cold chisel (Fig. 1.15).

2 Hold the flywheel in a soft jawed vice.

⚠️ ***Warning: Beware of flying fragments. A piece of cloth draped over the whole assembly will protect the operator from possible injury.***

3 Split the starter ring gear with a hammer and chisel.

36.7 Starter ring gear in position on flywheel

4 The new starter ring gear must be heated uniformly. The expansion of the metal permits it to fit over the flywheel and against the flange. Heat to between 338 degrees and 347 degrees Fahrenheit (170 and 175 degrees Centigrade). **Do not exceed the specified temperature.**

5 Place the flywheel on a flat surface with the flanged side downwards.

6 Offer up the heated ring to the flywheel with the chamfered inner diameter downwards, pressing it firmly against the flange until the ring contracts sufficiently to grip the flywheel.

7 Allow cooling to take place naturally and do not attempt to hasten cooling in any way as this could cause weakening by setting up internal stresses in the ring gear, leading to later break-up. Where the ring gear is chamfered on both sides it may be fitted either way round (photo).

37 Crankshaft spigot bearing - renewal

1 The spigot bearing, which is located in the rear end of the crankshaft and carries the front end of the gearbox input shaft, can only be removed when the engine is out of the vehicle.

2 With the engine removed from the vehicle, first remove the clutch assembly as described in Chapter 5.

3 Remove the old bearing which is a push fit into the crankshaft end flange.

4 Push in the new bearing which should finish flush with the end face of the crankshaft. Below this level is acceptable provided it does not recess more than 0.063 in (1.6 mm). (See Fig. 1.16).

5 The inside diameter of the bearing should be 0.7504 + 0.001 in (19.177 + 0.025 mm). Reamer out if necessary.

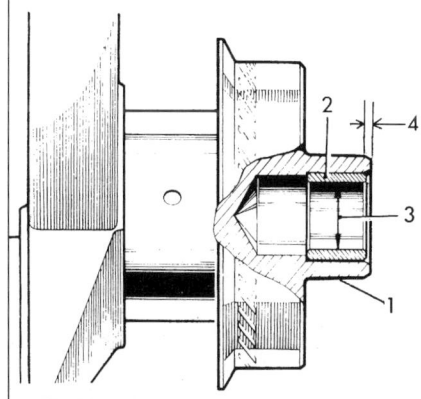

Fig. 1.16 Spigot bearing location (Sec 37)

1 End of crankshaft
2 Spigot bearing
3 Inside diameter of bearing
4 Maximum seating position below end face of crankshaft

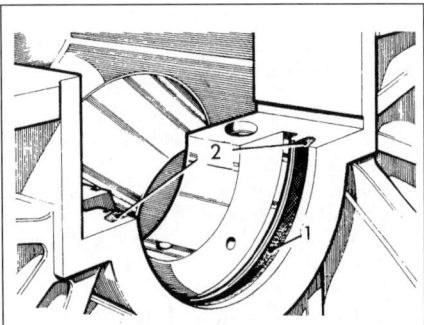

Fig.1.17 A new half oil seal (early type) fitted to the crankcase (Sec 39)

1 Oil seal   2 Seal ends trimmed off

38 Engine reassembly - general

To ensure maximum life with minimum trouble from a rebuilt engine, not only must everything be correctly assembled, but everything must be spotlessly clean, all the oilways must be clear, locking washers and spring washers must always be fitted where indicated and all bearing and other working surfaces must be thoroughly lubricated during assembly.

Before assembly begins renew any bolts or studs, the threads of which are in any way damaged, and whenever possible use new spring washers.

Gather together a torque wrench, oil can and clean rag, also a set of engine gaskets, crankshaft front and rear oil seals and a new oil filter element.

39 Crankshaft, main bearings and rear oil seal - refitting

1 Fit the upper main bearing shells to the crankcase. The inner shells have oil holes and grooves. Make sure that the tongue locates in the slot in the crankcase (photo).
2 The centre main bearing (No 3) has a

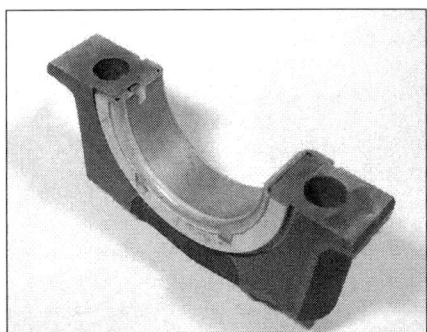

39.10 The tags must locate in the grooves. This is the flanged shell for No 3 bearing

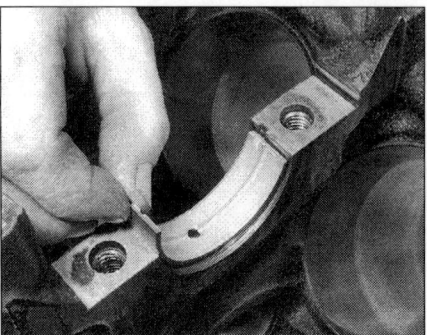

39.1 Refitting a main bearing upper shell

special flanged bearing shell as it takes the crankshaft endthrust.
3 There are two different types of rear oil seal fitted to the Range Rover engine. The earlier type consists of a rubber strip in two halves; one half is embedded into a groove in the crankcase (behind the rear main bearing location) and the other half is embedded into a groove in the combined oil seal carrier and rear main bearing cap. Later models have a standard round lip type oil seal which is clamped in place by the rear main bearing cap. Both types also incorporate rubber strip seals in the side faces of the rear main bearing cap, although they are of different design. The early type have a single straight strip whereas the later ones are of a cruciform pattern.
4 In the earlier type engines the oil seal has by its design to be fitted in two operations, one before the crankshaft is refitted and one after. The later type is fitted after the crankshaft has been refitted.

Early models

5 Fit a new half oil seal to the crankcase groove. The ends should project above the mating face. Force the seal into the groove using a hammer handle to rub it down. The seal should not project more than 0.031 in (1.5 mm) above the groove.
6 When the seal has been forced right into the groove, cut off the ends level with the packing face.

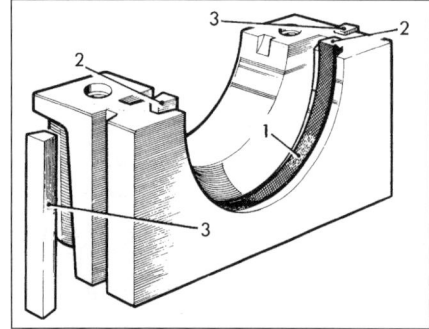

Fig. 1.18 Early type rear main bearing cap and oil seal carrier (Sec 39)

1 Seal   3 Side strip seals
2 Seal ends

39.8 Lubricate the main bearing shells generously

7 Apply heavy engine oil to the oil seal.

All models

8 Lubricate the upper shell bearings and main bearing journals with engine oil. Inject some into the oilways too (photo).
9 Lift the crankshaft and lower it evenly into position in the inner bearing shells.
10 Fit the lower bearing shells, which are plain, to the main bearing caps, ensuring that the tags locate correctly in the grooves in the caps (photo).
11 Lubricate the shells in the caps for numbers 1 to 4 main bearings and refit them in the correct order. The caps are marked 1 to 4 from front to rear and the arrows on them should all point the same way to the front of the engine.
12 Refit the retaining bolts but only do them up finger tight at this stage.
13 The next task is to refit the rear main bearing cap and oil seal carrier. As already described the rear oil seals differ. so here again the procedure varies.

Early models

14 Fit the other half seal to the groove in the rear main bearing cap as described in paragraphs 5 and 6.
15 Fit new seals to the side of the bearing cap. Do not cut them as they must protrude 1/16 in (1.5 mm) above the packing face of the cap.
16 Lubricate the rear oil seal strip with heavy engine oil and the side seals with light engine oil.
17 Fit and lubricate the lower bearing shell in the bearing cap and then fit the assembly to the crankcase. Refit the bolts finger tight.
18 Use a blunt instrument to drive the side seals into the bearing cap channels as far as they will go.
19 Use a mallet to tap the crankshaft first as far to the rear and then as far forward as it will travel. This is to align the centre main bearing thrust faces.
20 Tighten the main bearing caps numbers 1 to 4 to the specified torque.
21 Tighten the rear main bearing cap to its specified torque, and trim any of the side seals protruding from the cap.

39.22 Checking the crankshaft endfloat at the centre bearing

39.24 Tightening the main bearing cap bolts

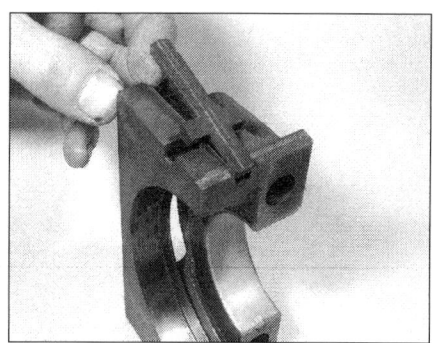

39.25 Fitting new side seals to the rear main bearing cap (later model)

22 Check that the crankshaft endfloat does not exceed that specified (photo). If it is not correct, check the assembly procedure or the components for faults.

Later models

23 In order to align the thrust faces of the centre main bearing tap the end of the crankshaft with a mallet, forward and rearward.

24 The securing bolts of the main bearing caps can now be tightened down evenly to the recommended torque setting (see Specifications) (photo).

25 Fit the new cruciform side seals to the grooves at the sides of the rear main bearing cap (photo).

26 Do not cut the cruiciform seals at this stage as they must project above the bearing cap mating faces approximately 0.062 in (1.5 mm).

27 Apply a coating of jointing compound to the rear half of the rear main bearing cap mating face, or alternatively apply the jointing compound to the equivalent area on the cylinder block (photo).

28 Lubricate the bearing shell and the cruciform side seals with clean engine oil and refit the bearing cap.

29 Do not fully tighten the two retaining bolts at this stage, but make sure that the cap is both fully home and squarely seated on the cylinder block.

30 Tighten the retaining bolts equally by one

quarter of a turn from finger tight to settle the cap. Now back off the bolts by one complete turn.

31 The crankshaft rear oil seal can now be fitted, but it is strongly recommended that the Rover service tool (RO.1014), which is a seal guide, be used when fitting the oil seal (Fig. 1.19).

32 If however the tool is unobtainable, it is possible to fit the seal provided that the greatest possible care is taken. Lightly oil the outer edge of the flange, ensuring that no oil is deposited on the seal housing surfaces, or the seal will not stay in position when clamped down. Lubricate the inner circumference of the seal, making sure that the outer edge remains absolutely dry and clean, or again it will not stay in position (photo).

33 Offer the seal to the flange, locating the lower edge in position and feeding the lip round under the flange. Then press the upper edge into position very gently. Push the seal home (photo).

34 If the tool can be obtained proceed as follows.

35 First make sure that the oil seal guide and the crankshaft journal are scrupulously clean and then coat the seal guide and crankshaft journal with clean engine oil. **Note:** *The lubricant must totally coat the outer surface of the oil seal guide to prevent the possibility of turning back the lip of the oil seal when fitting it.*

36 In respect of handling the oil seal, avoid

touching the seal lip at any time. Visually inspect the seal for damage and make sure that the outer diameter of the seal remains clean and dry at all times.

37 Position the oil seal, onto the seal guide tool, with the lip of the oil seal facing towards the engine.

38 Position the seal guide tool on the end of the crankshaft and push the seal, by hand, into the recess formed in the main bearing cap and cylinder block. The seal must fit squarely and abut the machined step in the recess.

39 With the seal so held in position, carefully withdraw the guide tool.

40 Once the seal is home in the recess, the

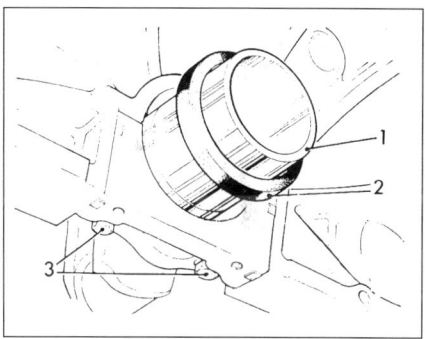

Fig. 1.19 Rover service tool RO.1014 – seal guide (Sec 39)

1 Seal guide   3 Main bearing cap bolts
2 Seal

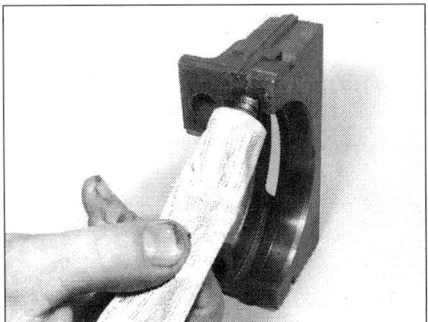

39.27 Applying jointing compound to the rear half of the cap mating face

39.32 Carefully lubricate the flange outer diameter

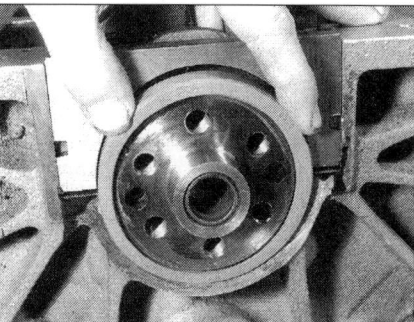

39.33 Feed the seal very carefully over the flange edge

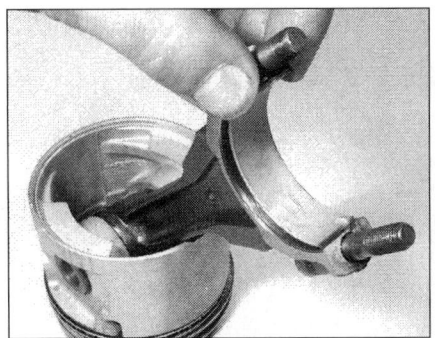

40.3 Fitting a new bearing shell to the connecting rod big-end

40.4 Don't forget to protect the connecting rod bolts

40.8 Using a hammer handle to push the piston into the bore

rear main bearing cap bolts can be tightened to the specified torque.

41 Check the crankshaft endfloat as described in paragraph 22.

42 Observe the rear main bearing seal whilst the piston assemblies are being refitted and before the flywheel is refitted. It has an unhappy knack of popping out under pressure if there is any trace of oil on the outer edge of the seal or the seal recess.

40 Pistons and connecting rods - refitting

1 As with removing the piston assemblies, the same comments apply on refitting. Refit

40.9 Lubricate the crankshaft journal as the connecting rod is drawn onto it

each one in sequence and make sure the correct assembly is fitted to the appropriate bore, unless new pistons are being fitted. Place the engine on one cylinder block and refit the four piston assemblies to the other side, then turn the block over and refit the other four. If the task is being done with the engine in the car, it is easier to work from front to rear, starting at No 1 cylinder.

2 Lubricate the bores and crankshaft big-end journals with oil.

3 Fit the upper big-end bearing shell to the connecting rod, ensuring that the tag slots into the groove (photo).

4 Fit the two plastic tubing pieces to the connecting rod bolts so they will not damage the bores or the journal (photo).

5 Lubricate the piston and rings. Using a piston ring compressor, clamp the piston rings, having checked that they are spaced correctly.

6 Lubricate the upper bearing shell and the piston and offer the assembly to its appropriate cylinder.

7 The domed boss on the connecting rod must face forwards for the right-hand bank of cylinders (2-4-6-8) and rearwards for the left bank (1-3-5-7). When the assemblies are refitted, the domed bosses should face each other on the crankshaft journals.

8 Push the piston into the bore as far as the ring compressor will allow. Then tap the piston into the bore using the wooden handle of a hammer (photo).

9 Guide the protected connecting rod bolts over the journal and then push the connecting rod and piston into position (photo).

10 Remove the protective plastic tubing from the bolts.

11 Refit the lower bearing shell to the bearing cap and ensure that the tag engages in the groove (photo). Lubricate the shell.

12 Refit the big-end bearing cap to the connecting rod (photo). Note that the rib on the edge of the cap faces in the same direction as the domed boss on the connecting rod, so that when the two connecting rods and caps are refitted to each of the four journals the ribs face each other.

13 Tighten the connecting rod cap nuts to the specified torque (photo).

14 Rotate the crankshaft so that the next journal is in the most convenient position and then refit the next assembly. Repeat the operation for the other piston and connecting rod assemblies.

41 Camshaft - refitting

1 Having inspected the camshaft it may now be refitted.

2 Take care when inserting the camshaft that the bearings are not damaged.

3 Check that the key is correctly located in

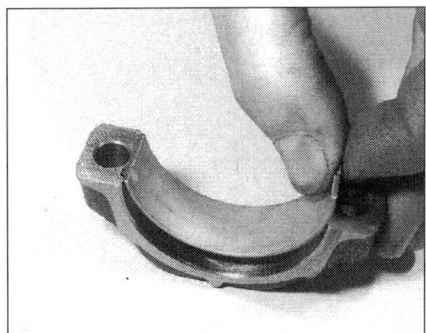

40.11 Engage the tag in the groove when fitting a shell to a cap

40.12 Refitting the big-end cap – note the rib on the cap

40.13 Tightening the big-end bearing cap nuts

41.3 Check that the key is correctly refitted to the camshaft keyway

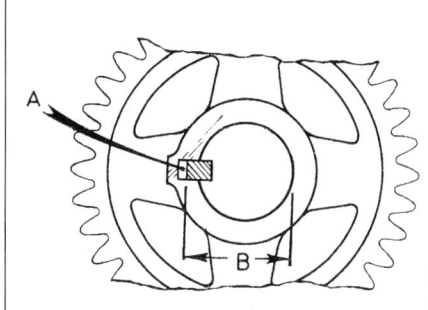

Fig.1.20 Camshaft key location and clearances (Sec 41)

A   Clearance that must exist as an oilway
B   1.187 (30.16 mm)

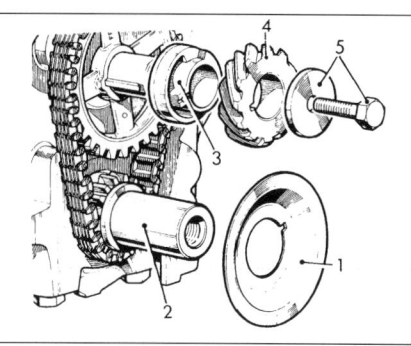

Fig. 1.21 Timing chain and gears assembly (Sec 42)

1   Oil thrower (very early models only)
2   Crankshaft
3   Fuel pump cam (mechanical fuel pump models)
4   Distributor drivegear
5   Retaining bolt and washer

the keyway (photo). It must be seated to its full depth and the key must be parallel with the shaft. The overall measurement of shaft and key must not exceed 1.187 in (30.16 mm) (Fig. 1.20). The reason for strict observance of the parallel attitude and seating of the key is that the remainder of the keyway in the camshaft gear acts as an oilway to feed the gears and chain. If it becomes blocked the results could be serious.

4 Two types of camshaft can be fitted. Make sure if the camshaft has been renewed that the correct one has been fitted. The early type has a spacer or cam which fits between the chainwheel and distributor drivegear to operate the mechanical fuel pump if one is fitted.

5 Refit the components and sub-assemblies that were removed for access to the camshaft in the reverse order to that described in Section 14.

42 Timing cover, chain and gears - refitting

Note: *This operation includes the renewal of the early type of oil seal.*

1 Rotate the crankshaft if the engine has been the subject of a full overhaul, so that No 1 piston is at top dead centre. If the engine has only been the subject of a partial strip-down it should have been left in this position.

2 Where the camshaft is not already aligned, refit the camshaft chainwheel temporarily with the FRONT marking facing outwards and rotate the camshaft so that the pointer on the chainwheel is at the 6 o'clock position with the engine vertical. (ie it is pointing directly at the crankshaft). If a full engine overhaul is being undertaken then the engine will probably still be upside-down on the bench, as this is the easiest method of reassembly. In this case the pointer will be at 12 o'clock, as shown in the photographs.

3 To check the correct alignment of the two shafts, temporarily refit the timing cover without its oil seal. Locate it on the crankcase dowels. Then refit the crankshaft pulley. Check the alignment of the TDC mark on the pulley with the pointer on the timing cover (photo). Rotate the crankshaft if necessary by rotating the flywheel, as it is possible to be several degrees out by visual checking of the No 1 for TDC.

4 Remove the crankshaft pulley and timing cover.

5 Fit the chain to the chainwheels with the timing marks aligned on both chainwheels. Remember the FRONT marking faces out.

6 Offer up the chainwheels and chain to both the camshaft and crankshaft simultaneously, ensuring that the timing marks stay in line.

7 Fit the chainwheels over the keys on both shafts and push them home. Check that the alignment is still correct (photo).

8 Check that the camshaft key is still parallel with the shaft and that the oilway is clear as described in the previous Section. Then refit the oil thrower (dished side out) to the crankshaft. This is only fitted to very early models.

9 Fit the fuel pump cam or spacer to the early type of camshaft, and ensure that the F marking faces outward (photo). The keyway oilway again must be clear.

10 Refit the distributor drivegear, washer and bolt (photo).

42.3 Check the alignment of the pointer and TDC mark on the pulley

42.7 Camshaft and crankshaft chainwheel alignment marks. Note FRONT marking on camshaft chainwheel

42.9 Refit the fuel pump cam – F marking faces out (early models)

42.10 The distributor drivegear, washer and bolt refitted

42.19 Locate the timing cover on the dowels

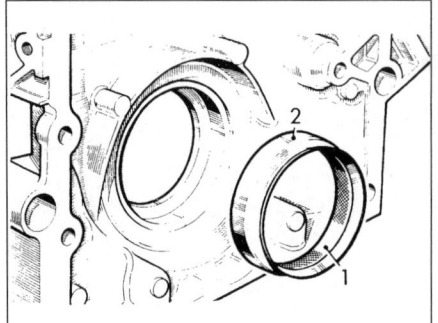

Fig. 1.22 Early type of timing cover oil seal and thrower (Sec 42)

1 Seal   2 Thrower

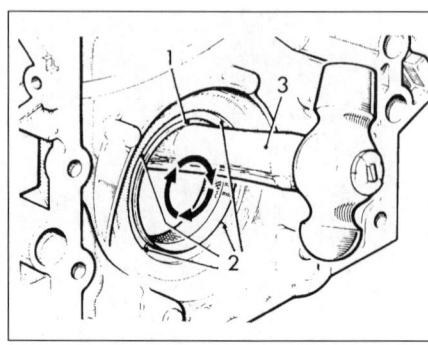

Fig. 1.23 Fitting an early type of oil seal (Sec 42)

1 Seal – ends at top   3 Hammer
2 Staking points

11 Tighten the bolt to the specified torque.

12 Fit a new timing cover oil seal. For the later 'lip' type of oil seal, this is covered in Section 26. For the earlier type follow these instructions.

Oil seal renewal (early type)

13 Drive the oil seal and oil thrower out of the casing to the rear. Both seal and thrower should then be discarded (Fig. 1.22).

14 Coil a new seal into a new oil thrower and fit the assembly into the cover from the rear, with the oil seal ends at the top (Fig. 1.23).

15 Stake the oil thrower in position at four opposite and equal points.

16 Run a hammer handle around the inside of the seal to seat it, until the crankshaft pulley can be inserted. The seal is now fitted.

Timing cover refitting

17 Fit a new gasket to the cylinder block mating face. Apply jointing compound to the gasket first to retain it in position. If the mating faces are rough, apply jointing compound to both sides.

18 If the job is being done with the engine in the vehicle, prime the oil pump with engine oil by injecting it through the suction port. Also apply jointing compound to the exposed part of the sump gasket.

19 Offer up the cover to the cylinder block and locate it on the dowels (photo).

20 If the bolt threads have not been cleaned,

clean them and apply 3MEC776 thread lubricant/sealant to them.

21 Fit the bolts and tighten to secure the cover. Ensure the correct bolts are in the correct holes, as they were removed. Tighten the bolts to the specified torque.

22 Refit the two sump bolts into the bottom face of the timing cover and tighten them (engine in the vehicle).

23 Refit the remainder of the components which were removed to reach the timing cover, in the reverse order to that described in Section 13, if the job is being done with the engine in the vehicle.

24 Check and adjust the ignition timing if necessary.

43 Sump - refitting

1 Refit the oil pick-up pipe and strainer. There is a small gasket between the flange and the crankcase. The flange is retained by two bolts.

2 Ensure that both the crankcase and sump mating surfaces are clean and free from old gasket or jointing compound.

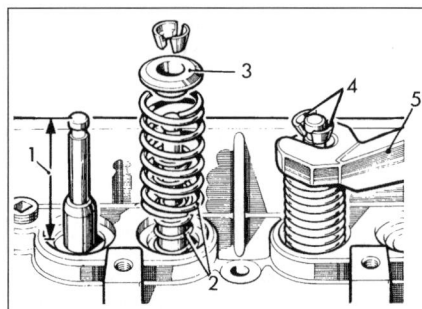

Fig. 1.24 Valve refitting sequence (Sec 44)

1 Height of valve   3 Cap
* stem above valve   4 Collets*
* spring seat   5 Valve spring*
2 Inner and outer   compressor
* valve springs*
* (earlier models)*

44 Cylinder heads - reassembly and refitting

1 Place the cylinder head on its side.

2 Fit each valve in turn into the guide from which it was removed, unless the valves are new ones.

3 Check the height of the valve stems above the valve spring seat surface. This distance **must not** exceed 47.63 mm (1.875 in). If necessary, grind the end of the valve stem to reduce the height. However, if this is going to entail too much grinding, new valves or even valve seat grinding may be required.

4 Remove the valves and lubricate both the valve stems and valve guides with engine oil, then refit them to their respective positions.

5 Refit the valve spring(s). Make sure that the bottom of the single valve spring (on later models) locates correctly in the recess in the cylinder head.

6 Refit the valve spring caps, compress the spring using a valve spring compressor and refit the split collets.

7 When all the valves and springs have been fitted, place the head face down on the bench and give each valve stem end a light tap with the butt end of a hammer handle or with a plastic-headed mallet to ensure that the

43.4 Refit the sump using a new gasket

44.7 Valve and springs assembly with collets correctly seated

44.9 Fit a new gasket and locate it on the dowels

44.10 Lowering a cylinder head into position

collets are well seated into their respective caps (photo).

8 Refit the oil dipstick tube to the left-hand cylinder block top face if it has been removed during overhaul.

9 Fit a new gasket to the cylinder block and engage it on the two small dowels. Note that the gasket is marked TOP to show which way up it should fit (photo). Do not use any sealant.

10 Lift up the cylinder head and lower it into position on the two dowels which ensure that it is aligned correctly (photo).

11 Clean the cylinder head bolts of all old sealant, if this has not already been done.

12 Apply thread sealant to each bolt in turn and refit it to its appropriate position. Rover recommend 3MEC776 thread lubricant and sealant for this purpose.

13 There are 3 long bolts, 7 medium length bolts, and 4 short ones. The long bolts fit in the three central holes in the cylinder head main section, the medium length bolts fit in the two outer holes on either side of the long bolts and the row immediately below the spark plugs, and the short bolts fit in the outer (lower edge) row - see Fig. 1.25. Note that there is a special short bolt which fits in the left-hand cylinder head immediately adjacent to the oil dipstick tube. This has a threaded head insert. The dipstick tube retaining clip bolt is screwed into it.

14 Tighten the cylinder head bolts gradually

in the correct sequence until they are at the specified torque (photo).

15 Repeat the procedure for the other cylinder head where it has been removed and overhauled.

16 Refit the rest of the components as they were removed.

45 Valve gear - refitting

1 This operation covers the refitting of the tappets, pushrods and rocker shaft assemblies, all of which have been inspected and overhauled or renewed as necessary.

2 Refit the tappets the right way up to the positions from which they were removed. New tappets must be fitted to the positions where tappets have been discarded for reasons of wear, etc. Check the tappet oilways before refitting.

3 Similarly refit the pushrods to their correct positions.

4 Refit the rocker shaft assemblies. Note that they are handed and must be fitted the correct way round to align the oilways. On the right-hand cylinder head the notch in the end of the shaft faces upwards and towards the front of the engine. On the left it faces upwards and towards the rear (photo).

5 As with the rocker shafts themselves, so the baffle plates are handed and fit on the

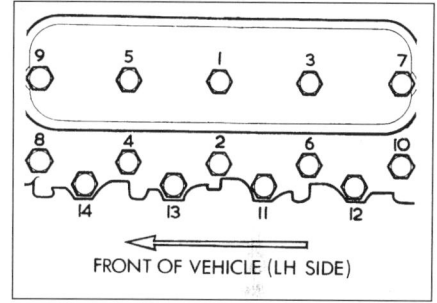

Fig. 1.25 Cylinder head retaining bolts tightening sequence (Sec 44)

Short bolts – sequence numbers
11, 12, 13 and 14
Medium bolts – sequence numbers
2, 4, 6, 7, 8, 9 and 10
Long bolts sequence numbers 1, 3 and 5

opposite ends of the assemblies to the notches in the shaft (ie at the front on the left-hand bank and at the rear on the right-hand bank).

6 Offer up the assembly complete with the retaining bolts in position through the pedestals.

7 Locate the pushrod ends in the rocker arm cups, then check the rocker pad alignment with the valves and ensure that they are correct. Gradually tighten the pedestal bolts in an even pattern. This must be done carefully as the varying tensions on the rockers must be taken up gradually.

8 Tighten the bolts finally to the specified torque (photo).

44.14 Tightening the cylinder head bolts – note special bolt (arrowed) for dipstick tube retaining clip

45.4 Left-hand rocker shaft refitted – notch to rear, baffle at front (viewed from rear of engine)

45.8 Tightening the rocker pedestal bolts

45.11 Rocker cover, with new gasket fitted, being offered up to the engine

46.4 Lining up the inlet manifold gasket – note the seals at each end

46.5 Refit the two gasket clamps

9 Rotate the crankshaft to ensure that all the valves, rockers and tappets function correctly.
10 Refit the rocker covers and secure them with the four cross-head screws.
11 Should the rocker cover gasket need renewing, note that it is stuck to the cover mating face using Bostik 1775 impact adhesive. Any old gasket and adhesive must be cleaned off before a new one is fitted. Before applying adhesive to the new gasket and cover check which way round it fits. It can only fit one way. Don't try to fit it in one go. Start at one end and push it firmly into the recessed face in the cover, then work the rest of the gasket into place. The gasket and cover should be left for fifteen minutes between applying the adhesive and fitting the gasket to the cover. Once fitted allow the gasket and cover to stand for about thirty minutes before refitting it to the engine (photo).
12 In the meantime refit the inlet manifold.

46 Inlet manifold - refitting

1 As the inlet manifold also serves to cover the pushrod cavities of the cylinder block, a single manifold gasket is fitted. Made from sheet metal, this gasket extends downwards over the inlet port face of each cylinder head and over each of the respective pushrod cavities. Rubber seals are fitted at each end to seal the manifold to the timing chest and rear flange. It is important that the gasket and seals are carefully fitted or oil leaks may develop.
2 Locate the new seals to the front and rear walls of the engine. The seals must be smeared on both sides with silicone grease and their ends must locate in the notches between the cylinder head and cylinder block joints.
3 Apply gasket sealing compound to the joints between the seals and cylinder heads, and around the manifold gasket cylinder head and inlet manifold water passages.
4 Fit the new gasket with the word FRONT at the front. The open notch should be at the right-hand side front (photo).
5 Refit the two gasket clamps but do not tighten the bolts fully. Note that the two clamps are different and can only fit at one end or the other (photo).
6 Refit the inlet manifold. Note that the open bolt hole aligns with the open hole in the gasket.
7 Refit the bolts. Again they should be cleaned and coated in 3MEC776 lubricant/sealant.
8 Tighten the bolts evenly and gradually, working on alternate sides from the centre to the ends. Do not exceed the specified torque (photo).
9 Tighten the gasket clamps front and rear.
10 Refit the remainder of the components removed to perform this operation.

11 When all the components are refitted, start the engine and check for oil and water leaks.

47 Ancillary components - refitting (engine out of car)

1 With the major components and sub-assemblies refitted to the engine, the ancillary components can now be refitted.
2 Always use new gaskets when refitting previously removed components and refer to the Chapter or Section concerned for the detailed instructions relating to any individual component.
3 The ancillary components listed below can be refitted in the order given:
(a) *Flywheel (Section 17) - unless it has already been refitted to rotate the crankshaft when refitting the timing gear or piston and connecting rod assemblies*
(b) *Crankshaft pulley and starter dog: engage the pulley on the crankshaft key. Screw in the starter dog bolt. Lock the flywheel to stop the crankshaft turning and tighten the starter dog to the specified torque. Remove the wedge or bracket from the flywheel (photos)*
(c) *Oil pump and oil filter (Section 19)*
(d) *Distributor and advance/retard vacuum pipe (Chapter 4)*
(e) *Rocker covers (Section 45)*

46.8 Tightening the inlet manifold bolts

47.3a Tightening the starter dog/crankshaft pulley bolt . . .

47.3b . . . with a wedge in position to stop the flywheel rotating

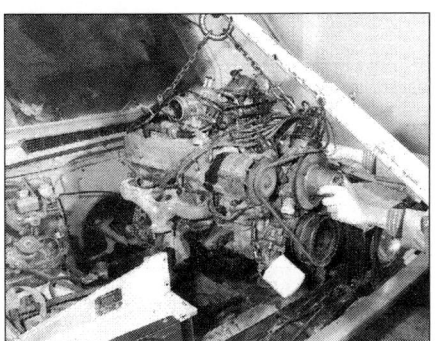

48.2 Clearing the front bodywork as the engine is refitted

(f) *Fuel pump (mechanical type - early models) (Chapter 3)*
(g) *Exhaust manifolds (Chapter 3)*
(h) *Clutch (Chapter 5)*
(j) *Spark plugs (Chapter 4)*
(k) *Crankcase breather valve (Chapter 3)*
(l) *Rocker breather pipes and flame traps (Chapter 3)*
(m) *Distributor cap and plug leads (Chapter 4)*
(n) *Starter motor (Chapter 10)*
(p) *Alternator and drivebelt (Chapter 10)*
(q) *Wiring loom and retaining brackets*

48 Engine - refitting

Note: *This is a 2-man operation.*

Basically the installation of the engine is the reverse procedure to the removal operation; however, mating the engine to the gearbox can be difficult unless the following method is used.

1 Make sure the clutch is centralised on the flywheel as described in Chapter 5.
2 Carefully lower the engine into the engine compartment using a suitable hoist until the flywheel housing is straight and level with the clutch housing. This can be tricky as the exhaust pipes tend to get in the way. Make sure the cables and wires do not snag (photo).
3 Push the engine rearwards, ensuring the gearbox input shaft enters the clutch assembly in a straight line and not at an angle.
4 If the engine begins to mate up and then stops with a couple of inches still to go, fit a spanner onto the crankshaft starter dog and turn it slowly while pushing the engine rearwards.
5 As soon as the flywheel and clutch

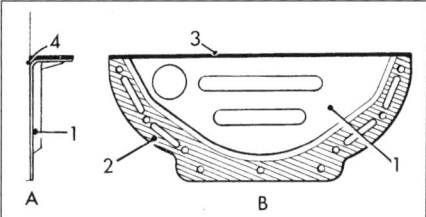

Fig. 1.26 Bellhousing cover plate gasket and sealant application points (Sec 48)

1 *Cover plate*
2 *Apply gasket sealant to shaded area*
3 *New gasket fits on top face*
4 *Apply a fillet of sealing compound along angled face*
A *Side-on view of plate*
B *Rear view of plate*

housings touch, line up and engage the bellhousing dowels. Insert a bolt finger tight to hold them together, and then refit and tighten all the bolts except the one that retains the clutch slave cylinder pipe joint brackets.
6 Raise the engine on the hoist sufficiently for the engine mounting rubbers to be inserted. Then lower the engine onto the mountings, ensuring that the exhaust pipes are in line with their manifolds.
7 Finally, lower the hoist completely and remove the engine slings and the jack or blocks from beneath the transmission. Reconnect all the controls, electrical leads, fuel pipes, exhaust pipe, etc, checking each item against the sequence given in Section 5.
8 When refitting the bellhousing cover plate, ensure that gasket sealing compound is applied to the vertical face and a new gasket is placed on the top horizontal face. The angled section across the top of the plate should have a good fillet of compound laid across it (Fig. 1.26). Do not forget the stiffening plate across the bottom of the cover plate (photo).
9 Do not forget to refill the cooling system, and refill the engine with the recommended grade and quantity of oil.

49 Engine - initial start-up after overhaul or major repair

1 Make sure that the battery is fully charged and that the oil, water and fuel are replenished.
2 If the fuel system has been dismantled it will require several revolutions of the engine on the starter motor to get the petrol up to the

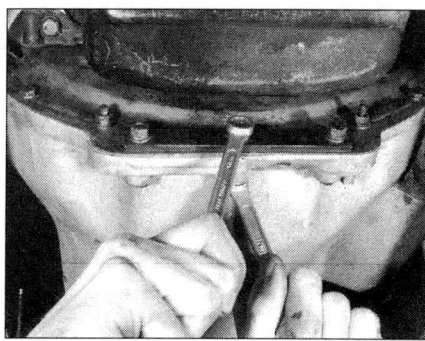

48.8 Tightening the bellhousing cover plate nuts and bolts – note stiffening plate

carburettor (models with mechanical fuel pump).
3 As soon as the engine fires and runs, keep it going at a fast tickover only (not faster) and bring it up to normal working temperature. **Do not** exceed 1000 rpm initially, or the crankshaft rear oil seal may be damaged.
4 Tappet noise will be experienced initially on starting up after an overhaul or major repair. This noise should vanish quite quickly as the tappets fill with oil. If excessive noise is apparent, run the engine at around 2500 rpm which should eliminate any tappet noise.
5 As the engine warms up there will be odd smells and some smoke from parts getting hot and burning off oil deposits. The signs to look for are leaks of oil or water which will be obvious, if serious. Check also the connections of the exhaust pipes to the manifolds as these do not always 'find' their exact gas-tight position until the warmth and vibration have acted on them and it is almost certain that they will need tightening further. This should be done, of course, with the engine stopped.
6 When normal running temperature has been reached adjust the idling speed as described in Chapter 3.
7 Stop the engine and wait a few minutes to see if any lubricant or coolant is dripping out when the engine is stationary.
8 Road test the car to check that the timing is correct and giving the necessary smoothness and power. Do not race the engine - when new bearings and/or pistons and rings have been fitted it should be treated as a new engine and run in at reduced revolutions for the first 500 miles. Change the engine oil and oil filter after the first 500 miles in order to get rid of the metallic particles which will have been created during the running-in process.

Fault finding - engine

Note: *When investigating starting and uneven running faults do not be tempted into snap diagnosis. Start from the beginning of the check procedure and follow it through. It will take less time in the long run. Poor performance from the engine in terms of power and economy is not normally diagnosed quickly. In any event the ignition and fuel systems must be checked first before assuming any further investigation needs to be made.*

Engine will not turn when starter switch is operated

- [ ] Flat battery
- [ ] Bad battery connections
- [ ] Bad connections at solenoid and/or starter motor
- [ ] Defective starter motor

Engine turns normally but fails to start

- [ ] No spark at plugs
- [ ] No fuel reaching engine
- [ ] Too much fuel reaching the engine (flooding)

Engine starts but runs unevenly and misfires

- [ ] Ignition and/or fuel system faults
- [ ] Sticking or leaking valves
- [ ] Burnt out valves
- [ ] Worn out piston rings

Lack of power

- [ ] Ignition and/or fuel system faults
- [ ] Burnt out valves
- [ ] Worn out piston rings

Excessive oil consumption

- [ ] Oil leaks from crankshaft oil seals, timing cover gasket, rocker cover gasket, oil filter gasket, sump gasket, sump plug
- [ ] Worn piston rings or cylinder bores resulting in oil being burnt by engine
- [ ] Worn valve guides and/or defective inlet valve stem seals

Excessive mechanical noise from engine

- [ ] Worn crankshaft bearings
- [ ] Worn cylinders (piston slap)
- [ ] Slack or worn timing chain and sprockets

Chapter 2 Cooling system

For modifications, and information applicable to later models, see Supplement at end of manual

Contents

Degrees of difficulty

Easy, suitable for novice with little experience	Fairly easy, suitable for beginner with some experience	Fairly difficult, suitable for competent DIY mechanic	Difficult, suitable for experienced DIY mechanic	Very difficult, suitable for expert DIY or professional

Specifications

General
System type .... Pressurised, spill return, thermostatically controlled, pump and fan assisted
System pressure .... 15 lbf/in² (1.05 kgf/cm²) maximum

Coolant pump
Type .... Centrifugal
Location .... In timing cover

Thermostat
Type .... Wax pellet
Location .... Front of inlet manifold
Jiggle pin position .... 12 o'clock
Opening temperature .... 173° to 182°F (78° to 83°C)

Coolant
Type .... Ethylene glycol based antifreeze to BS 3150, 3151, or 6580
Capacity .... 20 Imp pints (11.3 litres)

Drivebelt tension .... 0.437 to 0.562 in (11 to 14mm) deflection midway between alternator and crankshaft pulleys

Torque wrench settings

	lbf ft	kgf m
Water pump cover bolts:		
Long	20 to 25	2.8 to 3.5
Short	6 to 8	0.8 to 1.0

1 General description

The engine cooling system is conventional, acting on the thermosyphon pump-assisted principle. The coolant flow is controlled by a thermostat which is fitted at the forward end of the inlet manifold casting and behind the outlet elbow. The purpose of this thermostat is to prevent the full flow of the coolant around the system before the most efficient operating temperature is reached.

The purpose of pressurising the cooling system is to prevent premature boiling in adverse conditions and also to allow the engine to operate at its most efficient running temperature.

The overflow pipe from the radiator is connected to an expansion tank which makes topping-up unnecessary. The coolant expands when hot, and instead of being forced down an overflow pipe and lost, it flows into the expansion tank. As the engine cools the coolant contracts and, because of the pressure differential, flows back into the top tank of the radiator. Excess pressure is vented to the atmosphere via a pressure relief valve fitted to the expansion tank filler cap.

The cooling system comprises the radiator, water pump, thermostat, interconnecting hoses and waterways in the cylinder block and heads. The water pump is driven from the engine crankshaft pulley by a V-belt.

On early models a five-bladed metal fan is fitted directly to the water pump pulley. Later models are fitted with a multi-bladed plastic fan which is connected to a Holset viscous coupling which limits the fan speed at high engine revolutions. This works in a similar manner to a torque converter, and provides a 'slipping clutch' effect; its aim is to reduce noise and engine loading.

2.3 The radiator filler plug removed

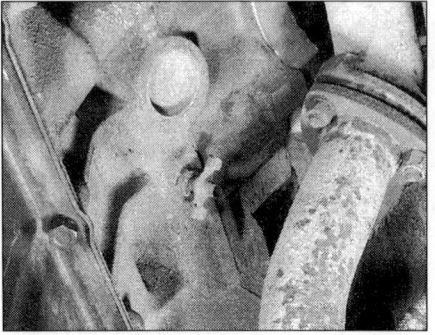

2.6 Left-hand cylinder block drain tap

4.6 Half-fill the expansion tank with coolant mixture

2 Cooling system - draining

⚠️ **Warning: Do not remove the expansion tank cap when the engine is hot, or the water will scald you.**

With the car on level ground, and the system cold, proceed as follows:

1 Move the heater control lever to the *Hot* position.
2 Depress and remove slowly the expansion tank filler cap.
3 Unscrew and remove the hexagon radiator filler plug (photo).
4 If antifreeze is used in the cooling system, and has been in use for less than two years, drain the coolant into a container of suitable capacity for re-use.
5 Remove the radiator drain plug from the bottom left-hand corner of the radiator.
6 Drain taps are provided in each of the cylinder banks and positioned directly beneath the exhaust manifolds (photo). Turn the taps in an anti-clockwise direction to drain the coolant.

3 Cooling system - flushing

1 With the passing of time, the cooling system will gradually lose its efficiency as the radiator becomes choked with rust, scale deposits from water and other sediment. To clear the system out, initially drain the system as described previously, then detach the lower radiator hose.
2 Using a garden hose, allow water to enter the radiator via the radiator filler plug. It will be necessary to close the cylinder block drain taps during this operation.
3 Allow the water from the hose to run through the radiator for several minutes until it emerges clean then refit the lower hose.
4 When it is desired to flush the cylinder block, simply remove the radiator filler plug and the cylinder block drain taps. The removal of the cylinder block drain taps will permit speedy clearance of the sediment and scale deposits. The garden hose can be inserted in the radiator filler plug hole as described in paragraph 2.
5 If when flushing the radiator the sediment and scale deposits are very dirty then it will be found desirable to remove the radiator and reverse flush it. Reverse flushing simply means feeding the clean flushing water into the lower radiator connection and expelling the sediment from the top radiator connection.
6 The alternative to the reverse flushing method, described in paragraph 5, is the use of a proprietary brand of radiator descaler available at most motor accessory shops or garages. The correct usage of the descaler compound is described on the container, but generally necessitates leaving it in the cooling system for a short period to free the deposits which can then be flushed out as described in paragraphs 3 and 4. Make sure that such a descaler is suitable for mixed metal (iron and aluminium) engines.

4 Cooling system - filling

1 The importance of refilling with the correct mixture of antifreeze/inhibitor and water, or inhibitor only with water, cannot be over-emphasised. Antifreeze solution conforming to British Standard No 3150, 3151, or 6580 should be used. Alternatively, where applicable, a Rover approved cooling corrosion inhibitor should be used. Antifreeze mixture can remain in the system for two years, provided that the specific gravity of the coolant is checked regularly, especially before the beginning of the second winter. If necessary it must be topped up with new antifreeze. After the second winter the system must be drained and flushed as described in Sections 2 and 3.
2 Before filling the system, check all hoses, clips and joints to make sure that they are in sound order. Renew any that are defective or cracked even if they are not actually leaking. This is a form of insurance and is in your best interest. Antifreeze has a very searching effect on hoses and joints.
3 When mixing water with the antifreeze inhibitor, or just inhibitor, it is better to use soft tap water or rain water, the mixture being carried out in a plastic bucket. It is not necessary to mix the whole amount required to fill the system, as further topping-up can be done once the initial coolant mix has been poured into the system.
4 Use the following table to ensure adequate protection according to the local climatic conditions:

Amount of antifreeze	Protection down to
7 pints (4 litres) (33%)	-25°F (-32°C)
10 pints (6 litres) (50%)	-33°F (-36°C)

5 Fill the system with the mixture through the radiator filler plug orifice then refit the filler plug.
6 Save a little of the mixture and half-fill the expansion tank and refit the cap (photo). There is a water level plate inside the tank.
7 Run the engine until the normal operating temperature is reached (ie the thermostat is open) and then switch off. Allow the system to cool, then check the coolant level. Top up as necessary.

5 Radiator - removal and refitting

1 For safety reasons disconnect the battery negative terminal.
2 Drain the cooling system as described in Section 2.

5.3a Disconnect the top hose at the radiator . . .

5.3b . . . the bottom hose and the two small hoses at the top of the photograph

5.5 Move the cowl back over the fan out of the way

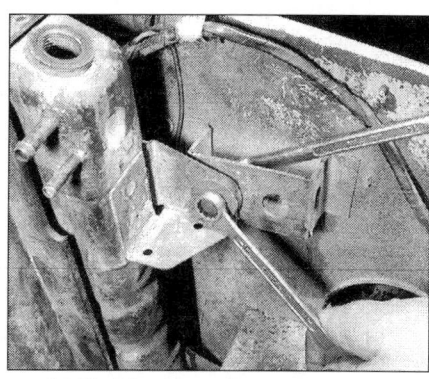

5.6 Undoing the radiator right-hand retaining nut and bolt

3 Disconnect the following hoses at the radiator (photos):

Top hose
Bottom hose
Manifold vent hose
Expansion tank bottom hose

4 Undo the two nuts and washers which retain the cowl to the top of the radiator brackets, as described in Section 6.

5 Lift the cowl straight up to release the lower edge from the clips on the bottom of the radiator. Then move the cowl back over the fan (photo).

6 Undo the two nuts and bolts which retain the radiator to the front body panels (photo).

7 Lift the radiator straight out to withdraw the pegs at the bottom corners from the grommets in the mounting brackets beneath. Take care that the fan does not catch the radiator matrix as it is removed, as the matrix is easily damaged (photo).

8 Refitting is the reverse procedure to removal. Check before refitting the radiator that the grommets into which the pegs fit are

in good condition and that the rubber mounting bushes for the radiator main fixing bolts are also in good order (photo).

9 After refitting, refill the cooling system as described in Section 4.

6 Fan cowl, blades, viscous coupling and pulley - removal and refitting

1 Undo the cowl retaining nuts and washers from the brackets on top of the radiator (photo).

5.7 The radiator removed – note the locating pegs and the cowl clips at the bottom

2 Lift the cowl straight up to release the lower edge from the clips on the bottom edge of the radiator (photo).

3 Carefully lift the cowl out, taking care that it does not catch on one of the fan blades and thereby damage the radiator matrix as it twists. The clearance is very limited for this.

4 Slacken the alternator adjusting bolt, push the alternator towards the engine and slip the belt from the pulley.

5 To remove the fan on early models, undo the four bolts and remove the fan (photo). Undo the four nuts and bolts which retain the fan to the viscous coupling (Fig. 2.1).

5.8 Check the grommets and bushes (arrowed) - left-hand side shown

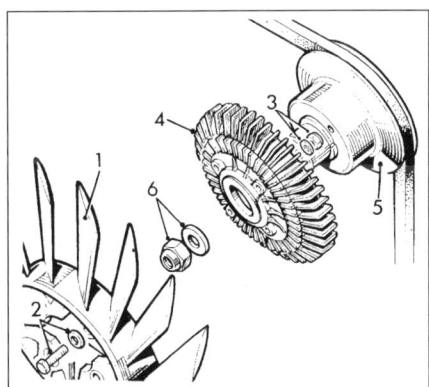

Fig. 2.1 Multi-bladed fan and viscous coupling assembly (later models) (Sec 6)

1 *Fan*
2 *Fan-to-coupling bolt and washer*
3 *Fan-to-coupling nut and washer*
4 *Viscous coupling*
5 *Pump/fan pulley*
6 *Coupling and pulley retaining nut and washer*

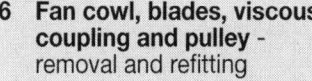

6.1 Undo the cowl retaining nuts (right-hand nut arrowed)

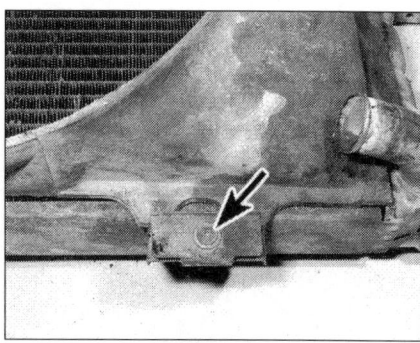

6.2 The cowl is retained by two clips at the bottom like the one arrowed (radiator and cowl out of the car for clarity)

6.5 Undo the four bolts to remove the fan (early models)

6.6 The pulley is secured to the fan hub by three bolts

7.1 Slacken the alternator adjuster bolt

6 To remove the water pump pulley on early models, undo the three bolts which retain it to the hub and remove it (photo). On later models remove the viscous coupling retaining nut from the pump shaft. The viscous coupling and pulley can now be pulled off the shaft in turn.

7 Refitting is the reverse procedure to removal. Note that the metal fan has a locating dowel on the pulley hub mounting face and the plastic fan has large diameter bosses on one side, which face forward to ensure that it is fitted the right way round.

8 Adjust the fanbelt when the belt has been refitted as described in Section 7.

7 Fan/alternator drivebelt - removal, refitting and adjustment

1 Loosen the alternator mounting and adjuster nuts and bolts (photo). If air conditioning is fitted, the alternator will be mounted on the left-hand side of the engine.

2 Tip the alternator towards the engine, slip the belt from the pulleys, and feed it over the fan blades to remove it.

3 Refitting of the drivebelt is the reverse of removal, but it is important to tension the belt correctly.

4 Pull the alternator away from the engine until the tension of the drivebelt is such that it can only be deflected by the specified amount

at a point midway between the alternator and crankshaft pulleys.

5 With the alternator so held, tighten the mounting and adjuster nuts and bolts, then recheck the tension (photo).

6 If a new drivebelt has been fitted then it will need to be retensioned after approximately 250 miles (400 km) owing to the fact that a certain amount of stretching occurs during the bedding-in stage.

8 Water pump - removal and refitting

1 Disconnect the battery negative terminal.

2 Drain the cooling system and remove the radiator as described in the previous Sections.

3 Remove the cooling fan blades, cowl, fan hub or viscous coupling and water pump pulley as described in Section 6.

4 Remove the bottom hose from the water pump inlet pipe.

5 Free the inner end of the alternator adjuster link from the water pump.

6 On later models with power steering, slacken the power steering pump mounting bolts, slip the belt off the pump pulley and then remove the mounting bolts and support the pump out of the way without straining the hoses.

7 Remove the water pump retaining bolts,

noting that four of them are much longer than the others. Note where those four fit. Note also where the power steering pump mounting brackets fit as they are removed (if applicable).

8 Pull the pump away from the locating dowels in the main casing section which is part of the timing cover.

9 Clean the threads of the pump securing bolts ready for reassembly. The threads of these bolts have a coating of thread lubricant sealant which will harden if left in contact with air.

10 It is in most cases cheaper and less frustrating to replace worn assemblies with an exchange unit. The water pump is no exception to this rule and though it is possible to renew bearings, shafts and seals, it is advised that the former course is adopted, since special tools including a press are required.

11 Refitting is mainly a matter of reversing the removal procedure. However, there are one or two points to note during the operation.

12 Ensure that the mating surfaces of pump and engine front cover are scrupulously clean.

13 Using a smear of light grease, secure the new gasket to the pump body.

14 Apply a light smear of grease to the other gasket surface and offer the unit to the engine taking care to ensure the dowels locate in the pump body holes (photo).

15 The pump securing bolts should be

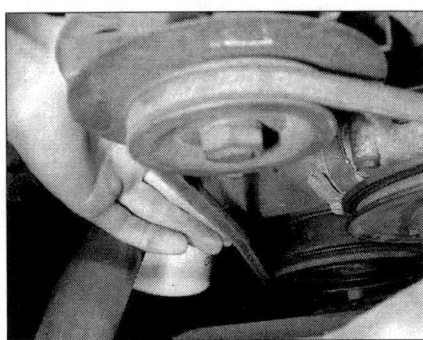

7.5 Checking the fanbelt tension

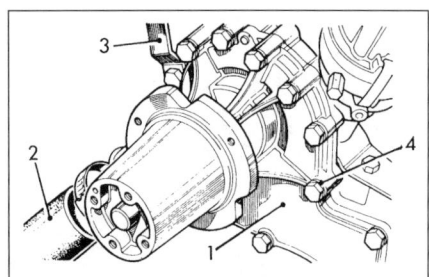

Fig. 2.2 Water pump assembly (Sec 8)

1 Pump housing
2 Water inlet hose
3 Alternator adjuster link
4 Water pump housing retaining bolt

8.14 Refit the water pump using a new gasket

cleaned, and treated with lubricant sealant 3M EC776 or equivalent.

16 Refit the bolts to their correct locations. Also ensure that the alternator adjuster link and the power steering pump mounting brackets (where fitted) are located in the correct positions.

17 Tighten the pump mounting bolts to the specified torque settings.

18 Do not forget to adjust the fanbelt and power steering pump drivebelt tensions, and refill the system with coolant as already described.

19 Run the engine and check for water leaks.

9 Thermostat -
removal, testing and refitting

1 If the engine tends to overheat, the cause is most likely to be a faulty thermostat that is failing to open at a predetermined temperature setting.

2 Conversely, where the thermostat is stuck permanently open. it will be found that the engine takes a long time to warm up. In cold weather, this results in having to drive considerable distances using the choke. If in doubt take out the thermostat and test it.

3 There is no need to drain the whole system, but simply drain enough so that the inlet manifold is empty. Then refit the drain plug.

4 Disconnect the thermostat bypass hose and the radiator top hose from the water elbow.

5 There are two bolts securing the thermostat housing elbow to the front of the engine.

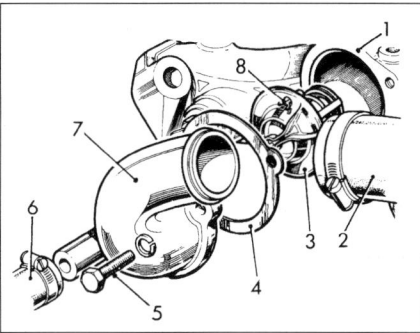

Fig. 2.3 Thermostat and water elbow assembly (Sec 9)

1 Inlet manifold	6 Thermostat bypass
2 Top hose	hose
3 Thermostat	7 Water elbow
4 Gasket	8 Jiggle pin
5 Bolt	

These should be removed, and the housing elbow lifted off (Fig. 2.3).

6 Remember to have a new gasket available for reassembly.

7 Carefully remove the thermostat, which should just lift out.

8 With the engine cold examine carefully to ascertain whether or not it is stuck open. If so, there is no point in making further tests; it should be renewed.

9 If the thermostat looks normal then proceed as follows.

10 Place the unit in a saucepan of cold water. Do not allow it to touch the bottom. Suspend it or support it with a piece of wire or string (Fig. 2.4).

11 Heat the saucepan and raise the

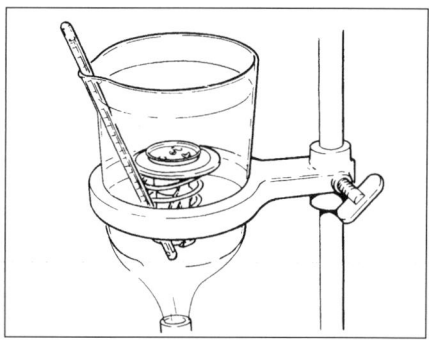

Fig. 2.4 Testing the thermostat (Sec 9)

temperature to that at which the thermostat is specified to open. The specified opening temperature is stamped on either the upper or lower face of the thermostat.

12 Should the thermostat fail to operate correctly, renew it with one of the correct type.

13 If it happens that you do not have a spare, the car will run quite well for a day or so without a thermostat until a replacement can be obtained, but the engine will take much longer to reach operating temperature.

14 Refit the elbow and thermostat housing cover using a new gasket.

15 When fitting the new thermostat, make sure that the small split pin, called a jiggle pin, which pokes through the valve face, is placed at the 12 o'clock position in the housing. This will prevent airlocks occurring in this area.

16 Finally reconnect the radiator and bypass hoses, top up the cooling system and check for leaks.

Fault finding - cooling system

Overheating
- [ ] Insufficient water in cooling system
- [ ] Fanbelt slipping (accompanied by a shrieking noise on rapid engine acceleration)
- [ ] Radiator core blocked or radiator grille restricted
- [ ] Thermostat not opening properly
- [ ] Ignition timing incorrectly set (accompanied by loss of power, and perhaps misfiring)
- [ ] Carburettors incorrectly adjusted (mixture too weak)
- [ ] Exhaust system partially blocked
- [ ] Oil level in sump too low
- [ ] Blown cylinder head gasket (water/steam being forced down the radiator overflow pipe under pressure)
- [ ] Engine not yet run-in
- [ ] Brakes binding

Overcooling
- [ ] Thermostat jammed on
- [ ] Incorrect thermostat fitted allowing premature opening of valve
- [ ] Thermostat missing

Loss of cooling water
- [ ] Loose clips of water hoses
- [ ] Top, bottom, or bypass water hoses perished and leaking
- [ ] Radiator core leaking
- [ ] Expansion tank pressure cap spring worn or seal ineffective
- [ ] Blown cylinder head gasket (pressure in system forcing water/steam down overflow pipe)
- [ ] Cylinder wall or head cracked

Notes

Chapter 3
Fuel, exhaust and emission control systems

For modifications, and information applicable to later models, see Supplement at end of manual

Contents

Degrees of difficulty

Easy, suitable for novice with little experience 	Fairly easy, suitable for beginner with some experience	Fairly difficult, suitable for competent DIY mechanic	Difficult, suitable for experienced DIY mechanic	Very difficult, suitable for expert DIY or professional

Specifications

Fuel pump

Type:
  Early models .... AC mechanical
  Later models .... AC or Bendix electrical
Location:
  Mechanical pump .... Left-hand side of engine at front
  Electrical pump .... Front chassis outrigger bracket on left-hand side, or beneath rear seat

Fuel filters

Main filter:
  Type .... AC, renewable paper element
  Location .... Left-hand chassis member in engine compartment
Auxiliary filter (where fitted):
  Type .... In-line, disposable
  Location .... Front of left-hand rocker cover

Carburettors

Number .... Two
Make .... Zenith/Stromberg
Type:
  Early models 175 CD2S
  Later models .... 175 CDSE
  Emission control models .... 175 CDSET
Spring colour (all models) .... Red
Jet orifice (all models) .... 1.75 mm with 2 mm washer
Metering valve
  175 CD2S B2AQ
  175 CDSE .... B2AS, B1DW or B1EJ
  175 CDSET B1EN
Float height (all models) .... 0.67 to 0.71 in (16 to 17 mm)

Carburettor tuning data

Dashpot oil:

		Idle	Fast idle
Type	SAE 20 engine oil		
Level	0.25 in (6 mm) below top of dashpot		
Engine idling speeds (rpm):		**Idle**	**Fast idle**
Pre-1972 models		600 to 650	1000 to 1200
1972 to 1976 models		650 to 750	1100 to 1300
1976 onwards		750 to 850	1100 to 1300
Full emission control models		850 to 950	1400 to 1500
Exhaust gas CO level	4% maximum at idle speed		

Fuel tank capacity .... 18 gallons (81.5 litres)

Emission control equipment

Equipment fitted .... Closed crankcase ventilation system (all models); thermostatically controlled air cleaner, air injection, exhaust gas recirculation system, fuel evaporative control system (according to model and market) Air pump drivebelt tension 0.016 in (0.4 mm) deflection per inch (25 mm) of belt run between pulley centres

Torque wrench settings

	lbf ft	kgf m
Exhaust manifold bolts	10 to 15	1.4 to 2.0
Inlet manifold bolts	20 to 25	3.5 to 4.0
Inlet manifold gasket clamp	10 to 15	1.4 to 2.0
Auto choke-to-carburettor screws	3.5	0.5

1	General description

Fuel system

The fuel system in the Range Rover varies depending on the age of the vehicle. Early vehicles have a mechanical fuel pump driven off the camshaft with an in-line fuel filter as well as a main fuel filter fitted with a renewable paper element. Later vehicles have an electric fuel pump located on the left-hand side of the chassis or under the rear seat and retain the main fuel filter. The fuel tank in all cases is mounted at the rear of the vehicle with the filler cap on the right-hand side.

The carburettors, twin Zenith Strombergs, vary also. Early ones have a mechanical choke whereas the later models, fitted with emission control equipment, have an automatic choke.

Exhaust system

The exhaust system is a straightforward, rugged assembly. Twin downpipes take the gases from the exhaust manifolds on either side of the engine and join together behind the gearbox to feed one main silencer box. A single pipe carries the exhaust gas to the left-hand side rear of the vehicle via a tail silencer on early models. Later vehicles have a similar arrangement but with twin pipes running all the way from the main silencer to the rear.

Emission control systems

All models have a crankcase breather valve and rocker cover breather pipes, providing crankcase emission control. Clean air is taken from the air cleaner and fed to the crankcase via the filter. Crankcase fumes rise via the hoses and flame traps.

Later models are fitted with an air intake temperature control system to warm up the engine quickly and reduce noxious gas output, while at the same time improving petrol consumption.

Vehicles with full emission control equipment are fitted with special twin air cleaners, air injection system (AIS), charcoal filter canister for absorbing petrol fumes, and an exhaust gas recirculation (EGR) system.

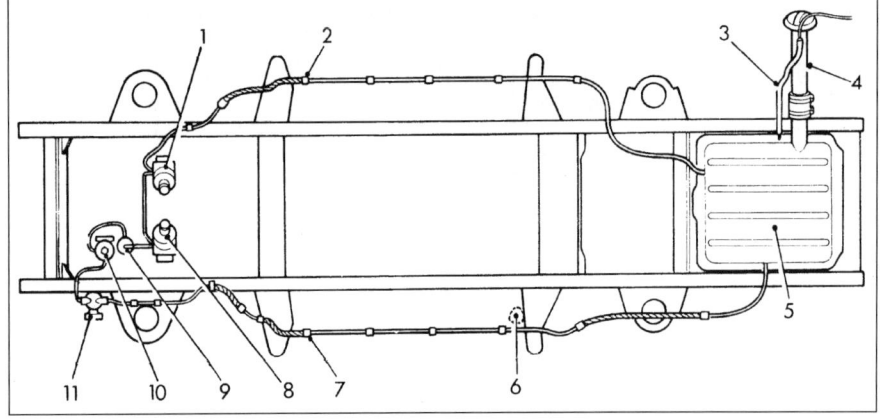

Fig. 3.1 The fuel system – typical component locations (Sec 1)

1 *Right-hand carburettor*
2 *Spill return fuel line*
3 *Fuel tank vent pipe*
4 *Fuel filler neck*
5 *Fuel tank*
6 *Location of electric fuel pump (later models)*
7 *Fuel supply pipe*
8 *Left-hand carburettor*
9 *In-line fuel filter (where fitted)*
10 *Mechanical fuel pump (early models)*
11 *Main fuel filter*

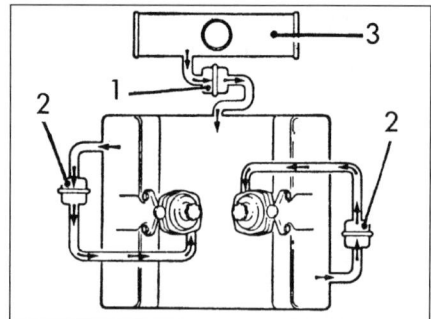

Fig. 3.2 Crankcase emission control system (Sec 1)

1 *Crankcase breather valve*
2 *Breather hoses and flame traps*
3 *Air cleaner*

⚠️ **Warning: Many of the procedures in this Chapter require the removal of fuel lines and connections, which may result in some fuel spillage. Before carrying out any operation on the fuel system, refer to the precautions given in Safety first! at the beginning of this manual, and follow them implicitly. Petrol is a highly-dangerous and volatile liquid, and the precautions necessary when handling it cannot be overstressed.**

2 Air cleaners - description

Standard type

1 The air cleaner is an oval metal cylinder. A paper disposable air filter is fitted into each end and alloy elbows feed the air to the twin

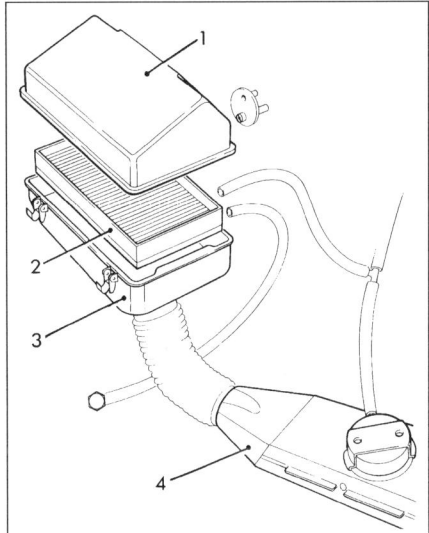

Fig. 3.3 Thermostatically controlled air cleaner components (Sec 2)

1 Air cleaner top half
2 Air filter element
3 Air cleaner bottom half
4 Air intake and valve

3.1 Removing the left-hand air intake elbow

carburettors. The air cleaner is located on mounting pegs attached to the rear of the inlet manifold and the air intake protrudes forward between the carburettors. On early models it is open-ended, but later vehicles have an air temperature control device mounted on the front of the intake pipe and attached to it by a short section of flexible hose.

Emission control equipment type

2 Some emission control equipment models are fitted with air cleaners of a different type to the standard one. These models have two separate air cleaners which are large rectangular containers with four clips, which retain the top to the bottom. One container is mounted onto each carburettor. Each container houses a flat element, rectangular in shape. The two air cleaners are linked together by balance pipes and each air cleaner has a separate air intake temperature control system attached to its intake connection at the front (Fig. 3.3). The temperature sensor is in the right-hand air cleaner.

3 Air cleaners - removal and refitting

Standard type

1 Undo the hose clips on each inlet pipe on either side of the air cleaner housing, then pull off the elbows. They are only retained by an O-ring to the carburettor (photo).
2 Release the choke cable from the clip on the air cleaner, and disconnect the two small pipes to the temperature sensor in the right-hand end of the air cleaner on models with air intake temperature control.
3 Lift the air cleaner assembly up to free it from the mounting pegs and detach the hose from the crankcase breather valve attached to the underside of the air cleaner as it is lifted. Release the air temperature intake valve flexible hose from the intake pipe (if applicable).
4 Place the air cleaner to one side.
5 Refitting is the reverse procedure to removal. Smear the carburettor intake O-rings

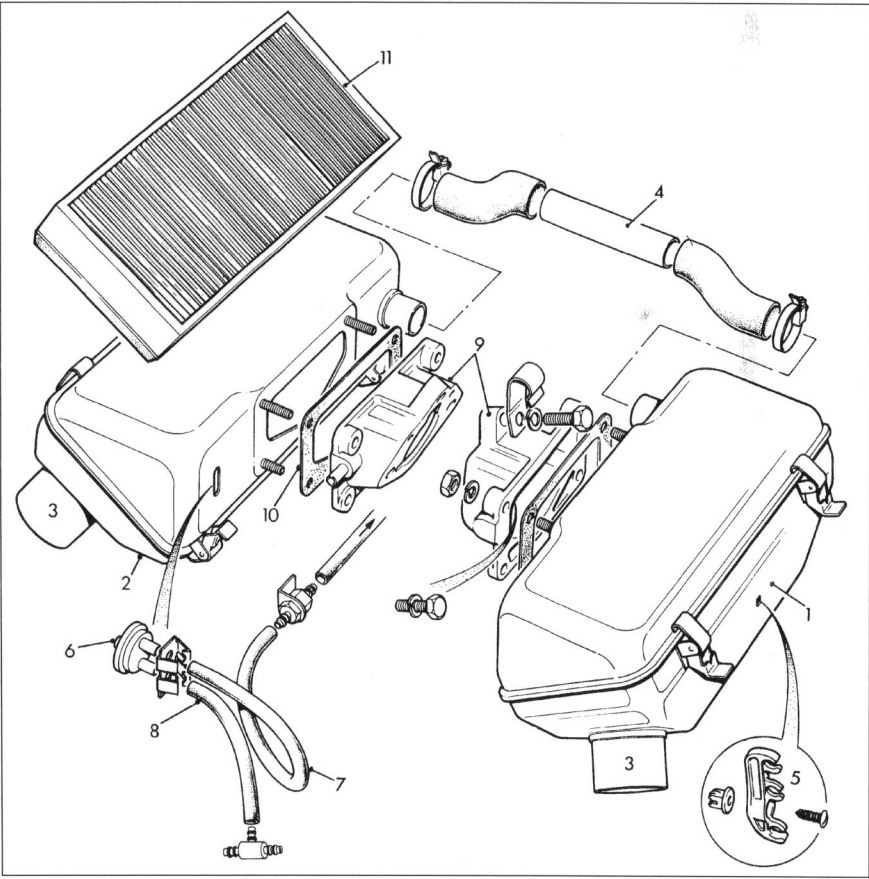

Fig. 3.4 Thermostatically controlled air cleaner layout (Sec 3)

1 Air cleaner container – left-hand	4 Balance pipe	manifold
2 Air cleaner container – right-hand	5 Spark plug lead clip assembly	8 Pipe to vacuum capsules
3 Air intakes	6 Temperature sensor	9 Carburettor adaptors
	7 Pipe to sensor from inlet	10 Gasket
		11 Air cleaner element

4.2 Removing the left-hand air filter element assembly

with molybdenum disulphide grease before refitting the elbows.

Emission control type

6 Disconnect the balance pipe between the two air cleaners.

7 Disconnect the rocker cover breather pipe and crankcase breather pipe from the right-hand air cleaner.

8 Slacken the hose clips and release both intake temperature control system flexible hoses from the air cleaner intakes.

9 Release the spark plug HT leads from the clips on the two air cleaners.

10 Disconnect the two pipes connected to the temperature sensor in the front inside face of the right-hand air cleaner.

11 Undo the four nuts which retain the air cleaner housings to their respective carburettor adaptor flanges.

12 Remove the air cleaners and gaskets from the carburettor adaptors.

13 Refitting is the reverse procedure to removal.

4 Air filter elements - renewal

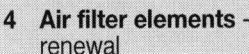

Standard type air cleaner

1 Slacken the hose clips on either end of the air cleaner and pull off the elbows.

2 Release the clips on each end of the air cleaner canister in turn and withdraw the endplate and air filter element from both ends (photo). Note that the air intake temperature control sensor pipes (if fitted) are attached to the right-hand assembly.

3 Remove the wing nut and retaining plate from the inner end of each assembly and remove the elements.

4 Fit a new element to each assembly and refit the retaining plate and wing nut. Check that the sealing washers on the end plate and retaining plate are in good condition, otherwise they must be renewed. Wipe clean the element housing.

5 Refit one assembly into the end of the housing and secure it with the spring clips. Refit the elbows and secure the hose clips.

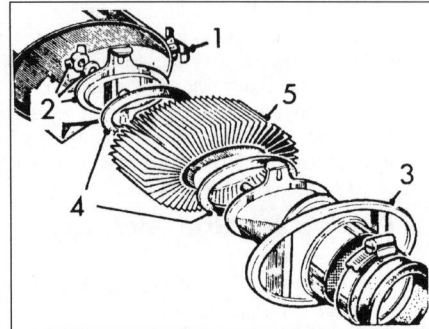

Fig. 3.5 Air filter element and endplate assembly (standard type) (Sec 4)

1 Canister clips
2 Wing nut and washer
3 Endplate
4 Sealing washers
5 Element

Emission control type (rectangular) air cleaners

6 Undo the four spring clips which retain the two halves of the air cleaner housing together, release the spark plug leads from the clip on the air cleaner and separate the air cleaner halves.

7 Lift the element out of the housing and place it to one side.

8 Fit a new element to the air cleaner. Note that the chamfered edge faces downwards.

9 Refit the two halves together and secure with the four spring clips. Refit the spark plug leads to the clip in the lower half of the air cleaner.

5 Air intake temperature control system - description

1 In order that the engine can operate at its most efficient air-to-fuel ratio, later vehicles have a system which is designed to achieve

an optimum running temperature of 38°C (100°F) as quickly as possible regardless of the outside air temperature.

2 The system comprises the following elements:

(a) A vacuum-operated thermostatically controlled flap valve in the air cleaner intake pipe(s)

(b) A hot box over the right-hand exhaust manifold connected to the air intake pipe by a flexible hose. Models with two air cleaners have a hot box over each exhaust manifold feeding their own air cleaners

(c) A temperature sensing device situated in the air cleaner on the clean side of the air filter element. In vehicles with two air cleaners it is located in the right-hand one

(d) A pipe from the inlet manifold attached to the temperature sensing device via a non-return valve

(e) A further pipe from the other side of the temperature sensing device to the vacuum capsule(s) operating the flap valve(s)

3 The flap valve controls the direction of the air supply. When the engine is cold the flap will cut off the cold air supply and will only draw air from the 'hot box' area. As the engine warms up, so the flap will gradually alter its setting so that a mixture of cold and hot air is drawn into the engine. When the engine is fully warmed up the flap will close off the hot air supply and allow only cold air to be drawn in. This, however, depends on the outside air temperature.

4 The optimum operating temperature is maintained by the sensing device in the air cleaner. The sensor allows the vacuum created in the inlet manifold to operate the flap valve. If the vacuum effect is changed suddenly (eg by depressing the accelerator hard to overtake), there will no effect on the flap valve because of the one-way valve that is fitted into the system.

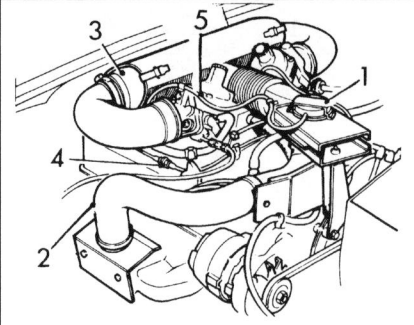

Fig. 3.6 The air intake temperature control system (Sec 5)

1 Flap valve and vacuum capsule
2 Hot box and flexible pipe to air intake
3 Air cleaner
4 Inlet manifold-to-sensor pipe
5 Vacuum pipe to vacuum capsule

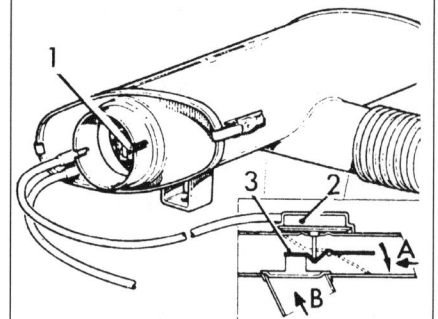

Fig. 3.7 Air cleaner sensor and flap valve assembly (Sec 5)

1 Temperature sensor located inside air cleaner
2 Vacuum capsule
3 Flap valve
A Cold air intake
B Hot air intake

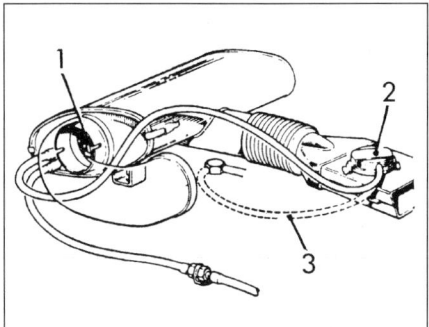

Fig. 3.8 Checking the temperature sensor or vacuum capsule (Sec 6)

1 *Temperature sensor*
2 *Vacuum capsule and flap valve*
3 *Temporary pipe connected directly to the inlet manifold*

6 Air intake temperature control system - operational check

1 Check the correct operation of the flap valve(s) in the air intake(s) by observing the valve(s) after starting the engine from cold.
2 The flap valve(s) should start to open slowly within a few minutes of starting up. They should continue to open until a steady position is reached. This position will be dependent on the outside air temperature.
3 If the valve(s) do not open at all then the fault can lie in two places. Either the vacuum capsule which operates the flap valve or the temperature sending device has failed, or both can be defective.
4 Failure of the temperature sensor or valve can be checked by connecting a pipe directly from the flap valve to the inlet manifold. If the flap valve now opens then the sensor is faulty. If the flap valve still does not move then the vacuum capsule operating the flap valve is at fault.
5 Renew the faulty part. The vacuum capsule and flap valve form an integral part of the air intake assembly.

7 Flap valve - renewal

Non-emission controlled models

1 The flap valve is an integral part of the front section of the air intake assembly, together with the vacuum capsule. The whole assembly has to be renewed if the valve becomes faulty or the vacuum capsule is defective.
2 Disconnect the vacuum pipe to the vacuum capsule.
3 Undo the two self-tapping screws on the top of the air intake box. One has a clip which retains the vacuum pipe and the other has a double clip which retains the carburettor-to-distributor vacuum pipe. The two screws also retain the front section of the air intake to the rear section.
4 Lift the air intake section upwards and release the rubber mounting from the pin. Release the pipe from the hot air box from the underneath of the air intake and remove the assembly.
5 Fit a new unit following the reverse procedure.

Emission controlled models

6 Disconnect the vacuum pipe from the vacuum capsule.
7 Slacken the hose clip which retains the air intake box to the hot box flexible pipe connector from the exhaust manifold.
8 Remove the two self-tapping screws which retain the intake box to the connector and withdraw the assembly.
9 Fitting the new unit follows the reverse procedure.

8 Temperature sensor - renewal

1 The temperature sensor for the air intake flap valve(s) is located in the right-hand end of the air cleaner in conventional systems, or in the inside face of the right-hand air cleaner where full emission control equipment is fitted.
2 If the standard air cleaner is fitted, remove the right-hand air filter element assembly as already described in Section 4. Disconnect the two tubes which run to and from the sensor.
3 With the assembly on the workbench, remove the sensor from the endplate.
4 With the rectangular air cleaner, remove the right-hand air cleaner as described in Section 3. Separate the two halves to remove the element. The sensor can then be extracted from the side of the air cleaner housing.
5 Fit a new sensor to the air cleaner and follow the reverse procedure to removal.

9 Crankcase breather valve - renewal

Vehicles with standard air cleaner

1 Remove the air cleaner as described in Section 3.
2 Undo the single self-tapping screw and slide the valve out of the retaining clamp (photo).
3 Pull the valve carefully out of the hose from the crankcase. Equally carefully pull off the short length of hose from the valve outlet end. With age the material from which the valve is made goes brittle and it is very easy to break off the two ends.
4 Fit a new filter with the end marked 'IN' facing forwards. If the filter is marked with arrows, they must point to the rear.
5 Clamp the retaining screw and fit the filter hoses.
6 Refit the air cleaner.

Vehicles with twin air cleaners

7 If the vehicle has full emission control equipment and two air cleaners, the valve can be renewed by simply disconnecting the tubes at either end of the valve which is easily reached. The points in paragraph 4 still apply. The location of the valve may vary according to equipment fitted.

10 Flame traps - removal, cleaning and refitting

1 Two flame traps are fitted. One is located on each side of the engine between the rocker cover and the carburettor in the rocker breather pipe.
2 Disconnect the pipe from the rocker cover and carburettor at either end and remove it. Separate the flame trap from the pipes (photo).

9.2 The crankcase breather valve

10.2 Disconnecting the breather pipe from the carburettor

11.2 The throttle cable is connected to the linkage by a clevis pin

11.3 Undo the adjuster nut to free the cable from the bracket

11.5 The cable is attached to the top of the pedal by a clevis pin (arrowed)

3 Place the flame trap and pipes in a petrol bath and clean them. Allow the flame trap to dry. Pull dry rag through the pipes.

4 Refitting is the reverse procedure to removal.

11 Throttle cable - removal, refitting and adjusting

1 Remove the air cleaner as described in Section 3.

2 Remove the split pin and clevis pin and disconnect the cable end from the carburettor linkage (photo).

3 Slide back the rubber cover and undo the adjuster nut so that the adjuster can be removed from the bracket (photo).

4 Inside the vehicle, remove the right-hand lower dash panel to reach the top of the accelerator pedal.

5 Remove the split pin and clevis pin so that the cable is freed from the pedal (photo).

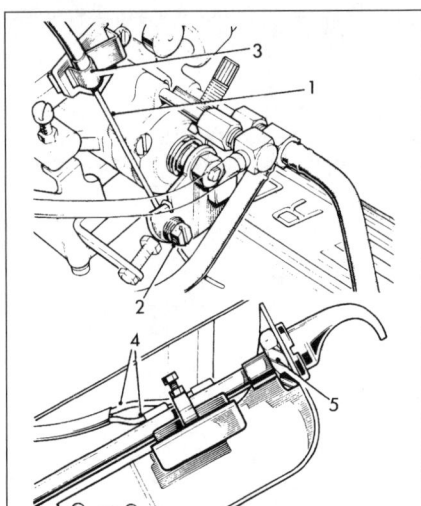

Fig. 3.9 Choke cable connections (Sec 12)

1 *Choke inner cable*
2 *Trunnion retaining screw*
3 *Cable retaining clip*
4 *Warning light wires*
5 *Retaining nut*

6 Undo the outer cable retaining nut and withdraw the cable and grommet into the engine compartment. The complete cable can now be removed.

7 Adjust the cable with the throttle pedal fully released. The adjustment should be such that the linkage moves with slight pressure on the pedal and not before. At the pedal end connection check that the cable yoke and clevis pin are not too tight a fit, and that the yoke can pivot freely.

12 Choke cable - removal and refitting

1 The choke cable is fitted to all vehicles which do not have an automatic choke.

2 The choke cable is attached to the trunnion at the front of the left-hand carburettor. Undo the screw to release it.

3 Disconnect the outer cable from the cable clip by the carburettor and the clip on the air cleaner housing.

4 Disconnect the choke warning light switch cables from the choke control assembly below the dashboard on the right-hand side of the steering column.

5 Undo the outer cable retaining nut and then withdraw the choke control knob and cable complete.

6 Refitting is the reverse procedure to removal. Ensure that the spring washer and nut are fitted over the cable before feeding it through the dashboard panel.

7 There should be approximately 1.5 mm (0.05 in) free play when the cable has been reconnected to the trunnion.

8 Run the engine and check the choke for correct operation.

13 Carburettors - general description

The carburettors are of the variable choke type. The fuel, which is drawn into the air passage through a jet orifice, is metered by a tapered needle which moves in and out of the

jet, thus varying the effective size of the orifice. This needle is attached to, and moves with, the air valve piston which controls the variable choke opening.

At rest, the air valve piston is right down, choking off the air supply, and the tapered needle is fully home with the jet virtually cutting off the fuel outlet from the jet.

For starting, the choke control is used except for the SET model which has an automatic starting device. The standard carburettor incorporates a disc valve for cold starting which allows additional fuel to flow into the mixture stream. The disc valve itself incorporates several orifices which are progressively uncovered as the disc is moved when the choke control is pulled. The throttle butterfly is also opened a small amount. Also included is a temperature controlled valve which weakens the mixture under light load and idling conditions when the engine is hot. The choke on SET models is operated automatically by a bi-metallic spring arrangement which is heated by water from the engine cooling system.

As soon as the engine fires, the suction from the engine (or manifold depression) is partially diverted to the upper side of the chamber in which the diaphragm attached to the air valve piston is positioned. This causes the valve to rise and provides sufficient airflow to enable the engine to run. As the throttle is opened further, manifold depression is reduced and now it is the speed of air through the venturi which causes the depression in the upper chamber, thus causing the piston to rise further. If the throttle is opened suddenly, the natural tendency of the air valve piston to rise - causing a weak mixture when it is least required (ie during acceleration) - is prevented by a hydraulic damper which delays the piston in its upward travel. The air intake is thus restricted and a proportionately larger quantity of fuel to air is drawn through.

The later types of carburettors with automatic choke (SET models) are fitted to enable the vehicle to conform to the prevailing emission control regulations, which vary from country to country. Tamperproof seals are also fitted to many carburettors so that adjustment, and therefore CO emissions, can

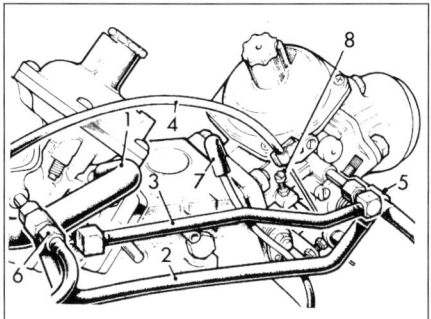

Fig. 3.10 Carburettor attachments (Sec 14)

1 Rocker breather pipe
2 Main fuel supply pipe
3 Choke fuel pipe
4 Choke cable
5 Main fuel supply union
6 Fuel spill return union
7 Vacuum pipe to distributor
8 Idle speed (throttle stop) screw

be controlled. The object is to prevent adjustment by unqualified mechanics. Satisfy yourself before removing a tamperproof seal that you are not breaking any local or national regulations by so doing.

14 Carburettors - removal and refitting

1 Remove the air cleaner(s) as described in Section 3.
2 Remove the air intake pipe(s), disconnecting the vacuum hoses (if applicable) first. Slacken the hose clip and separate the hose from the hot air box as the assembly is lifted away.
3 Disconnect the rocker breather pipes from the carburettors.
4 Disconnect the main fuel supply pipe which runs between the carburettors.
5 Disconnect the choke fuel supply pipe which runs between the carburettors.

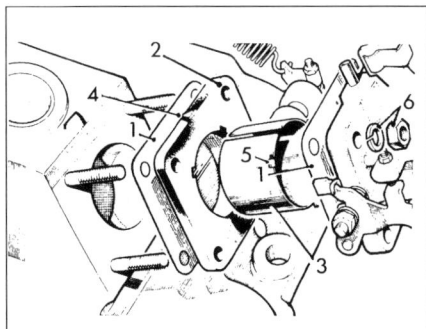

Fig. 3.12 Gaskets, insulator and liner assembly (Sec 14)

1 Gaskets	5 Lug
2 Insulator	6 Carburettor
3 Liner	retaining nuts and
4 Arrow	washers

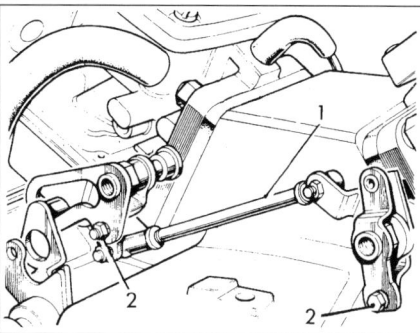

Fig. 3.11 Carburettor linkage connection (Sec 14)

1 Adjustable link
2 Throttle lever securing nuts

6 To remove the left-hand carburettor, disconnect the following:
(a) Throttle cable (Section 11)
(b) Choke cable (Section 12) or auto choke coolant pipes (as applicable)
(c) Fuel supply pipe at the front of the carburettor
(d) Throttle linkage between the carburettors
(e) Vacuum pipe to the distributor
7 To remove the right-hand carburettor, disconnect the following:
(a) Fuel return pipe from the union in front of the carburettor
(b) Throttle linkage between the carburettors
(c) Coolant pipes to automatic choke housing (where fitted)
(d) Brake vacuum servo hose from inlet manifold (for convenience)
8 Undo the four retaining nuts and washers for each carburettor and lift it away.
9 The gaskets and insulator can then be removed if necessary. Note that there is a liner fitted inside the insulator on some models.
10 Refitting of the carburettors is the reverse of the removal procedure, but the following points should be noted.
11 Clean the mating faces of the carburettor and the inlet manifold.
12 Fit the inner gasket, followed by the insulator, making sure that the arrow points towards the centre of the manifold.

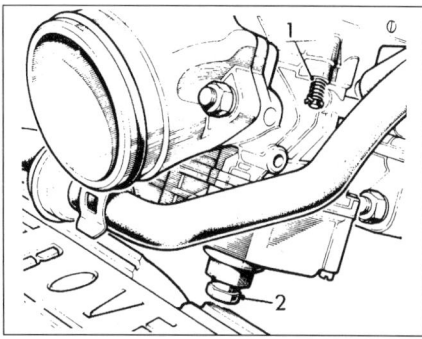

Fig. 3.13 Carburettor mixture adjustment (early models) (Sec 15)

1 Piston lifting pin
2 Jet adjusting screw

13 Refit the liner taking care to ensure that the lugs locate properly in the insulator recesses and do not stand proud. **Note:** *The liner can only be fitted one way round, that is with the tabs engaged in the slots.*
14 The remainder of the fitting procedure is a direct reversal of the removal sequence.
15 After installation it will be found necessary to tune and adjust the carburettors as described in Section 15.

15 Carburettors - tuning and adjusting

Before attempting to tune and adjust the carburettors, it is important to realise that certain items of equipment will be required. If these are not available, the job should not be attempted, but should be carried out by a suitably equipped Rover dealer. For those motorists intending to do the job themselves, it is essential that service tool number 'S.353' or a similar item is purchased beforehand to enable the later type of jet needle to be repositioned. An airflow balancing meter is also a very useful device for tuning and balancing, although listening carefully at the end of a rubber or plastic tube of about 1/4 in (6mm) diameter may be sufficient. It is also highly desirable that an exhaust gas analyser is used to check the CO content of the exhaust gas.

Before any attempt is made to adjust the carburettors, the ignition timing, spark plugs and distributor dwell angle should be checked and adjusted as necessary.

Manual choke carburettors

1 Check the throttle cable adjustment as described in Section 11. Also check that the linkage and cable move freely without any tendency to stick.
2 Start the engine and run it until warm.
3 The thermostat must be open (indicated by the radiator becoming warm) before switching off.
4 Slacken off the throttle adjusting lever securing nuts on both carburettors.
5 Start the engine and check that the idling speed is as specified. If necessary, adjust the throttle stop screws. On some models a tamperproof sleeve is fitted and this setting can only be adjusted by an authorized dealer with special tools.
6 Check the mixture in each carburettor in turn. Raise the piston very slightly (0.8 mm/ 0.031 in) using a long thin screwdriver, or by means of the piston lifting pin on early models. If the engine speed immediately increases, the mixture is too rich. If the engine speed immediately decreases, the mixture is too weak. No change, or a very slight fall in engine speed, indicates a correct mixture.
7 To correct the mixture strength, screw the jet adjusting screw (below the carburettor) into the carburettor to weaken or out of the carburettor to enrich the mixture.

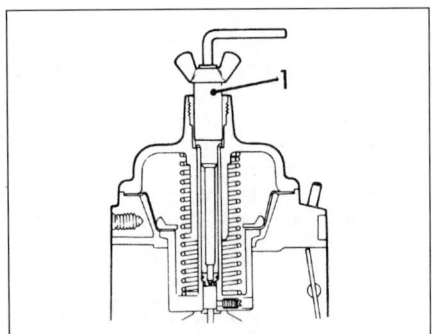

Fig. 3.14 Mixture adjustment, later models (Sec 15)

1 Special tool S.353

Fig. 3.15 Balancing meter in position (Sec 15)

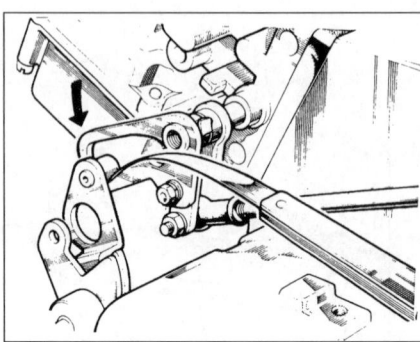

Fig. 3.16 Adjusting the left-hand throttle lever. Press in direction arrowed (Sec 15)

8 In later models tool S.353 has to be employed to adjust the mixture. Remove the piston damper from each carburettor in turn (Fig. 3.14).

9 Carefully insert the special tool S.353 into the dashpot until the outer part engages in the air valve, and the inner part engages in the hexagon of the needle adjuster plug.

10 Whilst preventing the outer part of the tool from moving (to prevent the diaphragm from rupturing) rotate the inner part either clockwise to enrichen the mixture or anti-clockwise to weaken the mixture.

11 When the mixture is correctly adjusted the engine speed will remain steady, or may drop very slightly, when the piston is lifted slightly.

12 Repeat this on the second carburettor, ensuring that the adjustment is made by the same amount. Remove the special tool.

13 The next stage is to balance the carburettors. The easiest way to do this is with an airflow balancing meter, although the rubber tube method can give a fairly accurate setting, depending on the experience of the person carrying out the task. Various proprietary balancing meters are available. The procedure described below relates to the Rover balancer, tool No 605330.

14 Zero the gauge on the meter and fit it to the carburettor adaptors. Ensure that there are no air leaks. If the engine speed falls or if the engine stalls when the gauge is fitted, the mixture is too rich. If the engine speed rises noticeably, the mixture is too weak.

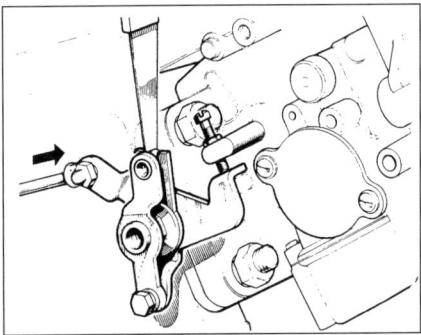

Fig. 3.17 Adjusting the right-hand throttle lever. Press in direction arrowed (Sec 15)

15 If necessary, remove the meter, adjust the mixture and then refit the meter. When correctly balanced the gauge should read in the central (zero) sector.

16 If the pointer moves to the left sector of the gauge, decrease the amount of air flow through the right-hand carburettor or increase the amount flowing through the left-hand one. Unscrew the idle speed (throttle stop) screw to decrease the airflow, or screw it in to increase it. If the pointer moves to the right reverse the procedure above.

17 If the idling speed rises too high or drops during these checks, adjust to the correct idle speed, maintaining the gauge needle in the zero area.

18 The difference in engine speeds set with and/or without the balancer in position will be negligible, being in the region of plus or minus 25 rpm. However, a wide variation in speeds would indicate a basic carburettor fault that may only be remedied by an overhaul, or replacement units.

19 Balancing the carburettors using a piece of rubber tubing is done by comparing the hiss in one carburettor intake with the hiss in the other (stick one end of the tubing in your ear). The noise is caused by the airflow through the carburettors and this is what you are trying to equalize.

20 Using a recognised type of CO meter, check the exhaust gas CO content.

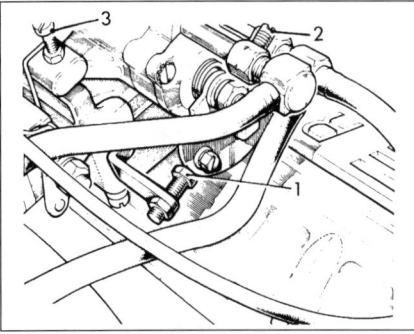

Fig. 3.18 Fast idle and cold start adjustment (Sec 15)

1 Fast idle adjustment screw
2 Cold start adjustment screw
3 Idle speed throttle stop screw

21 Insert the probe into the end of the exhaust pipe. The reading should not exceed the maximum given in the Specifications. Adjust the mixture if necessary to correct.

22 The next stage is to adjust and secure the throttle adjusting levers. Insert a 0.006 in (0.15 mm) feeler gauge between the throttle lever and the underneath of the roller on the countershaft lever. Apply pressure to the throttle lever to hold the feeler gauge and tighten the securing screw (Fig. 3.16).

23 Fit the feeler gauge between the pin on the right-hand throttle lever and the left leg of the fork on the adjusting lever on the right-hand carburettor. Apply light pressure to the linkage to hold the feeler gauge and tighten the screw. Withdraw the feeler gauge (Fig. 3.17).

24 Refit the air cleaner as described in Section 3.

25 To set the fast idle adjustment, which is pre-set on the left-hand carburettor and should not normally require adjustment, set the fast idle adjustment screw against the cam to give a fast idle speed within the specified limits when the choke warning light just goes out. On some carburettors this can only be adjusted by an authorised dealer with special tools.

26 The final step is to set the cold start adjuster screw. Where the vehicle is being used with an ambient temperature of -18°C (0°F) and above, push the cold start adjuster screw fully inwards and turn it through 90° to lock it in position. Should the vehicle be subjected to ambient temperatures below -18°C (0°F), the adjuster must be positioned fully outward.

Automatic choke carburettors

27 The following components must not be changed or modified in any way, or compliance with legal requirements relating to exhaust emissions may not be fulfilled.
(a) The fuel jet assembly
(b) The piston assembly
(c) The depression cover
(d) The temperature compensator
(e) The piston assembly return spring
The last two items if faulty must be replaced by new factory set components.

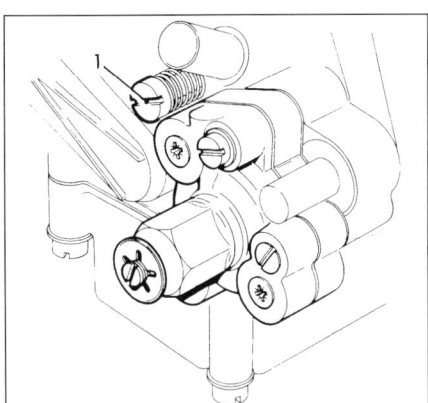

Fig. 3.19 CO content adjustment - auto choke carburettors (Sec 15)

1 Idle trim screw

Note: *During the following procedure do not allow the engine to idle for longer than three minutes without purging for one minute's duration at 2000 rpm.*

28 Run the engine until the normal operating temperature is attained, then remove the air cleaner(s) (refer to Section 3 if necessary).

29 Disconnect the throttle linkage so that each carburettor operates independently.

30 Ensure that the fast idle screw is clear of the fast idle cam, then check the balance of the carburettor inlet air flow using an airflow meter. If this is not available, listen to the airflow hiss using the small bore tube referred to in the introduction to this Section.

31 The procedure for adjusting the airflow balance is the same as that described for manual choke vehicles. But note that the adjustment screws are different. On auto choke carburettors the fast idle adjusting screw is in the place occupied by the idle speed (throttle stop) adjusting screw on manual choke types. The idle speed screw is adjacent.

32 Increase the engine speed to 1600 rpm and check the airflow balance. if necessary, turn the idle speed adjusting screws by equal amounts to achieve the balance.

33 Recheck the balance at idling speed.

34 Disconnect and plug the air pump outlet hose (if fitted).

35 With the engine still at normal operating temperature, check that the idle speed is as specified, then use an exhaust gas analyser to check that the CO content is within the specified maximum, or in accordance with the engine compartment emission control decal.

36 If slight adjustment is required, the idle trim screw on each carburettor may be rotated by equal amounts until the correct CO reading is obtained (Fig. 3.19).

37 If further adjustment is required, remove the piston damper from each carburettor and adjust the mixture as described in paragraphs 9 to 12.

38 Top up the carburettor piston dampers using engine oil. Fully raise each piston using a finger, and add oil until it is 1/4 in (6 mm)

below the top of the damper tube. Release the piston and refit the damper. Screw down the plug, then raise and lower the piston to ensure correct location of the oil retaining cup in the damper tube.

39 Recheck the CO content and idle speed as already described, then switch off the ignition. Unplug the air injection hose and reconnect it to the pump (if applicable).

40 Remove the auto choke housing and adjust the fast idle setting as described in Section 17.

41 All that remains is to adjust the throttle linkage. With the throttle lever clamp bolt slackened, disconnect the ball end link.

42 Unscrew both idle speed (throttle stop) screws away from the stops.

43 Adjust each screw until the lever and fast idle screw meet, then screw in a further three turns.

44 Check the airflow balance again and adjust if necessary.

45 Set the throttle link to a length of 3.452 in (77.68 mm).

46 Refit the ball end link. This will cause the left-hand carburettor throttle to open slightly.

47 Whilst holding the left-hand carburettor throttle lever in the fully closed position, take up the clearance with the spring lever screw.

48 Tighten the lever clamp bolt. Check and adjust the idle speed by turning the adjustment screws equal amounts on each carburettor.

16 Carburettors - overhaul

Diaphragm, piston assembly and metering needle

1 Unscrew and remove the oil cap and damper plunger.

2 Mark the installed position of the top cover, then remove the four screws and spring washers (photo).

3 Carefully lift off the cover, then remove the spring, retaining plate, diaphragm and piston, together with the metering needle (photos).

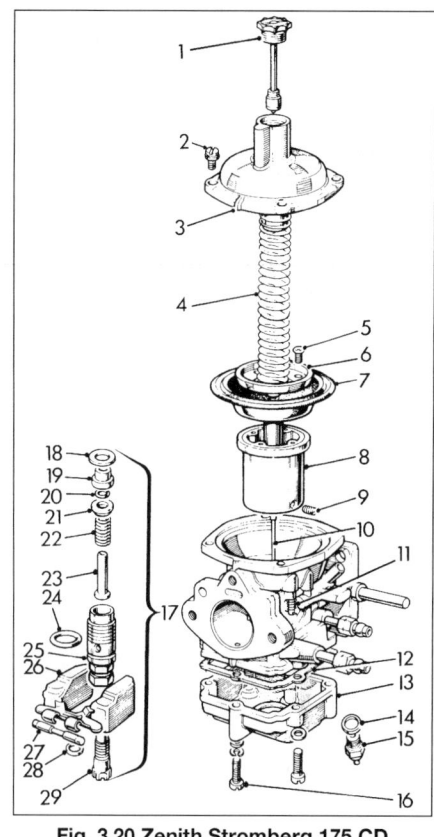

Fig. 3.20 Zenith Stromberg 175 CD carburettor – exploded view (Sec 16)

1 Oil cap and damper	15 Needle valve
2 Cover retaining screw	16 Float chamber screw
3 Top cover	17 Jet and float assembly
4 Spring	18 Washer
5 Screw	19 Top bush
6 Retaining plate	20 O-ring
7 Diaphragm	21 Guide bush
8 Piston	22 Spring
9 Grub screw	23 Jet orifice
10 Needle	24 O-ring
11 Piston lifting pin	25 Jet carrier
12 Float chamber gasket	26 Float
13 Float chamber	27 Float spindle
14 Washer	28 O-ring
	29 Jet adjusting screw

16.2 Undo the screws

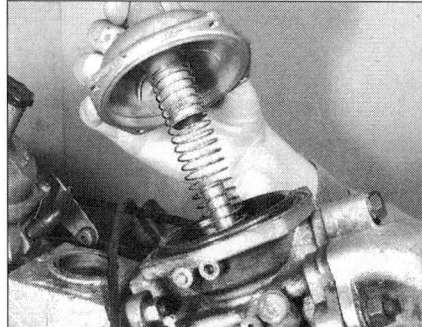

16.3a Lift off the cover and spring . . .

16.3b . . . then lift out the diaphragm and piston

16.4 The diaphragm retaining plate is retained by four screws

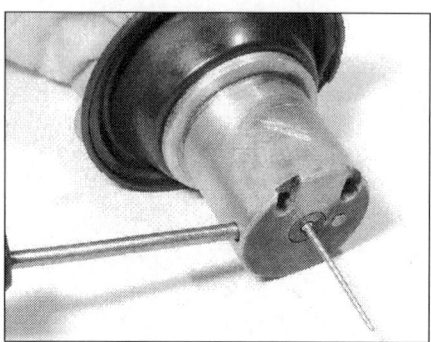

16.5 Undo the grub screw to remove the needle on early models

4 The diaphragm is retained to the top of the piston by a retaining plate and four small cross-head screws. Remove these and lift the diaphragm away. Fit a new diaphragm in the reverse order (photo).

5 To remove the needle from the base of the piston in early models, undo the locking screw in the side of the piston and remove it (photo). Refit the needle in the reverse order, but ensure that the shoulder of the needle is level with the face of the piston before locking the grub screw. The needle must be checked for centralisation during refitting.

6 Installation is the reverse of the removal procedure, but ensure that the inner and outer tags of the diaphragm locate in the air valve and body recesses respectively.

7 To centralise the metering needle in the jet orifice, refit the spring and top cover with the piston and diaphragm in position.

8 Lift the piston up and tighten the jet assembly fully. Then slacken it off half a turn. Release the piston and allow it to fall. This will automatically centralise the jet orifice. Slowly tighten the jet assembly, making sure that the needle is still free. Check by lifting the piston 6 mm (1/4 in) and letting it fall. The piston should stop firmly on the bridge.

9 Refill the dashpot with engine oil to within 6 mm (1/4 in) of the top (photo). Refit the damper plunger and screw in the cap.

10 Later model carburettors have fixed jets and sprung needles which cannot be removed or adjusted.

Float chamber needle valve - removal and installation

11 Remove the carburettors as described in Section 14.

12 Remove the jet assembly on earlier models only. Later models have a one-piece jet pressed into the body.

13 Remove the six screws and spring washers, and take off the float chamber and gasket.

14 Prise the spindle out of the locating clips, then remove the needle valve and washer.

15 Installation is the reverse of the removal procedure. Use a new washer on the float needle valve and ensure that the spindle is firmly secured in the locating clips. It is recommended that the float level is checked as described in the following paragraphs before fitting the float chamber.

Float level - checking and adjustment

16 Remove the carburettors as described in Section 14.

17 Remove the float chamber as described above.

18 With the carburettor in the inverted position, measure the distance between the carburettor body face to the highest point on the float. Bend the tab that contacts the needle valve, if necessary, to obtain a float height as given in the Specifications. Ensure

that the tab remains at right angles to the valve for satisfactory operation.

19 Install the float chamber using a new gasket. With early models, do not fully tighten the screws yet.

20 Refit the jet assembly to earlier models. One O-ring fits into the guide bush. Another O-ring fits over the jet carrier, and a third O-ring fits over the jet adjusting screw. Place the spring over the jet orifice and fit the guide bush onto it. Then fit the top bush to the jet orifice as well, with a plain washer on top. The jet assembly fits into the carrier. With the jet and carrier assembly together, insert it through the bottom of the float chamber and tighten it fully. Then tighten the float chamber retaining screws.

Temperature compensator - removal and installation

21 Remove the air cleaner (refer to Section 3 if necessary).

22 Remove the two screws and shakeproof washers, and detach the compensator. No repairs can be carried out; if defective, a new unit must be obtained (Fig. 3.22).

23 Installation is the reverse of the removal procedure. Ensure that the mating faces are clean and use new O-rings if the existing ones are hardened, distorted or cracked.

16.9 Refilling the dashpot with engine oil

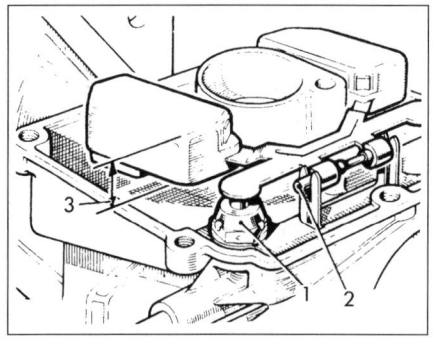

Fig. 3.21 Float level setting (Sec 16)

1 Float needle valve
2 Spindle
3 Float height – 0.67 to 0.71 in (17 to 18 mm)

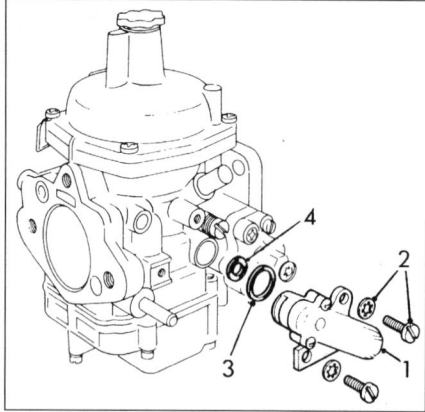

Fig. 3.22 Temperature compensator (Sec 16)

1 Compensator assembly
2 Retaining screw and washer
3 O-ring
4 O-ring

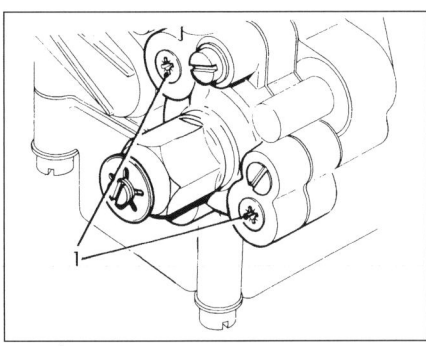

Fig. 3.23 Deceleration bypass valve (Sec 16)

1 Countersunk cross-head screws must not be touched

Deceleration bypass valve - removal and installation

24 Remove the carburettors as described in Section 14.

25 Remove the two cheesehead screws and the single countersunk head slotted screw. Do not touch the countersunk head cross-slotted screws (Fig. 3.23).

26 Withdraw the valve assembly and remove the gasket. No repairs can be carried out: if defective, a new unit must be obtained.

27 Installation is the reverse of the removal procedure. Ensure that the mating faces are clean and use a new gasket. Before the air cleaner is fitted, check the deceleration bypass valve(s) as follows.

28 With the engine idling at normal operating temperature, disconnect the vacuum pipe from the distributor.

29 Plug the end of the pipe with the finger and check that the idle speed increases to around 1300 rpm.

30 Should the speed increase to 2000 to 2500 rpm, it indicates that one or both of the deceleration bypass valves is floating off its seat. In this condition, if the throttle is momentarily opened; the additional increase in rpm will be slow to fall.

31 If adjustment is required, screw the bypass valve adjusting screw fully anti-

clockwise onto its seat **on the carburettor not being adjusted.** (This procedure will not need to be repeated when adjusting the second carburettor).

32 With the vacuum pipe still plugged, turn the bypass valve adjusting screw clockwise until the speed increases abruptly to 2000 to 2500 rpm.

33 Turn the screw anti-clockwise until the engine speed falls to around 1300 rpm.

34 Momentarily open, then release the throttle. The engine speed should increase then fall to around 1300 rpm. If this does not occur, repeat the adjusting sequence.

35 Repeat the adjustment for the second carburettor, then turn each bypass adjusting screw, 1/2 turn anti-clockwise to seat the valves.

36 Reconnect the vacuum pipe and refit the air cleaner.

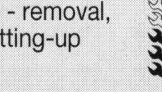

17 Automatic choke - removal, installation and setting-up

1 Remove the air cleaner from the carburettor.

2 Remove the carburettor from the engine.

3 Hold the throttle in the open position by inserting a suitable wooden plug between the throttle bore and butterfly.

4 Remove the three retaining screws and lift off the automatic choke and gasket. No repairs can be carried out: if defective, a new unit must be obtained.

5 Clean the carburettor and choke mating faces.

6 Remove the bolt and washer, and take off the water jacket and rubber sealing ring.

7 Remove the clamp ring (three screws and washers).

8 Carefully remove the heat mass, ensuring that the bi-metal coil is not strained.

9 Take off the heat insulator.

10 Using a new gasket, fit the choke body to the carburettor. Progressively and evenly tighten the screws to the specified torque; note that the lower screw is the shortest.

11 Adjust the fast idle screw to obtain a gap of 0.035 in (0.889 mm) between the base circle of the cam and the fast idle pin (dimension A in Fig. 3.26).

12 Position the heat insulator so that the bi-metal lever protrudes through the slot. Provided that the choke is in the ON position, the insulator can only be fitted in one position; the back of it locates in the choke body when the three holes are aligned.

13 Position the heat mass with the ribs facing outwards so that the bi-metal rectangular loop fits over the bi-metal lever.

14 Without lifting the heat mass, rotate it 30° to 40° only, in each direction, and check that it returns to the static position under spring action. If this does not occur, repeat paragraph 13.

15 Loosely fit the clamp ring, screws and spring washers.

16 Rotate the heat mass anti-clockwise 30° to 40° to align the scribed line on its edge with the datum mark on the insulator and choke body. Hold it in this position while tightening the clamp ring screws.

17 Fit the sealing ring and water jacket, but do not fully tighten the screw and washer.

18 Refit the carburettor to the engine. After connecting the water pipes, tighten the water jacket screw.

19 Top up the damper oil level as described in Section 16.

20 Operate the throttle before attempting to start the engine. This must be done in order to rest the auto choke.

21 Fit the air cleaner, then run the engine up to normal operating temperature and adjust the idle speed to the specified value by means of the throttle adjusting screw.

22 Stop the engine, allow it to cool, then top up the cooling system as necessary.

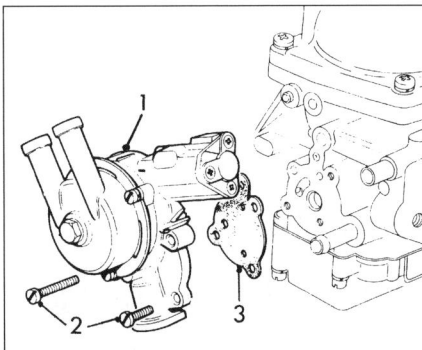

Fig. 3.24 Automatic choke assembly (Sec 17)

1 Automatic choke unit   3 Gasket
2 Screws

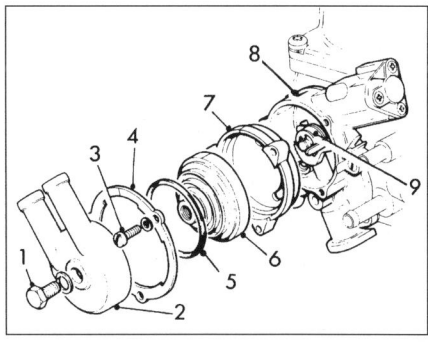

Fig. 3.25 Automatic choke – exploded view (Sec 17)

1 Centre bolt	*6 Heat mass*
2 Water jacket	*7 Heat insulator*
3 Screw	*8 Choke body*
4 Clamp ring	*9 Bi-metallic spring*
5 Rubber sealing ring	

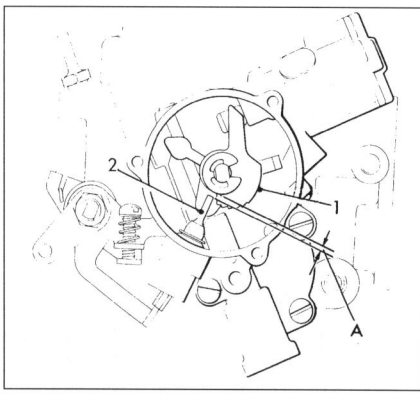

Fig. 3.26 Automatic choke adjustment (Sec 17)

1 Cam	*A = 0.035 in (0.9 mm)*
2 Fast idle pin	

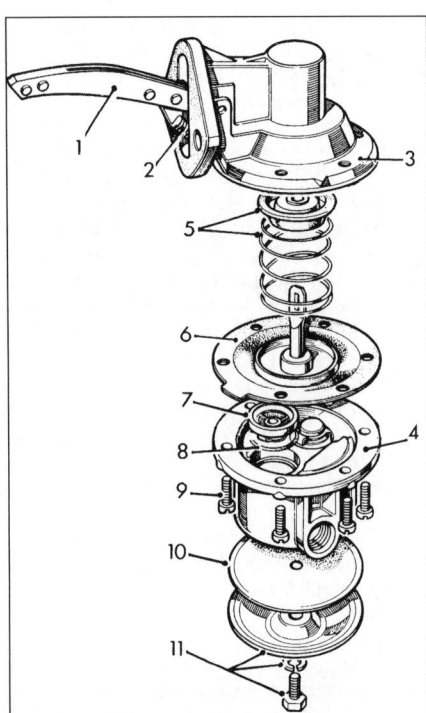

Fig. 3.27 Mechanical fuel pump (AC) – exploded view (Sec 18)

1 Operating lever
2 Spring
3 Top half of pump
4 Bottom half of pump
5 Diaphragm spring and oil seal
6 Diaphragm
7 Valve
8 Gasket
9 Screw
10 Pulsator diaphragm
11 Cover, screw and washer

18 Mechanical fuel pump - removal, overhaul and refitting

1 Remove the inlet and outlet pipe connections at the fuel pump. Plug the ends of the pipes to prevent fuel leaking out and dirt getting in (photo).

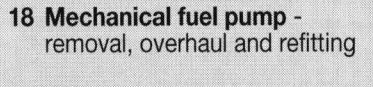

18.1 Fuel pump in situ – inlet pipe removed

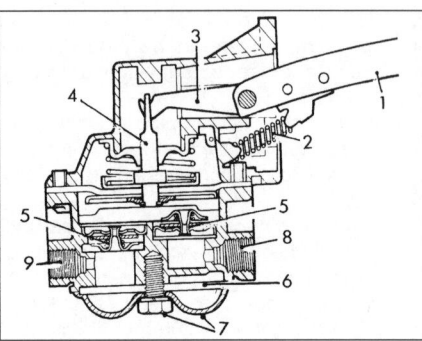

Fig. 3.28 Sectional view of mechanical fuel pump (Sec 18)

1 Operating lever
2 Lever return spring
3 Link
4 Diaphragm operating rod
5 Valves
6 Pulsator diaphragm
7 Cover and screw
8 Inlet connection
9 Outlet connection

2 Undo the two bolts securing the fuel pump to the timing cover.
3 Withdraw the fuel pump and remove the gasket (photo).
4 Undo the single screw from the bottom cover. Remove the cover and pulsator diaphragm (photo).
5 Scribe the two halves of the pump body and remove the retaining screws.
6 Separate the two halves of the pump. The diaphragm will still be attached to the upper half with the operating lever. 7Remove the operating bar return spring and hold the lever down.
8 Push the diaphragm into the body and tilt it to release the diaphragm operating rod from the link on the end of the operating lever.
9 Withdraw the diaphragm, spring and oil seal.
10 If the operating lever needs to be removed, use a parallel pin punch to drive the pivot pin and its end caps out. The lever and link can then be withdrawn.
11 If the valves need renewing, smooth out the staking marks and prise out the valve gaskets.

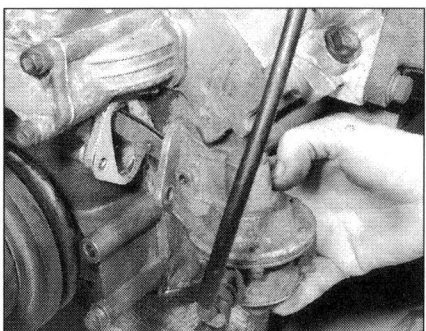

18.3 Withdrawing the fuel pump

12 Clean all the parts to be re-used in petrol and blow out all the passages with an air line.
13 Inspect the body of the pump and cover for cracks or damage. Examine screw holes and unions for worn or stripped threads.
14 Inspect the operating lever contact surface at the end for wear, and the lever and link for lateral play on the pivot pin.
15 If the unit is suspect then it is advisable to fit a replacement unit on an exchange basis, especially if the pivot pin is loose.
16 Reassembly and refitting are the reverse procedures to dismantling and removal, but note the following points.
17 When fitting the pivot pin, smear jointing compound on the end caps before refitting them.
18 When fitting the new diaphragm, make sure the spring and oil seal are located over the pull-rod before engaging the end of the pull-rod on the link hook.
19 Make sure that the valves are fitted the correct way round (Fig. 3.28). Stake them into place at four points evenly spaced around the valve.
20 Fit a new pulsator diaphragm as well as a new main diaphragm when overhauling a fuel pump.
21 Keep the operating lever fully depressed whilst tightening the fuel cover screws alternately and evenly. Make sure the holes in the diaphragm are correctly lined up before refitting the other half of the pump body, and line up the marks previously scribed.
22 When refitting the pump to the vehicle, remember that the operating lever fits under the operating cam on the end of the camshaft.
23 Use a new gasket when refitting the pump to the vehicle.

19 Electric fuel pump - removal, overhaul and refitting

1 The electric type of fuel pump is fitted to later vehicles and may be found in one of two places, It is located either on the chassis outrigger on the left-hand side of the car in front of the rear wheel, or beneath the rear passenger seat under the car.

18.4 Screw, cover and pulsator diaphragm removed

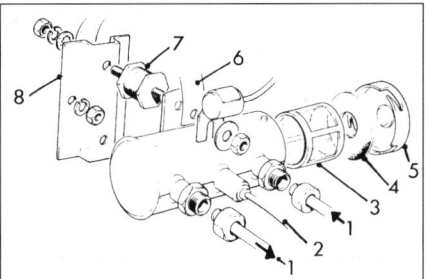

Fig. 3.29 Electric fuel pump – horizontally mounted model (Sec 19)

1 Fuel pipes
2 Electrical feed from ignition
3 Filter
4 Gasket
5 End cap
6 Earth strap
7 Rubber mounting
8 Pump mounting bracket

2 The pump may be mounted either vertically or horizontally and may or may not have a protective cover.

3 Disconnect the battery negative lead before starting work.

4 Remove the protective cover (where fitted).

5 Disconnect the electrical leads at the pump.

6 Undo the fuel pipe unions at the pump and plug the ends to prevent loss of fuel and ingress of dirt.

7 Undo the fuel pump mounting bracket nuts and washers and remove the pump and bracket together.

8 Remove the bracket from the pump, if necessary.

9 Only very limited overhauling is possible with an electrical fuel pump.

10 Remove the end cap (twist and pull off).

11 Withdraw the filter and gasket. Remove the magnet from the end of the cap and clean it.

12 Renew the filter and gasket and refit the end cap, having refitted the magnet in the centre of the cap.

13 Refit the pump in the reverse order to removal. Do not forget to reconnect the battery lead.

14 No further overhaul of the electrical fuel pump is possible. If cleaning as described fails to remedy any malfunction, the pump must be renewed.

20 Fuel main filter – element renewal

1 Unscrew the centre bolt which retains the filter bowl. Withdraw the bowl complete with filter, bolt, spring and seals.

2 Remove the small and large sealing rings from underneath the mounting bracket.

3 Remove the paper element from the bowl. Empty any petrol from the bowl and clean out any sediment.

4 Withdraw the seals and spring from the retaining bolt.

5 Fit a new element, small hole downward, to

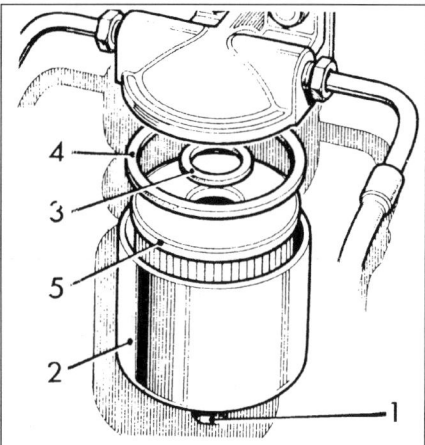
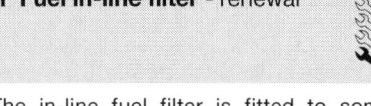
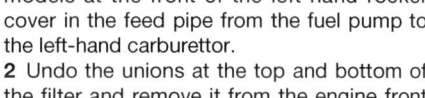

Fig. 3.30 Main fuel filter assembly (Sec 20)

1 Centre bolt
2 Bowl
3 Small sealing ring
4 Large sealing ring
5 Paper element

the filter bowl over the bolt with spring and new seals fitted.

6 Fit a new small sealing ring to the top of the element and a new large sealing ring to the mounting face.

7 Refit the filter bowl and tighten the bolt.

21 Fuel in-line filter - renewal

1 The in-line fuel filter is fitted to some models at the front of the left-hand rocker cover in the feed pipe from the fuel pump to the left-hand carburettor.

2 Undo the unions at the top and bottom of the filter and remove it from the engine front lifting eye after undoing the two small crosshead screws.

3 Fit a new filter with the end marked IN downwards. Alternatively, if marked with arrows they must point upwards.

4 Connect the fuel lines top and bottom, and connect the filter bracket to the lifting eye.

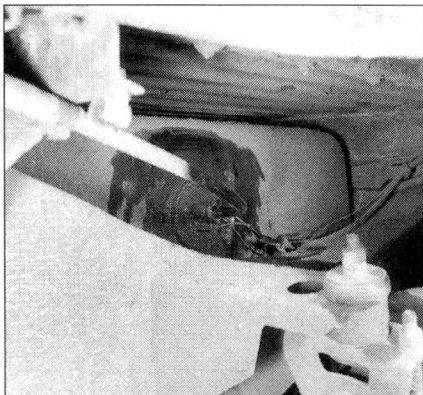

22.3 Tank gauge unit wiring and fuel feed pipe viewed through wheel arch

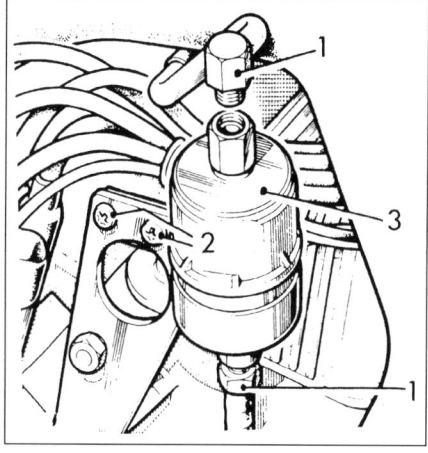

Fig. 3.31 In-line fuel filter (Sec 21)

1 Fuel pipe unions
2 Retaining screws
3 Filter

22 Fuel tank and tank gauge unit - removal and refitting

⚠️ *Warning: This operation must be carried out in a well ventilated area.*

1 Disconnect the battery negative lead for safety.

2 Remove the drain plug on the front right-hand side of the fuel tank and drain the petrol into a suitable (non-plastic) sealed container.

3 Disconnect the wires from the tank gauge unit (photo).

4 Undo the fuel outlet pipe union on the tank gauge unit.

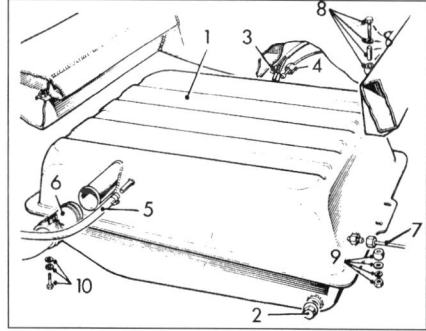

Fig. 3.32 Fuel tank installation (Sec 22)

1 Fuel tank
2 Drain plug
3 Gauge sender unit electrical leads
4 Fuel supply pipe
5 Vent pipe
6 Filler pipe flexible connector
7 Spill return fuel pipe
8 Tank retaining bolt washer, sleeve and bush
9 Tank retaining nut, washers, and bush
10 Mounting bolt

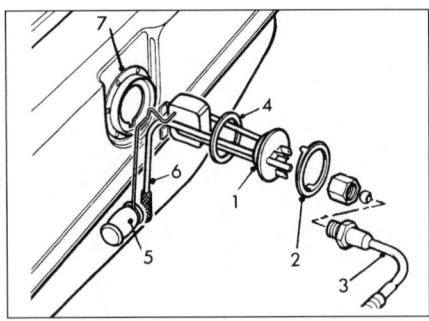

Fig. 3.33 Fuel gauge sender unit (Sec 22)

1 *Gauge sender unit*   5 *Float*
2 *Locking ring*   6 *Petrol pick-up*
3 *Petrol pipe*   *filter*
4 *Sealing ring*   7 *Mounting plate*

5 Release the breather pipe from the fuel tank next to the filler neck.
6 Undo the hose clips and release the filler neck from the tank.
7 Undo the pipe union and release the spill return pipe from the front of the tank.
8 Support the fuel tank and undo the tank mounting nuts and bolts front and rear.
9 Withdraw the fuel tank from under the vehicle.
10 With the tank removed from the vehicle the tank gauge unit can be removed.
11 Undo the locking ring and remove it. Withdraw the tank gauge unit with float, fuel pick-up strainer and seal.
12 Refit the assembly using a new seal and secure the locking ring tightly.
13 Refit the tank in the reverse order to removal.
14 Fill the tank with petrol and check for leaks.
15 Reconnect the battery lead.
16 Never be tempted to solder or weld a leaking fuel tank unless it has been thoroughly steamed out beforehand. This work should be left to the professionals. Temporary repairs are seldom satisfactory for long.

23 Exhaust manifolds - removal and refitting

Note: *The exhaust manifolds are handed. Check that any replacement parts are correct.*
1 Allow the exhaust system to cool down sufficiently if the engine has just been running.
2 Undo the hose clip and pull off the hot air intake/hose from the hot air box (where fitted).
3 Remove the bolts and washers, and lift away the hot air box (where fitted).
4 Bend back the ends of the locking tabs on the eight manifold retaining bolts (photo).
5 Raise the front of the vehicle and undo the three nuts securing the downpipe to the manifold flange (photo).
6 Lower the vehicle, undo the eight manifold retaining bolts and lift the manifold away (photo).

23.4 The manifold bolts have locking tabs or plates

7 Refitting is the reverse of removal, but the following points should be noted.
8 Clean the cylinder head and manifold faces scrupulously, as no gasket is used between the two parts.
9 Discard the two copper O-rings fitted to the downpipe flange and use new O-rings on reassembly.
10 Discard the old locking tabs and use new ones.
11 Fit the manifold and reconnect the downpipe, but do not turn back the ends of the tab washers at this stage, or refit the hot air box.
12 Start the engine, allow it to warm up and check for exhaust gas leakage.
13 Stop the engine and allow the exhaust system to cool down. Now check the tightness of the exhaust manifold bolts and the downpipe flange nuts.
14 Turn back the ends of the locking tabs on to the bolt heads.
15 The hot air box can now be refitted and the hot air hose reconnected to it (if applicable).

24 Exhaust system - renewal

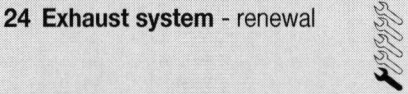

1 The exhaust system is of conventional design and comes in five sections:
(a) *Right-hand downpipe*

23.6 Lifting the right-hand exhaust manifold away

23.5 The downpipe is secured by three nuts to the manifold

(b) *Left-hand downpipe*
(c) *Front Y-section*
(d) *Main silencer box*
(e) *Tailpipe and silencer*
2 Early systems have a single pipe running from the main silencer box to the rear, later systems have twin pipes.
3 All the main pipe joints are flanged connections with three bolt locking collars, except for the two front downpipes (photo).
4 The system is supported by tough brackets with rubber bushes to allow flexing and U-bolt clamps.
5 When removing any section, apply penetrating oil liberally to the flange nuts and bolts before unscrewing them, and obtain new joint gaskets before reassembly.
6 When assembling the exhaust system do not tighten the flange coupling bolts any more than finger tight until the whole system has been connected.
7 Commencing at the manifold flange, proceed to secure the exhaust system, but take care that undue strain is not placed on any part of the system due to misalignment. Incorrect fitting will shorten the life of the system by causing fractures at the connecting points.
8 After fitting the system start the engine and check for exhaust gas leakages from the couplings and flanges.
9 Allow the system to cool down, then recheck the security of the entire system as some settling is bound to have occurred due to expansion and contraction.

24.3 Flanged pipe joint and U-bolt mounting bracket

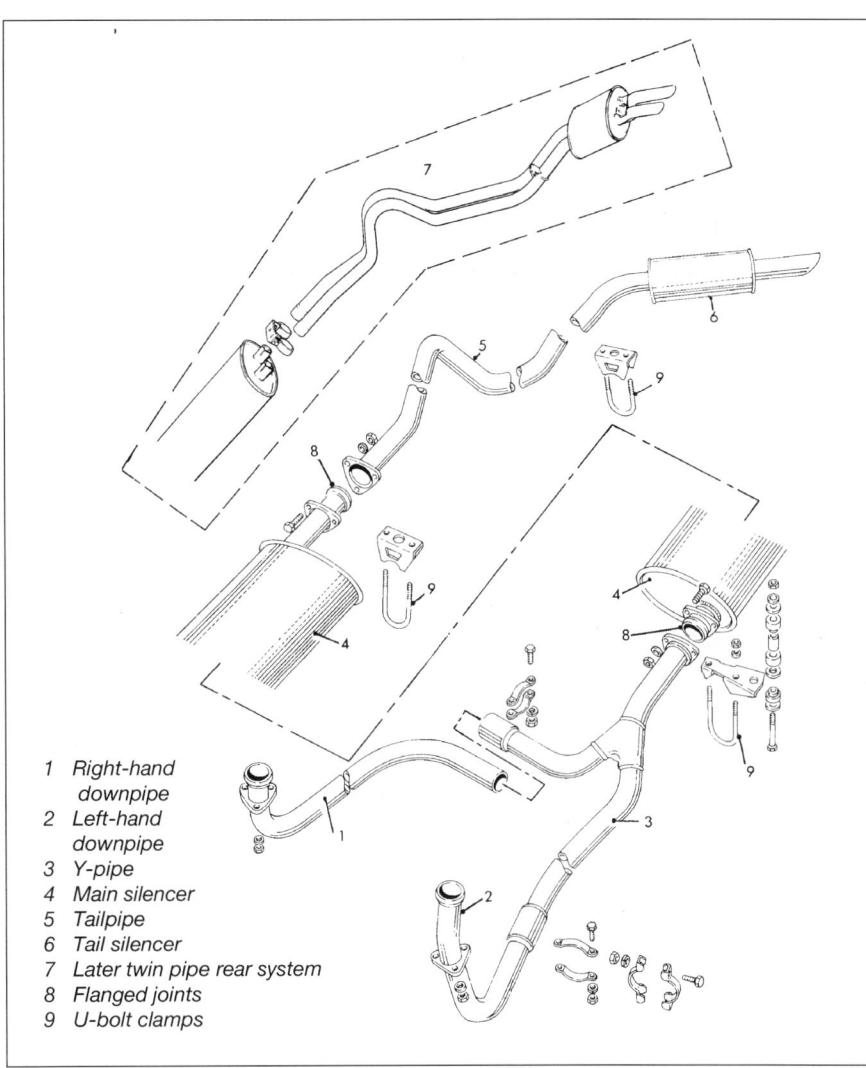

1 Right-hand downpipe
2 Left-hand downpipe
3 Y-pipe
4 Main silencer
5 Tailpipe
6 Tail silencer
7 Later twin pipe rear system
8 Flanged joints
9 U-bolt clamps

Fig. 3.34 Typical exhaust systems (Sec 24)

25 Emission control systems - general description

1 The standard emission control systems include the crankcase breather valve, rocker cover breather pipes and air intake temperature control systems.
2 This Section deals with the components which are fitted to vehicles with full emission control equipment.

Air injection system

3 This system is used to reduce the emission of hydrocarbons, nitric oxide and carbon monoxide in the exhaust gases, and comprises an air pump, a combined diverter and relief valve, a check valve and an air manifold.
4 The rotary vane type pump is belt-driven from the engine and delivers air to each of the exhaust ports.

5 The diverter and relief valve diverts air from the pump to atmosphere during deceleration, being controlled in this mode by manifold vacuum. Excessive pressure is discharged to atmosphere by operation of the relief valve.
6 The check valve is a diaphragm-spring operated non-return valve. Its purpose is to protect the pump from exhaust gas pressure both under normal operation and in the event of the drivebelt failing.
7 The air manifold is used to direct the air into the engine exhaust ports.

Air intake control air cleaner

8 Refer to Section 2 for further information on the air cleaner and temperature sensor.
9 The control system for the air cleaner incorporates a one-way valve so that full vacuum influence on the flap valve is maintained during sudden acceleration when the manifold vacuum is temporarily destroyed. The valve is installed in the vacuum line.

Evaporative control system

10 This system uses an activated absorption canister through which the fuel tank is vented, and incorporates the following features:
(a) The carburettor float chambers are vented to the engine when the throttle is open and to the absorption canister when the throttle is closed
(b) The carburettor constant depression is used to induce a purge condition through the canister. The crankcase breathing is also coupled into this system
(c) A separator tool is used to prevent fuel surges from reaching the canister which could otherwise saturate the system
(d) A sealed filler cap is used to prevent loss by evaporation
(e) The fuel filler tube extends into the fuel tank to prevent complete filling; this permits the fuel to expand in hot weather

Exhaust gas recirculation (EGR) system

11 To minimise nitric oxide exhaust emission, the peak combustion temperatures are lowered by recirculating a metered quantity of exhaust gas through the inlet manifold.
12 A control signal is taken from the throttle edge tapping of the left-hand carburettor. At idle or full load no recirculation is provided, but under part load conditions a controlled amount of recirculation is provided according to the vacuum signal profile of the metering valve. The EGR valve is mounted on the rear end of the left-hand exhaust manifold.

26 Emission control systems - repair and maintenance

1 This Section is similar to the previous one in that it covers only that equipment found on vehicles with full emission control systems.

Air pump - removal and installation

2 Detach the battery earth lead.
3 Disconnect the air pump hoses.
4 Remove the adjusting nut and bolt, and the pivot nut and bolt.

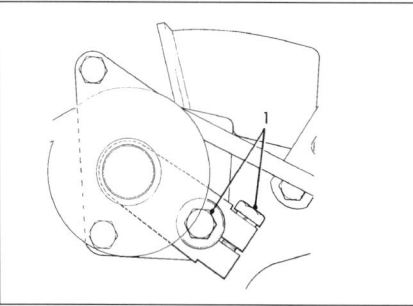

Fig. 3.35 Air pump drivebelt idler pulley (Sec 26)

1 Idler pivot and pinch-bolts

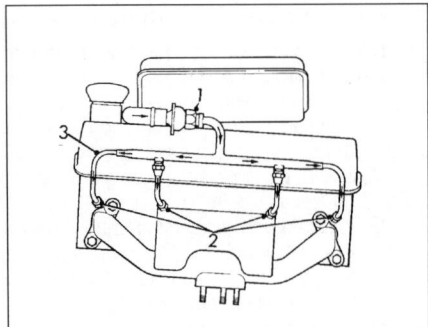

Fig. 3.36 Air distribution manifold – right-hand side (Sec 26)

1 Check valve
2 Manifold union nuts
3 Air distribution manifold

5 Remove the pump.
6 Installation is the reverse of the removal procedure. Refer to the following paragraphs for belt tensioning.

Air pump drivebelt - removal, installation and tensioning

7 Detach the battery earth lead.
8 Remove the alternator drivebelt, power steering pump drivebelt and air conditioning pump drivebelt (as applicable) in order to reach the air pump drivebelt.
9 Slacken the idler pulley mountings.
10 Push the idler pulley towards the engine and free the belt from the pulleys.
11 Fit a new belt and apply leverage to the idler pulley; then tighten the mounting nuts.
12 Check that the tension is correct (see Specifications).
13 Connect the battery earth lead.

Air distribution manifold - removal and installation

14 Remove the air cleaners as described in Section 3.
15 Uncouple the manifold pipework at the check valve union.

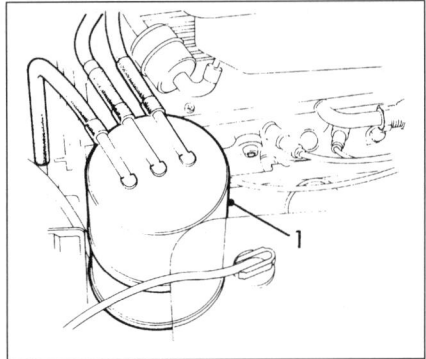

Fig. 3.39 Absorption canister (1) (Sec 26)

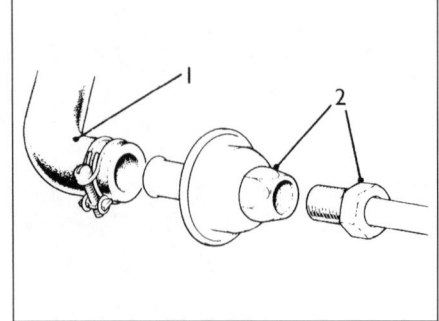

Fig. 3.37 Check valve installation (Sec 26)

1 Air hose
2 Air manifold/check valve union

16 Unscrew the four union nuts, one on each manifold, and withdraw the complete manifold. Alternatively the centre branches and the two outer unions can be released.
17 Refitting is the reverse of the removal procedure.

Check valve - removal, testing and installation

18 Disconnect the air hose at the check valve.
19 Using two open-ended spanners, unscrew the check valve whilst preventing strain on the air manifold.
20 If necessary the valve can be checked by blowing air (by mouth only) through the valve. Air should pass through from the hose connection end but not from the manifold end. Renew a defective valve.
21 Installation is the reverse of the removal procedure.

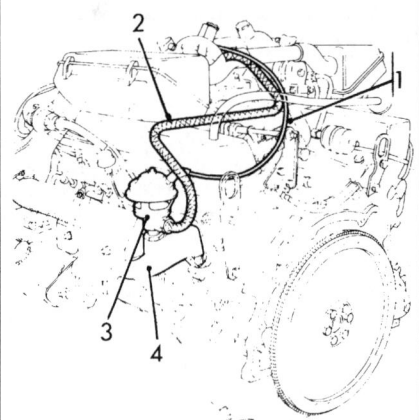

Fig. 3.40 EGR valve installation (Sec 26)

1 Vacuum pipe
2 Asbestos lagged pipe
3 EGR valve
4 Left-hand exhaust manifold

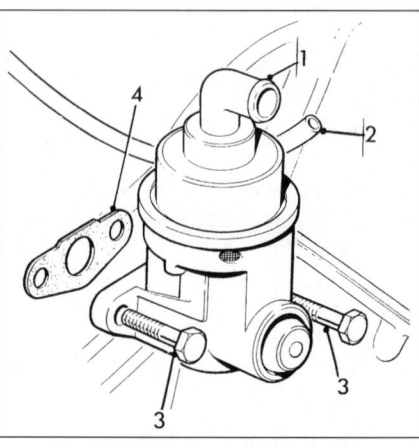

Fig. 3.38 Diverter and relief valve installation (Sec 26)

1 Air hose connection   3 Retaining bolts
2 Vacuum line   4 Gasket

Diverter and relief valve - removal and installation

22 Detach the battery earth lead.
23 Detach the hose and vacuum line from the diverter and relief valve.
24 Remove the two bolts which retain the valve to the air pump.
25 Remove the valve.
26 Installation is the reverse of the removal procedure; it is recommended that a new gasket is used between the valve and bracket.

Absorption canister - removal and installation

27 Disconnect the bottom pipe leading to the anti-run-on valve (if fitted).
28 Disconnect the three top pipes, noting their installed positions.
29 Loosen the clamping screw and lift out the canister.
30 Installation is the reverse of the removal procedure.

⚠️ **Warning: Do not use compressed air to clean out the absorption canister or clear a blockage. Explosive gas in the canister could be ignited by the heat generated by the compressed air passing through the canister.**

Exhaust gas recirculation (EGR) valve - removal and installation

31 Disconnect the vacuum pipe from the valve.
32 Disconnect the asbestos-lagged pipe from the valve.
33 Unscrew the valve from the exhaust manifold.
34 Refitting is the reverse of the removal procedure. Ensure that the valve is securely sealed to the exhaust manifold.

Fault finding - fuel system

Unsatisfactory engine performance and excessive fuel consumption are not necessarily the fault of the fuel system or carburettor(s). In fact they more commonly occur as a result of ignition faults. Before acting on the fuel system it is necessary to check the ignition system first. Even though a fault may /ie in the fuel system it will be difficult to trace unless the ignition is correct. The table below therefore assumes that the ignition system is in order.

Smell of petrol when engine is stopped

☐ Leaking fuel lines or unions
☐ Leaking fuel tank

Smell of petrol when engine is idling

☐ Leaking fuel line unions between pump and carburettor(s)
☐ Overflow of fuel from float chamber due to wrong level settings, ineffective needle valve or punctured float

Excessive fuel consumption for reasons not covered by leaks or float chamber faults

☐ Worn needle
☐ Sticking needle

Difficult starting, uneven running, lack of power, cutting out

☐ Incorrectly adjusted carburettor(s)
☐ Float chamber fuel level too low or needle sticking
☐ Fuel pump not delivering sufficient fuel
☐ Intake manifold gasket leaking, or manifold fractured
☐ Carburettor diaphragm split

Fault finding - emission control systems

Low CO content of exhaust gases (weak or lean mixture)

☐ Fuel level incorrect in carburettor(s)
☐ Incorrectly adjusted carburettor(s)
☐ Induction air leak

High CO content of exhaust gases (rich mixture)

☐ Incorrectly adjusted carburettor(s)
☐ Choke sticking
☐ Absorption canister blocked
☐ Fuel level incorrect in carburettor(s)
☐ Air injection system fault

Noisy air injection pump

☐ Belt tension incorrect
☐ Relief valve faulty
☐ Diverter faulty
☐ Check valve faulty

Notes

Chapter 4 Ignition system

For modifications, and information applicable to later models, see Supplement at end of manual

Contents

Degrees of difficulty

| Easy, suitable for novice with little experience | Fairly easy, suitable for beginner with some experience  | Fairly difficult, suitable for competent DIY mechanic  | Difficult, suitable for experienced DIY mechanic 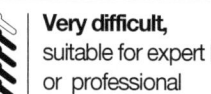 | Very difficult, suitable for expert DIY or professional  |

Specifications

General

System type	Contact breaker and coil with ballast resistor
Firing order	1-8-4-3-6-5-7-2
Location of No 1 cylinder	Front of left-hand bank
Cylinder numbering (from front):	
Left-hand bank	1-3-5-7
Right-hand bank	2-4-6-8

Distributor

Make and type	Lucas 35D8
Serial number:	
Pre-1972	41325
1972 to 1976	41487
1976 onwards	41680A
Full emission control models	41681A
Direction of rotation	Clockwise viewed from above
Contact breaker points gap (initial setting only)	0.014 to 0.016 in (0.35 to 0.40 mm)
Dwell:	
Angle	26 to 28°
Percentage	58 to 62%
Condenser capacity	0.18 to 0.25 microfarad

Ignition coil

Make and type	Lucas 16C6 and BA 16C6 with ballast resistor
Primary resistance	1.2 to 1.4 ohms at 20°C (68°F)
Consumption at 2000 rpm	1 amp approximately

Spark plugs

	Type	Electrode gap
3528 cc engine	Bosch WR 7 D+	0.8 mm
3947 cc engine	Bosch WR 9 D+	0.8 mm

Ignition timing

Distributor serial number	41326	41487	41680A	41681A
Static timing, and dynamic at idle speed:				
For 91 to 93 octane fuel	3° BTDC	5° ATDC	7° BTDC	5° ATDC
For 85 octane fuel	0° (TDC)	8° ATDC	5° BTDC	-
Centrifugal advance (decelerating check, vacuum pipe disconnected, initial advance/retard not included):				
4800 rpm	27° to 31°	23° to 27°	24° to 28°	22° to 26°
1800 rpm	15° to 19°	10° to 14°	12° to 16°	2.5° to 6.5°
1000 rpm	5° to 9°	0° to 5°	1° to 5°	No advance

1 General description

In order that the engine may run correctly, it is necessary for an electrical spark to ignite the fuel/air charge in the combustion chamber at exactly the right moment in relation to engine speed and load. The ignition system is based on supplying the low tension voltage from the battery to the ignition coil where it is converted to high tension voltage by virtue of contact breaker operation. The high tension voltage is powerful enough to jump the spark plug gap in the cylinder many times a second under high compression pressure, providing that the ignition system is in good working order and that all adjustments are correct.

The ignition system comprises two individual circuits. known as the low tension circuit and the high tension circuit.

The low tension (or primary) circuit comprises the lead from the positive terminal of the 12 volt battery, the ignition/starter switch, a ballast resistor wire, the primary winding of the 6 volt ignition coil, the contact breaker points of the distributor (which are bridged by the condenser) and an earth connection. Since the negative terminal of the battery is also earthed, current will flow in the low tension circuit when the distributor contacts are closed and a magnetic field will be set up in the primary winding of the coil.

The high tension (or secondary) circuit comprises the secondary winding of the ignition coil (one end of which is connected internally to the output terminal of the primary winding), the heavily insulated ignition lead from the centre of the coil to the centre of the distributor cap, the rotor arm, the spark plug leads and the spark plugs.

When the contacts open, the magnetic field in the primary coil winding collapses rapidly and induces a voltage in the secondary winding. At this instant, the distributor rotor is bridging the coil output terminal and one of the spark plug connections in the distributor caps, and a spark therefore jumps the electrode gap. The condenser across the contacts serves the dual purpose of assisting the rapid collapse of the magnetic field in the primary winding and acting as a spark suppressor for the contacts.

The whole cycle is repeated when the contacts open again which will be when the distributor shaft has turned through 45°, but this time the next spark plug in the ignition sequence will fire.

During the starting sequence, the ballast resistor or resistor wire in series with the coil primary winding is bypassed so that the full battery voltage (which will be low anyway due to the high current drawn by the starter motor) is passed to the 6 volt coil. In this way a bigger secondary voltage will be induced and therefore a bigger spark will result.

Whilst the above sequence is apparently satisfactory, in that the distributor can be physically set to provide a spark when it is needed, some variation of ignition timing is required to obtain optimum efficiency under varying conditions of engine load and speed. A centrifugal advance mechanism is used inside the distributor body which will give an increasing amount of spark advancement (ie, firing earlier in the cycle) as the engine speed increases. Additionally, a vacuum device is fitted, which is operated by the depression in the inlet manifold and will give additional spark advancement at low and moderate throttle openings, eg when the car is cruising. At wide throttle openings, eg when hill climbing, there is less suction in the inlet manifold and hence there will be little or no additional advancement. The combination of the two devices will provide a wide range of ignition advancement or retardation according to the engine requirements at any particular time.

2 Condenser - removal, testing and refitting

1 The purpose of the condenser (sometimes known as the capacitor) is to ensure that when the contact breaker points open, there is no sparking across them which would waste voltage and cause wear. It also boosts the HT voltage.

2 The condenser is fitted in parallel with the points. If it develops a short circuit, ignition failure will result as the points will be prevented from interrupting the low tension circuit.

3 If the engine becomes very difficult to start or begins to 'miss' after several miles running and the points show sign of excessive wear or burning, then the condition of the condenser must be suspect.

4 Without special equipment the only way to check whether the condenser is faulty is to fit a new one and observe the results.

5 To remove the condenser from the distributor, take off the distributor cap and rotor arm. Now remove the condenser locating screw and lead connection (photo).

6 Refitting the condenser is the reverse of the removal procedure, but take care that the lead cannot contact the moving parts or become trapped when the cap is refitted.

3 Contact breaker points - checking and adjustment

1 At the intervals specified in Routine Maintenance, or whenever new contact breaker points have been fitted, the points should be checked and adjusted as described below. For best results the use of a dwell meter is indispensable, but if one is not available, setting the contact breaker gap with feeler gauges will enable the engine to run until the dwell angle can be checked professionally.

Points gap adjustment

2 The contact breaker points gap should be adjusted as follows when fitting new points to enable the engine to be run.

3 With the distributor cap and rotor arm removed, turn the engine on the starting handle until the heel of the contact breaker is on a cam peak, ie, points opened by the cam as far as they will go.

4 Insert a clean feeler gauge between the point faces and check the gap. The correct gap is given in the Specifications. Take care not to contaminate the point faces with oil from the feeler gauge.

5 If adjustment is necessary, turn the adjusting nut on the side of the distributor clockwise to increase the gap or anti-clockwise to reduce it (photo). If much adjustment is required, it may be necessary to loosen the points retaining screw.

6 If no external adjuster is fitted, slacken the points retaining screw and move the fixed contact plate as necessary until the correct gap is achieved. Tighten the screw on completion.

7 Refit the rotor arm and distributor cap, then check the dwell angle as described below.

Dwell angle adjustment

8 Dwell angle is the angle through which the distributor cam turns between the instants of closure and opening of the contact breaker

2.5 Removing the condenser (points removed)

3.5 Insert a feeler gauge and adjust the hexagonal nut

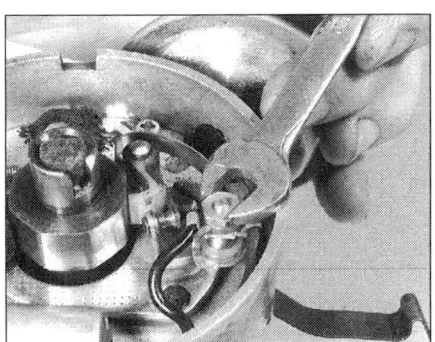

4.4a Removing the nut on the terminal post . . .

4.4b . . . and the fixed contact screw

5.5 Mark the alignment of the distributor rotor arm to the body

points. Reducing the points gap increases the dwell angle: increasing the gap reduces the dwell angle. The correct dwell angle is given in the Specifications.

9 Various proprietary instruments are available to measure dwell angle. Some operate with the engine running at idle speed, others require the engine to be cranked on the starter motor.

10 Connect the dwell meter to the engine in accordance with the maker's instructions. It may be necessary to zero it first.

11 Start the engine or crank it on the starter motor, as applicable, and read the dwell angle on the meter. (If an 8-cylinder scale is not provided, use the 4-cylinder scale and double the specified angle). If adjustment is necessary, turn the adjuster screw on the outside of the distributor clockwise to reduce the dwell angle or anti-clockwise to increase it. If no adjustment screw is fitted, adjust the points gap as described in paragraph 6.

12 Check the ignition timing as described in Section 8 and adjust if necessary.

4 Contact breaker points - removal, cleaning and refitting

1 At the intervals specified in Routine Maintenance, or if ignition trouble is suspected, the points should be removed for cleaning or renewal as described below.

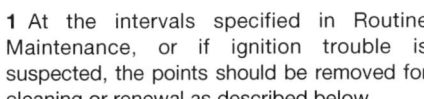

5.6 Scribe the relationship of the distributor body to the timing cover (arrowed)

2 Unclip and remove the distributor cap.
3 Remove the rotor arm.
4 Remove the nut on the contact breaker terminal post (photo) and the fixed contact securing screw (photo).
5 Remove the plastic washer, LT lead and condenser lead, and lift off the spring and moving contact. Recover the other plastic washer if it is not attached to the top one.
6 Remove the fixed contact.
7 On models with 'Quickfit' contact breaker points, remove the securing screw, relieve the spring tension at the terminal connection, unclip the leads and remove the contact set. Note the arrangement of any spacers, insulators, etc.
8 If the points are to be cleaned and re-used, then rub the faces of the contacts on fine emery cloth or fine carborundum paper (400 grade wet and dry). It is important that the faces are kept flat and parallel otherwise they will not meet properly when refitted and ignition problems may easily recur.
9 Refitting of the now cleaned set of points or the fitting of a new set, is simply the reverse procedure to removal. Remember to clean any preservative off a new set of points before fitting them, and apply a smear of grease to the heel of the moving contact.
10 Set the points gap and then check the dwell angle, as described in Section 3. (If new points have been fitted it is necessary to check the dwell angle again after 1000 miles (1600 km) have been covered).
11 Check the ignition timing as described in Section 8.

5.7 Removing the clamp plate bolt

5 Distributor - removal and refitting

1 Disconnect the battery negative lead.
2 Disconnect the vacuum pipe from the vacuum unit.
3 Undo the two clips and remove the distributor cap.
4 Disconnect the low tension lead from the coil.
5 It is not necessary to set the engine to TDC on No 1 cylinder (on compression stroke) to remove the distributor, unless the engine is to be rotated whilst the distributor is off the engine. Instead, mark the alignment of the rotor arm to the distributor body (photo).
6 Scribe the body of the distributor to show its relationship to the timing cover (photo).
7 Undo the clamp plate bolt and remove the plate (photo).
8 Withdraw the distributor from the timing cover.
9 Refitting is a straightforward procedure as long as the engine has remained static. If however it has been turned, follow the procedure from paragraph 15.
10 Fit a new O-ring to the distributor shaft casing.
11 Rotate the distributor driveshaft until the rotor arm is 30° anti-clockwise from the mark scribed on the body. This will allow the distributor drivegear to engage correctly as the distributor is refitted. As the distributor is pushed home, so the gear will rotate and the marks will be correctly aligned.

5.12 Aligning the oil pump driveshaft

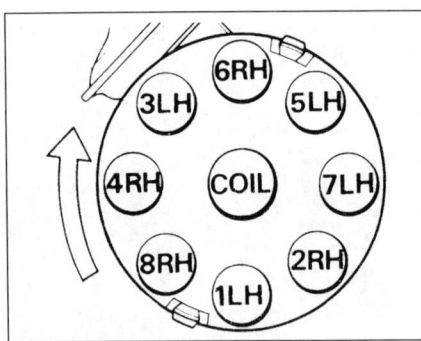

Fig. 4.1 Plan view of distributor from above showing spark plug lead positions (Sec 5)

Fig. 4.2 HT lead locations numbered for cylinders (Sec 5)

R   Right-hand bank viewed from driver's seat
L   Left-hand bank viewed from driver's seat

12 Refit the distributor with the marks scribed on the body and timing cover correctly aligned. Check as the distributor is offered up, that the oil pump driveshaft slot is correctly lined up to accept the end of the distributor driveshaft. If it is not in alignment, insert a screwdriver and set it to the correct position (photo).

13 Fit the clamp plate and bolt and secure the distributor in its original location.

14 Reconnect the low tension lead to the coil and the vacuum pipe to the vacuum unit. Refit the distributor cap. Reconnect the battery and set the dwell angle and ignition timing as

described in Sections 3 and 8 respectively.

15 If the timing has been lost completely (eg after engine rebuild), first set the engine so that No 1 piston (front, left-hand) is at TDC on its compression stroke.

16 Turn the distributor driveshaft so that the rotor arm position is 30° anti-clockwise from the No 1 cylinder HT lead position in the distributor cap (Fig. 4.1).

17 Fit the distributor to the engine, ensuring that the oil pump driveshaft slot engages in the end of the distributor driveshaft.

18 Check that the rotor arm is now aligned to the No 1 cylinder HT lead position in the distributor cap. If necessary rotate the body of the distributor to align it correctly so that the contact breaker points are just about to open.

19 Push the distributor fully home and refit the clamp plate and bolt, but do not tighten them yet.

20 Check the static timing as described in Section 8.

21 Reconnect the low tension lead to the coil and the vacuum pipe to the distributor. Refit the distributor cap.

22 Reconnect the battery negative lead.

23 Set the dwell angle and then the ignition timing dynamically, as described in Sections 3 and 8 respectively.

6 Distributor - dismantling, overhaul and reassembly

Check that spares are available before deciding to overhaul the distributor.

1 Although the distributors fitted to the Range Rover vary through the years of manufacture, the same basic instructions apply to all models, except where a different or alternative procedure is indicated. All photographs are of the earlier type of distributor.

2 Remove the distributor as described in the previous Section.

3 Remove the rotor arm (photo).

4 Remove the contact breaker points as described in Section 4.

5 Remove the condenser.

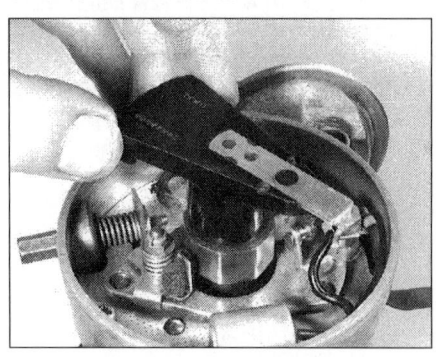

6.3 Remove the rotor arm

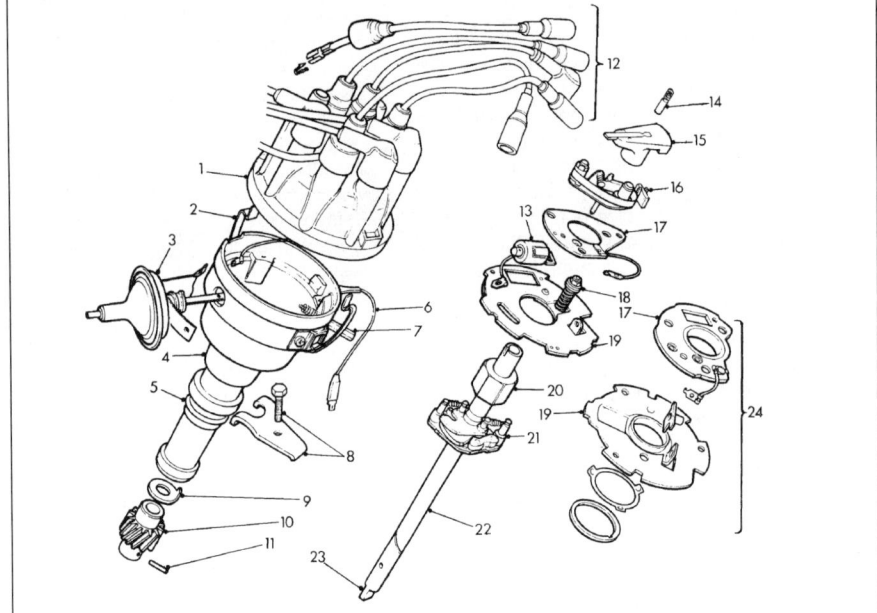

Fig. 4.3 Distributor (up to engine suffix 'E' inclusive) – exploded view (Sec 6)

1 Distributor cap	11 Roll pin	19 Centrifugal advance mechanism cover plate
2 Clip	12 HT leads	
3 Vacuum unit	13 Condenser	20 Cam
4 Distributor body	14 Carbon brush and spring	21 Centrifugal advance weights and springs assembly
5 O-ring	15 Rotor arm	
6 Low tension (LT) lead	16 Contact breaker set	
7 Dwell angle adjuster screw	17 Contact breaker baseplate	22 Distributor driveshaft
8 Clamp plate and bolt	18 Pivot pin with nut, spring and washer	23 Oil pump driving end
9 Locking hub washer		24 Central section of distributor for later models
10 Driving gear		

6.6a Undo the nut . . .

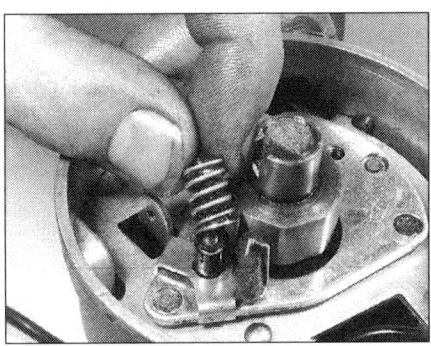

6.6b . . . and remove the washer and spring

6.8 Disconnecting the earthing lead

6.9a Removing the contact breaker baseplate

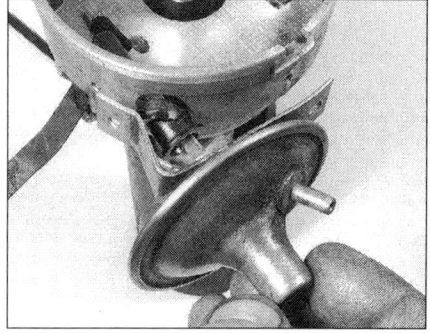

6.9b Unhook and withdraw the vacuum unit

6 Release the nut, spring and washer from the pivot pin on the contact breaker baseplate on early models (photos).

7 Unscrew and remove the dwell angle adjuster screw and spring. Note its relationship before removing it.

8 Disconnect the earthing lead from the centrifugal advance mechanism cover plate (photo).

9 Remove the contact breaker base plate. Then remove the vacuum unit and grommet. Note that this operation has to be reversed for later models (photos).

10 Remove the centrifugal advance mechanism cover plate (photo).

11 Withdraw the two springs very carefully so as not to stretch or damage them.

12 Remove the felt lubricating pad and undo the screw inside the top of the distributor cam shaft. The cam and foot can be lifted away (photo).

13 Remove the centrifugal advance weights if necessary.

14 To remove the drivegear from the end of the shaft, drive out the roll pin using a pin punch and remove the gear and tab washer (photo).

15 Remove the O-ring from the distributor body.

16 Clean the mechanical parts carefully in petrol, then examine them for wear as described in the following paragraphs.

17 Check the fit of the balance weights on the distributor shaft. If the pivots are loose or the holes excessively worn, the relevant parts

must be renewed. The springs are best renewed anyway (if available).

18 Examine the drivegear teeth for wear and renew if necessary.

19 Check the fit of the driveshaft in the housing. If excessive wear is present, the parts must be renewed.

20 Check that the vacuum unit is working correctly by sucking through the tube and checking that the linkage moves.

21 Check the metal contact on the distributor rotor for security of fixing and burning. Small burning marks can be removed with a smooth file or very fine emery paper, but if anything else is wrong the rotor should be renewed. Look also for cracks in the plastic moulding.

22 Check the distributor cap in a similar manner, renewing it if necessary.

23 Reassembly is essentially the reverse of the dismantling procedure, but the following points should be noted:

(a) *Lubricate the weight assembly with a dry lubricant*

(b) *Lubricate the shaft with a dry lubricant*

(c) *Lubricate the moving plate pin with a dry lubricant*

(d) *Don't stretch the centrifugal weight springs*

(e) *With later types of distributor it helps if the vacuum advance lever is located to the baseplate by the 'Quick fit' contact set before the vacuum unit is secured to the body of the distributor*

(f) *Screw in the dwell angle adjuster screw halfway. Any further adjustment can be*

made once the contact breaker points have been refitted.

24 With the distributor reassembled, set the points gap as described in Section 3.

25 Once the distributor has been refitted to the vehicle, check the static ignition timing, then check the dwell angle and the dynamic ignition timing as described in Sections 3 and 8 respectively.

7 Distributor - lubrication

1 During routine maintenance and where otherwise stated in this Chapter, the distributor should be lubricated as follows.

6.10 Removing the centrifugal advance mechanism cover plate

6.12 Removing the felt lubricating pad to reveal the screw

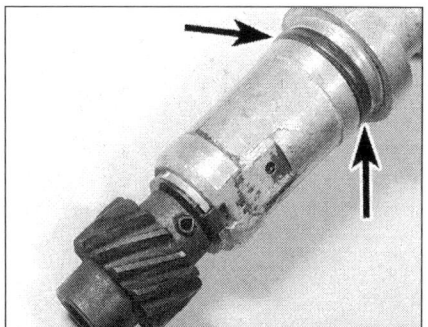

6.14 The drivegear is retained by a roll pin. Note the O-ring (arrowed)

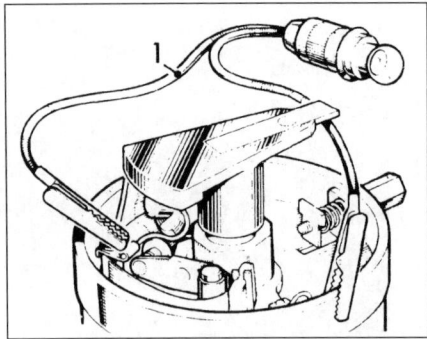

Fig. 4.4 Timing light (1) connected (Sec 8)

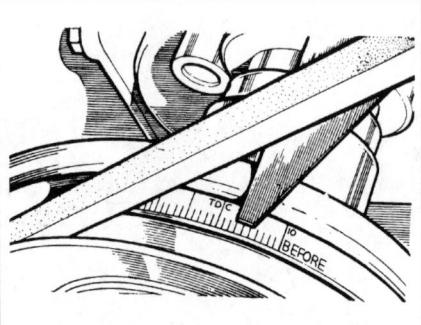

Fig. 4.5 Check that the scale and pointer are correctly aligned (Sec 8)

2 Remove the distributor cap and rotor arm.

3 Apply a few drops of engine oil to the felt pad to lubricate the cam spindle bearing.

4 Squirt a few drops of engine oil through the lubrication holes to oil the centrifugal timing control.

5 Lubricate the contact plate bearing by putting one drop of engine oil in each of the oil holes in the plate.

6 Grease the cam with a light smear of general purpose grease.

7 The contact post may be lubricated in the same manner.

8 Wipe up any excess lubricant and take care not to get any on the contact breaker point faces. Oil contamination of the point faces will cause burning, misfiring or total ignition failure.

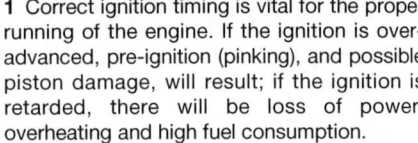

8 Ignition timing - checking and adjustment

1 Correct ignition timing is vital for the proper running of the engine. If the ignition is over-advanced, pre-ignition (pinking), and possible piston damage, will result; if the ignition is retarded, there will be loss of power, overheating and high fuel consumption.

2 Methods are given below for both static and dynamic timing. Static timing should be regarded only as a basic method for getting the engine running, and should be followed as soon as possible by a dynamic check. If the engine is known to be running reasonably well, dynamic timing is all that is necessary.

Static timing

3 Remove the distributor cap and rotor arm.

4 Connect a test lamp (12 volts, up to 5 watts - a sidelight or panel light bulb will do) between the contact breaker points LT terminal and earth (Fig. 4.4). Switch on the ignition. When the points are open, the lamp will light.

5 Turn the engine on the starting handle, observing the timing scale on the crankshaft pulley (Fig. 4.5). When the correct number of degrees before or after TDC is aligned with the pointer, the test lamp should just come on. Refer to Specifications for the correct static timing value for your model.

6 If the lamp lights too soon, the ignition timing is advanced. If the lamp does not come on when the relevant marks are aligned, the timing is retarded. In either case, slacken the distributor clamp bolt and rotate the distributor body slightly in the appropriate direction to correct the timing (clockwise to retard, anti-clockwise to advance).

7 Turn the engine 360° and recheck the timing.

8 Switch off the ignition, disconnect the test lamp and refit the rotor arm and distributor cap.

Dynamic timing

9 If not already done, check and adjust the dwell angle as described in Section 3.

10 The engine must be at normal operating temperature. Disconnect and plug the distributor vacuum hose.

11 Connect a timing light (strobe) into the ignition system in accordance with the manufacturer's instructions - usually to the No 1 HT lead. Some lights also require a connection to be made to the battery or to a mains power supply.

12 Depending on the brightness of the timing light and the ambient light level, it may be necessary to highlight the specified timing mark (on the scale on the pulley) and the pointer with quick-drying white paint. Typist's correcting fluid is ideal.

13 Start the engine and allow it to idle. Point the timing light at the timing marks and pointer. The timing marks will appear stationary, and if the timing is correct, the specified mark on the scale will be aligned with the pointer. Take care not to let the lamp or its leads come into contact with moving parts of the engine.

14 If the timing is incorrect, stop the engine, slacken the distributor clamp bolt and move the distributor in the required direction (clockwise to retard, anti-clockwise to advance) to correct the timing. Tighten the clamp bolt and recheck the timing.

15 Note that if the engine idle speed is too high, it will be impossible to set the timing correctly since the centrifugal advance mechanism in the distributor will have started

to operate. Connect a tachometer to the engine if in doubt. Refer to Chapter 3 for the specified idle speeds.

16 If it is wished to check the operation of the centrifugal advance mechanism, connect a tachometer to the engine and refer to the Specifications for centrifugal advance data. As the engine speed is increased, the timing scale will appear to drift relative to the pointer in the advanced (BTDC) direction. Accurate checking is difficult without special equipment, but any jerkiness or sticking in the movement of the scale should be regarded with suspicion.

Timing for low octane fuels

17 Suggested ignition timing settings for 85 octane fuel are given in the Specifications. Where fuel of even lower, or unknown, octane rating is to be used, the ignition should be retarded to the point where pinking on acceleration just disappears. Engine power and efficiency will be reduced, and the standard ignition timing should be restored when normal fuel is again available.

9 Spark plugs and HT leads

Note: There is very little clearance between the body of the spark plug and the cylinder head. The best tool is the box spanner and tommy-bar supplied in the vehicle tool kit as this is thin enough to fit.

1 The correct functioning of the spark plugs is vital for the correct running and efficiency of the engine. It is essential that the plugs fitted are appropriate for the engine (the suitable type is specified at the beginning of this Chapter). If this type is used and the engine is in good condition, the spark plugs should not need attention between scheduled replacement intervals. Spark plug cleaning is rarely necessary, and should not be attempted unless specialised equipment is available, as damage can easily be caused to the firing ends.

2 If the marks on the original-equipment spark plug (HT) leads cannot be seen, mark the leads 1 to 8, according to which number cylinder the lead serves (number 1 cylinder is at the front of the left-hand bank refer also to Fig. 4.2). Pull the leads from the plugs by gripping the end fitting, not the lead, otherwise the lead connection may be fractured.

3 It is advisable to remove the dirt from the spark plug recesses using a clean brush, vacuum cleaner or compressed air before removing the plugs, to prevent dirt dropping into the cylinders.

4 Unscrew the plugs using either the tool supplied in the vehicle tool kit (mentioned in the note above), a spark plug spanner, suitable box spanner, or a deep socket and extension bar. Keep the tool aligned with the

spark plug if it is forcibly moved to one side, the ceramic insulator may be broken off.

5 Examination of the spark plugs will give a good indication of the condition of the engine.

6 If the insulator nose of the spark plug is clean and white, with no deposits, this is indicative of a weak mixture or too hot a plug (a hot plug transfers heat away from the electrode slowly, a cold plug transfers heat away quickly).

7 If the tip and insulator nose are covered with hard black-looking deposits, then this is indicative that the mixture is too rich. Should the plug be black and oily, then it is likely that the engine is fairly worn, as well as the mixture being too rich.

8 If the insulator nose is covered with light tan to greyish-brown deposits, then the mixture is correct and it is likely that the engine is in good condition.

9 The spark plug electrode gap is of considerable importance as, if it is too large or too small, the size of the spark and its efficiency will be seriously impaired. The gap

should be set to the value given in the Specifications at the beginning of this Chapter.

10 To set it, measure the gap with a feeler gauge, and then bend the outer plug electrode open or closed until the correct gap is achieved. The centre electrode should never be bent, as this may crack the insulator and cause plug failure, if nothing worse.

11 Specialised spark plug electrode gap measuring and adjusting tools are available from most motor accessory shops.

12 Before fitting the spark plugs, check that the threaded connector sleeves on the plug tops are tight, and that the plug exterior surfaces and threads are clean. To make removal of the plugs easier for next time, apply a smear of copper-based brake grease to the plug threads.

13 Refit the spark plugs.

14 Wipe the spark plug (HT) leads clean over their entire length, then reconnect them in their correct order.

It's often difficult to insert spark plugs into their holes without cross-threading them. To avoid this possibility, fit a short piece of rubber hose over the end of the spark plug. The flexible hose acts as a universal joint, to help align the plug with the plug hole. Should the plug begin to cross-thread, the hose will slip on the spark plug, preventing thread damage.

Fault finding - ignition system

Engine fails to start

1 If the engine fails to start and the car was running normally when it was last used, first check there is fuel in the fuel tank. If the engine turns over normally on the starter motor and the battery is evidently well charged, then the fault may be in either the high or low tension circuits. **Note:** *If the battery is known to be fully charged the ignition light comes on and the starter motor fails to turn the engine check the tightness of the leads on the battery terminal and also the secureness of the earth lead to its connection to the body. It is quite common for the leads to have worked loose even if they look and feel secure. If one of the battery terminal posts gets very hot when trying to work the starter motor this is a sure indication of a faulty connection to that terminal.*

2 One of the commonest reasons for bad starting is wet or damp spark plug leads and distributor. Remove the distributor cap; if condensation is visible internally, dry the cap with a rag and also wipe the leads. Refit the cap.

3 If the engine still fails to start, check that current is reaching the plugs by disconnecting each plug lead in turn at the spark plug end and holding the end of the cable with an insulated tool or rubber glove about 1/8 in (3 mm) away from the cylinder block. Spin the engine on the starter motor.

4 Sparking between the end of the cable and the block should be fairly strong with a regular blue spark. If current is reaching the plugs, remove, clean and regap them. The engine should now start.

5 If there is no spark at the plug leads, take off the HT lead from the centre of the distributor cap and hold it to the block as before. Spin the engine on the starter once more. A rapid succession of blue sparks between the end of the lead and block indicates that the coil is in order and that the distributor cap is cracked, the rotor arm faulty, or the carbon brush in the top of the distributor cap is not making good contact with the spring on the rotor arm.

6 If there are no sparks from the end of the lead from the coil, check the connections at the coil end of the lead. If it is in order, start checking the low tension circuit. First check the contact breaker points for correct gap and cleanliness (Sections 3 and 4).

7 Use a 12 volt voltmeter, or a 12 volt bulb and two lengths of wire. With the ignition switched on and the points open, test between the low tension wire to the coil connection (+ ve) and earth. No reading indicates a break in the supply from the ignition switch. Check the connections at the switch to see if any are loose. Refit these and the engine should run. A reading shows that electricity is reaching the coil.

8 Take the condenser wire off the points assembly and with the points open, test between the moving points and earth. If there now is a reading, the fault is in the condenser. Fit a new one and the fault should be cleared.

9 With no reading from the moving point to earth, take a reading between earth and the negative (– ve) terminal of the coil. A reading here shows a broken wire (which will need to be renewed) between the coil and distributor.

No reading confirms that the coil has failed and must be renewed. Remember to refit the condenser wire to the points assembly. For these tests it is sufficient to separate the points with a piece of dry paper whilst testing with the points open.

Engine misfires

10 If the engine misfires regularly, run it at a fast idling speed. Pull off each of the plug caps in turn and listen to the note of the engine. Hold the plug cap in a dry cloth or with a rubber glove as additional protection against a shock from the HT supply.

11 No difference in engine running will be noticed when the lead from the defective circuit is removed. Removing the lead from one of the good cylinders will accentuate the misfire.

12 Remove the plug lead from the end of the defective plug and hold it with an insulated tool or rubber glove about 1/8 in (3 mm) away from the block. Restart the engine. If the sparking is fairly strong and regular, the fault must lie in the spark plug.

13 The plug may be loose, the insulation may be cracked, or the electrodes may have burnt away, giving too wide a gap for the spark to jump. Worse still, one of the electrodes may have broken off. Either renew the plug or clean it; reset the gap, and then test it.

14 If there is no spark at the end of the plug lead, or it is weak and intermittent, check the ignition lead from the distributor to the plug. If the insulation is cracked or perished, renew the lead. Check the connections at the distributor cap.

15 If there is still no spark, examine the distributor cap carefully for tracking. This can be recognised by a very thin black line running between two or more electrodes or between an electrode and some other part of the distributor. These lines are paths which conduct electricity across the cap thus letting it run to earth. The only remedy is a new distributor cap.

16 Apart from the ignition timing being incorrect, other causes of misfiring have already been dealt with under the section dealing with the failure of the engine to start. To recap - these are that:

(a) *the coil may be faulty giving an intermittent misfire*

(b) *there may be a damaged wire or loose connection in the low tension circuit*

(c) *there may be a mechanical fault in the distributor*

17 If the ignition timing is too far retarded, it should be noted that the engine will tend to overheat and there will be a quite noticeable drop in power. If the engine is overheating and the power is down and the ignition timing is correct, then the carburettors should be checked, as it is likely that this is where the fault lies.

Engine fires but will not run

18 If the engine fires when the starter motor is cranking but cuts out as soon as the starter switch is released, the ballast resistor or resistance wire must be suspect, since this is bypassed only when the starter motor is operating (See Section 1).

19 Do not be tempted by bypass a failed ballast resistor or resistance wire with ordinary wire, or coil overheating and possible failure may result.

Chapter 5 Clutch

For modifications, and information applicable to later models, see Supplement at end of manual

Contents

Degrees of difficulty

Easy, suitable for novice with little experience 	**Fairly easy,** suitable for beginner with some experience	**Fairly difficult,** suitable for competent DIY mechanic 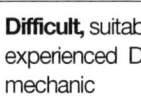	**Difficult,** suitable for experienced DIY mechanic	**Very difficult,** suitable for expert DIY or professional

Specifications

General

Make	Borg and Beck
Type	Diaphragm
Clutch plate diameter	10.5 in (266.5 mm)
Actuation	Hydraulic
Clutch fluid type/specification	Hydraulic fluid to SAE J1703

Torque wrench setting	lbf ft	kgf m
Clutch cover bolts	35 to 38	4.9 to 5.2

1 General description

The clutch which is fitted to the Range Rover is a single dry plate diaphragm spring type and is hydraulically operated.

The unit comprises a steel cover which is dowelled and bolted to the rear face of the flywheel and contains the pressure plate, diaphragm spring and fulcrum rings.

The clutch disc is free to slide along the splined input (primary) shaft and is held in position between the flywheel and the pressure plate by the pressure of the pressure plate spring. Friction lining material is riveted to the clutch disc and it has a spring cushioned hub to absorb transmission shocks and to help ensure a smooth take-off.

The circular diaphragm spring is mounted on shoulder pins and held in place in the cover by two fulcrum rings. The spring is also held to the pressure plate by three spring steel clips which are riveted in position.

The clutch release mechanism consists of a hydraulic master cylinder and slave cylinder and the interconnecting pipework, a release arm and sealed ball type release bearing - the latter being in permanent contact with the fingers of the pressure plate assembly.

As the friction linings on the clutch driven plate wear, the pressure plate automatically moves closer to the driven plate to compensate. This makes the centre of the diaphragm spring move nearer to the release bearing, so decreasing the release bearing clearance. Depressing the clutch pedal actuates the clutch release arm by means of hydraulic pressure. The release arm pushes the release bearing forwards to bear against the release fingers, so moving the centre of the diaphragm spring inwards. The spring is sandwiched between two annular rings which act as fulcrum points. As the centre of the spring is pushed in, the outside of the spring is pushed out, so moving the pressure plate

backwards and disengaging the pressure plate from the clutch disc.

When the clutch pedal is released, the diaphragm spring forces the pressure plate into contact with the friction linings on the clutch disc and at the same time pushes the clutch disc a fraction of an inch forwards on its splines so engaging the clutch disc with the flywheel. The clutch disc is now firmly sandwiched between the pressure plate and the flywheel so the drive is taken up.

 Warning: Dust created by clutch wear and deposited on the clutch components may contain asbestos which is a health hazard. DO NOT blow it out with compressed air or inhale any of it. DO NOT use petrol or petroleum based solvents to clean off the dust. Brake system cleaner or methylated spirit should be used to flush the dust into a suitable receptacle. After the clutch components are wiped clean with rags, dispose of the contaminated rags and cleaner in a sealed, marked container.

2 Maintenance

1 This consists of occasionally checking the security of the bolts which retain the master and slave cylinders and applying a little engine oil to the operating rod clevis joints.

2 Periodically check the hydraulic pipes and unions for leaks, corrosion or deterioration.

3 At weekly intervals remove the clutch master cylinder cap and check the fluid level. Before unscrewing the cap wipe it clean to prevent the ingress of dirt. Use only the recommended type of clutch fluid. If topping-up becomes a common occurrence, then carry out a visual inspection of the clutch hydraulic system. Any leakage of fluid would then be evident.

4 The clutch is self-adjusting, so periodic adjustment is not required.

3 Master cylinder - removal and refitting

1 From within the car remove the pivot bolt and bushes securing the clutch master cylinder pushrod to the clutch pedal.

2 From the engine compartment disconnect the metal hydraulic pipe at the master cylinder union. Plug the end of the pipe and the hole in the master cylinder to prevent the escape of the fluid. Remember that the fluid is corrosive and will have a detrimental effect on paintwork. If you should spill any fluid wipe it up immediately (photo).

3 Remove the two bolts, spring washers and plain washers securing the master cylinder to the scuttle/pedal assembly.

4 The master cylinder can now be withdrawn.

5 Refitting is the reverse of the removal

procedure, but the following points should be noted.

6 Check the brake pedal setting as described in Chapter 9.

7 Unscrew the upper and lower stop bolts for the clutch pedal.

8 Refit the master cylinder to the bulkhead and refit the pivot bolt but do not tighten it.

9 Set the clutch pedal to the same level as the brake pedal. This is achieved by rotating the pivot bolt with its integral cam.

10 Tighten the pivot bolt and nut.

11 Adjust the upper stop bolt by screwing it until it is just touching the pedal arm, then continue another 1/2 turn.

12 Depress the clutch pedal fully, and then adjust the lower stop bolt. This time continue for a full turn after touching the pedal. The lower stop bolt should protrude from the pedal box by a distance of 1.75 to 2.00 in (45 to 50 mm).

13 Refill the hydraulic system and bleed it as described in Section 8.

4 Master cylinder - overhaul

1 Remove the master cylinder as described in the previous Section.

2 Unscrew the reservoir cap and drain out the fluid.

3 Refer to Fig. 5.3, slide the rubber boot off the master cylinder and ease it down the pushrod.

4 From the pushrod end of the master cylinder extract the circlip retaining the pushrod.

5 Withdraw the pushrod assembly. The rubber boot can now be removed from the inner end of the pushrod.

6 Invert the master cylinder and bump the pushrod end into the palm of your hand to

3.2 The clutch fluid pipe is attached to the front of the unit

dislodge the piston assembly, or alternatively apply air supplied from a tyre foot pump to the outlet port.

7 Remove the piston seal.

8 Withdraw the piston washer.

9 Remove the main seal using a low pressure air jet.

10 Invert the master cylinder and tip out the spring and seat.

11 Discard all the old seals as they must not be used again.

12 Examine all the components for scores or 'bright' wear areas and if evident, renew the complete master cylinder. Wash all components in methylated spirit or clean hydraulic fluid.

13 If the master cylinder is serviceable, obtain a repair kit which includes new seals and other components.

14 Use rubber grease to coat the new seals. The remaining parts should be smeared with hydraulic fluid.

15 Reassembly is the reverse procedure to removal. Note that care must be taken to ensure that the main seal lip does not fold over when inserted into the cylinder bore.

16 The convex face of the piston washer faces the piston.

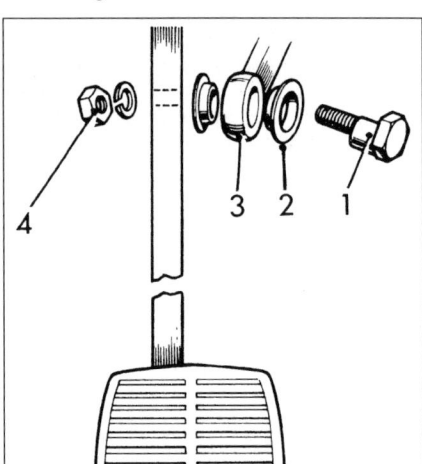

Fig. 5.1 Master cylinder pushrod-to-pedal linkage (Sec 3)

1	*Pivot bolt*	*3*	*Pushrod*
2	*Bush*	*4*	*Nut*

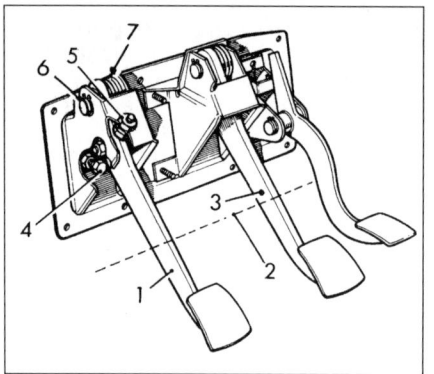

Fig. 5.2 Clutch pedal adjustment (Sec 3)

1 Clutch pedal
2 Clutch and brake pedal alignment
3 Brake pedal
4 Lower stop bolt
5 Upper stop bolt
6 Pedal spindle and circlip
7 Clutch pedal return spring

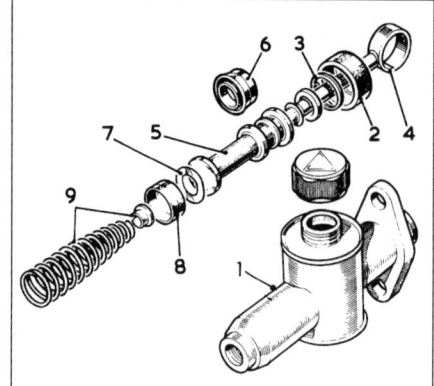

Fig. 5.3 Master cylinder – exploded view (Sec 4)

1	*Body and reservoir*	*6*	*Piston seal*
2	*Rubber boot*	*7*	*Piston washer*
3	*Circlip*	*8*	*Main seal*
4	*Pushrod*	*9*	*Spring and seal*
5	*Piston*		

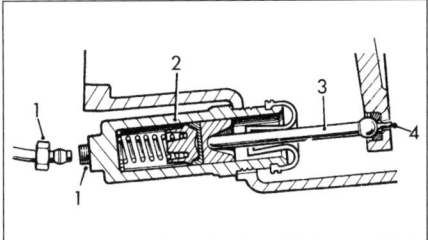

Fig. 5.4 Slave cylinder installation (Sec 5)

1 Hydraulic pipe and union
2 Slave cylinder
3 Pushrod
4 Release arm sear

17 Fill the rubber boot with rubber grease before refitting it to the end of the master cylinder.

18 Having rechecked that all the operations have been correctly carried out and there are no components left on the workbench, the unit can now be refitted to the car.

5 Slave cylinder - removal and refining

1 Unscrew the clutch master cylinder reservoir cap and place a thin sheet of polythene over the reservoir then refit the cap. This measure prevents the fluid syphoning out when the slave cylinder is removed.

2 Raise the car and support it securely.

3 Clean the external surface of the slave cylinder, especially in the region of the fluid pipe and union nut.

4 Undo the union nut, pull aside the fluid pipe and plug the end.

5 Remove the two bolts and spring washers securing the slave cylinder to the bellhousing (photo).

6 Withdraw the slave cylinder, leaving the pushrod in place (photo).

7 Apply gasket jointing compound to the slave cylinder and bellhousing mating surfaces.

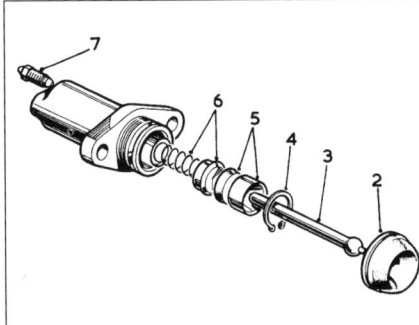

Fig. 5.5 Slave cylinder – exploded view (Sec 6)

2 Dust cover
3 Pushrod
4 Circlip
5 Piston and seal
6 Spring and seat
7 Bleed nipple

5.5 The clutch slave cylinder in position (viewed from beneath)

8 Position the plate (if fitted) and locate the end of the pushrod into the slave cylinder.

9 Make sure that the bleed nipple is located above the fluid pipe union as it is possible to install the slave cylinder in an upside down position.

10 After refitting it will be necessary to bleed the clutch hydraulic system as described in Section 8.

6 Slave cylinder - overhaul

1 Remove the slave cylinder as detailed in Section 5.

2 Clean the exterior of the unit, prior to dismantling, using clean brake fluid or methylated spirit.

3 Obtain the necessary servicing kit of spares which will include the required seal and dust cover. In the case of a high mileage vehicle, the piston return spring should also be renewed.

4 Remove the dust cover from the end of the pushrod.

5 Remove the circlip from the cylinder bore and remove the piston and seal from the cylinder.

6 Withdraw the spring and seat.

7 Unscrew the bleed valve from the cylinder.

8 Clean all the components in methylated spirit or clean brake and clutch fluid, then allow them to dry.

9 Examine the cylinder bore for wear or ridging. Renew the cylinder complete if evident.

10 All seals must be discarded and new ones used.

11 When reassembling, lubricate all the seals using rubber grease, and lubricate all the other components using brake and clutch fluid.

12 Fit a new seal, flat side first, to the piston.

13 Fit the smaller end of the spring into the seat and assemble it to the piston.

14 Offer the complete assembly to the cylinder bore, spring first. Make sure that the seal lip does not fall back.

5.6 Withdrawing the slave cylinder (viewed from beneath)

15 Secure the assembly in position with the circlip.

16 Fill the dust cover with rubber grease before refitting it to the end of the slave cylinder.

17 Refit the pushrod and then refit the cylinder to the car as described in Section 5.

7 Clutch pedal assembly - removal and refitting

1 Remove the lower facia panel from inside the cab.

2 Undo the pivot nut and bolt and withdraw the bushes which connect the clutch master cylinder pushrod to the pedal arm.

3 Remove the right-hand pedal spindle circlip and push out the spindle. Reclaim the return spring.

4 Remove the pedal.

5 Refit in the reverse order. Refer to Section 3 for aligning and setting the clutch pedal.

8 Bleeding the hydraulic system

Whenever the clutch hydraulic system has been overhauled, a part is renewed, or the level in the reservoir is too low, air will have entered the system necessitating its bleeding. During this operation the level of hydraulic fluid in the reservoir should not be allowed to fall below half full, otherwise air will be drawn in again.

1 Obtain a clean, dry, glass jar, a length of plastic or rubber tubing which will fit the bleed nipple of the clutch slave cylinder and which is about 12 in (300 mm) long, a supply of the correct type of fluid and the services of an assistant.

2 Check that the master cylinder reservoir is full and, if not. fill it to within 1/4 in (6.5 mm) of the top. Also add about one inch of fluid to the jar.

3 Remove the rubber dust cap from the slave cylinder bleed nipple, wipe the nipple clean then attach the bleed tube.

4 With the other end of the tube immersed in the fluid in the jar and the assistant ready inside the car, unscrew the bleed nipple one full turn.

5 The assistant should now pump the clutch pedal up and down until the air bubbles cease to emerge from the end of the tubing. Tighten the bleed nipple at the end of each downstroke. Check the reservoir frequently to ensure that the hydraulic fluid does not drop too far, so letting air into the system.

6 When no more air bubbles appear, tighten the bleed nipple at the bottom of a downstroke.

7 Fit the dust cap over the bleed nipple.

8 If a one-man bleeding kit is available, refer to Chapter 9 for details of its use.

9 Discard hydraulic fluid from the system as it is likely to be contaminated and unfit for re-use.

9 Clutch - removal, inspection and refitting

1 Remove the engine, as described in Chapter 1, unless the gearbox is to be removed anyway, in which case the clutch can be removed once the gearbox has been withdrawn. There is no easy way to tackle the task of clutch renewal with the Range Rover.

2 The clutch cover is secured to the flywheel by a peripheral ring of bolts. Mark the position of the clutch cover in relation to the flywheel.

3 Unscrew the securing bolts evenly, a turn at a time in diametrically opposite sequence, to avoid distortion. The three bolts located in the deep recesses of the cover should not be disturbed.

4 When the bolts are finally removed, withdraw the pressure plate assembly from the flywheel and catch the driven plate as it is released from the face of the flywheel. Note which way round the plate is fitted.

5 The pressure plate assembly should not be dismantled but if worn, cracked or distorted, it should be renewed on an exchange basis.

6 Examine the driven plate for wear. If the linings are worn almost down to the rivets then a factory reconditioned unit should be obtained on an exchange basis - do not waste your time trying to reline the plate, it seldom proves satisfactory.

7 If there is evidence of oil staining, find and rectify the cause which will probably be a faulty gearbox input shaft oil seal or a crankshaft rear oil seal.

8 Check the machined surfaces of the flywheel and pressure plate; if grooved or scored then the flywheel should be machined (within the specified limits - see Chapter 1) and the pressure plate assembly renewed.

9 Check the release bearing for smooth operation. There should be no harshness or slackness in it and it should spin reasonably freely bearing in mind that it is grease sealed (Refer to next Section). Renew the release bearing as a matter of course at time of major overhaul.

10 It is important that no oil or grease gets on the clutch plate friction linings of the pressure plate and flywheel faces. It is advisable to refit the clutch with clean hands and to wipe down the pressure plate and the flywheel faces with a clean rag before assembly begins.

11 Place the clutch plate against the flywheel, ensuring that it is the correct way round. The flywheel side of the driven plate is marked accordingly (photos).

12 Refit the clutch cover assembly loosely on the dowels. Refit the six bolts and spring washers and tighten them finger tight so that the clutch plate is gripped but can still be moved. The clutch disc must now be centralised so that the engine and gearbox are mated, the gearbox input shaft splines will pass through the splines in the centre of the driven plate (photo).

13 Centralisation can be carried out quite easily by inserting a round bar or long screwdriver through the hole in the centre of the clutch, so that the end of the bar rests in the small hole in the end of the crankshaft containing the spigot bush. Ideally a mandrel should be used.

14 Using the input shaft spigot bush as a fulcrum, moving the tool sideways or up and down will move the clutch disc in whichever direction is necessary to achieve centralisation.

15 Centralisation is easily judged by removing the tool and viewing the driven plate hub in relation to the hole in the centre of the clutch cover plate diaphragm spring. When the hub appears exactly in the centre of the hole, all is correct.

16 Tighten the clutch bolts firmly in a diagonal sequence to ensure that the cover plate is pulled down evenly and without distortion of the flange. Finally tighten the bolts to the recommended torque setting (photo).

9.11a Ensure that the driven plate markings are the right way round

9.11b Using a mandrel, the driven plate can be located easily

9.12 Refitting the clutch cover plate with centralising tool in position

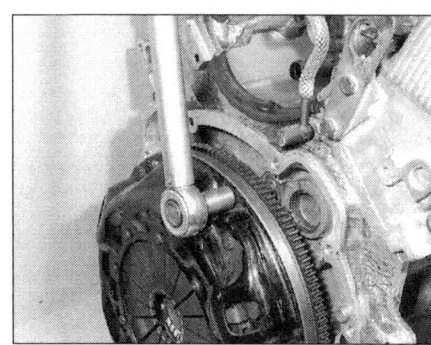

9.16 Tightening the clutch cover bolts

10 Clutch release mechanism - removal and refitting

1 The clutch release mechanism, which is operated by the slave cylinder and pushrod, consists of the release arm and pivot and the release bearing and sleeve assembly (Fig. 5.6).

2 Should the fault diagnosis indicates that the release bearing needs renewal then the engine or gearbox will have to be removed first. The easiest task is to remove the engine, unless the gearbox is being removed anyway.

3 With the engine removed as described in Chapter 1 work can proceed.

4 Withdraw the staple which links the release bearing sleeve to the release arm (photo).

5 Withdraw the bearing and sleeve assembly from the input shaft (photo).

6 Remove the spring clip retaining bolt and then remove the clip (photo).

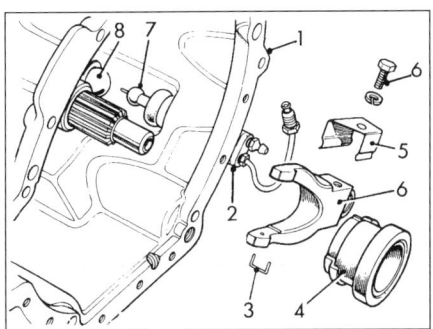

Fig. 5.6 Clutch release mechanism components (Sec 10)

1 Bellhousing
2 Slave cylinder
3 Staple
4 Release bearing and sleeve
5 Spring clip
6 Clip retaining bolt
7 Slave cylinder pushrod end
8 Pivot post

10.4 Withdrawing the staple

10.5 Withdrawing the release bearing and sleeve

7 The release arm can now be slid off the pivot post (photo).

8 Inspect the bearing and sleeve. The bearing should rotate smoothly. It is packed with grease and sealed for life. Renew the assembly if necessary. If in doubt, consider the work which will be entailed if the bearing fails in a relatively short time.

9 Grease the pivot post bolt and refit the release arm. Engage the pushrod into its seat at the outer end.

10 Refit the spring clip and secure it in position. The clip fits over the washer behind the pivot ball.

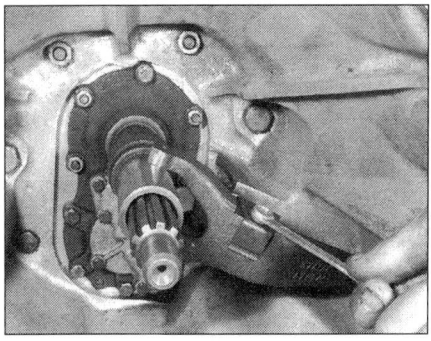

10.6 Undo the bolt

10.7 Withdrawing the release arm

11 Lubricate the release bearing sleeve inner surface with a thin film of molybdenum disulphide based grease and fit it to the front cover sleeve.

12 Line up the holes in the release arm and sleeve and refit the staple.

13 Check that the release bearing and sleeve slide smoothly on the input shaft assembly.

14 Refit the engine or transmission to the vehicle as applicable.

Fault finding - clutch

Judder when taking up drive

☐ Loose engine mountings
☐ Worn or oil-contaminated driven plate friction linings
☐ Worn splines on driven plate hub or first input (primary) shaft
☐ Worn crankshaft spigot bush (pilot bearing)

Noise as clutch pedal is released

☐ Distorted driven plate
☐ Broken or weak driven plate hub cushion coil springs
☐ Distorted or worn input (primary) shaft
☐ Release bearing loose

Clutch slip

☐ Damaged or distorted pressure plate assembly
☐ Driven plate linings worn or oil-contaminated

Noise on depressing clutch pedal

☐ Dry, worn or damaged clutch release bearing
☐ Excessive play in input (primary) shaft splines

Difficulty in disengaging clutch for gearchange

☐ Fault in master cylinder or slave cylinder
☐ Air in hydraulic system
☐ Driven plate hub splines rusted on shaft

Notes

Chapter 6 Transmission

For modifications, and information applicable to later models, see Supplement at end of manual

Contents

Degrees of difficulty

Easy, suitable for novice with little experience	**Fairly easy,** suitable for beginner with some experience 	**Fairly difficult,** suitable for competent DIY mechanic 	**Difficult,** suitable for experienced DIY mechanic 	**Very difficult,** suitable for expert DIY or professional 

Specifications

Main gearbox

Type	Four forward speeds and one reverse with synchromesh on all forward gears
Ratios:	
4th	1.00 to 1
3rd	1.50 to 1
2nd	2.44 to 1
1st	4.06 to 1
Reverse	3.66 to 1
Oil type/specification:	
Early gearbox with limited slip differential	Hypoid gear oil, viscosity SAE 80EP to API GL4
Later gearbox	Multigrade engine oil, viscosity SAE 20W/50 to API SF or SG
Oil capacity	4.5 Imp pints (5.5 US pints) (2.6 litres)

Transfer gearbox

Type	2-speed on main gearbox output (high or low ratio)	
Ratios:	**Early models**	**Later models**
High	1.174 to 1	1.113 to 1
Low	3.321 to 1	3.321 to 1
Oil type/specification:		
Early gearbox with limited slip differential	Hypoid gear oil, viscosity SAE 90EP to API GL4	
Later gearbox	Multigrade engine oil, viscosity SAE 20W/50 to API SF or SG	
Oil capacity	5.5 Imp pints (6.5 US pints) (3.1 litres)	

Overall ratios

	High Transfer		Low Transfer
	Early models	**Later models**	
4th	4.16 to 1	3.94 to 1	11.76 to 1
3rd	6.25 to 1	5.93 to 1	17.69 to 1
2nd	10.17 to 1	9.64 to 1	28.78 to 1
1st	16.91 to 1	16.03 to 1	47.83 to 1
Reverse	15.23 to 1	14.43 to 1	43.07 to 1

Main gearbox tolerances

Primary pinion endfloat (maximum)	0.002 in (0.05 mm)
Layshaft rolling resistance	6.0 to 8.5 lb (3.0 to 3.8 kg)
Transfer gear endfloat (maximum)	0.002 in (0.05 mm)
Mainshaft transfer gear endfloat (maximum)	0.002 in (0.05 mm)
Mainshaft gears endfloat	0.001 to 0.006 in (0.025 to 0.150 mm)

Transfer gear tolerances

Selectors clearance .... 0.010 in (0.25 mm)
Intermediate gears endfloat .... 0.006 to 0.009 in (0.15 to 0.23 mm)

Torque wrench settings

	lbf ft	kgf m
Main gear lever securing bolts	11	1.5
Output flange nut (front)	85	11.7
Output flange nut (rear)	85	11.7
Gearbox case-to-bellhousing studs/bolts:		
Large diameter	120	16.6
Small diameter	70	9.6
Reversing light switch	15 to 20	1.4 to 2.0

1 General description

The Range Rover transmission gives four forward speeds and one reverse in either high or low ratio gearing, thus giving a total selection of eight forward and two reverse speeds. Where the situation demands it, the two ranges can be used progressively when changing up.

The transmission unit houses three main assemblies, these being the main gears, the intermediate gears and the transfer gears. The main gearbox section provides the normal road use gears which are fitted with synchromesh units. The rear end of the mainshaft carries a transfer gear which is meshed with the intermediate transfer gears, which are in turn meshed with the output shaft differential gears.

The differential unit enables the vehicle to have a permanent four-wheel drive and prevents the possibility of transmission 'wind-up' under certain conditions. The differential can be locked to provide a positive four-wheel drive motion whereby all roadwheels rotate at the same speed. This is only normally used to provide the maximum traction when operating in severe conditions. The differential is locked by means of a switch mounted on the floor next to the main gear lever. The differential lock can only be operated when the engine is running and should only be engaged when the vehicle is being driven in the straight-ahead position, or the differential unit could suffer damage.

The gear assemblies and shafts run in ball or roller bearings, and the endthrusts are adjusted by means of shim washers which are available in varying thicknesses to suit.

The main gearbox and transfer gearbox each have their own oil supply and are therefore individually drained and topped up as and when necessary.

The main gearbox components are lubricated by means of a gear-driven oil pump attached to the front of the unit within the clutch bellhousing. The oil pump drive is direct from the end of the layshaft. The transfer gearbox components are splash fed with lubricant.

Although an overdrive unit has been available as an optional fitting to the Range Rover since 1978, at the time of writing no maintenance or overhaul procedures are available and this is not therefore included.

2 Transmission removal - special notes

1 As the transmission unit is removed upwards through the interior of the vehicle, the seats, flooring and heater unit must be removed to allow access and clearance for lifting the unit out.

2 Although no special Rover tools or equipment are required to perform the removal, you will need to have a suitable mobile hoist and this is most probably available from a tool hire dealer.

3 The removal and refitting procedures are more time-consuming than difficult, and therefore plenty of time should be allowed when starting. The aid of an assistant will not only help to speed things up but is almost essential during the actual removal and refitting procedures.

4 Some items of the transmission can be withdrawn without having to completely remove the transmission and these are mainly in the transfer gearbox. If a fault is suspected to be in the transfer gearbox, refer to Section 7, which lists those items which can be removed with the transmission in position.

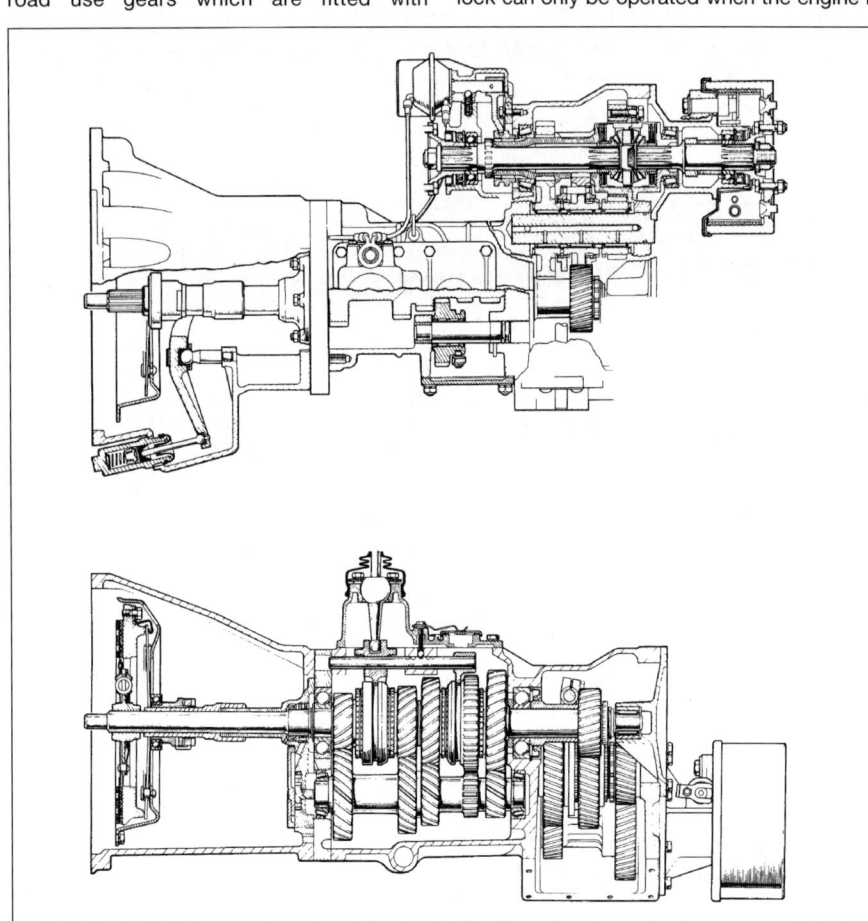

Fig. 6.1 Plan and side elevation views of the transmission (Sec 1)

3.2 General view of transmission with vehicle seats and floor panels removed

3.6 Detach the reversing light switch wires

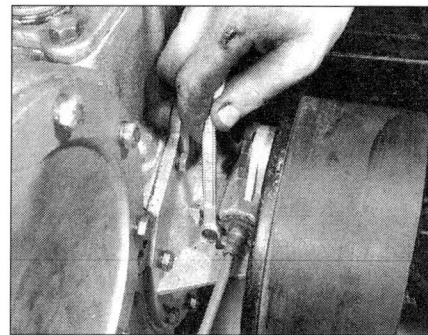

3.9 Disconnect the speedometer cable

3 Transmission - removal and refitting

1 Raise and support the bonnet and then disconnect the battery earth lead.

2 Remove the front seats and floor panel as described in Chapter 12 (photo).

3 Position a suitable container of sufficient capacity under the gearbox drain plugs and drain the oils from the gearboxes.

4 Unbolt and detach the front propeller shaft universal joint at the gearbox drive flange. Mark the shaft mating flanges for correct realignment on assembly.

5 Unbolt and detach the rear propeller shaft joint in a similar manner.

6 Disconnect the two wires at the reversing light switch, noting their respective positions (photo).

7 Disconnect the differential lock actuator wires, noting their respective positions. Also detach the handbrake warning light switch wire. Early models have only one wire to the differential lock actuator.

8 Undo the right-hand front bolt from the gearbox top cover and detach the cable bracket.

9 Detach the speedometer cable retaining clips, one on the left-hand chassis and one on the rear end of the gearbox. Withdraw the cable from the gearbox (photo).

10 Undo the exhaust pipe clamp mounting bolt and detach the mounting bracket, noting the rubber bushes. If the bushes are worn, damaged or perished they must be renewed on assembly (photo).

11 Support the gearbox with a jack and then undo and remove the three left-hand mounting bolts (photo).

12 Undo and remove the right-hand mounting bolts and nuts of which there are also three, mounted through the chassis.

13 Working underneath the vehicle, remove the bellhousing cover plate and stiffening plate (photo).

14 Disconnect the clutch hydraulic hose at the slave cylinder. Plug the end of the hose to prevent leakage and dirt ingress.

15 Position a jack under the engine and raise to support it.

16 To lift the gearbox out, either arrange a lifting sling around it (photo) or fabricate a lift bracket similar to that shown in Figs. 6.2 and 6.3, attached to the top cover.

17 Insert the jib of the hoist through the passenger side doorway. (If working from the driver's side, the steering wheel must be removed before lifting the gearbox out).

18 With the hoist attached to the sling or lifting bracket eye, raise to support the gearbox and then remove the gearbox bellhousing-to-engine retaining bolts (photo).

19 Check that all gearbox attachments are disconnected, then carefully pull the gearbox

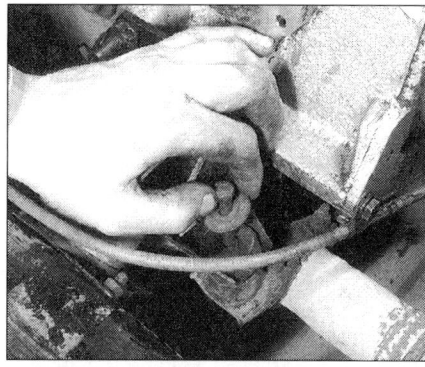

3.10 Remove the exhaust pipe clamp bolt

3.11 Remove the left-hand mounting bolts and bracket nut

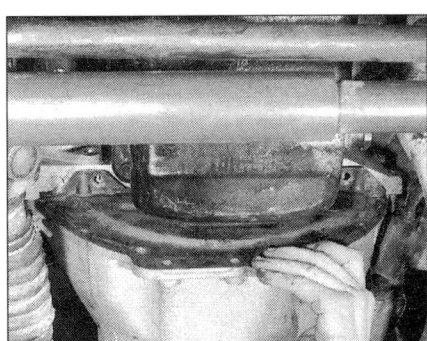

3.13 Remove the bellhousing cover plate underneath

3.16 Lifting sling in position

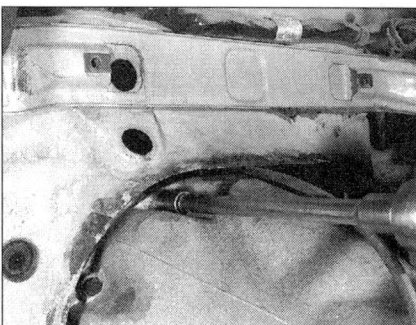

3.18 Remove the bellhousing-to-engine bolts

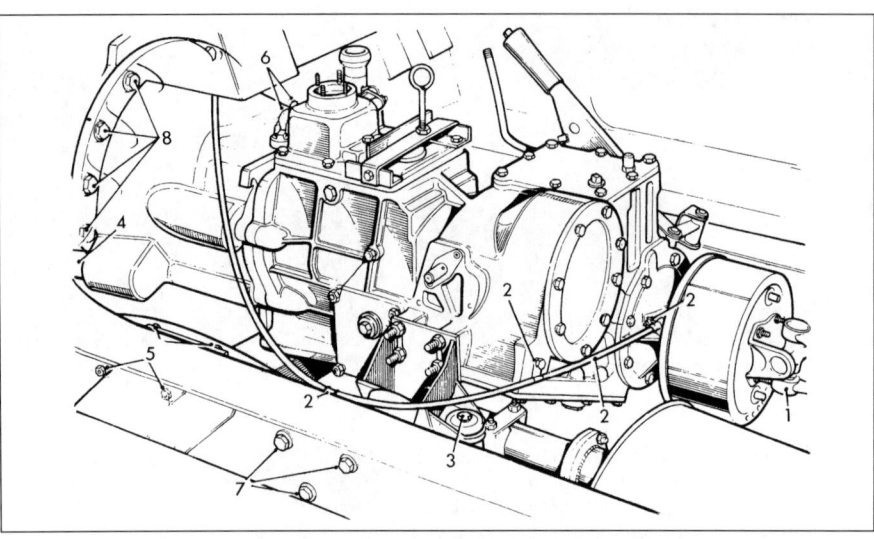

Fig. 6.2 Items to be disconnected - left side (Sec 3)

1 Rear propeller shaft
2 Speedometer cable and location clips
3 Exhaust mounting
4 Clutch slave cylinder
5 Cross ember-to-chassis side-member bolts
6 Reversing light switch wires
7 Mounting bolts
8 Bellhousing bolts

rearwards to disengage it from the engine. When the primary (input) shaft is clear of the clutch unit, lift the gearbox, pushing the front end down in order that the bellhousing can clear the bulkhead and crossmember. Assist by lifting at the rear end. An assistant will be required during this operation to ensure that the gearbox is manouvered as required and to avoid it damaging the surrounding fittings.

20 Once clear of its location aperture, level the gearbox and carefully withdraw it through the side doorway. Transport it to the work area.

21 Refitting the transmission unit is a reversal of the removal sequence. In order to engage the primary pinion with the clutch splines it will probably be necessary to select a gear and then turn the transmision brake drum whilst pushing on the rear face of the gearbox. When the splines are in alignment the gearbox will slide forwards over the shafts.

22 Smear the vertical joint face of the bellhousing cover plate with jointing compound before fitting. The cover plate and seal fillet must also be fitted with sealing compound.

23 After refitting, check that all fastenings are tightened to the specified torque wrench settings and then top up the gearbox and transfer box oil levels.

Fig. 6.3 Items to be disconnected - right side. Note lifting bracket and eye on top cover (Sec 3)

1 Front propeller shaft
2 Crossme ber-to-chassis side-member bolts
3 Bellhousing bolts
4 Mounting bolts

4 Transmission dismantling - special notes

1 When viewed as a complete assembly, the transmission may appear to be a rather complex mechanism. However, providing the three basic units are dealt with separately, the mechanic with a well equipped workshop and a reasonable engineering knowledge, should not experience any major problems in overhauling part, or all of the transmission assembly.

2 Before deciding to dismantle the transmission, an assessment should be made of the possible cause of the fault in question that has necessitated its removal. Removal of the top cover, end cover, side and bottom covers will enable you to make an initial inspection of the various sub-assemblies and you will then be able to assess the extent of any damage or wear that has occurred. If there is major damage or extensive wear in all components, serious consideration should be given to getting a replacement transmission unit complete. as the cost of individual parts, not to mention your time, could well be prohibitive. If you choose to dismantle the transmission, you will require a bearing puller, circlip pliers and a selection of tube drifts apart from your normal workshop tools.

5 Front cover and oil pump - removal and refitting

1 The front cover and the oil pump unit are located within the bellhousing and attached to the gearbox front bearing plate. The front cover houses the primary shaft bearing seal to prevent oil running down the shaft (from the gearbox) into the clutch assembly. The primary shaft extension sleeve is an interference fit on the front of the cover.

2 The lower half of the cover houses the gearbox oil pump and this is driven by means of its central gear, the shaft of which engages with and is driven by the layshaft.

3 The two main reasons for removal of the front cover and oil pump unit are to renew the primary shaft seal or to inspect and overhaul the oil pump.

4 Although no special tools are required to remove or refit the pump and/or cover unit, access to them is only available after removing either the engine or transmission units. Refer to Chapter 1 or to Sections 2 and 3 of this Chapter for information on their respective removal.

5 With the engine or transmission removed, refer to Chapter 5 and remove the clutch withdrawal mechanism and release lever.

6 The front cover can now be withdrawn having removed its retaining nuts and bolts. As the cover is withdrawn from the bearing plate, recover the shim washer which is

5.7 Extractor in position for withdrawal of
the oil feed ring

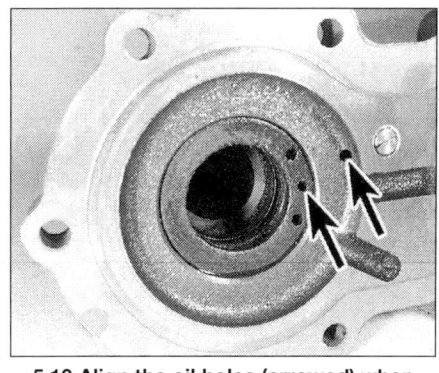

5.10 Align the oil holes (arrowed) when
fitting the feed ring

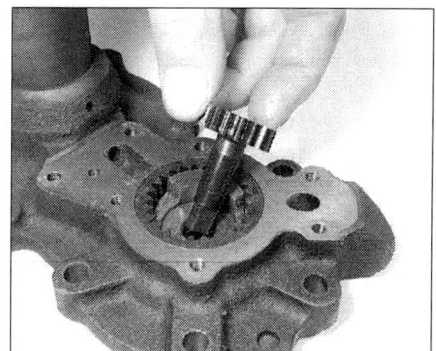

5.11a Withdraw the inner . . .

housed in the layshaft recess. This washer is
of a selected thickness to adjust the bearing
endplay and must therefore be refitted on
reassembly.

7 If the primary shaft oil seal is to be removed
for replacement, you will need to fabricate or
have the use of a suitable extractor with which
to withdraw the oil feed ring (photo).

8 With the oil feed ring removed, the oil seal
may be extracted in a similar manner.

9 Press or drift the new seal into position with
its plain side inwards.

10 When refitting the oil feed ring, first align
the centre hole in the ring with the oil feed
hole in the cover, then press it into position
(photo).

11 The oil pump assembly comprises an inner
and outer gear, both of which can be removed
from the front face of the cover, having
removed the pump cover (photos). A relief
valve unit is fitted into its rear face. To remove
the relief valve, spring and ball, unscrew and
remove the retaining screw (photos).

12 Inspect the oil pump components for
signs of excessive wear and/or damage and
renew any defective components (Fig. 6.4).

13 Reassemble in the reverse order to
dismantling, and lubricate the components
with gearbox oil. When the oil pressure ball
and spring are inserted (in that order), tighten
the retaining screw so that it is flush with, or
not more than 0.010 in (0.25 mm) below, the
face of the cover.

14 The cover gasket must be renewed and all
traces of the old gasket removed from the
mating faces of the cover and endplate.
Smear the gasket surfaces with grease and
locate it onto the endplate. Reinsert the
layshaft bearing thrust washer into its
recess. Do not refit the oil pump gear cover
yet.

15 Reposition the cover assembly into
position on the front endplate, taking care not
to damage the primary shaft oil seal as it is
slid down the shaft. With the cover in position
loosely fit the retaining nuts and bolts (with
spring washers).

16 Insert the oil pump drivegears, engaging
the inner gear shaft square section with the
laygear.

17 Refit the oil pump cover with a new gasket
and tighten its retaining bolts.

18 Prior to tightening the front cover retaining
bolts and nuts, the front cover position should
be checked to ensure that it is concentric with
the primary pinion. As the pinion is liable to a
small amount of radial movement, it should be
aligned with the bellhousing using the Rover
special tool number R0 1005 if this is available
(Fig. 6.5). If necessary adjust the cover
position and then tighten the cover retaining
nuts and bolts to secure.

19 The clutch withdrawal mechanism and
engine or transmission unit can now be
refitted in the reverse sequence to removal as
given in the respective Chapters.

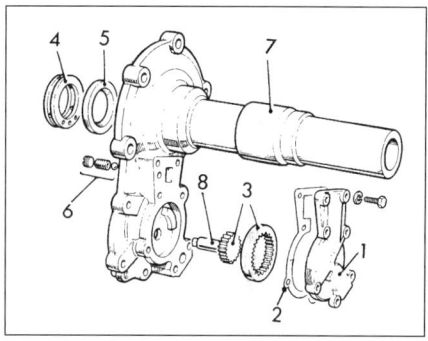

Fig. 6.4 The front cover and oil pump
components (Sec 5)

1 Pump cover	6 Relief valve ball,
2 Cover gasket	spring and plug
3 Pump gears	7 Front cover
4 Oil feed ring	8 Inner pump gear
5 Seal	shaft

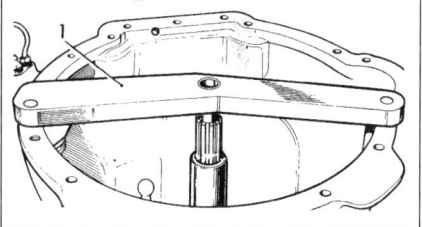

Fig. 6.5 Primary shaft centralising tool (1)
in position on the bellhousing (Sec 9)

5.11b . . . and outer gears for inspection

5.11c Removing the relief valve screw,
spring . . .

5.11d .. and relief valve ball

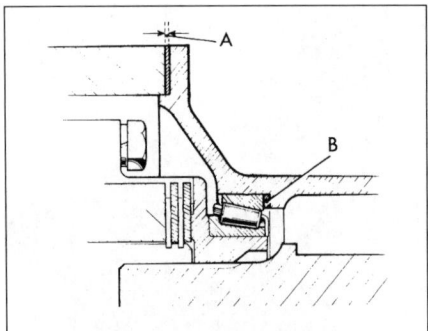

Fig. 6.6 Check the drive housing-to-gearbox flange faces clearance (A) to select gasket of the required thickness. Adjust joint face clearance by shimming behind the bearing at (B) (Sec 6)

6 Speedometer drive housing - removal, overhaul and refitting

1 Remove the transfer gearbox drain plug and drain the oil into a suitable container.
2 Disconnect the rear propeller shaft from the transmission brake attachment (Chapter 7).
3 Extract the split pin and withdraw the handbrake linkage clevis pin at its transmission brake connection.
4 Detach the speedometer drive cable from the drive housing and move the cable back out of the way.
5 Unscrew the speedometer housing-to-gearbox retaining bolts and supporting the housing and transmission brake assembly, withdraw and lower it.
6 Clean the exterior of the housing, but do not allow any cleaning fluid used to enter the transmission brake assembly.
7 Extract the speedometer cable/spindle housing followed by the driven gear and spindle. Prise free the O-ring seal and on later models observe which way round the seal lip is. Withdraw the thrust washer and the small oil seal from the spindle housing.
8 Unscrew and remove the output coupling flange-to-shaft retaining locknut and washer, then withdraw the brake drum and coupling flange complete.

6.18 Speedometer housing oil seal. oil shield and catcher fitted to the housing

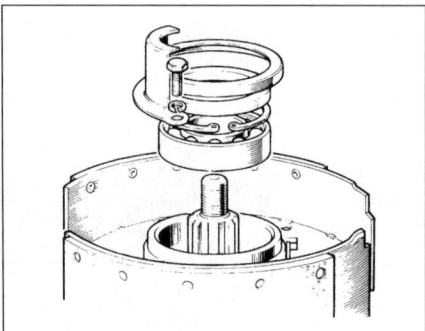

Fig. 6.7 Speedometer drive housing showing the bearing, circlip, oil seal and oil shield (Sec 6)

9 The new output shaft can now be withdrawn by pressing or driving out (use a hide mallet) forwards through the housing.
10 The spacer collar and speedometer worm can now be withdrawn along the shaft (if required).
11 Unbolt and remove the oil catcher and the oil shield and then withdraw the oil seal.
12 To remove the ball-bearing, extract the retaining clip and press or drift the bearing out using a suitable tube drift.
13 Clean and carefully inspect the housing components and renew any found to be worn or defective. If a new speedometer drive housing is to be fitted then the differential bearing preload should be checked as follows. **Note:** *This check should also be made if the gearbox, differential unit (transmission) or differential bearings are being renewed.*
14 Position the speedometer housing against the gearbox, but do not fit the gasket at this stage. The differential shaft taper roller bearing cone and cup should be in contact. Measure the clearance between the gearbox and the drive housing joint faces using feeler gauges to establish the gasket thickness requirement (Fig. 6.6). When assembled, the gasket will be compressed a given amount (under the retaining nut torque) to give the correct bearing preload of 0.002 to 0.004 in (0.050 to 0.100 mm).
15 The joint face clearance is adjusted by fitting the required thickness of shim behind the rear bearing cup. The bearing cup must be

6.19 Insert the shaft fitted with speedometer drivegear and spacer

removed using a suitable puller, then with the shim adjustment made to allow the correct joint face clearance, press or drive the bearing cup back into its housing and recheck the clearance.
16 To reassemble the housing, press or drive the ballbearing into its housing recess so that it is flush with the shoulder inside, then make secure by refitting the circlip.
17 Carefully insert the coupling oil seal, with its cavity section inwards, to the point where its plain face is just clear of the chamfer in the housing bore (Fig. 6.7).
18 Relocate the oil shield so that is a close fit on the housing, then fit the oil catcher, smeared with sealant, to seal between the catcher and brake backplate (photo).
19 Refit the speedometer worm gear and spacer onto the shaft, then insert the shaft into the housing (photo).
20 Refit the brake drum and coupling flange.
21 Fit the plain washer and locknut onto the output shaft and tighten the nut to the specified torque.
22 Lubricate and reassemble the speedometer driven gear seals and housing in the reverse sequence to dismantling and then refit it into the main housing.
23 Refit the speedometer housing, reversing the procedures given in paragraphs 1 to 5. Refit the drain plug and top up the transfer gearbox with the recommended grade and quantity of oil.

7 Transfer gearbox - dismantling and repairs (general)

1 Complete dismantling of the transfer gearbox can only be achieved with the transmission unit removed from the vehicle as described in Section 3.
2 The following sub-assemblies can however be removed and refitted from the transfer gearbox without having to remove the transmission unit:
(a) Gear lever and cross-shaft
(b) Gear selectors and shaft
(c) Differential lock actuator
(d) Differential unit
(e) Front output shaft and housing
(f) Transmission output shaft oil seals
3 The intermediate shaft gear assembly can only be removed with the transmission out of the vehicle.

8 Transmission shaft oil seals - renewal

Rear seal

1 Raise and support the vehicle at the rear using strong axle stands. Chock the front wheels.

2 Refer to Chapter 7 and disconnect the rear propeller shaft at the transmission brake coupling.

3 Unscrew the central locknut and remove it together with its washer and (on later models) the felt/rubber oil seal.

4 Remove the transmission brake drum retaining screws and withdraw the brake drum. If necessary further information on its removal is given in Chapter 9.

5 Withdraw the oil catcher, prise free the oil shield and withdraw the oil seal.

6 The new seal is pressed or drifted into position with its cavity face leading. When in position the plain face must be just clear of the seal housing bore chamfer.

7 Refit the oil shield so that it fits closely to the speedometer housing and then insert the oil catcher, which should be smeared with a suitable sealant so that when fitted it is sealed against the brake backplate.

8 Other reassembly procedures are a direct reversal of the removal sequence. Tighten the locknut to the specified torque and ensure that the propeller shaft is correctly realigned with its coupling flange.

Front seal

9 Raise the vehicle at the front end, support with axle stands and chock the rear wheels.

10 Refer to Chapter 7 and detach the front propeller shaft at the transmission coupling.

11 Unscrew and remove the coupling shaft locknut and remove it with its washer.

12 Withdraw the coupling flange together with its mud shield.

13 Prise free and extract the oil seal.

14 The new seal is fitted with its cavity side inwards (towards the transmission). Drift or press it into position using a suitable size tube.

15 Refit the coupling and attach the propeller shaft in the reverse order to removal. Tighten the coupling nut to the specified torque and be sure to correctly align the propeller shaft with the coupling flange.

9.4 Top cover removed, showing clamp bolt of selector finger (A) and lever retaining pin position (B)

9 Gear lever and cross-shaft (transfer gearbox) - removal and refitting

1 Refer to Chapter 12 and remove the front floor.

2 Refer to Chapter 9 and remove the transmission brake lever and its linkage.

3 Unbolt and remove the top cover from the transfer gearbox. Care must now be taken not to drop tools and fittings into the transfer gearbox, or the gearbox will have to be drained and the bottom cover removed as well.

4 Loosen the clamp bolt of the selector finger and then drive out the cross-shaft-to-gear lever retaining pin using a suitable diameter drift. Remove the gear lever from the end of the shaft (photo).

5 Support the distance collar and selector finger within the gearbox and then withdraw the cross-shaft. Lift out the collar and selector finger.

6 Remove the retaining screws, detach the endplates and extract the seal rings (photo).

7 On early models the damper is removed by unscrewing the knob and removing it with its rubber sleeve. Unscrew the upper rod and withdraw the metal and rubber sleeve

9.6 Remove the endplates and extract the seal rings

assembly. Note the rubber spacer which can be withdrawn (Fig. 6.8).

8 Examine the various components for signs of wear and renew as necessary. The shaft seals and the top cover gasket should always be renewed.

9 Commence reassembly by locating the selector finger into position in the gearbox, engaging with the fork.

10 Insert the cross-shaft and locate the spacer collar onto it as it is pushed through, then slide the shaft through the selector finger and into its opposing location housing.

11 Lubricate and fit the right-hand seal ring and its retaining plate, securing with the cross-head screws.

12 Refit the gear lever and make secure on the shaft by drifting the retaining pin through the lever and shaft location holes.

13 Lubricate and fit the opposing seal ring and retaining plate.

14 Tighten the selector finger clamp bolt with the gear lever positioned 10° forward of its vertical position (photo).

15 Refit the top cover using a new gasket (photo) and secure.

16 The gear lever damper unit of the early models is reassembled in the reverse order to removal.

17 Refit the transmission brake lever and linkage as given in Chapter 9.

18 Refit the floor as given in Chapter 12.

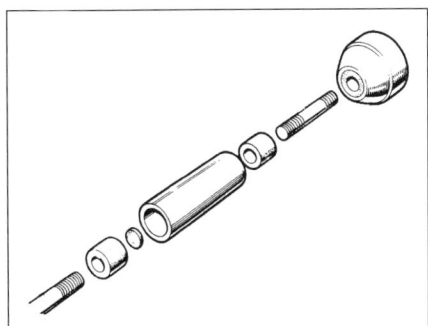

Fig. 6.8 Early selector lever damper components (Sec 9)

9.14 Tighten the selector finger clamp bolt with lever positioned 10° forwards of vertical

9.15 Refit the top cover

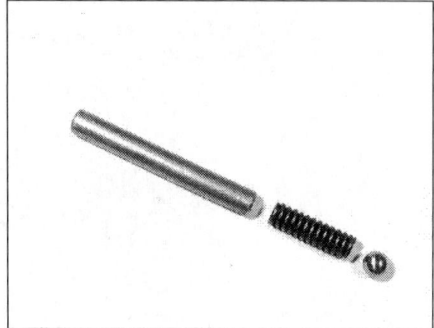

10.8a Remove the selector rod . . .

10.8b . . . spacer rod, spring and ball

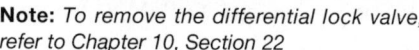

10.13 Inserting the spacer rod into the vertical port

10 Gear selectors and shaft (transfer gearbox) - removal and refitting

1 Refer to Chapter 12 and remove the front floor section.
2 Refer to Section 6 and remove the speedometer drive housing.
3 Unbolt and remove the transfer gearbox top cover and gasket. Care must be taken not to drop tools or fittings into the transfer gearbox once the cover is removed.
4 Select transfer gear low range, then drive out the front selector fork retaining pin just sufficiently to enable the fork to slide along the shaft when required.
5 Pull the differential unit rearwards.
6 Press the front selector fork forwards and pull the rear selector fork rearwards to enable the selector shaft to be disengaged from the detent balls located in the gearbox rear face.
7 Remove the rear selector fork clamp bolt, then withdraw the selector shaft sufficiently to allow the two selector forks to be lifted out of their locations in the gearbox.
8 If the shaft is to be withdrawn completely from the gearbox, seal the housing aperture as the shaft is extracted to prevent the detent balls from dropping down into the gearbox (photo). With the shaft removed, extract the balls and then withdraw the spacer rod and spring (photo).
9 Unscrew and remove the side plug and

extract the detent spring from the cross port.
10 Clean and examine the components for excessive wear and renew as necessary. Clean the detent ball and spring ports using a pipe cleaner if they are sludged up. A new top cover gasket should be fitted on reassembly and all traces of the old gasket cleaned off the mating faces.
11 Commence reassembly by inserting the cross port inner detent spring into position, followed by its ball. Lubricate them with grease to prevent them from rolling out.
12 Insert the selector shaft and compress the selector ball against its spring to enable the shaft to pass through.
13 Locate the detent ball, spring and spacer rod into the vertical port (photo).
14 Lower the rear selector fork into position with its plain face rearwards, then insert the front fork with its extended boss rearwards.
15 Push the shaft through to engage in the selector forks and align the retaining pin holes. Drive the front fork retaining pin into position to secure (photo).
16 Engage the transfer gears in the neutral position, then adjust the rear fork to allow 0.010 in (0.25 mm) clearance between the input gear inner member rear face and the front face of the fork. Tighten the fork retaining bolt to secure in this position (photo).
17 Refit and tighten the detent cross port end plug.
18 Refit the top cover using a new gasket and secure with retaining bolts.

19 Refit the speedometer drive housing as given in Section 6.
20 Refit the front floor panels and seats to complete.

11 Differential lock actuator (transfer gearbox) - removal and refitting

Note: *To remove the differential lock valve, refer to Chapter 10, Section 22*

1 Referring to Chapter 12, remove the front seats and floor panels, then proceed as follows.
2 Take a note of the fitted position of the vacuum supply hoses and detach the hoses from the actuator unit. Detach the wiring connection from the warning switch.
3 Unscrew and remove the actuator unit retaining nuts and bolts, or screws, and withdraw it from the transmission. On later models, remove the heat shield as well.
4 Extract the detent spring and ball from the flange port.
5 To dismantle the actuator unit, unscrew and remove the differential lock warning switch. Retain any shims fitted.
6 Drive out and extract the actuator fork-to-shaft retaining pin (photo).
7 Unscrew and remove the retaining bolts securing the actuator valve unit to the main housing and separate the two. Remove the O-ring seal and gasket.

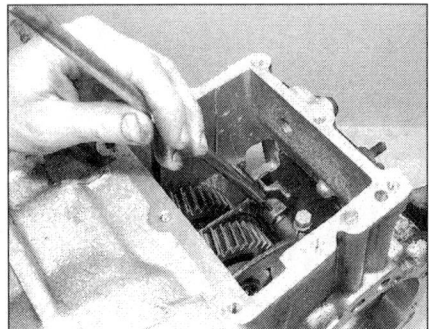

10.15 Drive the retaining pin into position to secure the front fork

10.16 Check the rear selector fork-to-input gear clearance

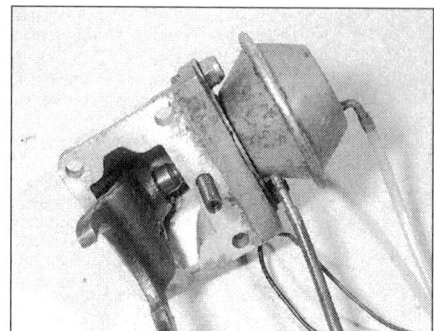

11.6 The actuator removed, showing the actuating fork and spring locations

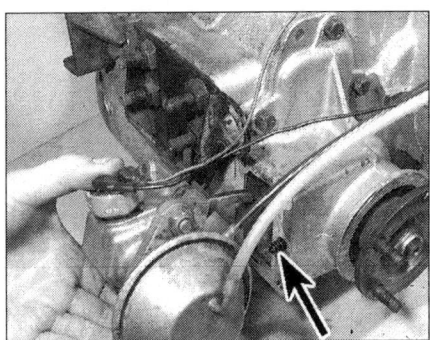

11.9 Refitting the actuator. Note spring location (arrowed)

12.5 Removing the differential unit

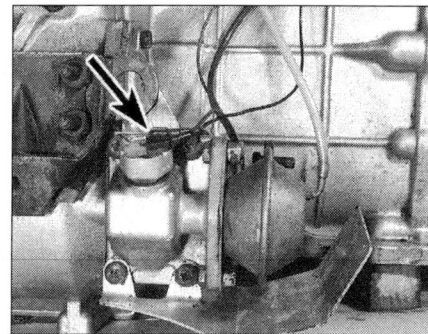

13.1 The differential lock actuator switch (arrowed)

8 Renew any excessively worn or defective components and then reassemble in the reverse order to dismantling. Smear the vacuum unit and main housing joint faces with a suitable sealant prior to fitting.

9 Refit the actuator unit in the reverse order to removal (photo). Smear the gasket faces with sealant before fitting. When in position reconnect the vacuum tubes, ensuring their correct fitting.

10 Refit the floor panels and seats in the reverse order to removal.

12 Differential unit (transfer gearbox) - removal and refitting

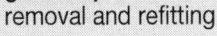

1 Refer to Chapter 12 and remove the front seats and floor panels, then proceed as follows.

2 Refer to the previous Section and remove (do not dismantle) the differential lock actuator unit.

3 Disconnect and remove the front output shaft and housing as given in Section 14.

4 Remove the speedometer drive housing as given in Section 6.

5 The differential unit can now be extracted from the housing (photo).

6 The dismantling, overhaul and reassembly of the transmission differential unit is a specialised operation and is therefore not recommended as a DIY task. If the differential is known to be faulty, or is suspected of malfunction, have it checked and if possible repaired by your Range Rover dealer, or renew the unit complete. Two different types have been fitted, the earlier models being equipped with a Salisbury unit.

7 Refitting is a reversal of the removal procedure, but note that if the differential unit, its bearings, the gearbox housing or speedometer drive housing have been renewed, then a differential bearing preload check must be made. This is described in Section 6 and is made before fully refitting the speedometer housing.

13 Differential lock actuator switch - removal and refitting

1 Located on the differential lock actuator housing, the switch is removed by detaching the wires and unscrewing the switch unit together with the shim washers (photo).

2 Correct setting is important during refitting and the following procedure should be taken.

3 Start the engine and locate the differential lock vacuum control valve in the 'up' position. Now reconnect the wires to the switch and screw the switch into its housing without the shim washers. As soon as switch contact is made, screw the switch in a further half turn.

4 Now measure the switch-to-housing flange face clearance using feeler gauges. Remove the switch and fit washers of the measured thickness. Reinsert the switch and tighten to secure.

5 Locate the differential lock vacuum control valve in the down position and switch off the engine to complete.

14 Front output shaft and housing - removal, overhaul and refitting

1 Remove the transfer gearbox drain plug and drain the oil into a suitable container.

2 Whilst the oil is being drained, refer to

14.6 Remove the lock-up dog clutch

Chapter 12 and remove the front seats and floor panel.

3 Unbolt and detach the front propeller shaft from the gearbox coupling. Scribe a line across the coupling flange and the propeller shaft for correct reassembly.

4 Refer to Section 11 and remove the differential lock actuator unit, but do not detach the vacuum, lines or wires to the switch.

5 Unscrew and remove the housing retaining bolts and detach the housing from the gearbox.

6 Withdraw the lock-up dog clutch unit (photo).

7 To dismantle the housing, support the shaft and unscrew the retaining nut at the front end. Remove the nut and washer and then withdraw the coupling flange with its mud shield.

8 Support the housing and press or drift the shaft out rearwards, then withdraw the oil seal.

9 Using circlip pliers, contract and remove the bearing retaining circlip. Press or drift the bearing out of the housing (photo).

10 Inspect the respective components and renew any excessively worn or damaged parts as required. The mud shield can be pressed free from the coupling if required.

11 Reassembly is a reversal of the removal sequence. Grease the bearing when fitted and ensure that the circlip is fully located. Lubricate the lips of the oil seal before inserting the shaft (photos).

14.9 Bearing and retaining circlip position in housing

14.11a Insert the oil seal and lubricate the lips, then . . .

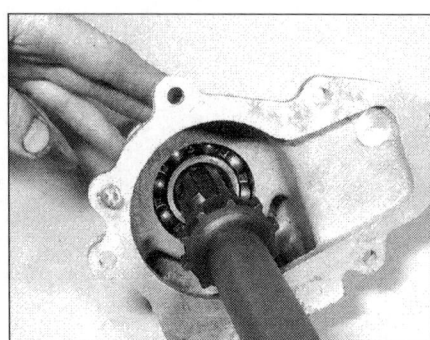

14.11b . . . insert the shaft

14.12a Location dowel position (arrowed)

14.12b Tighten the housing retaining bolts

14.13 Temporary plate attached to prevent coupling from turning

15.3 Reversing light switch location in front of the main gear lever turret. It is not necessary to remove the lever

12 When refitting the housing to the gearbox, ensure that the location dowel is in position (photo) for correct housing alignment. Do not forget to fit and tighten the housing retaining bolt located within the actuator location aperture (photo).

13 Tighten the coupling locknut to the specified torque. This can be achieved by temporarily attaching a plate to one of the coupling studs as shown (photo) which will prevent the shaft from turning as the nut is tightened. Remove the plate when the nut has been tightened.

15 Reversing light switch - removal and refitting

1 Disconnect the battery earth lead.
2 Peel back and remove the main gear lever rubber grommet from its retaining flange on the floor.
3 The reversing light switch is now accessible. Disconnect the lead(s), unscrew the switch unit using a suitable box spanner and lift it clear (photo). Note the shim washers.

4 Engage reverse gear and refit the switch, without the shim washers, with the leads connected. With the ignition switched on and the battery reconnected, screw the switch down until switch contact is made. Screw the switch in a further half turn and then using a feeler gauge, measure the switch lower flange-to-gearbox clearance.
5 Remove the switch, fit shim washers of the measured thickness, then refit the switch and tighten it to the specified torque.
6 Recheck the switch operation and then refit the rubber grommet, engaging with the floor plate flange to secure in position.

Fault finding - transmission

Note: *It is sometimes difficult to decide whether it is worthwhile removing and dismantling the gearbox for a fault which may be nothing more than a minor irritant. Gearboxes which howl, or where the synchromesh is worn but double declutching can overcome the problem, may continue to perform for a long time in this stage. A worn gearbox usually needs a complete rebuild to eliminate noise because the various gears, if re-aligned on new bearings, will continue to howl when different wearing surfaces are presented to each other.*

The decision to overhaul therefore, must be considered with regard to time and money available, relative to the degree of noise or malfunction that the driver can tolerate.

Difficult engagement of gears

☐ Clutch fault (see Chapter 5)
☐ Worn or damaged synchromesh units

Jumps out of gear (on overrun or drive)

☐ Weak detent springs, worn selector forks or worn synchro sleeves

Gear lever engages reverse gear instead of 1st too easily

☐ Reverse stop hinge plate spring weak or broken

Noisy gearbox

☐ Low oil level or incorrect oil grade
☐ Worn bearings and/or gears
☐ Gear trains/bearing endfloats incorrectly set (after rebuild)

Difficult disengagement of gears

☐ Worn synchromesh
☐ Damaged or distorted splines or gear dogs

Oil leaks

☐ Defective input or output oil seals
☐ Defective gasket or gearbox/transfer box cover plates
☐ Loose drain or level plug
☐ Cracked or broken casing

Chapter 7 Propeller shafts

For modifications, and information applicable to later models, see Supplement at end of manual

Contents

Degrees of difficulty

Easy, suitable for novice with little experience	**Fairly easy,** suitable for beginner with some experience	**Fairly difficult,** suitable for competent DIY mechanic 	**Difficult,** suitable for experienced DIY mechanic	**Very difficult,** suitable for expert DIY or professional

Specifications

General

Propeller shaft type	Tubular, splined joint
End joints	Hardy Spicer universal joint couplings with needle bearings
Lubricant type/specification	Multi-purpose lithium based grease to NLGI 2

Dimensions

Shaft diameter	2.0 in (50.8 mm)
Shaft lengths (overall - flange face-to-flange face with splined joint midway):	
Front shaft	25.33 in (643.4 mm)
Rear shaft	34.937 in (887.4 mm)

Torque wrench setting

	lbf ft	kgf m
Drive flange bolts and nuts	35	4.8

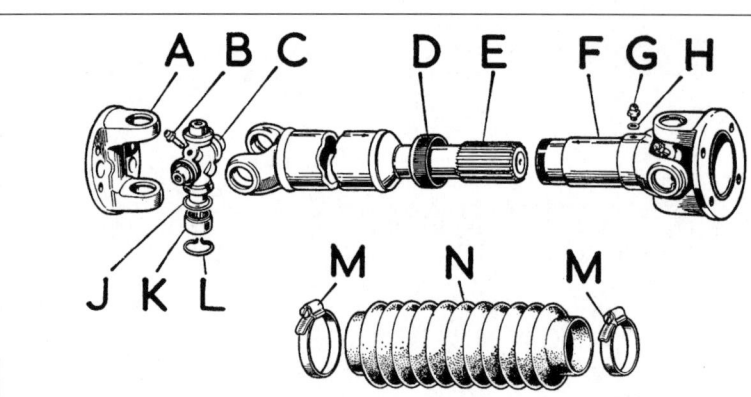

A Flanged yoke
B Grease nipple for
   universal joint
C Spider for bearings
D Dust cap
E Splined shaft
F Splined sleeve
G Grease nipple for
   splined joint
H Washer for nipple
J Seal for spider

K Needle roller bearing
   assembly
L Circlip retaining
   bearing
M Clips fixing rubber
   bellows (front shaft
   only)
N Rubber bellows for
   sliding joint (front shaft
   only)

Fig. 7.1 Propeller shaft components (Sec 1)

1 General description

The drive from the transmission assembly to the front and rear axles is transmitted by two tubular propeller shafts fitted with a universal joint at each end. The universal joints cater for the varying angle between the axle and transmission, caused by road spring deflection, while any fore-or-aft variation is taken care of by means of a splined sleeve in each shaft.

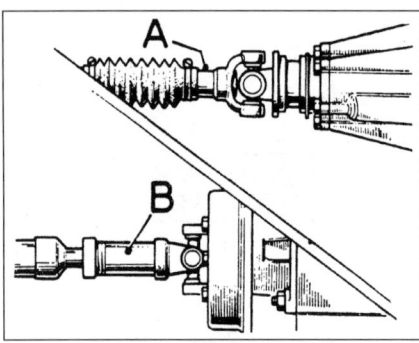

Fig. 7.2 Propeller shaft splined sleeve locations (Sec 1)

A Sleeve end of front propeller shaft
B Sleeve end of rear propeller shaft

Although of different lengths, the front and rear propeller shafts are virtually identical in construction with the exception of the position of the splined sleeve which is on the transmission end of the rear shaft and the axle end of the front shaft.

2 Propeller shafts - removal and refitting

1 The method of removing either the front or rear propeller shaft is almost the same. Any differences in procedure will be mentioned where necessary.
2 Depending on the shaft to be removed, jack up the appropriate end of the vehicle until the wheels are just clear of the ground. Place heavy duty axle stands beneath the chassis.
3 Scribe a line across the side of the axle coupling flange and the propeller shaft, remove the four nuts and bolts and lower the end of the shaft to the ground (photo).
4 If the rear propeller shaft is being removed, undo the four nuts securing the shaft flange to the brake drum. Pull the shaft rearwards to clear the studs and remove the complete shaft assembly from beneath the vehicle (photo).
5 In the case of the front propeller shaft, remove the four nuts and bolts securing the rear end of the shaft to the front output shaft

flange on the transfer box and remove the shaft assembly from the vehicle (photo).
6 Refitting the propeller shafts is the reverse sequence to removal. Note that the splined sleeve on the front shaft must be towards the front axle while the sleeve on the rear shaft must be adjacent to the transmission brake.

3 Universal joints - inspection and repair

1 Wear in the universal joint needle roller bearings is characterised by vibration in the transmission, clonks on taking up the drive and in extreme cases of lack of lubrication, metallic squeaking and ultimately grating and shrieking sounds as the bearings break up.
2 To test the universal joints for wear prior to removing the propeller shaft(s) from the vehicle, apply the handbrake and chock the wheels. Working under the vehicle, apply leverage between the yokes using a large screwdriver or flat metal bar. Wear is indicated by movement between the shaft yoke and coupling flange yoke. Check all four universal joints in this way.
3 To check the splined sleeve on the front of both shafts, attempt to push the shafts from side to side and note any excessive movement between the sleeve and shaft. A further check can be made by gripping the

2.3 The rear axle/rear propeller shaft coupling flange

2.4 The rear propeller shaft front coupling to the transmission brake drum

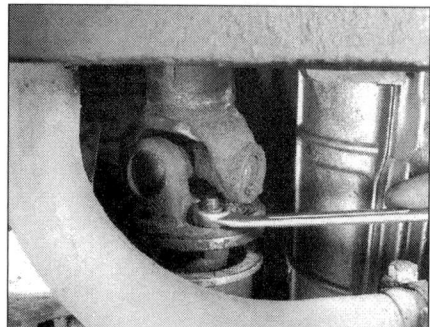

2.5 Undoing the front shaft coupling flange bolts at the transfer box from underneath

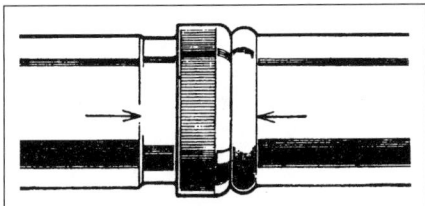

Fig. 7.3 Alignment marks on shaft and
splined sleeve (Sec 4)

shaft and sleeve and turning them in opposite
directions, noting any excessive movement.

4 If the universal joint is worn, a repair kit
comprising a new spider, bearings, cups and
seals should be purchased prior to removing
the affected shaft.

5 If excessive wear is apparent on the
propeller shaft splined sleeve, a new shaft will
have to be obtained.

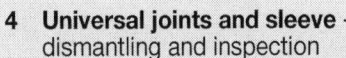
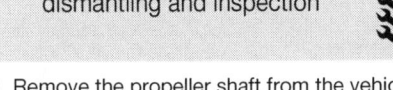

4 Universal joints and sleeve -
dismantling and inspection

1 Remove the propeller shaft from the vehicle
as described in Section 2.

2 If a protective rubber boot is fitted over the
sleeve section, slacken the securing clips and
slide the boot rearwards. A rubber boot
should be fitted to the front shaft but not the
rear.

3 Check that alignment marks are visible on
the sleeve and shaft (two arrows). If no marks
can be found, scribe a line along the sleeve
and shaft to ensure the splined shaft and
sleeve are reassembled in the original
position. This is most important.

4 Unscrew the dust cap and withdraw the
front universal joint and sleeve assembly from
the splined end of the shaft.

5 Clean away all the traces of dirt and grease
from the circlips located on the ends of the
spiders, and using a pair of circlip pliers
compress their open ends and hook them out
with the aid of a screwdriver. If they are
difficult to remove, place a drift between the
circlip and tap the top of the bearing cup to

4.9 Universal joint bearing components

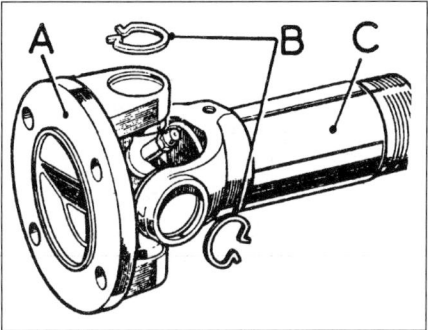

Fig. 7.4 Universal joint (Sec 4)

A Yoke flange   C Shaft yoke
B Circlips

ease the pressure on the circlip. Remove the
grease nipple.

6 Support the shaft in a vice with the yoke in
a vertical plane. Using a hammer and drift of
suitable diameter, tap the uppermost bearing
cup until the bearing cup at the bottom
protrudes from the yoke by approximately 1/4
in (6 mm) (photo). Remove the shaft and
securely grip the protruding bearing cup in the
vice jaws. Turn the shaft from side to side
while at the same time lifting the shaft until it
comes free of the bearing cup.

7 Replace the shaft in the vice with the
exposed spider uppermost. Tap the spider
with the hammer and drift until the lower
bearing cup protrudes and then remove the
cup as previously described.

8 The flange and spider can now be removed
from the shaft and the remaining two bearing
cups dismantled in the previously described
manner.

9 With the universal joint dismantled, carefully
examine the needle rollers, bearings cups and
spider for wear, scoring and pitting of the
surface finish. If any wear is detected the joint
must be renewed (photo).

10 Temporarily fit the splined end of the shaft
into the sleeve with the alignment marks
adjacent. Grip the sleeve in a soft-jawed vice
and ascertain the amount of spline wear by
turning the shaft in either direction. The

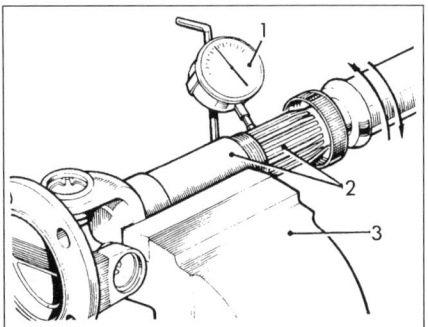

Fig. 7.5 Checking spline wear using a dial
indicator (Sec 4)

1 Dial indicator
2 Sleeve and shaft splined sections
3 Vice

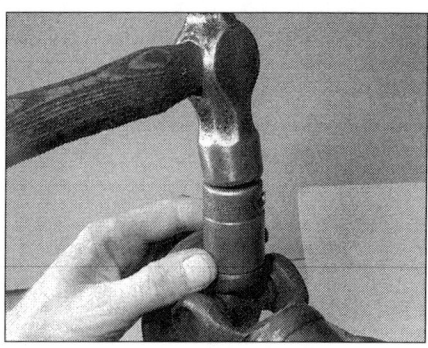

4.6 Tap the uppermost bearing cup

maximum permissible movement is 0.004 in
(0.10 mm) and this can only be accurately
checked using a dial indicator. As a rough
guide, if you can see any movement as the
shaft is turned then it is worn and should be
renewed.

11 If there is any sign of ovality in any one of
the eight yoke holes in any one propeller shaft
assembly, then a new complete propeller
shaft assembly must be fitted.

5 Universal joints and sleeve -
reassembly

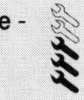

1 Before fitting the new bearing caps and
spider, check that the bearing caps are half
full of fresh lubricant, and that all the needle
rollers are present and properly positioned. If
necessary use a smear of grease to keep
them in place during the refitting operation.

2 Insert the new spider complete with seals
into the flange yoke. Ensure that the grease
nipple hole faces away from the flange.

3 Partially insert one of the bearing cups into
the yoke and enter the spider trunnion into the
bearing cup, being careful not to dislodge the
needle rollers.

4 Partially insert the other bearing cup into
the flange yoke. Using a vice carefully press
both cups into place, but ensure that the
spider trunnion does not dislodge any of the
needle rollers (photo).

5 Using a socket which is small enough to fit

5.4 Press the cups into place using a vice
and socket

5.5 Refitting a circlip

5.6 Inserting the bearing cups with the spider in position in the shaft yoke

5.7 Using a vice and socket to press the bearing cups into place

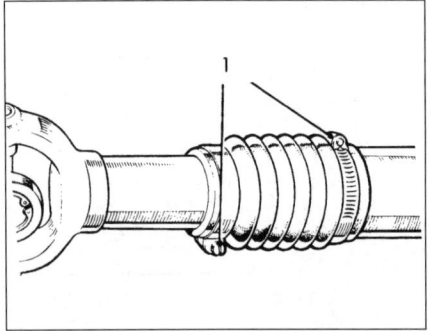

Fig. 7.6 Refit the rubber boot to the shaft with worm drives (1) 180° apart (Sec 5)

6.1 The rear shaft grease nipple for the splined section

inside the yoke press one of the bearing cups in just far enough to allow the circlip to be fitted (photo). Repeat this operation with the other bearing cup.

6 Insert the spider into the yokes of the propeller shaft. Partially insert both bearing cups, being careful to ensure that the spider trunnions do not dislodge any of the needle rollers (photo).

7 Using a vice carefully press both bearing cups into place but ensure that none of the bearing rollers are dislodged. Repeat the operation given in paragraph 5 (photo).

8 Fit the grease nipple to the spider.

9 Smear the splines on the end of the shaft with grease. Carefully match up the alignment

mark and slide the shaft into the sleeve. Tighten the dust cap. **Note:** *Do not pack grease into the sleeve prior to fitting the shaft as it may prevent the shaft being pushed fully home.*

10 If the front propeller shaft is being serviced, pull the rubber boot over the sleeve and tighten the clips. Ensure that the worm drives on the clips are 180° apart from each other to retain the balance of the shaft.

11 Refit the shaft to the vehicle as described in Section 2 and lubricate the bearings using a grease gun applied to the universal joint and sleeve nipples. **Note:** *If the sleeve is fitted with a plug instead of a grease nipple, replace it with a nipple to enable lubrication of the*

sleeve splines. Do not overfill the sleeve splines with grease. These should be sufficient to lubricate the splines only.

6 Propeller shaft sliding sleeves - lubrication

1 The rear propeller shaft splined sleeve is fitted with a grease nipple and this should be greased every 6000 miles (10 000 km) with the specified lubricant (photo).

2 The front propeller shaft does not have a grease nipple fitted to its splined sleeve because of its exposed location. A plug is fitted instead. Every 24 000 miles (40 000 km) or 2 years, the splined sleeve should be lubricated as follows.

3 Undo the front end of the propeller shaft as directed in Section 2.

4 Remove the plug from the splined sleeve greasing point and fit a grease nipple.

5 Compress the sliding joint as far as possible and then lubricate it with the specified grease. Compressing the joint first will ensure that too much grease is not injected.

6 Remove the grease nipple and refit the plug.

7 Refit the propeller shaft as directed in Section 2.

Fault finding - propeller shafts

Vibration

☐ Wear in sliding sleeve splines
☐ Worn universal joint bearings
☐ Propeller shaft out of balance
☐ Distorted propeller shaft

Knock or clunk when taking up drive

☐ Worn universal joint bearings
☐ Worn axle drive pinion splines
☐ Loose drive flange bolts
☐ Excessive backlash in axle gears

Chapter 8 Front and rear axles

For modifications, and information applicable to later models, see Supplement at end of manual

Contents

Degrees of difficulty

Easy, suitable for novice with little experience	Fairly easy, suitable for beginner with some experience	Fairly difficult, suitable for competent DIY mechanic 	Difficult, suitable for experienced DIY mechanic	Very difficult, suitable for expert DIY or professional

Specifications

Axle type
Front	Spiral bevel with enclosed CV joint
Rear	Spiral bevel with fully floating halfshafts
Final drive ratio	3.54 : 1

Adjustment data
Hub-to-stub axle endfloat (front and rear)	0.002 to 0.004 in (0.05 to 0.10 mm)
Endfloat on CV joint	0.025 in (0.64 mm) maximum
Swivel pin adjustment shims available	0.003, 0.005, 0.010 and 0.030 in (0.076, 0.127, 0.254 and 0.762 mm)
Differential pinion pre-load	7 to 12 lb (3.2 to 4.5 kg) measured at flange
Crownwheel-to-bevel gear backlash	0.008 to 0.010 in (0.20 to 0.25 mm)

Lubricant
Type/specification:	
Differentials and swivel pin housings	Hypoid gear oil, viscosity SAE 90EP to API GL4
Front and rear hubs	Multi-purpose lithium based grease to NLGI 2
Capacities:	
Differentials	3 Imp pints (1.7 litres)
Swivel pin housings	0.5 Imp pint (0.25 litre)

Torque wrench settings
	lbf ft	kgf m
Differential carrier-to-axle casing	28	3.8
Propeller shaft flanges	25	3.5
Halfshaft and hub cap	38	5.2
Drive flange - differential pinion	85	11.7
Crownwheel retaining bolts:		
Early models - cross-shaft with pin fixing	35	4.8
Later models - cross-shaft retained by circlips	45	6.2
Crownwheel bearing cap bolts	60	8.3
Self-levelling load adjuster - pivot bracket	30	4.0
Track rod end balljoint retaining nut	30	4.0
Brake caliper-to-front swivel	60	8.5
Front axle swivel housing-to-axle casing bolts	44	6.0
Stub axle-to-swivel housing (front)	44	6.0
Stub axle-to-axle casing (rear)	44	6.0
Front axle swivel pin retaining bolts	60	8.5
Front swivel-to-housing oil seal retainer plate bolts	10	1.4

1 General description

Both the front and rear axles of the Range Rover are of a similar design, comprising a one-piece steel casing housing the differential assembly and two driveshafts (halfshafts). The rear shafts are of solid steel construction, the inner ends of which are splined into the differential assembly, while the outer ends are attached to integral limbs.

To enable the front wheels to turn from lock-to-lock while being driven, the front halfshafts incorporate a CV joint on the outer end. The CV joint runs inside an oil-filled swivel pin housing, the swivel pins being located in tapered roller bearings.

Both the front and rear axle assemblies are attached to the chassis via coil springs and telescopic shock absorbers. Other methods of location are also employed; radius arms and a Panhard rod at the front, with the rear also incorporating a self-levelling ride unit in the centre of the axle and trailing lower links beneath.

2 Rear axle halfshaft - removal and refitting

1 Chock the front wheels securely, jack up the rear of the vehicle and remove the roadwheels. **Note:** *The handbrake will be ineffective once a halfshaft has been removed.*
2 Undo and remove the 5 bolts securing the halfshaft hub to the wheel hub and place a container beneath the hub to catch any oil.
3 Withdraw the hub and halfshaft from the wheel hub as a complete assembly. If the hub is initially tight, gently tap its circumference with a soft-faced mallet.
4 The halfshaft and hub are a one-piece assembly and cannot be separated.
5 Refitting the halfshafts is the reverse sequence to removal, noting the following additional points:
(a) Fit a new gasket between the halfshaft nut and the wheel hub, lightly coated on both sides with medium grease
(b) Check and if necessary top up the rear axle oil
(c) Tighten the halfshaft hub retaining bolts to the specified torque

3 Rear axle differential assembly - removal and refitting

1 The task of overhauling the differential assembly is a highly skilled operation requiring a considerable number of special tools. Taking into consideration the cost and non-availability of many of the parts involved, overhaul of a worn unit is not really an economical proposition.

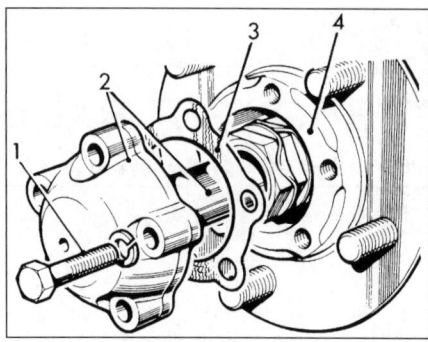

Fig. 8.1 Rear axle halfshaft assembly (Sec 2)

1 Bolt
2 Halfshaft and hub
3 Gasket
4 Wheel hub

2 Often the best course of action is to replace the complete differential with a new or reconditioned assembly or carefully selected unit from a breaker's yard.
3 Jack up the rear of the vehicle and support the axle on heavy duty stands. Check the remaining roadwheels.
4 Drain the axle lubricating oil into a suitable container as described in Section 14.
5 Undo and remove the four bolts and locknuts securing the propeller shaft flange to the rear differential pinion flange and lower the propeller shaft to the ground.
6 Withdraw the rear halfshafts as described in Section 2. It is only necessary to withdraw the shafts sufficiently to disengage from the differential unit.
7 Undo and remove the nuts and washer securing the differential to the axle casing. Support the unit with both hands and carefully withdraw the complete housing from the axle casing. Remove the gasket. Note that the brake pipe distribution bracket is mounted on one of the upper mounting studs. Hold it out of the way when withdrawing the differential unit (photo).
8 Refitting the differential is the reverse sequence to removal. Use a new gasket smeared on both sides with jointing compound when refitting the housing to the axle casing and refill the axle with the correct oil.
9 Tighten all retaining nuts and bolts to the specified torques.

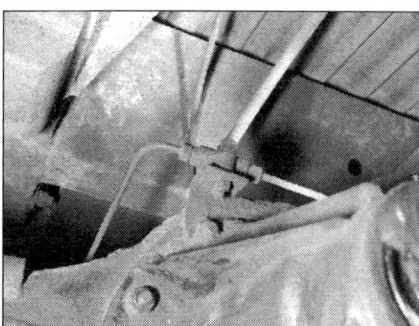

3.7 Rear brake pipe 3-way junction and bracket are secured to the rear axle casing

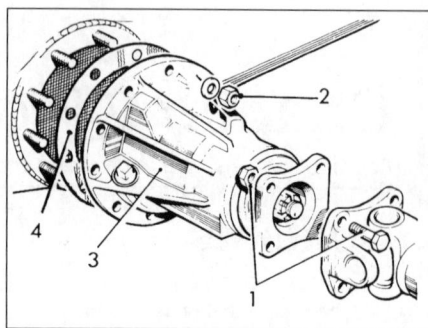

Fig. 8.2 Rear axle differential unit (Sec 3)

1 Rear propeller shaft nut and bolt
2 Differential unit retaining nut
3 Differential unit
4 Gasket

4 Rear axle - removal and refitting

1 Chock the front roadwheels, slacken the rear roadwheel nuts, jack up the rear of the vehicle and support it on strong axle stands.
2 Place a jack under the rear axle to take the weight off the suspension.
3 Remove the rear roadwheels.
4 Undo the lower rear shock absorber retaining nuts and remove the washer, the outer bush and the cone.
5 Remove the top of the brake fluid reservoir and place a piece of polythene over the top before refitting the cap. This will prevent loss of fluid when the brake pipes are disconnected.
6 Undo the flexible brake hose union at the three-way junction on top of the rear axle. Plug the end of the pipe to prevent ingress of dirt and loss of fluid.
7 Undo the nuts and drive out the bolts to release the trailing lower suspension links from the rear axle brackets.
8 Undo the bolts and nuts and separate the propeller shaft from the pinion drive flange, as described in Chapter 7.
9 Undo the nut which retains the self-levelling unit pivot bracket balljoint to the bracket on the top of the rear axle casing.
10 Undo the two bolts which retain the bottom endplates for each coil spring.
11 Lower the axle carefully on the jack and withdraw both coil springs when there is adequate clearance.
12 Lower the jack further so that the complete axle assembly can be removed from the vehicle.
13 Refitting is a straightforward procedure, but not quite the same as for removal.
14 Begin by lining up the axle beneath the vehicle with the weight on the jack, raise the axle so that the lower suspension links can be refitted to their mounting brackets.
15 Refit the coil springs and lock them in place with their respective retaining plates.

16 Jack the axle up into position, locating the top of the coil springs in their seats.

17 Reconnect the balljoint on the end of the pivot bracket and tighten it to the specified torque.

18 Refit the shock absorber lower ends to their mounting points. Refit the cone, bush and washer, and tighten the nut.

19 Refit the propeller shaft flange to the drive pinion as described in Chapter 7.

20 Reconnect the brake flexible hose to the three-way junction and then bleed the rear brakes as described in Chapter 9.

21 Refit the roadwheels and remove the axle jack and the chassis stands. Remove the wheel chocks and tighten the roadwheel nuts.

5 Front and rear wheel hubs and bearings - renewal

1 If the front hub bearings are to be renewed, first drain the oil from the swivel pin housing and from the front differential casing as described in Sections 13 and 14. Then remove the front stub driveshaft and integral hub as described in Section 8.

2 If the rear hub bearings are to be renewed, remove the appropriate halfshaft from the rear axle as described in Section 2.

3 Remove the brake caliper assembly as described in Chapter 9 and tie it up out of the way without straining the brake pipes.

4 Undo the wheel hub central locking nut, having first knocked back the locking plate, and remove them both (photo).

5 Remove the inner hub nut and keyed washer.

6 The wheel hub and brake disc can now be slid off the stub axle as a complete assembly with the hub bearings.

7 Hold one hand over the end of the hub to prevent the outer bearing from falling out and withdraw the hub and bearings from the stub axle.

8 Withdraw the outer roller bearings from the hub. Carefully prise out the oil seal from the rear of the hub and remove the inner roller bearing.

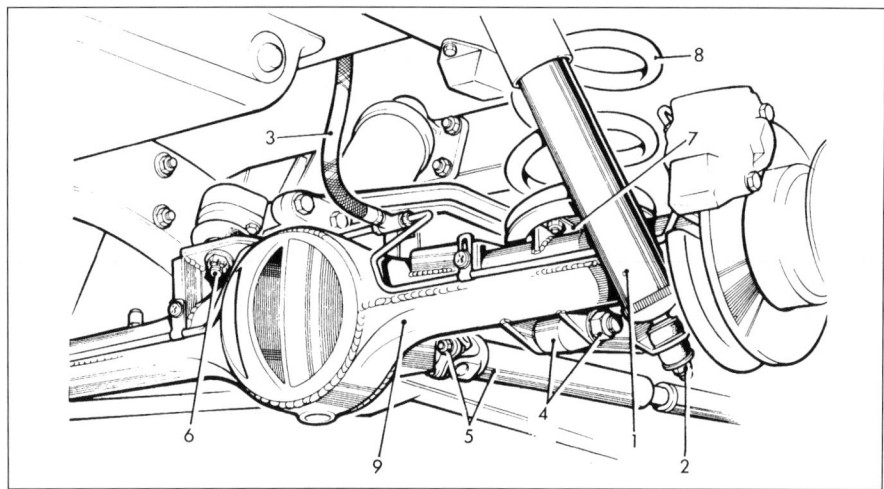

Fig. 8.3 Rear axle assembly (Sec 4)

1 Rear shock absorber	4 Lower suspension link and nut
2 Shock absorber lower retaining nut	5 Propeller shaft and retaining nut
3 Flexible brake pipe	6 Self-levelling unit balljoint and nut
	7 Retaining plate
	8 Coil spring
	9 Rear axle

9 Examine the bearings for wear. If there is any sign of scoring or pitting of the rollers or roughness of the bearings generally they must be renewed. If badly damaged or broken up, then examine also the stub axle sleeve.

10 If new bearings are being fitted, support the hub in a vice or on wooden blocks and drive out the bearing outer track using a hammer and suitable drift.

11 Clean all the old grease out of the casing and wash it out with paraffin. Dry it thoroughly before reassembly.

12 Carefully tap the new outer bearing track into the hub with the smaller inside diameter toward the centre of the hub. Ensure that the track is kept square to the hub during fitting. If it jams do not force it. Tap it out from the other end of the hub and start again.

13 Pack the inner bearing with medium grease and place it in position on the hub. Smear the outside diameter of a new oil seal with jointing compound and gently tap it into position using a flat block of wood. Ensure

that the seal is fitted with the lip facing towards the bearing. The outer flat face of the oil seal should be flush with the edge of the hub when fitted.

14 Fill the hub to half its capacity with medium grease and pack the outer bearing. Place the outer bearing in position on the hub.

15 Holding the outer roller bearing in position, slide the hub assembly onto the stub axle.

16 Refit the keyed washer and inner hub nut. Tighten the hub nut securely until there is no endfloat of the hub assembly. Rotate the hub several times to settle the bearings. Back off the hub nut until it is just possible to detect a trace of endfloat in the hub assembly. If a dial gauge is available set the endfloat to between the limits given in the Specifications. Rotate the hub and ensure that it turns freely with no harshness.

17 When the hub is adjusted correctly, fit the lockwasher and outer nut and tighten the outer nut. Recheck that the hub turns freely.

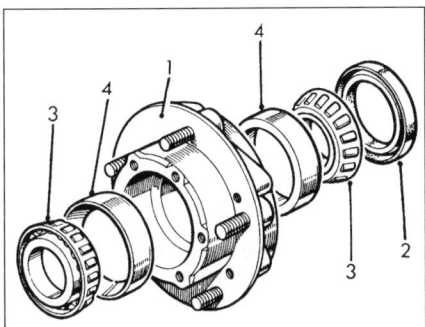

Fig. 8.4 Hub and bearing assembly (exploded view) (Sec 5)

1 Hub	3 Roller bearing races
2 Oil seal	4 Outer bearing tracks

5.4 Knock back the locking plate and remove nut and plate

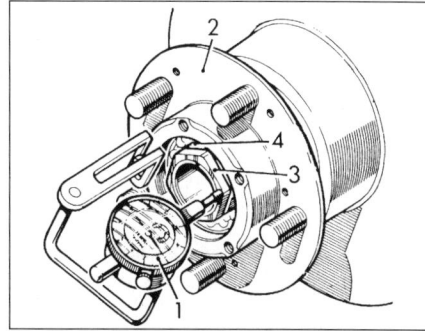

Fig. 8.5 Checking the hub bearing endfloat (Sec 5)

1 Dial gauge	3 Inner nut
2 Hub	4 Keyed washer

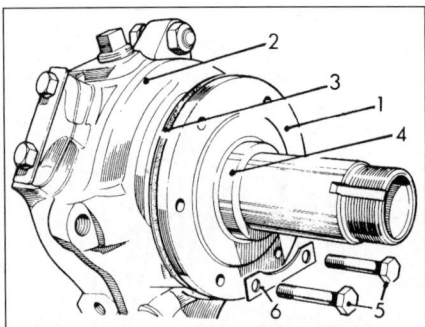

Fig. 8.6 Front wheel hub stub axle (Sec 6)

1 Stub axle	4 Distance piece
2 Steering swivel hub	5 Retaining bolts
3 Gasket	6 Locking plate

Bend over an edge of the lockwasher to secure the hub nut.

18 Refit the hub and driveshaft, referring to the Section(s) used when removing them.

19 Refit the brake caliper assembly as described in Chapter 9.

20 Refill the front swivel pin housing and front differential with oil of the specified grade to the correct level, as described in Sections 13 and 14 (if applicable).

6 Front and rear stub axles - removal, overhaul and refitting

1 When renewing the wheel hub bearings as described in the last Section, it may be found that not only are the bearings in need of renewal but that damage has been caused to the stub axle itself and that it too requires replacement.

2 Remove the hub as described in the previous Section.

3 Remove the six retaining bolts and the locking plates and then withdraw the stub axle and gasket from the end of the rear axle casing, or from the front steering swivel in the case of the front stub axle.

4 If a new stub axle is to be fitted, or if the old one is serviceable but is being overhauled, the distance piece on the inner end of the stub axle will have to be renewed, or a new one fitted to the new stub axle.

5 To renew the distance piece on an existing stub axle, secure the stub axle in a vice with protected jaws. Split the distance piece using a cold chisel and then remove it from the shaft (Fig. 8.7).

6 To fit a new distance piece, apply sealing compound to the seating face of the distance piece. Drive it onto the stub axle so that it seats against the flange. Remove any excess sealant from the shaft or flange.

7 The front stub axle has a bush fitted into the rear of the sleeve. On a new stub axle, press a new bush into the rear of the sleeve with the stub axle firmly supported in a vice with protected jaws (Fig. 8.8). If the original stub axle is to be used then the old bush must first

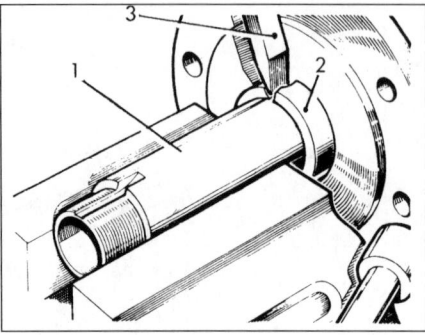

Fig. 8.7 Renewing the distance piece (Sec 6)

1 Stub axle	3 Cold chisel
2 Distance piece	

be removed and then a new one can be fitted as above.

8 Fit the new gasket to the mating surface of the stub axle, having smeared it with grease on both sides.

9 Offer up the stub axle to the swivel housing or rear axle casing, line up the bolt holes and refit the bolts and locking plates.

10 Tighten the bolts evenly in diagonal sequence to the specified torque.

7 Differential pinion oil seal - renewal

1 This procedure covers the renewal of the differential pinion oil seal for both front and rear differential units.

2 Remove the plugs and drain the oil from the differential casing into a container, as described in Section 14.

3 Detach the propeller shaft from the pinion drive flange as described in Chapter 7.

4 Remove the split pin and make up a bracket to stop the pinion drive flange rotating so that its retaining nut can be undone. Alternatively use the help of an assistant to apply the footbrake to lock the axle.

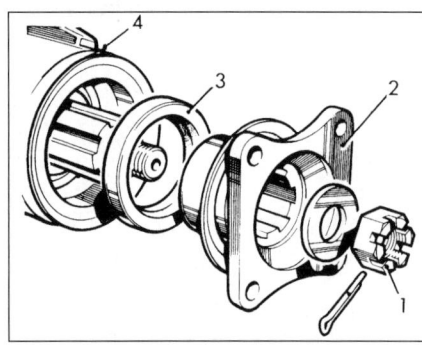

Fig. 8.9 Differential pinion oil seal renewal (exploded view) (Sec 7)

1 Castellated nut
2 Pinion drive flange
3 Oil seal
4 Differential pinion housing

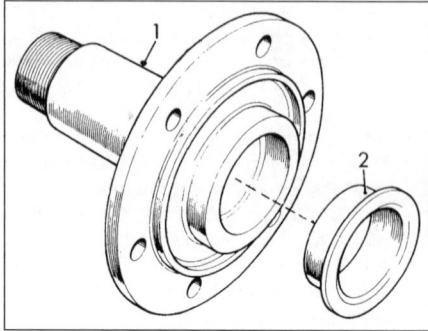

Fig. 8.8 Front stub axle and bush (Sec 6)

1 Stub axle   2 Bush

5 Remove the retaining nut and washer and use a soft-faced mallet to tap the drive flange off the pinion shaft.

6 Prise the oil seal from the housing front end using a screwdriver or a similar pointed tool. Take care not to damage the seal housing.

7 Smear the outside diameter of the new oil seal with the jointing compound, and the inside diameter with oil and tap it into position in the housing with the lips facing inwards.

8 Smear the outside diameter of the pinion drive flange sleeve with oil, checking it for any roughness or damage which may have damaged the last oil seal. Engage it on the splines of the shaft and push it carefully into position, taking care not to damage the new seal.

9 Refit the washer and castellated nut and tighten the nut to the specified torque. Insert a new split pin.

10 Refill the propeller shaft and secure with the bolts and locknuts.

11 Refill the axle with the correct grade of oil and check that the axle breather is clear. Remove the axle stands and lower the vehicle to the ground.

8 Front axle halfshafts and constant velocity joints - removal and refitting

1 Apply the handbrake and chock the rear wheels.

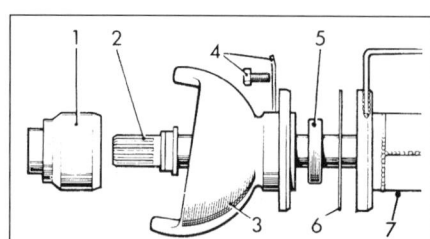

Fig. 8.10 Front axle halfshaft, constant velocity joint and axle casing oil seal assembly (exploded view) (Sec 8)

1 Constant velocity joint	4 Bolt and lockplate
2 Inner section halfshaft	5 Oil seal
	6 Gasket
3 Swivel housing	7 Axle casing

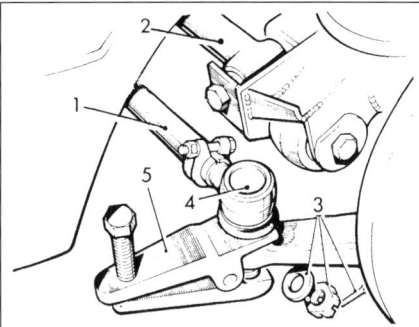

8.5 Withdrawing the front stub driveshaft and hub

2 Slacken the front roadwheel nuts, jack up the front of the vehicle and remove the roadwheels.

3 Drain the oil from the swivel pin housing as described in Section 13.

4 Undo the five bolts which retain the front stub driveshaft and its integral hub to the wheel hub.

5 Tap the integral hub loose and withdraw it and the stub driveshaft from the constant velocity joint in the swivel housing (photo). This is the outer section of the jointed driveshaft. The constant velocity joint is located in the swivel housing and is jointed to the main section of the halfshaft in the front axle casing. The left-hand inner driveshaft is larger than the right-hand one due to the location of the differential housing on the axle.

6 Remove the front wheel hub and bearing assembly as described in Section 5.

7 Remove the front wheel stub axle as described in Section 6.

8 Remove the constant velocity joint from the end of the inner section of the halfshaft assembly.

9 Withdraw the inner section halfshaft, taking care not to damage the oil seal in the outer end of the axle casing with the splined inner end of the halfshaft.

10 Lubricate the halfshaft inner section with oil and carefully feed the splined inner end through the oil seal, taking care not to damage it.

11 Engage the splined inner end in the differential side gear and push it right home.

12 Check the condition of the constant velocity joint and fit a new one if in any doubt.

13 Refit the stub axle as described in Section 6.

14 Refit the front wheel hub and bearing assembly as described in Section 5.

15 Fit a new gasket to the mating face of the stub driveshaft hub and offer the driveshaft to the stub axle sleeve. Engage the splines into the constant velocity joint and align the holes in the shaft hub with the holes in the wheel hub.

16 Refit and tighten the hub bolts to the specified torque.

17 Refill the swivel pin housing with oil to the correct level and refit the plug.

18 Refit the roadwheel, lower and remove the jack and tighten the roadwheel nuts.

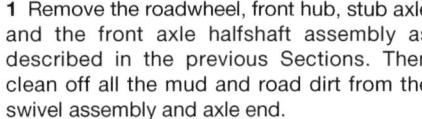

Fig. 8.11 Drag link removal from left-hand steering swivel (Sec 9)

1 Drag link	4 Balljoint
2 Panhard rod	5 Balljoint extractor
3 Split pin, nut and washer from balljoint	

9 Front axle casing oil seals - removal and refitting

1 Remove the roadwheel, front hub, stub axle and the front axle halfshaft assembly as described in the previous Sections. Then clean off all the mud and road dirt from the swivel assembly and axle end.

2 Separate the track rod balljoint from the front swivel.

3 In the case of the left-hand swivel, disconnect the drag link balljoint as well from the swivel front arm (Fig. 8.11).

4 Knock back the locking tabs, undo the swivel housing retaining bolts and remove the swivel and housing assembly from the axle casing.

5 Remove the gasket and withdraw the oil seal from the inner end of the swivel housing.

6 Fit a new seal to the swivel housing with the lipped face outwards.

7 Fit the swivel housing assembly and a new

gasket to the axle casing. Tighten the bolts to the specified torque evenly and diagonally. Then knock down the tabs to secure them.

8 Reconnect the steering arm balljoint(s) to the swivel and tighten the nut(s) to the specified torque.

9 Refit the front axle halfshaft assembly, stub axle, front hub and roadwheel as directed in the previous Sections.

10 Front steering swivel and housing assembly - removal, overhaul, adjustment and refitting

1 Remove the front axle halfshaft assembly, front wheel hub and bearing assembly and stub axle as described in Sections 5, 6 and 8.

2 Remove the complete steering swivel and housing assembly and oil seal as described in Section 9. Clean the outside of the assembly thoroughly using a proprietary degreasing agent before dismantling begins.

3 Undo the bolts which retain the swivel and housing oil seal retainer plate.

4 Withdraw the retainer plate and the large oil seal.

5 Knock back the locking plate and undo the two bolts which retain the upper swivel pin and shim(s). Remove the complete swivel pin assembly.

6 Undo the two lower swivel pin assembly retaining bolts and remove the lower pin assembly in the same way.

7 Separate the steering swivel from the housing.

8 Remove the swivel bearing races from the top and bottom positions in the swivel housing.

9 Examine the general condition of the steering swivel and swivel housing surfaces. The swivel surface of the housing must be free from corrosion, pitting and damage, otherwise the main swivel oil seal will become damaged and begin to leak.

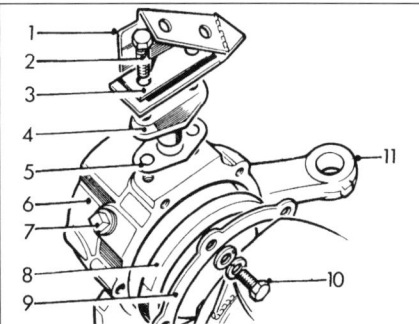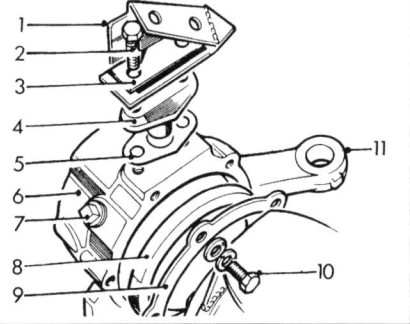

Fig. 8.12 Front steering swivel and housing assembly (Sec 10)

1 Brake pipe bracket	7 Filler plug
2 Swivel pin retaining bolt	8 Oil seal
3 Locking plate	9 Oil seal retainer plate
4 Swivel pin	10 Retainer plate bolt
5 Shim	11 Steering arm
6 Steering swivel	

Fig. 8.13 Swivel housing assembly (exploded view) (Sec 10)

1 Roller bearing race - top	5 CV joint
2 Outer bearing track	6 Roller bearing race - bottom
3 Inner halfshaft section	7 Swivel housing
4 Bush	8 Housing retaining bolt

Fig. 8.14 Front axle differential location (Sec 11)

1 Differential unit
2 Flexible brake pipes
3 Front steering swivel
4 Swivel housing bolt and locking plate
5 Radius arm
6 Differential housing nuts
7 Steering damper retaining nut
8 Pinion drive flange
9 Track rod

10 Examine the roller bearing races for wear, damage and fit on the swivel pins. They should be a light push fit onto the pins. If necessary renew the bearings, as follows.
11 Drive the outer bearing tracks from the swivel housing using a hammer and suitable drift from inside the housing.
12 Fit a new bearing track to each bearing location in turn. Drive the track in squarely using a block of hardwood. Make sure that the swivel housing is adequately supported.
13 Reassemble the swivel housing assembly as follows. Fit the lower swivel pin to the steering swivel and position the bearing race on the pin. Fit the other bearing race to the upper bearing track in the housing. Secure the housing flange in a vice with projected jaws with the bearings in a vertical plane, so that the swivel area is clear of the vice.
14 Offer the steering swivel to the swivel housing and engage the lower swivel pin and bearing into the lower bearing track. As the bearing enters the location, tilt the steering swivel so that the upper swivel pin location is over the upper bearing position.
15 Refit the upper swivel pin and shim(s).
16 Check that the swivel pin bolts are tightened to the correct torque.
17 Connect a spring balance to the balljoint eye of the steering arm on the rear of the steering swivel in order to measure the resistance of the swivel to rotation in a horizontal plane. After overcoming the initial inertia, it should require a steady pull of 2.5 to 3 lb (1.2 to 1.3 kg) to turn the steering swivel on its pins.
18 To adjust the resistance where necessary, the shims beneath the top swivel pin can be changed. Shims range from 0.003 to 0.030 in (0.076 to 0.762 mm) as shown in the Specifications.
19 If adjustments have been made to the shims, refit the swivel pin bolts and tighten

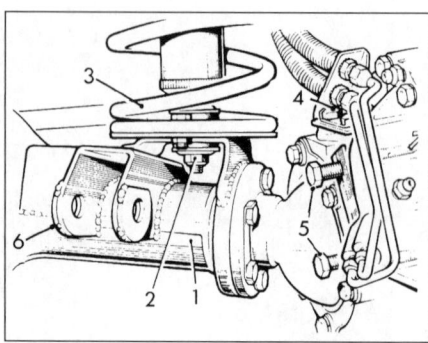

11.11 The front differential unit viewed from above with the engine removed

them. Then recheck that the rotational resistance is acceptable. Knock over the locktabs when it is satisfactory.
20 Pack the new large oil seal with heavy grease and fit it to the assembly with the flat face to the rear.
21 Refit the seal retainer plate and refit the retaining bolts, flat and spring washers. Tighten the bolts to the specified torque.
22 Refit the steering swivel and housing assembly to the front axle using a new gasket, having renewed the axle casing oil seal, as described in Section 9.
23 Rotate the steering swivel before reconnecting the track rod balljoint, and the drag link balljoint in the case of the left-hand swivel, and check that the oil seal wipes evenly over the surface of the swivel housing.
24 Refit the remainder of the removed assemblies in the reverse order to removal as described in Sections 5, 6 and 8.
25 Check the front wheel alignment and the setting of the steering stop bolts as described in Chapter 11.

11 Front axle differential assembly - removal and refitting

Note: *Refer to paragraphs 1 and 2 of Section 3 as they apply equally here.*

1 Slacken the front roadwheel nuts, jack the vehicle up, place strong axle stands under the chassis side-members and remove the roadwheels. Chock the rear roadwheels.
2 Remove the drain plug from the front differential casing and drain the oil into a suitable container.
3 Remove the steering track rod by undoing the balljoints at each end and use a separator to free them from the swivel arms. Note which way round the track rod fits before placing it to one side.
4 Remove the steering telescopic damper as described in Chapter 11.
5 Detach the drag link balljoint from the left-hand steering swivel.
6 Remove the cap from the brake fluid reservoir. Place a sheet of polythene over the neck and then refit the cap to help prevent

Fig. 8.15 Front axle removal (Sec 12)

1 Front axle
2 Shock absorber lower retaining nut
3 Coil spring
4 Brake pipe bracket/swivel pin bolt
5 Brake caliper bolts
6 Radius arm mounting bracket

loss of fluid when the brake hoses are undone.
7 Undo the flexible brake hoses to the front calipers at the wing valance brackets, and cover the open ends of the hoses to prevent the ingress of dirt.
8 Undo the steering swivel housing retaining bolts from the front axle casing, having knocked down the locktabs.
9 Pull the wheel hubs gently outwards just far enough to disengage the inner halfshaft sections from the differential unit side gears.
10 Remove the front propeller shaft from the front pinion drive flange as described in Chapter 7. Move the shaft to one side out of the way.
11 Undo the differential unit retaining nuts and washers while supporting the unit using a jack (photo).
12 Remove the unit carefully from the axle casing using both hands. Recover the gasket.
13 Refitting the differential unit is the reverse of the removal procedure. Note that the braking system will have to be bled when the brake hoses have been connected. Details are given in Chapter 9.
14 Refit the differential drain plug and fill the casing with the correct grade of oil to the correct level.
15 Tighten all nuts and bolts to the specified torque settings.

12 Front axle - removal and refitting

1 Should it be necessary, the complete front axle assembly with steering swivels, track rod and differential unit can be removed in one operation.
2 Slacken the front roadwheel nuts, jack up the front of the vehicle, and support it securely with axle stands under the chassis side-members.
3 Support the weight of the front axle and

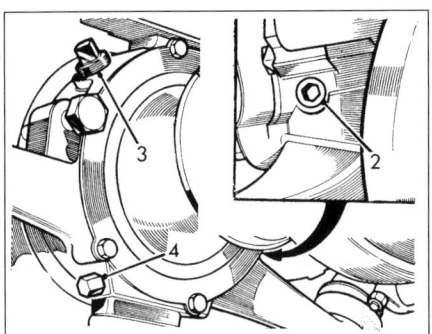

Fig. 8.16 Steering swivel pin housing –
drain, level and filler plugs (Sec 13)

2 Level plug   3 Filler plug   4 Drain plug

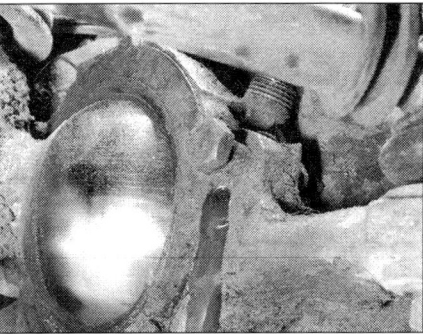

13.2 Check the steering swivel oil level by
removing the front plug (this is too full)

13.3 Remove the filler plug

remove the front roadwheels. Chock the rear
roadwheels.

4 Remove the front radius arms and front
shock absorber lower mounting nuts as
described in Chapter 11.

5 Knock back the locking tabs and remove
the brake pipe bracket retaining bolts from the
steering swivel.

6 Move the bracket to one side and refit the
bolts.

7 Remove the front brake caliper as
described in Chapter 9 and tie it up out of the
way. Do not strain the brake pipes.

8 Separate the drag link balljoint from the left-
hand steering swivel front arm using a balljoint
separator. Move the drag link out of the way.

9 Disconnect the Panhard rod from the
bracket on the axle casing as described in
Chapter 11.

10 Disconnect the front propeller shaft from
the pinion drive flange as described in
Chapter 7.

11 Lower the axle carefully on the jack and
withdraw the two front coil springs.

12 Lower the axle and remove it from under
the vehicle.

13 Refitting is straightforward. With the axle
in position under the vehicle, reconnect the
Panhard rod to it.

14 Place the coil springs over the shock
absorbers, then raise the axle and support the
left hand-side on a jack. Reconnect the radius
arms to the axle and chassis.

15 Reconnect the shock absorber lower
mountings as described in Chapter 11.

16 Reconnect the propeller shaft to the front
pinion drive flange and the drag link to the
left-hand steering swivel front arm. Tighten
the bolts and nuts.

17 Refit the brake calipers and brake pipe
brackets. Tighten the mounting bolts to the
specified torque.

18 Remove the jack from beneath the axle.

19 Refit the roadwheels, jack up and remove
the axle stands supporting the chassis, and
lower the vehicle to the ground. Remove the
jack.

20 Tighten the roadwheel nuts and remove
the chocks from the rear wheels.

13 Steering swivel pin housing - oil changing and level checking

1 The front wheel drive CV joints and the
swivel pins are lubricated by oil in the swivel
housings.

2 To check the level, remove the recessed
level plug (Fig. 8.16) or the square-headed
plug at the front of the swivel (photo), as
applicable. The oil should be level with the
bottom of the hole. Do not overfill or the oil
seals may be damaged and start to leak.

3 To top up the oil, remove the filler plug from
the top of the steering swivel at the front
(photo). If considerable amounts of oil are
required, check the oil seals and gaskets for
leakage. Also check that the level and drain
plugs are screwed in tightly.

4 To renew the oil in the swivel housings,
remove the level and filler plugs as above and
remove the drain plug from the housings at
the lower front side of the steering swivels,
preferably after a run when the oil is warm.
Drain the oil, approx half a pint (one quarter of
a litre), into a container.

5 Refit the drain plugs tightly.

6 Fill the housings with fresh gear oil, as
specified, to the bottom of the level plug and
no higher.

7 Refit the level plug and filler plug tightly.

8 Wipe off any excess oil from the steering
swivel and housing.

14 Front and rear axle oil - changing and level checking

1 Both differential units have the same
lubricant type and capacity. The filler level and
drain plugs are also similar.

Checking

2 Remove the combined filler and level plug
from the differential casing. This is located on
the right-hand side of the differential at the

rear, and on the left-hand side of the
differential at the front, since the positions are
reversed.

3 The plug fitted in the front axle casing at the
front can be disregarded.

4 The oil level should be at the bottom of the
level plug hole and no higher, or oil seals may
suffer.

5 If significant topping-up is required,
check the oil seals (pinion and axle casing
ends) drain plug and gaskets for signs of
leakage.

Oil changing

6 When changing the oil, do so after a run
when it is warm as it flows better.

7 Remove the filler/level plug.

8 Place a container beneath the differential,
large enough to hold 3 pints (1.7 litres), and
remove the drain plug from the bottom of the
differential housing.

9 Allow the axle to drain thoroughly, then refit
the drain plug tightly.

10 Fill the axle with the specified quantity of
fresh oil, to the bottom of the level plug hole.
Do not overfill the axle or damage to the oil
seals will result.

11 Refit the level/filler plug and wipe off any
excess oil from the axle and casing.

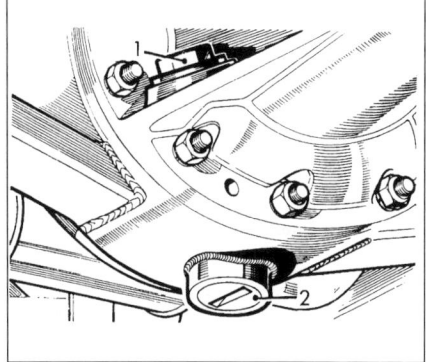

Fig. 8.17 Differential drain and level/filler
plugs (Sec 14)

1 Filler and level plug   2 Drain plug

Fault finding - front and rear axles

Vibration

- [ ] Out of balance propeller shaft
- [ ] Worn hub bearings
- [ ] Wheels out of balance
- [ ] Universal joints or constant velocity joints worn

See also *Fault finding - suspension and steering*

Noise on drive and overrun

- [ ] Worn crownwheel and pinion gears
- [ ] Worn differential bearings
- [ ] Lack of lubrication in axle or swivel pin housings

See also *Fault finding - transmission*

Noise consistent with road speed

- [ ] Worn hub bearings
- [ ] Worn differential bearings
- [ ] Lack of lubricant in axle or swivel pin housings

See also *Fault finding - transmission*

'Clonk' on drive or overrun

- [ ] Excessive crownwheel and pinion backlash
- [ ] Worn propeller shaft or halfshaft universal joints
- [ ] Worn halfshaft splines
- [ ] Hub flange or roadwheel securing bolts loose
- [ ] Broken, damaged or worn suspension or axle fittings

See also *Fault finding - transmission*

Oil leakage

- [ ] Faulty differential pinion or halfshaft oil seals
- [ ] Blocked axle breather valve
- [ ] Damaged swivel housing or oil seal

Chapter 9 Braking system

For modifications, and information applicable to later models, see Supplement at end of manual

Contents

Degrees of difficulty

Easy, suitable for novice with little experience		Fairly easy, suitable for beginner with some experience		Fairly difficult, suitable for competent DIY mechanic		Difficult, suitable for experienced DIY mechanic		Very difficult, suitable for expert DIY or professional	

Specifications

System type
Footbrake . . . . Disc brakes front and rear, dual hydraulic system, servo-assisted
Handbrake . . . . Mechanically-operated drum brake transmission rear output shaft

Brake fluid type/specification . . . . Hydraulic fluid to SAE J1703

Front brakes
Disc diameter . . . . 11.75 in (298.17 mm)
Disc thickness . . . . 0.510 in (13.0 mm) minimum
Disc run-out . . . . 0.006 in (0.15 mm) maximum
Pad minimum thickness . . . . 0.125 in (3.0 mm)
Number of caliper pistons . . . . 4 (2 per circuit)

Rear brakes
Disc diameter . . . . 11.42 in (290.0 mm)
Disc thickness . . . . 0.460 in (12.0 mm) minimum
Disc run-out . . . . 0.006 in (0.15 mm) maximum
Pad minimum thickness . . . . 0.062 in (1.5 mm)
Number of caliper pistons 2

Handbrake (transmission brake)
Lining width . . . . 3.0 in (76.2 mm)
Drum internal diameter . . . . 7.25 in (184.05 mm)
Refinishing limit . . . . +0.030 in (0.76 mm)

Torque wrench settings

	lbf ft	kgf m
Brake disc retaining bolts	38	5.0
Brake caliper retaining bolts	60	8.3
Brake caliper halves retaining bolts	60	8.3
Transmission output flange	120	16.6
Transmission brake backplate bolts	25	3.5
Transmission brake pivot bolt	43	5.9
Brake failure warning switch end plug	16	2.2

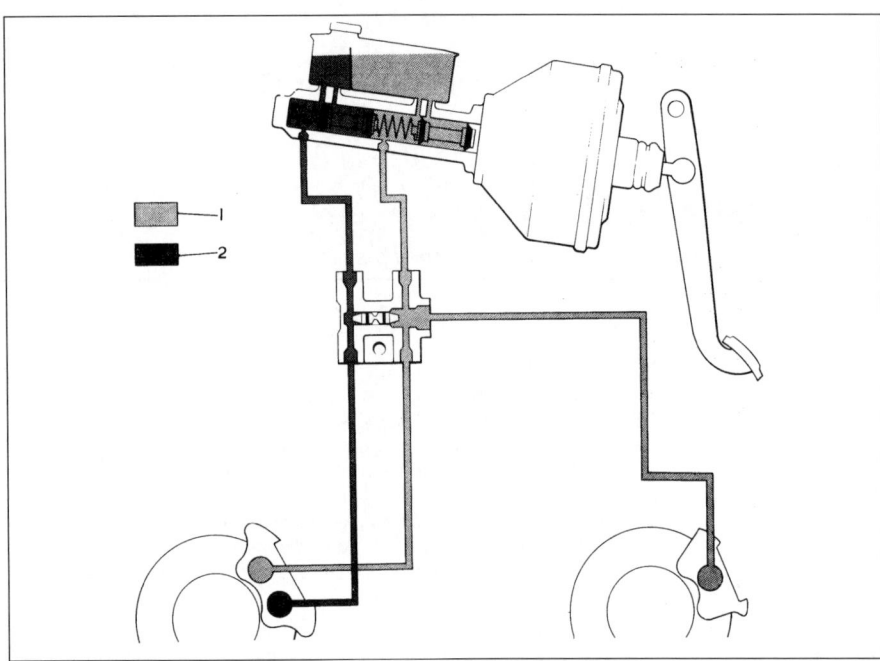

Fig. 9.1 Hydraulic system layout (Sec 1)

1 Primary circuit   2 Secondary circuit

1 General description

The Range Rover is equipped with self-adjusting servo-assisted disc brakes at the front and rear. A dual-line hydraulic system is employed. This has primary and secondary circuits. The primary circuit is connected to all four disc brake calipers whereas the secondary circuit is connected to the front brakes alone. A brake failure warning switch is incorporated in the system so that in the event of failure of either circuit, a warning light will be illuminated on the dashboard.

In order that there is no connection between the primary and secondary circuits in the front brakes, each front caliper has four pistons. The primary circuit is connected to the upper pair of pistons and the secondary circuit to the lower pair. The rear brake calipers have only two pistons each.

The brake fluid reservoir is divided with an internal partition so that the rear section feeds the primary circuit and the front section feeds the secondary circuit.

In the event of a failure in the primary system, the secondary system will still function and will operate the front brakes. Although this will still stop the vehicle adequately, it will inevitably take longer to do so.

Should the vacuum servo unit fail, the brakes will still function, although greater effort will be required to push the brake pedal down. The purpose of the vacuum unit is to reduce the effort required by the driver to operate the brakes.

The handbrake operates independently of the footbrake. A central lever operates a drum brake, which is mounted on the rear end of the transfer gearbox output shaft. via a mechanical linkage. Since the effect of operating the handbrake is to lock the rear propeller shaft, the Range Rover being a four-wheel drive vehicle has effectively a handbrake which operates on all four wheels. There is however a certain amount of slack in the system and before any work is done under the car the wheels should be chocked.

The handbrake, or transmission brake, has two brake shoes and is adjustable externally. Since it is mounted high up under the vehicle it is in a well-protected position from flying dirt and water, unless deep wading is being undertaken.

Warning: Dust created by the braking system may contain asbestos, which is a health hazard. Never blow it out with compressed air, and don't inhale any of it. An approved filtering mask should be worn when working on the brakes. DO NOT use petroleum-based solvents to clean brake parts. Use brake cleaner or methylated spirit only.

2 Brake hydraulic system - bleeding

1 If any of the hydraulic components in the braking system have been removed or disconnected, or if the fluid level in the master cylinder has been allowed to fall appreciably, it is inevitable that air will have been

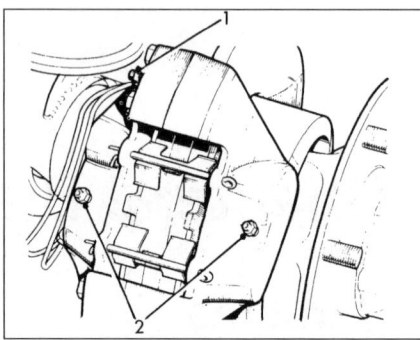

Fig. 9.2 Front caliper bleed nipples (Sec 2)

1 Primary circuit bleed nipple
2 Secondary circuit bleed nipples

introduced into the system. The removal of all this air from the hydraulic system is essential if the brakes are to function correctly, and the process of removing it is known as bleeding.

2 There are a number of one-man, do-it-yourself, brake bleeding kits currently available from motor accessory shops. It is recommended that one of these kits should be used whenever possible as they greatly simplify the bleeding operation and also reduce the risk of expelled air and fluid being drawn back into the system.

3 If one of these kits is not available, then it will be necessary to gather together a clean jar and suitable length of clear plastic tubing which is a tight fit over the bleed screw, and also to engage the help of an assistant. If the complete system is to be bled, two lengths of tubing will be required.

4 Before commencing the bleeding operation, check that all rigid pipes and flexible hoses are in good condition and that all hydraulic unions are tight.

HAYNES HiNT *Take great care not to allow hydraulic fluid to come into contact with the vehicle paintwork, otherwise the finish will be seriously damaged. Wash off any spilled fluid immediately with cold water.*

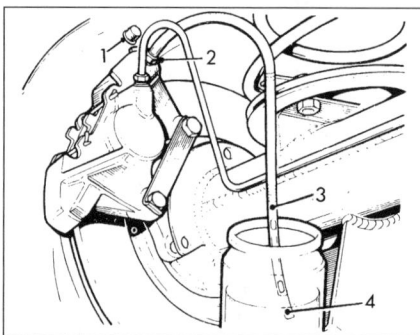

Fig. 9.3 Brake bleeding – the traditional method (Sec 2)

1 Bleed nipple dust cap   3 Tube
2 Bleed nipple   4 Jar

5 If hydraulic fluid has been lost from the master cylinder, due to a leak in the system, ensure that the cause is traced and rectified before proceeding further or a serious malfunction of the braking system may occur.

6 To bleed the system, clean the area around the bleed screw at the wheel cylinder to be bled. If the hydraulic system has only been partially disconnected and suitable precautions were taken to prevent further loss of fluid, it should only be necessary to bleed that part of the system. However, if the entire system is to be bled, start at the wheel furthest away from the master cylinder.

7 If the secondary circuit only is being bled, start at the caliper furthest from the master cylinder, first bleeding the screw on the same side as the fluid pipes. Then bleed from the other secondary bleed screw on the same caliper. Repeat on the other front caliper.

8 If the entire system is being bled, the primary and secondary bleed screws on the same side of the front caliper must be bled simultaneously, followed by the secondary bleed screw on the other side of the caliper. Obviously two lengths of bleed tubing will be required for this, and a T-piece adaptor if a one-man bleeding kit is being used.

9 Remove the master cylinder filler cap and top up the reservoir. Periodically check the fluid level during the bleeding operation and top up as necessary.

10 If a one-man brake bleeding kit is being used, connect the outlet tube to the bleed screw (photo) and then open the screw half a turn. If possible position the unit so that it can be viewed from the car, then depress the brake pedal to the floor (or as far as it will go) and slowly release it. The one-way valve in the kit will prevent dispelled air from returning to the system for 5 seconds, between each stroke. Repeat this operation until clean hydraulic fluid, free from air bubbles, can be seen coming through the tube. Now tighten the bleed screw and remove the outlet tube.

11 If a one-man brake bleeding kit is not available, connect one end of the plastic tubing to the bleed screw and immerse the other end in the jar containing sufficient clean hydraulic fluid to keep the end of the tube submerged. Open the bleed screw half a turn and have your assistant depress the brake

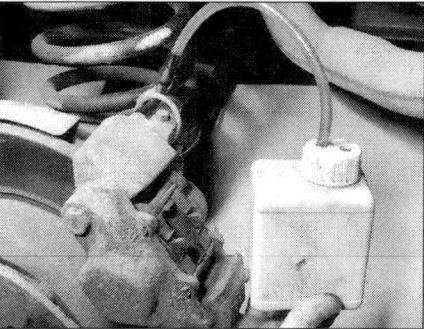

2.10 Connecting the one-man bleeding kit to the rear caliper

pedal to the floor (or as far as it will go) and then slowly release it. Pause for 5 seconds between each stroke. Tighten the bleed screw at the end of each downstroke to prevent expelled air and fluid from being drawn back into the system. Repeat this operation until clean hydraulic fluid, free from air bubbles, can be seen coming through the tube. Now tighten the bleed screw and remove the plastic tube.

12 If the entire system is being bled the procedures described above should now be repeated at each wheel, finishing at the wheel nearest the master cylinder. Do not forget to recheck the fluid level in the master cylinder at regular intervals and top up as necessary. See also paragraph 8.

13 When completed, recheck the fluid level in the master cylinder, top up if necessary and refit the cap. Check the 'feel' of the brake pedal which should be firm and free from any 'sponginess' which would indicate air still present in the system.

14 Discard any expelled hydraulic fluid as it is likely to be contaminated with moisture, air and dirt which makes it unsuitable for further use.

3 Brake pads - removal and refitting

1 Apply the handbrake, slacken the appropriate roadwheel nuts and jack up the front or rear of the vehicle. Chock the roadwheels still on the ground.

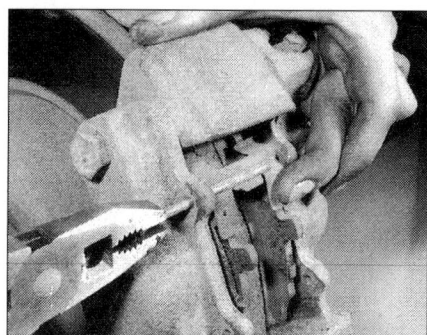

3.3 Withdraw the upper split pin and hold the retaining spring

2 Remove the roadwheel.

3 Withdraw the split pins from the caliper (photo).

4 Lift the pad retaining springs away.

5 Withdraw the pads, and the shims as well at the rear. Note which way the shims fit (photo).

6 Carefully press the caliper pistons back into their bores (photo). **Note:** *This will cause the reservoir fluid level to rise. Prevent it from overflowing by loosening the caliper bleed nipple as the piston is being moved then close it when movement is complete.*

7 Refitting is the reverse of the removal procedure, but the following points should be noted:

(a) *Ensure that the pad location area in the caliper is free from dust and dirt. Smear a little disc brake lubricant on the metal-to-metal contact arms*

(b) *If the shims are corroded, obtain new ones; they should be inserted with the D-shaped cut-out downwards (rear brakes only)*

(c) *Use new split pins. Fold back one leg of each split pin (photo)*

(d) *Depress the brake pedal several times on completion to correctly locate the pads*

(e) *Check the reservoir fluid level on completion*

8 If new brake pads are being fitted remember that the pads in both calipers on any one axle must be renewed at the same time, otherwise unbalanced braking will be the result.

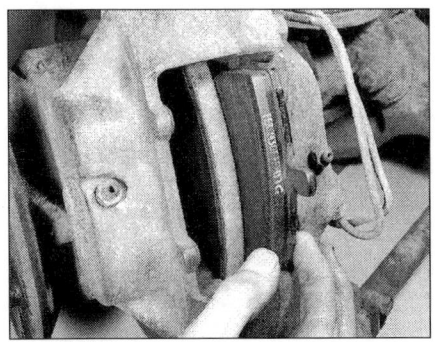

3.5 Withdrawing a front brake pad

3.6 When the pads have been withdrawn the pistons must be pushed back

3.7 Use new split pins when refitting the pads

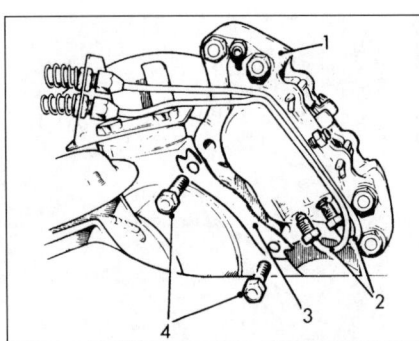

Fig. 9.4 Front brake caliper (Sec 4)

1 Caliper assembly
2 Primary and secondary circuit brake fluid pipes
3 Locking plate (early models only)
4 Caliper mounting bolts (and spring washers – later models)

4 Brake caliper - removal and refitting

Note: *The brake caliper can be unbolted from the axle casing and tied up out of the way without undoing the brake pipes but the pipes must not be strained. On the rear axle undo the brake pipe clips to ease the strain.*

1 Slacken the roadwheel nuts, jack up the front or rear of the vehicle and remove the appropriate roadwheel(s). Chock the roadwheels still on the ground. Place axle stands beneath the raised axle to support it.
2 Clean off the road dirt from the caliper, hub and disc assembly.
3 Place a film of polythene over the neck of the brake fluid reservoir and refit the cap to reduce the fluid loss when the brake pipes are disconnected at the calipers.
4 Disconnect the brake pipe(s) from the caliper at the connector(s). There are two pipes feeding each of the front calipers and one pipe feeding each of the rear calipers. Wipe up any spilled fluid that cannot be collected in a container.
5 On early models knock back the locking plates used to retain the caliper mounting bolts. Later models have spring washers instead.
6 Undo the two mounting bolts and withdraw them so that the caliper can be lifted away. Note that the later types have splash guards on the rear brake calipers and these can be lifted away with the caliper.
7 Remove the brake pads from the calipers, referring to Section 3 if necessary.
8 Refitting is the reverse procedure. Do not fit the pads until after the calipers have been refitted.
9 Tighten the caliper mounting bolts to the specified torque. Knock up the locking plates (where fitted).
10 Refit the brake pads as described in Section 3.

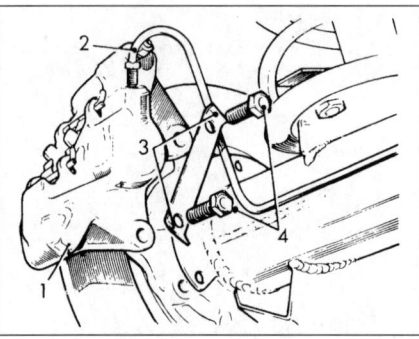

Fig. 9.5 Rear brake caliper assembly (Sec 4)

1 Caliper assembly
2 Brake fluid pipe
3 Locking plate
4 Caliper mounting bolts

11 Connect the brake fluid pipes and bleed the brakes in accordance with the instructions given in Section 2. Refit the roadwheels and lower the vehicle. Check the brakes for correct operation.

5 Brake caliper - overhaul

1 The overhaul procedure for both front and rear brake calipers is basically the same. The differences that occur are due to the fact that the front caliper has four pistons for the primary and secondary braking circuits while the rear caliper has only two pistons, since it is only connected to the primary circuit.
2 Remove the brake caliper as directed in Section 4.
3 The overhaul procedure given here is for the renewal of the piston seals and the inspection of the pistons, bores, and seal grooves. **Do not** separate the two halves of the caliper, as the whole overhaul procedure can be carried out without doing so.
4 Having removed the caliper from the vehicle and withdrawn the brake pads,

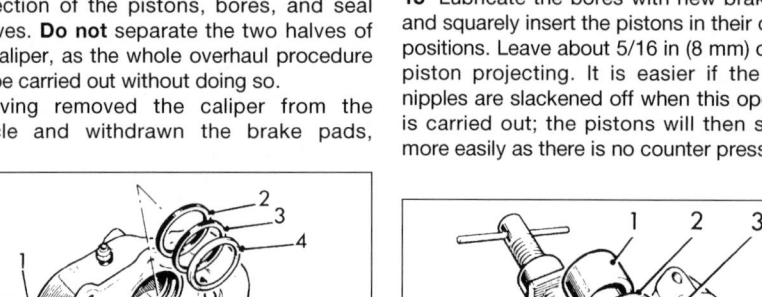

Fig. 9.6 Front brake caliper overhaul (Sec 5)

1 Piston	4 Retainer
2 Fluid seal	5 Clamp
3 Wiper seal	

thoroughly clean the outside of the caliper using methylated spirits.
5 Using a small G-clamp and a thin flat piece of wood, clamp the piston(s) on the inside half of the caliper (i.e. the half with the mounting bracket).
6 Apply a low pressure air line or alternatively a tyre foot pump to the fluid port(s) and eject the piston(s) from the outer half of the caliper.
7 Take great care when doing this that the pistons and bores do not become scratched.
8 Having removed the piston(s) from one half of the caliper, remove the G-clamp and place the flat piece of wood over the hole(s) vacated by the piston(s) that have just been removed. Carefully clamp the piece of wood in position.
9 Apply the low pressure air source to the fluid port and eject the other piston(s), then remove the G-clamp.
10 Note the exact positions of the pistons. Under no circumstances change their caliper positions. Should one of the pistons be seized in the caliper. the whole caliper must be renewed.
11 Using a blunt screwdriver, carefully prise out the wiper seal retainers. Do not scratch any metal parts.
12 Extract the wiper dust seals and fluid seals from the bores.
13 Thoroughly clean the metal parts using clean brake fluid, methylated spirit or isopropyl alchohol. Inspect the caliper bores and pistons for wear, scoring and corrosion, renew parts as necessary. *Do not attempt to separate the two halves of the calipers.*
14 To reassemble the caliper and pistons, first coat the fluid seal with clean brake fluid or disc brake lubricant. Then using your fingers only, position new fluid seals in the caliper bores, ensuring that they are properly located. They will stand proud of the bore at the edge furthest away from the mouth of the bore.
15 Lubricate the bores with new brake fluid and squarely insert the pistons in their original positions. Leave about 5/16 in (8 mm) of each piston projecting. It is easier if the bleed nipples are slackened off when this operation is carried out; the pistons will then slide in more easily as there is no counter pressure.

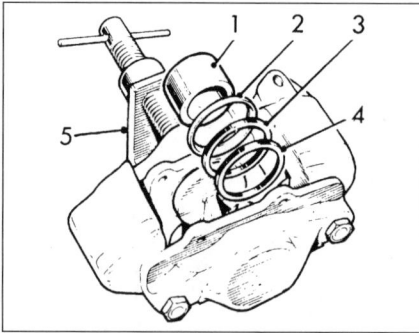

Fig. 9.7 Rear brake caliper overhaul (Sec 5)

1 Piston	4 Fluid seal
2 Retainer	5 Clamp
3 Wiper seal	

16 Smear the wiper seal with disc brake lubricator brake fluid. Fit a new wiper seal into each seal retainer, and slide an assembly into each bore, seal side first. Use the piston as a guide.

17 Press the seals and pistons fully home, using the G-clamp if necessary.

18 Refitting of the caliper is now the reverse of the removal procedure. Fit the remaining bolts only finger tight at first and reconnect the fluid pipe(s).

19 Tighten the retaining bolts to the recommended torque setting and, where fitted on earlier models, bend back the ends of the tab washers. The fluid coupling can now be fully tightened.

20 On completion of this installation the brakes will have to be bled as described in Section 2. Fitting of the brake pads is covered in Section 3.

6 Brake disc - removal and refitting

1 Remove the brake caliper as described in Section 4.

2 Remove the wheel hub assembly as described in Chapter 8.

3 Undo and remove the bolts which retain the brake disc to the wheel hub.

4 Using a soft-faced mallet tap the disc off the wheel hub.

5 Refit the disc to the wheel hub and secure it with the retaining bolts. Tighten them to the specified torque.

6 Use a dial gauge to check the disc run-out. This must not exceed that specified. If necessary undo the bolts, remove the disc and fit it with the holes aligned differently. Tighten the bolts and recheck the run-out, until correct. If the run-out is excessive with the disc in all possible positions, renew the disc.

7 Refit the wheel hub assembly as described in Chapter 8 and the brake caliper as described in Section 4.

7 Brake disc - inspection and refacing

1 Remove the roadwheel.

2 Check the surfaces of the disc for wear, scoring, ridging or breaking up. As a vehicle gets older there is a tendency for the disc to break up from the outer edge. Less of the effective braking area is left and the rough edges quickly ruin the brake pads. A disc in this condition must be renewed.

3 If however the disc is slightly scored or ridged it may be refaced, provided that in so doing the thickness of the disc is not reduced below that specified.

4 Refacing of the disc is done by machining equal amounts off both sides of the disc. This

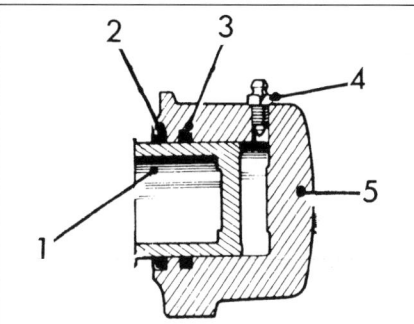

Fig. 9.8 Sectional view of caliper and piston assembly (Sec 5)

1 Piston   4 Bleed nipple
2 Wiper seal   5 Caliper housing
3 Fluid seal

is a specialist job and must be done properly, or there is a good chance that the braking efficiency of the vehicle will be worse than before. Check the cost of refacing against the cost of a new disc before deciding to go ahead.

5 The disc original thickness is marked on the disc boss. Using this value, the amount that can be removed before the minimum thickness is reached can be worked out.

6 Also check the disc for run-out as described in Section 6. If the disc is in the vehicle, be sure that excessive run-out is not due to worn hub bearings.

8 Brake failure warning valve and switch - removal, overhaul and refitting

1 The brake failure warning valve and switch are located beneath the brake master cylinder in the engine compartment.

2 Unplug the electrical connector at the switch (photo).

3 Remove the brake fluid reservoir cap, place a piece of polythene film over the filler opening and refit the cap, to reduce the loss of fluid when the brake fluid pipes are disconnected from the switch.

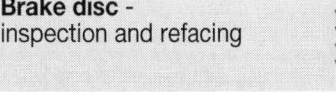

Fig. 9.10 Brake failure warning valve and switch assembly (exploded view) (Sec 8)

1 Switch   4 Shuttle valve
2 Valve body   5 Copper washer
3 O-rings   6 Plug

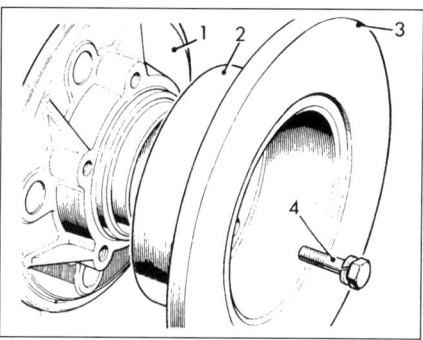

Fig. 9.9 Brake disc and hub (Sec 6)

1 Wheel hub   3 Disc
2 Boss   4 Retaining bolt

4 Undo the five brake pipe connectors and plug the ends of the pipes to prevent ingress of dirt or foreign matter.

5 Undo the single central bolt and remove the switch and valve unit from the inner wing panel.

6 To overhaul the unit, first clean the outside with methylated spirit.

7 Remove the end plug and copper washer. The washer should be discarded.

8 Unscrew and remove the switch itself.

9 The shuttle valve can now be removed. Use a low pressure air line or tyre pump if necessary.

10 Remove the O-rings from the shuttle valve.

11 Clean all the components in brake fluid or methylated spirit and inspect the valve and its bore for any signs of scratching, corrosion, or wear. They must be in perfect condition. If they are not, fit a new complete assembly.

12 Check the operation of the warning light switch by reconnecting the leads to the switch. Press the switch plunger against any earthing point on the vehicle and the warning light should be illuminated (ignition on). If not, then check the warning light bulb and renew it if necessary; alternatively renew the switch, having checked the circuit for continuity first.

13 To reassemble the valve and switch unit, first fit two new O-rings to the shuttle. Lubricate them with disc brake lubricant or clean brake fluid.

14 Lubricate the shuttle bore with brake fluid and refit the shuttle.

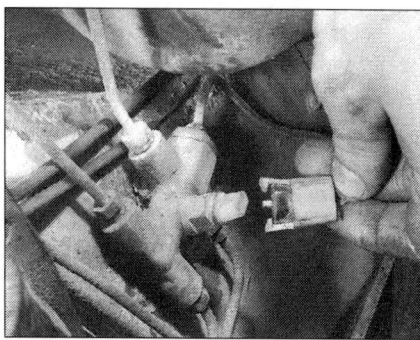

8.2 Unplug the electrical connector

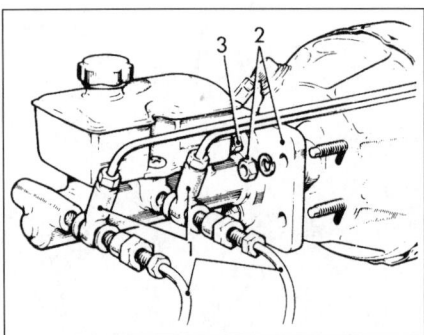

Fig. 9.11 Early type of master cylinder (Sec 9)

1 Brake pipes
2 Adaptor and retaining nut
3 Master cylinder-to-adaptor nut

15 Refit the end plug using a new copper washer. Tighten the plug to the specified torque.

16 Screw in the warning switch tightly.

17 Refit the unit to the inner wing with the plug facing to the rear. Secure it with the single bolt.

18 Unplug and refit the five brake pipes to the unit. Make sure that they are fitted to their correct locations.

19 Refit the warning light switch lead.

20 Bleed the complete braking system, both primary and secondary circuits, as described in Section 2.

9 Master cylinder and servo unit - general

1 There are three different types of master cylinder and servo unit assemblies fitted to the Range Rover. On the early type the master cylinder is secured to an adaptor plate, which is then attached to the servo unit by four nuts. On the later models the master cylinders are attached directly to the servo unit with two nuts. In all cases a tandem master cylinder is fitted.

2 Individual components are not interchangeable between the three different

10.3 The later type of master cylinder – up to 1986

types, nor can the later master cylinder be fitted to the early servo unit.

3 If either the master cylinder or servo unit of the early pattern requires renewal, then it will be necessary to replace both with a complete master cylinder and servo unit of the later type.

4 With the later type, individual components or assemblies can be renewed.

10 Master cylinder - removal, overhaul and refitting

Note: *Read Section 9 before overhauling the master cylinder.*

1 Disconnect the brake pipes from the master cylinder. Note their installed positions. Plug the ports and cover the ends of the pipes to prevent the ingress of dirt or foreign matter and loss of fluid.

2 Early models: undo the master cylinder and adaptor plate nuts and remove the master cylinder from the adaptor plate.

3 Later models: undo the two units which secure the master cylinder directly to the servo unit on later models and remove the unit (photo).

4 Remove the fluid reservoir cap and invert the unit. Drain the fluid into a container.

5 Undo the two screws which secure the reservoir unit to the master cylinder. Lift the reservoir away.

6 Remove the inlet port seals.

7 Remove the circlip from the rear end of the cylinder bore and apply low air pressure to the rear fluid outlet to push out the primary piston.

8 With the piston removed, recover the guide and spring.

9 Push the secondary piston down the bore against its spring using a copper or brass rod so that the locating pin can be withdrawn from the forward inlet port.

10 Release the secondary piston and remove it, using air pressure if necessary. Both inlet ports will have to be blocked off temporarily to do this.

11 Withdraw the secondary piston spring and guide.

12 Separate the seals and shim washers from the two pistons. Note which type fits where and how it fits.

13 Wash all components in methylated spirit, isopropyl alcohol or clean fluid, and examine the surfaces of the pistons and cylinder bore for scoring or 'bright' wear areas. Where these are evident renew the complete master cylinder.

14 If the components are in good condition, discard all seals and obtain the appropriate repair kit.

Later models up to 1986

15 Install a shim washer to the primary and secondary pistons, with the concave face towards the seal.

16 Using the fingers only, manipulate the two identical piston seals into place on the primary and secondary piston (lips facing away from the washers).

17 Of the two remaining seals contained in the repair kit, fit one to the primary piston (lip towards primary spring seat). Fit the other to the secondary piston (lip towards rear).

18 Fit the shorter return spring and cup to the secondary piston, dip the assembly into clean hydraulic fluid and insert it into the master cylinder body. Take care not to turn back the lip of the seal.

19 Depress the secondary piston and insert the stop pin after the head of the piston has been seen to pass the feed port.

20 Fit the return spring and cup to the

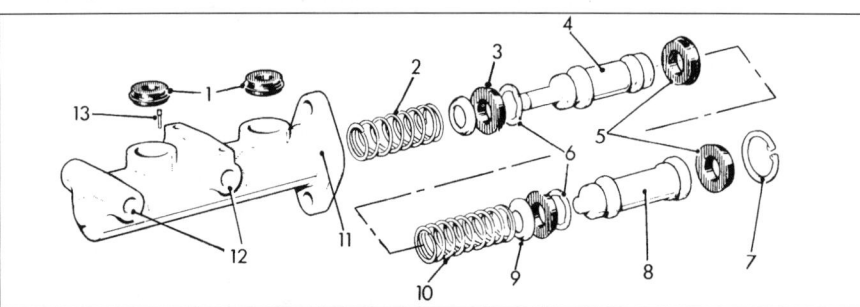

Fig. 9.12 Brake master cylinder up to 1986 – exploded view (Sec 10)

1 Inlet port seals	6 Shim washers	10 Piston spring
2 Piston spring	7 Circlip	11 Master cylinder housing
3 Seal	8 Primary piston	12 Brake pipe connections
4 Secondary piston	9 Guide	13 Locating pin
5 Seals		

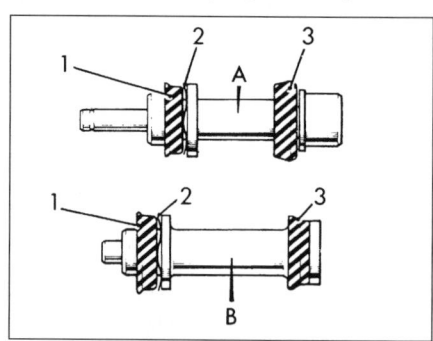

Fig. 9.13 Master cylinder piston seal assembly – up to 1986 (Sec 10)

A Secondary piston
B Primary piston
1 Front seal

2 Shim washer
3 Rear seal

primary piston, dip the assembly into clean hydraulic fluid and insert it into the master cylinder body. Take care not to turn back the seal lips. Refit the retaining circlip.

Models from 1986

21 Install the secondary piston washer, seal retainer and spring as shown. Note the seal orientation.

22 Install the primary piston washer, seals, seal retainer, circlip, spring, spring retainer and screw as shown. Note the seal orientation.

23 Dip the secondary piston assembly into clean hydraulic fluid and insert it into the master cylinder body. Take care not to turn back the lip of the seal.

24 Depress the secondary piston and insert the locating pin after the head of the piston has been seen to pass the feed port.

25 Dip the primary piston assembly into clean hydraulic fluid and insert it into the master cylinder body. Take care not to turn back the seal lips. Depress the primary piston and refit the retaining circlip.

All models

26 Fit new seals to the inlet ports.

27 Refit the reservoir and secure it with the two screws.

28 Refit the master cylinder to the servo unit and secure it with four nuts (early models with adaptor plate) or two nuts (later models).

29 Reconnect the brake pipes to their correct locations on the master cylinder.

30 Refit the brake fluid reservoir with brake fluid of the specified type.

31 Bleed the complete braking system as described in Section 2.

---

11 Servo unit - removal, filter renewal and refitting

Note: *Read Section 9 before removing the servo unit*

1 The vacuum servo unit on early models cannot be repaired. If it has to be renewed then the master cylinder will have to be renewed as well.

2 Remove the master cylinder as described in Section 10, unless the complete early type assembly is being replaced by the complete later type.

3 Disconnect the servo vacuum pipe from the servo valve.

4 On later models (1979 on), disconnect the vacuum loss warning switch lead.

5 Separate the servo operating rod from the brake pedal, undo the servo and brake pedal mounting bracket nuts and release the stoplight switch wiring from the brake pedal bracket as described in Section 12.

6 Withdraw the servo unit from the engine compartment.

7 To renew the servo air filter, slide the rubber boot and end cap along the operating rod.

8 Prise the old filter from the diaphragm housing neck.

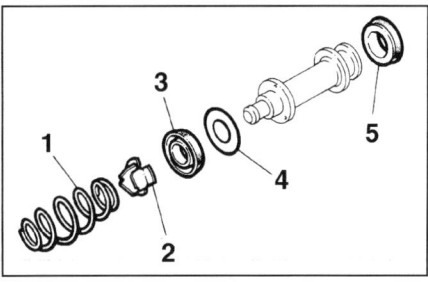

Fig. 9.14 Secondary piston - 1986-on

1 Spring   4 Washer
2 Seal retainer 5 Seal
3 Seal

Fig. 9.15 Primary piston - 1986-on

1 Retaing screw   5 Seal retainer
2 Spring retainer 6 Seal
3 Spring   7 Washer
4 Circli   8 Seal

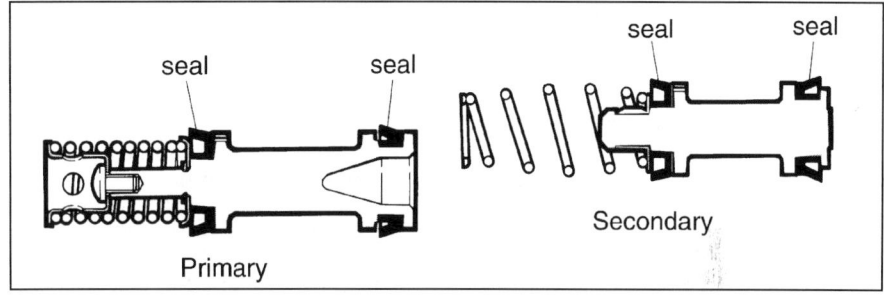

Fig. 9.16 Master cylinder piston seal orientation - 1986-on

9 Cut the filter from the outside to the inside diameter to remove it from the rod.

10 Cut the new filter obliquely from the outer edge to the centre to fit it over the operating rod.

11 Fit the new filter into the neck of the diaphragm housing.

12 Refit the seal end cap and rubber boot.

13 Refitting is the reverse procedure to removal. Note that the servo pushrod should be reconnected to the brake pedal with the cam on the bolt facing forward. Do not tighten it immediately.

14 On the early type of servo there should be some free play in the pedal action. Adjust the sleeve and locknut if necessary to achieve this.

15 Rotate the pivot bolt to pull the brake

pedal back until it just touches the rubber buffer. Then tighten the nut.

16 Reconnect the brake pipes to the master cylinder and the vacuum servo hose to the unit. Reconnect the vacuum loss switch lead and brake failure switch lead, (as applicable).

17 Bleed the complete braking system as described in Section 2.

---

12 Brake pedal assembly - removal, overhaul and refitting

1 Remove the trim panel below the dashboard on the driver's side of the car (photo).

2 Undo the nut and remove the pivot bolt which attaches the servo operating rod to the brake pedal.

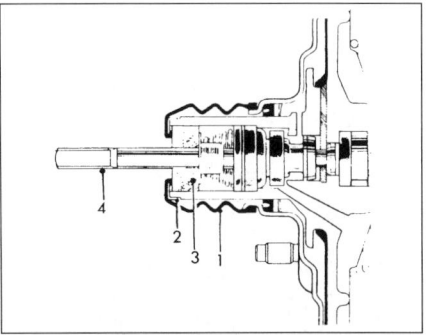

Fig. 9.17 Brake servo air filter assembly (Sec 11)

1 Rubber boot   3 Filter
2 End cap   4 Operating rod

12.1 View of brake pedal assembly with trim removed

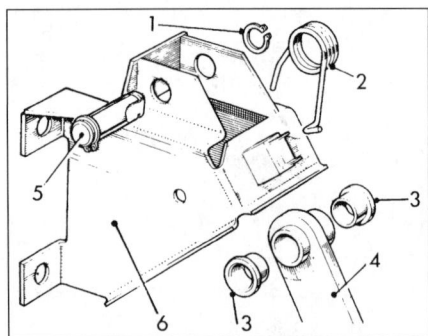

Fig. 9.18 Brake pedal mounting – exploded view (Sec 12)

1 Circlip
2 Pedal return spring
3 Bushes
4 Pedal
5 Pivot pin
6 Pedal box

3 Disconnect the two wires from the stop-light switch on the brake pedal box.
4 Undo and remove the four nuts and washers which attach the brake pedal box and servo unit to the bulkhead.
5 Withdraw the brake pedal and box assembly from the car.
6 To remove the brake pedal from the pedal box, unhook the pedal return spring from the pedal and remove the circlip from the flattened end of the pedal pivot shaft. Withdraw the shaft, and the pedal and return spring can be separated from the pedal box.
7 Remove the pivot bushes from the pedal.
8 Fit new bushes to the pedal pivot. Press them in squarely and evenly.
9 Offer the pedal and return spring to the pedal box and refit the pivot shaft. Secure the shaft with the circlip.
10 The assembly can now be refitted to the car, the procedure being the reversal of the removal sequence. Refer to Section 11 for servo pushrod adjustment (early models) and pivot bolt adjustment.

13 Brake pipes and hoses - inspection, removal and refitting

1 Inspection of the braking system hydraulic pipes and flexible hoses is part of the maintenance schedule. Carefully check the rigid pipes along the rear axle, underbody and in the engine compartment, not forgetting the short runs to the front wheel calipers. Any pipes showing signs of corrosion or damage should be renewed, following which it will be necessary to bleed the system as described in Section 2.
2 Carefully inspect the flexible hoses. There is one flexible pipe to the rear axle and two to each of the front calipers. Look for any signs of swelling, cracking and/or chafing. If any of these maladies is evident, renew the hoses straight away. Remember that your life could depend on it.
3 Where flexible hoses are to be renewed,

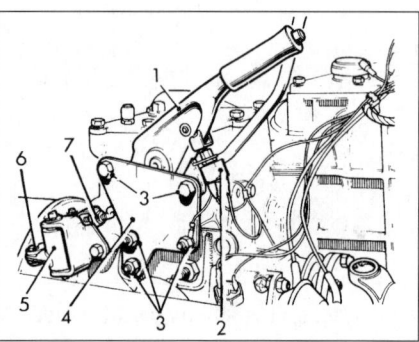

Fig. 9.19 Handbrake, mounting bracket and linkage (Sec 14)

1 Handbrake lever
2 Warning light switch
3 Mounting bracket retaining nuts and bolts
4 Mounting bracket
5 Main pivot
6 Clevis pin
7 Adjuster

unscrew the metal pipe union nut from its connection to the hose, and then holding the hexagon on the hose with a spanner, unscrew the attachment nut and washer.
4 The body end of the flexible hose can now be withdrawn from the chassis mounting bracket and will be quite free.
5 Refitting is the reverse of the removal procedure, following which it will be necessary to bleed the appropriate part of the system, as described in Section 2.

14 Handbrake lever and linkage - removal and refitting

Note: *This operation is complicated by the location of the linkage which is attached to the right-hand side of the transfer gearbox and requires the removal of the front section of the floor of the vehicle in order to reach and remove it. The rear end of the linkage which is connected to the handbrake lever can be reached from underneath the vehicle in the normal way.*

1 Remove the carpet or rubber matting from the front of the vehicle and remove the floor as described in Chapter 12.

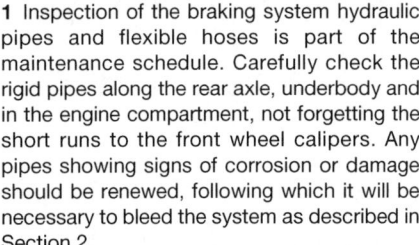

14.5 Undoing the handbrake mounting bracket (gearbox removed)

14.4 Withdrawing the pivot pin

2 The linkage is in two parts. The main section consists of a mounting bracket for the handbrake lever and ratchet assembly, and to the rear of this is the bracket which holds the main pivoting part of the handbrake linkage.
3 Remove the split pins and clevis pins from the main linkage pivot arms.
4 Remove the split pin from the main pivot pin and withdraw the pivot pin. The main pivot can now be removed from its bracket (photo).
5 Undo and remove the retaining nuts and bolts for the handbrake mounting bracket (photo).
6 Lift the assembly away, disconnecting the warning light switch wiring as this is done.
7 Refitting is the reverse procedure to removal. Once the linkage has been reconnected at the pivot end, the slack in the linkage can be taken up in the screw adjuster to the rear of the handbrake lever.

15 Transmission brake (handbrake) - dismantling, overhaul, shoe renewal and reassembly

1 Jack the rear of the vehicle up and support it securely on strong axle stands. If the front of the vehicle is not jacked up, chock the front wheels.
2 Disconnect the propeller shaft from the transmission brake as described in Chapter 7 (photo).
3 Remove the clevis pin at the rear of the handbrake linkage pivot (photo).

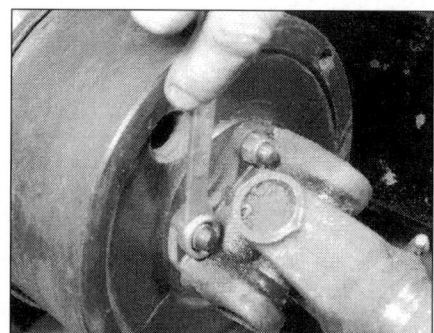

15.2 Disconnecting the propeller shaft

15.3 Removing the linkage clevis pin

15.4 Pull off the brake drum

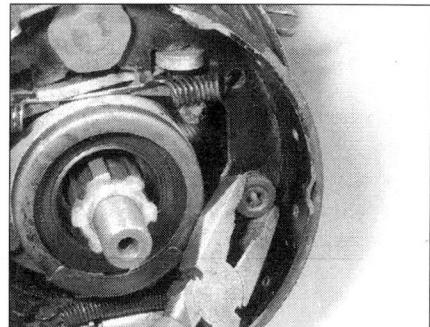

15.6 Removing the steady cup and spring for the trailing shoe

4 Remove the two countersunk cross-head screws in the rear face of the brake drum and pull off the drum (photo).

5 If the drum is difficult to remove, slacken the shoe adjuster as described in Section 16.

6 Note the positions of the brake shoes and springs. Remove the steady cups and springs from the shoes and withdraw the steady pins from the rear of the backplate (photo).

7 Slacken the adjuster completely to relieve the tension on the brake shoes and springs, and withdraw the adjuster (photo).

8 Unhook the tensioner spring (lower one) and remove it.

9 Unhook and remove the upper spring (photo).

10 Remove the left-hand (leading) shoe and the right-hand (trailing) shoe, which has to be freed from the actuating lever (photo).

11 Remove the actuating lever and shim by withdrawing them through the backplate towards the rear of the vehicle, should this be necessary.

12 To remove the transmission backplate, have an assistant apply the footbrake and engage a low gear to stop the output flange rotating, and remove the output flange retaining nut. Withdraw the flange.

13 Undo and remove the brake shoe pivot bolt (photo).

14 Undo the backplate and oil catcher retaining bolts and remove them. Lift the oil catcher away (photo).

15 Carefully remove any brake lining dust from the backplate, taking care not to inhale it as it can be injurious to health. Remove the backplate (photo).

16 Examine the brake shoes for wear. If the

linings are worn down to or near the rivets they must be renewed, or new brake shoes must be fitted.

17 Check that the brake shoes are not contaminated with oil. Renew them if necessary and correct the leakage.

18 Examine the brake drum for scoring, uneven wear or cracks. If the drum is scored then it can be skimmed to the maximum oversize listed in the Specifications.

19 Reassembly is basically the reverse procedure to dismantling.

20 Refit the backplate and oil catcher, but do not tighten the bolts until the pivot bolt has been refitted and the backplate aligned. The threads of the pivot bolt should be coated with sealant.

21 Tighten the pivot bolt and backplate/oil catcher bolts to the specified torques.

15.7 Pull the brake shoes apart to remove the adjuster

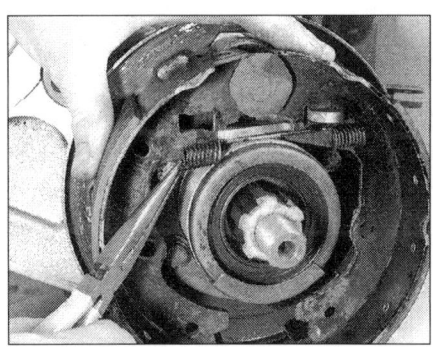

15.9 Unhook and remove the upper spring

15.10 Disconnect the actuating lever from the trailing shoe as it is removed

15.13 Removing the pivot bolt

15.14 Undo the oil catcher and backplate bolts

15.15 Lifting the backplate away

15.28 Refitting the coupling flange

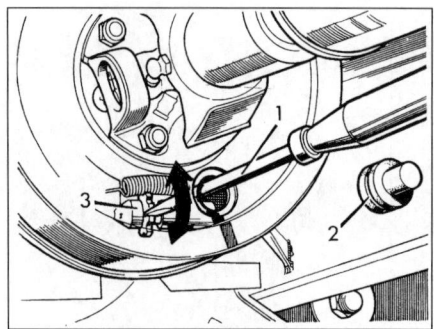

Fig. 9.20 Handbrake adjustment (Sec 16)

1 Screwdriver   2 Rubber bung   3 Adjuster

16.7 Insert a screwdriver to rotate the adjuster notched wheel

22 Refit the actuator lever and the sealing shim together if they were removed.
23 Refit the trailing (right-hand) shoe first and engage the actuator lever in the slot in the shoe.
24 Refit the steady pin, spring and cup for that shoe.
25 Refit the other shoe, steady pin, spring and cup.
26 Refit the upper spring and then the lower spring.
27 Pull the shoes apart to refit the adjuster with the wheel facing to the left.
28 Refit the coupling flange and tighten its retaining nut to the specified torque (photo).
29 Refit the brake drum and secure it.
30 Adjust the brake shoes as described in Section 16.
31 Reconnect the handbrake linkage.
32 Operate the handbrake several times to centralise the brake shoes.
33 Recheck the handbrake shoe adjustment.

34 Refit the rubber bungs to the brake drum, reconnect the propeller shaft and remove the axle stands and chocks.

16 Transmission brake (handbrake) - adjustment

1 The transmission brake is located beneath the vehicle and is attached to the rear output end of the transfer gearbox shaft. Because of the high ground clearance the brake can be reached by sliding underneath the vehicle.
2 Chock the front and rear road wheels, having positioned the vehicle on level ground.
3 Release the handbrake fully.
4 Remove the rubber bungs from the face of the brake drum.
5 Rotate the drum if necessary so that one of the adjuster holes is at the bottom. The

easiest way to do this is to move aside the wheel chocks and move the vehicle forwards or backwards the small amount required.
6 Put the chocks back in position.
7 Insert a screwdriver through the hole in the brake drum and engage it in the notches of the adjuster (photo).
8 Lever the screwdriver downwards to tighten the shoes, or upwards to slacken them off.
9 If new shoes have just been fitted, or if taking up the slack due to normal wear, turn the adjuster wheel until the brake shoes are touching the drum.
10 Slacken the adjuster by two notches.
11 With new brake shoes it will be necessary to centralise the brake shoes by operating the handbrake lever several times. Then recheck the adjustment.
12 Refit the rubber bungs.
13 Check the operation of the handbrake lever. Remove the chocks and check that it holds the vehicle.

Fault finding - braking system

Pedal travels almost to floorboards before brakes operate
☐ Brake fluid too low
☐ Caliper leaking
☐ Master cylinder leaking (bubbles in master cylinder fluid)
☐ Brake flexible hose leaking
☐ Brake line fractured
☐ Brake system unions loose

Brakes uneven and pulling to one side
☐ Pads and discs contaminated with oil, grease
☐ or hydraulic fluid
☐ Tyre pressures unequal
☐ Brake caliper loose
☐ Brake pads fitted incorrectly
☐ Different type of pads fitted at each wheel
☐ Anchorages for front suspension or rear suspension loose
☐ Brake discs badly worn, cracked or distorted

Brake feels spongy and soggy
☐ Caliper piston seals leaking
☐ Master cylinder leaking (bubbles in master cylinder reservoir)
☐ Brake pipe line or flexible hose leaking
☐ Unions in brake system loose
☐ Air in hydraulic system

Brake pedal feels springy
☐ New pads not yet bedded-in
☐ Brake discs badly worn or cracked
☐ Master cylinder securing nuts loose

Excessive effort required to brake car
☐ Pads badly worn
☐ New pads recently fitted - not yet bedded-in
☐ Harder pads fitted than standard causing increase in pedal pressure
☐ Pads and discs contaminated with oil, grease or hydraulic fluid
☐ Servo unit inoperative or faulty
☐ One half of dual brake system inoperative

Brakes tend to bind, drag or lock-on
☐ Air in hydraulic system
☐ Wheel cylinders seized

Handbrake will not hold vehicle
☐ Shoes worn or need adjustment
☐ Linkage too slack
☐ Shoes and drum contaminated with oil

Transmission judder when moving off
☐ Brake shoes too tight, need adjustment
☐ Brakes shoes sticking in 'on' position

Chapter 10 Electrical system

For modifications, and information applicable to later models, see Supplement at end of manual

Contents

Degrees of difficulty

Easy, suitable for novice with little experience	Fairly easy, suitable for beginner with some experience 	Fairly difficult, suitable for competent DIY mechanic 	Difficult, suitable for experienced DIY mechanic 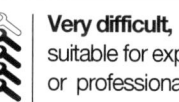	Very difficult, suitable for expert DIY or professional

Specifications

General

System type .... 12 volt, negative earth
Battery capacity (typical) .... 60 Ah at 20-hour rate

Alternator

Type:
    Early models .... Lucas 16ACR
    1975 to 1979 models .... Lucas 18ACR
    1980 models .... Lucas 20ACR or 25ACR

Test data:	16ACR	18ACR	20/25ACR
Maximum output (nominal)	34A	45A	66A
Regulating voltage	14.1 to 14.5	13.6 to 14.4	13.5 to 14.4
Field resistance (ohms)	4.33	3.2	3.6
Minimum brush length	0.2 in (5 mm)	0.3 in (8 mm)	0.3 in (8 mm)

Drivebelt tension .... 0.4 to 0.5 in (11 to 14 mm) deflection under firm thumb pressure at mid-point of longest run

Starter motor

Make	Lucas M45 or 3M100PE	
Type	Pre-engaged	
Repair data:	**M46**	**3M100PE**
Minimum brush length	0.3 in (8 mm)	0.375 in (9.5 mm)
Armature endfloat	0.005 to 0.015 in (0.12 to 0.40 mm)	0.010 in (0.25 mm)
Minimum copper thickness on commutator after refinishing	-	0.14 in (3.5 mm)

Horns

Number	2
Make and type	Lucas 6H or Mixo TR89

Wiper motors

Make and type:	
Windscreen	Lucas 17W 2-speed
Tailgate and headlamps (as applicable)	Lucas 14W single speed
Armature endfloat	0.002 to 0.008 in (0.05 to 0.20 mm)
Minimum brush length	0.187 in (4.8 mm)

Bulbs

	Wattage	Type
Headlamps:		
Tungsten	75/50	Butlers 1967/4 DE
Quartz halogen	60/55	-
Sidelamps	4	Lucas 233
Stop/tail lamps	21/6	Lucas 380
Reversing lamps	21	Lucas 382
Direction indicator lamps	21	Lucas 382
Number plate lamps	4	Lucas 233
Instrument illumination and warning lamps	2.2	Smiths capless
Hazard warning switch illumination	2	Lucas 281
Clock illumination	2	Lucas 281
Interior lamp	10	Lucas 585 (festoon)

Fuses

Location:	
Main fuse box	Under bonnet, on left-hand bulkhead
In-line fuses	Heated rear window, heater blower motor
Rating:	
Main fuse box	35 amp
Heater rear window	50 amp
Heater blower motor	10 amp

Torque wrench settings

	lbf ft	kgf m
Starter motor securing bolts	30 to 35	4.0 to 4.4
Alternator pulley nut	25 to 30	3.5 to 4.2
Wiper motor yoke bolt	12 to 16	1.6 to 2.2

1 General description

The electrical system is of the 12 volt type and the major components comprise a 12 volt battery, of which the negative terminal is earthed. A Lucas alternator is fitted to the front right-hand side of the engine and is driven from the engine crankshaft pulley. A pre-engaged Lucas starter motor is mounted on the rear right-hand side of the engine.

The battery supplies current for the ignition, lighting and other electrical circuits, and provides a reserve of electricity when the current consumed by the electrical equipment exceeds that being produced by the alternator. Normally, the alternator is able to meet any demand placed upon it. In later models there is an option available to provide a split charging facility. With this option, two batteries can be fitted instead of the normal single unit. When equipment such as an electric winch is being used the power will be provided by the second battery leaving the main one untouched for normal usage.

When fitting electrical accessories to cars with a negative earth system, it is important, if they contain silicon diodes or transistors, that they are connected correctly, otherwise damage may result to the components concerned. Before purchasing any electrical accessory check that it has or can be adjusted to the correct polarity to suit the car.

It is important that the battery leads are always disconnected if the battery is to be boost charged, or if any body or mechanical repairs are to be carried out using electric arc welding equipment, otherwise serious damage can be caused to the more delicate instruments, especially those containing semi-conductors.

Apart from carrying spare fuses in the vehicle as a normal precaution, it is wise to carry space bulbs as well. In many countries this is required by law. One of the most important bulbs is the ignition (charge) warning light bulb. This is connected into the charging circuit and if it fails, no charge will be made by the alternator. If this bulb fails it must therefore be renewed immediately.

Fig. 10.1 Location of electrical equipment (Sec 1)

1	Battery
2	Alternator
3	Brake warning switch (circuit failure)
4	Stop-light switch
5	Windscreen wiper motor
6	Windscreen/tailpate washer reservoir and motors (later models)
7	Starter relay
8	Instrument housing
9	Roof lamp
10	Hazard warning switch
11	Reversing light switch
12	Differential lock switch
13	Handbrake switch
14	Clock
15	Door pillar switch
16	Fuse box
17	Windscreen washer reservoir and motor (earlier models)
18	Starter relay
19	Ignition coil
20	Starter motor
21	Thermostat
22	Oil pressure switch
23	Thermostat switch
24	Horns

2 Battery - removal and refitting

1 Detach the negative battery lead followed by the positive battery lead from the battery terminal lugs. Disconnecting the leads in this order reduces the possibility of 'shorting' the battery (photo).
2 Remove the wing nuts and lift off the frame.
3 Lift out the battery.

2.1 The battery in position. Negative (earth) lead is the one connected to the strap

4 Before refitting the battery, clean the battery tray thoroughly.
5 Fit the battery, then connect the terminal leads, positive first. Do not hammer them on. They may jam or at worst the battery will crack.
6 Finally, smear the battery terminals and lead ends with a little petroleum jelly or a proprietary brand of battery corrosion inhibitor. Do not use regular lubricating grease as a substitute.
7 Never disconnect the battery while the engine is running or the alternator semi conductors will be damaged.

3 Battery - maintenance and inspection

1 Normal battery maintenance consists of checking the electrolyte level of each cell to ensure that the separators are covered by 1/4 in (6 mm) of electrolyte, If the level has fallen, top up the battery using distilled water only. Do not overfill. If a battery is overfilled or any electrolyte spilled, immediately wipe away the excess as electrolyte attacks and corrodes any metal it comes into contact with very rapidly.

2 If the battery has the 'Auto-fill' device fitted, a special topping-up sequence is required. The white balls in the 'Auto-fill' battery are part of the automatic topping-up device which ensures correct electrolyte level. The vent chamber should remain in position at all times except when topping-up or taking specific gravity readings. If the electrolyte level in any of the cells is below the bottom of the filling tube, top up as follows:
(a) Lift off the vent chamber cover
(b) With the battery level, pour distilled water into the trough until all the filling tubes and trough are full
(c) Immediately refit the cover to allow the water in the trough and tubes to flow into the cells. Each cell will automatically receive the correct amount of water.
3 As well as keeping the terminals clean and covered with petroleum jelly, the top of the battery, and especially the top of the cells, should be kept clean and dry. This helps prevent corrosion and ensures that the battery does not become partially discharged by leakage through dampness and dirt.
4 Once every three months remove the battery and inspect the battery securing bolts, the battery clamp plate, tray and battery leads for corrosion (white fluffy deposits, on the metal, which are brittle to the touch). If any corrosion is found, clean off the deposits with ammonia or a solution of bicarbonate of soda and warm water, and paint over the clean metal with anti-rust and anti-acid paint.
5 At the same time inspect the battery case for cracks. If a crack is found, clean and plug it with one of the proprietary compounds marketed for this purpose. If leakage through the crack has been excessive then it will be necessary to refill the appropriate cell with fresh electrolyte as detailed later. Cracks are frequently caused to the top of the battery case by pouring in distilled water in the middle of winter *after* instead of *before* a run. This gives the water no chance to mix with the electrolyte and so the former freezes and splits the battery case.
6 If topping-up the battery becomes too frequent and the case has been inspected for cracks that could cause leakage, but none are found, the battery is being overcharged and the alternator will have to be checked. Generally, this indicates that the regulator (housed within the alternator end cover) is at fault thus allowing the alternator to operate uncontrolled, delivering full output even when the battery is fully charged. A fairly basic check can be carried out (See Section 7), but as a general principle this sort of job is best left to a competent auto-electrician or your Rover dealer.
7 With the battery on the bench at the three-monthly interval check, measure the specific gravity with a hydrometer to determine the state of charge and condition of the electrolyte. There should be very little variation between the different cells, and, if a variation in excess of 0.025 is present, it will be due to either:

(a) *Loss of electrolyte from the battery at some time caused by spillage or a leak resulting in a drop in the specific gravity of the electrolyte when the deficiency was replaced with distilled water instead of fresh electrolyte.*

(b) *An internal short-circuit caused by buckling of the plates or similar malady pointing to the likelihood of total battery failure in the near future.*

8 The specific gravity of the electrolyte for fully charged and fully discharged conditions at the electrolyte temperature indicated, is listed below.

Fully discharged	Electrolyte temperature	Fully charged
1.098	38°C (100°F)	1.268
1.102	32°C (90°F)	1.272
1.106	27°C (80°F)	1.276
1.110	21 ° C (70°F)	1.280
1.114	16°C (60°F)	1.284
1.118	10°C (50°F)	1.288
1.122	4°C (40°F)	1.292
1.126	-1.5°C (30°F)	1.296

4 Battery electrolyte - replenishment

1 With the battery fully charged, check the specific gravity of the electrolyte in each of the cells. If one or more of the cells reads 0.025, or more, below the others, it is likely that some electrolyte has been lost. Check each cell for short-circuits with a voltage meter. A four to seven second test should give a steady reading of between 1.2 and 1.8 volts. (This test is only possible if the cell connectors are exposed on the top of the battery).

2 Top up the cell with a solution of 1 part sulphuric acid to 2.5 parts of water. If the cell is already fully topped up draw some electrolyte out of it with a pipette.

3 When mixing the sulphuric acid and water, *NEVER ADD WATER TO SULPHURIC ACID -* always pour the acid slowly onto the water in a glass container. *IF WATER IS ADDED TO SULPHURIC ACID IT WILL EXPLODE.*

4 Continue to top up the cell with the freshly made electrolyte and then recharge the battery and check the hydrometer readings.

5 Battery - charging

Note: *Before charging the battery disconnect the terminal leads, check the electrolyte level and, if possible, remove the battery from the car.*

1 In winter time when heavy demand is placed upon the battery, such as when starting from cold and much electrical equipment is continually in use, it is a good idea to occasionally have the battery fully charged from an external source at the rate of 3.5 to 4 amps.

2 Continue to charge the battery at this rate until no further rise in specific gravity is noted over a four-hour period.

3 Alternatively, a trickle charger, charging at the rate of 1.5 amps, can be safely used overnight.

4 Specially rapid 'boost' charges which are claimed to restore the power of the battery in 1 to 2 hours are most dangerous as they can cause serious damage to the battery plates through overheating.

5 Whilst charging the battery note that the temperature of the electrolyte should never exceed 100°F (38°C).

6 Always disconnect both battery cables before the external charger is connected, otherwise serious damage to the alternator may occur.

6 Alternator - general description, maintenance and precautions

1 Briefly, the alternator comprises a rotor and stator. Voltage is induced in the coils of the stator as soon as the rotor revolves. This is a 3-phase alternating voltage which is then rectified by diodes to provide the necessary current for the electrical system. The level of the voltage required to maintain the battery charge is controlled by a regulator unit.

2 Maintenance consists of occasionally wiping away any oil or dirt which may have accumulated on the outside of the unit.

3 No lubrication is required as the bearings are sealed for life.

4 Check the drivebelt tension at intervals given in the 'Routine Maintenance' Section. Refer to Section 8, for the procedure.

5 Due to the need for special testing equipment and the possibility of damage being caused to the alternator diodes if incorrect testing methods are adopted, it is recommended that overhaul or major repair is entrusted to a Lucas or Rover dealer. Alternatively, a service exchange unit should be obtained.

6 Alternator brush renewal is dealt with in Section 9.

7 Take extreme care when connecting the battery to ensure that the polarity is correct, and never run the engine with a battery charger connected. Do not stop the engine by removing a battery lead as the alternator will almost certainly be damaged. When boost starting from another battery ensure that it is connected positive to positive and negative to negative.

7 Alternator - testing in situ

If the alternator is suspected of being faulty, a test can be carried out which can help in isolating any such fault. A dc voltmeter (range 0 to 15V) and a dc ammeter (suitable for the nominal output current - see Specifications) will be required.

1 Cheek the alternator drivebelt tension and adjust if necessary - see Section 8.

2 Disconnect the brown cable which runs from the alternator at the starter motor solenoid. Connect the ammeter between this cable and the starter motor solenoid terminal.

3 Connect the voltmeter across the battery terminals.

4 Run the engine at 3300 rpm (6000 rpm of the alternator): the ammeter reading should stabilize.

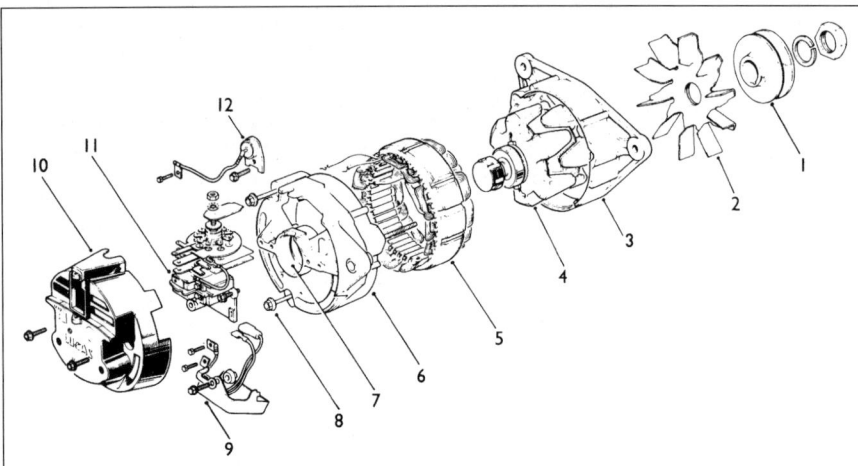

Fig. 10.2 Lucas 16 ACR alternator – exploded view (Sec 6)

1 *Pulley*	6 *End bracket*	10 *Cover*
2 *Fan*	7 *O-ring*	11 *Rectifier*
3 *Drive end bracket*	8 *Retaining bolts*	12 *Anti-surge protection*
4 *Rotor*	9 *Regulator*	*device*
5 *Stator*		

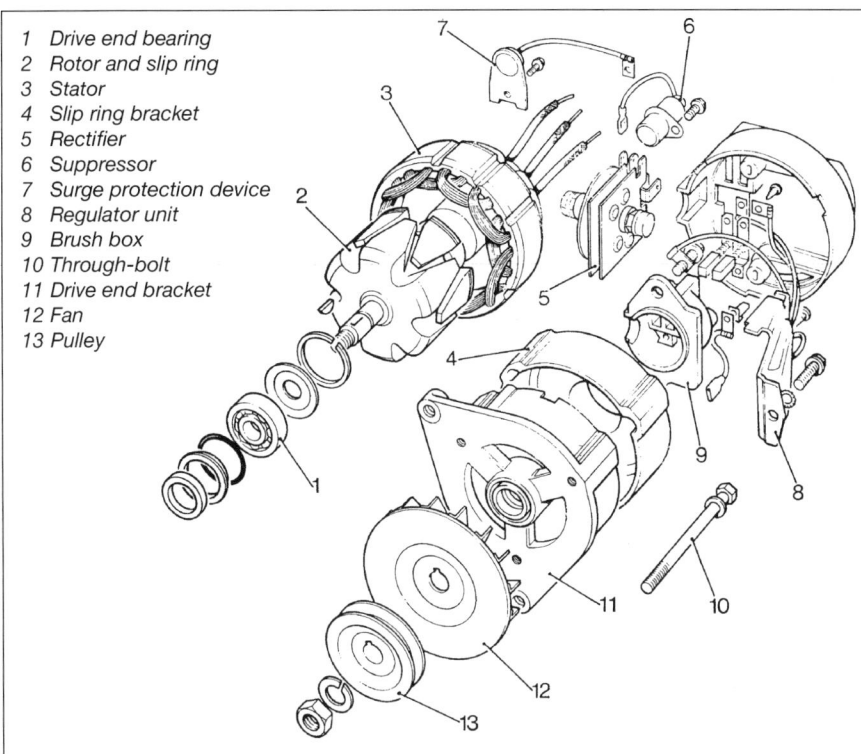

1 Drive end bearing
2 Rotor and slip ring
3 Stator
4 Slip ring bracket
5 Rectifier
6 Suppressor
7 Surge protection device
8 Regulator unit
9 Brush box
10 Through-bolt
11 Drive end bracket
12 Fan
13 Pulley

Fig. 10.4 Lucas 18 ACR alternator – exploded view (Sec 6)

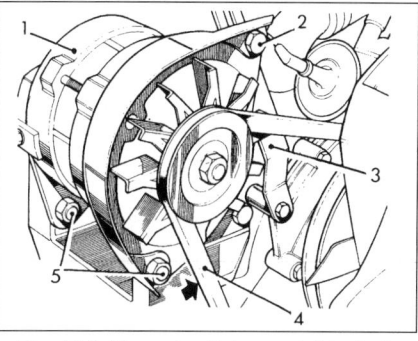

Fig. 10.3 Alternator fixing and drivebelt tensioning (Sec 8)

1 Alternator	4 Drivebelt
2 Adjustment bolt	5 Pivot bolts
3 Adjustment bracket	

10 Tighten the mounting bolts on completion.

11 If a new belt has been fitted, the belt tension should be rechecked after about 150 miles (250 km) of travelling.

12 On later vehicles which are fitted with air conditioning systems, the alternator is located beneath the vehicle on the left-hand side of the engine. Access to the alternator, adjustment bracket and mounting bolts is from underneath the vehicle. Otherwise the main instructions still apply.

5 If the ammeter reads zero, an internal fault in the alternator is indicated.

6 If less than 10 amps is indicated, and the voltmeter shows 13.6 to 14.4 volts, where it is known that the battery is in a low state of charge, the alternator is suspect and should be checked by an auto electrician. The nominal output is given in the Specifications. (If the battery is fully charged, a low current reading is normal).

7 If the ammeter reads less than 10 amps and the voltmeter reads less than 13.6 volts, a fault in the alternator internal regulator is indicated. A fault in the regulator is also indicated when the voltage exceeds 14.4 volts.

8 On 18ACR models a surge protection unit is fitted. This can be checked by removing the rear cover from the alternator and then disconnecting the device from the terminal marked IND. Reassemble and test the unit. If

8.2 Disconnecting the alternator plug

the alternator functions correctly when run, renew the surge protection unit.

8 Alternator - removal, refitting and drivebelt adjustment

1 Detach the battery earth lead.

2 Disconnect the plug-in connector(s) and wiring from the rear of the alternator (photo).

3 Slacken the adjustment bolt and the mounting bolts in that order.

4 Push the alternator towards the engine so that the drivebelt can be removed.

5 Remove the adjustment bolt and washer, and the main mounting bolts, nuts and washers.

6 Support the alternator and withdraw the main mounting bolts and washers. The alternator can now be lifted clear.

7 Refitting is basically the reverse of the removal procedure, but do not tighten the nuts and bolts until the drivebelt tension has been checked as described below.

8 Where necessary, slacken the adjustment bolt, and the mounting bolts (Fig. 10.3).

9 Pull the alternator away from the engine and tighten the adjustment bolt. Check the total movement of the belt (see Specifications) under firm thumb pressure at the midpoint of the longest belt run, between the alternator and crankshaft. Re-adjust, if necessary. **Note:** *It is permissible to apply leverage at the drive and bracket, if necessary to obtain the correct tension, but only a softwood lever or similar item may be used.*

9 Alternator - brush renewal

1 With the alternator removed from the car, remove the two setscrews retaining the plastic end cover.

2 Remove the end cover and disconnect, where applicable, the radio interference suppressor (capacitor) lead.

3 Remove the four small setscrews positioned in the centre of the brush box. When removing the setscrews, take a note of the exact positions of the various wires located by the screws.

4 Remove the single setscrew retaining the regulator unit and lift away the flat metal connector strip coupling the regulator to one of the smaller setscrews (referred to in paragraph 3).

5 The brushes can be lifted out of their locations in the brush box.

6 Examine the slip rings for discoloration before fitting the new brushes.

7 Where necessary the slip rings can be cleaned by polishing them with fine glass paper, crocus paper or metal polish. Ensure that no residue is left afterwards.

8 Better access to the slip rings can be achieved after removing the brush box which is retained by two setscrews. Note that the black wire from the regulator unit is located under the head of one of these setscrews.

9 Reassemble the alternator by reversing the dismantling procedure.

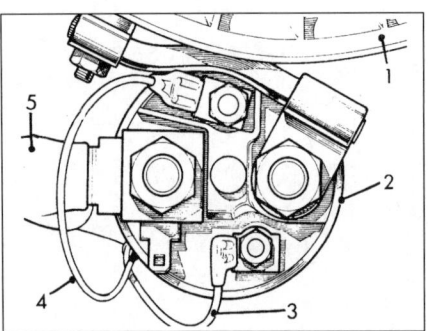

Fig. 10.5 Starter motor solenoid wiring (Sec 11)

1 Starter motor
2 Solenoid
3 Small lead
4 Small lead
5 Battery feed cable

10 Starter motor - general description

When the ignition switch is turned, current flows through the solenoid pull-in winding on the starter motor, moving the solenoid armature. At the same time a much smaller current flows through the solenoid hold-in winding directly to earth.

The movement of the solenoid armature causes the drive pinion to move and engage with the starter ring gear on the flywheel. At the same time the main contacts close and energise the motor circuit. The pull-in winding now becomes ineffective and the solenoid remains in the operated condition by the action of the hold-in winding only.

A special one-way clutch is fitted to the starter drive pinion, so that when the engine commences to fire there is no possibility of it driving the starter motor.

When the ignition key is released, the solenoid is de-energised and returns to its original position. This breaks the supply to the motor and returns the drive pinion to the disengaged position.

11 Starter motor - removal and refitting

1 Detach the battery earth lead and raise the front of the vehicle to a suitable working height for access to the starter motor. A pit or ramp is best.
2 Remove the nut and spring washer, then disconnect the heavy battery feed cable to the starter motor solenoid.
3 Disconnect the two smaller wires at the solenoid by removing the two cross-head screws. Note the locations of the wires. Some have spade connector fittings.
4 Using a socket extension and ratchet spanner, remove the starter motor mounting flange bolts, and the exhaust heat shield on later models.

11.5 Withdrawing the starter motor (engine removed from vehicle)

5 Lift the starter motor out and downwards from the engine (photo).
6 Refitting is the reverse of removal, but check that the solenoid wires are connected correctly.
7 Tighten the starter motor mounting bolts to the specified torque.

12 Starter motor - overhaul

3M100PE type

1 Slacken the nut which secures the connecting link to the solenoid terminal 'STA'.
2 Remove the two screws which secure the solenoid to the drive end bracket.
3 Lift the solenoid plunger upwards and separate it from the engagement level. Extract the return spring seat and dust excluder from the plunger body.
4 Withdraw the block from between the drive end bracket and the starter motor yoke.
5 Remove the armature end cap from the commutator end bracket.
6 Chisel off some of the claws from the armature shaft spire nut so that the nut can be withdrawn from the shaft.
7 Remove the two tie-bolts and then withdraw the commutator end cover and starter motor yoke from the drive end bracket.
8 Separate the commutator end cover from the starter motor yoke, at the same time disengaging the field coil brushes from the brush box to facilitate separation.
9 Withdraw the thrust washer from the armature shaft.
10 Remove the spire nut from the engagement lever pivot pin and then extract the pin from the drive end bracket.
11 Withdraw the armature and roller clutch drive assembly from the drive end bracket.
12 Using a piece of tubing, drive back the thrust collar to expose the jump ring on the armature shaft. Remove the jump ring and withdraw the thrust collar and roller clutch.
13 Remove the spring ring and release the engagement lever, thrust washers and spring from the roller-clutch drive.
14 Remove the dust-excluding seal from the bore of the drive end bracket.
15 Inspect all components for wear. If the armature shaft bushes require renewal, press them out or screw in a 1/2 in tap to withdraw

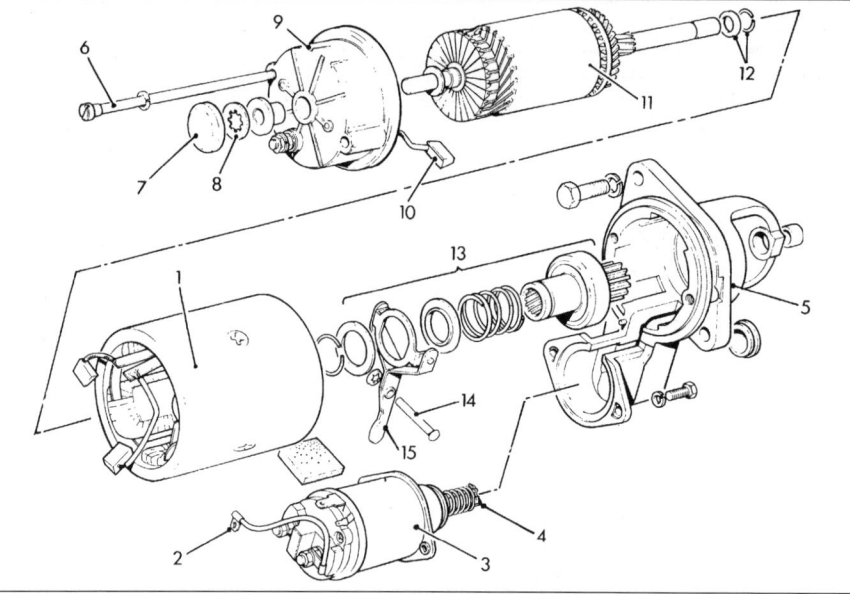

Fig. 10.6 3M100PE type starter motor - exploded view (Sec 12)

1 Yoke
2 Connecting link
3 Solenoid
4 Solenoid plunger
5 Drive end bracket
6 Through-bolt
7 End cap
8 Spire nut
9 Commutator end cover
10 Field coil brush
11 Armature
12 Collar and circlip
13 Engagement lever, thrust collar and roller clutch
14 Pivot pin
15 Engagement lever

them. Before inserting the new bushes, soak them in engine oil for 24 hours.

16 If the brushes have worn below the minimum specified length, renew them by cutting the end bracket brush leads from the terminal post. File a groove in the head of the terminal post and solder the new brush leads in to the groove. Cut the field winding brush leads about 1/4 in (6 mm) from the joint of the field winding. Solder the new brush leads to the ends of the old ones. Localise the heat to prevent damage to the field windings.

17 Check the field windings for continuity using a torch battery and test bulb. If the windings are faulty, removal of the pole shoe screws should be left to a service station having a pressure screwdriver, as they are very tight.

18 Check the insulation of the armature by connecting a test bulb and torch battery. Use probes placed on the armature shaft and each commutator section in turn. If the test bulb lights at any position then the insulation has broken down, and the armature must be renewed. Discoloration of the commutator should be removed by polishing it with a piece of glass paper (not emery cloth). Do not undercut the insulation.

19 Reassembly is a reversal of dismantling, but apply grease to the moving parts of the engagement lever, the outer surface of the roller clutch housing and to the lips of the drive end bracket dust seal. Fit a new spire nut to the armature shaft, positioning it to give the specified shaft endfloat. Measure this endfloat by inserting feeler blades between the face of the spire nut and the flange of the commutator end bush.

M45 type

20 With the starter motor on the bench unscrew and remove the nut that secures the solenoid link wire or tag to the terminal on the starter motor body, lift off the link.

21 Mark the relative positions of the solenoid and drive end bracket, then undo and remove the two securing nuts (bolts on early models) and spring washers.

22 Withdraw the solenoid rearwards and disengage the solenoid plunger from the operating lever. Remove the solenoid from the starter motor.

23 Remove the rubber sealing grommet from the slot in the drive end bracket.

24 On later models, undo and remove the two nuts and rubber seals and lift off the commutator end cover and cover band. On early models, slacken the clamp screw and slide the cover band off the rear of the starter .

25 Using a hook-shaped length of wire, lift off the brush springs and withdraw the brushes from their holders.

26 Unscrew and withdraw the two long through-bolts that secure the commutator end bracket and lift off the end bracket from the starter body and armature.

27 Remove the drive end bracket complete with armature from the starter body.

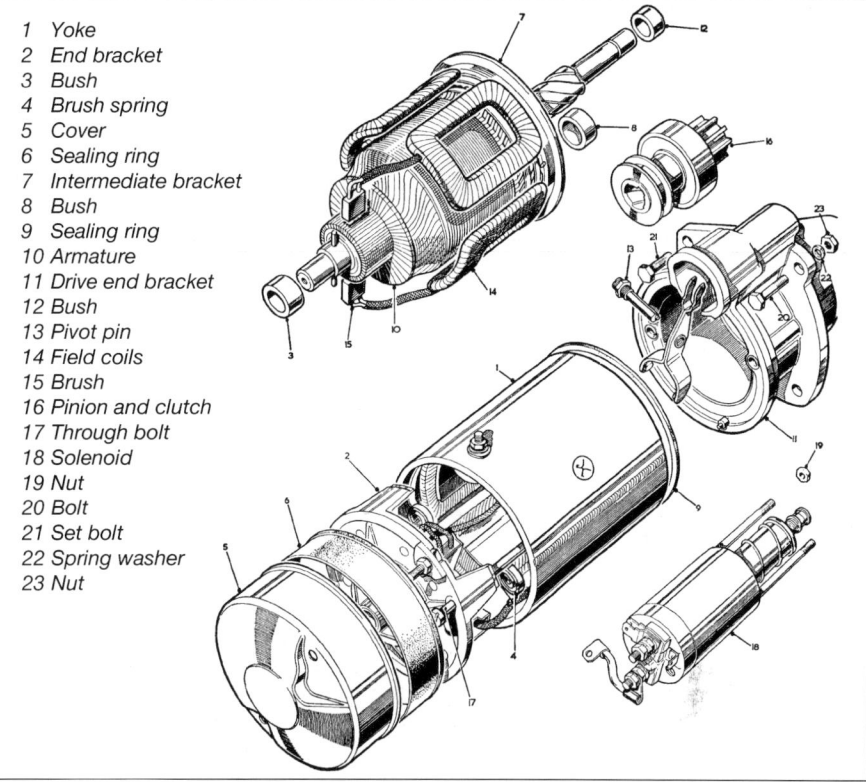

1   Yoke
2   End bracket
3   Bush
4   Brush spring
5   Cover
6   Sealing ring
7   Intermediate bracket
8   Bush
9   Sealing ring
10 Armature
11 Drive end bracket
12 Bush
13 Pivot pin
14 Field coils
15 Brush
16 Pinion and clutch
17 Through bolt
18 Solenoid
19 Nut
20 Bolt
21 Set bolt
22 Spring washer
23 Nut

Fig. 10.7 M45 type starter motor – exploded view (Sec 12)

28 Slacken the locknut and undo and remove the eccentric engagement lever pivot pin from the end bracket.

29 Withdraw the armature and intermediate bracket from the drive end bracket and lift off the engagement lever.

30 Push back the lockring cover on the end of the armature shaft and prise off the lockring.

31 Withdraw the drive assembly and intermediate bracket from the armature shaft. Note any shims that may be fitted behind the intermediate bracket.

32 On later models, remove the brake ring, steel and tufnol washers from the commutator end bracket.

33 With the starter motor dismantled, check that the brushes move freely in their holders. If necessary, they may be cleaned with a petrol moistened cloth or by very light rubbing with a smooth file.

34 If the brushes are worn they should be renewed.

35 The brush wires are soldered or crimped to terminal tags and must be unsoldered to remove. New brush wires may then be resoldered onto the tags.

36 Clean the commutator with a petrol-moistened rag, and if necessary wrap a piece of glass paper around the commutator and rotate the armature to remove any burnt areas or high spots.

37 If the commutator is badly worn, mount the armature in a lathe and with the lathe turning at high speed, take a very fine cut out of the commutator. Finish the surface by

polishing with glass paper. Do not undercut the insulation between the commutator segments.

38 Check that the roller clutch rotates freely in one direction and locks up in the other. If not, the clutch must be renewed.

39 The field coil continuity may be tested as follows: Connect a 12 volt battery with a 12 volt bulb in one of the leads between the field terminal post and the tapping point of the field coils to which the brushes are connected. An open-circuit is proved by the bulb not lighting.

40 If the bulb lights, it does not necessarily mean that the field coils are in order, as there is a possibility that one of the coils will be earthed to the starter yoke or pole shoes. To check this, remove the lead from the brush connector and place it against a clean portion of the starter yoke. If the bulb lights, the field coils are earthing.

41 If the armature is damaged, this will be evident on inspection. Look for signs of burning, discoloration and for conductors that have lifted away from the commutator.

42 To reassemble the starter motor is the reverse sequence of dismantling. The following additional points should be noted:

(a) *When refitting the solenoid plunger to the engagement lever, turn the eccentric pin until the engagement lever is in its lowest and most forward position*

(b) *With the starter motor reassembled, reset the drive pinion engagement positions as described below.*

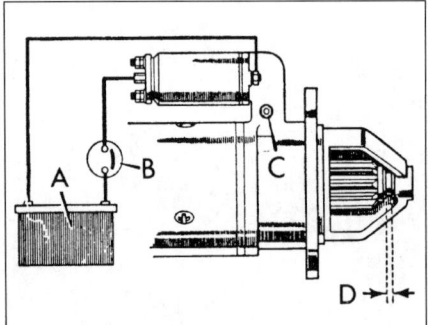

Fig. 10.8 Drive pinion clearance adjustment (Sec 12)

A *Battery*   B *Switch*   C *Pivot pin*
D *Clearance = 0.005 to 0.015 in*
(0.12 to 0.40 mm)

43 Connect one lead from a 12 volt battery to the small unmarked terminal on the starter solenoid.
44 Using a switch in the circuit, connect the other battery terminal lead to one of the solenoid fixing studs.
45 With the switch closed, the drive pinion will move forward to the engaged position. Measure the distance between the end of the pinion and the lockring cover on the end of the armature shaft (Fig. 10.8).
46 A clearance within the limits given in the Specifications should exist with the drive pinion pushed gently back to take up any free play in the operating linkage.

13.6 Withdrawing the complete headlamp unit

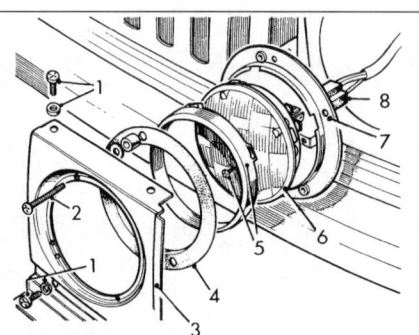

Fig. 10.9 Headlamp assembly – exploded view (Sec 13)

1 *Headlamp retaining screws*
2 *Headlamp adjuster screw*
3 *Headlamp retainer*
4 *Seal*
5 *Rim and retaining screw*
6 *Sealed beam unit*
7 *Mounting ring*
8 *Wiring connectors*

47 If the clearance is incorrect, slacken the locknut and rotate the engagement arm fulcrum one way or the other until the correct clearance is obtained. Note that the adjustment arc is 180° and the arrow marked on the head of the fulcrum pin must be within 90° of either side of the cast arrow on the end casing.
48 When the clearance is correct, tighten the locknut.

Testing the solenoid (all models)

49 To test the solenoid contacts for correct opening and closing, connect a 12 volt battery and a 60 watt test lamp between the main battery feed terminal and the 'STA' terminal. The lamp should not light.
50 Energize the solenoid with a separate 12 volt supply connected to the small unmarked Lucar terminal and a good earth on the solenoid body.
51 As the coil is energized the solenoid should be heard to operate and the test lamp should light with full brilliance.
52 No attempt should be made to repair a faulty solenoid. If it is faulty it must be renewed as a complete unit.

13.4 Removing one of the headlamp retainer screws

13 Headlamp unit - removal and refitting

Tungsten filament type

1 The headlamp is of the sealed beam type and has no separate bulb.
2 Disconnect the battery negative lead as a safety precaution.
3 Open the bonnet and prop it securely.
4 Undo and remove the four cross-head screws which secure the headlamp retainer to the body (photo).
5 If the headlamp washers and wipers are fitted, disconnect the washer tubing to the jet and withdraw the wiper rack and the motor as described in Sections 37 and 40.
6 Withdraw the headlamp unit and retainer and disconnect the wiring at the rear of the unit (photo).
7 Remove the two adjusting screws to separate the lamp unit from the retainer. Later models have a clamp in addition to the adjusting screws (photo).
8 Remove the rubber seal.
9 Slacken the three rim retaining screws, turn the rim anti-clockwise and lift it away. The headlamp unit can now be separated from the mounting ring (photos).
10 Refitting is the reverse of the removal procedure.

13.7 One of the headlamp adjusting screws almost removed

13.9a Slackening a rim retaining screw so that . . .

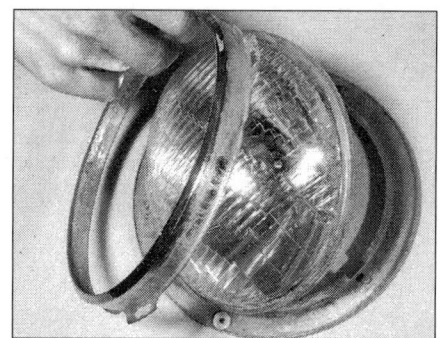

13.9b . . . the headlamp unit, rim, and mounting ring can be separated

Fig. 10.10 Front side and flasher lamp unit - exploded view (Sec 15)

1 *Lens retaining screw*
2 *Lens*
3 *Seal*
4 *Flasher bulb*
5 *Sidelamp bulb*
6 *Washer between lens and lamp unit at screw hole*
7 *Lamp unit retaining screw and washer*
8 *Wiring to lamp unit*

11 The headlamps should be checked for alignment as soon as possible after refitting (Section 14).

Quartz halogen type

12 Bulb renewal can be achieved without removing the headlamp unit provided that access can be gained from the rear.
13 Unplug the connector from the bulb and remove the bulb from the rear of the reflector unit. Take care if the bulb is hot.
14 Refitting is the reverse of the removal procedure. Do not touch the bulb envelope with bare fingers, or it will become blackened in use where it has been touched.
15 Note that headlamp wipe/wash systems cannot be fitted in conjunction with quartz

> **HAYNES HiNT**
> *If a bulb is accidentally touched, clean it using methylated spirit and a lint-free cloth.*

halogen headlamps, due to the high temperature at which the lamps run.

14 Headlamp beam alignment

1 Each headlamp is equipped with two adjusting screws. By screwing these two screws in or out, the alignment of the headlamps can be altered.
2 The owner or driver of the vehicle who wants to alter the beam alignment must remember that it is an offence not to have the vehicle lights set correctly.
3 Any setting that is carried out without the correct beam setting equipment should only be regarded as a temporary measure.

15.2 Removing the front lamp lens cover and seal

4 If, after headlamp renewal, or after an accident, the beam alignment has to be reset, then the vehicle should be taken to a Range Rover dealer to have the headlamp beams correctly set as soon as possible.

15 Front side and flasher lamps - bulb renewal, removal and refitting

Bulb renewal

1 Remove the four cross-head screws which secure the combined lens cover.
2 Lift away the lens cover and seal. Recover the rubber washers between the lens and lamp unit screw holes (photo).
3 Remove the bulb. The top bulb is the flasher, the bottom is sidelight. Both bulbs have a bayonet 'push-and-twist' type fitting.
4 Ensure that the new bulb is of the correct wattage.
5 Refit the lens and seal. Make sure the seal fits correctly so that water cannot enter the lamp unit.
6 Refit the four screws but do not overtighten them.

Removal and refitting

7 Remove the bulbs as described above.
8 Open the bonnet and prop it securely.
9 Remove the two screws in the top of the lamp unit which secure the unit to the front panel.

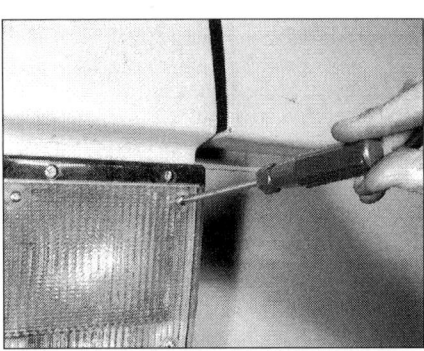

16.1 Removing the lens retaining screws (rear combination light)

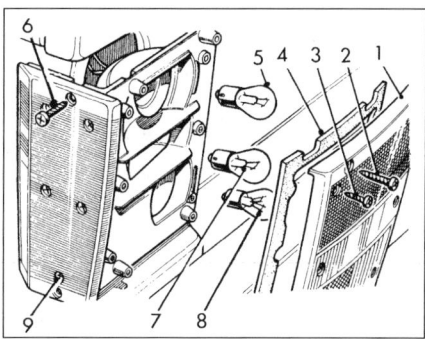

10.11 Rear lamp assembly – exploded view (Sec 16)

1 *Lens*
2 *Lamp unit retaining screw*
3 *Lens retaining screw*
4 *Seal*
5 *Flasher bulb*
6 *Lamp unit retaining screw*
7 *Reversing bolt*
8 *Stop/fail bulb*
9 *Side reflector retaining screw*

10 Lift the lamp unit up and forwards to clear the mounting pegs at the bottom.
11 Disconnect the wiring at the rear of the lamp unit and lift it away.
12 Refitting is the reverse of the removal procedure.

16 Rear lamp assembly - bulb renewal, removal and refitting

Bulb renewal

1 Remove the six lens retaining screws (photo).
2 Lift the lens and seal away (photo).
3 The bulbs are identified as follows: Top - flasher, centre - reversing lamp, bottom - tail/stop-lamp.
4 All bolts are of the bayonet 'push-and-twist' type.
5 Remove the required bulb.
6 Fit another bulb of the correct wattage and type.

16.2 Lifting the lens and seal away (rear combination light)

17.1 Removing the number plate light lens cover

7 Refit the lens and seal.
8 Refit the six screws; do not overtighten them.

Removal and refitting

9 Remove the lens and bulbs only if necessary (see below).
10 Remove the four cross-head screws which retain the lamp unit to the body. (It is possible to remove the nut without removing the lens and bulbs as the screws are accessible through the lens cover).
11 Remove the top and bottom screws in the side reflector unit.
12 Withdraw the lamp unit and disconnect the leads at the connectors.
13 The reflector can be removed from the lamp unit by removing the five screws which retain it. Note that there is a rubber seal behind it.
14 Refitting is the reverse of the removal procedure.

17 Number plate lamp - bulb renewal, removal and refitting

Bulb renewal

1 Remove the two lens cover retaining screws and lower the cover, lens and seal (photo).
2 The bulb is a bayonet 'push-and-twist' fitting.
3 Renew the bulb with one of the correct type and wattage.
4 Refit the seal, lens and cover and secure it with the two screws.

Removal and refitting

5 Remove the bulb as directed.
6 Remove the two screws and nuts which secure the lamp base to the number plate. Lift the number plate up to reach the nuts more easily.
7 Disconnect the leads from the lamp base as it is withdrawn.
8 Refitting is the reverse procedure.

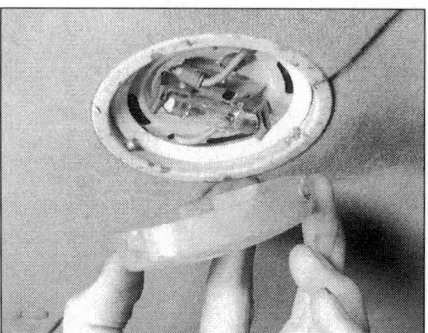

18.2 Removing the interior lamp lens cover (single bulb type lamp)

18 Interior lamp (roof-mounted) - bulb renewal, removal and refitting

1 The interior roof-mounted lamp(s) may have one or two festoon bulbs. The lamp is operated by switches on both door pillars and also by a switch on the steering column.

Bulb renewal

2 To remove the lens cover, press and rotate it anti-clockwise (photo).
3 Remove the bulb(s) from the holder.
4 Fit a new bulb of the correct wattage.
5 Refit the lens cover.

Removal and refitting

6 Remove the bulb(s) as directed. Disconnect the battery earth lead.
7 Prise the cable ends from the connectors.
8 Remove the screws which secure the lamp holder to the roof panel.
9 Withdraw the lamp holder, feeding the cables through the lamp holder base.
10 Refitting is the reverse of the removal procedure.

19 Cigar lighter - bulb renewal, removal and refitting

Bulb renewal

1 The cigar lighter is illuminated only when the sidelights are switched on.
2 From behind the centre console pull out the bulb and holder from the mounting position.
3 Prise the bulb and socket from the holder.
4 The bulb is of the bayonet 'push-and-twist' fit type.
5 Renew the bulb with one of the correct type and wattage.
6 Fit the bulb and socket into the holder.
7 Refit the holder to the cigar lighter.

Removal and refitting

8 Remove the console unit as described in Section 29.
9 With the wiring disconnected, hold the back

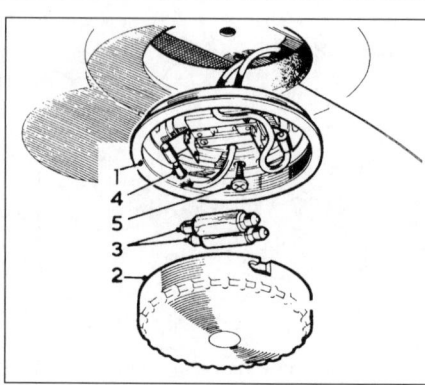

Fig. 10.12 Interior roof-mounted courtesy lamp (Sec 18)

1 Lamp holder   4 Cable end
2 Cover   5 Screw
3 Bulbs

of the lighter using a pair of pliers. Unscrew the centre barrel and pull it out of the front of the console complete with chromed ring (Fig. 10.13).
10 Refitting is the reverse of the removal procedure.

20 Instrument panel - illumination and warning lamp renewal

1 All the illumination and warning lamp bulbs are housed in the instrument panel binnacle, on top of the dashboard in front of the steering wheel.
2 To remove the instrument binnacle rear cover, press in the bottom rear edge (towards the windscreen) and lift it off the mounting clips, but do not disconnect any wiring to it.
3 Separate the binnacle from the instrument panel; there is no need to detach the speedo trip cable from the binnacle to do this.
4 All the warning and illumination lamp bulbs

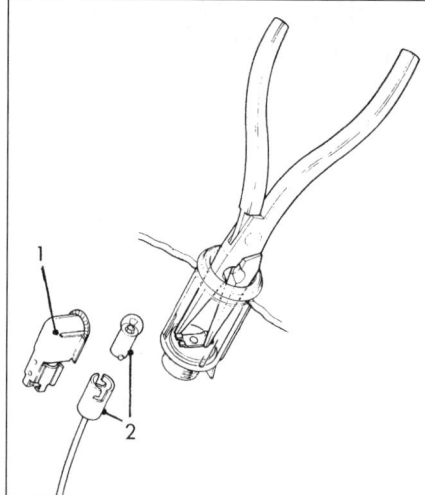

Fig. 10.13 Cigar lighter removal (Sec 19)

1 Bulb holder   2 Bulb and socket

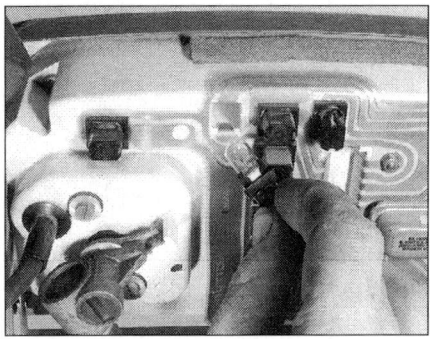

20.4 Bulb and holder removed from instrument panel

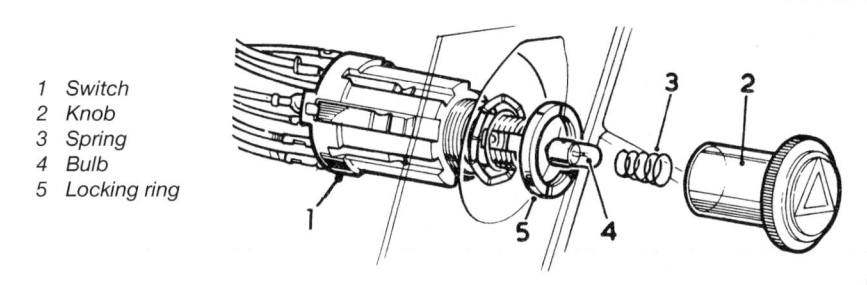

1 Switch
2 Knob
3 Spring
4 Bulb
5 Locking ring

Fig. 10.14 Hazard flasher switch – exploded view (Sec 21)

are of the capless type, held in position in small plastic holders (photo).

5 Identify the bulb, pull the holder and bulb out of the panel and renew the bulb. Ensure it is of the same type and wattage as that specified.

6 Refit the bulb and holder to the panel.

7 Refit the rear binnacle cover to the instrument panel and secure it on the clips.

21 Hazard flasher and heated rear screen switches - bulb renewal, removal and refitting

Bulb renewal

1 Unscrew the knob from the end of the switch.

2 Be careful not to lose the spring inside the knob.

3 Withdraw the bulb from the switch body.

4 Renew the bulb with one of the same type and wattage.

5 Refit the spring and knob. Note that the spring fits with the large diameter end towards the knob.

Removal and refitting

6 Remove the bulb as directed. Disconnect the battery earth lead.

7 Undo the locking ring which retains the switch to the facia or console.

8 To remove the hazard flasher switch, remove the facia panel below the steering column to which the switch is attached.

9 Withdraw the switch from the rear of the facia.

10 Note the wiring connectors and remove them.

11 To remove the heated rear screen switch remove the centre console, as described in Section 29.

12 Withdraw the switch, note the wiring connections and remove them.

13 Refitting of both switches is the reverse of the removal procedure.

22 Differential lock valve and warning light - bulb renewal, removal and refitting

1 The differential lock control valve is located on the floor to the right of the main gear lever. On early models the warning light is incorporated in the top of the knob itself, but from October 1973 onwards the warning light has been fitted to the bottom of the instrument panel. To remove the differential lock actuator switch refer to Section 27.

Bulb renewal

Early models

2 Undo the chrome locking ring in the top of the knob.

3 Remove the ring and lens and then withdraw the spring and bulb assembly.

4 Unscrew the spring and seat from the bulb.

5 Fit the spring and seat to a new bulb of the correct type and wattage.

6 Refit the bulb spring and seat assembly to the knob, and screw in the lens and locking ring.

Later models

7 Prise the warning light holder, lens and bulb from the facia.

8 Pull the bulb holder out of the lens cover and remove the bulb.

9 Fit a new bulb of the correct wattage to the holder and refit the holder to the lens.

10 Refit the lens to the facia and locate the two pins on the lens to the holes in the facia.

Control valve - removal and refitting

11 Remove the rubber boot surrounding the main gear lever and differential lock control valve.

12 Undo the two bolts which retain the differential lock control valve to the top of the gearbox (photo).

13 Disconnect the vacuum tubing from the control valve, noting which tube fits onto which connector.

14 Disconnect the wiring from the warning light connectors, noting which wire fits where.

15 Remove the complete valve assembly.

16 Refitting is the reverse of the removal procedure.

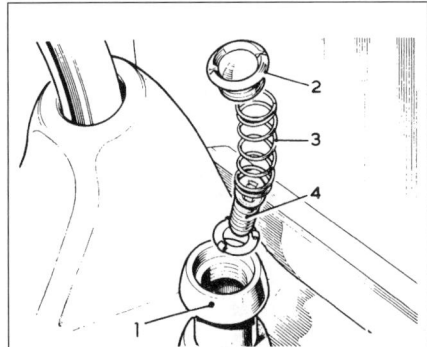

Fig .10.15 Early differential lock warning light assembly (Sec 22)

1 Knob
2 Locking ring and lens
3 Spring
4 Bulb

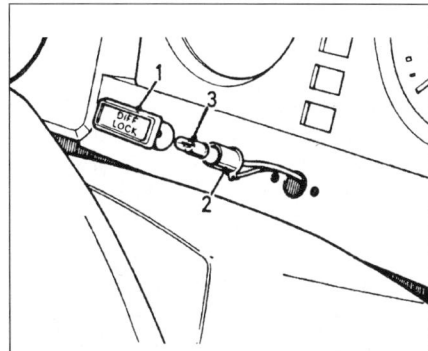

Fig. 10.16 Later type differential lock warning light (Sec 22)

1 Lens cover
2 Bulb holder
3 Bulb

22.12 Undo the differential lock valve retaining bolts (gear lever removed)

23.1 The hazard flasher can be seen (arrowed) below the round heavy duty flasher fitted for towing

23 Relays and flasher units - removal and refitting

Hazard flasher unit/Direction indicator flasher unit

1 The hazard flasher unit is located with the twin signal flasher unit on the steering column support bracket. The hazard flasher is the right-hand unit (photo).
2 Disconnect the battery earth lead and remove the lower facia panel. Pull the flasher unit from its spring mounting clip and disconnect the electrical leads, noting the locations of the leads for refitting.
3 Fit a new unit and reconnect the leads to the flasher, ensuring that they are correctly located.
4 Refit the flasher to the spring clip.
5 Refit the lower facia panel and reconnect the battery earth lead.

Starter motor relay

6 Disconnect the battery as a safety precaution
7 The starter motor relay is located on the left-hand side of the rear engine compartment bulkhead, next to the windscreen washer reservoir on early models.
8 Disconnect the wiring from the relay, noting the wiring positions.
9 Remove the two self-tapping screws and lift the relay away.
10 Refitting is the reverse of the removal procedure. Do not forget the earthing wires.

24 Fuses - general

1 The main fuse box is located in the engine compartment on the left-hand side of the bulkhead (photo).
2 The fuse box has a plastic push-on cover and the protected circuits are shown on it. Normally two spare fuses are located inside the fuse box.
3 All the fuses are of the 35 amp rating.

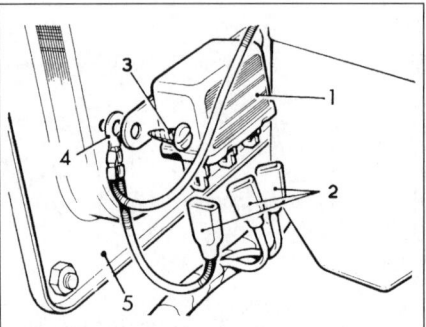

Fig. 10.17 Starter relay (Sec 23)

1 Relay
2 Wiring connectors
3 Mounting screw
4 Earth wires
5 Bulkhead panel

4 Some of the circuits such as the heater and heated rear screen are protected by in-line fuses in the appropriate circuit. Other auxiliary circuits such as the radio (where fitted) are protected in the same way.
5 If any item of electrical equipment fails to operate, first check the appropriate fuse. If the fuse has blown the first thing to do is to find the cause, otherwise it will merely blow again - (fuses can blow through age fatigue, but this is the exception rather than the rule). Having found the faulty fuse, switch off the electrical equipment and then fit a new fuse. From the wiring diagrams note which circuits are served by the blown fuse and then start to switch each one on separately in turn. (It may be necessary to have the ignition circuit switched on at the same time). The fuse should blow again when the faulty item is switched on. It the fuse does not blow immediately, start again, but this time leave the circuits switched on and build up the cumulative total lead on the fuse. If and when it blows you will have an indication of which circuits may be causing the problem. If a new fuse does not blow until the car is moving then look for a loose, chafed or pinched wire.
6 When fitting a new fuse always use a fuse of the correct rating. Do not, under any circumstances, fit a fuse of a higher rating or use a piece of tin foil as a substitute. It should be clearly understood that fuses are the weakest link in a circuit. Any fault causing

25.4 Lower the bottom half shroud and switches away from the steering column

24.1 Fuse box location on rear bulkhead

shorting or an overload of a particular circuit will cause the fuse wire to melt and thus break the circuit. A higher rated fuse or a piece of tin foil will not break the circuit and in such cases overheating and the risk of fire at the fault source, could easily occur.
7 If a fault occurs in one accessory or component and its rectification defies all efforts, always remember that it could be a relay at fault. Relays cannot be repaired or adjusted and, if faulty, should be renewed as a unit.

25 Column-mounted switches - removal and refitting

1 Disconnect the battery as a safety precaution.
2 Undo the four screws which retain the bottom half of the steering column shroud to the top half.
3 Remove the single screw which retains the top half of the shroud to the column bracket, and lift it away.
4 Lower the bottom half of the shroud and switches away from the steering column (photo).

Ignition/starter switch

5 Remove the two self-tapping screws which retain the ignition/starter switch to the left-hand end of the steering column lock bracket.

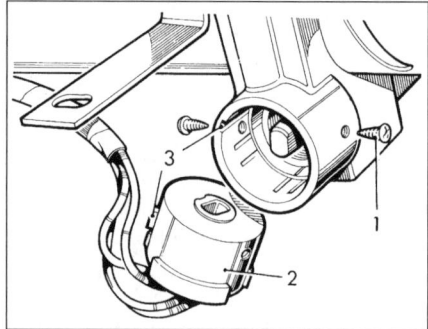

Fig. 10.18 Ignition starter switch (Sec 25)

1 Self-tapping screw
2 Switch
3 Lug and groove

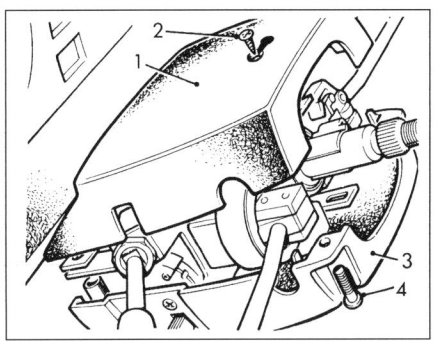

Fig. 10.19 Steering column shrouds (Sec 25)

1 Top half
2 Top half retaining screw
3 Bottom half shroud
4 Bottom half retaining screw

6 Pull the switch out of its mounting and disconnect the wiring at the plug-in connector block.

7 Refitting is the reverse procedure to removal. Note that there is a lug on the side of the switch body which has to locate in the groove in the mounting bracket.

8 Should the steering column lock require renewal, this task must be undertaken by a Range Rover dealer with the necessary equipment.

Main lighting switch

9 This is located on the right-hand side of the steering column and is the front stalk switch.

10 With the lower shroud away from the column, undo the locking ring on the switch and free it from the bracket.

11 Disconnect the wiring from the switch at the snap connectors, noting the wiring locations.

12 Refitting is the reverse of the removal procedure.

Combination dipswitch, direction indicator, horn and flasher switch

13 This is located on the right-hand side of

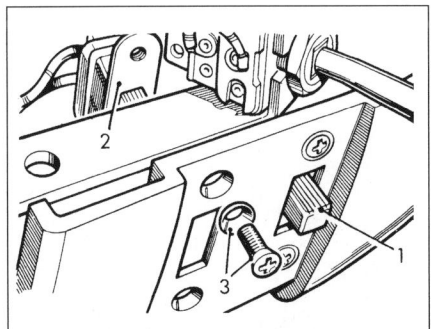

Fig. 10.22 Panel light and interior light switches (Sec 25)

1 Interior light switch
2 Panel light switch removed
3 Retaining screw and cup washer

Fig. 10.20 Bottom half shroud – switch mounting (Sec 25)

1 Mounting bracket   3 Switch
2 Locking ring

the steering column and is the rear stalk switch.

14 Remove the column shrouds as already described.

15 Remove the wiper/washer switch as described below.

16 Undo the two screws which retain the column switch to the mounting bracket.

17 Disconnect the wiring to the switch, noting the wiring colours and locations.

18 Refitting is the reverse of the removal procedure.

Auxiliary driving lamps/foglamps switch

19 This is located on the left-hand side of the steering column and is the front stalk switch.

20 With the lower half of the column shroud lowered as already described, undo the locking ring and remove the switch from its mounting bracket.

21 Disconnect the switch wiring at the snap connectors, noting the wiring colours and locations.

22 Refitting is the reverse of the removal procedure.

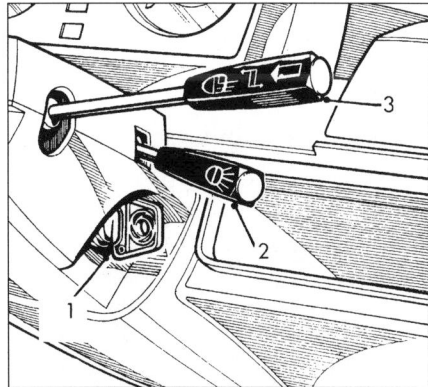

Fig. 10.23 Switch identification – right-hand side of column (Sec 25)

1 Ignition/starter
2 Headlamp/sidelamp main switch
3 Dip, indicator, horn and flasher switch

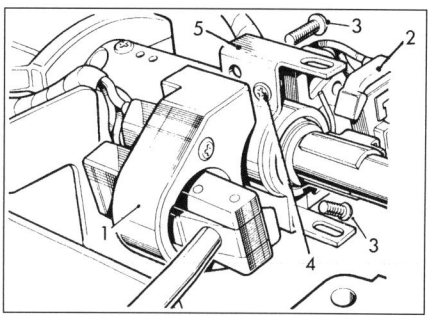

Fig. 10.21 Rear column-mounted switches (Sec 25)

1 Windscreen wiper/washer switch
2 Dip, indicator, horn and flasher switch
3 Retaining screws for left-hand switch
4 Retaining screw for right-hand switch
5 Mounting bracket

Windscreen wiper/washer switch

23 This is located on the left-hand side of the steering column and is the rear stalk switch. If headlamp wash/wipe facilities are fitted, this switch operates them at the same time as the main windscreen wash/wipe system. However, this only operates when the headlamps are switched on.

24 Remove the steering column shrouds as described above.

25 Remove the two cross-head screws which retain the switch to the column bracket.

26 Lift the switch away and disconnect the wiring. Note the colours and locations of the wires.

27 Refitting is the reverse of the removal procedure.

Panel light switch

28 The panel and instrument lighting switch is the front switch located in the lower half of the steering column shroud on the left-hand side of the column.

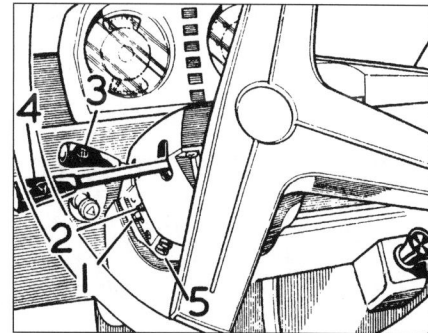

Fig. 10.24 Switch identification – left-hand side column (Sec 25)

1 Panel lights switch
2 Interior light switch
3 Auxiliary lamps switch
4 Wiper/washer for windscreen (and headlamps if fitted)
5 Plug-in sockets

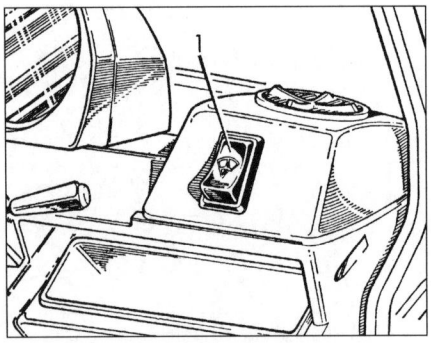

Fig. 10.25 Tailgate wash/wipe switch location (1) (Sec 26)

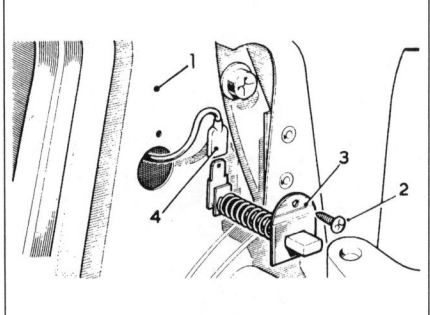

Fig. 10.26 Door-operated courtesy light switch (Sec 27)

1 Door pillar 3 Switch
2 Screw 4 Wiring connector

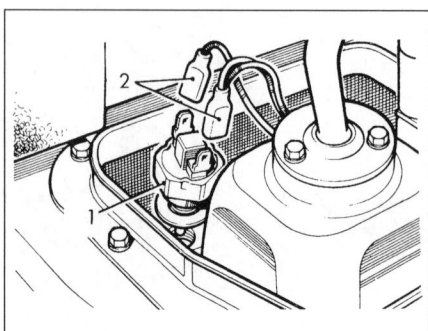

Fig. 10.27 Reversing light switch (Sec 27)

1 Switch 2 Wiring connectors

29 Remove the lower half shroud retaining screws and lower the shroud.
30 Disconnect the wiring from the switch, noting the wiring colours and locations.
31 Undo and remove the two screws and cup washers that retain the switch, and remove the switch from the shroud.
32 Refitting is the the reverse of the removal procedure.

Interior light switch

33 This is located next to the panel lighting switch on the left-hand side of the lower half shroud, and is the rearmost of the two toggle switches.
34 Removal and refitting is identical to the procedure given above for the panel light switch.

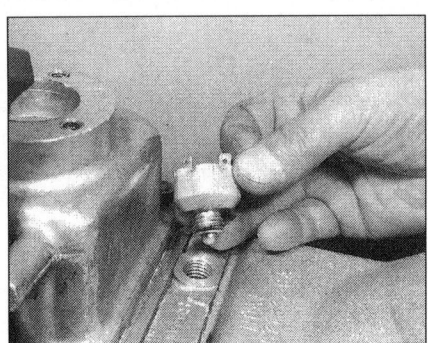

27.6 Removing the reversing light switch (gearbox removed)

26 Tailgate wiper/washer switch - removal and refitting

1 The tailgate wiper/washer switch (on models so equipped) is located on the facia to the right of the instrument binnacle.
2 Prise the rocker type switch out of the facia.
3 Disconnect the wiring from the rear of the switch, noting colours and locations.
4 Remove the switch.
5 Refitting is the reverse of the removal procedure..

27 Automatic switches and coolant temperature transmitter

Door switch (courtesy lights)

1 With the door open, remove the single screw, withdraw the switch and detach the wiring connector.
2 Refitting is the reverse of the removal procedure.

Reversing light switch

3 Disconnect the battery earth lead.
4 Remove the main gear lever rubber cover to gain access to the switch.

5 Disconnect the electrical leads from the switch and note their positions.
6 Unscrew and remove the switch and shim washer (photo).
7 Refitting is the reverse of the removal procedure.

Handbrake warning light switch

8 Disconnect the battery earth lead.
9 Remove the retaining screws and lift off the handbrake rubber boot and retaining plate (photo).
10 Pull the handbrake fully on.
11 Remove the hexagonal nut which retains the switch to its mounting bracket (photo).
12 Withdraw the switch and disconnect the leads as it is removed.
13 Refitting is the reverse of the removal procedure.

Differential lock actuator switch

14 Remove the front floor of the vehicle as described in Chapter 12.
15 Disconnect the wiring from the switch (photo).
16 Unscrew the switch and remove the switch and shim washers.
17 Refitting the switch is the reverse procedure to removal. Do not forget the shim washers. Refer to Chapter 6, Section 18 for details of the switch setting adjustment.

Oil pressure warning light switch

18 Disconnect the battery as a safety precaution.

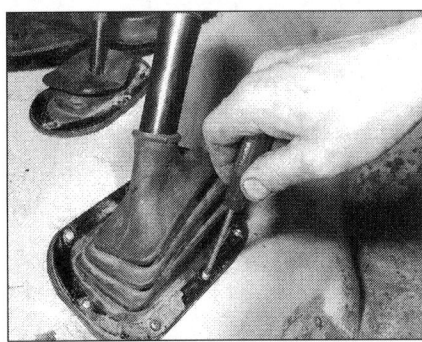

27.9 Removing the handbrake rubber boot and retaining plate

27.11 Handbrake warning light switch (gearbox removed)

27.15 View of differential lock actuator switch (gearbox removed)

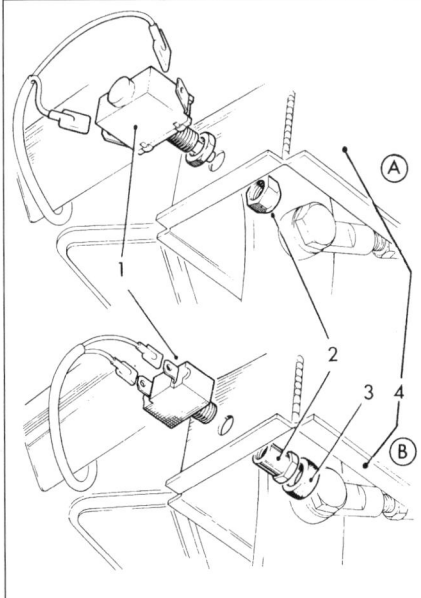

27.24 Coolant temperature transmitter (arrowed)

19 Disconnect the lead from the switch on the oil filter housing.
20 Unscrew the switch unit and remove it and the washer.
21 Refitting is the reverse of the removal procedure.

Coolant temperature transmitter

22 Disconnect the battery as a safety precaution.
23 Drain the coolant from the inlet manifold as described in Chapter 2.
24 Disconnect the electrical wiring from the transmitter in the front end of the manifold (photo).
25 Unscrew the transmitter from the manifold and remove it and the washer.
26 Refitting is the reverse procedure, but use a new washer. Refill the cooling system as described in Chapter 2.

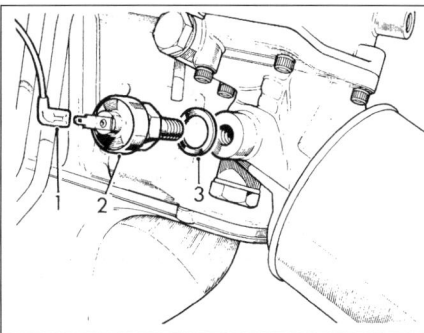

Fig. 10.28 Oil pressure warning light switch (Sec 27)

1 Head   2 Switch   3 Washer

Choke warning light switch

27 Remove the switch cover, which is retained by one screw on later models.
28 Disconnect the wiring from the switch.
29 Remove the screw and clip which retain the switch to the choke cable, and remove the switch.
30 Refitting is the reverse of the removal procedure.

Stop-light switch

31 Disconnect the battery as a safety precaution.
32 Remove the lower facia panel beneath the steering column.
33 Depress the footbrake and remove the rubber cover (if fitted) from the operating end of the switch.
34 Undo the locking nut and withdraw the switch from the pedal box.
35 Disconnect the wiring and remove the switch.
36 Refitting is the reverse of the removal procedure. Check the correct operation of the switch on completion.

28 Instrument panel housing - removal and refitting

Note: *To remove the instrument panel illuminating bulbs and the warning light bulbs it is not necessary to remove the instrument*

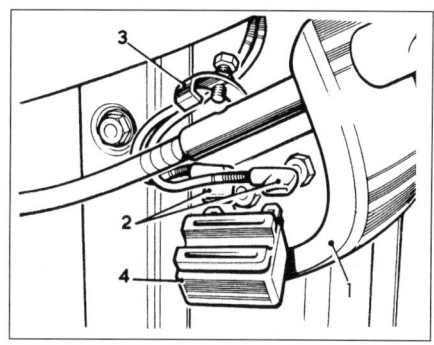

Fig. 10.29 Choke warning light switch (Sec 27)

1   Choke mounting bracket
2   Wiring connectors
3   Screw and retaining clip
4   Switch

panel housing completely. The rear of the binnacle can be removed by pressing inwards on the rear lower edge of the housing and releasing it from the mounting clips.
1 Disconnect the battery negative lead.
2 Remove the binnacle rear casing.
3 Disconnect the speedometer cable from the speedometer as described in Section 31.
4 Unplug the electrical connector from the rear of the printed circuit (photo).
5 Remove the facia panel below the steering column.
6 Remove the four nuts and washers which secure the instrument panel housing to the dashboard.
7 Lift the instrument housing away complete with instruments (photo).
8 Refitting is the reverse of the removal procedure.

29 Instruments - removal and refitting

Instruments mounted in the instrument panel

1 Remove the instrument panel housing as described in Section 28.
2 Unscrew the knurled nut which secures the

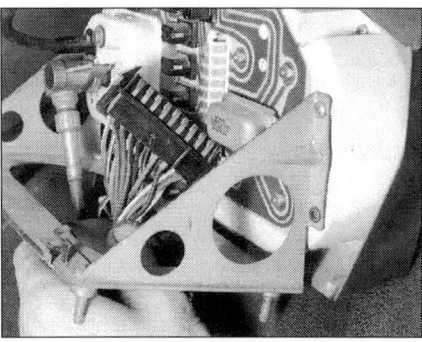

Fig 10.30 Stop-light switch (different types fitted) (Sec 27)

1   Switch   *4   Pedal box*
2   Locking nut   *A   Early type*
3   Rubber cover   *B   Later type*

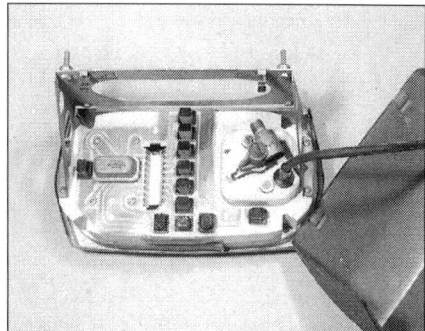

28.4 Unplug the electrical connector from the printed circuit

28.7 The complete instrument housing removed

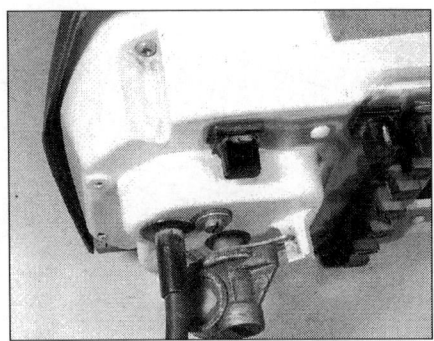

29.6 The angled speedometer drive is retained by the captive knurled nut

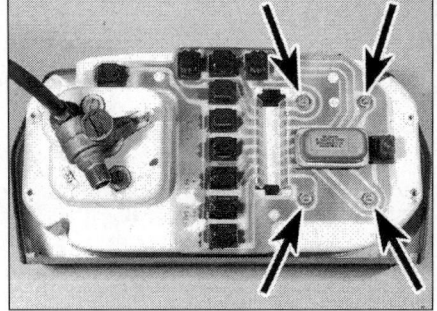

29.10 Fuel and water temperature gauge retaining nuts (arrowed)

29.23 Pull the console forward to reach the instruments

speedometer trip reset control to the left-hand side of the binnacle rear cover.

3 Undo the four screws which retain the mounting bracket to the instrument panel, and remove it.

4 Remove the screws which retain the front of the instrument panel to the panel itself.

5 Separate the panel from the front cover.

Speedometer

6 Remove the angle drive from the rear of the speedometer by undoing the captive knurled nut (photo).

7 Remove the two screws, washers and bushes from the rear of the speedometer.

8 Withdraw the speedometer from the front of the panel.

9 Refitting is the reverse of the removal procedure.

Fuel gauge

10 Remove the two nuts and washers from the rear of the fuel gauge whilst holding the fuel gauge in the instrument panel (photo).

11 Withdraw the gauge, taking care that the pins do not damage the printed circuit as they are withdrawn.

12 Refitting is the reverse of the removal procedure.

Coolant temperature gauge

13 Hold the gauge and undo the two retaining nuts on the rear of the printed circuit panel.

14 Withdraw the temperature gauge, taking care not to damage the printed circuit with the mounting bolts.

15 Refitting is the reverse procedure.

Instruments mounted in the facia

16 The same basic procedures apply to all the facia-mounted instruments.

17 Disconnect the battery negative lead.

18 Undo the grub screws and remove the heater control lever knobs.

19 Undo the screws and remove the heater control plate.

20 Undo the four heater console upper retaining screws.

21 Remove the centre face level louvre.

22 From inside the glovebox remove the lower centre console retaining screw.

23 Move the console forwards to gain access to the instruments (photo).

24 Disconnect the wiring from the appropriate instrument.

25 Remove the illuminating bulb holder and bulb from the rear of the instrument.

26 Remove the knurled nut(s) from the mounting arm(s) for the instrument. Some have one, others have two.

27 Withdraw the instrument from the console.

28 Refitting is the reverse of the removal procedure.

---

30 Voltage stabiliser (instruments) - removal and refitting

1 Disconnect the battery as a safety precaution.

2 Remove the rear of the instrument binnacle.

3 Withdraw the instrument voltage stabilizer from the rear of the printed circuit panel.

4 Plug in the new stabilizer unit.

5 Refit the rear of the instrument binnnacle and reconnect the battery.

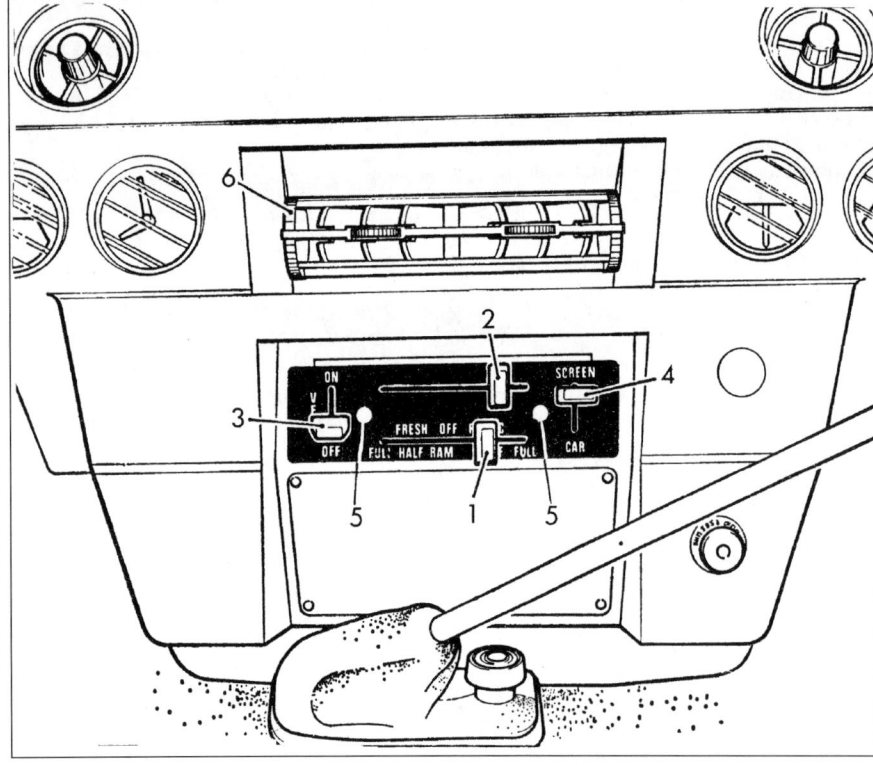

Fig. 10.31 Heater panel/console removal (Sec 29)

1 Main air control	3 Vent control	5 Plate securing screws
2 Temperature control	4 Screen/car control	6 Centre face level louvre

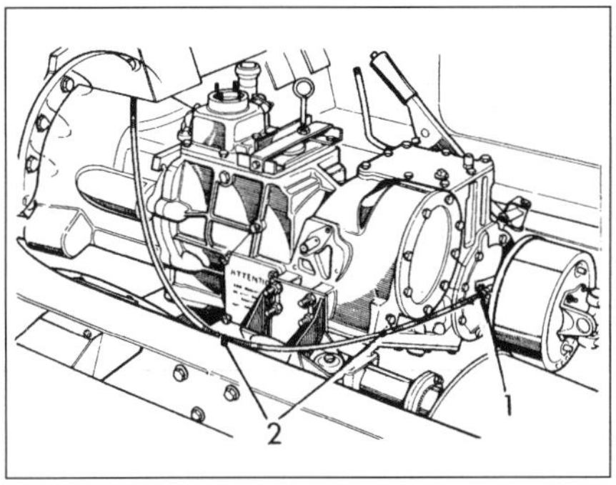

Fig. 10.32 Speedometer cable location at gearbox (Sec 31)

1 Cable retainer and nut 2 Cable clips

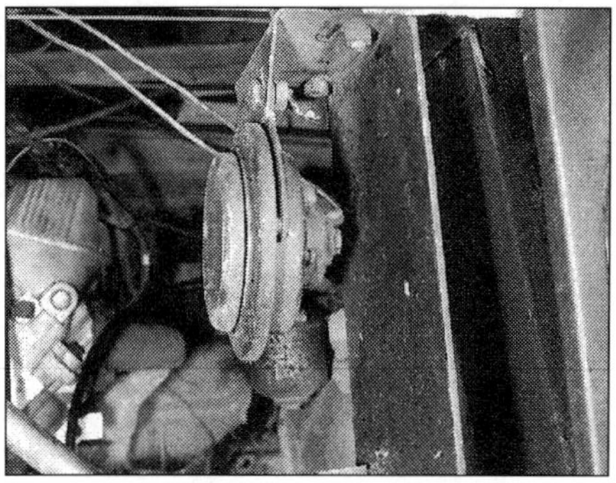

32.3 Left-hand horn location

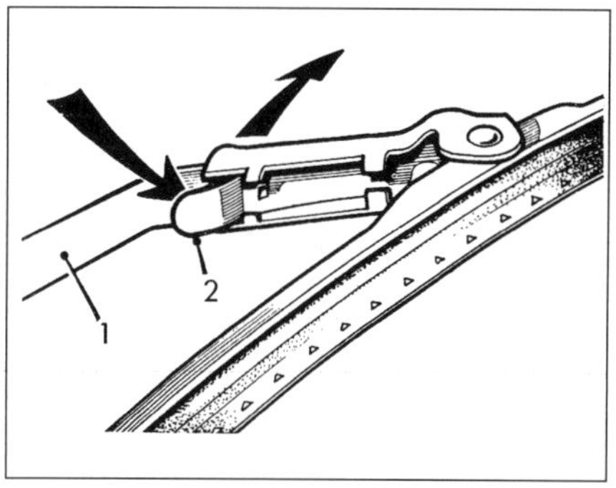

Fig. 10.33 Wiper blade removal (Sec 33)

1 Arm 2 Clip

31 Speedometer cable - removal and refitting

1 Disconnect the battery earth lead. Remove the rear of the instrument binnacle by pressing in on the rear lower edge to free it from the mounting clips.

2 Undo the knurled collar and free the cable from the speedometer angle drive.

3 From underneath the vehicle at the rear of the gearbox remove the cable retainer and nut.

4 Pull the cable from the speedo drive housing.

5 Release the cable retaining clips from the rear of the gearbox and the chassis side-member.

6 Withdraw the cable and grommet through the bulkhead.

7 Refit the cable from the top, as it is easier to feed it downwards.

8 Reconnect the ends of the cable and secure it with the clips.

9 Refit the rear of the instrument binnacle and reconnect the battery earth lead.

32 Horns - removal and refitting

1 Disconnect the battery.
2 Remove the radiator grille.
3 Undo the two nuts and bolts securing the horn to its mounting bracket. One horn is fitted to either side of the grille opening (photo).
4 Withdraw the horn, disconnecting the wiring.
5 Identify the horn if it is to be renewed. An identification letter is stamped on the front outer rim. The high note horn has a letter 'H', the low note 'L'.
6 Refitting is the reverse of the removal procedure.

33 Windscreen and tailgate wiper arms and blades - removal and refitting

Wiper blade

1 Pull the wiper away from the windscreen.
2 Lift up the spring clip and withdraw the blade from the arm.
3 Refitting is the reverse of the removal procedure.

Wiper arm

4 Prise the retaining clip on the wiper arm boss away from the shoulder of the splined spindle.
5 Pull the wiper arm off the spindle.
6 To refit the wiper arm, first make sure the wiper motor is in the 'off' or parked position.
7 Push the boss of the wiper arm onto the spindle so that the wiper arm is correctly aligned.
8 Push the boss home so that the spring clip engages behind the shoulder of the spindle.

34 Windscreen wiper motor and drive assembly - removal and refitting

1 Remove both wiper arms as described in Section 33.
2 Remove the locknuts and washers from the wiper spindles.
3 Remove the rubber grommets from the spindle bases.
4 Remove the bonnet and front decker panel as described in Chapters 12 and 13 respectively.

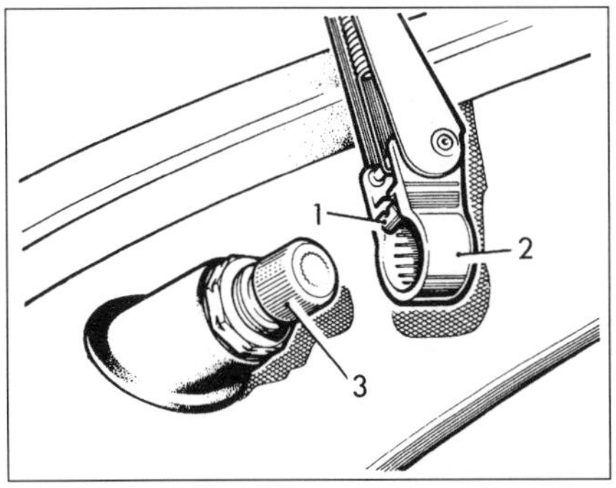

Fig. 10.34 Wiper arm removal (Sec 33)

1 Retaining clip 3 Splined spindle
2 Wiper arm boss

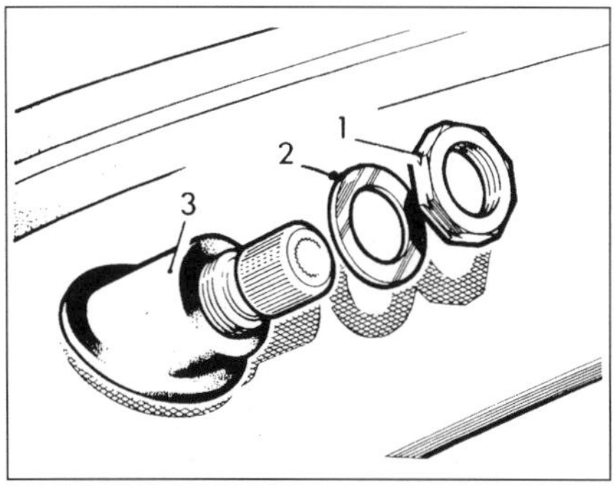

Fig. 10.35 Wiper spindle assembly (Sec 34)

1 Locknut 3 Grommet
2 Washer

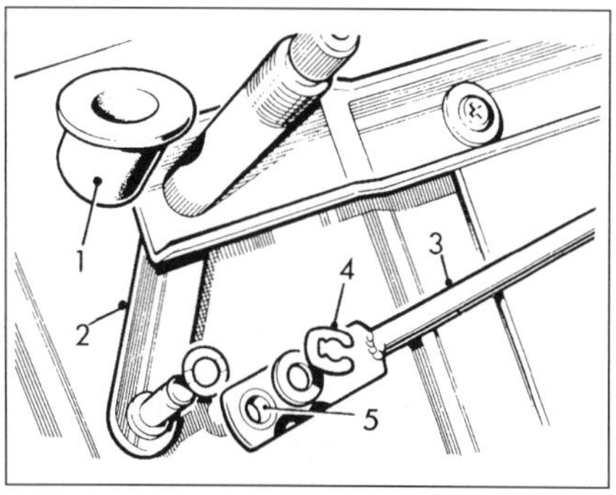

Fig. 10.36 Spindle and linkage assembly (Sec 34)

1 Grommet 4 Circlip
2 Spindle link arm 5 Bush
3 Main link arm

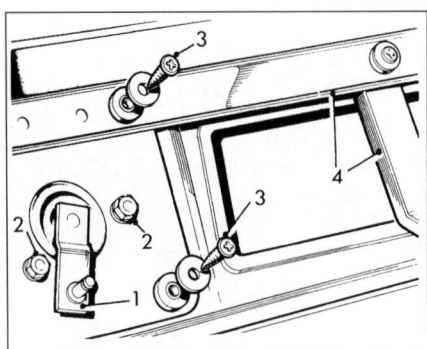

Fig. 10.37 Wiper motor and linkage mounting (Sec 34)

1 Wiper motor crank
2 Wiper motor mounting bolts
3 Linkage mounting screws
4 Linkage assembly

5 Prise off the spring clips and separate the main link arms from the spindle link arms.

6 Prise off the spring clips and separate the main link arms from the wiper motor crank. Note which way the bushes fit.

7 Remove the inner wiper spindle grommets.

8 Undo the screws which secure the wiper motor and linkage to the bulkhead.

9 From underneath the dashboard above the steering column withdraw the wiper motor. Disconnect the electrical plug-in connector (photo).

10 Refitting is the reverse of the removal procedure. Remember that the shorter link fits on the driver's side.

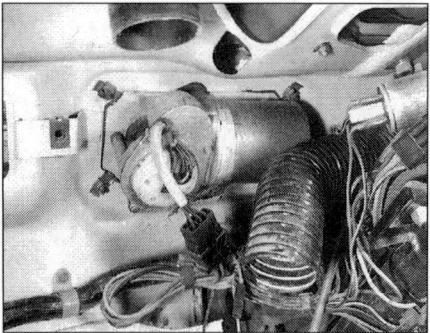

34.9 Disconnect the wiper motor plug-in connector

35 Windscreen wiper motor - overhaul

1 Remove the wiper motor as described in Section 34.

2 Remove the three bolts which secure the motor to its mounting plate.

3 Withdraw the motor crank through the grommet to separate the motor from the mounting plate.

4 Mark the gearbox cover adjacent to the arrowhead on the limit switch cover.

5 Undo the screws that retain the gearbox cover and lift it off.

6 Make sure that the end of the wiper motor shaft is free from burrs, then withdraw it and extract the dished washer.

7 Remove the thrust screw, or thrust screw and locknut, from the side of the wiper body.

8 Remove the through-bolts and slowly withdraw the cover and armature. The

brushes will drop clear of the commutator, but do not allow them to become contaminated with grease from the worm gear.

9 Pull the armature out of the cover.

10 Undo the three screws that retain the brush assembly.

11 Lift and slide the limit switch sideways, to release it from the spring clip.

12 The brush assembly and limit switch can now be lifted away together.

13 Examine the various components for wear and renew as necessary.

14 Commence the reassembly procedure by sliding the limit switch in position and securing it with the clip.

15 Refit the brush assembly and secure it with the three screws.

16 Lubricate the cover bearing and soak the cover bearing felt washer with Shell Turbo 41 oil.

17 Refit the armature to the cover, lubricate the self-aligning bearing with Shell Turbo 41 oil, then insert the armature shaft through the bearing whilst restraining the brushes. Take care when inserting the armature shaft to prevent the brushes from becoming contaminated with grease.

18 Position the cover against the gearbox casing so that the datum lines are correctly aligned.

19 Insert the cover through-bolts and tighten them.

20 Refit the thrust screw, or the thrust screw and locknut, and then check the armature endfloat.

21 On types with an adjustable thrust screw, loosen the locknut and screw the adjustment screw inwards until resistance is felt. Turn the screw back by a quarter of a turn and tighten the locknut.

22 On types with a non-adjustable thrust screw, push the armature towards the cover and place a feeler gauge between the armature shaft and thrust screw. The endfloat at this point should be within the limits given in the Specifications. Where the endfloat is insufficient, the only solution is to place a packing washer under the head of the thrust screw. If the endfloat is excessive, then have metal machined from under the head of the thrust screw.

23 Lubricate the final gear bushes with Shell Turbo 41 oil and apply Ragosine Listate grease to the final gear cam.

24 Fit the dished washer with its concave surface facing the final drive gear then insert the shaft.

25 Pack the area around the worm and final gear with Ragosine Listate grease.

26 Reposition the gearbox cover and fit the rubber seal.

27 The wiper motor can now be refitted to the mounting plate by reversing the removal procedure.

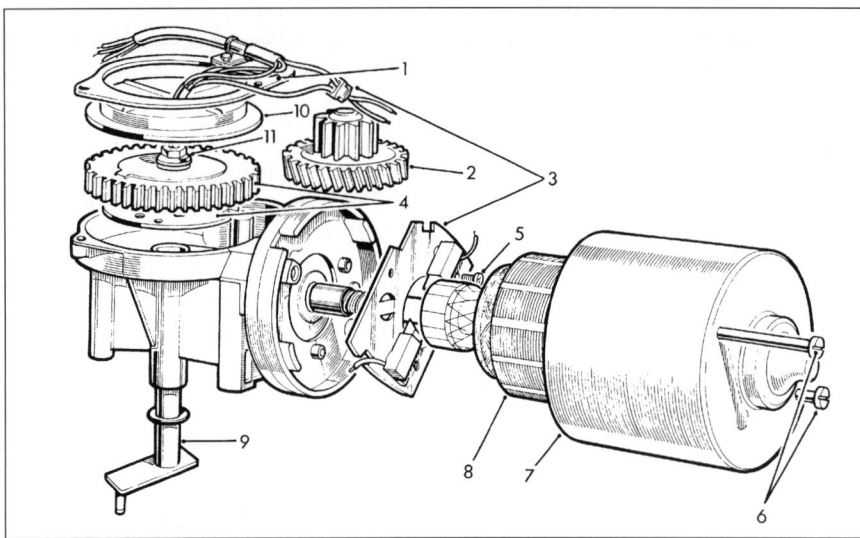

Fig. 10.38 Windscreen wiper motor – exploded view (Sec 35)

1 Gearbox cover
2 Intermediate gear wheel
3 Wiring – to brush assembly
4 Gear wheel and driving plate
5 Brush assembly retaining screws
6 Through-bolts
7 Yoke
8 Armature
9 Wiper motor crank
10 Limit switch
11 Locknut

36 Tailgate wiper motor and drive assembly - removal and refitting

Note: *Two different wiper systems have been fitted. On early models the wiper motor is located behind the right-hand rear quarter trim panel and is secured to the body by a two-bolt mounting. On later models the wiper motor is located high up behind the left-hand rear quarter panel. This motor is retained to the body by a split bracket with a bolt and captive nut.*

1 Remove the appropriate quarter panel.
2 Pull the rear headlining away in order to reach the wiper wheelbox.
3 Remove the wiper arm complete as described in Section 33.
4 Remove the nut and spacer from the wiper spindle.
5 Disconnect the wiper rack tube clips from the body.
6 Disconnect the wiring plug connector at the wiper motor.
7 Remove the wiper motor retaining bolt(s) and support the unit.
8 Remove the wiper motor, withdrawing the rack tube and wheelbox with it as one assembly.
9 The wheelbox and end tube assembly can be removed by slackening the two bolts and nuts which retain it. Then slide it off the end.
10 The tube can be slid off the rack by undoing the nut at the wheelbox.
11 Refitting is the reverse procedure. Ensure that the wheelbox is correctly aligned on the rack before tightening the nuts.

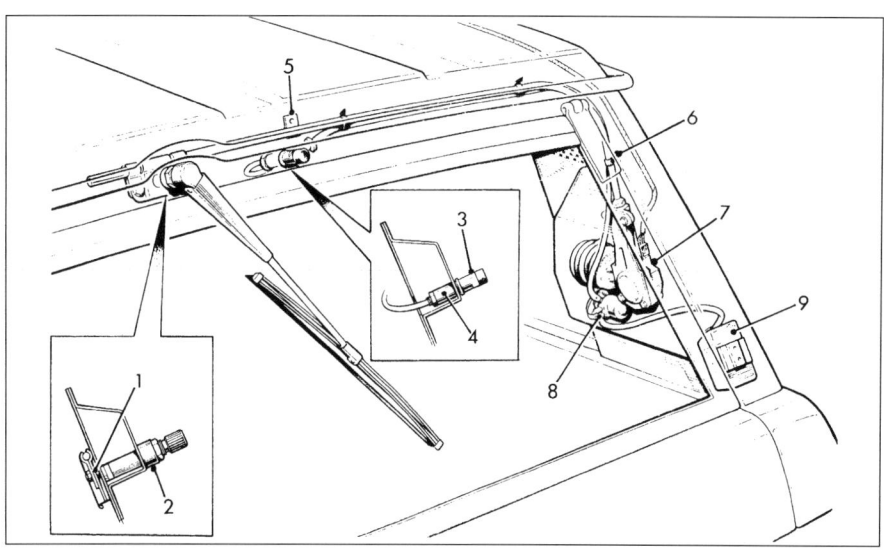

Fig. 10.39 Tailgate wiper/washer layout (early type) (Sec 36)

1 *Wiper wheelbox*	4 *Sleeve*	7 *Wiper motor*
2 *Nut and spacer*	5 *Wiper rack clip*	8 *Washer motor*
3 *Washer jet*	6 *Wiper rack*	9 *Washer reservoir*

37 Headlamp wiper motor and drive racks - removal and refitting

1 Unplug the wiring connector from the headlamp wiper motor, which is located on the right-hand inner front wing.
2 Undo the rack tube collar nuts at the motor.
3 Support the wiper motor, undo the two nuts and remove the clamp.
4 The wiper motor is now free.
5 With the help of an assistant to gently rotate the wiper blades, free the wiper racks from the wheelboxes.
6 Withdraw the motor and racks from the flexible rack tubes.
7 Do not move the wiper blades on the headlamps, or refitting is made more difficult.

8 Refitting is the reverse of the removal procedure. When refitted, the headlamp wiper blades must be aligned with the centre frame when the rack has been fully engaged.

38 Headlamp wiper arm and blade - removal and refitting

Note: *The headlamp wiper arm and blade are serviced as one unit.*

1 Using only finger pressure to prevent the wiper arm from rotating, undo the centre screw.
2 Ease the centre frame away from the headlamp. The wiper arm and blades can then be withdrawn.
3 Refitting is the reverse of the removal procedure. Ensure that the arm is aligned with the centre frame.

39 Tailgate and headlamp wiper motors - overhaul

Brush renewal

1 Unscrew the through-bolts and remove the yoke and armature assembly. Keep the yoke in a clean area, away from any metallic dust or swarf.
2 Note the position and colour coding of the wiring and disconnect it at the switch.
3 Withdraw the brush and plate assembly.
4 Remove the brushes from the insulating plate.
5 Renew the brushes if they are worn below the specified minimum.
6 Reassembly is the reverse of the dismantling procedure.

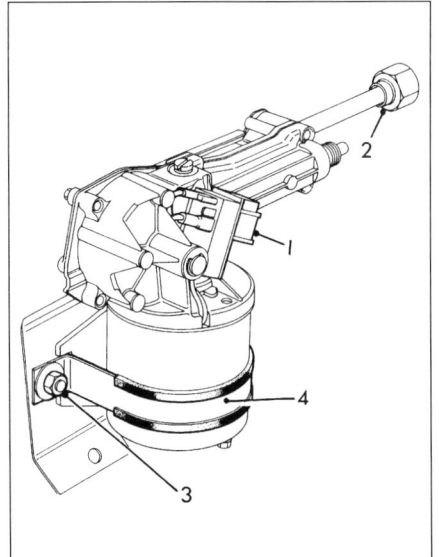

Fig. 10.40 Headlamp wiper motor mounting (Sec 37)

1 *Electrical connector socket*
2 *Rack tube retaining nut*
3 *Mounting nut*
4 *Clamp*

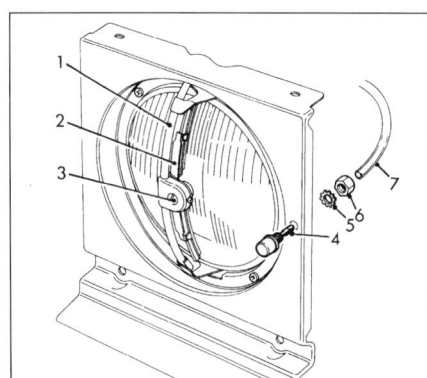

Fig. 10.41 Headlamp wiper/washer jet assembly (Sec 38)

1 *Centre frame*	5 *Washer*
2 *Wiper blade*	6 *Nut*
3 *Centre screw*	7 *Tubing*
4 *Jet*	

Dismantling

7 Unscrew the gearbox cover screws and remove the cover.

Headlamp motor

8 Remove the circlip and washer in order to disconnect the racks from the driving gear. Then remove the racks from the motor.

Tailgate motor

9 Remove the circlip and washer which secure the connecting rod to the crankpin.

10 Lift away the connecting rod. Note the flat washer fitted beneath it.

11 Lift out the cable rack with the cross-head and outer casing threaded connector.

All motors

12 Remove the circlip and washer which retain the drivegear and shaft.

13 Make sure the gear shaft is free from burrs and withdraw it. Do not lose the dished washer underneath it.

14 Pull downwards and outwards to release the switch retaining clip.

Inspection

15 The resistance between adjacent commutator segments should be 0.34 to 0.41 ohms.

16 Carefully examine the internal wiring for signs of breaks or chafing which would lead to a short-circuit. Insulate or renew any damaged wiring.

17 Measure the value of the field resistance which should be between 12.8 and 14 ohms.

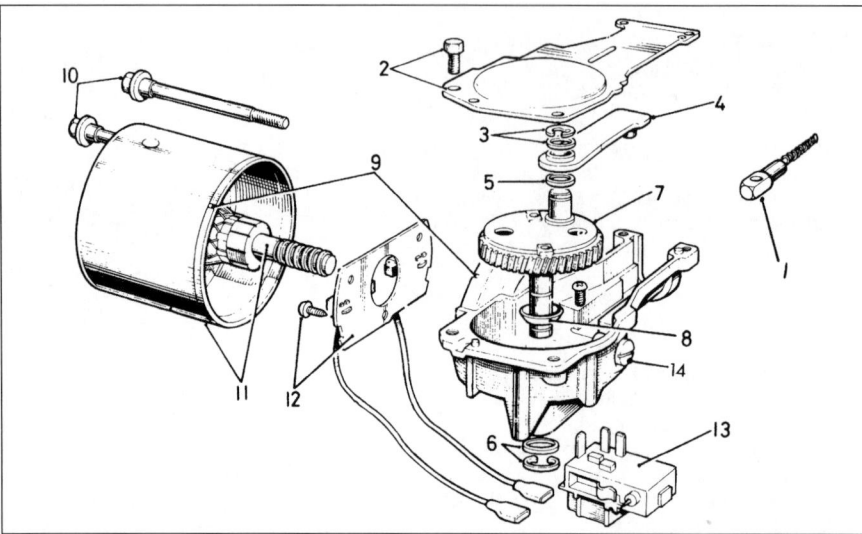

Fig. 10.42 Tailgate and headlamp wiper motors (exploded view) (Sec 39)

1 Drive cable	5 Washer	10 Retaining bolts
2 Cover and securing bolt	6 Circlip and washer	11 Yoke and armature
3 Circlip and washer	7 Drive gear	12 Brush gear
4 Connecting rod	8 Dished washer	13 Limit switch
	9 Yoke and gearbox	14 Adjuster screw

If a lower reading than this is obtained it is likely that there is a short-circuit and a new field coil should be fitted.

18 Renew the gearbox gear if the teeth are damaged, chipped or worn.

Reassembly

19 Reassembly is a straightforward reversal of the dismantling sequence, but ensure the following items are lubricated:

(a) *Immerse the self-aligning armature bearing in engine oil for 24 hours before assembly*

(b) *Oil the armature bearings with engine oil*

(c) *Soak the felt lubricator in the gearbox with engine oil*

(d) *Grease generously the wormwheel bearings, crosshead, guide channel, connecting rod, crankpin, worm cable rack and wheelboxes and the final gear shaft, using Ragosine Listate grease*

20 To set the armature endfloat, hold the yoke vertically with the adjuster screw uppermost. Screw the adjuster in very carefully until resistance is just felt. Then unscrew it one quarter of a turn.

---

40 Windscreen, tailgate and headlamp washer systems - description, component removal and refitting

Description

1 On early vehicles, only the windscreen washer is standard equipment. The reservoir is located in the engine compartment on the left-hand side. Where a tailgate washer is fitted, this may have a separate reservoir and pump mounted behind the right-hand rear quarter panel, or it may be fed via a second cap on the screen washer reservoir.

2 On later models a combined reservoir unit is mounted on the right-hand side of the engine compartment. Separate caps and pump units are fitted for the windscreen, tailgate and (if applicable) headlamp washers.

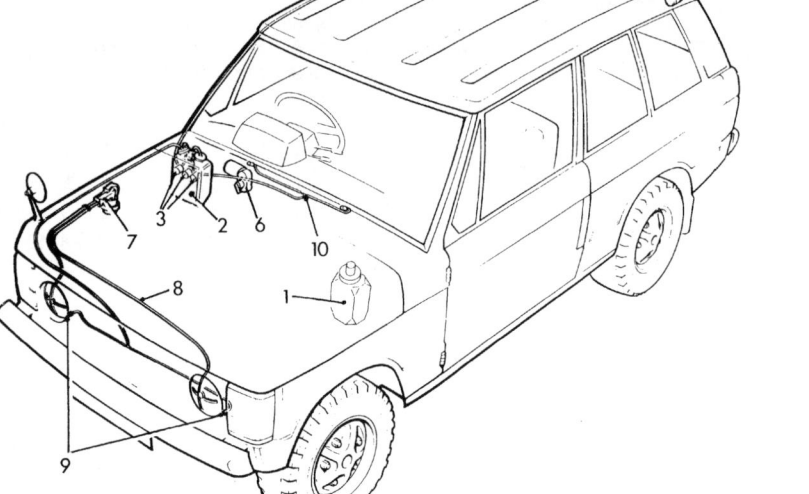

Fig. 10.43 Wiper/washer system layout (Sec 40)

1 Early windscreen washer reservoir	4 Tailgate wiper motor – later type	7 Headlamp wiper motor
2 Later type reservoir for all washers	5 Tailgate washer jet	8 Headlamp wiper rack/tube
3 3 separate pump units	6 Windscreen wiper motor	9 Headlamp washer jets
		10 Windscreen washer jets

40.3 The early type of windscreen washer reservoir with integral pump

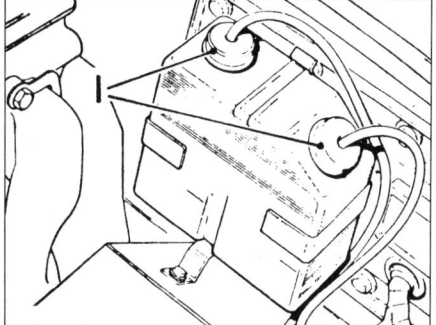

Fig. 10.44 Early type of combined screen and tailgate reservoir (Sec 40)

1 Reservoir caps

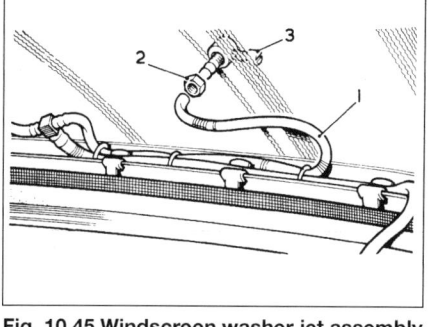

Fig. 10.45 Windscreen washer jet assembly (Sec 40)

1 Tubing   2 Retaining nut   3 Jet

Removal and refitting

Reservoirs

3 On models with pump integral with the cap, disconnect the electrical leads and hose connections (photo).
4 Remove the cap(s) from the reservoir.
5 Lift the reservoir out of its bracket.
6 Refitting is the reverse of the removal procedure.

Pump units

7 The early type pump unit is removed with the reservoir cap.
8 The later type pump units are each secured by two mounting screws. Remove the screws and disconnect the tubes to remove the pump.
9 Refitting is the reverse of the removal procedure.

Windscreen washer jet

10 Pull off the pipe, then remove the nut and anti-vibration washer, taking care that they are not dropped.
11 Remove the jet and sealing washer.
12 Refitting is the reverse of this procedure. If necessary, rotate the jet using a screwdriver to direct the jet satisfactorily.

Tailgate washer jet and sleeve

13 Pull the rear headlining away sufficiently to reach the jet securing nut and tube connection.

14 Disconnect the washer jet feed tubing from the pump, and drain any water in the tubing to avoid damaging the trim.
15 Hold the jet sleeve and undo the retaining nut.
16 Remove the nut and distance piece.
17 Detach the jet and remove it from the sleeve.
18 Disconnect the tubing from the jet.
19 Withdraw the sleeve and washer from the tubing.
20 Withdraw the tubing inside the vehicle and remove the distance piece, seal and nut.
21 Refitting is the reverse of the removal procedure.

Headlamp washer jet

22 Remove the headlamp and holder from the body for access.
23 Disconnect the washer tubing from the jet.
24 Undo the nut and lockwasher and withdraw the jet from the front of the headlamp assembly.
25 Refitting is the reverse of the removal procedure.

41 Split charging facility - description

1 The purpose of having a split charging facility is to provide a separate source of

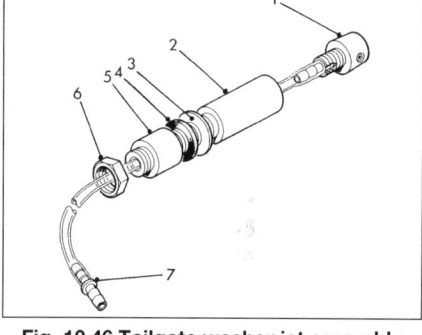

Fig. 10.46 Tailgate washer jet assembly (Sec 40)

1 Jet	*5 Distance piece*
2 Sleeve	*6 Nut*
3 Washer	*7 Tubing end*
4 Seal	

12 volt current to power auxiliary equipment, without discharging the vehicle main battery.
2 To achieve this a diode is located between the alternator and auxiliary terminal bracket. A second battery can then be fitted and connected to the terminals. This will be charged by the alternator when the engine is running.
3 When this battery is being used without the engine in use, it is effectively isolated from the main vehicle electrical system.
4 A wiring diagram for this facility is provided at the end of the Chapter.

Fault Finding overleaf

Fault finding - electrical system

Starter motor fails to turn engine

- [ ] Battery discharged
- [ ] Battery defective internally
- [ ] Battery terminal leads loose or earth lead not securely attached to body
- [ ] Loose or broken connections in starter motor circuit
- [ ] Starter motor switch or solenoid faulty
- [ ] Starter brushes badly worn or brush wire loose
- [ ] Commutator dirty, worn or burnt
- [ ] Starter motor armature faulty
- [ ] Field coils earthed

Starter motor turns engine very slowly

- [ ] Battery in discharged condition
- [ ] Starter brushes badly worn sticking. or brush wires loose
- [ ] Loose wires in starter motor circuit

Starter motor operates without turning engine

- [ ] Pinion or flywheel gear teeth broken or worn

Starter motor noisy or excessively rough engagement

- [ ] Pinion or flywheel gear teeth broken or worn
- [ ] Starter motor retaining bolts loose

Battery will not hold charge for more than a few days

- [ ] Battery defective internally
- [ ] Electrolyte level too low or electrolyte too weak due to leakage
- [ ] Plate separators no longer fully effective
- [ ] Battery plates severely sulphated
- [ ] Fanbelt slipping
- [ ] Battery terminal connections loose or corroded
- [ ] Alternator regulator unit not working correctly
- [ ] Short in lighting circuit causing continual battery drain

No charge light fails to go out, battery runs flat in a few days

- [ ] Fanbelt loose and slipping, or broken
- [ ] Brushes worn, sticking, broken or dirty
- [ ] Brush springs weak or broken
- [ ] Slip rings dirty, greasy, worn or burnt
- [ ] Alternator stator coils burnt, open, or shorted

Horn operates all the time

- [ ] Horn switch either earthed or stuck
- [ ] Horn cable to horn switch earthed

Horn fails to operate

- [ ] Blown fuse
- [ ] Cable or cable connection loose, broken or disconnected
- [ ] Horn has an internal fault

Horn emits intermittent or unsatisfactory noise

- [ ] Cable connections loose or horn needs adjusting

Lights do not come on

- [ ] If engine not running, battery discharged
- [ ] Light bulb filament burnt out or bulbs broken
- [ ] Wire connections loose, disconnected or broken
- [ ] Light switch shorting or otherwise faulty

Lights come on but fade out

- [ ] If engine not running, battery discharged

Lights work erratically - flashing on and off especially over bumps

- [ ] Battery terminals or earth connection loose
- [ ] Lights not earthing properly
- [ ] Contacts in light switch faulty

Wiper motor fails to work

- [ ] Blown fuse
- [ ] Wire connections loose, disconnected or broken
- [ ] Brushes badly worn
- [ ] Armature worn or faulty
- [ ] Field coils faulty

Wiper motor works very slowly and takes excessive current

- [ ] Commutator dirty, greasy, or burnt
- [ ] Armature bearings dirty or unaligned
- [ ] Armature badly worn or faulty

Wiper motor works slowly and takes little current

- [ ] Brushes badly worn
- [ ] Commutator dirty, greasy, or burnt
- [ ] Armature badly worn or faulty

Wiper motor works but wiper blades remain static

- [ ] Wiper motor gearbox parts badly worn

Chapter 11 Suspension and steering

For modifications, and information applicable to later models, see Supplement at end of manual

Contents

Degrees of difficulty

Easy, suitable for novice with little experience	**Fairly easy,** suitable for beginner with some experience	**Fairly difficult,** suitable for competent DIY mechanic	**Difficult,** suitable for experienced DIY mechanic	**Very difficult,** suitable for expert DIY or professional

Specifications

Suspension

Front suspension	Coil springs with hydraulic telescopic shock absorbers. Axle located by radius arms and Panhard rod
Rear suspension	Coil springs with hydraulic telescopic shock absorbers and Boge self-levelling ride unit. Axle located by radius arms
Balljoint grease type/specification	Multi-purpose lithium based grease to NLGI 2

Steering

Type:		
Early models (up to 1980)	Burman, recirculating ball, manual	
Optional from 1973	Power-assisted steering	
Standard fitting, 1980 models	Adwest Varamatic, power-assisted steering	
	Manual	**Power-assisted**
Number of turns, lock to lock	4 3/4 (early), 5 1/2 (later)	3 1/2
Ratio - straight-ahead	18.2 : 1	17.5 : 1
Steering wheel diameter	17 in (431.8 mm)	
Manual steering box lubricant type/specification	Hypoid gear oil, viscosity SAE 90EP to API GL4	
Power steering fluid type	Dexron IID type ATF	

Steering/front suspension geometry

Front wheel alignment	0.046 to 0.094 (1.2 to 2.4 mm) toe-out
Camber angle - unladen*	0°
Castor angle - unladen*	3°
Swivel pin inclination - unladen*	7°

*Unladen condition means vehicle empty but with water, oil and 5 gallons (25 litres) of fuel. Rock the vehicle up and down at the front to allow it to assume a static position

Wheels

Type	Pressed steel - enamelled
Fixing type	5 stud
Size	600 JK x 16

Tyres

Size	205 x 16 (tubed) radial ply	
Tyre pressures (cold) in lbf/in^2 (kgf/cm^2)	**Front**	**Rear**
Normal use - on and off-road		
All speeds - loads up to 500 lb (226 kg)	25 (1.8)	25 (1.8)
All speeds - loads above 500 lb (226 kg)	25 (1.8)	35 (2.5)
Off-road - emergency soft use:		
Max speed 40 mph - up to 500 lb (226 kg) loads	15 (1.1)	15 (1.1)
Max speed 40 mph (64 kph) - loads in excess of 500 lbs		
(226 kg)	15 (1.1)	25 (1.8)

Power steering pump drivebelt tension

Power steering pump drivebelt tension . . . . 0.4 to 0.5 in (11 to 14 mm) deflection at midpoint of longest run

Torque wrench settings

	lbf ft	kgf m
Balljoint nuts	30	4
Steering joint pinch-bolt	25	3.5
Drop arm nut	125	17.9
Steering box cover bolts (manual)	17	2.3
Track rod clamp bolts	10	1.4
Steering wheel nut	28	3.8
Power steering pulley bolt	12	1.6
Self-levelling unit balljoint collar	50	7.0
Rear radius arm - stem end	90	12.4
Self-levelling unit-to-axle bracket	130	17.9
Power steering sector cover bolts	16 to 20	2.2 to 2.8
Steering pump valve cap	30 to 35	4.0 to 4.9

1 General description

The live front and rear axles are both located by radius arms and in addition the front axle has the benefit of a Panhard rod. The heavy duty coil springs and double-acting hydraulic shock absorbers allow the suspension amazingly long vertical travel which enables it to give a smooth ride even over rough terrain. At the rear there is also a centrally mounted A-frame incorporating a Boge gas-filled self levelling unit. This keeps the vehicle level when it is fully loaded or when towing a trailer.

Steering in early models was by a manual recirculating ball, worm and nut system with a safety steering column. Power steering by Adwest was not available until 1973, but even then only as an optional extra. From the advent of the 1980 model, in September 1979, power steering has been fitted as standard equipment. The power steering pump is belt-driven from the crankshaft.

In manual steering models the system is aided by a steering damper unit fitted between the track rod mounting bracket and the front axle casing.

The steering and suspension is relatively maintenance-free apart from (on models so equipped) periodically checking the tension of the steering pump drivebelt, power steering fluid level and renewing the power steering fluid reservoir filter. It is advisable to periodically inspect the entire steering and suspension systems.

2 Panhard rod - removal and refitting

1 The Panhard rod locates the front axle laterally. It is mounted onto a bracket on the axle casing at the left-hand end and onto a bracket below the right-hand chassis side-member.
2 Undo the nuts on the end of both bolts.
3 Drive out the left-hand bolt and then the right-hand bolt and remove the rod.
4 Bushes are fitted to both ends of the Panhard rod and these can be pressed out and renewed if required.
5 Ensure if new bushes are fitted that they are centrally located in the eyes at the end of the rod.
6 Refitting is the reverse of the removal procedure. Make sure the rod is fitted with the cranked section in front of the front axle differential case, facing forwards (Fig. 11.1).

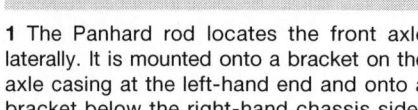
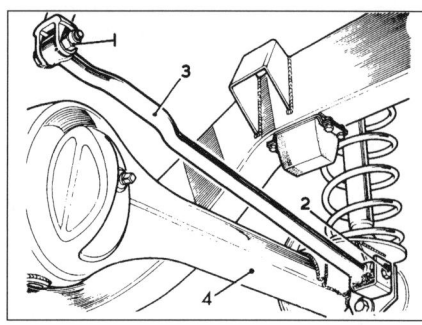

Fig. 11.1 Panhard rod assembly (Sec 2)

1 Chassis mounting 3 Panhard rod
2 Axle mounting   4 Front axle

3 Front radius arm - removal and refitting

1 Jack up the front of the vehicle on the appropriate side and support it securely with axle stands under the front axle. Chock the other wheels.
2 Remove the roadwheel on the side being worked on.
3 Undo the nut and remove the washer and bush on the rear end of the radius arm (Fig. 11.2).

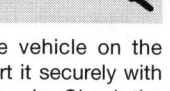
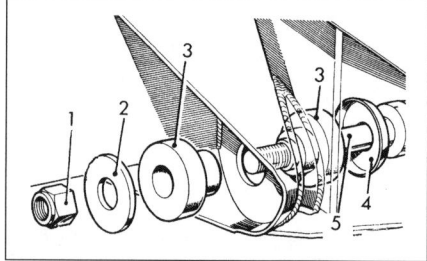

Fig. 11.2 Front radius arm – rear mounting (exploded view) (Sec 3)

1 Nut   4 Cup washer
2 Washer   5 Radius arm
3 Bushes

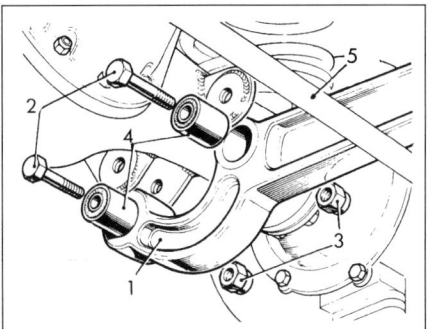

Fig. 11.3 Front radius arm – axle mounting (exploded view) (Sec 3)

1 Radius arm   4 Bushes
2 Bolts   5 Track rod
3 Nuts

4 Disconnect the track rod balljoint, at the side of the vehicle being worked on, as described in Section 14.
5 Undo the nuts on the ends of both bolts which retain the radius arm to the axle mounting bracket.
6 Drive out the bolts while supporting the arm.
7 Lower the radius arm from the axle and withdraw the rear end from the chassis mounting bracket.
8 The bushes can be pressed out of the front end of the radius arm and renewed if required. When fitting new bushes, ensure that they are centrally located in the eyes.
9 Renew the bushes on the rear end of the radius arm also if required.
10 Refitting is the reverse of the removal procedure. Tighten the track rod balljoint nut to the specified torque.

4 Front shock absorber - removal, refitting and bush renewal

1 Jack up the front of the vehicle and support it on axle stands under the chassis side-members and under the front axle. Chock the roadwheels and open the bonnet.
2 Remove the roadwheel on the appropriate side.

4.7 On some models the shock absorber is retained by a single locknut

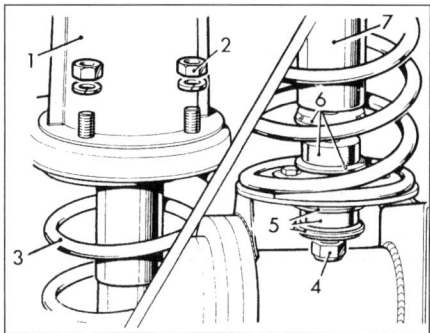

Fig. 11.4 Front shock absorber mountings (Sec 4)

1 Shock absorber   5 Washer, bush and
   carrier   seating washer
2 Retaining nut   6 Washer, bush and
3 Coil spring   cup washer
4 Shock absorber   7 Shock absorber
   lower retaining nut

3 Undo the shock absorber lower retaining nut, and remove the washer, seating bush and seating washer.
4 Undo and remove the nuts which retain the shock absorber carrier to the coil spring housing. Note that on the left-hand side unit there are two petrol pipe brackets beneath the inner nuts (photo).
5 The shock absorber and carrier can now be lifted straight out and removed from the car.
6 Recover the sealing washer, rubber bush and cup washer from the lower mounting point inside the coil spring.
7 Undo the locknut(s) and retaining nut from the top end of the shock absorber and withdraw the shock absorber from the carrier (photo).
8 Recover the cup washer, flat washer and top bush from the carrier, and withdraw the lower bush, flat washer and cup washer from the top of the shock absorber.
9 Check the condition of all four bushes, which are the same top and bottom. Renew them if necessary.
10 Refitting is the reverse of the removal procedure. Make sure that the washers and bushes are fitted in the correct order.

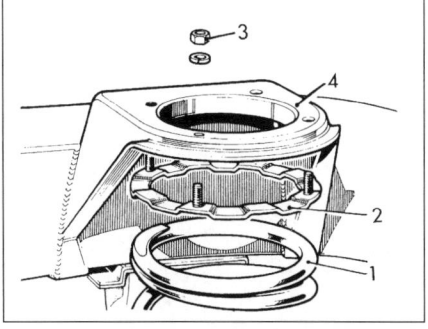

Fig. 11.5 Front coil spring upper mounting point (Sec 5)

1 Coil spring   3 Retainer nut
2 Carrier retainer   4 Mounting bracket

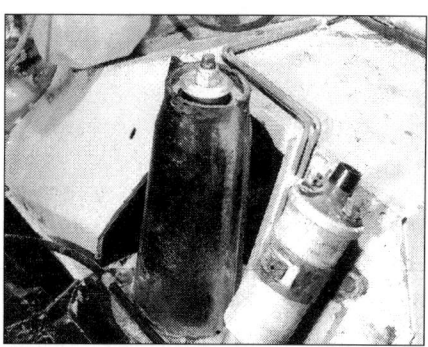

4.4 Front shock absorber carrier location – left-hand side

5 Front coil spring - removal and refitting

1 Remove the front shock absorber as described in Section 4, then refit the nuts to the carrier mounting bolts.
2 With the chassis securely supported, carefully lower the jack beneath the front axle just enough to allow the coil spring to be withdrawn. Take care that the brake hoses are not stretched during this operation.
3 Refitting is the reverse of the removal procedure. Ensure the bottom of the coil spring is securely seated on its mounting plate, and that the top locates correctly under the carrier retainer as the axle is raised (Fig. 11.5).

6 Bump stops - removal and refitting

1 Bump stops are fitted front and rear beneath the chassis side members directly above the axle location. At the front they are each retained by two bolts and nuts front and rear of the bump stop, while at the rear each bump stop is retained by single bolt and nut front and rear.
2 Jack up the vehicle and remove the

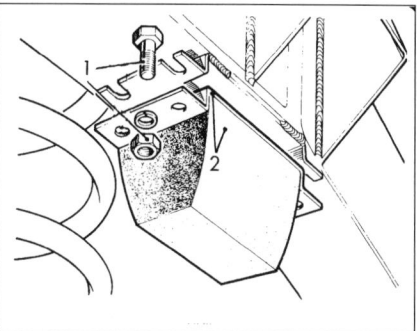

Fig. 11.6 Front bump stop (Sec 6)

1 Nut and bolt
2 Bump stop rubber and carrier

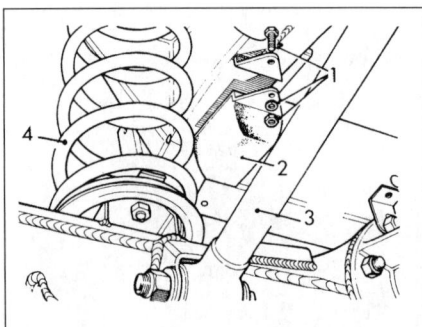

Fig. 11.7 Rear bump stop and suspension layout (Sec 6)

1 Nut, bolt and washer
2 Sump stop
3 Radius arm
4 Coil spring

appropriate roadwheel. Support the chassis side-member with axle stands, leaving the weight of the axle unsupported.

3 Undo the bump stop nuts and bolts and remove it.

4 Fit a new bump stop in position and secure it with the appropriate nuts and bolts.

5 Refit the roadwheel and lower the vehicle to the ground.

7 Rear shock absorber - removal, refitting and bush renewal

1 The rear shock absorbers are fitted to opposite sides of the rear axle casing, but the procedure is the same for both sides (photo).

2 Jack up the rear of the vehicle on the appropriate side.

3 Remove the roadwheel.

4 Place a jack under the rear axle to support it.

5 Undo the lower mounting nut and withdraw the cup washer, bush and flat washer (photo).

6 Undo the split pin in the upper mounting and remove the flat washer (Fig. 11.8).

7 Draw the shock absorber off the upper mounting. The inner bush may stay behind on the mounting pin. Pull it off as well for inspection.

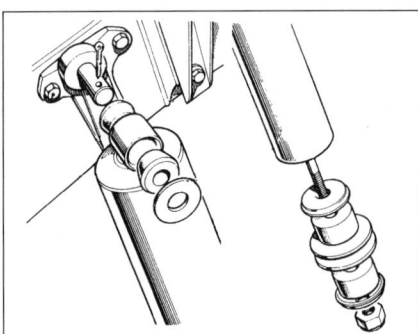

Fig. 11.8 Rear shock absorber assembly (Sec 7)

7.1 The right-hand rear shock absorber is located to the rear of the axle

8 Lift the shock absorber up to withdraw the bottom mounting from the axle bracket. Then withdraw the complete unit from the vehicle.

9 Recover the lower washer and bush if they become separated as the unit is removed.

10 inspect the rubber bushes and renew them if cracked, damaged, worn or hard.

11 Refitting is the reverse of the removal procedure.

8 Rear coil springs - removal and refitting

1 This operation is designed to replace both coil springs together. The operation has to be performed on the complete axle. It is not advisable to attempt one end of the axle only, due to the difficult angles that would be involved and uneven pressure on the springs and axle.

2 Jack up the rear of the vehicle and support it securely on axle stands under the chassis. Place a support jack under the axle casing.

3 Remove the rear roadwheels and chock the front ones.

4 Disconnect the lower ends of both rear shock absorbers as described in Section 7.

5 Undo the retaining nut on the A-frame pivot balljoint. Use a balljoint separator to free it from the axle mounting bracket.

6 Lower the axle carefully, avoiding strain on the rear flexible brake hose above the axle.

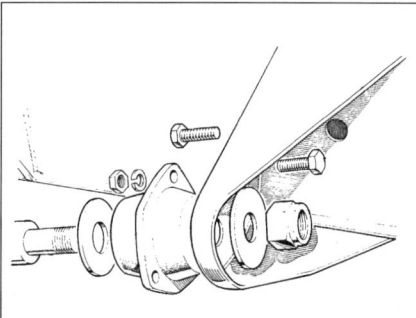

Fig. 11.9 Rear radius arm-to-bracket mounting. Either nuts and washers or self-locking nuts may be found (Sec 9)

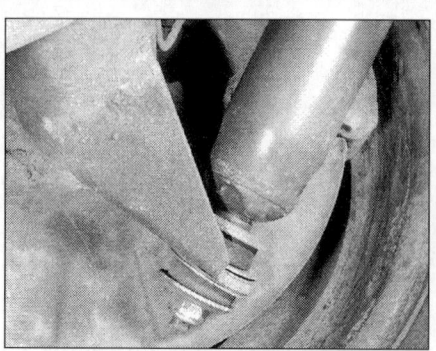

7.5 The rear shock absorber lower mounting point, showing its bushes

The axle only needs to be lowered far enough to free the coil springs from their upper seats.

7 Undo the bolts and withdraw the lower spring retainer plates from the axle casing brackets.

8 Lift the coil springs away from the lower seats.

9 Remove the seats.

10 Refitting is the reverse procedure. Tighten the A-frame pivot balljoint retaining nut to its specified torque.

9 Rear radius arm - removal and refitting

1 Jack up the rear of the vehicle on the appropriate side. Place axle stands beneath the rear axle.

2 Remove the roadwheel, and chock the other wheels.

3 On the left-hand side, where the shock absorber is mounted in front of the rear axle casing, undo the lower mounting from the shock absorber and free it from the mounting bracket.

4 Undo the radius arm front end retaining nut and remove the washer.

5 Undo the rear retaining nut and withdraw the bolt.

6 Lower the radius arm from the rear bracket on the underneath of the axle casing and withdraw it from the front mounting bush. If difficulty is experienced, unbolt the front bush from the bracket and remove it with the arm (Fig. 11.9).

7 If the front bush is to be removed or renewed, undo the three nuts and bolts which retain it to the forward mounting point on the chassis side-member.

8 If the rear mounting bush is worn, press it out of the arm and fit a new bush, ensuring that it is located centrally.

9 If the front mounting bush has been removed, refit it to the front end of the radius arm before fitting the assembly to the vehicle. Do not tighten the front locknut.

10 Refit the front end of the radius arm and secure it lightly with one bolt, then refit and secure the rear end with its bolt and nut.

10.4 The self-levelling unit

11 Fit the remaining front bolts and nuts and tighten them.
12 If applicable, refit the left-hand shock absorber lower mounting.
13 Refit the roadwheel and lower the vehicle.
14 Finally tighten the front locknut on the radius arm to its specified torque.

10 Self-levelling unit - removal and refitting

⚠️ *Warning: Do not attempt to strip the self-levelling unit in any way as it contains pressurised gas.*

1 Jack up the rear of the vehicle and support the chassis side-member using axle stands.
2 Take the weight of the rear axle on a jack.
3 Remove the two bolts and nuts that retain the lower ends of the A-frame suspension unit to the lower pivot.
4 Pull up the rubber boot on the bottom of the self-levelling unit (photo).
5 Unscrew the lower balljoint from the levelling unit pushrod.
6 Undo the four mounting bolts and nuts which retain the upper mounting bracket to the chassis crossmember.
7 The self-levelling unit and upper mounting bracket may be withdrawn from the vehicle as one unit.
8 To separate the self-levelling unit from the upper mounting bracket, pull back the rubber boot and use a spanner to unscrew the upper balljoint from the unit.
9 Undo the retaining clips and remove the rubber boots at either end of the unit.
10 Refitting is the reverse procedure. Tighten all mounting bolts to their specified torque. Use thread sealant on both balljoint threads before screwing them into the self-levelling unit.

11 Self-levelling unit balljoints - renewal

1 Remove the self-levelling unit as described in Section 10.

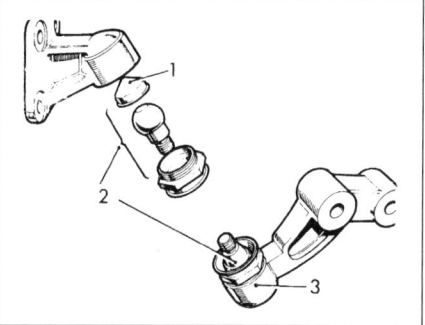

Fig. 11.10 Levelling unit balljoint components (Sec 11)

1 Joint seat 3 Levelling unit
2 Joint assembly

2 Each balljoint is retained by a hexagonal collar. Undo the collar and withdraw the balljoint and seat.
3 Clean the balljoints and inspect them. If obviously worn they must be renewed. If however they are serviceable they may be re-used.
4 Clean out the balljoint seat and housing (Fig. 11.10).
5 Fit the seat and ensure that it is square.
6 Fill the housing with multi-purpose lithium-based grease.
7 Refit the balljoint and screw in the collar. Tighten the collar to the specified torque.
8 Wipe off any excess grease.
9 Refit the self-levelling unit as described in Section 10.

12 Upper suspension A-frame and pivot - removal and refitting

1 Jack up and support the rear of the vehicle securely. Place axle stands beneath the chassis side-members.
2 Take the weight of the axle on another jack.
3 Disconnect the lower end of the self-levelling unit from its bottom balljoint, as described in Section 10.
4 Remove the split pin and nut which retain the rear A-frame pivot balljoint to the mounting bracket on top of the rear axle casing.
5 Lower the axle on the jack and if necessary use a balljoint extractor wedge to separate the rear pivot from the bracket. Do not strain the brake hoses.
6 Undo the nuts and bolts which retain the front ends of the A-frame arms. Withdraw the bolts.
7 Lift the whole A-frame and pivot assembly from beneath the vehicle.
8 The pivot assembly and A-frame arms may now be separated. Undo the two nuts and bolts and withdraw them.
9 If required, the bushes in the front ends of the arms may be renewed. Press out the old bushes and fit new ones, ensuring that they are centrally located in the mountings.

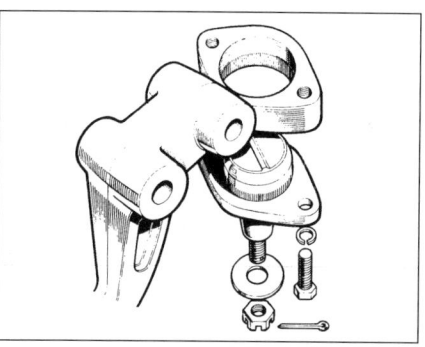

Fig. 11.11 Pivot bracket balljoint unit. Do not dismantle the joint (Sec 13)

10 Refitting is the reverse procedure. Do not fully tighten all mounting bolts and nuts until the complete assembly is refitted. Then tighten all nuts and bolts to their specified torques.

13 A-frame rear pivot balljoint - renewal

1 Follow the procedure given in the previous Section from paragraphs 1 to 5.
2 Undo the two bolts and nuts which retain the pivot bracket between the A-frame arms.
3 Remove the pivot bracket complete with A-frame pivot balljoint and the lower self-levelling unit balljoint.
4 Undo the two nuts and bolts and remove the rear pivot balljoint from the pivot bracket.
5 The balljoint assembly must not be dismantled. A replacement comes as a complete unit, pre-packed with grease.
6 Press the new balljoint into the pivot bracket.
7 Refit the two bolts and nuts.
8 Refit the pivot bracket complete assembly to the A-frame arms, fit the rear pivot balljoint to the axle bracket and reconnect the lower ends of the self-levelling unit.
9 Tighten all nuts and bolts to their specified torques.

14 Steering track rod and drag link balljoints - removal and refitting

1 Excessive play in the steering or a tendency for the vehicle to wander or follow undulations in the road surface, often indicates wear in the track rod or drag link balljoints. This may be confirmed by observing the balljoints from beneath the front of the vehicle whilst an assistant turns the steering wheel rapidly half a turn either way from the straight-ahead position. If there is any visible side-to-side movement of the balljoint it must be removed.
2 Slacken the front wheel nuts, jack up the front of the vehicle and support it on heavy duty stands. Chock the rear wheels and remove the appropriate front wheel.

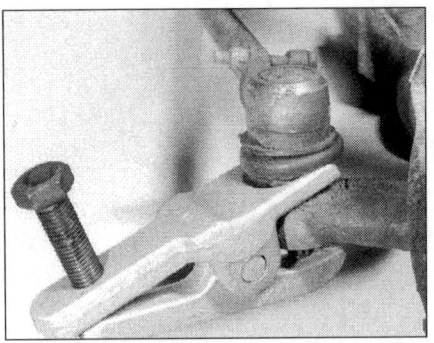

14.4 Balljoint separation method using a universal separator

3 Withdraw the split pin and undo and remove the castellated nut that secures the balljoint to the steering arm.
4 Using a universal balljoint separator, detach the balljoint shaft from the steering arm (photo).

 If a balljoint separator is not available, refit the castellated nut one or two turns to protect the threads and using a medium hammer, strike the end of the steering arm with a few sharp blows until the joint separates from the steering arm. Remove the castellated nut and lift off the balljoint.

5 Make a note of the number of threads on the shank of the balljoint protruding from the track rod or drag link. Slacken the nut and bolt that secure the clamp to the track rod or drag link and unscrew the balljoint. Note that the balljoints on one end of the track rod and drag link have left-hand threads.
6 Refitting the balljoint is the reverse sequence to removal, bearing in mind the following points:
(a) *Refit the balljoint to the track rod or drag link with the same number of threads exposed as were previously noted. Adjust the link-to-balljoint so that it is dimensionally as shown in Fig. 11.12*
(b) *Referring to Fig. 11.13, tap each balljoint in the direction indicated so that the angular plane of each ball-pin is identical*
(c) *Tighten the securing castellated nut to the torque setting given in the Specifications and secure with a new split pin*
(d) *Turn the steering from lock to lock and*

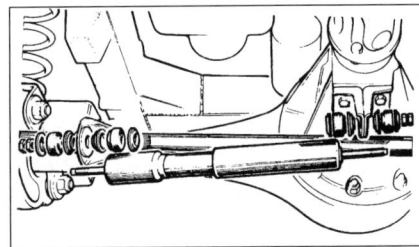

Fig. 11.14 The steering damper and mounting bushes (Sec 15)

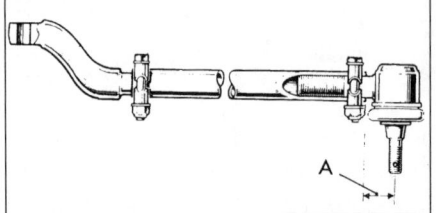

Fig. 11.12 Set the balljoint-to-drag link dimension (A) to 1.25 in (28.5 mm) (Sec 14)

check that full travel is available. If necessary adjust the lock stops as given in Section 33
(e) *If a balljoint on the track-rod has been renewed or its position altered, the front wheel alignment must be reset. Refer to Section 32*

15 Track rod and steering damper - removal and refitting

1 Jack up the front of the vehicle and use axle stands to support the chassis.
2 Chock the rear and remove the front roadwheels.
3 Undo the steering damper locknuts and retaining nuts at the track rod and axle casing mounting brackets and withdraw the outer bush assembly from either end (Fig. 11.14).
4 Compress the damper and withdraw one end from one of the mounting brackets. Then lift the unit away.
5 Refit the outer bush assemblies to each end temporarily.
6 Undo the balljoints on either end of the track rod as described in the previous Section.
7 Lift the complete track rod away.
8 Refit the track rod and tighten the balljoint retaining nuts to the specified torque. Make sure that both balljoint pins are in the same plane.
9 Check the front wheel alignment as described in Section 32.

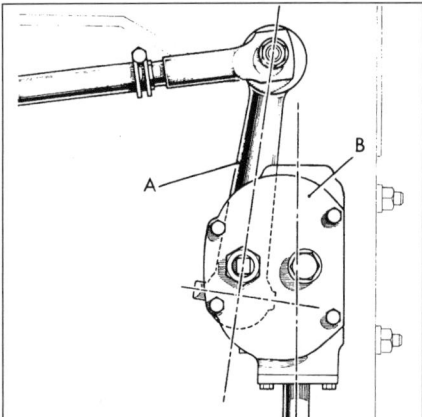

Fig. 11.15 Drop arm fitting position (A) to steering box (B) (Sec 17)

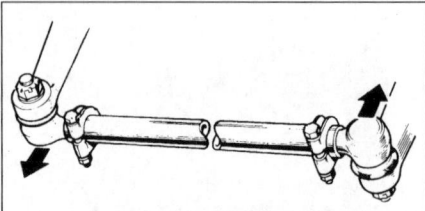

Fig. 11.13 Tap the balljoints in the direction of the arrows (Sec 14)

10 Before refitting the steering damper, check the condition of the bushes at either end. If they are cracked, hard or if a lot of play was noticed on removal, they should be renewed.
11 Fit new bushes, if necessary, to the inner ends of the damper mounting bolts.
12 Refit the damper to the track rod and axle casing brackets.
13 Fit new bushes and washers to the outer ends of the mounting bolts and refit the retaining and locknuts.

16 Drag link - removal and refitting

1 The drag link is the rod that connects the front steering arm on the passenger side front wheel swivel to the drop arm from the steering box.
2 Jack up the front of the vehicle and support it securely on axle stands.
3 Remove the front passengers side roadwheel. Chock the rear wheels.
4 Disconnect the drag link balljoint from the front steering arm and the drag link from the drop arm balljoint as described in Section 14.
5 Remove the drag link from beneath the vehicle.
6 Refitting is the reverse procedure. Check that the balljoint pins are in the same plane before tightening them.

17 Drop arm - removal and refitting

1 Jack up the front of the vehicle and support it securely on axle stands.
2 Separate the drag link from the drop arm balljoint as directed in Section 14.
3 Undo the drop arm retaining nut and washer.
4 Use a puller to remove the drop arm from the splines on the steering box rocker shaft.
5 To refit the drop arm set the steering box so that it is in the mid-travel position (Fig. 11.15).
6 Refit the drop arm and align the blank splines.
7 Refit the drop arm retaining washer and nut and tighten the nut to the specified torque.
8 Refit the drag link to the drop arm and tighten the retaining nut to the specified torque. Refit the split pin.

18 Manual steering box - removal and refitting

1 Jack up the front of the vehicle and support it securely using axle stands.
2 Chock the rear wheels and remove the driver's side front roadwheel.
3 Open the bonnet and prop it securely.
4 Disconnect the drag link from the steering drop arm as described in the previous Section.
5 Slacken the pinch-bolt on the steering column lower universal joint (photo).
6 Undo the four bolts and nuts which retain the steering box to the chassis sidemember (photo).
7 Lift the steering box and drop arm off its mounting bolts and disengage the splined shaft from the bottom universal joint on the steering column as it is lifted away.
8 To refit the steering box, align the steering wheel centre spoke so that it points downwards to the 6 o'clock position.
9 Set the steering box in the mid-travel position.
10 Offer up the steering box to its mounting position and engage the shaft splined end into the lower universal joint.
11 Refit the steering box mounting bolts and nuts.
12 Check the steering wheel and drop arm alignment, then tighten the pinch-bolt on the universal joint to the specified torque.
13 Tighten the steering box mounting nuts and bolts.
14 Refit the drag link to the drop arm and tighten it to the specified torque.

18.5 The steering column lower (A) and upper (B) joint clamps

19 Manual steering box - overhaul

1 Remove the drop arm using a puller as described in Section 17.
2 Remove the top cover and gasket and drain the oil into a suitable container.
3 Lift out the rocker shaft.
4 Slide the roller from the main nut assembly.
5 Undo the four bolts and remove the wormshaft end cover, seal plate and shims.
6 Withdraw the wormshaft by rotating it, and lift out the main nut. Recover any balls that fall out.
7 Remove the bearing balls and outer bearing race.
8 Tap the casing to free the inner bearing race.
9 Examine the rocker shaft and bush for wear and if necessary, remove the washer and oil seal. Press the bush out of the steering box

18.6 The steering box-to-chassis retaining nuts (arrowed)

and fit a new one. A new oil seal should be fitted as a matter of course.
10 Examine the inner track on the main nut and the wormshaft for signs of pitting or scaling and renew them where necessary. Check the upper and lower ball-bearings and races for similar signs of wear.
11 If the wormshaft, main nut and bearings are all worn, the most sensible solution is to obtain a replacement steering box assembly.
12 Fit a new oil seal, lipped side first, to the wormshaft end cover.
13 To reassemble the steering box first fit the wormshaft inner bearing race to the casing and coat it with grease. Refit the ten ballbearings (smaller size) to the race.
14 Reassemble the main nut bearing assembly. There should be 28 larger ballbearings. Hold them in place with grease.
15 Position the main nut assembly in the casing and refit the wormshaft. Ensure that it fits correctly into the bearing race.
16 Grease the outer race and fit thirteen of

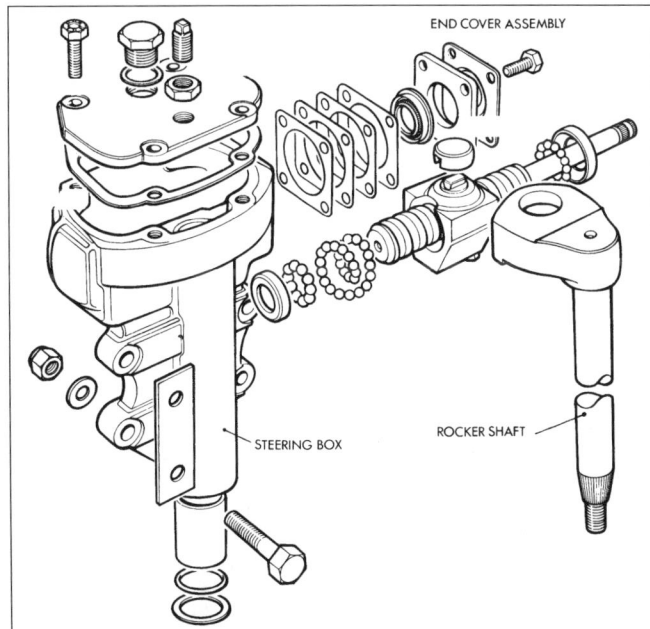

Fig. 11.16 The manual steering box assembly as fitted to earlier models (non-tie-bar type) (Sec 19)

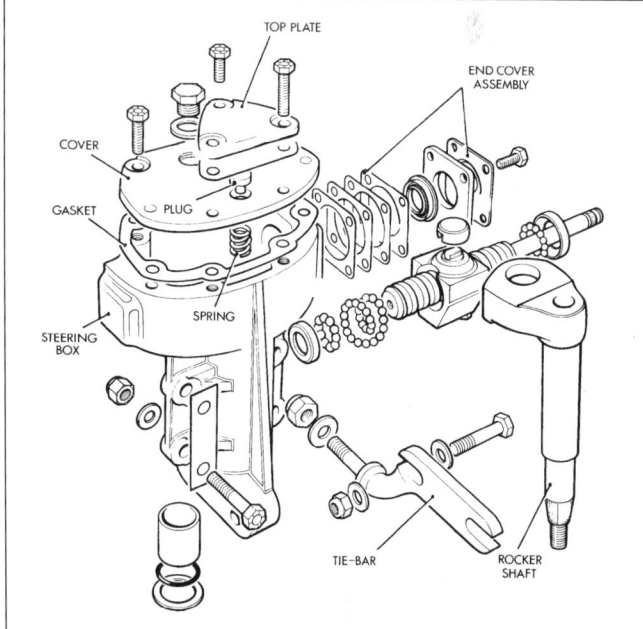

Fig. 11.17 The manual steering box fitted to later models (tie-bar type) (Sec 19)

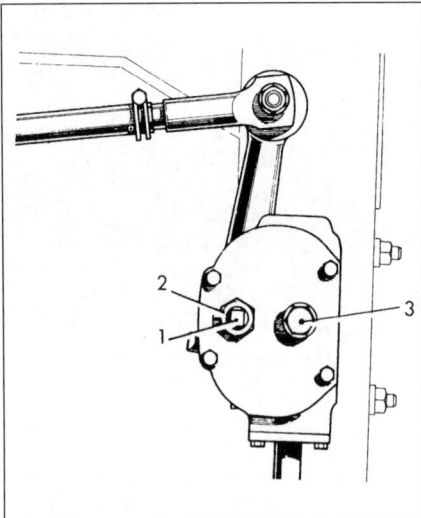

Fig. 11.18 Early steering box adjuster screw (1), locknut (2) and filler plugs (3) (Sec 20)

the smaller ball-bearings to it. Then offer it up to the wormshaft.

17 Refit the shims, seal and end cover and check that there is no wormshaft endfloat. It should be loaded by 0.003 in (0.07 mm) but should still be free to rotate. Remove or fit shims as necessary.

18 Tighten the end cover bolts to the specified torque and check that the shaft is still free to rotate.

19 Fit a new O-ring to the rocker shaft bore.

20 Rotate the wormshaft so that the main nut is central, then refit the roller.

21 Insert the rocker shaft and engage it in the roller.

22 Smear both mating faces of the top cover and steering box with non-hardening sealant, fit a new gasket and refit the top cover.

23 Set the adjusting screw with the gear in the straight-ahead driving position so that the gear is free to rotate with no backlash between the worm and rocker shafts. There should be no endfloat on the rocker shaft either.

24 On later models fitted with the tie-bar type steering box, see Fig. 11.17, the rocker shaft is spring-loaded and the spring pressure (and thus the endfloat) is adjusted by means of selected shims which are fitted between the cover and its top plate. When the plate retaining bolts are tightened, the shims fitted affect the plate-to-spring (and its top plug) pressure, which in turn bears onto the sector end.

25 Refit the drop arm and secure it as described in Section 17.

26 Refit the steering box to the vehicle as described in the previous Section.

27 Fill the steering box with the correct type of oil to the bottom of the filler plug hole in the cover plate. Refit the filler plug.

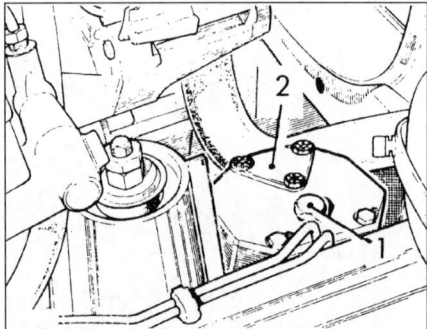

Fig. 11.19 Later model manual steering box showing the filler plug (1) and top plate (2) (Sec 20)

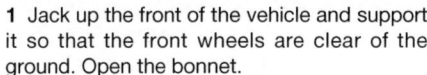

20 Manual steering box - adjustment

1 Jack up the front of the vehicle and support it so that the front wheels are clear of the ground. Open the bonnet.

2 Set the roadwheels straight-ahead.

3 On early models fitted with the non-tie-bar steering box, slacken the adjuster locknut on the steering box and then loosen the adjuster screw (Fig. 11.18). Retighten the adjuster screw until there is a minimum amount of backlash between the steering shaft and drop arm. Return the screw in this set position and retighten the locknut. Recheck the backlash.

4 On later models the adjustment is made in inserting or extracting shims as required under the top plate. The plate is secured to the steering box cover by three bolts (Fig. 11.19). Shims are available in a number of thicknesses as required.

5 On completion of adjustment on both steering box types, turn the steering from lock to lock to check for tight spots or excessive slack. If satisfactory, lower the vehicle and close the bonnet to complete.

21 Power steering system - special precautions

1 Whenever any repairs are carried out or the flexible hoses are disconnected in the power steering system, particular care must be taken to ensure utmost cleanliness.

2 Clean components externally before detaching and when disconnected, seal off to prevent the entry of dirt. If any part of the system contains metallic sediment it must be completely checked, the defective part(s) renewed, and the system thoroughly cleaned out.

3 Do not start the engine until the power steering reservoir has been refilled to the correct level as given in Section 31. If the power steering pump is operated dry it will be damaged.

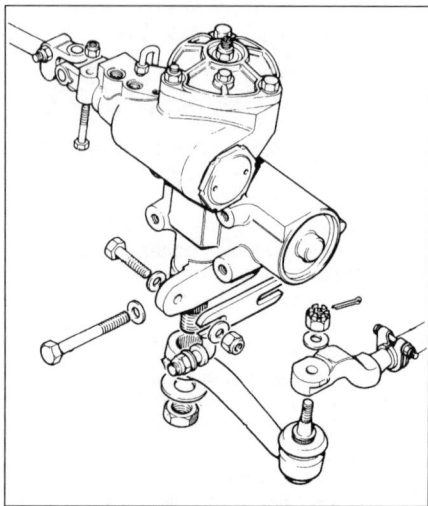

Fig. 11.20 The power steering box and associated fittings (Sec 22)

22 Power steering box - removal and refitting

1 Jack up the front of the vehicle and support it securely on axle stands, and chock the rear wheels. Open the bonnet and prop it securely.

2 Separate the drag link from the drop arm balljoint as described in Section 16.

3 Remove the drop arm as described in Section 17.

4 Slacken the pinch-bolt on the lower universal joint on the steering column.

5 Remove the filler cap from the power steering fluid reservoir. Disconnect the fluid pipes from the pump and drain the fluid into a suitable container.

6 Disconnect the fluid pipes from the steering box and drain any fluid left in them. Refit the power steering reservoir cap. Cover the ends of the hoses to protect them.

7 The fluid which has been drained off must not be re-used under any circumstances.

8 Slacken the nut which secures the tie-bar to the chassis.

9 Undo the nuts which secure the steering box to the tie-bar and move the tie-bar to one side.

10 Remove the power steering box mounting bolts from the chassis sidemember.

11 Remove the steering box disengaging the splined end of the wormshaft from the universal joint.

12 Refitting is basically the reverse procedure to removal. Note that the steering wheel must be set in the straight-ahead position before the universal joint is reconnected to the steering box.

13 Fill and bleed the power steering system as described in Section 31.

14 Check the system and if necessary adjust the steering box as described in Section 24.

15 Test the system for leaks. With the engine running, hold the steering wheel on full lock in

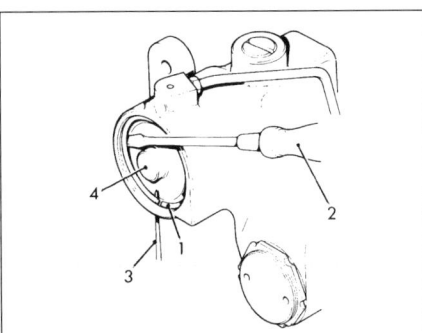

Fig. 11.21 Remove the retaining ring (1) with screwdriver (2) and pin punch (3) to extract the end cover (4) (Sec 23)

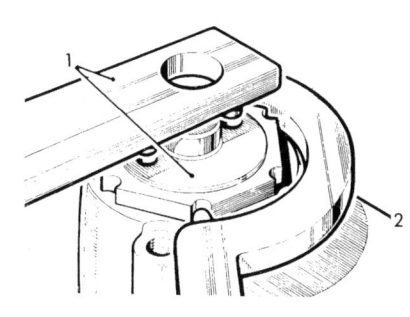

Fig. 11. 22 Peg spanner (1) and C-spanner (2) used to remove worm adjuster screw and locknut (Sec 23)

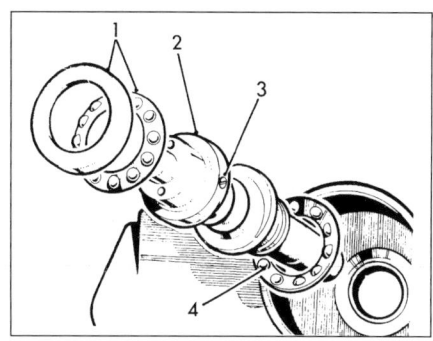

Fig. 11.23 Valve and worm unit components (Sec 23)

1 *Bearing cup and caged ball-bearing*
2 *Valve and worm assembly*
3 *Trim screw – do not disturb it!*
4 *Inner bearing assembly*

both directions. Do not exceed this pressure for more than 30 seconds in any one minute or the oil will overheat and seal damage will result.

16 Check the front wheel alignment as described in Section 32.

23 Power steering box - overhaul

Before starting to dismantle the power steering box, it should be noted that you will need the use of a suitable spring balance and special Rover tool number 801016 with which to check and make adjustments during assembly. Other special tools required include a C-spanner (606600), peg spanner (606601), circlip pliers and some suitable tube drifts. You will also need to have a modicum of general engineering practice to access the setting adjustments on reassembly. With this in mind you should first read through the various overhaul procedures before starting, to fully assess what is required.

If all the tools required are available and you decide to carry out the overhaul, prepare a suitable work area and as the components are dismantled, lay them out in order of appearance for inspection and reassembly.

1 Remove the steering box as described in Section 22.

2 Mark the steering drop arm position on the splined shaft and then withdraw it, using a puller if necessary.

3 Turn the retaining ring to locate one end approximately 0.5 in (12 mm) from the extractor hole in the housing. Insert a suitable pin punch or similar through the hole to lift the retaining ring clear of its groove and then prise it free using a screwdriver as shown in Fig. 11.21.

4 Turn to right lock (RHD) or left lock (LHD) to enable the piston to be pushed out of the end cover.

5 Loosen the rack pad adjuster retaining screw (in the side of the boss) and unscrew and remove the pad adjuster.

6 Unscrew and remove the sector shaft locknut.

7 Remove the sector shaft cover retaining bolts and then tighten the sector shaft adjuster to remove the cover. Withdraw the sector shaft

8 The piston is extracted by inserting a 1/2 in UNC bolt into the tapped hole in the end face of the piston, and pulling it out.

9 Using a C-spanner, unscrew and remove the worm adjusting screw locknut.

10 You now need the use of Rover special tool number 606601 which is a peg spanner for removing the worm adjuster screw (Fig. 11.22). It should not be too difficult to fabricate a suitable spanner for this purpose if the Rover tool is not available.

11 To free the bearing, tap the splined end of the shaft using a soft hide mallet and withdraw the bearing.

12 Extract the valve and worm, but **do not** loosen or remove the trim screw (Fig. 11.23) or the calibration will be upset.

13 Extract the inner bearing and shims.

14 Prise free and remove the circlip and then withdraw the oil seal from the sector shaft housing.

15 Remove the input shaft circlip and oil seals in a similar manner.

16 If the sector shaft bush is to be renewed, extract the old one with a suitable tube drift.

17 If the input shaft needle bearing is to be renewed, remove it from its location housing.

18 With the main assemblies dismantled, they can be cleaned and examined for signs of wear and damage.

19 Check the steering box inlet tube seat, piston bore and feed pipe for signs of damage, wear or score marks in the bore and seat. Renew or repair as necessary.

20 Inspect the sector shaft unit. Check for side play in the rollers and the adjuster screw retainer, which should be secured by staking to the shaft. The endfloat of the adjuster screw must not exceed 0.005 in (0.12 mm): if it does, relieve the staking, rotate the adjuster retainer to suit and then restake to secure. Inspect the sector shaft gear teeth for signs of wear or damage and also look for signs of wear caused by the bearings on the shaft. Renew as necessary.

21 Examine the valve and worm unit. If the valve rings are scratched, damaged or loose in their grooves, they must be renewed. This is a task best entrusted to your Range Rover dealer as the fitting method is critical and requires the use of special tools. Check the bearings and worm for excessive wear and renew if necessary. Check the worm-to-valve sleeve endfloat which must not exceed 0.005 in (0.12 mm). Check that there is no free movement between the worm and the input shaft. If excessive endfloat or wear exists the valve and worm assembly complete must be renewed.

22 Inspect the bearing assemblies and if worn or damaged renew them, but don t lose the shim washers.

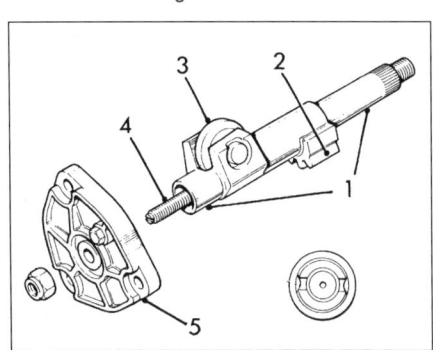

Fig. 11.24 Check the sector shaft (1), gear teeth (2), rollers (3), adjusting screw retainer (4) and end cover (5) (Sec 23)

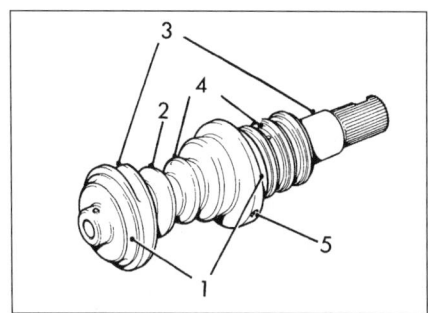

Fig. 11.25 Check the bearings (1), worm track (2) and torsion bar pins (3) for wear. Check worm-to-sleeve endfloat (4). Note the trim pin (5) (Sec 23)

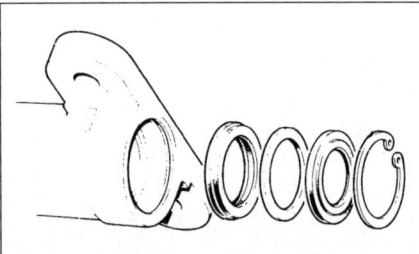

Fig. 11.26 Sector shaft seal assembly (Sec 23)

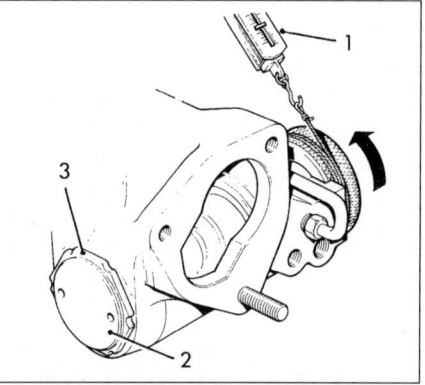

Fig. 11.27 Check the valve and worm setting using a spring balance (1). Adjust worm (2) and lock with nut (3) (Sec 23)

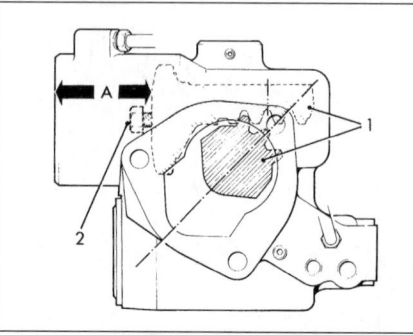

Fig. 11.28 View showing piston fitting position (A) which is about 2.5 in (65 mm) from end of bore. Note correct rack-to-sector shaft engagement position (1) and slave bolt (2) (Sec 23)

23 Examine the rack thrust pad and adjuster for wear or damage and renew if necessary.
24 Check the rack and piston, and if damaged or excessively worn, renew. A new rubber ring must be fitted to the piston. The white nylon seal should be warmed before fitment to the piston. When in position, slide the piston into the cylinder (rack tube outwards) and let it cool off.
25 If the input needle bearing is being renewed, insert the new bearing with its numbered face upwards. It must be flush with the top of the bore and just clear of the bottom of the bore.
26 All oil seals, and this includes the rubber seal at the rear of the plastic ring on the rack piston, must be renewed on reassembly. The plastic ring must also be renewed.
27 Lubricate the bearings and seals with petroleum jelly prior to fitment.
28 Start reassembly by inserting the input shaft oil seal into its housing with its lipped side inwards. When fitted, the seal backing must be flat on the bore shoulder. Locate the washer and retaining circlip to secure.
29 Refit the sector shaft seal with its wide flange inwards, followed by the washer and second seal, which has its lipped side facing outwards. Insert the circlip to secure (Fig. 11.26).
30 Where the valve and worm unit inner bearing was removed, refit together with the shims which were removed on dismantling. If the original shims cannot be fitted, insert shims of a nominal thickness of 0.030 in (0.76 mm).
31 Refit the valve and worm unit, taking special care not to damage the seal lips as it is pushed through.
32 Locate the outer bearings and cup, then locate the new worm adjuster seal ring and tighten the screw into the housing. Fit but do not tighten the locknut.
33 Tighten the worm adjuster to take up most of the endfloat. The shaft rolling resistance must now be checked and this can only be achieved using a spring balance, cord and special torque setting tool number R01016. If these tools are not available, entrust the checking and setting to your Range Rover dealer. If the tools are available, coil the cord around the torque setting tool which should be located on the shaft. and measure and record the rolling resistance by

pulling the balance and uncoiling the cord (Fig. 11.27). Rotate the adjuster to increase the recorded amount by 4 to 5 lb (1.8 to 2.2 kg) at 1.25 in (31.75 mm) radius in order to settle the bearings, then unscrew the adjuster so that the originally recorded figure is increased by 2 to 3 lb (0.9 to 1.3 kg). Tighten the locknut using the peg spanner and C-spanner to retain the setting.
34 Reassemble the piston and rack and locate the piston 2.5 in (63.5 mm) from the bore outer end (use the 1/2 in UNC slave bolt). Carefully insert the sector shaft, aligning the central gear pitch of the rack with the centre tooth of the sector shaft (Fig. 11.28). Push the sector shaft in whilst rotating the input shaft slightly to allow the roller to engage with the worm.
35 Locate the seal ring on the rack adjuster and insert the adjuster and thrust pad to the point where they touch the rack, then unscrew by a half turn. Insert the nylon pad and the grub screw but do not fully tighten it yet, simply engage it with the rack adjuster.
36 The selector shaft cover is now fitted. Locate the seal ring onto the cover and then

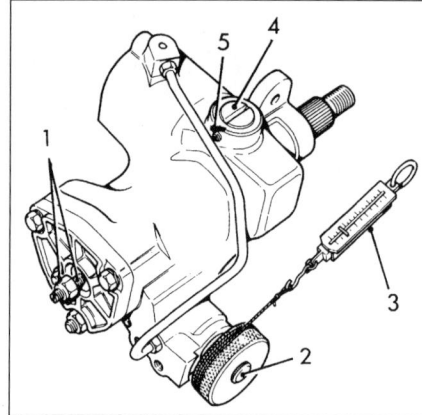

Fig. 11.29 Sector shaft adjustment (Sec 23)

1 Sector shaft adjustment screw and locknut	3 Spring balance
	4 Rack adjuster
	5 Rack adjuster grub screw
2 Worm	

screw the cover onto the sector shaft adjustment screw so that it is flush with the casing. Tap the cover fully home, and if necessary loosen the adjustment screw to enable the cover joint to be fully flush with the case. Before tightening the cover retaining bolts, turn the input shaft through a small arc to ensure that the sector roller is free. Tighten the retaining bolts to the specified torque.
37 Locate the square sectional seal into the groove in the cylinder cover, extract the slave bolt and then press the cover into the cylinder just enough to clear the retainer ring groove. The retainer ring can then be fitted and located so that one end of the ring is approximately 0.5 in (12 mm) from the extractor hole.
38 With the steering box assembled, the sector shaft adjustment must be checked and rack adjustment made. To adjust the sector shaft, centrally position the worm by turning it 1.5 rotations from either full lock position. Turn the sector shaft adjuster screw anti-clockwise to get backlash between the sector shaft and the input shaft, then turn the screw clockwise until the backlash in taken up (Fig. 11.29).
39 The input shaft maximum rolling resistance must now be measured using the spring balance, cord and torque tool R01016 previously mentioned. Locate a new locknut whilst retaining the sector shaft adjuster screw in position, but do not tighten the nut yet. Now turn the adjuster screw to provide 2 to 3 lb (0.9 to 1.3 kg) additional resistance to the maximum figure previously noted. Under no circumstances must the final torque figure exceed 16 lb (7.25 kg). When set, tighten the grub screw to set the adjuster in the selected position.
40 The final check to be made before refitting the steering box is a torque peak check. When the input shaft is turned from lock to lock, a greater torque resistance should be found equally disposed across the centre of travel. This torque resistance depends on the amount of shims fitted between the casing and bearing of the valve and worm unit. The original shim or nominal shim (paragraph 30)

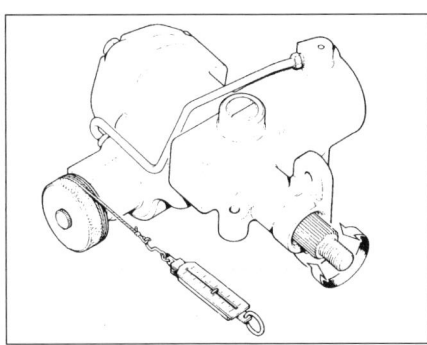

Fig. 11.30 Method of checking the torque peak (Sec 23)

should give the required torque peak but if major components have been renewed, further adjustment may be necessary.

41 To make this check, point the input shaft towards you and turn it fully anti-clockwise. Now use the previously mentioned spring balance, cord and torque tool (R01016) to check the torque figures (Fig. 11.30). If the highest torque figure readings are not in the centre of travel, adjust as follows. If the torque peak occurs before the central position, a thinner washer must be fitted between the casing and the valve and worm unit, whilst a greater torque figure after the central position necessitates fitting a thicker washer. As a guide to adjustment, a 0.003 in 10.07 mm) washer difference will move the torque peak area by about a quarter of a turn on the shaft.

24 Power steering box - backlash adjustment

1 Jack up the front of the vehicle and support it securely, with the wheels clear of the ground. Check the rear wheels.
2 Set the wheels to the straight-ahead position.
3 Rock the steering wheel to get the 'feel' of the backlash that is present. It should not be more than 0.375 in (9.5 mm) measured at the rim of the steering wheel.
4 With the help of an assistant, unlock the steering box adjuster nut and slacken off the

adjuster screw whilst still rocking the steering wheel gently.
5 Screw the adjuster in until the backlash is reduced to the correct amount (Fig. 11.31).
6 Tighten the locknut and then turn the steering wheel from lock to lock, checking for any tight spots.
7 Close the bonnet, lower the vehicle to the ground and remove the rear wheel chocks.

25 Steering wheel - removal and refitting

1 Set the steering wheel in the straight-ahead position with the spokes at 9, 3 and 6 o'clock, or on 1980 models with the centre pad lettering horizontal.
2 Remove the central motif from the three-spoke steering wheel (photo) or remove the centre safety pad from the later type of steering wheel. It is retained by a single screw underneath and at the rear of the steering wheel.
3 Undo the retaining nut and washer from the top of the steering column.
4 Remove the steering wheel with a suitable puller. **Do not** hammer on the steering wheel to remove it, or the shear pins in the steering column may be broken.
5 Refitting is the reverse of the removal procedure. Ensure that the front roadwheels are correctly set in the straight-ahead position before offering up the steering wheel, correctly aligned.
6 Tighten the retaining nut to the specified torque, and refit the central motif or centre pad.

26 Steering column - removal and refitting

1 Open the bonnet and disconnect the battery negative lead.
2 Remove the steering wheel as described in the previous Section.
3 Remove the lower facia panel below the steering column, as described in Chapter 12.

4 Disconnect the electrical multi-plug connectors beneath the dashboard for the steering column switches, noting their locations.
5 Undo and remove the lower universal joint pinch-bolt at the steering box wormshaft.
6 Undo and remove the two bolts which secure the steering column to the interior floor of the vehicle (Fig. 11.32).
7 Undo the steering column support bracket nuts and free the steering column from the bracket.
8 Withdraw the steering column through the bulkhead into the interior of the vehicle, with the help of an assistant to guide the lower jointed end. Ensure that it does not snag any cables or brake pipes.
9 Recover the gasket from the column lower flange.
10 Refitting is the reverse procedure. Fit all the couplings and retaining nuts and bolts loosely to start with, then when the whole assembly is located correctly, tighten the mounting nuts and bolts. Leave the lower pinch-bolt till last. Retighten it to the specified torque.

27 Power steering pump - removal and refitting

1 Open the bonnet and remove the filler cap of the power steering reservoir.
2 Place a suitable receptacle underneath the power steering pump. Detach the inlet hose from the pump and drain the fluid.
3 After draining the fluid, seal the end of the hose to prevent the ingress of dirt and refit the reservoir cap.
4 Disconnect the outlet hose from the pump and seal its end to prevent the ingress of dirt.
5 Slacken and remove the adjustment and pivot nuts and bolts. Undo the two bolts securing the front bracket to the water pump.
6 Lift the drivebelt forward from the pulley and lift the pump away.
7 Refitting is the reverse of the removal procedure, but before installing the drivebelt carry out the initial bleeding operation (as

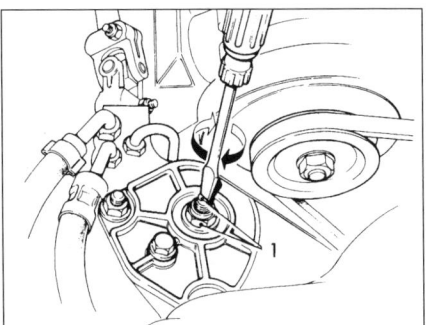

Fig. 11.31 Power steering box backlash adjuster and locknut (1) (Sec 24)

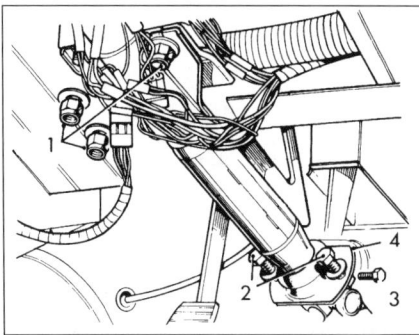

Fig. 11.32 Steering column upper (1) and lower (2) mountings, clamp bolt (3) and gasket (4) (Sec 26)

25.2 Remove the central motif to expose the retaining nut – early models

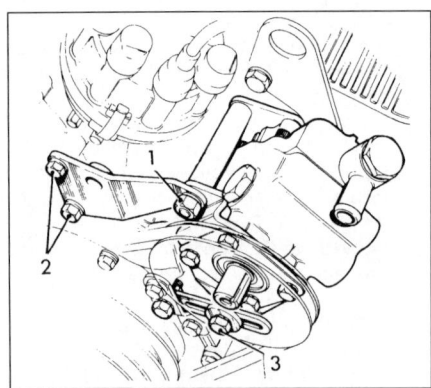

Fig. 11.33 Power steering pump and fixings (Sec 27)

1   Front mounting bracket nut
2   Front mounting bracket-to-water pump bolts
3   Pump adjuster strap bolt

described in Section 31) after refilling the hydraulic reservoir. The drivebelt adjustment procedure is described in Section 29 and the remainder of the bleeding operation is covered in Section 31.

28 Power steering pump - servicing

1   Thoroughly clean the pump exterior surfaces.
2   Remove the pulley by removing its centre bolt, spring washers and plain washers.
3   Remove the front mounting bracket and body endplate, also the rear bracket.
4   Secure the pump body in a vice and remove the adaptor screw, adaptor, fibre washer and rubber seal. Do not remove the venturi flow director which is pressed into the cover.
5   Remove the six Allen screws which secure the cover to the pump body and remove the pump from the vice, holding it vertically as the cover is removed so that the internal components do not fall out.
6   Remove the O-ring seals from the groove in the pump body and discard them.

7   Tilt the pump and extract the six rollers.
8   Draw the carrier off the shaft and remove the drive pin. Withdraw the shaft, the cam and the cam lock peg. If essential, remove the shaft key and draw off the sealed bearings.
9   Extract the shaft seal from the pump body and then withdraw the valve cap, valve and valve spring.
10 Wash all components in methylated spirit or clean pump hydraulic fluid and renew all seals.
11 Examine all components for wear or damage and renew as appropriate.
12 Reassembly is a reversal of dismantling, but observe the following points. The shaft seal is fitted to the pump body so that its lip is towards the carrier pocket. The vane carrier is fitted to the shaft so that the greater vane angle is as shown in Fig. 11.35.

13 Check the end clearance of the carrier and rollers in the pump body using a straight-edge and feeler gauges. If it is more than 0.002 in (0.05 mm), renew carrier and rollers.
14 Tighten the valve cap to the specified torque.

29 Power steering pump drivebelt - removal, refitting and adjusting

1   Remove the fan and alternator drivebelt as described in Chapter 2.
2   Slacken the power steering pump pivot bolt and adjuster nut and bolt (Fig. 11.37).

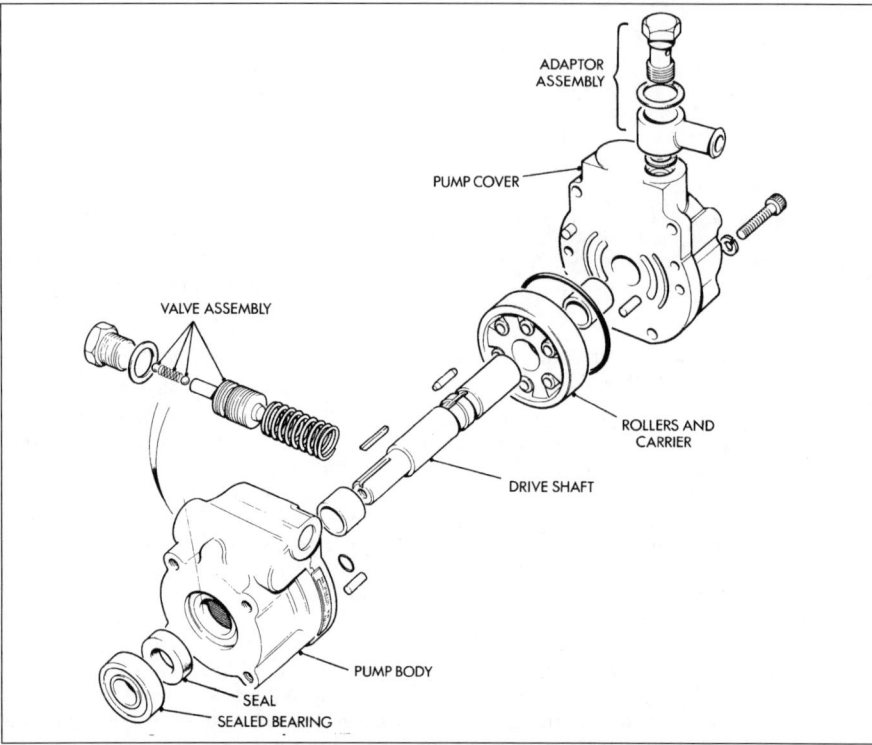

Fig. 11.34 Power steering pump components (Sec 28)

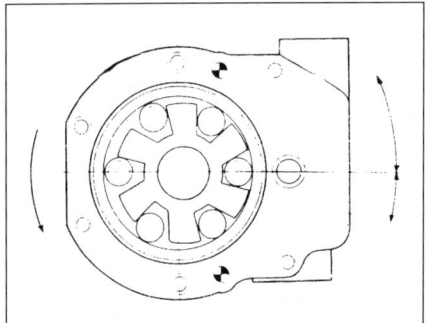

Fig. 11.35 Vane angle to be as shown (Sec 28)

Fig. 11.36 Check the carrier and roller endfloat clearance with rule and feeler gauges as shown (Sec 28)

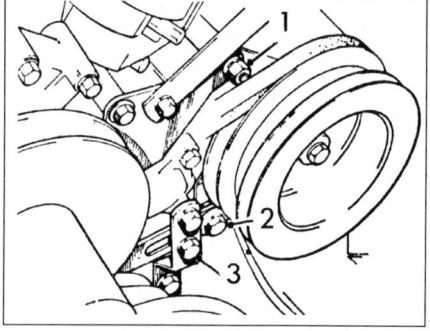

Fig. 11.37 Power steering pump adjustment (Sec 29)

1   Pivot bolt
2   Pump lower bracket bolt
3   Adjuster link bolt

3 Push downwards on the pump and free the belt from the pulley.
4 Remove the belt over the crankshaft pulley.
5 Refitting of the drivebelt is basically the reverse of the removal procedure, but it will be necessary to adjust the drivebelt before tightening the pivot and adjuster nuts and bolts.
6 Check the deflection at a point midway between the crankshaft and pump pulleys. The total deflection should be as given in the Specifications. Adjust by carefully levering the pump towards or away from the engine until the belt deflection is correct, then tighten the adjuster and pivot nuts and bolts.
7 When a new drivebelt has been fitted it will be necessary to check its adjustment and tension after approximately 1000 miles (1500 km) of motoring, unless squealing is heard when the steering is operated at low speeds, in which case adjust it at once.

30 Power steering reservoir filter element - renewal

1 Rover recommend that the power steering reservoir filter be renewed at intervals of 20 000 miles (32 000 km) or where the steering rack or pump assemblies have been overhauled or renewed.
2 Unscrew the reservoir cap and remove the retaining bar, spring and filter from the reservoir.
3 Withdraw and discard the filter and reassemble using a new filter.
4 After installation check the fluid level and top up as necessary.

31 Power steering system - filling and bleeding

1 Turn the steering wheel so that the roadwheels are pointing in the straight-ahead position.
2 Before filling the fluid reservoir check the system completely to ensure that all the pipes, hoses and unions are satisfactory.
3 Fill the hydraulic reservoir with the recommended type of fluid (see Specifications) to a point 1 in (25 mm) below the base of the filler neck.
4 Loosen the pump adjuster/pivot bolts and nuts and relieve the drivebelt tension.
5 Rotate the hydraulic pump pulley, by hand, several times in a clockwise direction to prime the system.
6 Retension the drivebelt as described in Section 29, recheck the fluid level and top up as necessary.
7 Start the engine and whilst allowing it to idle, turn the steering wheel so that the roadwheels are deflected, from the straight-ahead position, to the full left-hand lock position. Return the roadwheels to the

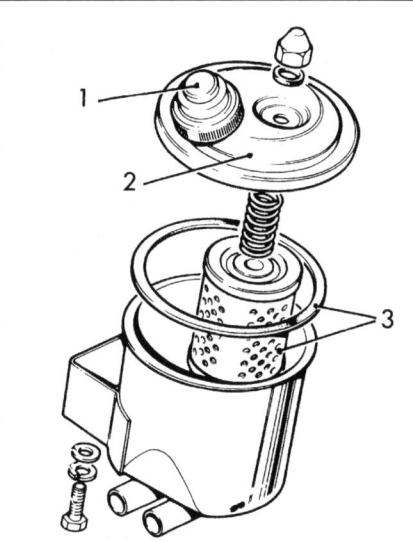

Fig. 11.38 The power steering fluid reservoir, filler cap (1) and top cover (2), element and seal washer (3) (Sec 30)

straight-ahead position and recheck the fluid level.
8 Repeat paragraph 7 but this time turn the steering to the right-hand lock position and then return it to the straight-ahead position. Recheck the fluid level and top up as necessary.
9 Repeat paragraphs 7 and 8 until all air is expelled. Finally recheck and top up the fluid level.

32 Front wheel alignment - checking and adjusting

1 In order to minimize tyre wear, and retain the correct steering and roadholding characteristics, it is essential that the front wheels are correctly aligned. Ideally, the alignment should be checked using special gauges. It is, therefore, recommended that the job is done by a Rover dealer. However, it is possible to do the check with a reasonable amount of accuracy if care is taken. Proprietary tracking gauges are available at car accessory stores.
2 The front wheels are correctly aligned when they are turning outwards at the front by the specified amount; this is the toe-out. This measurement is made with the wheels in the straight-ahead position, with the steering box in the mid-position of its travel, the ball centres of the tie-rod equal and the steering wheel correctly aligned as for steering wheel removal (Section 25).
3 Push the vehicle backwards and then forwards a short distance in order to settle the linkage. The vehicle must be on level ground.
4 Measure the distance between the insides of the wheel rims at hub height at the front and rear of the wheels. The distance at the

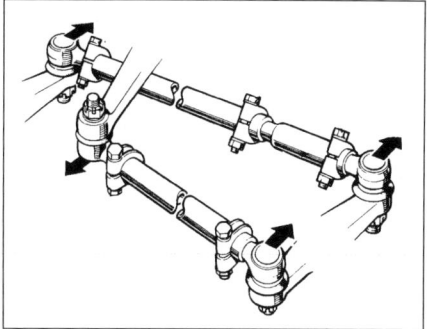

Fig. 11.39 Tap the balljoints in the direction of the arrows (Sec 32)

front should be greater than the distance at the rear by the amount given in Specifications for toe-out.
5 To adjust the toe-out, jack up the front of the vehicle and support the chassis using axle stands. Chock the rear wheels.
6 Slacken the adjuster sleeve clamp bolts on both the track rod and the drag link.
7 Rotate the adjusters as necessary to shorten or lengthen the track rod or drag link, then re-check the toe-out.
8 When the setting is correct, clamp the sleeve bolts and tap the balljoints lightly in the directions shown in Fig. 11.39 as far as they will go to ensure that their travel is unrestricted.
9 Lower the front of the vehicle and remove the chocks.

33 Steering lock stop - checking and adjustment

1 Steering lock stops are fitted to the steering swivels to stop the swivels over-rotating and straining the main swivel-to-housing oil seals.
2 The bolts should protrude 1.59 in (40.5 mm) as shown (photo).
3 To adjust the lock stop, slacken the locknut on the rear of the bolt.
4 Screw the bolt in or out as required, then re-tighten the locknut.
5 Check the wheel positions at full lock.

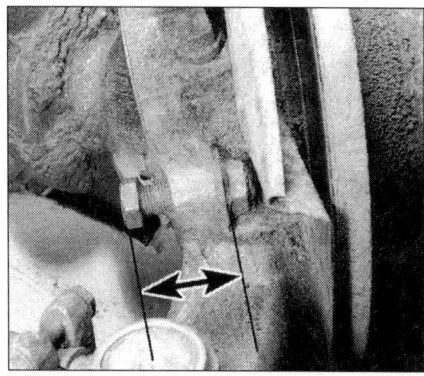

33.2 Measure the stop bolt protrusion between the points shown

34 Roadwheels and tyres

1 Whenever the roadwheels are removed it is a good idea to clean the insides to remove accumulations of mud and disc pad dust.

2 Check the condition of the wheel for rust and repaint if necessary.

3 Examine the wheel stud holes. If these are tending to become elongated or the dished recesses, in which the nuts seat, have worn or become overcompressed, then the wheel will have to be renewed.

4 With a roadwheel removed, pick out any embedded flints from the tread and check for splits in the sidewalls or damage to the tyre carcass generally.

5 Where the depth of tread pattern is below the current legal limit, the tyre must be renewed.

6 Rotation of the roadwheels to even out wear may be a worthwhile idea if the wheels have been balanced off the car. Include the spare wheel in the rotational pattern. Do not move wheels from side to side, only from front to rear.

7 Wheel balancing should only be carried out with the wheels off the vehicle.

⚠️ **Warning: If the wheels have to be balanced on the vehicle, the differential lock must be engaged and the propeller shaft to the stationary wheels (axle) must be disconnected.**

8 If the wheels have been balanced on the car then they cannot be moved round the car as the balance of the wheel, tyre and hub will be upset. In fact their exact fitting positions must be marked before removing a roadwheel so that it can be returned to its original inbalance state.

9 It is recommended that wheels are re-balanced halfway through the life of the tyres to compensate for the loss of tread rubber due to wear.

10 Finally, always keep the tyres (including the spare) inflated to the recommended pressures and always refit the dust caps on the tyre valves. Tyre pressures are best checked first thing in the morning when the tyres are cold.

Fault finding - suspension and steering

Steering feels vague, car wanders and 'floats' at speed

☐ Tyre pressures incorrect
☐ Dampers (shock absorbers) worn
☐ Steering gear balljoints badly worn
☐ Steering mechanism free play excessive
☐ Front/rear suspension pick-up points out of alignment

Stiff and heavy steering

☐ Tyre pressures too low
☐ No grease in steering gear
☐ Front wheel toe-out incorrect
☐ Steering gear incorrectly adjusted
☐ Steering column badly misaligned
☐ Power steering pump defective
☐ Power steering drivebelt slack or missing

Wheel wobble and vibration

☐ Wheel nuts loose
☐ Front wheels and tyres out of balance
☐ Steering balljoints badly worn
☐ Hub bearings badly worn
☐ Steering gear free play excessive
☐ Front springs weak or broken

Chapter 12 Bodywork and fittings

For modifications, and information applicable to later models, see Supplement at end of manual

Contents

Degrees of difficulty

Easy, suitable for novice with little experience	**Fairly easy,** suitable for beginner with some experience	**Fairly difficult,** suitable for competent DIY mechanic	**Difficult,** suitable for experienced DIY mechanic	**Very difficult,** suitable for expert DIY or professional

1 General description

The backbone of the Range Rover is the box section chassis frame. Although the base and main body structural points are manufactured in steel, the majority of body panels are of magnesium-aluminium alloy known as 'Birmabright'. This alloy has the advantage of being stronger than pure aluminium and it will not corrode or rust under normal operating conditions.

The station wagon style body has a single wide door at each side, hinged at the front. Wind-down windows and quarter vents are fitted to them.

At the rear the lower tailgate is manufactured in steel for additional strength whilst the rear body floor is corrugated aluminium. The rear seat can be folded forward for greater load area when required.

The information given in this Chapter refers to Range Rover models fitted with the standard body style and not to the various specialised bodies which can be fitted to suit individual requirements.

2 Maintenance - body and chassis

1 Because most of the bodywork on the Range Rover is constructed from an aluminium alloy, rust is not a great problem. However, if the vehicle is being used in wet, muddy conditions, the worst of the dirt should be washed off at least once a month using a hosepipe and brush. The hidden portions of the body, such as the wheel arches, the chassis and the engine compartment are equally important, though obviously not requiring such frequent attention as the immediately visible paintwork.

2 Once a year or every 12 000 miles, it is sound advice to visit your local main agent and have the underside of the body steam cleaned. All traces of dirt and oil will be removed and the underside can then be inspected carefully for rust, damaged hydraulic pipes, frayed electrical wiring and other faults.

3 At the same time, the engine compartment should be cleaned in the same manner. If steam cleaning facilities are not available

brush a grease solvent over the whole engine and engine compartment with a stiff paintbrush. working it well in where there is an accumulation of oil and dirt. As the solvent is washed away it will take with It all traces of dirt, leaving the engine looking clean and bright.

3 Minor body damage - repair

Repair of minor scratches in the vehicle's bodywork

If the scratch is very superficial, and does not penetrate to the metal of the bodywork, repair is very simple. Lightly rub the area of the scratch with a paintwork renovator or a very fine cutting paste to remove loose paint from the scratch and to clear the surrounding bodywork of wax polish. Rinse the area with clean water.

Apply touch-up paint to the scratch using a thin paint brush, continue to apply thin layers of paint until the surface of the paint in the scratch is level with the surrounding paintwork. Allow the new paint at least two weeks to harden; then, blend it into the surrounding paintwork by rubbing the paintwork in the scratch area with a paintwork renovator or a very fine cutting paste. Finally apply wax polish.

Where the scratch has penetrated right through to the metal of the bodywork, a different repair technique is required. Remove any loose paint, etc, from the bottom of the scratch with a penknife. Using a rubber or nylon applicator, fill the scratch with bodystopper paste. If required, this paste can be mixed with cellulose thinners to provide a very thin paste which is ideal for filling narrow scratches. Before the stopper-paste in the scratch hardens, wrap a piece of smooth cotton rag around the top of a finger. Dip the finger in cellulose thinners and then quickly sweep it across the surface of the stopper-paste in the scratch: this will ensure that the surface of the stopper-paste is lightly hollowed. The scratch can now be painted over as described earlier in this Section.

Repair of dents in the vehicle's bodywork

The alloy body panels on the Range Rover are easier to work on than steel, and minor dents or creases can be beaten out fairly easily. However, if the damaged area is quite large, prolonged hammering will cause the metal to harden and to avoid the possibility of cracking, it must be softened or 'annealed'. This can be done easily with a gas blowlamp but great care is required to avoid actually melting the metal. The blowlamp must always be kept moving in a circular pattern whilst being held a respectable distance from the metal.

One method of checking when the alloy is hot enough is to rub down the surface to be annealed and then apply a thin film of oil over it. The blowlamp should be played over the rear side of the oiled surface until the oil evaporates and the surface is dry. Turn off the blowlamp and allow the metal to cool naturally, the treated areas will now be softened and it will be possible to work it with a hammer or mallet. After panel beating, the damaged section should be rubbed down and painted as described later in this Section.

When deep denting of the vehicle's bodywork has taken place, the first task is to pull the dent out until the affected bodywork almost attains its original shape. There is little point in trying to restore the original shape completely, as the metal in the damaged area will have stretched on impact and cannot be reshaped to its original contour. It is better to bring the level of the dent up to a point which is about 1/8 in (3 mm) below the level of the surrounding bodywork. In cases where the dent is very shallow anyway, it is not worth trying to pull it out at all.

If the underside of the dent is accessible, it can be hammered out gently from behind using the method described earlier.

Should the dent be in a section of the bodywork which has a double skin or some other factor making it inaccessible from behind, a different technique is called for. Drill several small holes through the metal inside the dent area, particularly in the deeper sections. Then screw long self-tapping screws into the holes just sufficiently for them to gain a good purchase in the metal. Now the dent can be pulled out by pulling on the protruding heads of the screws with a pair of pliers.

The next stage of the repair is the removal of the paint from the damaged area and from an inch or so of the surrounding 'sound' bodywork.

Note: *On no account should coarse abrasives be used on aluminium panels in order to remove paint. The use of a wire brush or abrasive on a power drill for example, will cause deep scoring of the metal and in extreme cases, penetrate the thickness of the relatively soft aluminium alloy.*

Removal of paint is best achieved by applying paint remover to the area, allowing it to act on the paintwork for the specified time and then removing the softened paint with a wood or nylon scraper. This method may have to be repeated in order to remove all traces of paint. A good method of removing small stubborn traces of paint is to rub the area with a nylon scouring pad soaked in thinners or paint remover.

Note: *If it is necessary to use this method, always wear rubber gloves to protect the hands from burns from the paint remover. It is also advisable to wear protection over the eyes as any paint remover that gets into the eyes will cause severe inflammation, or worse.*

Finally, remove all traces of paint and remover by washing the area with plenty of clean fresh water.

To complete the preparations for filling, score the surface of the bare metal with a screwdriver or the tang of a file, or alternatively, drill small holes in the affected area. This will provide a really good 'key' for the filler paste.

To complete the repair, see the Section on filling and respraying.

Repair of holes or gashes in the vehicle's bodywork

Remove all the paint from the affected area and from an inch or so of the surrounding 'sound' bodywork, using the method described in the previous Section. With the paint removed you will be able to gauge the severity of the damage and therefore decide whether to replace the whole panel (if this is possible) or to repair the affected area. It is often quicker and more satisfactory to fit a new panel than to attempt to repair large areas of damage.

Remove all fittings from the affected area except those which will act as a guide to the original shape of the damaged bodywork (eg. headlamp shells, etc). Then, using tin snips or a hacksaw blade remove all loose metal and

other metal badly affected by damage. Hammer the edges of the hole inwards in order to create a slight depression for the filler paste.

Before filling can take place it will be necessary to block the hole in some way. This can be achieved by the use of zinc gauze or aluminium tape.

Zinc gauze is probably the best material to use for a large hole. Cut a piece to the approximate size and shape of the hole to be filled, then position it in the hole so that its edges are below the level of the surrounding bodywork. It can be retained in position by several blobs of filler paste around its periphery.

Aluminium tape should be used for small or very narrow holes. Pull a piece off the roll and trim it to the approximate size and shape required, then pull off the backing paper (if used) and stick the tape over the hole; it can be overlapped if the thickness of one piece is insufficient. Burnish down the edges of the tape with the handle of a screwdriver or similar, to ensure that the tape is securely attached to the metal underneath.

Bodywork repairs - filling and respraying

Before using this Section, see the Section on dent, deep scratch, hole and gash repairs.

Many types of bodyfiller are available, but generally speaking those proprietary kits which contain a tin of filler paste and a tube of resin hardener are best for this type of repair. A wide, flexible plastic or nylon applicator will be found invaluable for imparting a smooth and well contoured finish to the surface of the filler.

Mix up a little filler on a clean piece of card or board. Use the hardener sparingly (follow the maker's instructions on the packet) otherwise the filler will set rapidly.

Using the applicator, apply the filler paste to the prepared area; draw the applicator across the surface of the filler to achieve the correct contour and to level the filler surfaces. As soon as a contour that approximates the correct one is achieved, stop working the paste; if you carry on too long the paste will become sticky and begin to 'pick-up' on the applicator. Continue to add thin layers of filler paste at twenty-minute intervals until the level of the filler is just 'proud' of the surrounding bodywork.

Once the filler has hardened, excess can be removed using a metal plane or file. From then on, progressively finer grades of abrasive paper should be used, starting with a 40 grade production paper and finishing with a 400 grade 'wet or dry' paper. Always wrap the abrasive paper around a flat rubber, cork, or wooden block, otherwise the surface of the filler will not be completely flat. During the smoothing of the filler surface, the 'wet-or-dry' paper should be periodically rinsed in water. This will ensure that a very fine smooth finish is imparted to the filler at the final stage.

At this stage, the 'dent' should be surrounded by a ring of bare metal, which in turn should be encircled by the finely 'feathered' edge of the good paintwork. Rinse and repair with clean water, until all the dust produced by the rubbing-down operation is gone.

Spray the whole area with a light coat of grey primer, this will show up any imperfections in the surface of the filler. If at all possible, it is recommended that an, etch-primer is used on untreated alloy surfaces, otherwise the primer may not be keyed sufficiently and may subsequently flake off. Repair imperfections with fresh filler paste or bodystopper and once more, smooth the surface with abrasive paper. If bodystopper is used, it can be mixed with cellulose thinners to form a really thin paste which is ideal for filling small holes. Repeat the spray and repair procedures until you are satisfied that the surface of the filler, and the feathered edge of the paintwork are perfect. Clean the repair area with clean water and allow it to dry fully.

The repair area is now ready for spraying. Paint spraying must be carried out in a warm dry, windless and dust free atmosphere. This condition can be created artificially if you have access to a large indoor working area, but if you are forced to work in the open, you will have to pick your day very carefully. If you are working indoors, dousing the floor in the work area with water will 'lay' the dust which would otherwise be in the atmosphere. If the repair is confined to one body panel, mask off the surrounding panels; this will help to minimise the effects of a slight mismatch in paint colours. Bodywork fittings will also need to be masked off. Use genuine masking tape and several thickness of newspaper for the masking operation.

Before commencing to spray, agitate the aerosol can thoroughly, then spray a test area (an old tin, or similar) until the technique is mastered. Cover the repair area with a thick coat of primer: the thickness should be built up using several thin layers of paint rather than one thick one. Using 400 grade 'wet or dry' paper, rub down the surface of the primer until it is really smooth. Whilst doing this the work area should be thoroughly doused with water, and the 'wet-or-dry' paper periodically

rinsed in water. Allow to dry before spraying on more paint.

Spray on the top coat, again building up the thickness by using several thin layers of paint. Start spraying in the centre of the repair area and then, using a circular motion, work outwards until the whole repair area and about 2 in of the surrounding original paintwork is covered. Remove all masking material 10 to 15 minutes after spraying on the final coat of paint.

4 Major chassis and body damage - repair

Major chassis and body repair work cannot successfully be undertaken by the average owner. Work of this nature should be entrusted to a competent body repair specialist who should have the necessary jigs, welding and hydraulic straightening equipment as well as skilled panel beaters to ensure that a proper job is done.

If the damage is severe, it is vital that on completion of repair the chassis is in the correct alignment. Less severe damage may also have twisted or distorted the chassis although this may not be visible immediately. It is therefore always best on completion of the repair to check for twist and squareness to ensure that all is correct.

If distortion of the chassis is suspected, the chassis dimensions must be checked. Again, this is something that must be done by a specialist.

5 Maintenance - hinges and locks

1 Periodically oil the hinges of the bonnet, tailgate and doors with a drop or two of light oil. A good time is after the vehicle has been washed.
2 Periodically oil the bonnet release catch pivot pin and the safety catch pivot pin.
3 Do not over-lubricate door latches and strikers. Normally a little oil on the catch alone is sufficient.

6 Door rattles - tracing and rectification

1 Check first that the door is not loose at the hinges and that the latch is holding the door firmly in position. Check also that the door lines up with the aperture in the body.
2 If the hinges are loose or the door is out of alignment, it will be necessary to reset the hinge positions as described in Section 10.
3 If the latch is holding the door properly, it should hold the door tightly when fully latched and the door should line up with the body. If it is out of alignment it needs adjustment as described in Section 10. If loose, some part of the lock mechanism must be worn out and requiring renewal.

7 Bonnet - removal and refitting

1 Open and support the bonnet.
2 Detach the windscreen washer feed pipe at the reservoir.
3 Mark an outline around the bonnet hinge positions, then unscrew the retaining bolts whilst an assistant helps to support the bonnet in the raised position. With the bolts removed, lift the bonnet clear.
4 Refit in the reverse order of removal, checking bonnet alignment before fully tightening the retaining bolts.

8 Front wing - removal and refitting

1 Remove the bonnet as described in the previous Section.
2 Referring to Chapter 3, remove the air cleaner unit.
3 Refer to Chapter 10 and remove the windscreen wiper arms.
4 Unbolt and remove the decker panel, the retaining bolt and screw positions of which are shown in Fig. 12.1.
5 Refer to Chapter 10 and remove the front side and indicator light unit from the wing to be removed.
6 The wing panel on the side concerned can now be removed after its retaining bolts and screws are removed. Their positions are shown in Fig. 12.2.
7 Refitting the wing is a direct reversal of the removal procedure. Before fully tightening its fastenings, check the panel alignment. When refitting the decker panel, engage it fully under the top of the windscreen rubber surround.
8 On completion ensure that the lights, indicators, windscreen wipers and washers are fully operational.

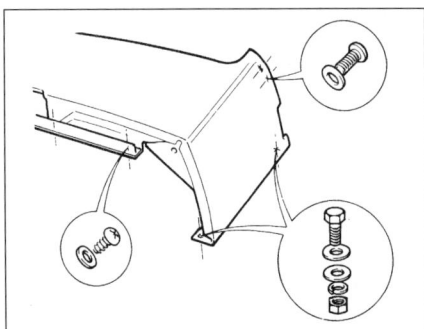

Fig. 12.1 the decker panel and fixings (Sec 8)

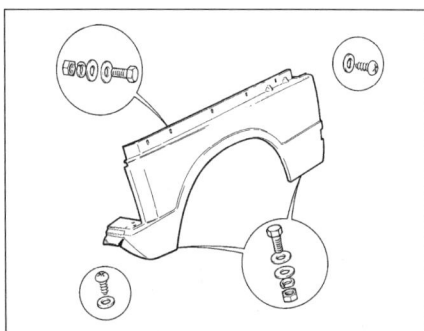

Fig. 12.2 The front wing panel and fixings (Sec 8)

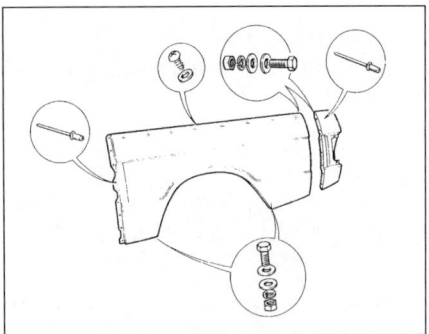

Fig. 12.3 The rear wing panel and fixings (Sec 9)

9 Rear wing panel - removal and refitting

1 The rear wing panels are attached on their rear corner edge by means of pop rivets and therefore unless you have a pop rivet gun this task must be left to your Rover dealer or local body repair shop. If you intend to remove a panel yourself, proceed as follows.

2 On the right-hand panel only, refer to Chapter 3 and remove the fuel tank filler cap and neck.

3 Remove the spare wheel if necessary.

4 Refer to Chapter 10 and remove the rear combination light unit on the side concerned.

5 The pop rivets securing the winy panel at its rear and front edges must now be drilled through to detach it.

6 Unbolt or unscrew the other fastenings shown in Fig.12.3 from the locations indicated and withdraw the complete panel. Detach the rear corner panel from the wing.

7 Refitting is a reversal of the removal procedure. Apply a suitable body sealant at the corner panel-to-rear wing joint. Ensure that the panel is correctly aligned before retightening the retainers and inserting the pop rivets.

8 On completion, check the operation of the rear combination lights.

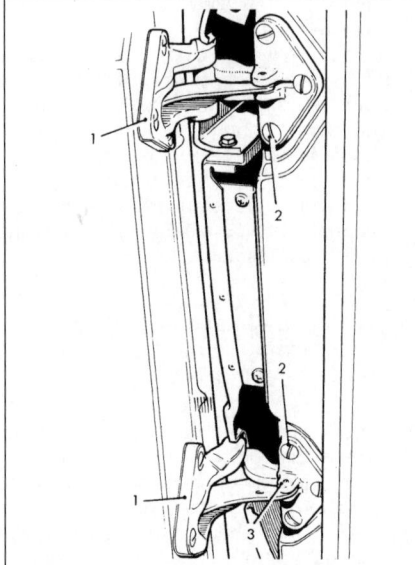
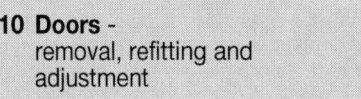

Fig. 12.4 The door hinges (1), retaining screws (2) and check strap retaining pin (3) (Sec 10)

10 Doors - removal, refitting and adjustment

1 Open the door concerned and get an assistant to hold it for support during its removal.

2 Use a pin punch and drive out the check strap retaining pin.

3 Mark an outline around the door hinges so that you have an alignment guide when refitting, then unscrew and remove the hinge screws. Lift the door clear and temporarily reinsert the retaining screws, together with any shims fitted between the hinge and door (or door pillar as applicable), so that they do not get mislaid.

4 Refit the door in the reverse order to removal, positioning the hinges to the alignment marks during removal. If adjustment is necessary proceed as follows.

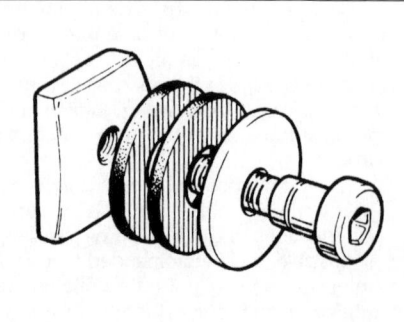

Fig. 12.5 Lock striker and packing shims (Sec 10)

Adjustment

5 The doors can be adjusted by any of three methods.

6 To move the door in or out, add or subtract shims as required to the door hinge at the door pillar.

7 To adjust the door forwards or rearwards, add or subtract shims as necessary between the door hinge and the body pillar.

8 Door vertical adjustment is made by loosening the hinge-to-door screws and lifting or lowering the door as required.

9 The lock striker can be adjusted by adding or subtracting packing shims as required.

11 Upper tailgate - removal and refitting

1 Raise the tailgate and detach the support stay at one end. On early models prise free the retaining cap at the stay pivot, remove the plain washer and detach the stay (Fig. 12.6). On later models simply prise the stay itself from the pivot.

2 Get an assistant to support the tailgate and then unscrew and remove the hinge-to-tailgate screws.

3 On later models disconnect the heated rear window lead at its connector and also the rear screen wiper before lifting the tailgate clear.

4 Refitting is a reversal of the removal procedure, but on later models check that the hinge fixing sealing washers are located correctly.

12 Lower tailgate - removal and refitting

1 Detach the rear number plate light wires at the connector.

2 Support the tailgate and then disconnect the check straps from the tailgate by prising free the retaining clip and removing the washers (Fig. 12.7).

3 Unscrew the tailgate hinge bolts and lift the tailgate clear.

4 Refit in reverse order to removal.

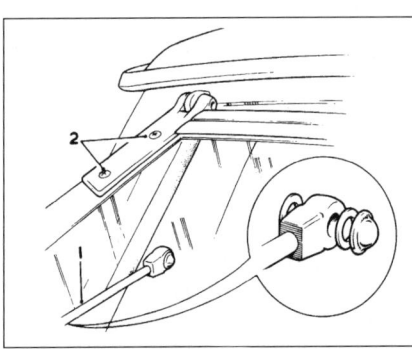

Fig. 12.6 The early model tailgate stay rod fixing (1) and hinge screws (2) (Sec 11)

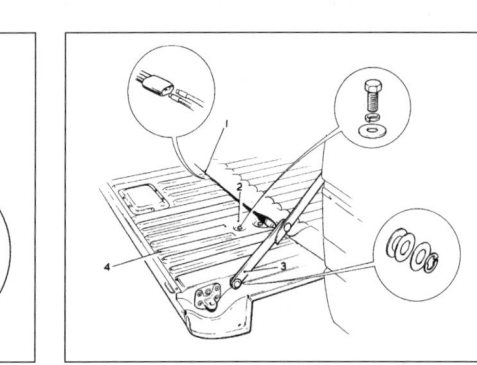

Fig. 12.7 The lower tailgate (4), stay rod fixing (3), hinge bolts (2) and number plate light leads (1) (Sec 12)

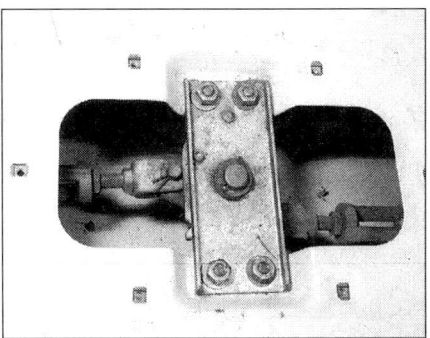

13.6 The lower tailgate lock mounting plate and adjusters

13 Lower tailgate lock - removal, refitting and adjustment

1 Remove the lock cover plate retaining screws and detach the plate.
2 Remove the retaining screws of the lock mounting plate.
3 Extract the split pin, withdraw the clevis pin and detach one of the bolt arms. The lock can now be withdrawn complete with the bolt arm still attached and this can be detached on removal.
4 Refitting of the lock is in the reversal of the removal process but on completion close the tailgate and check the lock operation. If adjustment is required, proceed as follows.

Adjustment

5 If the cover plate is in position, remove it.
6 Loosen the lock end adjuster locknuts off and also the locknuts at the bolt end of the adjuster (photo). The latter nuts have a *left-hand thread*.
7 Rotate the adjuster in the required direction to move the bolt outwards or inwards the necessary amount. Tighten the locknuts and recheck the operation before refitting the cover plate.
8 If the eye brackets on each side of the tailgate need adjusting, simply loosen the retaining screws and move the bracket accordingly. Retighten the screw to secure.

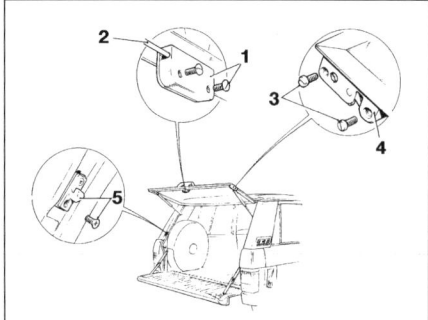

Fig. 12.8 The upper tailgate lock cover screws (1), bolt arms (2), side lock mechanism and retaining screws (3 and 4) and striker plate location (5) (Sec 14)

14 Upper tailgate lock - removal, refitting and adjustment

1 On earlier models, remove the rear cover from the lock. On later models, remove the side covers from the lock.
2 Detach the bolt arms (early models) or free the centre lock (later models).
3 Remove the lock retaining screws each side and remove the lock with bolt arms.
4 Refit in the reverse order to removal.
5 If adjustment is required, screw the bolt arms in or out as required. The striker plate(s)

15.1 Remove the window regulator handle

can be adjusted by loosening the retaining screws, repositioning the plate as necessary and then retightening the screws.

15 Door glass - removal and refitting

1 Remove the retaining screws and withdraw the window regulator handle (photo).
2 Remove the armrest retaining screws and lift the armrest clear, disengaging its upper location pegs from the door pull handle brackets (photo).
3 Remove the door handles, which are retained by a screw on the trim side (photo).
4 Remove the door pull handle retaining bolt and rotate the handle 90° to detach it (photos). Repeat the procedure with the other handle.
5 Carefully prise free the upper and lower trim panels from the door.
6 Remove the door top edge seals.
7 Unbolt and remove the glass frame channel. The frame securing bolts and screws are shown in Fig. 12.9.
8 The door glass can now be carefully lifted out of the door. On later models fitted with a door-mounted mirror, you may find removal and installation of the glass easier if the mirror is removed.
9 Refit the glass and assemble the various components in the reverse order to removal. Before reassembling the trim panels and

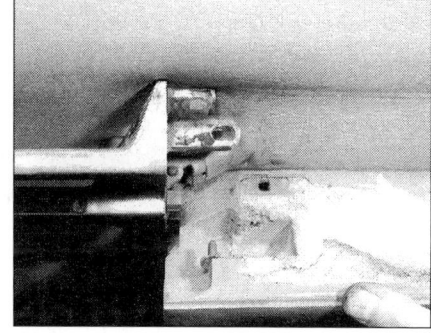

15.2 Disengage the armrest location peg to remove

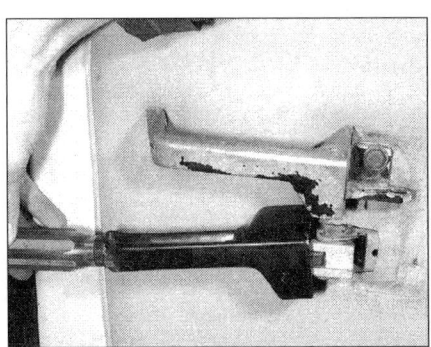

15.3 Remove the door handle retaining screw

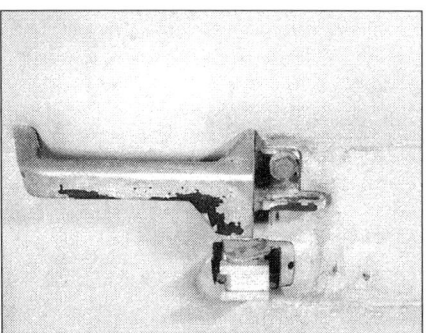

15.4a Remove the pull handle retaining bolt . . .

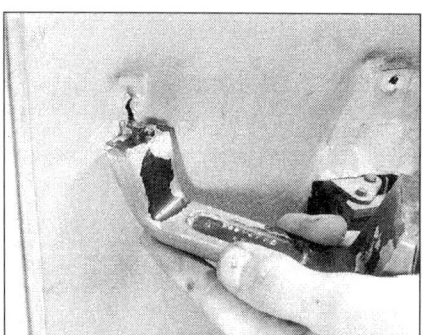

15.4b . . . then twist handle to disengage

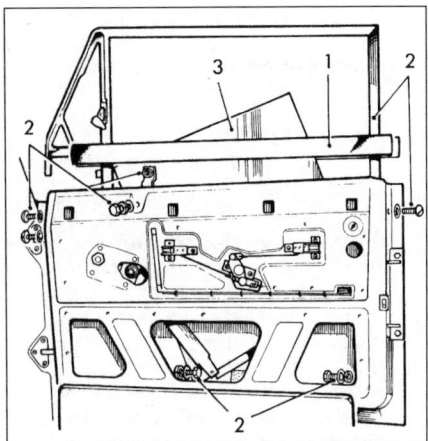

Fig. 12.9 Door glass removal showing top seal (1), glass frame channel and retainers (2) and glass (3) (Sec 15)

fittings, check that the window winds up and down in a satisfactory manner. Minor frame adjustment may be required. Renew the upper seals if they are perished or damaged.

16 Door quarter vent - removal and refitting

1 Refer to the previous Section and remove the door glass.
2 Unscrew and remove the quarter vent lower pivot nut and withdraw the spring and washers.
3 The vent can now be pivoted, slightly tilted and lifted clear of the door.
4 Refit in the reverse order to removal. Check the operation of the vent before refitting the door glass and trim assembly.

17 Door glass regulator - removal and refitting

1 Refer to Section 15 and remove the door glass.
2 Unbolt and remove the regulator retaining bolts (photo) and then withdraw the regulator through the lower aperture.

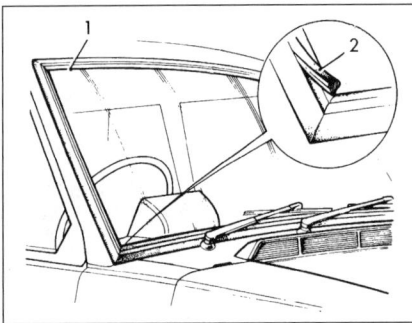

Fig. 12.11 Windscreen surround rubber (1) and expander strip (2) (Sec 19)

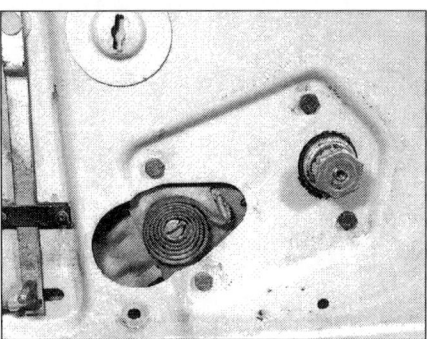

17.2 Window regulator retaining bolt positions

3 Refitting is a direct reversal of the removal procedure. Lubricate the assembly prior to fitting and when the window is refitted, check that the winding mechanism is satisfactory before assembling the trim.

18 Door lock unit - removal and refitting

1 Refer to Section 15 and remove the door glass.
2 Unbolt and detach the door external handle, then remove the lever-to-lock operating rod (Fig. 12.10).
3 Detach the operating rod from the private (key) lock.
4 Detach the rod from the internal door handle relay at the lock end and then withdraw the lock.
5 Refit in the reverse order to removal.

19 Windscreen - removal and refitting

Windscreen renewal is one job which the average owner is advised to leave to a specialist. The fitting charge is insignificant compared with the expense which will be incurred if a new screen is accidentally broken. For the owner who wishes to attempt the work himself, the following instructions are given.
1 Referring to Chapter 10, remove the windscreen wiper arms and blades.
2 Prise free and remove the expander strip from the channel in the screen surround moulding (Fig. 12.11).
3 Gently ease the windscreen lower edge from the moulding and carefully lift it clear.
4 To refit the windscreen first smear the moulding screen location channel with wet soap to ease refitting.
5 Fit the windscreen bottom edge into the lower moulding channel, then using some suitable wood or plastic levers (with a tapered edge), progressively prise free the moulding and gradually insert the windscreen.

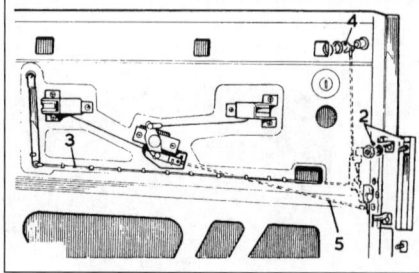

Fig. 12.10 Door lock operating mechanism components (Sec 18)

2 Door handle retaining nuts
3 Operating rod (lever-to-lock)
4 Key lock
5 Inner handle operating rod

6 With the windscreen fully located into the moulding, refit the expander strip into the outer channel of the moulding and then refit the windscreen wiper arms and blades.
7 Any leakage around the screen can be repaired by squeezing some suitable waterproof 'screen sealant' between the glass and moulding or body and moulding as required.

20 Tailgate glass - removal and refitting

1 Refer to Section 11 and remove the tailgate, then remove the tailgate lock as described in Section 14.
2 Remove the tailgate lift handle and trim.
3 The glass and frame are now renewed as a unit - they are not supplied separately.
4 Refit in the reverse order to removal.

21 Body side glass - removal and refitting

1 Refer to Section 18 in Chapter 10 and remove the interior light.
2 Detach and remove the rear quarter trim panels.
3 Disconnect the gear handles each side at their rear end, or at the central fixings in later models.
4 Prise free the headlining at the rear so that it is clear of the rear location bracket and withdraw it to the rear, taking special care not to damage or tear it.
5 Prise free the expander strip from the moulding channel of the glass surround (Fig. 12.12).
6 Raise the front glass runner spring clip tongue and slide the runners clear of the glass.
7 Lift out the front then the rear side windows.
8 Refitting is a reversal of the removal procedure.

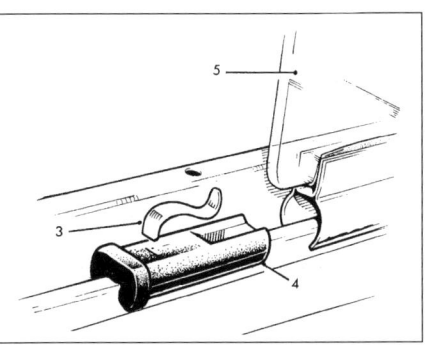

Fig. 12.12 The side window (5), runner (4) and clip (3) (Sec 21)

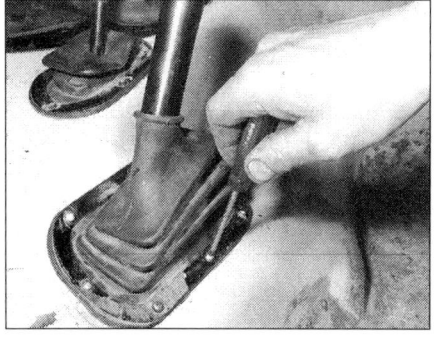

22.3a Remove the grommet retaining plate screws (handbrake shown)

22.3b Remove the retaining plates (main gear lever shown)

22 Front seats and floor panel - removal and refitting

1 To remove the front seats, unscrew and remove the seat runner check bolt, release the stop mechanism and withdraw the seat. Remove the floor carpets.
2 To remove the seat base unscrew the respective retaining bolts, disengage the eye bolts and detach the seat base unit from the chassis. Lift the base out of the vehicle.
3 Remove the retaining screws and release the grommet retainers from the handbrake, transfer and main gear levers, then remove the grommets (photos).
4 Unbolt and remove the main gear lever from its turret location in the main gearbox cover.
5 Unbolt and remove the differential lock vacuum control switch from its gearbox mounting. If the vacuum tubes are being disconnected make a note of their locations at the switch to ensure correct reassembly.
6 Unbolt and remove the exhaust system heat shield from the floor.
7 Detach the handbrake linkage by withdrawing a convenient clevis pin so that full lever movement is available.
8 Unscrew and remove the respective floor retaining bolts and screws. Two of the retaining bolt nuts are only accessible from the engine compartment side. You will need

to remove the air filter assembly (see Chapter 3) to gain access to these two nuts/bolts.
9 The floor pan can now be removed. As it is withdrawn, move the handbrake lever upwards to enable the panel to clear it.
10 Refitting of the panel is a reversal of the removal process. As the panel is relocated apply some suitable waterproof sealant to the seal lip,
11 When relocating the main gear lever unit, tighten the retaining bolts to the specified torque setting of 11 lbf ft (1.5 kgf m).

23 Console unit - removal and refitting

1 Disconnect the battery earth lead.
2 Unscrew and remove the lower facia panel retaining screws, the positions of which are shown in Fig. 12.13.
3 Lower the facia panel just enough to enable the hazard warning switch wires to be detached from the multi-connector, then lift the panel clear.
4 Open the glovebox and detach the glovebox check strap (as given in Section 25).
5 Remove the facia finisher.
6 Unscrew and remove the respective heater knob retaining screws, then pull the knobs free. Remove the panel retaining screws and then withdraw the panel (photos).
7 Remove the console unit retaining screws,

withdraw the unit far enough to enable the console instrument wire connections to be detached, then withdraw the console unit.
8 Refitting the console unit is a direct reversal of the removal procedure. Ensure that the wiring connections are securely made.

24 Top facia panel - removal and refitting

1 Disconnect the battery earth lead.
2 Refer to the previous Section and remove the console unit.
3 Refer to Chapter 10, Section 28, and remove the instrument panel housing.
4 Unscrew and remove the top facia panel

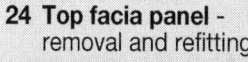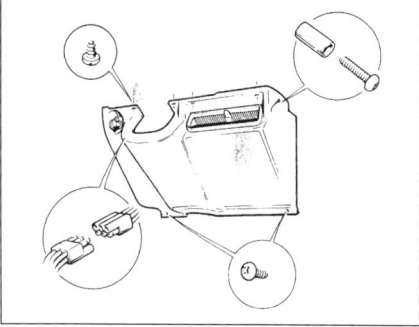

Fig. 12.13 Lower facia panel and fixings (Sec 23)

23.6a Remove the heater control knob screws . . .

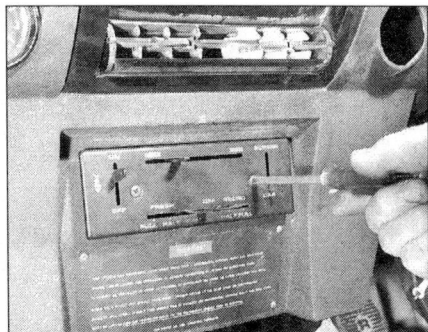

23.6b . . . and panel screws to . . .

23.6c . . . remove the panel

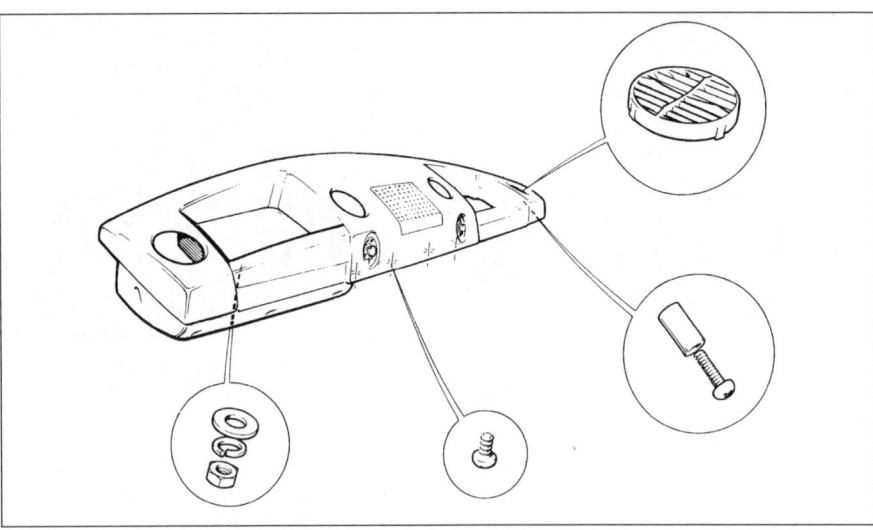

Fig. 12.14 Top facia panel and fixing points (Sec 24)

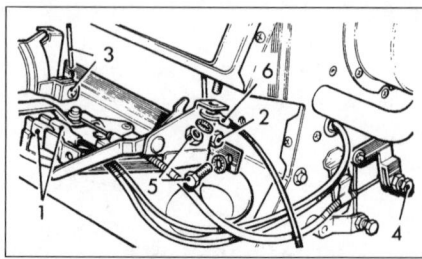

Fig. 12.15 The heater control connections (Sec 26)

1   Wire connectors
2   Relay rod (Screen/Car lever)
3   Relay rod (Vent lever)
4   Control cable connection
5   Control unit fixings
6   Earth wire connection

retaining nut and screws from underneath the panel and lift the panel clear, disconnecting the heater trunking and fresh air ducts as it is withdrawn.

5   Refit in the reverse order to removal.

25 Glovebox -
removal and refitting

1   Unscrew and remove the glovebox hinge screws on each side underneath.
2   Open and withdraw the glovebox sufficiently to detach the check strap. Remove the glove box.
3   Refit in the reverse order to removal.

26 Heater controls -
removal and refitting

1   Disconnect the battery earth lead.
2   Remove the lower facia panel, the glovebox and the console unit, referring to Sections 23 and 25 for the removal details.
3   Detach the switch wires.

4   Detach the relay rods from the 'Screen-Car' and 'Vent' levers.
5   Detach the control cables on each side of the heater unit then remove the controls, which are secured by a retaining bolt and nut on each side (Fig. 12.15).
6   Refitting the controls is a reversal of the removal procedure, but when attaching the unit, do not forget to locate the earth lead to the right-hand fixing stud before fitting the retaining nut and washer.
7   When retracting the control rods, adjust them to allow the flaps full movement,
8   Ensure that the control switch leads are connected correctly with the black/white lead to the front terminal.

27 Heater unit -
removal and refitting

1   Disconnect the battery earth lead.
2   Refer to Section 2 in Chapter 2 and drain the cooling system.
3   Remove the carburettor air cleaner unit as given in Section 3 of Chapter 3.
4   Unscrew the inlet and outlet hose retaining clips on the heater unit pipes protruding

through the engine compartment bulkhead and detach the pipes (Fig. 12.16).
5   Remove the lower facia panel, the glovebox and the console unit, referring to Sections 23 and 25 for details.
6   Detach the four demister hoses from their heater unit connections (two on each side) (photo).
7   Detach and remove the fresh air duct facia panel (photo).
8   Loosen the top facia panel retaining screws and lift the panel sufficiently to allow the fresh air duct to be withdrawn (photo).
9   Detach the heater unit wires at their connectors.

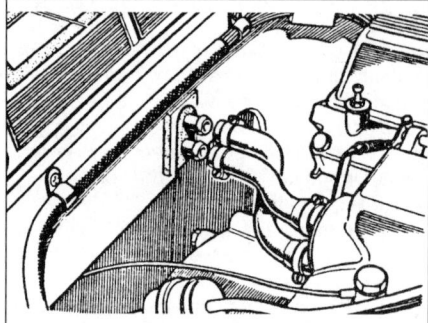

Fig. 12.16 The heater inlet and outlet coolant hose connections (Sec 27)

27.6 Detach the demister hoses

27.7 Remove the facia panel . . .

27.8 . . . and fresh air ducting

10 Unscrew and remove the heater unit retaining bolts (photo) and withdraw the unit (photo). Be prepared for some loss of coolant.

11 Refitting of the heater unit is a direct reversal of the removal procedure. Ensure that the fresh air intake seal is in position at the back of the unit and also the heater radiator seal on the pipes. Refill the cooling system as described in Chapter 2.

28 Heater radiator -
removal and refitting

1 Refer to the previous Section and remove the heater unit.

2 Unscrew and remove the fresh air flap cam control bracket retaining screws. Detach the bracket.

3 Prise free the lockwashers from the four flap spindles.

4 Unscrew and remove the remaining left side cover retaining screws and withdraw the cover complete with the air flap.

5 Extract the radiator together with its seals from the heater unit.

6 Refit in the reverse order to removal, but when locating the left-hand side cover, seal its edge with a suitable sealing compound.

29 Heater fan motor -
removal and refitting

Early models

1 Refer to Section 27 and remove the heater unit.

27.10a Unscrew the heater unit retaining bolts ..

2 Detach the wiring and air cooling hoses from the unit, noting their connections.

3 Unscrew and remove the fan unit retaining bolts, pull the motor and fan out sufficiently to enable the fan-to-motor grub screw to be loosened, then extract the fan motor.

4 Refit in the reverse order to removal. When locating the fan motor, engage its spindle in the fan bearing then holding the unit in position, spin the motor to ensure that the fan can rotate freely. It may be necessary to readjust the fan-to-motor position to suit.

5 When reconnecting the wires, the green wire must be attached to the terminal next to the air hose.

Later models

6 Remove and dismantle the heater fan motor unit as given in paragraphs 1 to 3. When the motor retaining bolts have been removed, drill out the pop rivets to remove the motor unit itself from the fan assembly.

7 Refit in the reverse order to removal, using new pop rivets to secure the fan.

27.10b . . . and remove the unit

30 Heater fan motor resistance
- removal and refitting

1 Refer to Section 27 and remove the heater unit.

2 Detach the wires from the fan motor, noting their locations.

3 Detach the air hose.

4 Referring to the previous Section, remove the heater fan motor and fan assembly and detach the electrical leads from the control switch.

5 The resistance unit retaining pop rivets can now be drilled out and the unit withdrawn together with its leads.

6 Refit in the reverse order to removal. The black/white resistance lead must be attached to the control switch front terminal and the green fan motor lead attached to the terminal next to the air hose. Use new pop rivets where necessary.

Notes

Chapter 13 Supplement:
Revisions and information on later models

Contents

Degrees of difficulty

Easy, suitable for novice with little experience	**Fairly easy,** suitable for beginner with some experience	**Fairly difficult,** suitable for competent DIY mechanic 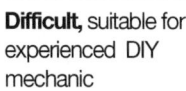	**Difficult,** suitable for experienced DIY mechanic	**Very difficult,** suitable for expert DIY or professional

1 Introduction

Since its introduction in 1970, the Range Rover has had a number of modifications and improvements made to it. Most of the modifications made upzcovered in the original text of Chapters 1 to 12 of this Manual. This Chapter covers modifications made from 1980 on, but in some instances items applicable to earlier models not covered in the previously mentioned Chapters are also included.

In order to use this Supplement to the best advantage, particularly with later models, it is suggested that it is referred to before the main Chapter(s) of the manual. This will ensure that any relevant information can be collated and accommodated into the procedures given in Chapter 1 to 12. Time and cost will therefore be saved and the particular job will be completed correctly.

Project vehicle

The vehicles used in the preparation of this Supplement, and appearing in many of the photographic sequences, were a 1986 model and 1987 model Vogue EFi, and a 1990 model Vogue SE.

A brief resume of the principal model changes and improvements made since 1980

August 1980	Fleeting Special introduced
February 1981	Vogue Estate, two-door limited edition introduced: fitted with a centre console, walnut door cappings, stainless steel rear tailgate cappings and air conditioning
September 1981	Four-door Station Wagon introduced
December 1981	Monteverdi four-door limited edition introduced, having leather seats and air conditioning
August 1982	Automatic transmission became an optional fitting
July 1983	Five-speed manual transmission introduced
August 1983	'325 In Vogue' special edition introduced with central door locking and other refinements
June 1984	Electronic ignition, revised facia and instrument display, improved heating/ventilation system
October 1985	Fuel injection system fitted to Vogue models. New front spoiler incorporating twin driving lamps. Four-speed automatic transmission introduced and five-speed manual gearbox selector linkage improved
December 1986	Fuel injected engine standard on all four-door models. Horizontal bar radiator grille and concealed bonnet hinges improve frontal appearance. Revised tailgate lock, and radio aerial incorporated in rear window de-mist element. New steering wheel and detailed interior improvements
October 1987	Hot-wire fuel injection system introduced.
March 1988	Vogue SE introduced. Features include air conditioning, electric sunroof, leather seats (electrically adjustable at front)
October 1988	New chain driven Borg Warner transfer box and viscous coupling. Variable delay front wipers. Upgraded central locking to include tailgate. Catalytic converter option. Heated front washer jets and improved heating/ventilation.
October 1989	3.9 litre (3950 cc) all-aluminium V8 engine introduced, replacing 3.5 litre engine. Anti-Lock Brakes optional, but standard on Vogue SE. Improved gearbox bearings. Ventilated front disc brakes on all models.
December 1990	Front and rear anti-roll bars introduced. New 3GA automatic transmission introduced. Larger fuel tanks. Cruise control added to SE models.
November 1991	Improved gearbox and audio system. Heated front seats introduced. Map reading lights introduced.

2 Specifications

The specifications listed below are revised or supplementary to the main specifications given at the beginning of each Chapter

Engine

Pre-1990 models (3528 cc)

Power output (DIN):
  Carburettor models (9.35 to 1, high compression) . . . . 126 BHP (92.6 kW) at 4000 rpm
  Fuel injected models (9.35 to 1 high compression) . . . . 165 BHP (123.0 kW) at 4750 rpm
Maximum torque (DIN):
  Carburettor models (9.35 to 1 high compression) . . . . 194 lbf ft (26.8 kgf m) at 2500 rpm
  Fuel injected models (9.35 to 1 high compression) . . . . 207 lbf ft (28.6 kgf m) at 3200 rpm

Valve timing:	Inlet	Exhaust
Carburettor models (pre-1988 9.35 to 1):		
Valve opens	36° BTDC	74° BBDC
Valve closes	64° ABDC	26° ATDC
Fuel injection models (9.35 to 1 and 8.13 to 1):		
Valve opens	24° BTDC	62° BBDC
Valve closes	52° ABDC	14° ATDC

1990-on models (3947 cc)

Bore . . . . 94 mm (3.700 in)
Stroke . . . . 71.12 mm (2.800 in)
Capacity . . . . 3947 cc (241 in³)
Power output:
  8.13 to 1 compression . . . . 127 kW at 4550 rpm
  9.35 to 1 compression . . . . 134 kW at 4750 rpm

1990-on models (3947 cc) (continued)

	Inlet	Exhaust
Valve timing:		
Valve opens	32° BTDC	70° BBDC
Valve closes	73° ABDC	35 ° ATDC

Piston clearance in bore, measured at the bottom of skirt at right
angles to piston pin .... 0.018 to 0.041 mm (0.0007 to 0.0016 in)
Number of compression rings 2
Number of oil control rings 1
No 1 compression ring .... Molybdenum, barrel-faced
No 2 compression ring .... Tapered and marked 'T' or 'TOP'
Width of compression rings .... 1.478 to 1.490 mm (0.058 to 0.059 in)
Compression ring gap .... 0.40 to 0.65 mm (0.016 to 0.026 in)
Oil control ring width .... 3.0 mm (0.118 in)
Oil control ring rail gap .... 0.38 to 1.40 mm (0.015 to 0.055 in)

Torque wrench settings

	lbf ft	Nm
Inlet manifold to cylinder head (fuel injection models)	35 to 40	48 to 55
Cylinder head bolts:		
Outer row	40 to 45	54 to 61
Centre and inner row	65 to 70	88 to 95
Transmission torque converter driveplate to crankshaft	55 to 60	75 to 81
Oil cooler adaptor to oil pump cover	30 to 37	41 to 50

Cooling system

Drivebelts

Tension (1987-on models) .... 4.0 to 6.0 mm

Thermostat

Opening temperature (high compression engine) .... 190°F (88°C)

Torque wrench settings

	lbf ft	Nm
Fan viscous coupling nut	27 to 30	37 to 41
Fan to viscous coupling unit	19 to 24	26 to 33
Water pump pulley to hub	17	23
Thermostat housing to inlet manifold	18 to 22	24 to 30
Oil cooler union nut	19 to 25	36 to 34

Fuel, exhaust and emission control systems

Carburettors (later models)

Zenith/Stromberg/Solex

Number fitted .... Two
Specification number .... 4104 or 4187
Needle .... BIFH (4104) or BIGG (4187)
Idle speed .... 650 to 750 rpm
Fast idle speed .... 1050 to 1150 rpm
CO content (at idle) .... 0.5 to 2.5%
Fuel octane rating (high compression engine) .... 97 RON (4-star)

SU HIF44

Number fitted .... Two
Specification number .... FZX 2006
Needle .... BGD
Idle speed .... 700 to 800 rpm
Fast idle speed .... 1100 to 1150 rpm
CO content (at idle) .... 0.5 to 2.5% (pulsair connected)
Fuel octane rating .... 97 RON (4-star)
Fuel level .... 0.5 to 1.5 mm below level of float chamber face

Fuel injection system

Lucas L

Idle speed .... 700 to 800 rpm
CO content (at idle) .... 0.5 to 1.0%
Fuel octane rating .... 97 RON (4-star)

Lucas Hot-wire

Fuel pump delivery pressure	34 to 38 lbf/in²
Idle speed	672 to 728 rpm
Fuel octane rating	95 RON unleaded
Air bypass valve resistance	48 to 58 ohms
Fuel system pressure	34 to 37 lbf/in²
CO content (at idle)	0.5 to 1.0%
Lambda sensor heater coil resistance	2.5 to 6.0 ohms

Torque wrench settings

	lbf ft	Nm
Plenum chamber to ram housing	16 to 21	22 to 28
Ram housing to inlet manifold	15 to 20	20 to 27
Lambda sensor	15	20
Air bypass valve	13 to 16	17 to 22
Fuel hose to fuel rail	16	22

Ignition system

Conventional ignition system - later models

Distributor type	Lucas 35 D8 sliding contact type
Dwell angle	26 to 28°
Contact breaker points gap	0.14 to 0.16 in (0.36 to 0.40 mm)

Ignition timing:

Static (and at idle speed with vacuum retard pipe detached)	5 to 7° BTDC
Dynamic (at idle speed with vacuum retard pipe attached)	4 to 8° ATDC

Electronic ignition system

Distributor type:

Pre-1987 models	Lucas 35 DM8
1987 models onwards	Lucas 35 DLM8
Pick-up air gap	0.008 to 0.014 in (0.20 to 0.35 mm)

Ignition timing:

June 1984 to 1986 models:

Static	6° BTDC
Dynamic	6° BTDC at 650 to 750 rpm
1987 fuel injection models (static or dynamic)	TDC ± 1°
1987 carburettor models (static or dynamic)	6° ± 1° BTDC at 750 rpm maximum (vacuum pipe disconnected)
1988 and 1989 Hot wire fuel injection models (dynamic)	6° ± 1° BTDC at 800 rpm maximum (vacuum pipe disconnected)

1990 models onwards (dynamic):

8.13 to 1 compression, non catalyst	2° ± 1° BTDC
8.13 to I compression, catalyst	6° ± 1° BTDC
9.35 to 1 compression, non catalyst	4° ± 1° BTDC

Clutch

Torque wrench settings

	lbf ft	Nm
Clutch cover bolts (1986-on)	18 to 22	25 to 29

Manual transmission (four-speed gearbox)

Vogue models

Transfer gearbox:

High range ratios (direct)	1.1 : 1

Overall ratios (final drive high transfer):

4th	3.54 : 1
3rd	5.33 : 1
2nd	8.67 : 1
1st	14.44 : 1
Reverse	13.00 : 1

Later models - general

Transfer gearbox - standard compression engines:

High ratio - from gearbox number 35594060 C	1.1227: 1

Transfer gearbox - high compression engines:

High ratio - from gearbox number 12C 01061 A	0.9962: 1

Overall ratios - high transfer:	Standard compression	High compression
4th	3.97 : 1	3.53 : 1
3rd	5.98 : 1	5.30 : 1
2nd	9.72 : 1	8.63 : 1
1st	16.16 : 1	14.34 : 1
Reverse	14.56 : 1	12.91 :1

Manual transmission (five-speed gearbox)

General

Type	Five forward speeds (all synchromesh) and reverse
Model	LT77

Ratios

5th	0.770 : 1
4th	1.00 : 1
3rd	1.397 : 1
2nd	2.132 : 1
1st	3.321 : 1
Reverse	3.429 : 1

Transfer gearbox

Type	Two-speed on main gearbox output (high or low ratio)	
Ratios:		
High	1.192 : 1	
Low	3.320 : 1	
Overall ratios:	**High transfer**	**Low transfer**
5th	3.25 : 1	9.05 : 1
4th	4.22 : 1	11.75 : 1
3rd	5.89 : 1	16.41 : 1
2nd	8.99 : 1	25.04 : 1
Ist	14.01 : 1	39.02 : 1
Reverse	14.46 : 1	40.26 : 1

Main gearbox

Synchromesh hub unit:	
Synchro cone-to-gear minimum clearance	0.025 in (0.64 mm)
1st gear bush sizes available	1.579 to 1.581 in (40.11 to 40.16mm)
	1.581 to 1.583 in (40.16 to 40.21 mm)
	1.583 to 1.585 in (40.21 to 40.26 mm)
	1.585 to 1.587 in (40.26 to 40.31 mm)
	1.587 to 1.588 in (40.31 to 40.34 mm)
1st gear bush endfloat	0.0002 to 0.0020 in (0.005 to 0.51 mm)
Mainshaft endfloat	0.0004 to 0.0020 in (0.010 to 0.051 mm)
Layshaft endfloat	0.0010 in (0.025 mm)
Layshaft preload	0.0010 in (0.025 mm)
5th gear-to-spacer clearance	0.0002 to 0.0020 in (0.005 to 0.051 mm)

Transfer gearbox

Input gear bearing preload	0.001 to 0.003 in (0.03 to 0.08 mm)
Intermediate gear cluster endfloat	0.003 to 0.014 in (0.08 to 0.36 mm)
Front output shaft bearing preload	0.001 to 0.003 in (0.03 to 0.08 mm)
Centre differential pinion backlash	Zero to 0.003 in (Zero to 0.08 mm)

Lubrication

Main gearbox	Dexron IID type ATF
Transfer gearbox	Hypoid gear oil, viscosity SAE 90EP to API GL4
Capacities:	
Main gearbox	3.9 Imp pints (2.2 litres)
Transfer gearbox	5.0 Imp pints (2.8 litres)

Torque wrench settings

	lbf ft	Nm
Main gearbox		
Oil drain plug	23	31
Oil filler plug	23	31
Oil filler plug (remote housing)	23	31
Oil level plug	23	31
Breather	7	10
Reverse switch hole blanking plug	17	23
Clutch housing-to-gearbox bolts	55	75
Front cover to gearcase	17	23
Attachment plate to gearcase	6	8
Attachment plate to remote housing	6	8
Clutch release lever clip	6	8
Extension case to gearbox	17	23

Torque wrench settings

	lbf ft	Nm

Main gearbox (continued)

	lbf ft	Nm
Remote selector housing to extension case	17	23
Gear lever housing to remote housing	17	23
Remote selector housing to extension case	17	23
Plunger housing to remote housing	17	23
Extension case blanking plug	6	8
Pivot plate	17	23
Oil pump to extension case	6	8
5th support bracket	17	23
Gear lever retainer	6	8
Selector shaft yoke	17	23
Gear lever unit retaining nut	37	50
Reverse pin-to-centre plate nut	37	50
Detent spring plug	17	23
Clutch release sleeve guide	17	23
Slave cylinder to clutch housing	17	23
Layshaft fifth driven gear retaining nut (late models)	160	217

Transfer gearbox

	lbf ft	Nm
Gearchange housing	18	24
End cover	6	8
Gearchange housing locating plate	5	7
Transfer case bottom cover	18	24
Front output housing to transfer case	18	24
Cross-shaft housing to front output housing	18	24
Front output housing cover	18	24
Extension housing bracket	18	24
Finger housing to front output housing	18	24
Mainshaft bearing housing	18	24
Operating arm pinch-bolt	6	8
Gate plate to grommet plate	6	8
Pivot shaft	18	24
Connecting rod	18	24
Retaining plate intermediate shaft	18	24
Speedometer cable retainer	6	8
Speedometer housing/rear output	6	8
Gearbox to transfer box	34	46
Bearing housing to transfer gearbox	34	46
Drain plug	23	31
Oil filler/level plug	23	31
Transfer breather	7	10
Gearbox to transfer case	34	46
Differential case	43	58
Output flange	120	163
Link arm and cross-shaft lever to balljoint	8	11
Transmission brake	55	75
Brake drum	18	24
Selector shaft high/low yoke	18	24
Selector fork high/low to shaft	18	24
Operating arm high/low	18	24
Speedometer housing to transfer case	34	46
Selector fork to cross-shaft	34	46

Gearbox/transfer box

	lbf ft	Nm
Bellhousing to engine	30	41
Gearbox housing-to-bellhousing studs/bolts (small diameter)	70	95
Gearbox housing-to-bellhousing studs/bolts (large diameter)	120	163
Output flange nuts and bolts (rear)	35	48
Output shaft nut (rear)	120	163
Output shaft nut (front)	120	163
Gear selector spherical seat bolts	11	15
Propeller shaft/flange bolts	35	48
Other nuts and bolts:		
M6	8	11
M8	20	27
M10	39	53

Automatic transmission (Chrysler three-speed)

General

Type number	A 727
Type	Fully automatic with three forward speeds and one reverse. Epicyclic type with fluid torque converter
Lubrication method	Rotor pump

Gear ratios

Top	1.00 : 1	
2nd	1.45 : 1	
1st	2.45 : 1	
Reverse	2.20 : 1	
Transfer gearbox:		
High	1.003 : 1	
Low	3.320 : 1	
Overall ratios:	**High transfer**	**Low transfer**
Top	3.55 : 1	11.75 : 1
2nd	4.16 : 1	17.04 : 1
1st	8.70 : 1	28.79 : 1
Reverse	7.81 : 1	25.86 : 1

Lubrication

Lubricant type:	
Automatic gearbox	Dexron IID type ATF
Transfer gearbox	Hypoid gear oil, viscosity SAE 90EP to API GL4
Capacity:	
Automatic gearbox	15 Imp pints (8.5 litres)
Transfer gearbox	5 Imp pints (2.8 litres)
Automatic gearbox - refill after draining	8 Imp pints (4.5 litres)

Torque wrench settings

	lbf ft	Nm
Breather tube banjo bolt	7	10
Torque converter-to-driveplate bolts	22.5	31
Throttle lever clamp bolt	4.5	6
Gearchange pivot self-locking nut	18	24
Tie-plate to gearbox sump	18	24
Tie-plate to engine sump	18	24
Gearbox sump	18	24
Lower bracket to gearbox	27.5	37
Adaptor housing to gearbox	33	45
Coupling shaft to mainshaft nut	54	73
Mainshaft special nut	100	136
Drain plug	22	30
Oil filter to spacer	3	4
Oil filter extension	3	4
Starter ring to driveplate	25	34
Spigot aligner to spacer	35	48
Spacer to crankshaft	60	81
Lower gearchange housing adaptor housing	18	24
Kickdown pivot bracket adaptor ring	18	24
Cover plate to adaptor ring	6	8
Torque converter housing packing	5	7
Oil cooler bridge pipe sleeve nuts	6	8
Oil cooler adaptors	8	11
Oil cooler elbow to adaptors	8	11
Valve body nuts	8	11
Kickdown band adjuster screw locknut	30	41
Low and reverse band adjuster screw locknut	30	41

Automatic transmission (ZF four-speed)

General

Type number	ZF 4HP 22
Type	Fully automatic with four forward speeds and one reverse. Epicyclic type with fluid torque converter and lock-up facility
Lubrication method	Rotor pump

Gear ratios

Top	. . . .	0.728 : 1
3rd	. . . .	1.000 : 1
2nd	. . . .	1.480 : 1
1st	. . . .	2.480 : 1
Reverse	. . . .	2.086 : 1

Transfer gearbox:	**Pre-1989 models**	**1989-on models**
High	1.192 : 1	1.206 : 1
Low	3.320 : 1	3.244 : 1

Overall ratios:

High transfer:		
Top	3.08 : 1	3.11 : 1
3rd	4.218 : 12	4.27 : 1
2nd	6.240 : 1	6.32 : 1
1st	10.458 : 1	10.59 : 1
Reverse	8.797 : 1	8.91 : 1

Low transfer:		
Top	8.553 : 1	8.36 : 1
3rd	11.747 : 12	11.48 : 1
2nd	17.380 : 1	17.00 : 1
1st	29.127 : 1	28.50 : 1
Reverse	24.501 : 1	23.96 : 1

Lubrication

Lubricant type:

Automatic gearbox	. . . .	Dexron IID type ATF
Transfer gearbox	. . . .	Hypoid gear oil, viscosity SAE 90EP to API GL4

Capacity:

Automatic gearbox		16 Imp pints (9.1 litres) - refill to MAX mark on dipstick after draining

	Pre-1989 models	**1989-on models**
Transfer gearbox	4.4 Imp pints (2.5 litres)	3.7 Imp pints (2.1 litres)

Torque wrench settings

	lbf ft	Nm

Pre-1989 models

	lbf ft	Nm
Filler tube to oil pan	25 to 30	34 to 41
Oil pan to gearbox	6	8
Oil pan drain plug	7	10
Converter housing cover	5 to 7	7 to 10
Bellhousing to engine	34	46
Gearchange lever to gearbox	16 to 21	22 to 29
Cooler pipe adaptor to gearbox	26 to 34	35 to 46
Torque converter to driveplate	25 to 30	74 to 41

1989-on models (Borg Warner)

	lbf ft	Nm
Brake drum backplate to rear output housing	48 to 59	65 to 80
Brake drum to drive flange	16 to 21	22 to 28
Centre differential (front to rear)	40 to 47	55 to 64
Drive flanges to transfer box	150 to 180	203 to 244
Driven gear to centre differential	30 to 45	41 to 61
Front cover to rear cover - main case	22 to 36	30 to 49
Front output housing to main case	18 to 30	24 to 41
Mounting brackets to chassis	29 to 39	40 to 50
Mounting bracket to gearbox	68 to 83	92 to 112
Neutral warning switch	25 to 35	34 to 47
Oil drain plug	14 to 22	19 to 30
Oil filler/level plug	14 to 22	19 to 30
Oil pump fixings	3 to 6	4 to 8
Rear output housing to main case	22 to 36	30 to 49
Selector lever shaft	5 to 7	7 to 9
Selector fork operating arm	5 to 7	7 to 9

Propeller shafts

Type

Models fitted with catalytic converter	. . . . Solid bar front, tubular rear

Front and rear axles

Adjustment data

Front and rear hub bearing endfloat	0.013 and 0.05 mm (0.0005 and 0.002in)
Front driveshaft constant velocity joint endfloat	0.64 mm (0.025 in) max
Front driveshaft endfloat	0.08 and 0.25 mm (0.003 to 0.010 in)
Swivel pin bearing preload	0.2 and 0.25 mm (0.008 and 0.010 in)

Lubricant

Swivel pin housing capacity	0.35 litres (0.6 pint)

Torque wrench settings (models with ABS only)

	lbf ft	Nm
Driving member to hub	44 to 52	60 to 70
Brake disc to hub	48 to 59	65 to 80
Stub axle	44 to 52	60 to 70
Disc backplate to rear axle	7 to 9	9 to 12
ABS rear sensor ring	5 to 7	8 to 10
Upper swivel pin	44 to 52	60 to 70
Lower swivel pin	16 to 21	22 to 28
Oil seal retainer	7 to 9	9 to 12
Swivel pin bearing housing	48 to 59	65 to 80
Rear brake caliper to axle case	55 to 65	75 to 88
Front brake caliper to swivel pin housing	55 to 65	75 to 88
Upper swivel pin to swivel pin housing	44 to 52	60 to 70
Disc shield to lower bracket	5 to 7	7 to 10

Braking system

Anti-lock brake system (ABS)

Type	Clayton Dewandre-Wabco

Torque wrench settings

	lbf ft	Nm
Non-ABS models		
Brake pressure warning switch	16	22
Servo unit	16 to 19	22 to 25
Hydraulic brake pipes to master cylinder	7 to 8	9 to 11
Master cylinder to servo	15 to 22	21 to 29
ABS models		
Hydraulic brake pipe connections:		
Hydraulic booster	9 to 12	12 to 16
M12	11 to 15	15 to 20
Calipers	7 to 8	9 to 11
Rear axle 4-way connector	7 to 8	9 to 11
Hydraulic hose brackets	8 to 10	11 to 13.5
Hydraulic hose female connector	8 to 10	11 to 13.5
Hydraulic pump and accumulator	9 to 12	12 to 16
PCRV-M10	8 to 10	11 to 13.5
PCRV M12	9 to 10	12 to 14
Hydraulic booster to pedal box	17 to 20	23 to 27
Fluid reservoir bracket	7 to 8	9 to 11

Electrical system

Alternator

Lucas A133/80

Nominal output	80 amps
Minimum brush length	10 mm (0.39 in)
Regulating voltage	13.6 to 14.4 volts
Field resistance	2.6 ohms
Drivebelt tension	4 mm to 6 mm (0.19 to 0.25 in) deflection under firm thumb pressure midway between pulleys

Lucas 127/65

Nominal output	65 amps
Minimum brush length	5 mm (0.20 in)
Regulating voltage	13.6 to 14.4 volts
Field resistance	3.2 ohms

Starter motor

Type .... Lucas 78R

Main fusebox - mid-1984 to 1985 models

Fuse number and circuit	Rating (amps)	Colour
1 RH headlamp - dipped	7.5	Brown
2 LH headlamp - dipped	7.5	Brown
3 RH headlamp - main	7.5	Brown
4 LH headlamp - main	7.5	Brown
5 RH sidelamps and illumination panel lamps	5	Tan
6 LH sidelamps	5	Tan
7 Front and rear wiper motors	15	Light blue
8 Heater motor	20	Yellow
9 Heated rear windows	15	Light blue
10 Electric mirror heater elements*	3	Violet
11 Interior lamps, clock, horns, cigar lighter, headlamp flasher, engine compartment lamp	15	Light blue
12 Rear foglamps (from headlamp dip)	10	Red
13 Indicators, stop-lamps, reversing lamps, electric mirror motors	15	Light blue
14 Trailer auxiliary circuit	15	Light blue
15 Air conditioning fan*	20	Yellow
16 Air conditioning fan*	20	Yellow
17 Air conditioning compressor clutch*	5	Tan
18 Air conditioning blower motor*	20	Yellow
19 Central door locking system*	10	Red
20 Electric window lifts*	25	White

*Optional fittings

Note: *In addition to the above fuses, an in-line fuse of 7 amp rating protects the radio/cassette circuit*

Main fusebox - 1985-on models

The fusebox is the same as for mid-1984 to 1985 models except for the following:

Fuse number and circuit	Rating (amps)	Colour
15 Auxiliary driving lamps	15	Light blue
16 Rear wash/wipe motor	10	Red
17 Cigar lighters	20	Yellow
18 Fuel pump	10	Red
19 Central door locking*	10	Red
20 Electric window lifts*	25	White

*Optional fittings

Auxiliary fusebox - models with air conditioning (1985-on)

Fuse number and circuit	Rating (amps)	Colour
A1 Air conditioning fan	20	Yellow
A2 Air conditioning fan	20	Yellow
A3 Air conditioning compressor clutch	5	Tan
A4 Air conditioning blower motor	20	Yellow
A5 Spare		
A6 Spare		

Main fusebox - 1989 models

Fuse number and circuit	Rating (amps)	Colour
1 RH headlamp low beam and power wash	7.5	Brown
2 LH headlamp low beam	7.5	Brown
3 RH headlamp high beam	7.5	Brown
4 LH headlamp high beam, auxiliary lamp switch	7.5	Brown
5 RH parking lamps and instrument illumination	5	Tan
6 LH parking lamps and radio illumination	5	Tan
7 Front wash/wiper motors, seat relay, window lift relay, aerial amplifier	15	Blue
8 Heater/air conditioning motor	30	Green
9 Heated rear screen	25	White
10 Window lifts rear - option	30	Green
11 Interior lamp delay, clock, radio, under-bonnet illumination	15	Blue
12 Rear fog guard (from dipped headlamps)	10	Red

Main fusebox - 1989 models (continued)

Fuse number and circuit	Rating (amps)	Colour
13 Direction indicators, stoplamps, reverse lamps, electric mirror pick-up point, low coolant, heated jets, interior lamp delay heater/air conditioning relay	15	Blue
14 Hazard lamp, horn, headlamps flash	20	Yellow
15 Auxiliary driving lamps	15	Blue
16 Rear wash/wipemotor,heated rear screen switch	10	Red
17 Cigar lighters (front and rear)	20	Yellow
18 Fuel pump	10	Red
19 Central door locking option	10	Red
20 Electric window lifts front option	30	Green

Main fusebox - 1990 models

Fuse number and circuit	Rating (amps)	Colour
A1 LH dipped beam	10	Red
A2 LH main beam, auxiliary lamp relay	10	Red
A3 LH sidelamps, radio illumination, trailer pick-up	5	Tan
A4 Rear fog guard (headlamp switch controlled)	10	Red
A5 Direction indicators, resistor, heated jets, thermostat, heated front screen timer, air conditioning low coolant, speed transducer, interior lamp delay, reverse lights, stop-lamps	20	Yellow
A6 Auxiliary driving lamps (from main beam)	10	Red
A7 RH sidelamps, rheostat controlled instrument/switch illumination, trailer pick-up	5	Tan
A8 RH main beam	10	Red
A9 RH dipped beam	10	Red
B1 Front wash/wipe, seat relays, window lift relays, aerial amplifier	20	Yellow
B2 Interior lamp, clock, under-bonnet illumination, electric seat relays, radio, door lamps	20	Yellow
B3 Hazard switch, alarm, main beam/dip flash, horns	20	Yellow
B4 Cigar lighters	20	Yellow
B5 Sunroof motor	20	Yellow
B6 Headlamp wash	20	Yellow
B7 Air conditioning compressor clutch	5	Tan
B8 Air conditioning/radiator cooling fan	20	Yellow
B9 Air conditioning/radiator cooling fan	20	Yellow
C1 Heated rear screen (voltage switch controlled)	30	Green
C2 Window lifts rear	30	Green
C3 Rear wash wipe motor, heated rear screen relay, mirror heaters	10	Red
C4 Fuel pump	10	Red
C5 Mirror motors, cruise control (option)	10	Red
C6 Not used	-	-
C7 Central locking	15	Blue
C8 Window lifts front	30	Green
C9 Heater/air conditioning motor	30	Green

Bulbs

	Wattage
Rear foglamps	21
Side repeater lamps	6
Differential lock warning lamp	2.2
Engine compartment lamp	5
Auxiliary driving lamps	55
Sidelamps	5
Stop/tail lamps	21/5
Number plate lamp	5
Instrument panel lamps	1.2
Ignition warning lamp	2
Cigar lighter illumination	1.2
Door edge/puddle lamps	5
Auxiliary switch panel illumination	1.2
Automatic graphics illumination	5

Suspension and steering

Road springs

Colour code	Rating - lb/in (kg/m)	Free length - in (mm)	No of coils
Yellow stripe	130 (2321.5)	16.34 (414.29)	7.11
Yellow stripe	170 (3035.86)	16.95 (430.53)	8.85
Green stripe	150 (2678.7)	16.13 (409.70)	7.63
Blue stripe	133 (2375.1)	15.4 (391.16)	7.18
Red/white stripe	170 (3035.86)	16.95 (430.53)	7.00
Red/yellow stripe	150 (2678.7)	17.18 (436.40)	7.65
Blue/white stripe	133 (2375.1)	16.44 (417.57)	7.65
Green/yellow stripe	170 (3035.86)	16.20 (411.48)	7.00

Maximum allowable spring free length contraction (under
that specified) .... 0.787 in (20 mm)
Rear axle bump stop-to-pad clearance (measured to front corner of pad):
    Average minimum allowable .... 2.8 in (67 mm)

Tyre pressures

Michelin 205 R 16 M + S - all loads under normal conditions:
    Front (cold) .... 25 lbf/in^2 (1.8 kgf/cm^2)
    Rear (cold) .... 35 lbf/in^2 (2.5 kgf/cm^2)
Michelin 205 R 16 M + S - sustained high speed above 60 mph
(100 kph) or when checked above ambient temperature of 77°F (25°C):
    Front .... 28 lbf/in^2 (2.0 kgf/cm^2)
    Rear .... 38 lbf/in^2 (2.7 kgf/cm^2)
All models from July 1979*:
    Normal use:
        Front .... 25 lbf/in^2 (1.8 kgf/cm^2)
        Rear .... 35 lbf/in^2 (2.5 kgf/cm^2)
    Emergency soft use:
        Front .... 15 lbf/in^2 (1.1 kgf/cm^2)
        Rear .... 25 lbf/in^2 (1.8 kgf/cm^2)
*Also suitable for earlier models fitted with heavy duty suspension

Torque wrench setting

	lbf ft	Nm
Alloy roadwheel nuts	90 to 95	122 to 129

3 General dimensions, weights and capacities

Heights

Overall height .... 70 in (1.78 m)
Maximum cargo height .... 40 in (1.01 m)
Rear opening height .... 40 in (1.01 m)

Weights

EEC kerb weight: **Total**
    Four-door .... 4248 lb (1927 kg)
    Two-door .... 4178 lb (1895 kg)
Maximum allowable towing weights (on road):
    Non-braked trailer .... 1100 lb (500 kg)
    Braked trailer .... 4400 lb (2000 kg)
    Four wheel trailer with continuous or semi- continuous (coupled)
    brakes .... 8800 lb (4000 kg)
Maximum allowable towed weights (off road):
    Non-braked trailer .... 1100 lb (500 kg)
    Braked trailer .... 2200 lb (1000 kg)
    Four wheel trailer with continuous or semi- continuous (coupled)
    brakes .... 2200 lb (1000 kg)
Maximum allowable roof rack load .... 165 lb (75 kg)

Capacities

Luggage capacity:
    Rear seat in position - four- door .... 36.18 cu ft (1.02 cu m)
    Rear seat in position - two- door .... 41.48 cu ft (1.17 cu m)
    Rear seat folded .... 70.8 cu ft (2.99 cu m)

4 Engine

Engine size (1990-on models) - description

1 As from October 1989 (ie 1990 models) all petrol version Range Rovers are fitted with a 3947 cc engine which replaces the 3528 cc engine. The specifications for the new engine are given at the beginning of this Supplement.

Oil cooler adaptor (1990-on models) - removal and refitting

2 If necessary apply the handbrake then jack up the front of the vehicle and support on axle stands. Alternatively position the vehicle over an inspection pit.
3 Place a suitable container beneath the oil filter position then unscrew and remove the filter. If it is tight use a filter removal strap wrench.
4 Unscrew the union nuts and disconnect the two oil cooler pipes from the adaptor.
5 Mark the adaptor in relation to the oil pump cover, then unscrew the centre mounting nut and withdraw the adaptor.
6 Clean the adaptor and filter mounting faces. Refit the adaptor to the oil pump cover and tighten the nut.
7 Re-connect the oil cooler pipes and tighten the union nuts.
8 Smear a little clean engine oil on the filter sealing ring. Screw on the filter until it just touches the adaptor face, then tighten it a further half turn only by hand. On completion, run the engine and check for oil leaks.

Inlet valve oil seals - general

9 On later models the inlet valves are fitted with an oil seal. These seals can be used on earlier models not previously having seals fitted.
10 When fitting the seals onto the valves, press the seal down until it abuts with the valve guide. When the engine is started the seal will automatically position itself on the valve stem (Fig. 13.2).

Engine (automatic transmission models) - removal and refitting

11 The engine removal and refitting details for automatic transmission models are basically the same as described for the manual transmission models in Chapter 1. As with the manual gearbox models, the engine must be removed separately from the transmission (see Section 4 in Chapter 1).
12 In addition to those items detailed in Chapter 1 for engine removal it will also be necessary to disconnect the oil cooler lines where they are attached to the side of the engine. These and other items which differ when disconnecting the engine from the automatic transmission are described in Sections 5, 10 and 11 of this Chapter.

Engine (fuel injection models) - removal and refitting

13 Removal of an engine equipped with fuel injection is essentially the same as described in Chapter 1 for carburettor models. The differences are largely self-evident, but the following points should be noted:
(a) *Depressurize the fuel system before disconnecting the battery*
(b) *When disconnecting fuel pipes, plug the openings after removal and take great care to prevent dirt ingress*
(c) *Remove ancillary components, delicate items and those likely to interfere with the lifting gear before removing the engine. These include the alternator, air conditioning compressor (if fitted), power steering pump, air cleaner, airflow meter, throttle linkage and brackets, and the plenum chamber, in addition to the items covered in Chapter 1*
(d) *Label the wiring harness connectors when removing them if there is any possibility of subsequent confusion*
14 Removal and refitting procedures applicable to the fuel injection system components will be found in Section 6, details of the air conditioning system in Section 17 and the power-assisted steering in Chapter 11.

Engine and associated components - air conditioned models

15 When removing the engine or any of its ancillary components which will necessitate disconnecting the air conditioning system hoses or components, reference should first be made to the special precautions concerning the air conditioning system in Section 17 of this Supplement.

Thread sealant specification - general

16 When refitting bolts to critical areas of the engine, cooling system and certain other applications, reference is made throughout this manual to the use of thread sealant type 3MEC 776. This has now been revised and the manufacturers currently specify Loctite 572 for this purpose.

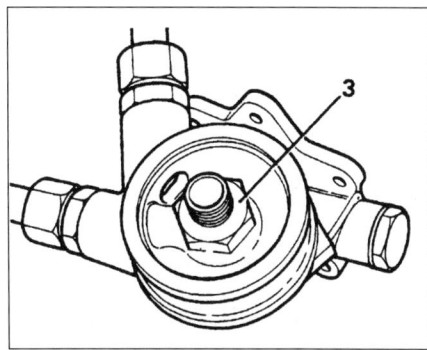

Fig. 13.1 Oil cooler adaptor retaining nut (3) fitted to 1990-on models (Sec 4)

Inlet manifold (pre-1988 fuel injection models) - removal and refitting

17 The following procedure assumes that the engine is in the vehicle If the engine has been removed some of the following will already have been carried out and can be ignored. Further information on removal and refitting of the applicable fuel injection system components is given in Section 6.
18 Depressurise the fuel system as described in Section 6.
19 Disconnect the battery negative terminal.
20 Refer to Chapter 2 and drain the cooling system.
21 Remove the plenum chamber and ram housing.
22 Remove the extra air valve.
23 Disconnect the wiring multi-plugs from the fuel injectors, cold start injector, thermotime switch and coolant sensor.
24 Release the wiring harness retaining clips and move the harness to one side.
25 Disconnect the top hose at the thermostat housing and the two hoses at the rear of the water pump.
26 Disconnect the water temperature sensor electrical lead.
27 On models equipped with air conditioning, disconnect the two electrical leads at the thermostat housing sensor.
28 Disconnect the two heater hoses at the rear of the inlet manifold.
29 Slacken the clip and disconnect the fuel pressure regulator flexible hose at the rigid fuel supply pipe (Fig. 13.3).
30 At the rear of the manifold unscrew the bolt securing the rigid fuel supply pipe clip.
31 At the other end of the rigid fuel supply pipe, unscrew the union nut and disconnect the fuel feed hose.
32 Slacken the clip and disconnect the fuel return hose at the fuel pressure regulator.

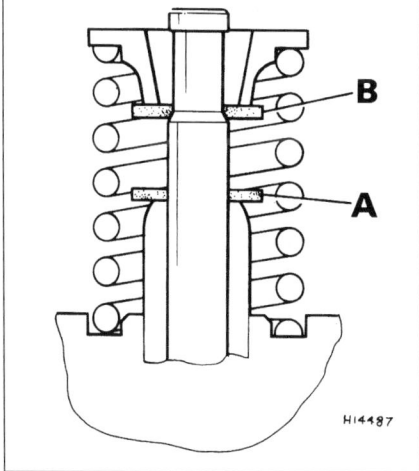

Fig. 13.2 Inlet valve oil seal - fitment to early models (Sec 4)

A Abut oil seal with valve guide
B Oil seal operating position

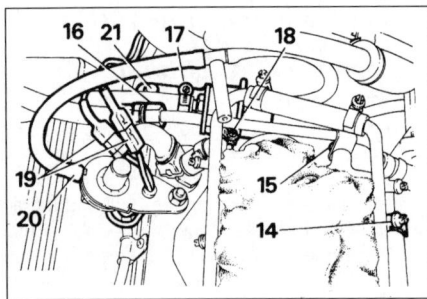

Fig. 13.3 Inlet manifold component attachments - fuel injection models (Sec 4)

14 *Fuel pressure regulator hose connection at rigid pipe*
15 *Rigid fuel supply pipe*
16 *Fuel feed hose union nut*
17 *Fuel return hose attachment*
18 *Fuel return hose attachment at side of regulator*
19 *Vacuum switch electrical leads*
20 *Vacuum switch hose*
21 *Fuel pressure regulator mounting bracket bolt*

33 Release the clip and remove the fuel return hose at the side of the fuel pressure regulator.
34 Disconnect the two electrical leads at the vacuum switch, followed by the vacuum hose.
35 Undo the fuel pressure regulator mounting bracket bolt and remove the regulator.
36 Release the spark plug HT leads from the two clips at the front of the inlet manifold.
37 Undo the twelve bolts and washers securing the manifold to the cylinder heads noting that the two bolts at the front are longer than the remaining ten.
38 Lift off the manifold, undo the two gasket clamp bolts and remove the gasket from the cylinder block.
39 Remove the gasket seals.
40 Before refitting the manifold ensure that all mating faces are clean with all traces of old gasket removed.
41 Smear both sides of the new gasket seals with silicone grease and locate the seals with their ends engaged in the notches formed between the cylinder heads and block.
42 Apply Hylomar sealant around the outside of the cylinder head, manifold gasket and manifold water passages then fit the gasket with the word FRONT at the front and the open bolt hole to the front right-hand side.
43 Fit the gasket clamps but tighten the clamp bolts finger-tight only at this stage.
44 Place the inlet manifold in position on the gasket, smear the threads of the retaining bolts with Loctite 572 and fit the bolts. Tighten the bolts progressively working from the centre outwards to the specified torque wrench setting.
45 Tighten the gasket clamp bolts to the specified torque wrench setting.
46 The remainder of the refitting procedure is a direct reversal of removal. Fill the cooling

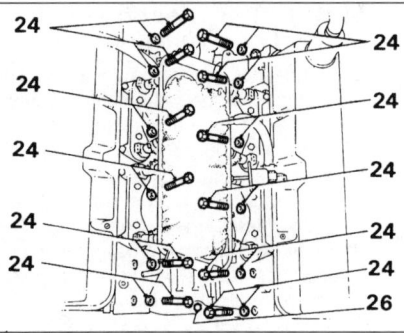

Fig. 13.4 Inlet manifold retaining bolt details (Sec 4)

24 *Retaining bolts and washers*
26 *Gasket clamps*

system with reference to Chapter 2 on completion.

Inlet manifold (1988-on fuel injection models) - removal and refitting

47 Depressurise the fuel system as described in Section 6.
48 Disconnect the battery negative lead.
49 Disconnect the radiator bottom hose and partially drain the cooling system until the level is below the thermostat housing. Refit the hose and tighten the clip. Refer to Section 5 if necessary.
50 Remove the plenum chamber and ram housing with reference to Section 6.
51 Disconnect the wiring multi-plugs to the fuel temperature thermistor, coolant temperature thermistor and injectors.
52 Unbolt the pressure regulator from the fuel rail. Remove it then seal the end of the fuel rail with suitable plastic plugs to prevent the ingress of dirt and foreign matter. It is not necessary to completely remove the fuel rail.
53 Disconnect the wiring plugs from the air conditioning engine coolant sensor located on the thermostat elbow.
54 Disconnect the wiring plug from the coolant temperature transmitter located at the front of the inlet manifold.

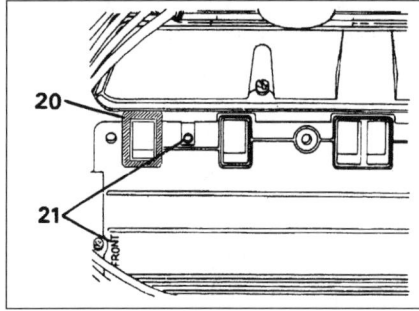

Fig. 13.5 Inlet manifold gasket location (Sec 4)

20 *Sealant around the water passage openings*
21 *Open bolt hole and 'FRONT' marking on gasket*

55 Release the injector harness from the rear of the fuel rail and place it to one side.
56 Loosen the clips and disconnect the heater hoses from the heater pipes at the front of the right-hand rocker cover. Unbolt the rigid heater pipes from the inlet manifold and remove the pipes out of the hoses. Place the heater pipe assembly to one side.
57 Unscrew the bolts securing the inlet manifold to the cylinder heads, then withdraw the manifold from the engine compartment.
58 Remove the clamps and withdraw the gasket and seals.
59 Clean away all sealing compound from the water passage openings of the cylinder heads.
60 Commence refitting by locating the new seals in position with their ends engaged in the notches formed between the cylinder heads and cylinder block.
61 Apply sealant to the outside of the water passage openings on the cylinder heads, manifold gasket and inlet manifold.
62 Locate the manifold gasket in position with the word 'FRONT' to the front and the open bolt hole to the front right-hand side.
63 Fit the gasket clamps but do not fully tighten them at this stage.
64 Locate the inlet manifold on the cylinder heads and clean the threads of the manifold securing bolts. Insert all the bolts and tighten them progressively from the centre outwards to the specified torque. Tighten the gasket clamps to the specified torque.
65 The remaining refitting procedure is a reversal of removal.
66 Fill the cooling system with reference to Section 5.
67 Start the engine and check for fuel and water leaks.

Exhaust manifold (1988-on fuel injection models) - removal and refitting

68 Unbolt the front exhaust downpipe from the exhaust manifold and support.
69 Bend back the lock tabs and unscrew the exhaust manifold mounting bolts. Remove the lock tabs and washers.
70 Withdraw the exhaust manifold from the cylinder head and recover the gaskets.
71 Clean the mating surfaces of the exhaust

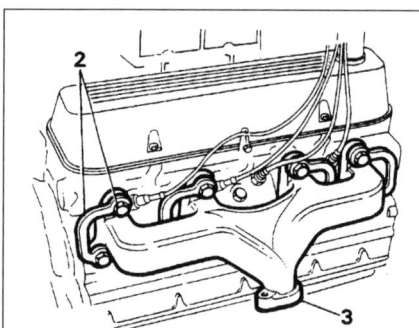

Fig. 13.6 Exhaust manifold (Sec 4)

2 *Bolt and locktab*   3 *Exhaust manifold*

manifold and cylinder head and apply anti-seize compound to the threads of the bolts.

72 Fit new gaskets to the cylinder head and locate the manifold in position. Fit the bolts, locktabs and plain washers noting that the plain washers are located between the manifold and the locktabs. Progressively tighten the bolts to the specified torque, then bend over the locktabs to secure.

73 Re-connect the front downpipe together with new gaskets and tighten the bolts to the specified torque.

5 Cooling system

Cooling system (pre-1990 models) - draining

1 Later models are not equipped with a drain plug on the radiator and it is therefore necessary to remove the bottom hose at its connection on the radiator to drain the system.

2 Apart from this, the procedures given in Chapter 2 are still applicable.

Cooling system (1990-on models) - general

3 The radiator fitted to the 3.9 litre engine incorporates oil coolers in both the left-hand and right-hand end tanks. The right-hand tank forms an engine oil cooler and the left-hand tank forms an automatic transmission fluid cooler. Where applicable, the manual gearbox oil cooler is still located in front of the radiator and air conditioning condenser fans.

4 The automatic transmission fluid temperature warning lamp sensor is now fitted beneath the bonnet next to the radiator end tank.

Cooling system (1990-on models) - draining

> ⚠ **Warning: Do not remove the expansion tank filler cap when the engine is hot or the water will scald you.**

5 With the engine cold slowly unscrew and remove the expansion tank filler cap taking care not to pull on the low level warning switch wiring. If necessary pull the plug from the switch first.

6 Unscrew and remove the hexagon radiator filler plug and O-ring.

7 Position a suitable container beneath the radiator bottom hose, then loosen the clip and disconnect the bottom hose from the radiator. Drain all of the coolant into the container.

8 Position the container beneath each of the cylinder banks, then unscrew the square-headed drain plugs located below the exhaust manifolds one at a time and drain the cylinder blocks.

9 It is not possible to drain all of the coolant from the heater system, so the heater system

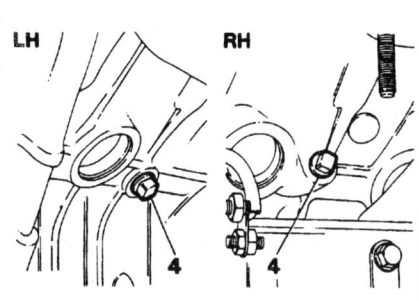

Fig. 13.7 Drain plugs (4) beneath each of the cylinder banks (Sec 5)

should be flushed with clean water by pouring water into the fill tower on top of the engine until it runs clear from the radiator bottom hose and cylinder block drain plug holes.

10 After all of the coolant has drained, reconnect the radiator bottom hose and tighten the cylinder block drain plugs.

Cooling system (1990-on models) - filling

11 It is important to carry out the following procedure as described in order to prevent air locks forming in the heater circuit. This is particularly relevant if the heater hoses on top of the rocker cover have been disconnected for any reason.

12 Refer to Chapter 2 paragraphs 1 to 4 inclusive.

13 Pour the mixture of water and antifreeze into the fill tower on top of the engine until the radiator is full (photo). The mixture should be poured in quickly to prevent the formation of air locks.

14 Before refitting the radiator filler cap, fill tower filler cap, or expansion tank filler cap, start the engine and run it until normal operating temperature is reached. During this period top up the coolant level in the radiator as necessary.

15 Switch off the engine, and refit the expansion tank and fill tower filler caps. If necessary renew the O-rings.

16 Allow the engine to cool over several hours then check the level in the expansion tank and top up if necessary to the mark on the seam. Refit and tighten the filler cap.

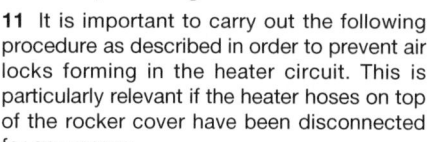

5.13 Coolant fill tower (arrowed) on the right-hand side of the plenum chamber

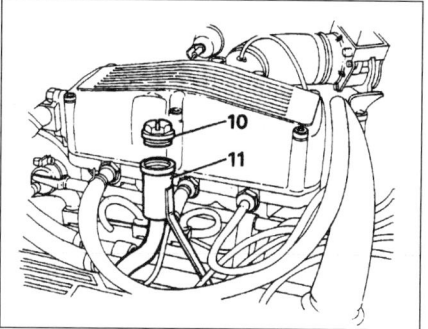

Fig. 13.8 Fill tower (11) and filler plug (10) (Sec 5)

Radiator (1990-on models) - removal and refitting

17 Disconnect the battery negative lead.

18 Drain the cooling system as previously described in this Section.

19 Remove the cooling fan assembly as described in this Section.

20 Remove the fan cowling.

21 Loosen the clips and disconnect the radiator top hoses.

22 Position suitable containers beneath each end of the radiator, then unscrew the union nuts and disconnect the transmission cooler and engine oil cooler pipes as applicable. Plug the ends of the pipes to prevent the ingress of foreign matter.

23 Disconnect the transmission oil temperature sensor plug.

24 Unscrew the nuts and remove the radiator mounting brackets from each side.

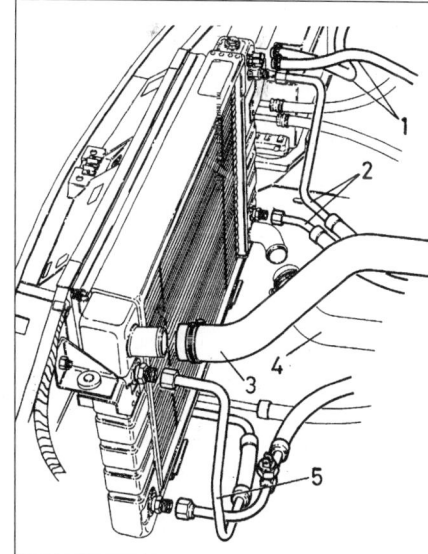

Fig. 13.9 Radiator fitted to 1990-on models (Sec 5)

1 *Expansion tank hoses*
2 *Engine oil cooler pipes*
3 *Radiator top hose*
4 *Radiator bottom hose*
5 *Automatic transmission fluid cooler pipes*

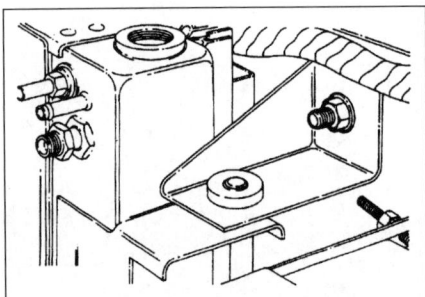

Fig. 13.10 Radiator mounting bracket (Sec 5)

25 Lift the radiator from its mounting rubbers taking care not to damage the radiator matrix on the cooling fan blades.

26 If a new radiator is being fitted transfer the oil cooler adaptors from the oil unit to the new one.

27 Refitting is a reversal of the removal procedure but tighten the union nuts to the specified torque. Top up the automatic transmission fluid and engine oil levels as necessary.

Fan cowl, blades, viscous coupling and pulley (1987-on models) - removal and refitting

28 Later models are equipped with a revised fan cowl and modified viscous coupling with either a seven blade or eleven blade fan. Removal and refitting is as follows.

29 Disconnect the battery negative terminal.

30 Undo the four fan cowl upper retaining screws and lift the cowl out of its lower mounting lugs.

31 Unscrew the central nut which secures the viscous coupling to the water pump spindle noting that the nut has a left-hand thread.

32 Release the nut and remove the viscous coupling/fan blade assembly.

33 Lift out the fan cowl.

34 If necessary separate the fan and viscous coupling by undoing the four bolts. If a seven blade fan is fitted undo the bolt securing the viscous coupling boss and remove the boss.

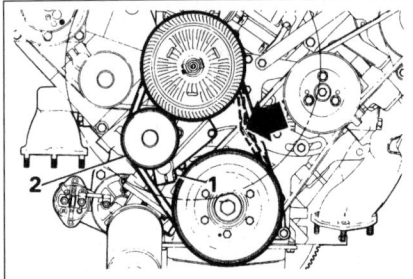

Fig. 13.13 Fanbelt adjustment - later models (Sec 5)

1 Jockey wheel clamp bolt
2 Jockey wheel
Arrow indicates tension checking point

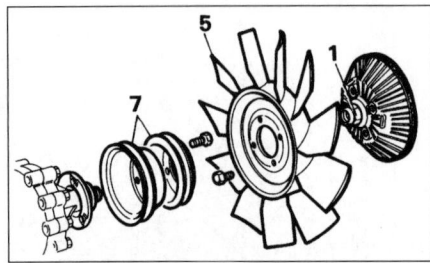

Fig. 13.11 Viscous coupling and eleven bladed fan components - later models (Sec 5)

1 Viscous coupling retaining nut
5 Fan
7 Pulley assembly

35 To remove the water pump pulley, remove the fanbelt as described in the next sub-section and, on models equipped with air conditioning, the compressor drivebelt (Sec 17).

36 Undo the pulley retaining bolts and remove the pulley.

37 Refitting is the reverse procedure to removal. Adjust the fanbelt as described in the following sub-section, and the compressor drivebelt, if fitted (Sec 17), on completion.

Fanbelt (1987-on) - removal, refitting and adjustment

38 On later models the water pump and cooling fan are driven by a separate belt from the crankshaft pulley and incorporate a jockey wheel to adjust the tension.

39 To remove the fanbelt, slacken the jockey wheel clamp bolt, move the jockey wheel toward the engine and slip the belt off the pulleys.

40 Fit the new belt and lever the jockey wheel outward to adjust the tension to the dimension given in the Specifications. Check the deflection at a point midway between the crankshaft and water pump pulleys.

41 Hold the jockey wheel in its correct position and tighten the clamp bolt.

6 Fuel, exhaust and emission control systems

PART A: CARBURETTOR MODELS (ZENITH/ STROMBERG/SOLEX)

> ⚠️ *Warning: Many of the procedures in this Section require the removal of fuel lines and connections which may result in some fuel spillage. Before carrying out any operation on the fuel system refer to the precautions given in 'Safety first!' at the beginning of this manual, and follow them implicitly. Petrol is a highly-dangerous and volatile liquid and the precautions necessary when handling it cannot be overstressed*

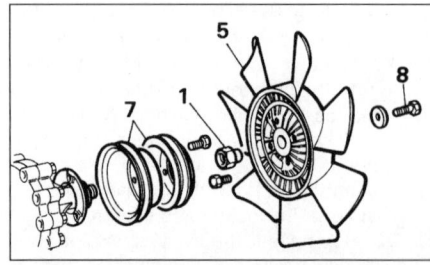

13.12 Viscous coupling and seven-bladed fan components - later models (Sec 5)

1 Viscous coupling retaining nut
5 Viscous coupling boss retaining bolt
7 Pulley assembly
8 Bolt

Air cleaner baffle - general

1 Some models may have a baffle fitted to the end of the air intake unit. The baffle will have been fitted to prevent backfiring on the overrun and can be fitted to models not so equipped to prevent this problem. Before fitting the baffle, first check that the vacuum pipes to the air intake temperature control unit are correctly located, are in good condition and securely fitted. The baffle is fitted to the intake, as shown in Fig. 13.14, and is secured by self-tapping screws.

Idle speed and mixture adjustment screws - general

2 The idle speed adjustment screw on later models is secured by a locking ring which is housed in a protective cover, and a special tool (Zenith part number B25243 or Rover tool MS 86) is necessary when making adjustments to the idle speed. The special tool is shown in Fig. 13.15. A similar tool

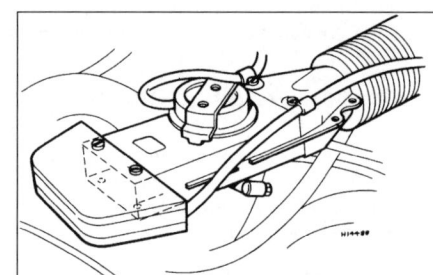

Fig. 13.14 Air cleaner baffle (Sec 6A)

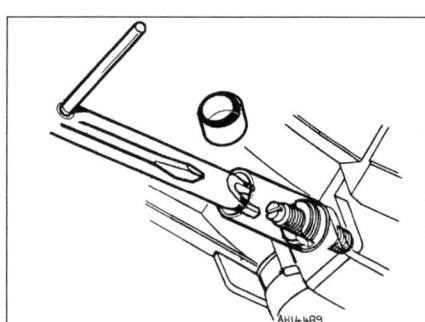

Fig. 13.15 Idle speed adjustment tool for later models (Sec 6A)

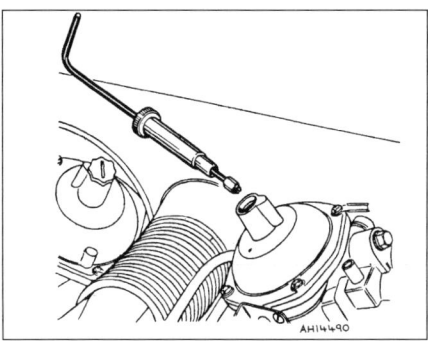

Fig. 13.16 Mixture adjustment tool for later models (Sec 6A)

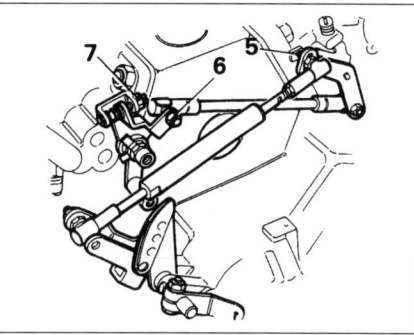

Fig. 13.17 Later type throttle linkage - automatic transmission models (Sec 6A)

5 *Kickdown cable interconnecting link nut*
6 *Interconnecting link attachment at left-hand carburettor*
7 *Lost motion adjusting screw*

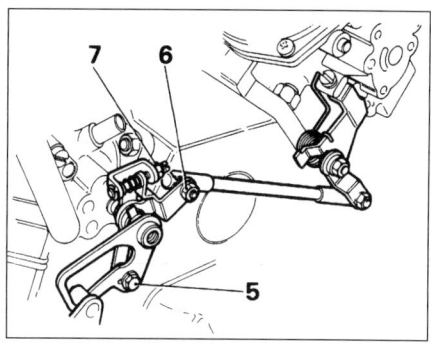

Fig. 13.18 Later type throttle linkage - manual transmission models (Sec 6A)

5 *Throttle cam securing nut*
6 *Interconnecting link attachment at left-hand carburettor*
7 *Lost motion adjusting screw*

would be easy to fabricate using a length of suitable diameter tube, shaped at one end. This would enable it to engage with the locking slots so that the ring can be held while adjustment is made using a screwdriver passed down through the tubing to turn the adjuster screw.

3 Any attempt to adjust the idle speed without this tool will result in damage to the adjuster screw and possibly the carburettor.

4 The carburettor mixture adjustment on later models (from 1979) differs from the earlier types described in Chapter 3 in that the later CD type carburettors have a raised blade type mixture needle adjuster instead of the Allen key socket.

5 Mixture adjustment on the later carburettor types will require the use of Zenith special tool B25860 or Rover tool MS 80 (shown in Fig. 13.16). The central socket engages over the tongue in the reservoir base and the external barrel locks into the air valve guide rod. When fitted in position to make any adjustments, ensure that the external barrel is correctly located to prevent the air valve from turning during adjustment which could damage the main diaphragm.

6 Turn the central socket clockwise to richen the mixture of anti-clockwise to weaken it.

Idle speed and mixture adjustment procedure - revisions

7 Automatic transmission models and later manual transmission versions (approximately 1986 onwards) are fitted with a modified throttle linkage necessitating a revised adjustment procedure, as follows.

8 Check the throttle cable adjustment as described in Chapter 3, Section 11. Also check that the linkage and cable move freely without any tendency to stick.

9 Start the engine and run it up to normal operating temperature.

10 Switch off the engine and remove the air cleaner (Chapter 3).

11 On automatic transmission models slacken the nut securing the kickdown cable to the interconnecting link on the right-hand carburettor lever.

12 On manual transmission models slacken

the nut securing the throttle cam to the left-hand carburettor lever.

13 Undo the nut and disconnect the interconnecting link between the two carburettors, at the left-hand carburettor linkage.

14 Slacken the locknut and turn the lost motion adjusting screw on the left-hand carburettor until it is well clear of the spring-loaded pad.

15 Place a suitable carburettor balancing tool across the carburettor intake apertures. Various proprietary balancing meters are available, but the following procedure relates to the use of the Rover balancer, tool No 605330.

16 Connect a tachometer to the engine in accordance with the manufacturer's instructions.

17 Remove the tamperproof caps over the idle speed adjustment screws on each carburettor and slacken the adjustment screw locknuts using Rover tool MS 86 or a suitable alternative.

18 Start the engine and observe the balancer gauge reading and the idle speed.

19 If the balancer gauge pointer is in the central (zero) sector of the gauge then the airflow through both carburettors is equal and correct.

20 If the gauge pointer moves to the right, decrease the air flow through the left-hand carburettor or increase the airflow through the right-hand carburettor by means of the idle speed adjustment screws. Reverse the procedure if the needle moves to the left.

21 Once the carburettors are balanced turn both idle speed adjustment screws by equal amounts in whichever direction is necessary to bring the idle speed to the specified setting. Ensure that, with the engine idling at the specified speed, the gauge pointer is still in the central sector of the gauge.

22 With this accomplished, tighten the idle speed adjustment screw locknuts.

23 Reconnect the interconnecting link to the left-hand carburettor linkage.

24 Hold the throttle lever against its stop on the right-hand carburettor and tighten the lost motion screw until contact is just made with the spring-loaded pad. Tighten the locknut.

25 Recheck the idle speed and balance; make any small corrections as necessary then switch off the engine and remove the balancer gauge.

26 On automatic transmission models make sure that the right-hand carburettor countershaft lever is against the idle stop and tighten the nut securing the kickdown cable to the interconnecting link.

27 On manual transmission models ensure that the roller on the left-hand carburettor throttle cam is seated in the corner of the cam slot then tighten the cam securing nut.

28 With the carburettor balance and idle speed correctly adjusted, check the mixture strength in each carburettor as follows.

29 Start the engine, run it at 2000 rpm for 30 seconds to clear the inlet manifold of excess fuel, then allow it to idle.

30 Using a long thin screwdriver, raise the piston in each carburettor in turn very slightly (0.03 in/0.08 mm) and note the change in engine speed. If the speed increases, the mixture is too rich. If the speed decreases, the mixture is too weak. No change, or a very slight fall in engine speed indicates a correct mixture.

31 If adjustment is necessary remove the piston damper from the top of the carburettor and adjust the mixture using Rover tool MS 80 (see paragraphs 4, 5 and 6). After every adjustment the tool should be removed from the carburettor and the engine speed increased to 2000 rpm for 30 seconds. Continue this procedure, making small corrections each time until the mixture strength in both carburettors is correct.

32 If a recognized type of CO meter is available this can be used to check the exhaust gas CO content. Insert the probe into the end of the exhaust pipe. The meter reading should not exceed the maximum figure given in the Specifications. Adjust the mixture as previously described if necessary.

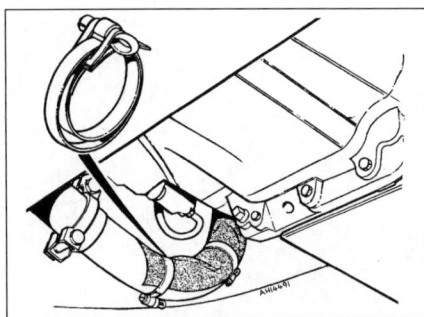

Fig. 13.19 Insulation pad location on the exhaust downpipe (Sec 6A)

33 Refit the piston dampers to each carburettor on completion.

34 If necessary, readjust the engine idle speed by turning the idle speed adjustment screws by equal amounts until the specified speed is obtained.

35 When all is correct switch off the engine, remove the tachometer and refit the air cleaner.

Fast idle speed - adjustment

36 On later models (approximately 1986 onwards) the fast idle speed adjustment procedure has been revised and is as follows.

37 Slacken the screw securing the choke cable to the fast idle cam on the left-hand carburettor.

38 From inside the vehicle pull the choke knob out to a distance of approximately 12.7 mm (0.5 in) and lock it in this position.

39 Rotate the fast idle cam, allowing the cable to slide through the trunnion, until the punch mark on the cam is in line with the centre of the fast idle adjusting screw on the throttle lever. Now tighten the choke cable clamping screw.

40 Slacken the fast idle adjusting screw locknut.

41 Start the engine and turn the fast idle adjusting screw as necessary until the specified fast idle speed is obtained then tighten the locknut.

42 Release the choke knob, push it fully in and check that the engine returns to normal idling speed.

Exhaust system - downpipe insulation

43 On some models an insulation pad may be found clipped to the exhaust downpipe adjacent to the clutch slave cylinder. The insulation is fitted to prevent the heat from the exhaust shortening the life of the slave cylinder seals.

44 When renewing the exhaust system, or the left-hand downpipe, the insulation pad must be fitted to the new system. The insulation pad is secured by three retaining clips.

45 The exhaust system fitted to models produced from 1980 was modified, but the downpipes and intermediate pipe sections on each side are interchangeable on earlier models.

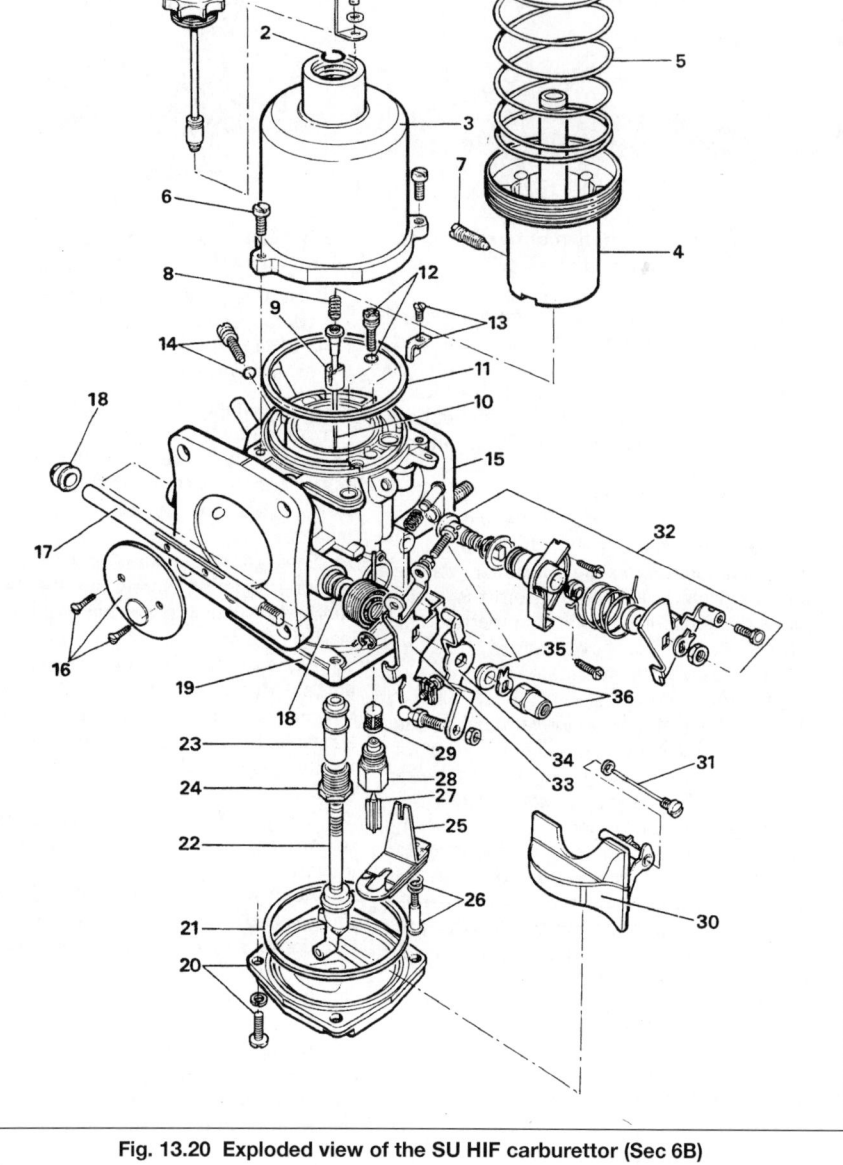

Fig. 13.20 Exploded view of the SU HIF carburettor (Sec 6B)

1 Piston damper	14 Mixture adjusting screw and seal
2 Spring clip	15 Carburettor body
3 Suction chamber	16 Throttle butterfly and retaining screws
4 Piston	17 Throttle spindle
5 Piston spring	18 Throttle spindle seals
6 Suction chamber retaining screws	19 Float chamber
7 Needle retaining screw	20 Float chamber cover and retaining screws
8 Needle bias spring	21 Seal
9 Needle guide	22 Jet assembly
10 Needle	23 Jet bearing
11 Suction chamber sealing ring	24 Jet bearing nut
12 Throttle adjusting screw and seal	25 Bi-metal jet lever
13 Piston key and retaining screw	

26 Jet retaining screw and spring
27 Float needle
28 Float needle seat
29 Float needle seat filter
30 Float
31 Float pivot spindle
32 Cold start and cam lever assembly
33 Throttle adjusting lever and lost motion assembly
34 Throttle actuating lever
35 Bush washer
36 Throttle lever assembly retaining nut and lock washer

PART B: CARBURETTOR MODELS (SU)

⚠️ *Warning: Many of the procedures in this section require the removal of fuel lines and connections which may result in some fuel spillage. Before carrying out any operation on the fuel system refer to the precautions given in 'Safety first!' at the beginning of this manual, and follow them implicitly. Petrol is a highly-dangerous and volatile liquid and the precautions necessary when handling it cannot be overstressed*

SU HIF carburettor- description

1 Carburettor models manufactured from 1987 onwards are fitted with SU HIF (Horizontal Integral Float chamber) carburettors. Each carburettor is of the variable choke, constant depression type incorporating a sliding piston which automatically controls the mixture of air and fuel supplied to the engine with respect to the throttle valve position and engine speed. In addition the carburettor is equipped with an electronically-operated mixture control device. This alters the mixture strength and engine speed when starting and during slow running, and also controls the operation of a fuel shut-off valve when decelerating or descending a hill.

2 The carburettor functions as follows. When the engine is started and is allowed to idle, the throttle valve passes a small amount of air. Because the piston is in a low position, it offers a large restriction, and the resultant pressure reduction draws fuel from the jet, and atomization occurs to provide a combustible mixture. Since the inside section of the tapered needle is across the mouth of the jet, a relatively small amount of fuel is passed.

3 When the throttle valve is opened, the amount of air passing through the carburettor is increased, which causes a greater depression beneath the sliding piston. An internal passageway connects this depression with the suction chamber above the piston, which now rises. The piston offers less of a restriction and the depression is reduced, with the result that a point is reached where the forces of depression, gravity, and spring tension balance out. The tapered needle has now been raised, and more fuel passes from the jet.

4 Incorporated in the jet adjusting (mixture) screw mechanism is a bi metal strip which alters the position of the jet to compensate for varying fuel densities resulting from varying fuel temperatures.

5 Fuel enrichment for cold starting is by an internal valve which admits more fuel into the airstream passing through the carburettor. This valve is operated by a stepper motor which also controls the engine idling speed. An electronic control unit (ECU) - which is a small microprocessor - receives inputs from the coolant thermistor, ambient air temperature sensor, accelerator pedal switch and ignition coil, and adjusts the engine idle speed and mixture accordingly. The ECU also controls the operation of a fuel shut-off valve which comes into operation when decelerating or descending a hill. If, during these conditions, the engine speed is in excess of 1300 rpm, the ambient air temperature and engine temperature are above a predetermined value, and the accelerator pedal switch is closed (pedal released), the valve will be opened and closed at half second intervals. This introduces a partial vacuum to the top of the float chamber thus weakening the mixture. The fuel shut-off circuit is de-activated if the engine speed suddenly drops, i.e. when declutching. When accelerating, a vacuum operated switch acts upon the mixture control, allowing more fuel to be drawn through, resulting in the necessary richer mixture.

6 The overall effect of this type of carburettor is that it will remain in tune during the lengthy service intervals and also under varying operating conditions and temperature changes. The design of the unit and its related systems ensures a fine degree of mixture control over the complete throttle range, coupled with enhanced engine fuel economy.

Carburettor (SU HIF) - overhaul

Note: *The following procedure is for the right-hand carburettor. The left-hand carburettor procedure is similar.*

7 Remove the carburettor from the engine and clean it with fuel or paraffin.

8 Remove the nuts and spring washers, and remove the air inlet adaptor and the gasket.

9 Unscrew the piston damper and drain the oil into a suitable container.

10 Mark the suction chamber and piston body in relation to each other with a pencil. Unscrew the screws and withdraw the suction chamber together with the piston and spring.

11 Extract the circlip from the top of the piston rod, and remove the piston and spring.

12 Unscrew the metering needle guide locking screw and remove the needle, guide and spring assembly from the piston. If difficulty is experienced, carefully grip the needle in a soft-jawed vice close to the piston and give the piston a sharp pull. Take care not to bend the needle.

13 Invert the carburettor then unscrew the screws and remove the float chamber cover plate and sealing ring from the bottom of the carburettor.

14 Unscrew the jet adjusting lever mounting screw and remove the spring.

15 Remove the jet together with the bi-metal lever and separate the lever from the jet.

16 Hold the float then unscrew and remove the pivot spindle and remove the washer. Withdraw the float.

17 Remove the needle valve from its seat.

18 Unscrew and remove the needle valve seat, and remove the filter.

19 Unscrew the jet bearing nut, then invert the carburettor and extract the jet bearing. If necessary tap the carburettor to release the bearing.

20 Unscrew the screw and remove the piston guide key. Remove the suction chamber sealing ring.

21 Unscrew and remove the mixture adjusting screw and seal using thin nosed pliers to withdraw the screw.

22 Bend back the tabs and remove the cam lever nut and lock washer. Remove the cam lever and spring.

23 Remove the end seal cover and seal.

24 Unscrew the screws and withdraw the cold start valve body and seal together with the valve spindle. Remove the gasket.

25 Note the positions of the throttle levers and the return spring, then bend back the tab and remove the throttle lever nut. Withdraw the lock washer, bush washer and the throttle actuating lever.

26 Release the throttle return spring and remove the throttle adjusting lever from the throttle butterfly spindle. Remove the return spring.

27 With the butterfly shut, mark the butterfly in relation to the carburettor flange. Unscrew the remaining screws and withdraw the butterfly from the spindle.

28 Remove the throttle butterfly spindle from the carburettor body together with the two seals.

29 Wash all components in fuel or paraffin, and examine them for wear and damage. In particular check the throttle spindle and bearing for excessive play, the float needle and seating for wear, the float for punctures, the carburettor body for cracks, the metering needle for wear and scoring, and the bi-metal jet for cracks. Check all springs and renew all seals. Clean the inside of the suction chamber and the piston, then locate the piston in the chamber without the spring. Hold the

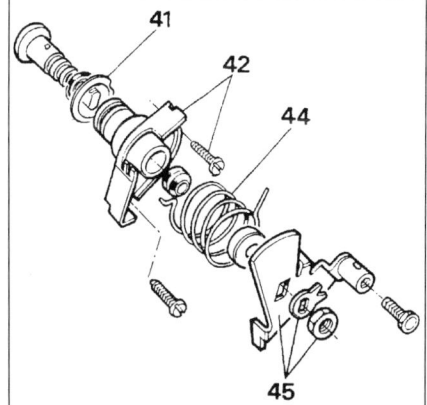

Fig. 13.21 Cold start valve components (Sec 6B)

41 Washer with half-moon cut-out
42 Body and screws
44 Return spring
45 Cam lever, lock washer and nut

assembly horizontal and spin the piston: it should spin freely in all positions. If there is any tendency to stick check for any foreign matter or for distortion and renew the components as necessary.

30 Commence reassembly by inserting the throttle spindle into the carburettor body, then insert the butterfly into the spindle in its correct position as noted on removal. Insert the screws but before tightening them close the throttle firmly to ensure that the butterfly is centred correctly. After tightening the screws, carefully splay the inner ends to lock them.

31 Locate the new seals on both ends of the throttle spindle making sure that they are the correct way round.

32 Locate a new O-ring to the cold start valve body and assemble the valve spindle to the valve body. Fit the new gasket to the valve noting that the half-moon cut-out in the washer is positioned for the top retaining screw.

33 Refit the cold start assembly to the carburettor body, and fit and tighten the screws.

34 Fit the end seal and cover followed by the spring.

35 Refit the cam lever and tension the spring, then fit a new lock washer and secure with the nut. Bend over the lock tab to secure. Check that the spring is located correctly and re-position the coils if necessary.

36 Refit the throttle lever return spring so that the longest leg rests against the throttle adjusting screw housing.

37 Refit the throttle adjusting lever and lost motion assembly, and tension the return spring.

38 Fit the throttle actuating lever then refit the bush washer and lock washer.

39 Refit the special nut and bend over the lock tabs to lock.

40 Refit the jet bearing with its long end towards the float, then refit the bearing nut.

41 Clean the filter and refit it followed by the float seat. Tighten securely.

42 Locate the needle valve in the seat with its spring loaded pin uppermost.

43 Locate the float in the carburettor body, then insert the pivot pin with the washer and tighten.

44 With the carburettor inverted and the needle valve closed by the weight of the float only, use a straight-edge as shown in Fig. 13.22 and check that the point on the float is 0.5 to 1.5 mm below the level of the float chamber face. if not, adjust the position by bending the brass pad until the correct dimension is achieved. Make sure that the float pivots correctly on the spindle.

45 Assemble the jet to the bi-metal jet lever and make sure that the jet head moves freely in the cut-out.

46 Refit the jet and bi-metal jet lever to the carburettor and secure with the spring loaded jet retaining screw.

47 Refit the mixture adjusting screw and adjust until the jet is flush with the carburettor bridge, then turn the screw 3 1/2 turns clockwise.

48 Refit the float chamber cover together with a new gasket. Insert the screw and washer and tighten.

49 Locate the needle, spring and guide assembly to the piston making sure that the, etched arrow head on the needle locating guide is aligned between the piston transfer holes as shown in Fig. 13.23. insert and tighten the screw making sure that the guide is flush with the piston and that the screw locates in the guide slot.

50 Locate the piston key on the body and tighten the screw. Splay its end to lock.

51 Locate a new sealing ring in the groove in the carburettor body.

52 Locate the piston and needle assembly in the carburettor body followed by the spring.

53 Hold the suction chamber over the spring in its correct position in relation to the body then lower the chamber onto the spring and

onto the body taking care not to rotate the chamber. Failure to observe this may result in the spring being 'wound up'. Insert and tighten the screws then check that the piston moves up and down freely.

54 With the piston held at the top of its stroke, refit the circlip.

55 Top up the piston with the correct quantity of oil, then insert the piston damper and tighten.

56 Refit the air inlet adaptor together with a new gasket and secure with the nuts and washers.

57 Refit the carburettors to the engine with reference to Chapter 3 and the following paragraphs.

Carburettors (SU HIF) - removal and refitting

58 The removal and refitting procedures are similar to those for the Zenith/Stromberg carburettors described in Chapter 3.

59 When refitting the carburettors to the engine make sure that the joint washers, deflector and insulator are fitted in their correct order. The insulator must be fitted with the arrow head uppermost and pointing inwards towards the inlet manifold. Refit the nuts and spring washers, and tighten evenly.

60 Re-connect the linkages and adjust the carburettors as described later in this Part.

Carburettors (SU HIF) - tuning and adjustment

61 Before commencing the procedure it will be necessary to obtain a carburettor balancer and an exhaust gas analyser. The ambient air temperature should be between 15°C and 26°C and an accurate tachometer should be used. The engine must be at normal temperature at least 5 minutes after the thermostat has opened and the adjustment should be preceded by running the engine at 2500 rpm for one minute. Run the engine at

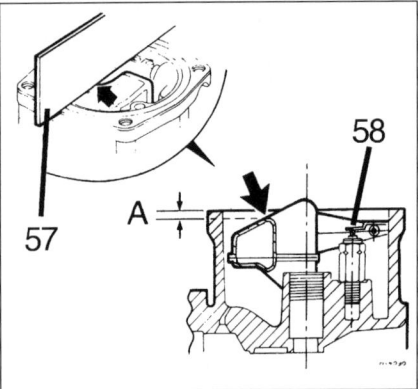

Fig. 13.22 Checking the float level (Sec 6B)

57 Straight edge   *A = 0.5 to 1.5 mm*
58 Brass pad

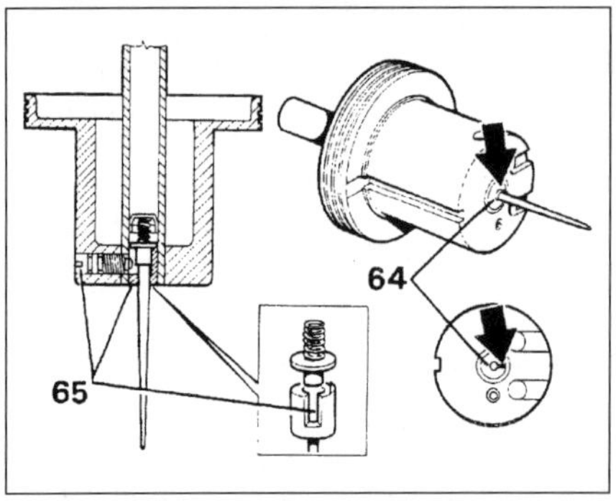

Fig. 13.23 Correct alignment of the needle, spring and guide assembly in the piston (Sec 6B)

64 Etched arrow location
65 Guide location

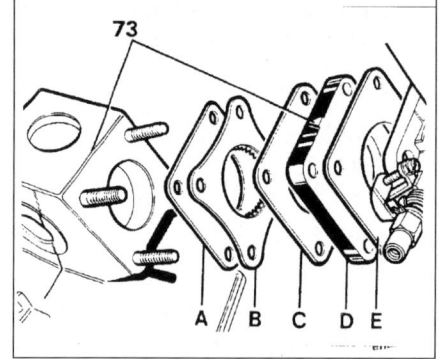

Fig. 13.24 Correct order of the carburettor joint washers, deflector and insulator (Sec 6B)

73 Arrow position

this speed every two minutes, to prevent the engine overheating. Make sure that the piston dampers are topped up before starting the procedure.

62 The idle speed and mixture adjustment screws are fitted with tamperproof plugs and these should be renewed after making the adjustments.

63 Disconnect the interconnecting throttle link between the two carburettors, then unscrew the idle adjusting screws on each carburettor until clear of the throttle levers. Now turn each adjusting screw until it just touches the throttle lever.

64 Start the engine and allow it to idle. Turn each adjusting screw clockwise by equal amounts until the idling speed is between 700 and 800 rpm.

65 Connect the carburettor balancer to each carburettor in turn in accordance with the equipment manufacturer's instructions, and if necessary adjust the idle screws to give the same reading on each carburettor. The idle speed must also be maintained.

66 With the carburettor balance set, re-connect the throttle interconnecting link.

67 Working on one carburettor at a time, remove the carburettor suction chamber, piston and spring as described previously and adjust the jet flush with the bridge. This provides a datum position for adjusting the mixture. Refit the suction chambers to the carburettors and make sure that the dampers are topped up with engine oil to the top of the hollow piston rod.

68 Turn each mixture adjustment screw 3 1/2 turns clockwise.

69 Insert the exhaust gas analyser probe into the end of the exhaust pipe as far as possible, then start the engine and allow it to stabilise for approximately 1 1/2 minutes.

70 With the engine idling, check the CO reading and if necessary adjust each mixture adjustment screw by equal amounts to achieve the CO reading of 0.5 to 2.5%. If the reading is not satisfactory after two minutes, run the engine at 2000 to 2500 rpm for a minute before proceeding.

71 Check the engine idling speed as follows making sure that it is at normal temperature.

72 On manual gearbox models loosen the nut, at the left-hand carburettor securing the interconnecting link ball to the throttle cam lever. On automatic transmission models loosen the lower nut, securing the interconnecting link ball to the throttle lever at the right-hand carburettor.

73 Disconnect the interconnecting link between the carburettors at the left-hand carburettor.

74 Working on the right-hand carburettor, unscrew the locknut and loosen the lost motion adjustment screw until it is well clear of the spring-loaded pad.

75 With the engine idling adjust the idle screw so that the specified idling speed is maintained, then re-check the CO reading and adjust if necessary.

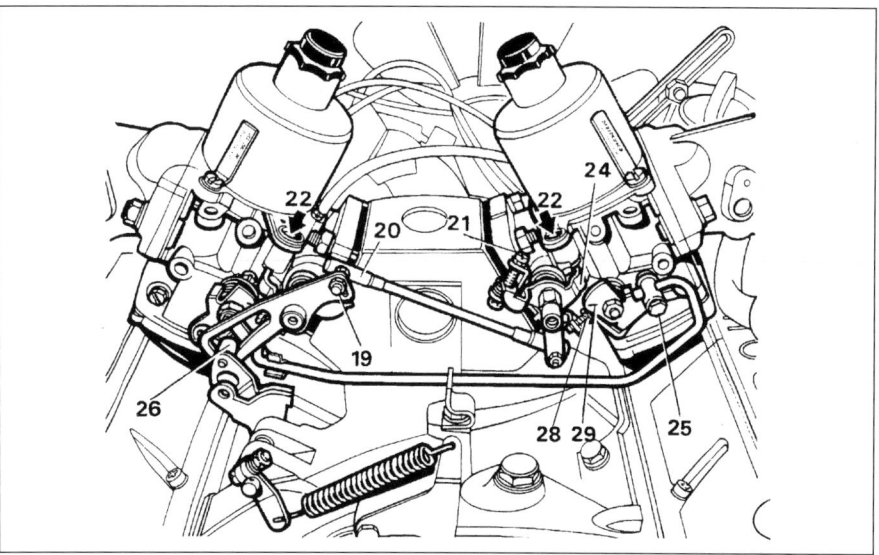

Fig. 13.25 Carburettor adjustment points and linkages for manual gearbox models (Sec 6B)

19 Interconnecting link nut
20 Interconnecting link
21 Lost motion adjustment screw
22 Idle speed adjustment screws
24 Throttle lever

25 Fast idle cam link rod screw
26 Roller
28 Fast idle adjustment screw
29 Scribed line

76 Re-connect the interconnecting link to the left-hand carburettor.

77 While holding the right-hand throttle lever against the idle screw stop, adjust the lost motion screw until contact is made with the spring loaded pad then tighten the locknut.

78 Check the idle speed and balance and adjust the lost motion screw if necessary to maintain balance.

79 On manual gearbox models ensure that the roller is firmly seated in the lower corner of the cam lever then tighten the nut securing the interconnecting link ball to the cam lever. On automatic transmission models ensure that the kickdown cable linkage is firmly on its idle stop then tighten the interconnecting link ball securing the nut to the right-hand carburettor.

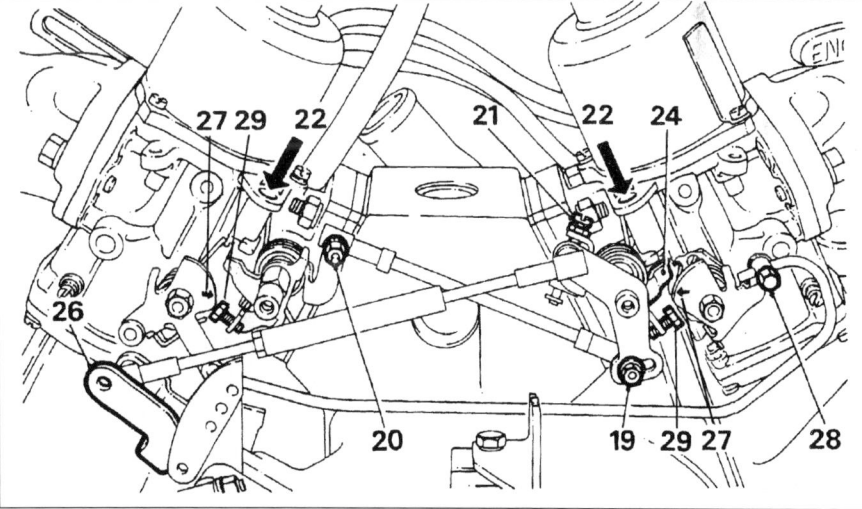

Fig. 13.26 Carburettor adjustment points and linkages for automatic transmission models (Sec 6B)

19 Interconnecting link lower nut
20 Interconnecting link nut
21 Lost motion adjustment screw
22 Idle speed adjustment screws
24 Throttle lever

26 Kickdown cable linkage
27 Scribed lines
28 Fast idle cam link rod screw
29 Fast idle adjustment screws

80 Switch off the engine and carry out the fast idle adjustment as follows. First pull out the choke control until the scribed line on the left-hand fast idle cam is aligned with the centre of the fast idle screw. Check that the scribed line on the right-hand fast idle cam is also aligned with the fast idle screw. If not, loosen the fast idle cam link rod screw at the right-hand carburettor and move the cam until the scribed line is aligned with the centre of the screw. Tighten the cam rod screw.

81 Turn each fast idle screw clockwise until just clear of the cam.

82 With the engine idling, turn the fast idle screw of the leading (left-hand) carburettor clockwise until a slight change in engine speed is noted. Working on the right-hand carburettor turn the fast idle screw down until a further slight change of engine speed is noted.

83 Adjust the fast idle screws of both carburettors by equal amounts to achieve a fast idle speed of 1100 to 1150 rpm.

84 Push the choke fully home, then pull it fully out again and re-check the fast idle speed.

85 Fit the new tamperproof caps to the mixture screw recess and the idling adjusting screw.

86 Refit the carburettor air inlet elbows and the air cleaner.

PART C: FUEL INJECTION SYSTEM (LUCAS L)

⚠️ **Warning: Many of the procedures in this section requires the removal of fuel lines and connections which may result in some fuel spillage. Before carrying out any operation on the fuel system refer to the precautions given in 'Safety first!' at the beginning of this manual, and follow them implicitly. Petrel is a highly-dangerous and volatile liquid and the precautions necessary when handling it cannot be overstressed.**

Electronic fuel injection system - description

1 The electronic fuel injection (EFI) system fitted to certain models may for descriptive purposes be divided into two parts: the injection system itself, and the electronic control system.

2 Fuel is drawn from the tank to an electric pump located in the fuel tank. Filtered fuel under pressure is fed to the eight injectors via a pressure regulator. Excess fuel is returned from the pressure regulator to the fuel tank.

3 The injectors are opened electrically. Their state is either fully open or fully closed, the amount of fuel delivered being controlled by the time for which they are open. On the Range Rover V8 engine the injectors are controlled in two groups of four, the groups opening alternately. There is no direct relationship between any one injector and one cylinder, and thus no need for injection timing to relate directly to ignition timing or valve timing.

4 A separate cold start injector, controlled by a temperature-sensitive switch, supplies extra fuel for cold starting enrichment when the engine is cranking.

5 The control system must be considered to include the fuel pump. The pump is wired in such a way that it is only energised when the ignition is switched on and the engine is running, or when the starter motor is cranking. An inertia switch, in series with the pump, stops the pump operating in the event of an accident involving impact.

6 The injectors are controlled by an electronic control unit (ECU) which receives information relating to engine speed, airflow into the engine, throttle position and coolant temperature. Injector output is thus matched very closely to engine and driver requirements.

7 Engine speed information is supplied to the ECU in the form of pulses from the LT side of the ignition system.

8 Airflow into the engine is measured by the deflection of a flap in the airflow meter, which alters the position of a potentiometer (variable resistance) to which it is connected. Because the mass as well as the volume of air is significant, the air temperature is also measured. A bypass channel, the size of which can be varied by an adjustment screw, allows fine adjustment of the quantity of air passing at idle speed.

9 Throttle position information is supplied to the ECU by a simple potentiometer, confusingly referred to as the throttle switch. The ECU can 'read' throttle position from the voltage at the potentiometer, and can determine the rate of change in throttle position by the rate of change in the voltage. A sudden 'foot down' signal will cause the ECU to pulse all the injectors once, so delivering extra fuel for acceleration.

10 The coolant temperature sensor is located between the cylinder head. A 'cold' signal to the ECU causes the injection pulses to be lengthened slightly, and activates the heater element in the extra air valve.

11 The extra air valve opens and so provides the additional air needed for smooth idling when the engine is cold. The valve is closed by increasing coolant temperature and by the heat generated by its own heater element, which is under the control of the ECU.

Electronic fuel injection system - maintenance

12 Maintenance of the fuel injection system consists of inspecting and renewing the air cleaner element at the specified intervals. At the same time the fuel line filter(s) should be renewed.

13 If suitable equipment is available, the idle speed and mixture may be checked and adjusted, if necessary. In the absence of the correct equipment, the task should be left to a competent specialist.

14 Apart from the above, regular inspection should be made to verify the security and good condition of all pipes, hoses, unions, connectors, injectors, etc.

15 Remember that the EFI system supplies fuel under considerable pressure and that even a small leak may be most dangerous.

Idle speed and mixture - adjustment

Note: *Before making any adjustments to the idle speed and mixture the engine must be at normal operating temperature with the air cleaner fitted the throttle potentiometer correctly set and all hoses in place and secure. Check also that the ignition timing is correct and that the spark plugs are in good condition with their gaps set as specified.*

16 Connect a tachometer and an exhaust gas analyser (CO meter) to the engine in accordance with the manufacturer's instructions.

17 Hook out the tamperproof cap (if still in place) over the idle speed adjustment screw on the side of the plenum chamber (photo).

18 Start the engine and allow it to idle.

19 Turn the idle speed adjustment screw as necessary, clockwise to decrease the speed and anti-clockwise to increase it, until the engine is idling at the specified rpm (photo).

20 To adjust the mixture, hook out the

6C.17 Hooking out the idle speed adjustment screw tamperproof plug

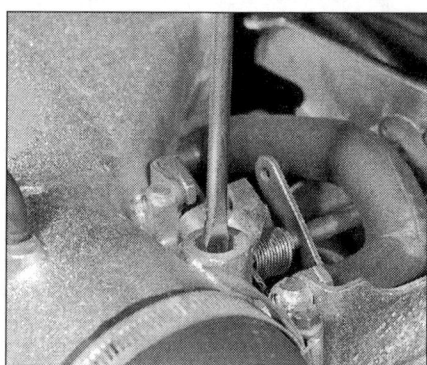

6C.19 Idle speed adjustment

6C.20 Hooking out the mixture adjustment screw tamperproof plug

6C.22 Idle mixture adjustment

6C.25 Using a feeler blade to measure the throttle butterfly clearance

tamperproof plug over the mixture adjustment screw on top of the airflow meter (photo).

21 Run the engine at 2000 rpm for 30 seconds to clear the manifold of excess fuel then return it to idle. Repeat this 'clear-out' burst every 3 minutes during adjustment.

22 Using a suitable Allen key in the mixture adjustment screw (photo) turn the screw as necessary until the specified idle CO emission is obtained.

23 On completion readjust the idle speed if necessary, then switch off and disconnect the instruments.

Throttle levers and throttle butterfly - adjustment

Note: *This is not a routine adjustment and will only be necessary if the position of the throttle stop screw is altered or if new components are fitted.*

24 Slacken the clips and remove the intake air hose from the airflow meter and plenum chamber.

25 Insert a 0.002 in (0.05 mm) feeler blade between the throttle butterfly and the intake bore (photo).

26 If fitted, remove the tamperproof cap from the throttle stop screw then, using a small Allen key inserted into the screw from below,

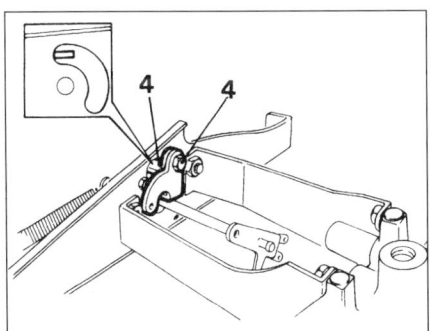

Fig. 13.27 Throttle lever adjustment (Sec 6C)

4 Throttle operating lever securing bolt and lever

Inset shows throttle lever in contact with top end of bracket slot

6C.26 Throttle stop screw location (arrowed)

turn the screw until contact is just made with the stop lever (photo).

27 Slacken the throttle operating lever securing bolt (photo) and reposition the lever until contact is just made with the top end of the slot in the throttle lever mounting bracket (Fig. 13.27). Hold the lever in this position and tighten the bolt.

28 Remove the feeler blade and refit the intake air hose.

29 Reset the throttle potentiometer as described later in this Section.

Fuel injection system relays - general

30 In addition to the ECU, control of the fuel injection system electrical circuits is carried

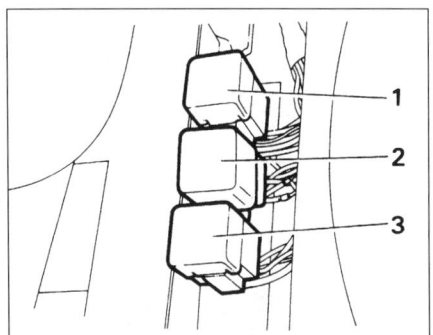

Fig. 13.28 Fuel injection system relay locations under front seat (Sec 6C)

1 Fuel pump relay   3 Main relay
2 Diode pack

6C.27 Throttle operating lever securing bolt (arrowed)

out by three relays and a current-steering diode pack.

31 Two of the relays and the current-steering diode pack are located under the front right-hand seat in front of the ECU. The remaining relay is located in the engine compartment attached to the airflow meter mounting bracket.

32 The relay locations and identification are shown in Figs. 13.28 and 13.29. Removal is carried out by simply pulling the relevant relay from its socket. To gain access to the three relays under the front seat remove the protective cover after releasing the quarter turn screw.

Fuel injection system components - testing

33 Most fuel injection components are tested by substitution of a known good unit; those

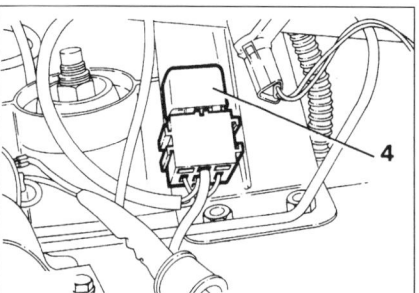

Fig. 13.29 Overrun fuel shut-off relay (4) location in engine compartment (Sec 6C)

items which can also be tested by the DIY mechanic with moderate equipment are listed below.

34 The reader is warned that various fuel injection control components are mechanically and/or electrically fragile. Improvised or clumsy testing procedures may cause more damage than was originally present.

35 Testing and fault diagnosis of the fuel injection system as a whole requires specially dedicated test equipment which will only be possessed by a dealer or fuel injection specialist.

Extra air valve

36 Check that when the engine is being cranked on the starter motor, battery voltage is present at the extra air valve connector terminals. If not, there is a supply fault.

37 With the voltage supply verified, check the electrical resistance between the terminals of the extra air valve. A reading of 33 ohms should be obtained; a short-circuit (zero) or open-circuit (infinity) reading means that the valve must be renewed.

Coolant temperature sensor

38 Disconnect the battery earth lead.

39 Unplug the coolant temperature sensor connector and connect an ohmmeter to the sensor terminals. The resistance measured between the terminals should vary according to coolant temperature as follows:

Coolant temperature	Resistance (ohms)
-10°C (+ 14°F)	9200
0°C (+ 32 °F)	5900
+ 20°C (+ 68 °F)	2500
+ 40°C (+ 104°F)	1180
+ 60°C (+ 140°F)	600
+ 80°C (+ 176°F)	330

40 Measure the resistance between each sensor terminal and the body of the sensor. An infinity (open-circuit) reading should result.

41 If the sensor fails any of the above tests, renew it.

Air temperature sensor

42 Proceed as described for the coolant temperature sensor, using ambient air temperature instead of coolant temperature in the table of resistance values. (The higher temperatures are unlikely to be encountered under normal conditions.)

Thermotime switch

43 Check the rated temperature of the thermotime switch (stamped on its body).

44 Measure the coolant temperature with a thermometer of known accuracy.

45 Disconnect the battery earth lead and unplug the electrical connector from the thermotime switch.

46 Measure the resistance between switch terminal W and earth. If the coolant temperature exceeds the switch rating, an infinity reading (open-circuit) should be

recorded; if the coolant temperature is lower than the switch rating, a zero or very low resistance (closed-circuit) should be recorded. Renew the switch if it fails this test.

47 If the above test is satisfactory, wait if necessary until the coolant temperature falls below the switch rating, then connect a switched 12 volt electrical supply to switch terminal G and earth. Leave the ohmmeter connected as before.

48 Switch on the electrical supply and record the time taken for the thermotime switch state to change from low to high resistance. The time taken will depend on the coolant temperature as follows.

Coolant temperature	Delay time
-10°C (+ 14°F)	8 sec
0°C (+ 32°F)	4 1/2 sec
+ 10°C (+ 50°F)	3 1/2 sec
+ 35°C (+ 95°F)	0 sec

49 Renew the switch if the recorded time differs widely from that specified.

Injector winding

50 The resistance of each injector winding (measured with the wiring disconnected from the injector) should be 2.4 ohms at 20°C (68°F). Such a low resistance will show up on most multi-meters as a zero reading; an infinity (open circuit) reading shows that the injector must be renewed.

51 The resistance between either terminal of an-injector and the injector body should be infinite (open circuit). If not, renew the injector.

52 Note that the injectors are designed to operate on a nominal 3 volt supply, the excess voltage being dropped across the power resistors. *Do not apply battery voltage directly to the injector terminals during testing or otherwise.*

Fuel pressure regulator

53 Depressurise the fuel system, as described later in this Section.

54 Disconnect the cold start injector pipe from the right-hand fuel rail and connect a suitable pressure gauge, of known accuracy, in its place.

55 Disconnect the coil LT negative lead.

56 Have an assistant crank the engine on the starter motor. Observe the pressure gauge

reading; it should stabilise at 35 to 37 lbf/in² (2.5 to 2.6 kgf/cm²). Have the assistant stop cranking and check that the fuel pressure remains steady or declines slowly. A rapid fall is not acceptable.

57 If the above test does not produce satisfactory results, it is wise to seek specialist advice before renewing the fuel pressure regulator. It is possible for a defective fuel pump or a leaky pump non-return valve to produce the same symptoms as a defective pressure regulator. Trial by substitution in such a case becomes prohibitively expensive unless spare parts can be obtained on a sale-or-return basis.

Fuel hoses - precautions

58 The fuel hoses fitted to the fuel injection system incorporates a special inner lining for the higher pressures and temperatures encountered compared with the carburettor fuel system. *Normal unlined hose* **must not** be used, and extra care is necessary when fitting the lined hose to prevent any damage to the inner lining.

59 The hoses must be fitted at least 1.0 in (25.4 mm) onto the pipes with the clip positioned between 0.04 and 0.12 in (1.0 and 3.0 mm) from the end of the hose.

Fuel injection system - fault finding

60 As mentioned previously, special equipment is needed for thorough fault diagnosis of the fuel injection system.

61 Before seeking professional assistance in tracing a fault, make sure that the battery is in good condition and fully charged, that all electrical connections are clean and tight, and that the fuel tank contains clean fuel of the correct grade.

Air cleaner and element - removal and refitting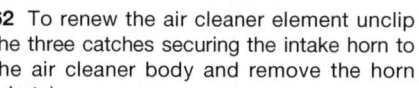

62 To renew the air cleaner element unclip the three catches securing the intake horn to the air cleaner body and remove the horn (photo).

63 Undo the nut and remove the end plate securing the element in position (photos).

6C.62 Air cleaner intake horn retaining catch

6C.63A Undo the retaining nut (arrowed) . . .

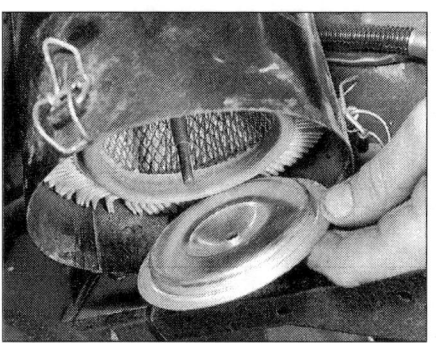

6C.63B . . . and remove the air cleaner element end plate

6C.64 Removing the air cleaner element

6C.72 Fuel filter location under rear wheel arch

64 Withdraw the element from the air cleaner body (photo).

65 Wipe out the inside of the air cleaner body then fit a new element using the reverse sequence to removal.

66 To remove the air cleaner body, slacken the connecting hose retaining clip, undo the two mounting bracket nuts and bolts, and remove the unit from the engine compartment.

67 Refitting is a reversal of removal.

Fuel filter - renewal

 Warning: Ensure that this operation is carried out in a well-ventilated area.

68 Depressurise the fuel system as described later in this Section.

69 Disconnect the battery negative terminal.

70 Jack up the rear of the vehicle and support it on stands.

71 Remove the right-hand rear roadwheel.

72 Clamp the inlet and outlet hoses at the fuel filter which is accessible through the rear right-hand wheel arch (photo).

73 Slacken the hose clips and disconnect the inlet and outlet hoses. Plug the hoses after removal to prevent dirt ingress.

74 Unscrew the filter clamp bolt and remove the filter from the clamp.

75 Refitting is the reversal of removal.

Throttle cable - removal and refitting

76 Disconnect the battery negative terminal.

77 Extract the split pin and remove the washer and clevis pin securing the cable to the throttle linkage.

78 Carefully prise the cable adjusting nut out of the linkage mounting bracket, then withdraw the cable from the bracket.

79 Release the cable from its retaining clips in the engine compartment.

80 Remove the lower facia panel from under the steering column.

81 Disconnect the cable at the throttle pedal then feed it through the bulkhead grommet into the engine compartment.

82 Refitting is a reversal of removal but adjust the cable by means of the adjusting nut to give 0.062 in (1.57 mm) free play.

Fuel system - depressurising

83 The fuel system must be depressurised as follows before any fuel line or union is disconnected.

84 From inside the vehicle remove the protective cover over the fuel system electronic control unit (ECU) located under the right-hand front seat.

85 Pull the fuel pump relay, located nearest the centre of the vehicle (photo) off its multi-plug connector.

86 Start the engine and allow it to run until it stops. This will occur when sufficient fuel has been used to cause the fuel line pressure to drop. After the engine stops switch off the ignition.

87 Undo the two screws securing the cold start injector to the side of the plenum chamber.

88 Place the cold start injector in a suitable container, slacken the hose clip and slowly pull off the fuel hose. This will release any remaining pressurised fuel from the system.

89 Disconnect the battery negative terminal.

90 On completion of the work for which the system was depressurised, refit the cold start injector using a new gasket if necessary and reconnect the fuel hose.

91 Refit the fuel pump relay, ECU cover and battery negative terminal. Start the engine in the normal way, it should fire within approximately six to eight seconds.

Fuel tank - removal and refitting

 Warning: This operation must be carried out in a well-ventilated area.

92 Depressurise the fuel system as described previously.

93 Disconnect the battery negative terminal.

94 Jack up the rear of the vehicle and support it on stands.

95 Remove the drain plug from the bottom of the tank and drain the fuel into a suitable container.

96 Disconnect the fuel inlet hose at the filter; plug the hose after removal.

97 Disconnect and plug the breather hose.

98 Slacken the two hose clips and disconnect the filler tube hose from the tank by sliding the hose up the pipe.

99 On vehicles fitted with a tow bar, remove the two tie-bars from the chassis to towing plate to provide sufficient clearance for removal of the tank.

100 Support the tank on a jack or on blocks and undo the four tank retaining bolts.

101 With the help of an assistant, tilt the left-hand side of the tank downward and disconnect the fuel feed pipe connection and fuel pump electrical leads. Plug the fuel pipe after removal.

102 Carefully lower the tank to the ground and remove it from under the vehicle.

103 Refitting is the reversal of removal. On completion repressurise the fuel system as previously described.

Fuel pump - removal and refitting

104 The fuel pump is located inside the fuel tank which must first be removed, as described in the previous sub-section, to gain access.

105 With the tank removed, unscrew the five screws securing the pump to the top of the tank.

106 Withdraw the pump and pump seal from the tank.

107 Refitting is a reversal of removal using a new seal between pump and tank.

6C.85 Fuel pump relay location (arrowed) under right-hand front seat

6C.116 Cold start injector wiring multi-plug (arrowed)

6C.122 Removing the intake air hose

6C.123A Removing the breather hose . . .

Fuel pressure regulator - removal and refitting

108 Depressurise the fuel system as previously described.
109 Disconnect the battery negative terminal.
110 Pull off the vacuum hose from the bottom of the fuel pressure regulator which is located behind the plenum chamber.
111 Release the clips and disconnect the fuel feed and return hoses from the regulator, noting their locations. Plug the hoses after removal.
112 Undo the single large nut securing the regulator to its mounting bracket and remove the regulator.

113 Refitting is the reversal of removal. Repressurise the fuel system as previously described on completion.

Cold start injector - removal and refitting

114 Depressurise the fuel system as previously described.
115 Disconnect the battery negative terminal.
116 Disconnect the wiring multi-plug from the cold start injector which is located on the right-hand side of the plenum chamber (photo).
117 Slacken the clip and disconnect the injector fuel hose. Plug the hose after removal.

118 Undo the two securing screws and remove the injector from the plenum chamber.
119 Refitting is the reversal of removal but use a new gasket between the injector and plenum chamber. Repressurise the fuel system as previously described on completion.

Plenum chamber - removal and refitting

120 Disconnect the battery negative terminal.
121 Remove the bottom hose and drain the radiator with reference to Section 5.
122 Slacken the clips and remove the intake air hose from the airflow meter and plenum chamber (photo).
123 Disconnect the breather hose and vacuum hose from the plenum chamber (photos).
124 Slacken the clips and release the two coolant hoses from beneath the plenum chamber intake neck (photo).
125 Disconnect the throttle potentiometer wiring harness multi-plug (photo).
126 Undo the two screws securing the cold start injector to the side of the plenum chamber (photos). Withdraw the cold start injector leaving the fuel hose and wiring multi-plug still attached. Recover the sealing gasket.
127 Disconnect the air hose from the side of the plenum chamber and extra air valve rail (photo).

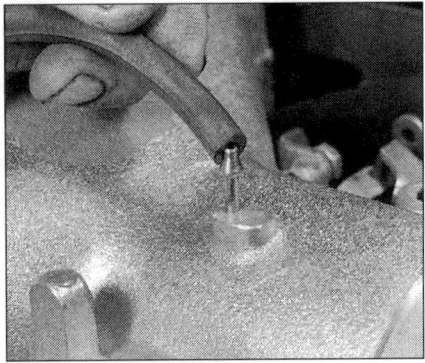

6C.123B . . . and vacuum hose from the plenum chamber

6C.124 Coolant hose attachments (arrowed) under the plenum chamber intake neck

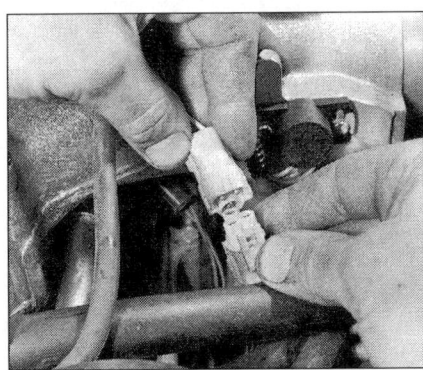

6C.125 Disconnecting the throttle potentiometer multi-plug

6C.126A Undo the two cold start injector retaining screws . . .

6C.126B . . . and remove the injector

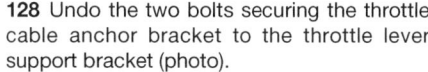

6C.127 Disconnecting the air hose from the plenum chamber

6C.128 Removing the throttle cable anchor bracket bolts

6C.129 Throttle lever return spring location (arrowed)

128 Undo the two bolts securing the throttle cable anchor bracket to the throttle lever support bracket (photo).

129 Unhook the small throttle lever return spring and remove it from the linkage (photo).

130 Disconnect the small vacuum hose from the rear of the plenum chamber (photo).

131 Undo the six socket-headed bolts securing the plenum chamber to the ram housing (photo).

132 Lift the plenum chamber up and off the ram housing (photo). After removal cover the ram pipes with a cloth to prevent dirty entry.

133 Refitting is the reversal of removal, bearing in mind the following points:

(a) Clean away all traces of previous sealing compound from all mating surfaces

(b) Apply Hylomar sealant to the plenum chamber and ram housing mating faces (photos)

(c) Tighten the plenum chamber retaining bolts to the specified torque

(d) Refill the cooling system as described in Chapter 2 and repressurise the fuel system as described previously in this Section

Ram housing - removal and refitting

134 Remove the plenum chamber as described in the previous sub-section.

135 Disconnect the brake servo vacuum hose and extra air valve hose at the right-hand side of the ram housing (photo).

136 Where a solenoid operated air valve is fitted, disconnect the hoses from the front left-hand side of the ram housing and from the rear of the extra air valve rail.

137 Disconnect the extra air valve hose from the air valve rail.

138 Undo the six bolts securing the ram housing to the inlet manifold (photo).

139 Lift the ram housing off the manifold and remove it from the engine compartment. After removal cover the inlet manifold with a cloth to prevent dirt entry.

140 Refitting is a reversal of removal, bearing in mind the following points:

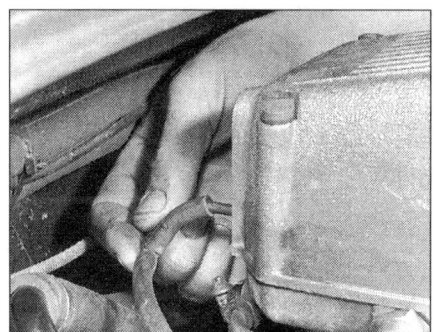

6C.130 Disconnecting the plenum chamber rear vacuum hose

6C.131 Undo the six socket-headed bolts . . .

6C.132 . . . and remove the plenum chamber from the ram housing

6C.133A Apply jointing compound to the mating faces prior to refitting . . .

6C.133B . . . and tighten the bolts to the specified torque

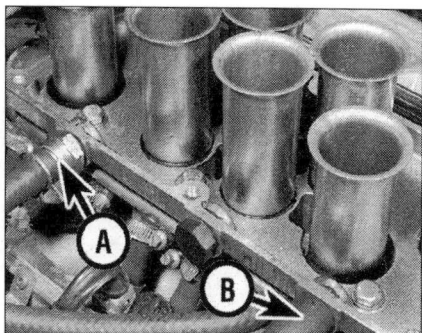

6C.135 Brake servo vacuum hose connection (A) and extra air valve hose (B) at the ram housing

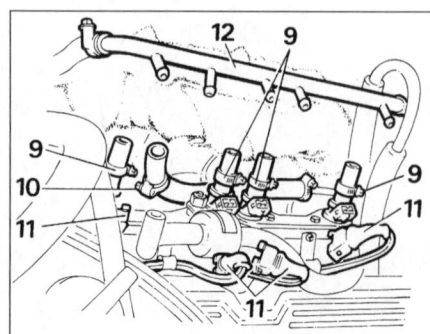

6C.138 Ram housing-to-inlet manifold retaining bolt locations (arrowed)

6C.147 Disconnecting the fuel injector wiring multi-plug

Fig. 13.30 Fuel injector attachments - left-hand bank (Sec 6C)

9 Injector fuel hose-to-fuel rail clips
10 Fuel feed pipe-to-fuel rail clip
11 Injector wiring multi-plugs
12 Fuel rail

(a) Clean away all traces of previous sealing compound from all mating surfaces
(b) Apply Hylomar sealant to the inlet manifold face, fit the ram housing and secure with the six bolts tightened progressively to the specified torque working diagonally outwards from the two centre bolts
(c) Refit the plenum chamber as described in the previous sub-section

Fuel rails - removal and refitting

141 Remove the plenum chamber and the ram housing as previously described.
142 Disconnect the fuel feed pipe, and the fuel return pipe from the fuel pressure regulator, at the fuel rail.
143 Slacken the eight hose clips securing the fuel injector fuel hoses to the fuel rail.
144 Withdraw the fuel rail from the injector hoses and remove it from the engine.
145 Refitting is the reversal of removal.

Fuel injectors - removal and refitting

146 Remove the left-hand or right-hand fuel rail as applicable using the procedure described in the previous sub-section.
147 Disconnect the wiring multi-plug(s) from the injector(s) to be removed (photo).
148 If the left-hand front pair of injectors is to be removed, undo the nut securing the solenoid operated air valve to the injector

retaining plate and remove the air valve for access.
149 If the right-hand rear pair of injectors is to be removed undo the nut securing the overrun shut-off valve to the injector retaining plate and remove the valve for access.
150 Undo the two bolts securing the injector retaining plate to the location plate and withdraw the injectors in pairs, complete with their retaining plates (photo).
151 Undo the screw securing the injector wiring harness retaining clip to the relevant location plate.
152 Undo the two bolts securing the location plate(s) to the manifold and remove the plate(s).
153 With the location plate(s) removed, hook out the small rubber sealing washers located in the injector bores in the inlet manifold.
154 Release the injectors from their retaining plate by removing the large rubber sealing washer from its register on each injector.
155 Refitting is a reversal of removal, bearing in mind the following points:
(a) Fit new sealing washers to the injectors and to the injector bores in the inlet manifold
(b) Fit the injectors with their wiring multi-plug sockets facing away from the inlet manifold
(c) Refit the fuel rails, ram housing and plenum chambers as described previously.

Overrun fuel shut-off valve - removal and refitting

156 Disconnect the battery negative terminal.
157 Disconnect the two electrical leads at their harness connectors.
158 Remove the vacuum hose from the side of the valve.
159 Undo the single nut and spring washer and remove the valve and mounting plate from the injector retaining plate (photo).
160 Refitting is a reversal of removal.

Solenoid operated air valve - removal and refitting

161 The solenoid operated air valve is only fitted to vehicles equipped with air conditioning and certain other optional equipment items.
162 Disconnect the battery negative terminal.
163 Disconnect the electrical lead at the wiring connector.
164 Detach the front air valve pipe at the plenum chamber and the rear air valve pipe from the extra air valve air rail.
165 Undo the single nut and spring washer securing the air valve to the injector retaining plate and remove the valve.

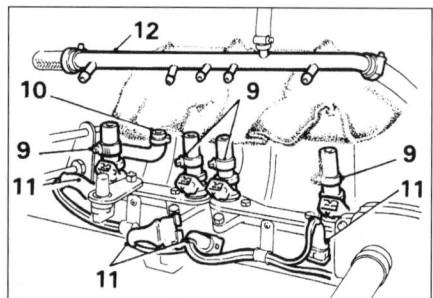

6C.150 Injector retaining plate bolt locations (arrowed)

6C.159 Overrun fuel shut-off valve mounting plate nut (arrowed)

Fig. 13.31 Fuel injector attachments - right-hand bank (Sec 6C)

9 Injector fuel hose-to-fuel rail clips
10 Fuel feed pipe-to-fuel rail clip
11 Injector wiring multi-plugs
12 Fuel rail

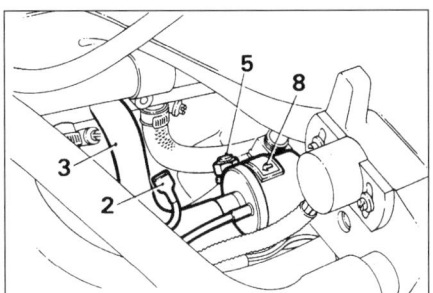

Fig. 13.32 Solenoid operated air valve attachments (Sec 6C)

2 *Electrical lead*
3 *Air valve pipe*
5 *Air valve retaining nut*
8 *Direction-of-flow arrow*

166 Refitting is the reversal of removal but note the direction-of-flow arrow on the air valve body. The direction of flow is from air rail to plenum chamber.

Extra air valve - removal and refitting

167 Slacken the clips and disconnect the two hoses at the extra air valve (photo).
168 Disconnect the wiring multi-plug at the harness connector.
169 Undo the two bolts securing the valve to the inlet manifold noting the location of the earth lead (where fitted).
170 Move the earth lead and spark plug lead support bracket to one side and remove the extra air valve.
171 Refitting is the reversal of removal but note that the arrow on the air valve body must point towards the short hose leading to the ram housing.

Throttle potentiometer - removal, refitting and adjustment

172 Disconnect the battery negative terminal.
173 Disconnect the wiring multi-plug at the harness connector.
174 Undo the two screws securing the throttle potentiometer to the side of the plenum chamber and carefully pull the switch off the throttle spindle (photo). Remove the gasket.

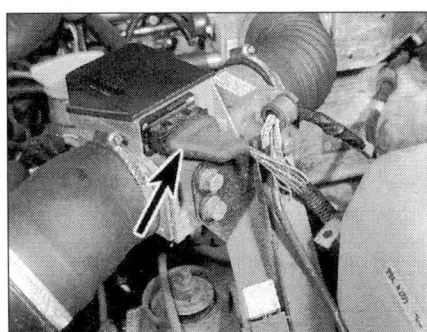

6C.182 Airflow meter wiring multi-plug attachment (arrowed)

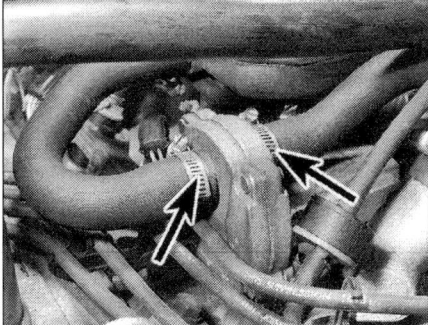

6C.167 Hose attachments (arrowed) at the extra air valve

175 Refit the unit using the reversal of removal sequence then adjust as follows.
176 To set the throttle potentiometer accurately a voltmeter capable of recording millivolts will be required. If this instrument is not available set the potentiometer to the mid-point of its elongated mounting slots and have the adjustment carried out by a Range Rover dealer.
177 Assuming a voltmeter is available, connect it between the red and green leads of the potentiometer multi-plug.
178 Slacken the potentiometer retaining screws and switch on the ignition.
179 Turn the potentiometer slightly as required until the reading on the voltmeter scale is 290 ± 20 millivolts.
180 Tighten the retaining screws, switch off the ignition and disconnect the voltmeter.

Airflow meter - removal and refitting

181 Disconnect the battery negative terminal.
182 Disconnect the wiring multi-plug from the side of the airflow meter (photo).
183 Slacken the hose clips and remove the air intake hoses on both sides of the airflow meter.
184 Undo the three mounting bolts and remove the airflow meter.
185 Refitting is the reversal of removal.

Thermotime switch - removal and refitting

186 With the engine cold remove the cooling

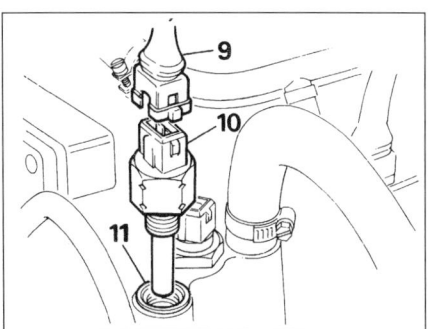

Fig. 13.33 Thermotime switch details (Sec 6C)

9 *Wiring multi-plug*   11 *Sealing washer*
10 *Thermotime switch*

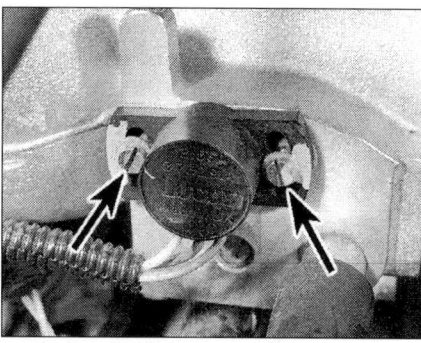

6C.174 Throttle potentiometer retaining screws (arrowed)

system expansion tank cap to relieve any pressure in the system.
187 Disconnect the wiring multi-plug from the switch.
188 Unscrew and remove the switch, noting that there may be some coolant spillage. Remove the copper sealing washer.
189 Refitting is the reversal of removal but use a new copper sealing washer. Tighten the switch securely but take care not to overtighten.
190 Top up the cooling system if necessary on completion.

Coolant temperature sensor - removal and refitting

191 The procedure is the same as described previously for the thermotime switch.

Power resistor unit - removal and refitting

192 The power resistor unit is situated below the airflow meter and attached to the airflow meter mounting bracket.
193 Disconnect the battery negative terminal.
194 Disconnect the wiring multi-plug from the bottom of the resistor unit.
195 Undo the two retaining bolts and remove the unit from the mounting bracket.
196 Refitting is the reversal of removal.

Electronic control unit - removal and refitting

197 The electronic control unit is located under the right-hand front seat and is accessible through an aperture in the front of the seat base.
198 Disconnect the battery negative terminal.
199 Release the quarter-turn screw and remove the cover over the ECU.
200 Mark the position of the three relays in front of the ECU and remove them by carefully pulling them out of their sockets.
201 Pull the ECU wiring multi-plug retaining clip towards the rear of the seat and pull the rear of the multi-plug out. Manoeuvre the rear of the plug towards the transmission tunnel so as to release the hooked front of the plug from its retaining peg.
202 Undo the three retaining screws and remove the ECU from under the seat.
203 Refitting is the reversal of removal.

PART D: FUEL INJECTION SYSTEM (LUCAS HOT-WIRE)

⚠️ **Warning: Many of the procedures in this Section require the removal of fuel lines and connections which may result in some fuel spillage. Before carrying out any operation on the fuel system refer to the precautions given in 'Safety first!' at the beginning of this manual, and follow them implicitly. Petrol is a highly-dangerous and volatile liquid, and the precautions necessary when handling it cannot be overstressed**

Description

1 A Lucas Hot-wire electronic fuel injection system is fitted to all 1988-on models. The system ensures that the correct air/fuel mixture is supplied to the engine under all engine operating conditions. This is achieved by using various sensors which send signals to the ECU, and this information is then computed and the injectors opened for the correct period. The injectors are operated on each bank separately (ie each set of four injectors is triggered together).

2 The ECU is located beneath the front left-hand seat and is connected to the main harness by a 40-pin multi-plug.

3 The injectors are located on a common fuel rail but electrically they are arranged in two banks of four.

4 On 1990-on models a tune select resistor is located next to the ECU.

5 A coolant temperature thermistor is located by the front left hand branch of the inlet manifold.

6 A fuel temperature thermistor is located on the front of the fuel distribution rail.

7 Engine idle speed is controlled by a by-pass air valve located on the rear of the air inlet plenum chamber. The by-pass air valve maintains the engine idle speed constant when differing loads are applied to the engine such as when the air conditioning system or headlamps are switched on.

8 On engines fitted with catalytic converters Lambda sensors are located just forward of the front converters to monitor the oxygen content of the exhaust gases. The sensors are heated by an internal element to improve their response time.

9 The fuel pressure regulator located on the rear of the fuel rail maintains the fuel pressure at 2.5 bars above the inlet manifold pressure.

10 The fuel pump is located in the top of the fuel tank.

11 The airflow sensor is of the hot wire type. A proportion of air flowing through the sensor is passed through a by-pass in which two wires are located. One wire is a sensing wire and the other is a compensating wire. An electronic module mounted on the side of the airflow sensor passes a small current through the sensing wire to produce a heating effect. The compensating wire is not heated but reacts to the temperature of the air passing through the meter. The electronic module monitors the reaction of the wires in proportion to the airflow and sends output signals to the ECU.

12 A throttle potentiometer is mounted on the side of the plenum chamber inlet neck and is attached to the throttle valve shaft.

13 A road speed transducer is located on a bracket beneath the left hand chassis side member. The transducer is operated by cable from the transfer box output shaft, and it sends signals to the ECU. It is also used to operate the electronic speedometer.

14 On 1990-on models an inertia switch is located beneath the front right-hand seat. In the event of an accident the switch opens and disconnects the fuel pump. The switch may be reset by pressing the button.

15 Two fuel injection relays are located beneath the front left-hand seat, and they are energized by the ECU. The main relay supplies current to the fuel injection system; the fuel pump relay energizes the fuel pump.

16 Should the fuel injection system develop a fault, a warning light on the instrument panel will illuminate and the fuel injection system should then be investigated to find the fault. However the system incorporates a limp home feature enabling the vehicle to be driven carefully to a garage.

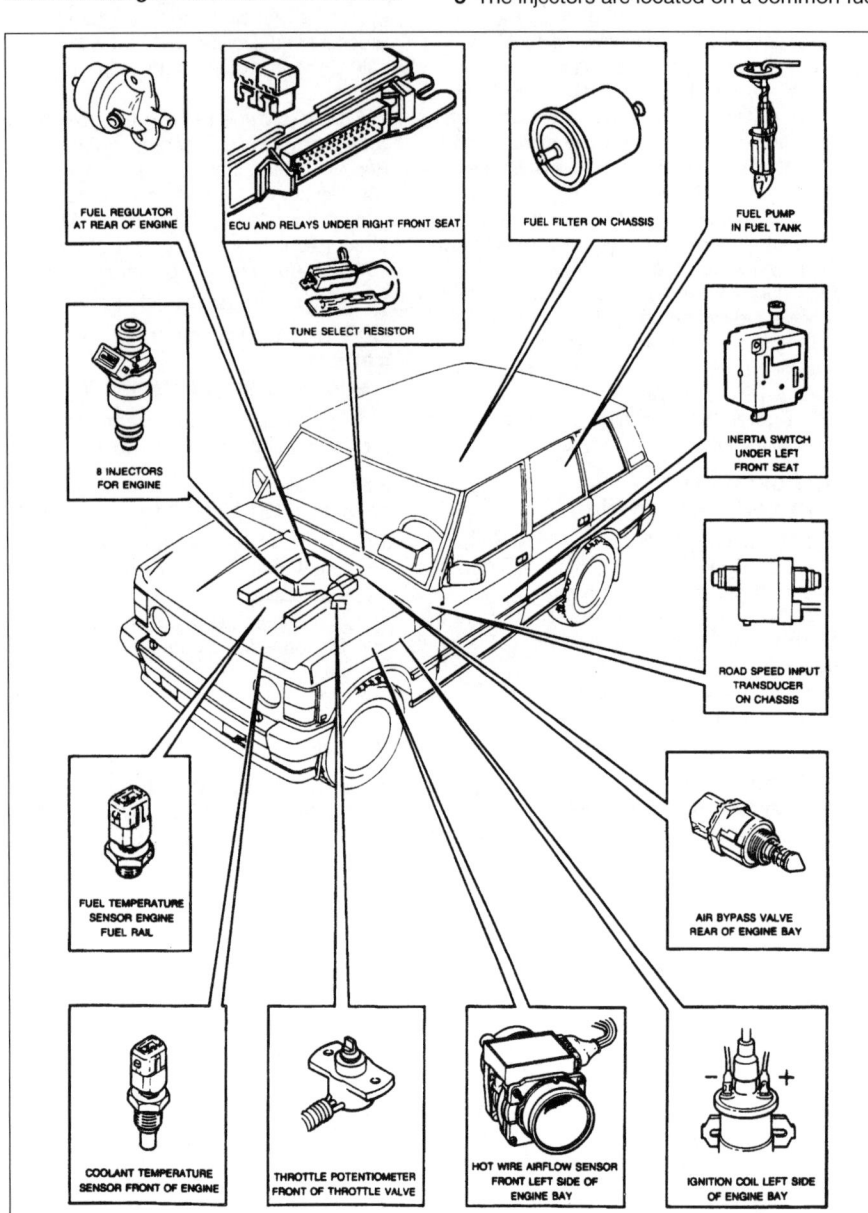

Fig. 13.34 Lucas Hot-wire electronic fuel injection system components (Sec 6D)

Tune select resistor and inertia switch not fitted to pre-1990 models
Left-hand drive model shown

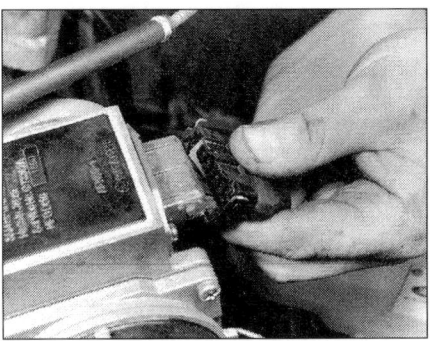

6D.19 Disconnecting the multi-plug from the air flow sensor

6D.20 Removing the airflow sensor from the air cleaner

6D.24 Disconnecting the wiring multi-plug from the by-pass air valve on the rear of the plenum chamber

Airflow sensor - removal and refitting

17 Disconnect the battery negative lead.
18 Loosen the clip and disconnect the hose from the rear of the airflow sensor.
19 Disconnect the multi-plug from the unit (photo).
20 Release the two clips securing the airflow sensor to the air cleaner then withdraw it from the engine compartment (photo).
21 Refitting is a reversal of the removal procedure but make sure that the multi-plug is secure, and that the hoses and clips are fitted correctly.

Throttle potentiometer - removal, refitting and adjustment

22 The procedure is the same as described earlier in Part C, but the adjustment setting is 325 ± 35 millivolts.

By-pass air valve (stepper motor) - removal and refitting

23 Disconnect the battery negative lead.
24 Disconnect the wiring multi-plug (photo).
25 Unscrew the valve from the rear of the plenum chamber and remove the washer.
26 Refitting is a reversal of the removal procedure, but clean the threads and apply locking fluid such as Loctite 241 before tightening the valve to the specified torque.

Speed transducer - removal and refitting

27 Disconnect the battery negative lead.
28 Jack up the front of the vehicle and support on axle stands.
29 The speed transducer is located on a bracket on the left-hand chassis side member adjacent to the rear engine mounting (photo). The two sections of the speedometer cable are connected to the transducer, one at each end. A faulty speed transducer would affect the idle speed of the engine.
30 Disconnect the speed transducer wiring plug.
31 Unscrew the collars and disconnect the cables from each side of the transducer.
32 Unbolt and remove the transducer from its mounting.
33 Refitting is a reversal of the removal procedure.

Fuel injection relays - removal and refitting

34 The two relays are located beneath the front right-hand seat next to the main ECU. The fuel pump relay is mounted on a blue terminal block and the main relay is mounted on a black terminal block.
35 Disconnect the battery negative lead.
36 Pull the relevant relay directly from its socket.
37 Refitting is a reversal of the removal procedure.

Electronic control unit (ECU) - removal and refitting

38 Disconnect the battery negative lead.
39 Move the front right-hand seat fully forwards, then remove the rear opening cover for access to the ECU.
40 Pull out and unhook the multi-plug from the ECU. An arrow on the plug indicates which way to remove it.
41 Unscrew the screws and release the ECU from the spring clip.
42 Refitting is a reversal of the removal procedure.

Fuel temperature thermistor- removal and refitting

43 Disconnect the battery negative lead.
44 Disconnect the multi-plug from the thermistor.
45 Unscrew the thermistor from the fuel rail. Note that it is not necessary to depressurise the fuel system as the thermistor is not in direct contact with the fuel.
46 Refitting is a reversal of the removal procedure.

Coolant temperature thermistor - removal and refitting

47 Partially drain the cooling system with reference to Section 5 of this Chapter.

6D.29 Speed transducer located on the left-hand chassis side member

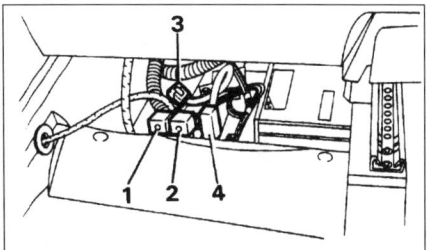

13.35 Fuel injection relay locations beneath the front right-hand seat (Sec 6D)

1 *Fuel pump relay*
2 *Main relay*
3 *Diagnostic plug*
4 *Condenser fan timer unit*

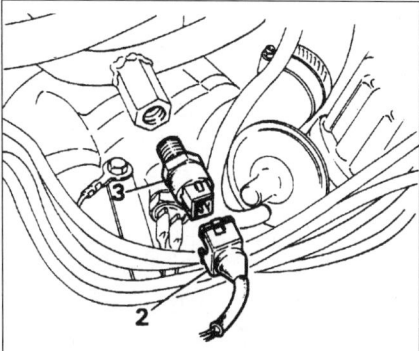

Fig. 13.36 Fuel injection thermistor (3) and plug (2) (Sec 6D)

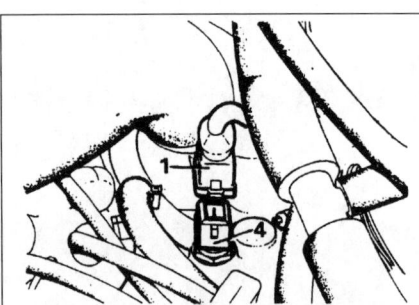

Fig. 13.37 Coolant temperature thermistor (4) and plug (1) (Sec 6D)

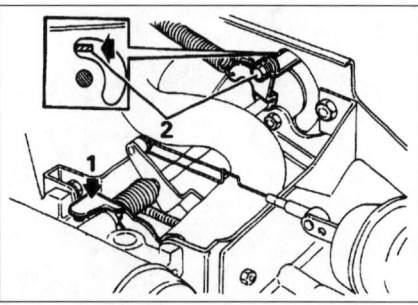

Fig. 13.38 Throttle lever adjustment (Sec 6D)

1 Stop lever and throttle/kickdown lever
2 Throttle operating lever securing screw

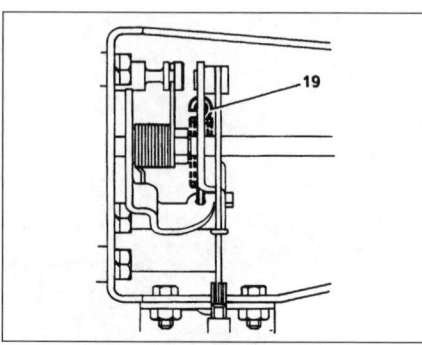

Fig. 13.39 Correct position of the small return spring (19) (Sec 6D)

48 Disconnect the multi-plug, and unscrew the thermistor from the left-hand front branch of the inlet manifold. Remove the copper washer.

49 Refitting is a reversal of the removal procedure, but fit a new copper washer and refill the cooling system with reference to Chapter 2.

Throttle levers - adjustment

Note: *Adjustment is made at the closed throttle position only. Do not alter the position of the factory-set adjustment screw in the plenum chamber casting which sets the throttle valve in the vertical position. The only time that this may need resetting is in the event of new throttle linkages and brackets being fitted.*

50 Refer to Fig. 13.38. Keep the throttle valve in the 90° vertical position during the adjustment by holding down the stop lever and throttle/kickdown lever.

51 Release the throttle lever securing screw, then adjust the lever until it contacts the top end of the slot in the throttle lever mounting bracket. With the lever in this position, tighten the throttle lever securing screw.

52 Lightly grease the throttle lever bearing surfaces and the torsion spring. Where applicable, check the cruise control actuator link adjustment as described in Part E of this Section.

Throttle cable - removal, refitting and adjustment

53 Refer to Part C.

Plenum chamber - removal and refitting

54 Disconnect the battery negative lead.

55 Partially drain the cooling system with reference to Section 5 of this Chapter.

56 Loosen the clips and remove the air hose between the airflow sensor and plenum chamber (photo).

57 Identify their locations then disconnect the coolant hoses from the bottom of the plenum chamber (photo).

58 Disconnect the distributor vacuum hose, crankcase ventilation hose and brake servo hose (photo).

59 Disconnect the multi-plugs from the throttle potentiometer and air by-pass valve.

60 Disconnect the small vacuum hose from the rear of the plenum chamber below the air by-pass valve location.

61 Disconnect the hose between the air by-pass valve and plenum chamber, then unhook the return spring below the throttle levers.

62 Unhook the throttle return springs.

63 Unbolt the throttle cable and kickdown cable bracket from the support bracket and position to one side.

64 Unscrew the socket-headed bolts and remove the plenum chamber from the ram housing. Cover the ram housing to prevent the ingress of foreign matter (photos).

65 Refitting is a reversal of the removal procedure but apply sealant to the mating faces, and tighten the bolts to the specified torque. Refer to Fig. 13.39 and make sure that

6D.56 Removing the air hose between the airflow sensor and plenum chamber

6D.57 Coolant hose locations on the bottom of the plenum chamber

6D.58 Disconnecting the distributor vacuum hose from the plenum chamber

6D.64A Unscrew the socket-headed bolts . . .

6D.64B . . . and remove the plenum chamber

6D.68A Disconnect the front vacuum hoses . . .

6D.68B . . . and rear vacuum hose from the ram housing

6D.69 Unscrewing the ram housing through- bolts

the hooked open end of the spring is facing the plenum chamber. Refill the cooling system with reference to Chapter 2.

Ram housing - removal and refitting

66 Disconnect the battery negative lead
67 Remove the plenum chamber as described previously.
68 Disconnect the hoses from the outer edges of the ram housing (photos).
69 Unscrew and remove the through-bolts and washers holding the ram housing to the inlet manifold (photo).
70 Withdraw the ram housing from the inlet manifold and cover the top of the inlet manifold to prevent the ingress of foreign matter (photos).
71 Refitting is a reversal of the removal

procedure but apply sealant to the mating faces and tighten the bolts progressively working diagonally outwards from the two centre bolts. Tighten the bolts to the specified torque.

Fuel system - depressurising

72 The procedure is the same as that described in Part C, but references to the cold start injector should be ignored. There will be some residual pressure remaining in the fuel system and therefore cloth should be placed beneath the component being removed to absorb the escaping fuel.

Fuel pressure regulator - removal and refitting

73 The procedure is the same as that described in Part C. Apply a little silicon

grease to the O-ring before refitting the regulator to the fuel rail.

Fuel rail and injectors - removal and refitting

74 Depressurise the fuel system as described previously.
75 Disconnect the battery negative lead.
76 Remove the plenum chamber and ram housing as described previously. Place clean cloth rags in the inlet ports to prevent ingress of dirt.
77 Slacken the clip and disconnect the fuel return hose from the pressure regulator. Also loosen the union nut and disconnect the fuel feed hose from the fuel rail (photos).
78 Disconnect the multi-plug from the fuel temperature thermistor on the front of the fuel rail (photo).

6D.70A Removing the ram housing from the inlet manifold

6D.70B Cover the inlet manifold or place clean cloth rags in the inlet ports

6D.77A Disconnecting the fuel return hose from the pressure regulator

6D.77B Fuel feed union on the rear of the fuel rail (arrowed)

6D.78 Disconnecting the multi-plug from the fuel temperature thermistor on the front of the fuel rail

6D.79 Disconnecting the multi-plugs from the injectors

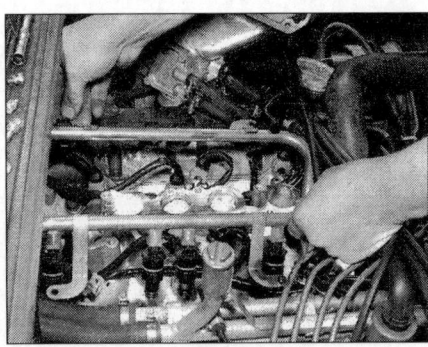

6D.81 Removing the fuel rail together with the injectors

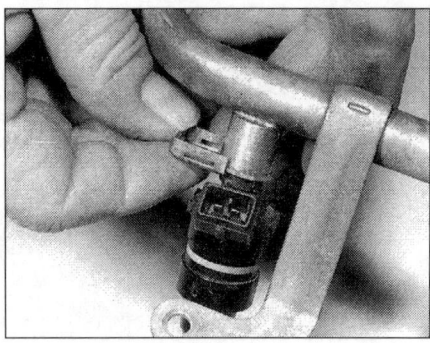

6D.82A Pull out the clips . . .

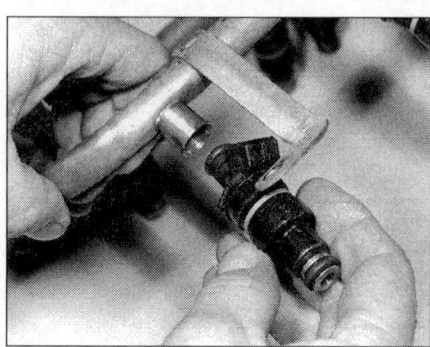

6D.82B . . . and ease the injectors from the fuel rail

79 Disconnect the multi-plugs from the injectors (photo).
80 Unscrew and remove the fuel rail mounting bolts noting the location of the heater pipe bracket. Move the heater pipes to one side.
81 Carefully ease the fuel rail together with the injectors from the inlet manifold and remove the assembly from the engine compartment (photo).
82 Pull out the clips securing the injectors to the fuel rail and ease the injectors from the rail (photos).
83 Unscrew the two nuts and bolts securing the pressure regulator to the fuel rail and ease the regulator from the rail.
84 Prise the O-rings from the injectors, clean the grooves and fit new O-rings. Also clean the injector locations in the fuel rail.

85 Apply a light coating of silicon grease to the O-rings then fit the injectors to the fuel rail with the multi-plug connections facing outwards. Secure with the clips.
86 Remove the O-ring from the pressure regulator, clean the location and fit a new O-ring. Apply a little silicon grease to the O-ring and press the regulator into the fuel rail. Refit and tighten the two nuts and bolts.
87 The remaining procedure is a reversal of removal. On completion switch on the ignition and check for leaks from the fuel rail.

Fuel filter - renewal

88 The procedure is the same as that described in Part C, but make sure that the fuel flow direction arrow is facing towards the front of the vehicle.

Air cleaner and element - removal and refitting

89 The procedure is similar to that for the Lucas L injection system described in Part C.

Fuel tank - removal and refitting

90 The procedure is similar to that for the Lucas L injection system described in Part C. On models fitted with the fuel evaporative emission control system it will be necessary to disconnect the additional hoses (photos).

Fuel pump - removal and refitting

91 Depressurise the fuel system as described earlier in this Part.
92 It will be necessary to fold the luggage compartment carpet back and this can be done either by disconnecting the seat belts at the front or by prising out the fasteners at the rear. With the carpet folded back lift the soundproof matting for access to the fuel pump cover.
93 Unscrew the screws and lift off the cover from the rear luggage compartment floor.
94 Clean any dirt from the top of the fuel pump and from the surrounding area on the tank.
95 Working through the left-hand rear wheel arch disconnect the fuel pump wiring at the connector and release the wiring from the clips (photo).
96 Loosen the clip and disconnect the fuel supply hose from the fuel pump.

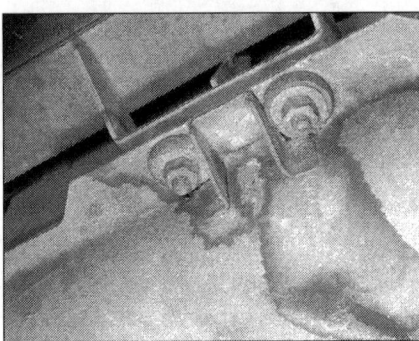

6D.90A Fuel tank front mounting nuts

6D.90B A fuel tank rear mounting nut

6D.95 Fuel pump wiring connector (arrowed) on the left-hand side of the fuel tank

6D.97A Unscrew the screws . . .

6D.97B . . . and lift the fuel pump out of the fuel tank

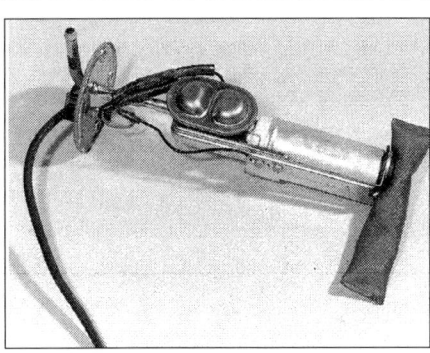

6D.97C View of the fuel pump on the bench

97 Unscrew the mounting screws and lift the fuel pump out of the fuel tank (photos). Take care not to allow any foreign material or pieces of the cork pump gasket to fall into the tank.

98 Remove the gasket and clean the top of the tank.

99 Refitting is a reversal of the removal procedure, but to prevent damage to the cork gasket as the pump is inserted into the tank it is suggested that the gasket is assembled to the pump first.

Fuel injection system components - testing

100 Most fuel injection system components are tested by substitution of a known good unit; those items which can also be tested by the DIY mechanic with moderate equipment are listed below.

101 The reader is warned that various fuel injection control components are mechanically and/or electrically fragile. Improvised or clumsy testing procedures may cause more damage than was originally present.

102 Testing and fault diagnosis of the fuel injection system as a whole requires specially dedicated test equipment which will only be possessed by a dealer or fuel injection specialist.

103 A good quality digital multi-meter should be used when carrying out the following procedures and it is important to set the meter correctly to the volts or ohms scale before connecting the probes.

104 Carry out the following preliminary checks.
(a) Check that fuse C4 in the fusebox is not blown
(b) Check that the inertia switch under the front seat is not tripped
(c) Make sure that there is adequate fuel in the fuel tank
(d) Check that the battery is in good condition
(e) Check that there are no induction air leaks particularly between the airflow meter and the cylinder head
(f) Check that all relevant electrical connections are clean, dry and secure

105 When connecting the probes to the ECU multi-plug, first remove the ECU without disconnecting the multi-plug as described earlier in this Part, then remove the screws and lift off the shroud so that the probes can be inserted onto the back of the pins. Do not connect the probes to the multiplug sockets as this practise will damage the terminals and result in poor connections.

106 The wire colours to the pins are as follows, and where applicable the last colour denotes the tracer:

1988 and 1989 catalyst models

1	Red/green	2	Brown/orange
3	Yellow	4	Black
5	Brown/purple	6	Yellow
7	Green/blue	8	Not used
9	White/light green	10	Black/yellow
11	Yellow/white	12	Blue/red
13	Yellow/blue	14	Black
15	Brown	16	Blue/purple
17	Not used	18	White/pink
19	White/grey	20	Red
21	Yellow/blue	22	Blue/red
23	Blue	24	Blue
25	Red/black	26	Green/white
27	Black/grey	28	Blue/grey
29	Orange	30	Not used
31	Not used	32	Grey/white
33	Not used	34	Black/orange
35	Blue/green	36	Not used
37	White/yellow	38	Not used
39	White/black	40	Black

1990-on models

1	Red/green	2	Brown/orange
3	Yellow	4	Black
5	Grey/black	6	Yellow
7	Green/blue	8	Purple/yellow
9	White/light green	10	Black/Yellow
11	Yellow/white	12	Blue/red
13	Yellow/blue	14	Black
15	Brown	16	Blue/purple
17	Grey/yellow	18	White/pink
19	White/grey	20	Red
21	Yellow/black	22	Blue/red
23	Blue	24	Blue
25	Red/black	26	Green/white
27	Black/grey	28	Blue/grey
29	Orange	30	Not used
31	Black/green	32	Grey/white
33	Black/grey	34	Orange/black
35	Blue/green	36	Black/green
37	Not used	38	Not used
39	White/black	40	Black

107 On 1990-on models test the tune select resistor first. Disconnect the multi-plug from the ECU and connect the ohmmeter across terminals 27 and 5. On non-catalyst models a reading of between 446 and 494 ohms should be obtained, but on catalyst models the reading should be between 3700 and 4100 ohms.

108 With the ignition off and the multi-plug connected to the ECU, connect the voltmeter between pin 15 and earth, and check that the battery supply to the ECU is a minimum of 10 volts.

109 With the ignition on and the multi-plug connected to the ECU, connect the voltmeter between pin 19 and earth, and check that the ignition supply to the ECU is a minimum voltage of 10 volts.

110 With the ignition on and the multi-plug connected to the ECU, connect the voltmeter between terminal 87 on the main relay and earth, and check that battery voltage is available.

111 If the reading is zero check the wiring to and from the main relay.

112 On 1990-on models check the engine speed signal, cable and resistor. With the ECU multi-plug connected and the ignition on, connect a voltmeter between terminal 39 and earth. Check that the reading is 9.5 volts ± 1 volt. This reading takes into consideration the resistance of the lead from the ignition coil negative terminal to terminal 39 on the multiplug.

113 To check the operation of the pump relay, connect a test lamp between the central terminal and earth. With the ECU multi-plug connected, switch on the ignition and check that the test lamp illuminates for approximately 1 second. The relay should also be heard to make an audible click.

114 With the ECU multi-plug disconnected temporarily earth pin 16 and connect a voltmeter between the central fuel pump relay

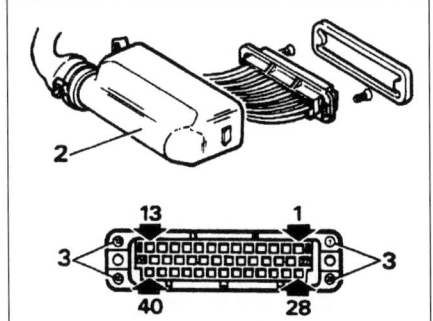

Fig. 13.40 ECU pin numbering for 1988 and 1989 models (Sec 6D)

2 Shroud   3 Screws

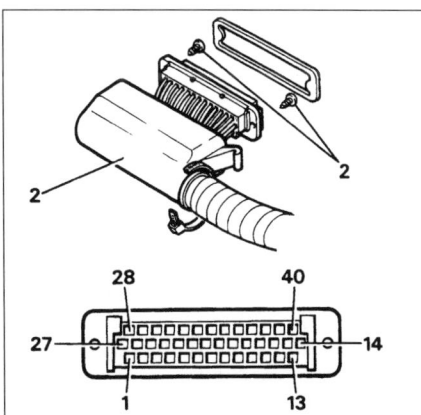

Fig. 13.41 ECU pin numbering for 1990-on models (Sec 6D)

2 Shroud and screws

and earth. Battery voltage should be read. If not, suspect the ECU.

115 With the ECU multi-plug still disconnected locate the fuel pump feed wiring plug accessible through the rear left-hand wheelarch and connect a voltmeter between the supply terminal and earth. Battery voltage should be available.

116 On 1990-on models check the purge valve by disconnecting the purge valve pipe at the plenum chamber and applying a vacuum of 2.5 in/Hg. With the ECU multi-plug disconnected and the ignition off the vacuum should hold for 2.5 minutes. Apply the vacuum again and connect pins 16 and 17 on the multi-plug to earth. Switch on the ignition and check that the vacuum is released, proving that the purge valve is off when the fuel pump is running with a vacuum of 2.5 in/Hg.

117 With the ECU multi-plug disconnected and the ignition off, connect an ohmmeter across pins 2 and 13. The reading should be between 4.0 and 4.5 ohms. If the reading is between 5.0 and 6.0 ohms suspect one left-hand bank injector. If the reading is between 8.0 and 9.0 ohms suspect two left-hand bank injectors. If the reading is between 16.0 and 17.0 ohms suspect three left-hand bank injectors.

118 With the ECU multi-plug disconnected and the ignition off, connect an ohmmeter across pins 2 and 11. The reading should be between 4.0 and 4.5 ohms. If the reading is between 5.0 and 6.0 ohms suspect one right-hand bank injector. If the reading is between 8.0 and 9.0 ohms suspect two right-hand bank injectors. If the reading is between 16.0 and 17.0 ohms suspect three right-hand bank injectors.

119 To check the fuel temperature thermistor disconnect the ECU multiplug and switch off the ignition, then connect an ohmmeter between pins 25 and 32. Refer to the following table to determine the correct resistance which will vary according to the fuel temperature.

°C	Ohms
- 10	9100 to 9300
0	5700 to 5900
20	2400 to 2600
40	1100 to 1300
60	500 to 700
80	300 to 400
100	150 to 200

120 To check the coolant temperature thermistor, disconnect the ECU multi-plug and switch off the ignition, then connect an ohmmeter
between pins 25 and 7. Refer to the table in the previous test to determine the correct resistance which will vary according to the coolant temperature.

121 With the ECU multi-plug disconnected and the ignition off, connect an ohmmeter between pins 1 and 26 to check the air bypass valve. A reading of between 48.0 and 58.0 ohms should be obtained for 1988 and

1989 catalyst models or between 40.0 and 60.0 ohms for 1990-on models. Now connect the ohmmeter between pins 28 and 29 and check that the same reading is obtained.

122 With the ECU multi-plug disconnected and the ignition off, connect an ohmmeter between pins 3 and 25 to check the throttle potentiometer. The reading should be between 4000 and 6000 ohms. With the ECU multi-plug connected and the ignition on connect a voltmeter between pin 20 and earth. With the throttle closed the reading should be between 0.29 and 0.36 volts for 1988 and 1989 catalyst models and between 0.085 and 0.545 volts for 1990-on models. With the throttle fully open the reading should be between 4.6 and 5.0 volts for 1988 and 1989 catalyst models and between 4.2 and 4.9 volts for 1990-on models. The movement of the throttle between the closed and open positions should be smooth with no signs of seizure of the switch.

123 With the ECU multi-plug connected and the ignition on, check the airflow sensor by connecting a voltmeter between pin 35 and earth. The reading should be between 0.3 and 0.6 volts for 1988 and 1989 catalyst models and between 0.2 and 0.7 volts for 1990-on models.

124 A fuel pressure gauge will be required for the following test. Depressurise the fuel system and connect the pressure gauge in the fuel feed line immediately after the fuel line filter located beneath the right-hand rear wheel arch. Disconnect the ECU multi-plug and temporarily connect an earth wire to pin 16. Switch on the ignition and check that the pressure is between 34 and 37 lbf/in² for 1988 and 1989 catalyst models and between 34 and 38 lbf/in² for 1990-on models. Now switch off the ignition and check that the pressure drop is a maximum of 10 lbf/in² in one minute.

125 Before examining the injectors remove all of the spark plugs and check them for discoloration. A leaking injector will blacken the corresponding spark plug due to a rich mixture.

126 Remove the injectors together with the fuel rail leaving the fuel hose still connected, then with the ECU multi-plug connected and the ignition on, check that the injectors do not leak more than 2 drops per minute. Any which do should be renewed.

127 If calibrated containers are available, position one under each of the injectors. Temporarily connect earthing wires between pins 16 and earth, and 13 and earth, then with the ECU multi-plug connected switch on the ignition. The fuel flow for each injector on the left bank should be 167 cc minimum per minute for 1988 and 1989 catalyst models, and between 180 and 195 cc minimum per minute for 1990-on models. Now connect temporary earth wires between pins 16 and earth, and 11 and earth, then repeat the test for the right-hand bank of injectors.

128 With the ECU multi-plug connected and

the ignition on, connect a voltmeter between pin 34 and earth to check the automatic transmission gear switch input. With the gear selector lever in Neutral or Park there should be zero volts, but with the lever in R,D,3,2 or 1 the reading should be between 4.5 and 5.0 volts for 1988 and 1989 catalyst models and between 2.5 and 5.0 volts for 1990-on models.

129 On models fitted with a manual gearbox check the gear switch signal as follows. With the ECU multi-plug connected and the ignition on connect a voltmeter between pin 34 and earth. A reading of between 1.5 and 3.5 volts should be obtained, and this takes into consideration the gearbox resistor of 510 ohms.

130 Chock the front wheels then jack up the rear of the vehicle and have an assistant slowly rotate the left-hand rear wheel. With the ECU multiplug disconnected and the ignition switched on, connect a voltmeter between pin 6 and earth. The voltmeter should fluctuate between 0 and 12 volts six times per minute.

131 To check the Lambda sensor heater coils on models fitted with a catalytic converter, with the ECU multi-plug connected and the ignition off, connect an ohmmeter between pin 4 and terminal 87A on the fuel pump relay (relay removed from its connector). A reading of between 2.65 and 3.35 ohms on 1988 and 1989 catalyst models and between 2.5 and 6.0 ohms on 1990-on models should be obtained.

132 To check the Lambda sensor supply voltage, temporarily connect a wire between terminal 30 and the centre terminal of the fuel pump relay. With the ignition off and the ECU multi-plug connected, connect a voltmeter between the Lambda sensor supply wire and earth, and check that the reading is 12 volts. Check both sensors in the same way.

133 To check the operation of the Lambda sensors, with the ECU multiplug connected and the ignition on, run the engine at 1000 rpm until it reaches normal operating temperature. Connect a voltmeter between pin 23 and 4, and check that the voltage fluctuates between 0.50 and 1.0 volts. A reading of 0.05 volts is incorrect and denotes an air leak, faulty or contaminated injectors, or low fuel pressure. If these faults are proved unfounded, suspect the left-hand Lambda sensor. A steady reading of 1.0 volt is also incorrect and denotes high fuel pressure, leaking injectors or a saturated carbon canister. Zero volts is also incorrect. If the faults are proved unfounded suspect the left-hand Lambda sensor. Repeat the test but connecting the voltmeter between pin 24 and 4 to check the right-hand Lambda sensor.

134 With the ECU multi-plug connected and the ignition on, connect a voltmeter between pin 21 and earth to check the air conditioning thermostat input. A reading of battery volts should be obtained. If not check the air conditioning wiring.

135 To check the heated front screen input proceed as follows. With the ECU multi-plug connected and the ignition on, start the engine and allow it to idle. Connect a voltmeter between pin 8 and earth. With the heated front screen switched on check that battery voltage is obtained. If not, check the wiring from the oil pressure switch, heated front screen timer unit and heated front screen switch.

Exhaust system - general

136 The exhaust system is shown in Fig. 13.42, and the removal and refitting procedures are similar to those given in Chapter 3 (photos). On models fitted with catalytic converters it will be necessary to disconnect the wiring from the Lambda sensors on the downpipes. Make sure that the engine is cold before starting work as the catalytic converters are very hot when in use. On some models a grass-shield may be fitted over the catalytic converters.

PART E: CRUISE CONTROL SYSTEM

Cruise control system - description

1 Cruise control may be fitted to models manufactured from 1990 onwards as an option. The system incorporates the following components:

(a) Electronic control unit located behind the instrument panel and attached to the instrument binnacle. The ECU receives information from the driver, brake pedal switch and road speed transducer, and activates the throttle vacuum pump accordingly

(b) Cruise control switches are located in the auxiliary switch panel and on the steering wheel. The steering wheel switches provide **set/accelerate** and **resume/decelerate** functions

(c) The brake pedal switch is mounted on the brake pedal bracket and, when the pedal is applied, the ECU disengages the cruise control system and releases the throttle levers to their idle position

(d) The road speed transducer is mounted beneath the left-hand side of the vehicle. Cruise control cannot be engaged at road speeds under 28 mph.

(e) The actuator is located in the engine compartment and moves the throttle levers as required

(f) The neutral lockout relay is located under the rear of the right-hand front seat and disengages the cruise control if neutral or park is selected in the main gearbox when the system is engaged

2 If the cruise control system develops a fault check all of the associated wiring and vacuum hoses.

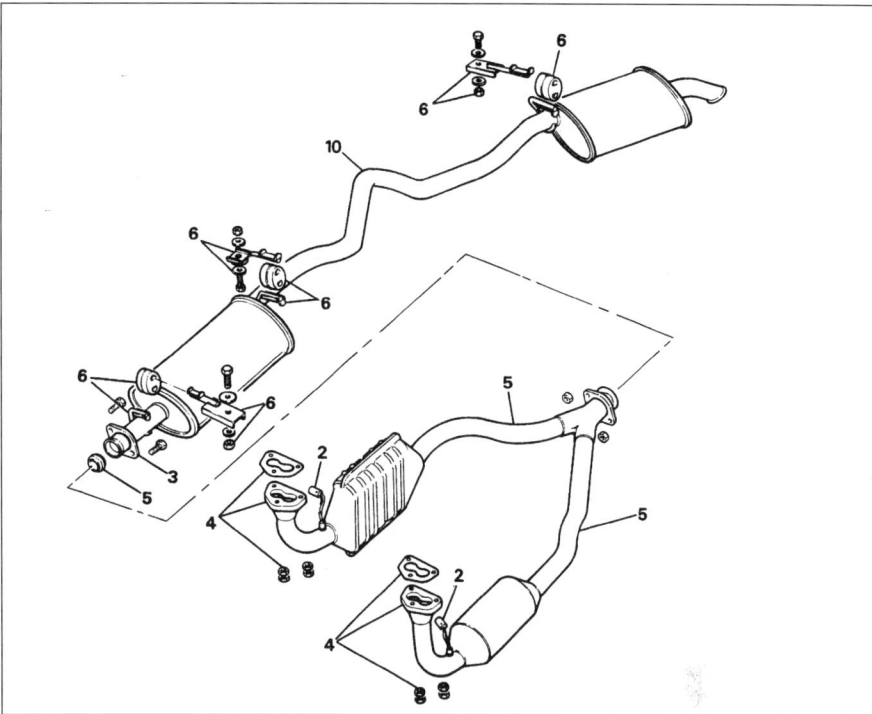

Fig. 13.42 Exhaust system fitted to 1990-on models (Sec 6D)

2 Lambda sensors (catalyst models only)
3 Flange
4 Downpipe gasket, flange and nuts
5 Exhaust front pipe, and silencers or catalytic converter
6 Exhaust system mountings
10 Exhaust rear section with silencers (on 1988 and 1989 catalyst models the front silencer is a catalytic converter, ie there are three catalytic converters)

6D.136A Front right-hand catalytic converter

6D.136B Front left-hand catalytic converter

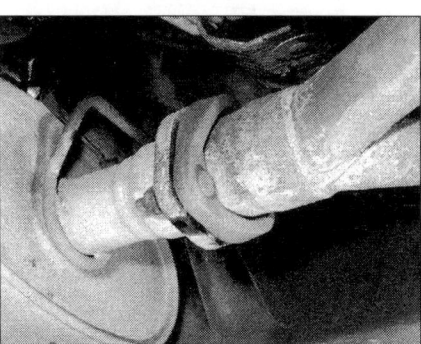

6D.136C Exhaust front pipe-to-main exhaust system connection

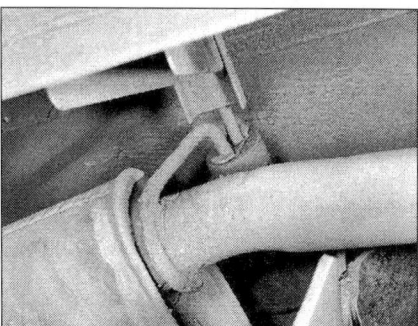

6D.136D Rear exhaust mounting

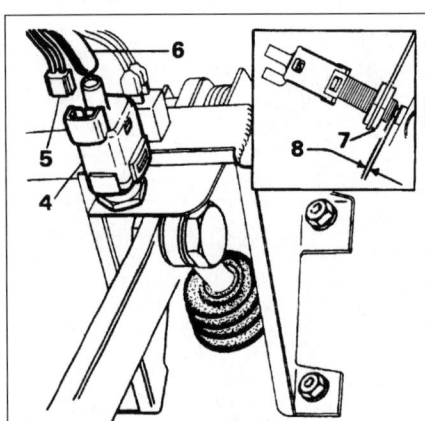

Fig. 13.43 Cruise control brake switch/vent valve removal (Sec 6E)

4 Brake switch/vent valve
5 Multi-plug
6 Vacuum hose
7 Adjusting nut
8 Adjustment clearance

Cruise control system components - removal, refitting and adjustment

Brake switch/vent valve

3 Disconnect the battery negative lead.
4 Remove the six screws and pull down the lower facia panel. Disconnect the rheostat switch multi-plug and remove the warning lamp control unit from the retaining clip. Remove the lower facia panel from inside the vehicle.
5 Disconnect the wiring from the brake switch/vent valve, then pull the hose unit, unscrew the nut, and withdraw the unit from the pedal bracket.
6 Refitting is a reversal of the removal procedure, but adjust to provide a clearance of 1.0 mm between the brake switch/vent valve body and the inside shoulder of the contact button.

Steering wheel switches

7 Disconnect the battery negative lead.
8 Pull the centre pad off the steering wheel, and disconnect the multi-plug located below the steering wheel retaining nut. Prise the switch(es) out of the steering wheel spoke(s). Prise the small switch button from the spoke(s).
9 Pull the switch and wiring leads through the spoke(s) to gain access to the electrical connections beneath the switch.
10 Disconnect the wiring from the switch and withdraw it.
11 Refitting is a reversal of the removal procedure.

Spiral cassette

12 Disconnect the battery negative lead.
13 Remove the steering wheel as described in Chapter 11. Apply adhesive tape to the upper and lower halves of the cassette to hold the upper half and prevent it turning. If this

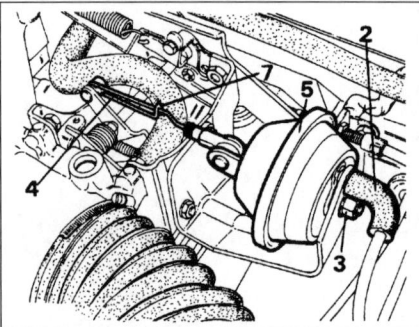

Fig. 13.44 Cruise control actuator and linkage (Sec 6E)

2 Rubber elbow
3 Actuator mounting nut
4 Operating link
5 Actuator
7 Position of hook on operating link

precaution is not taken the flexible tape inside the cassette will be damaged.
14 Unscrew the shroud lower mounting screws, then unscrew the left or right-hand upper screw and carefully separate the two halves until the multi-plug can be disconnected.
15 Remove the cassette from the steering column.
16 Refitting is a reversal of the removal procedure, but make sure that the two driving pegs locate in the holes on the underside of the steering wheel. Make sure that the wiring is not trapped between the upper and lower shroud.

Actuator

17 Disconnect the battery negative lead.
18 Remove the rubber elbow, and unscrew the nut holding the actuator to the throttle bracket.
19 Detach the actuator and disconnect the operating link from the throttle lever. Remove the actuator from the engine compartment.
20 Examine the rubber diaphragm for wear and damage, and renew the actuator if necessary.
21 Refitting is a reversal of the removal procedure.

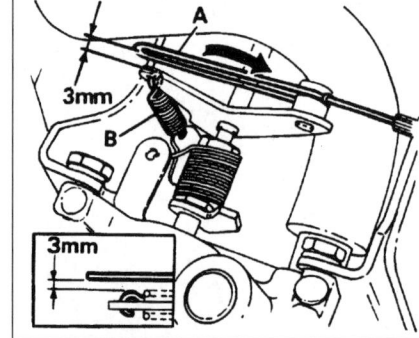

Fig. 13.46 Cruise control actuator adjustment (Sec 6E)

A Actuator link   B Small spring (see text)

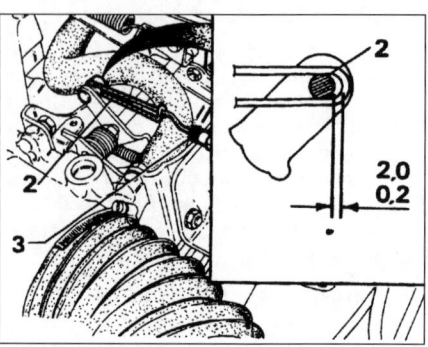

Fig. 13.45 Cruise control actuator link clearance (Sec 6E)

2 Actuator link   3 Socket joint

Actuator link adjustment

22 With the ignition off, check the clearance between the inside edge of the actuator link and the recessed diameter of the throttle lever. This should be between 0.2 and 2.0 mm.
23 To adjust the setting remove the link from the actuator and rotate the socket joint on the link as required to increase or decrease the length of the link. Refit the link to the actuator and recheck the adjustment.
24 Open the throttle fully and check that a gap of 3.0 mm minimum exists between the side of the actuator link and the side of the small spring which connects the inner throttle lever to the outer throttle lever. Bend the link to achieve the correct gap if it is less than 3.0 mm. Check the clearance again at closed throttle and open throttle and check that the actuator link slides smoothly in the groove of the throttle lever.

Vacuum pump

25 Disconnect the battery negative lead.
26 Disconnect the vacuum pump multi-plug and vacuum pipe, then remove the rubber mountings and withdraw the pump.
27 Refitting is a reversal of the removal procedure.

Cruise control electronic control unit (ECU)

28 The ECU is located behind the facia below the steering column. First disconnect the battery negative lead.
29 Unscrew the screws and pull down the lower facia panel.
30 Disconnect the multi-plug from the rheostat switch and detach the warning lamp control unit from the retaining clip.
31 Remove the lower facia panel.
32 Unscrew the mounting screws and withdraw the cruise control ECU so that the wiring multi-plugs can be disconnected.
33 Refitting is a reversal of the removal procedure.

Neutral lockout relay

34 The neutral lockout relay is located under the rear of the front right-hand seat and access to it is gained by moving the seat fully

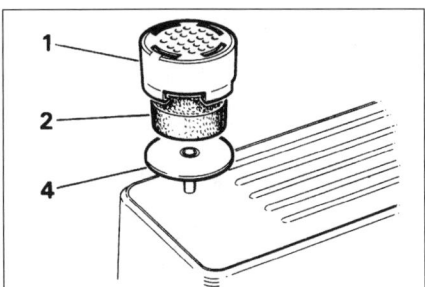

Fig. 13.47 Cruise control neutral lockout relay (3) location (Sec 6E)

forwards and reaching up underneath. First disconnect the battery negative lead.

35 With the seat fully forwards, reach up and pull the relay from its terminal block.

36 Refitting is a reversal of the removal procedure.

PART F: EMISSION CONTROL SYSTEMS

⚠️ *Warning: Many of the procedures in this Section require the removal of fuel lines and connections which may result in some fuel spillage. Before carrying out any operation on the fuel system refer to the precautions given in 'Safety first!' at the beginning of this manual, and follow them implicitly. Petrol is a highly-dangerous and volatile liquid, and the precautions necessary when handling it cannot be overstressed*

Pulsair air injection system (carburettor models) - description

1 This emission control feature was introduced in 1981. The system operates by drawing air from the air cleaner unit under manifold depression, passing the air through gulp valves and pipes, and then injects the air into the exhaust manifold. The injected air mixes with the exhaust gases and reduces the CO (carbon monoxide) emission to atmosphere.

2 Very little in the way of maintenance to the system is required, apart from checking the condition and security of the hoses, pipes and air valves at the specified intervals.

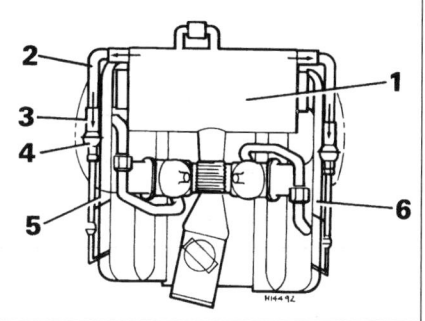

Fig. 13.48 Pulsair injection system layout (Sec 6F)

1 Air cleaner unit	5 Air manifold
2 Connecting pipes	(right-hand)
3 Connecting hoses	6 Air manifold
4 Gulp valves	(left-hand)

Crankcase breather filter (fuel injection models) - renewal

3 At the intervals given in Routine Maintenance the crankcase breather filter must be renewed as follows.

4 The breather filter is located on the rear of the left-hand rocker cover beneath the throttle linkage.

5 Prise the filter cover off the base and take out the sponge filter element.

6 Place a new filter in the cover then press the cover firmly onto the base until it clips in position.

Engine flame trap (fuel injection models) - removal and refitting

7 The flame trap is located on the front of the right-hand rocker cover.

8 Slacken the clip and disconnect the breather hose from the top of the flame trap.

9 Unscrew the flame trap from the rocker cover and retrieve the sealing O-ring.

10 Examine the wire gauze inside the flame trap. If the gauze is in poor condition or heavily contaminated, renew the flame trap. If the gauze is acceptable, immerse the flame trap in petrol and allow time to soak.

11 Remove the flame trap from the petrol bath, shake off excess petrol, and allow it to air-dry. Do not use compressed air to dry the gauze.

12 Refit the flame trap using the reversal of removal but with a new sealing O-ring.

Charcoal canister and purge valve - description, removal and refitting

13 As from 1988-on an evaporative emission control system is fitted incorporating a vented charcoal canister. The charcoal canister absorbs fuel vapour from the sealed fuel tank when the engine is not running. Compared to a vented fuel tank, the system prevents fuel vapour pollution to the atmosphere. The vapour is drawn into the engine by inlet manifold vacuum. For 1990-on purging of the canister is controlled by a solenoid valve when the engine speed is above idle and the vehicle is in motion (photo). The rate of purge will depend on engine speed, road speed and throttle position.

14 The system incorporates an expansion tank located between the inner right-hand body side and the rear right-hand wing. This tank is fitted in the line from the fuel tank to the charcoal canister.

15 To remove the canister disconnect the battery negative lead, disconnect both purge lines and release the canister from its mounting brackets. Note the location of the purge lines and identify them if necessary.

16 To remove the purge valve disconnect the battery negative lead, purge lines, and wiring plug, then unclip the valve.

17 Refitting of the canister and purge valve is a reversal of the removal procedure. Ensure that the restrictor in the short flexible connection is not blocked.

Fuel expansion tank (models fitted with a charcoal canister) - removal and refitting

18 Depressurise the fuel system as described earlier in this Part.

19 Disconnect the battery negative lead.

20 Remove the rear lamp cluster with reference to Chapter 10.

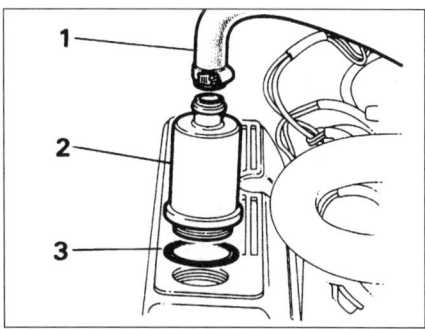

Fig. 13.49 Crankcase breather filter components - fuel injection models (Sec 6F)

1 Filter cover	4 Filter base
2 Sponge element	

6F.13 Charcoal canister (A) and purge valve (B)

Fig. 13.50 Engine flame trap details - fuel injection models (Sec 6F)

1 Breather hose	3 O-ring seal
2 Flame trap	

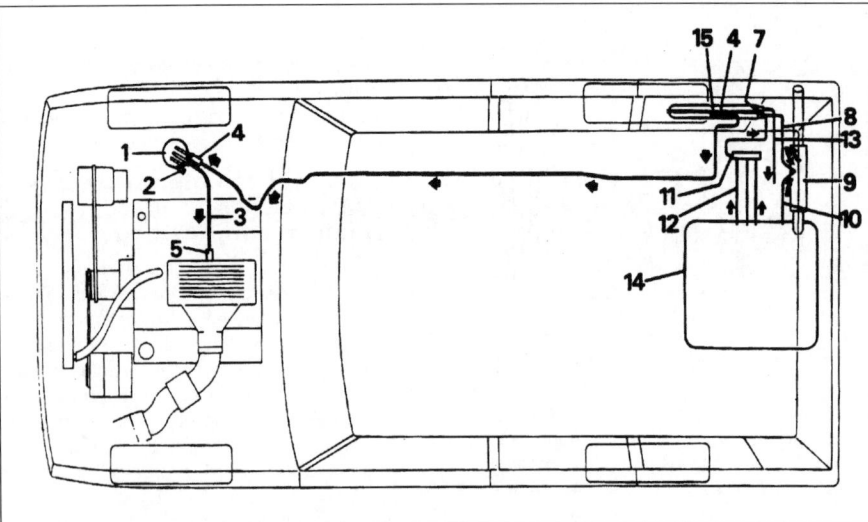

Fig. 13.51 Fuel evaporative emission control system layout (Sec 6F)

1 *Charcoal canister*
2 *Air inlet*
3 *Purge line to plenum chamber*
4 *Connector hoses with restrictors*
5 *Restrictor in purge line*
7 *Fuel vapour pipe from manifold*
8 *Breather hose with anti-surge valve*
9 *Fuel tank filler neck*
10 *Filler neck breather hose*
11 *Manifold*
12 *Fuel vapour pipes from fuel tank*
13 *Pressure relief valve and hose*
14 *Fuel tank*
15 *Float/rollover valve*

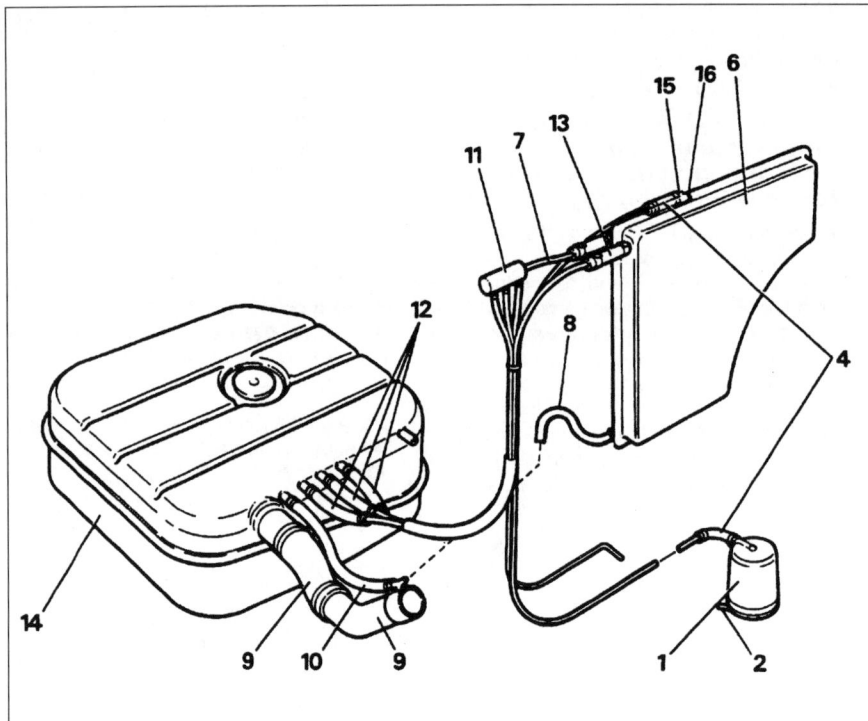

Fig. 13.52 Fuel evaporative emission control system components (Sec 6F)

1 *Charcoal canister*
2 *Air inlet*
4 *Connector hoses with restrictors*
6 *Fuel expansion tank*
7 *Fuel vapour pipe from manifold*
8 *Breather hose with anti-surge valve*
9 *Fuel tank filler neck*
10 *Filler neck breather hose*
11 *Manifold*
12 *Fuel vapour pipes from fuel tank*
13 *Pressure relief valve and hose*
14 *Fuel tank*
15 *Float/rollover valve*
16 *Rubber grommet*

21 Remove the wrap around bumper end cap.
22 Remove the rear wing and corner panel assembly.
23 Loosen the hose clamps and disconnect the three hoses from the expansion tank.
24 Loosen the clamp and disconnect the hose from the float valve located on top of the expansion tank.
25 Unscrew the bottom mounting bolts.
26 Access to the upper mounting bolts is gained by lifting the trim covering the vehicle tool kit. With the bolts removed, lift out the tank and remove it from the vehicle.
27 Disconnect the short hose connection from the top vapour hose and check that the restrictor in the hose is free from blockages.
28 With the expansion tank removed, check the float/rollover valve as follows. Plug the two upper outlet pipes, then apply air pressure of 2.0 lbf/in² to the bottom pipe. With the tank upright air should flow through the valve but with the tank turned 90° onto its side the air flow should cease. Disconnect the air supply from the tank, then with the bottom pipe sealed fill the tank with white spirit. Hold the tank in its upright position and check that the float valve shuts off and prevents fluid passing through the valve.
29 Disconnect the breather hose from the top of the filler neck and shake the hose. It should be possible to hear the valve ball but if not renew the hose assembly. Drain the white spirit on completion, and flush with clean fuel.
30 Refitting is a reversal of the removal procedure.

Lambda sensor - description, removal and refitting

31 Lambda sensors are fitted to vehicles equipped with catalytic converters. One sensor is located in the exhaust downpipe for each bank of cylinders, just forward of the front catalytic converter (photo), and its purpose is to monitor the quantity of oxygen present in the exhaust gases and send a corresponding signal to the fuel injection system ECU. The ECU then computes the correct fuel/air mixture and makes any adjustment necessary to the injector opening period for the relevant bank of cylinders.

6F.31 Lambda sensor (arrowed) viewed from below the vehicle

32 The engine should be cold before attempting to remove the Lambda sensors.

33 Disconnect the battery negative lead.

34 Disconnect the wiring plug from the sensor, then unscrew and remove the sensor from the exhaust downpipe.

35 Apply a little anti-seize compound to the threads of the sensor but take care not to allow the compound to contact the nose of the sensor, otherwise its efficiency may be impaired. If there is any contamination of the sensor nose by any other substance the sensor should be renewed.

36 Screw the sensor into the exhaust downpipe and tighten to the specified torque. Rover technicians use an adaptor as shown in Fig. 13.53 since the sensor is located on top of the downpipe, but it may be possible to fabricate a similar tool if this tool is not readily available.

37 Reconnect the wiring and battery negative lead.

Catalytic converters - description

38 On 1990-on models catalytic converters are fitted to the exhaust system, one on each exhaust downpipe. On 1988 and 1989 catalyst models a further catalytic converter is fitted just to the rear of the point where the downpipes join the main part of the exhaust system.

39 The catalytic converters reduce the emission of carbon monoxide, oxides of nitrogen and hydrocarbon.

40 Only unleaded fuel must be used in engines fitted with catalytic converters. The use of leaded fuel will seriously damage or destroy the internal parts of the catalytic converter.

7 Ignition system

Sliding contact breaker point distributor - description

1 The Lucas 35 D8 distributor fitted to models produced from 1981 differs in that it has sliding contact type breaker points fitted. These have the advantages of increased reliability and longer contact life, renewal being necessary at less frequent intervals.

2 In all other respects, the distributor is the same as that fitted to earlier models; the removal, cleaning and refitting details are identical to those described in Section 4 of Chapter 4. However, the following special points must be noted.

(a) Only sliding contact type breaker points must be fitted

(b) When removing the contact breaker points, clean the contact faces with petrol to remove the protective coating

(c) When fitting the contact points, lubricate the actuator ramps, the contact breaker

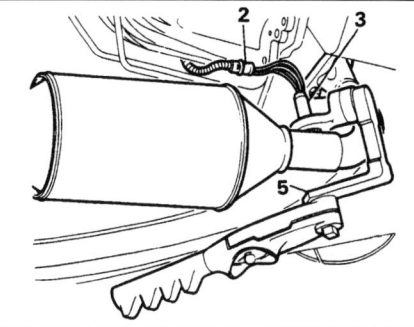

Fig. 13.53 Using the Rover tool to remove a Lambda sensor (Sec 6F)

2 Wiring plug   5 Rover tool
3 Lambda sensor

heel ribs, the heel actuator base and the fixed pin and actuator fork with grease (Fig. 13.55)

(d) On fitting the contact points into position, the sliding actuator fork must engage over the baseplate pin, and the pegs on the underside of the contact set engage with holes in the movable plate

(e) When new contact breaker points have been fitted, check the dwell angle after 1000 miles (1500 km) have been covered

Ignition timing - 8.13:1 and 9.35:1 compression ratio engines with contact breaker ignition

3 In addition to those details mentioned in Sections 3 and 8 in Chapter 4, the following items should be noted for these engine types.

4 Prior to checking the ignition timing, it is essential that the contact breaker points are correctly adjusted. If adjustment is necessary due to the gap being too small, the adjuster screw should be unscrewed beyond that required, then retighten to set the clearance specified. This method will avoid the possibility of backlash in the screw mechanism.

5 Run the engine up to its normal operating temperature.

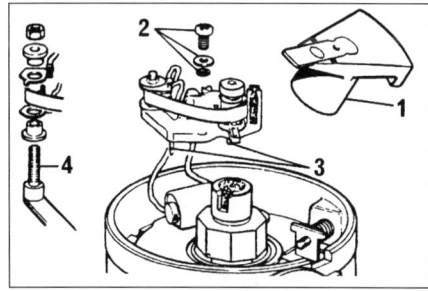

Fig. 13.54 Sliding contact breaker points (Sec 7)

1 Rotor arm
2 Retaining screw and washers
3 Movable plate pegs
4 Terminal post connections (red lead fits over bottom plastic bush)

6 On 8.13:1 compression ratio engines set the engine idle speed at 600 to 650 rpm, leaving the vacuum pipes connected.

7 On 9.35:1 compression ratio engines set the idle speed at 550 to 650 rpm, leaving the vacuum pipes connected. With the idle speed adjusted, detach both vacuum pipes from the distributor vacuum unit, the engine idle speed will then increase and must be reduced to 750 rpm by disconnecting a breather pipe from one of the carburettors. Further equal adjustment of the idle speed setting screws of the carburettors may be required to achieve this speed.

8 On both engine types the swell angle can then be checked and adjusted, as described in Section 8 of Chapter 4.

9 After the dwell angle check is completed, the ignition timing should be checked dynamically, as described in Section 8 of Chapter 4.

10 On 9.35:1 compression ratio engines, complete the timing checks by reconnecting the vacuum retard pipes and the carburettor breather pipe, then recheck the engine idle speed.

11 If necessary readjust the idle speed to that specified, then recheck the dynamic timing which should be between 4 and 8° ATDC. If not then the vacuum system is at fault.

12 Check the vacuum unit, detach the vacuum retard pipe at the distributor. The idle speed should increase and the timing advance to between 6 and 14° BTDC.

Electronic ignition system - general

⚠️ *Warning: The HT voltage generated by an electronic ignition system is extremely high and in certain circumstances, could prove fatal. Take care to avoid receiving electric shocks from the HT side of the ignition system. Do not handle HT leads, or touch the distributor or coil, when the engine is running. If tracing faults in the HT circuit, use well-insulated tools to manipulate live leads. Persons with surgically-implanted cardiac pacemaker devices should keep well clear of the ignition circuits, components and test equipment*

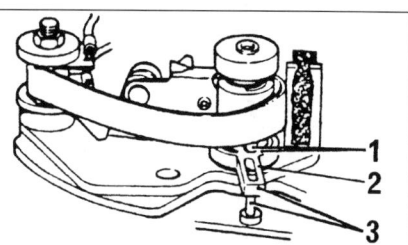

Fig. 13.55 Sliding contact breaker points lubrication areas (Sec 7)

1 Actuator ramps and breaker heel ribs
2 Heel actuator base
3 Fixed pin and fork

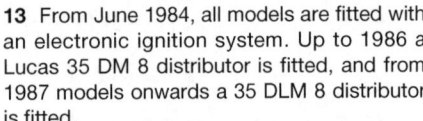

7.14 Ignition coil and electronic control unit location

7.25 Removing the distributor

7.26 Plastic insulation cover retaining screws (arrowed)

13 From June 1984, all models are fitted with an electronic ignition system. Up to 1986 a Lucas 35 DM 8 distributor is fitted, and from 1987 models onwards a 35 DLM 8 distributor is fitted.

14 The electronic ignition functions in a similar manner to a conventional system, but the contact points and condenser are replaced by a magnetic sensor in the distributor and a control unit (amplifier). Up to 1986 the amplifier is mounted separately next to the ignition coil on the left-hand side of the engine compartment, but as from 1987 the amplifier is mounted on the side of the distributor body (photo). As the distributor driveshaft rotates, the magnetic impulses are fed to the amplifier which switches the primary circuit on and off.

15 No condenser is necessary as the circuit is switched electronically with semi-conductor components.

16 The ignition advance is controlled mechanically by centrifugal weights and by a vacuum capsule mounted on the side of the distributor.

Electronic ignition system - precautions

17 To prevent personal injury and damage to the ignition system, the following precautions must be observed when working on the ignition system.

18 Do not attempt to disconnect any plug lead or touch any of the high tension cables when the engine is running, or being turned by the starter motor.

19 Ensure that the ignition is turned OFF before disconnecting any of the ignition wiring.

20 Ensure that the ignition is switched OFF before connecting or disconnecting any ignition testing equipment such as a timing light.

21 If the HT cable is disconnected from the distributor the cable must immediately be connected to earth and remain earthed if the engine is to be rotated by the starter motor (for example if a compression test is to be done).

22 If an electric arc welder is to be used on any part of the vehicle, the vehicle battery

must be disconnected while welding is being done.

Electronic ignition system - maintenance

23 At the intervals given in Routine maintenance at the beginning of this Supplement, remove the distributor cap, withdraw the rotor arm and wipe clean the inner components using a clean dry cloth, but

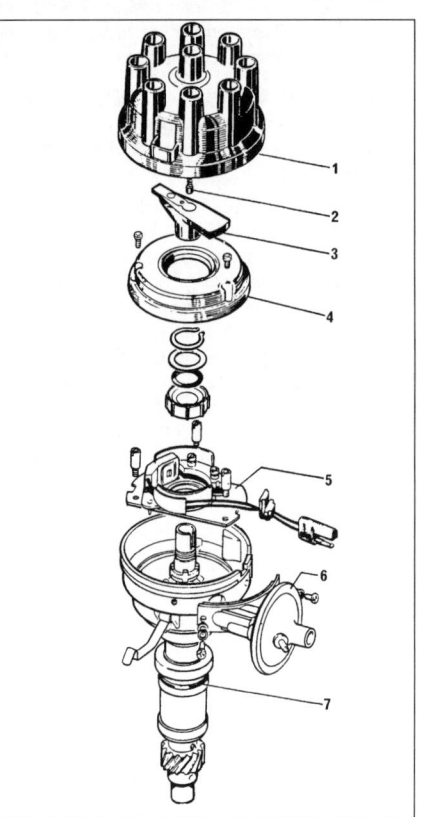

Fig. 13.56 Electronic ignition distributor components for pre-1987 models (Sec 7)

1 Cap	5 Pick-up and
2 HT brush and	baseplate
spring	assembly
3 Rotor arm	6 Vacuum unit
4 Insulation cover	7 O-ring oil seal
(flash shield)	

do not remove the plastic insulating cover protecting the magnetic pick-up module.

24 Wipe clean the ignition HT and LT leads and check that their respective connections are secure.

Electronic ignition distributor - removal, overhaul and refitting

25 The distributor can be removed and

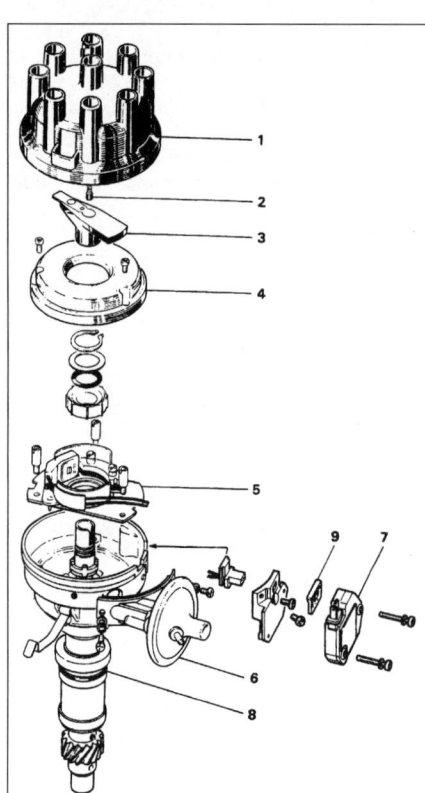

Fig. 13.57 Electronic ignition distributor components for 1987-on models (Sec 7)

1 Cap	5 Pick-up and
2 HT brush and	baseplate
spring	assembly
3 Rotor arm	6 Vacuum unit
4 Insulation cover	7 Amplifier module
(flash shield)	8 O-ring oil seal
	9 Gasket

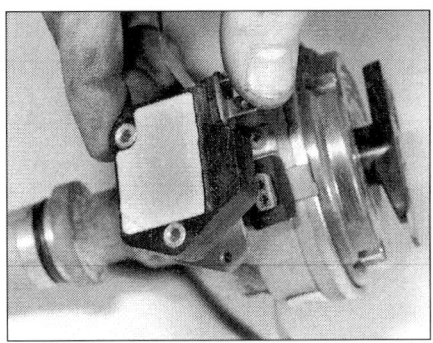

7.28A Removing the amplifier from the side of the distributor . . .

7.28B . . . followed by the gasket

7.28C Removing the cast heat sink from the side of the distributor

refitted in the same manner as that described for the conventional type in Section 5 of Chapter 4 (photo).

26 Commence dismantling by withdrawing the rotor arm, then undo the three retaining screws (photo) and lift clear the plastic insulation cover (flash shield).

27 Undo the two screws securing the vacuum unit and withdraw the unit, disengaging the connecting rod from the pick-up baseplate peg as it is removed.

28 On 1987 models onwards, unscrew the two screws and withdraw the amplifier from the side of the distributor together with the gasket. Unscrew the two screws and remove the cast heat sink from the side of the distributor (photos).

29 On all models, using a pair of circlip pliers, release the circlip securing the reluctor on the driveshaft, then withdraw the reluctor complete with the flat washer and O-ring. To assist with the removal of the reluctor, insert a small screwdriver blade under it and prise it up the shaft. Note the coupling ring located underneath the reluctor.

30 To remove the pick-up module and baseplate unit, unscrew and remove the three support pillars, but take care not to undo the two barrel nuts. These retain the pick-up module and if disturbed the air gap will have to be reset. Do not dismantle the distributor any further.

31 Clean and renew as necessary any items which are worn or suspected of malfunction.

32 Reassembly is a reversal of the dismantling procedure, but note the following special points.

(a) When refitting the pick-up and baseplate unit locate the pick-up leads in the plastic channel (Fig. 13.58)

(b) When refitting the reluctor, slide it down the shaft as far as possible then turn the reluctor so that it engages with the coupling ring underneath the baseplate

(c) Before refitting the amplifier on 1987 models onwards, apply MS4 Silicone grease or an equivalent heat-conducting compound to the amplifier module backplate, the seating face on the distributor body and to both faces of the heat sink casting

(d) Apply three drops of clean engine oil to the felt pad in the top end of the rotor shaft

(e) Apply grease to the vacuum unit connecting rod seal (within the unit)

(f) Apply grease to the automatic ad vance mechanism, the pick-up plate centre bearing, pre-tilt spring and contact area, the vacuum unit connecting peg and corresponding connecting rod hole

(g) Prior to refitting the insulation cover check, and if necessary adjust, the pick-up air gap

33 Refer to Chapter 4 Section 5 when refitting the distributor.

Electronic ignition distributor - air gap adjustment

34 The air gap should only need checking and adjusting when the distributor has been dismantled and either the original or a new pick-up and baseplate assembly have been fitted.

35 The air gap is checked by inserting a non-ferrous feeler gauge of the specified thickness between the pick-up limb and a reluctor tooth (photo).

36 Where adjustment is necessary, loosen the two barrel nuts retaining the pick-up module (these will already be loosened on a new unit) and move the module/pick-up to adjust the gap. Retighten the nuts.

37 Refit the plastic cover, rotor arm and distributor cap (photo).

Ignition timing - electronic ignition

38 The ignition timing and adjustment methods on models fitted with electronic ignition are the same as those described for the contact breaker type. When making a dynamic timing check, disconnect the vacuum pipe at the distributor and check that the idle speed does not exceed 750 rpm for pre-1987 models, 600 rpm for 1987 and 1988 models, or 800 rpm for 1989-on models (Hot-wire fuel injection system). Disconnect a breather hose to achieve this speed, if necessary, as the speed must not be regulated by adjusting the

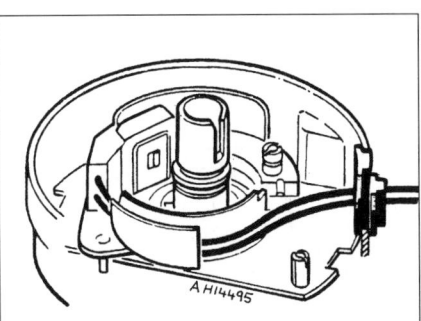

Fig. 13.58 Electronic ignition distributor pick-up leads arrangement (Sec 7)

7.35 Checking the air gap

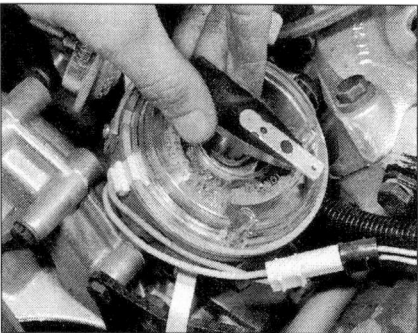

7.37 Refitting the rotor arm

idle speed screws. Do not allow the engine speed to exceed 3000 rpm during the check. Refer to the Specifications in this Chapter for the static and dynamic ignition timing settings.

Ignition system HT leads

39 Further to the information given concerning HT leads in Chapter 4, it is important to note that if the leads are detached for any reason, they must be refitted and arranged as shown in Figs. 13.59 or 13.60. This arrangement ensures that there is no cross firing (arcing) between the leads which will cause misfiring. Note that the distributor position is slightly different for 1989-on models.

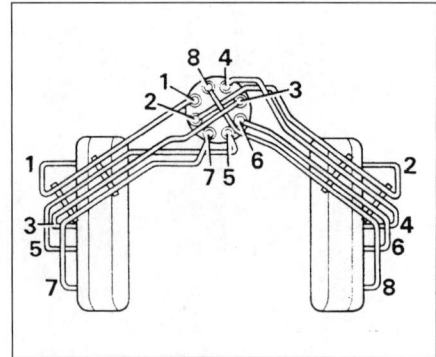

Fig. 13.59 HT lead arrangement for pre-1987 models (Sec 7)

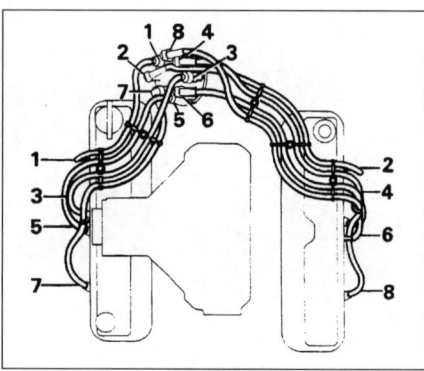

Fig. 13.60 HT lead arrangement for 1987-on models (Sec 7)

Electronic ignition system - fault finding

If a fault occurs in the electronic ignition system first check the wiring and ensure that connections are clean, dry and secure. Check the battery state of charge. Check the HT leads for correct routing and condition.

Remove the distributor cap and check the reluctor air gap as described earlier in this Section.

Check the HT circuit by disconnecting the coil-to-distributor HT lead at the distributor and holding it approximately 6 mm away from the cylinder block using well insulated pliers. Have an assistant switch on the ignition and turn the engine on the starter motor. If there is a regular stream of sparks then the fault must be in the distributor cap or HT leads; however if there are no sparks, continue to check the LT circuit as follows.

Connect a voltmeter across the battery terminals and check that the reading is at least 12 volts. If it is less than this the battery is discharged and should be re-charged.

Connect the voltmeter between the battery negative terminal and the positive terminal on the ignition coil. Switch on the ignition and check that the reading is a maximum of 1 volt below that of the battery. If it is lower than this the ignition switch or wiring should be checked.

Connect the voltmeter between the battery negative terminal and the negative terminal

on the ignition coil. With the ignition switched on check that the reading is a maximum of 1 volt below that of the battery. If it is lower than this the ignition switch, wiring, coil, or amplifier should be checked. If the coil or amplifier is suspected at this stage, disconnect the amplifier wire from the coil and make the check again. If the voltage is now correct either the LT lead or the amplifier is at fault. If the voltage is no different a new coil should be fitted.

Connect the voltmeter between the amplifier mounting screw and a good earthing point on the engine. The reading on the voltmeter should be between zero and 0.1 volt. If it is higher than this the amplifier mounting screw is not making a good earth with the distributor body.

With the ignition switched off, connect the voltmeter between the battery positive terminal and the ignition coil negative terminal. Zero volts should be registered. If there is a reading a fault is indicated in the amplifier. Now switch on the ignition and crank the engine, and check that the voltage increases indicating that the amplifier is switching the LT circuit.

If there is no increase in voltage in the previous test, remove the amplifier from the side of the distributor and connect an

ohmmeter across the pick-up module terminals. The ohmmeter should register between 2000 and 5000 ohms. If correct, check the wiring connections and, if good, renew the amplifier. If the resistance is incorrect renew the pick-up module.

If the engine will still not run, fit a known good HT lead between the ignition coil and the distributor cap and, using well insulated pliers, hold it approximately 6 mm away from the cylinder block while an assistant turns the engine on the starter. If the spark is weak renew the ignition coil and repeat the test.

To check the rotor arm, remove the distributor cap and disconnect the coil-to-distributor HT lead at the cap. Using well insulated pliers hold the end of the lead approximately 3 mm away from the centre of the rotor arm electrode. Have an assistant crank the engine, then check that there is no sparking onto the rotor arm. If there is, the rotor arm is conducting current to earth through the distributor driveshaft, and the rotor arm should therefore be renewed.

Check the distributor cap for signs of tracking or cracking before refitting it. Also check the ignition coil tower for similar signs.

If the HT circuit is in good order, but the engine still refuses to start, remove the spark plugs and check them.

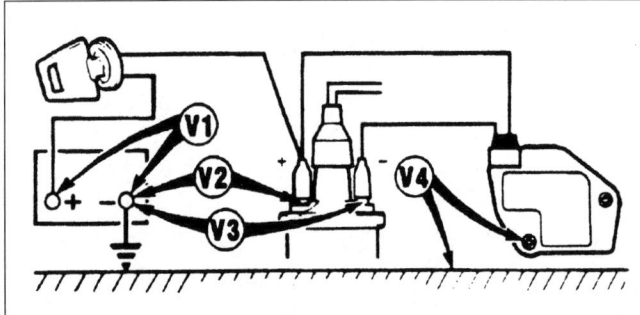

Fig. 13.61 Ignition system checks with the engine stationary (Sec 7)

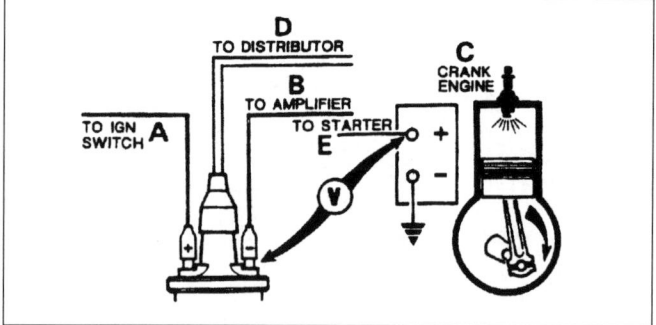

Fig. 13.62 Ignition system checks with the engine cranking (Sec 7)

8 Clutch

Master cylinder - removal and refitting

1 The clutch pedal upper stop bolt is not fitted to later models and therefore its adjustment procedure described in Chapter 5 is not applicable.

Master cylinder - overhaul

2 On later models manufactured from approximately 1985, the master cylinder primary seal is improved. The later master cylinder is interchangeable as a complete unit with the earlier type, although the overhaul kit of seals is different.

9 Manual transmission

PART A: FOUR-SPEED TRANSMISSION - MODIFICATIONS

Gearbox mainshaft bearing

1 From 1979 the gearbox mainshaft bearing arrangement was modified by having a semi-circular groove machined in the periphery of the bearing outer race. A roll pin driven through a hole in the gearbox bearing housing engages with the groove in the bearing to prevent any possible lateral movement of the bearing in the housing. It therefore follows that when removing this bearing (fitted from

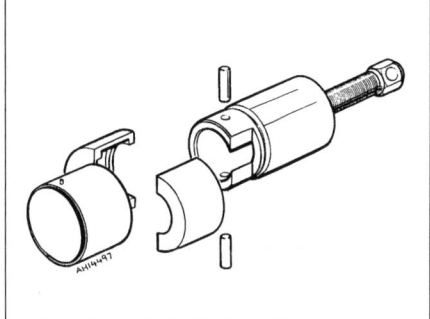

Fig. 13.63 Special tool 18G 1388 for removal of the transfer gear and spacer on later models (Sec 9A)

gearbox number 35574323) it will first be necessary to remove the roll pin.

2 When fitting the bearing, align the peripheral groove with the pin hole in the housing, then drive a new roll pin in to secure.

Mainshaft and transfer gear

3 On later models (1983-on), the mainshaft spacer and transfer gear are assembled using Loctite 275 (or similar) and because of this it is essential to use a later type special service tool number 18G 1388, instead of the special extractor RO 1004 suggested for earlier gearbox types in Section 5 of Chapter 6.

Reverse selector shaft

4 From late 1980 onwards, a longer roll pin was fitted to secure the reverse selector to the shaft. When fitted, ensure that the roll pin is driven fully into position and is located as shown in Fig. 13.64.

Main gearbox-to-transfer gearbox oil seal - renewal

5 From gearbox type numbers 35600623C and 12C15923A (later 9.35:1 compression

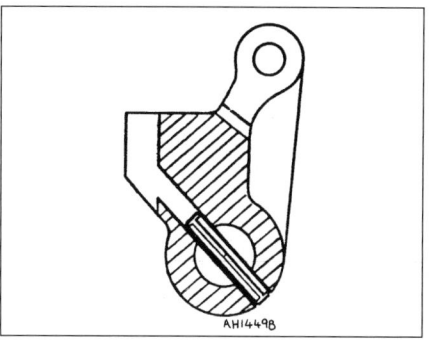

Fig. 13.64 Reverse selector-to-shaft roll pin location on later models (Sec 9A)

engines), it is possible to renew the main gearbox-to-transfer gearbox oil seal without removing the gearbox or the selector lever cross-shaft. However, if attempting this operation, two Rover service tools will be required, these being 18G 1388 (mainshaft output gear and spacer remover) and 18G 1426 (interbox oil seal replacer).

6 Remove the drain plug, and drain the oil from the transfer gearbox into a suitable container.

7 Refer to Chapter 6 and remove the speedometer drive housing.

8 Unbolt and remove the transfer gearbox bottom cover. It may be necessary to remove the intermediate exhaust pipe section to allow bottom cover removal.

9 Unbolt and remove the mainshaft rear bearing cover and gasket. Withdraw the roller bearing (See Fig. 6.4).

10 Screw a suitable (8 mm) bolt into the end of the intermediate gear shaft. Support the intermediate gear cluster from underneath and withdraw the shaft.

11 Keep the intermediate gears together during removal by inserting a suitable slave shaft through them - use Rover special tool number RO 1003 if available. Withdraw the intermediate gear cluster.

12 If dismantling of the gear cluster is necessary, this is dealt with in Section 12 of Chapter 6.

13 Before removing the mainshaft output (transfer) gear it should be noted that the gear, selective washer and snap-ring control the mainshaft endfloat.

14 If during the removal of these items the mainshaft is allowed to move forward, the 1st gear needle roller bearing thrust washer will become dislodged. To prevent this it is necessary to engage 3rd gear and then secure the main gear lever in this position during the subsequent operations until the output gear assembly is refitted.

15 With the 3rd gear securely engaged, and the gear lever held under tension, release the snap-ring and remove it, together with the selective washer and the mainshaft output gear. Remove the output gear using Rover special tool 18G 1388.

16 Use this tool to remove the mainshaft

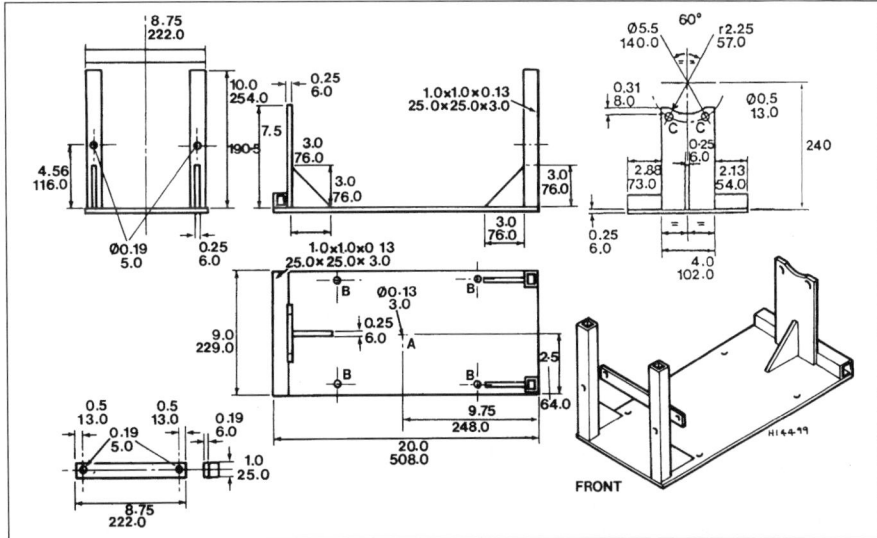

Fig. 13.65 Special cradle required when removing/refitting the five-speed transmission from underneath the vehicle (Sec 9B)

Dimensions in inches and millimetres

spacer sleeve, but check that the extractor pins are fully engaged prior to withdrawal.

17 The interbox oil seal can now be levered out, but take care not to damage the housing bore.

18 Clean the mainshaft, output gear and spacer sleeve, ensuring that no traces of old Loctite are present on them.

19 Wrap some plastic insulation tape over the splined sections of the mainshaft so that the oil seal lip is protected from damage as it is located over the shaft.

20 Carefully locate the oil seal over the shaft and beyond the cross-shaft, then fit it into the housing using Rover special tool 18G 1426. When the seal is fully fitted into the housing bore, remove the special tool and unwind the protective tape from the shaft. Smear the oil seal lip with clean oil to provide initial lubrication.

21 Temporarily refit the spacer sleeve, output (transfer) gear and selective washer. Locate the snap-ring then measure the endfloat clearance between the snap-ring and the washer. If necessary obtain a selective thrust washer to adjust the clearance to that specified (Chapter 6).

22 Remove the washer, gear and spacer sleeve.

23 Smear the inner bores of the spacer sleeve and gear with Loctite 275 (paying attention to the manufacturer's instructions), but ensure that no sealant is allowed to contact the external surfaces and the spacer sleeve seal track.

24 Refit the spacer sleeve, gear and selective washer, and secure in position with the snap-ring, ensuring that it is fully engaged in its groove (without forcing it). Third gear can now be disengaged. If the washer and snap-ring prove difficult to fit it is probable that the 1st gear needle roller thrust washer is dislodged, in which case pull and simultaneously rotate the mainshaft until the thrust washer is correctly relocated and the shim washer and snap-ring can be fitted.

25 Refit the intermediate gears and shaft, reversing the removal procedure and referring to Section 12 in Chapter 6.

26 When refitting the speedometer drive housing, coat the gasket with Hylomar PL32 sealant or equivalent.

27 On completion top up the transfer gearbox with the recommended quality and quantity of oil.

Top cover

28 From gearbox numbers 35596645L (standard compression engine) and 12C04252A (high compression engine), the top cover has an adjustable stop and locknut to provide a positive stop position for the reserve selector hinge unit.

Selector jaw roll pin

29 From gearbox number 35589427C, the selector jaw roll pin fitted is both larger in diameter and longer than the roll pin fitted to earlier gearbox types. This modification was made to improve the 1st/2nd and reverse selector jaw location on the selector shafts.

PART B: FIVE-SPEED TRANSMISSION AND TRANSFER GEARBOX - REMOVAL AND REFITTING

Special notes

Before any attempt is made to remove the transmission unit, the Special notes in Section 2 of Chapter 6 should be read.

The five-speed transmission unit complete (main gearbox and transfer gearbox) is best removed upwards through the vehicle in circumstances where limited workshop tools and facilities are available. This method is described in this Chapter.

If for any reason a different removal procedure is used, whereby the transmission unit is disconnected and then lowered on a jack for removal underneath the vehicle, it will be necessary to suitably support the gearbox. To do this you will need to make up a special transmission support cradle to the dimensions shown in Fig. 13.65. Alternatively you may be able to borrow this tool from your local Range Rover dealer. An industrial trolley jack will also be required to support, lower and manoeuvre the transmission unit clear of the vehicle, when using this method. Any attempt to remove the transmission from underneath without using the recommended cradle and a

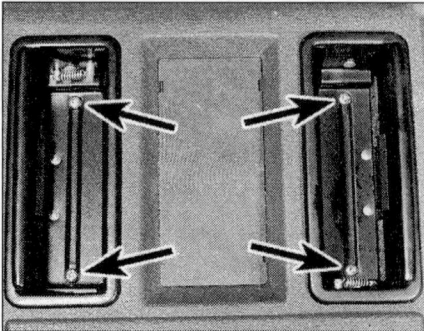

Fig. 13.66 Remove the ashtray holder retaining screws (arrowed) (Sec 9B)

suitable jack could result in both personal injury and damage to the transmission; therefore this method is not recommended for the DIY mechanic.

Pre-1986 models

1 Disconnect the battery earth lead.

2 Select the low range transfer gear then remove the high/low and main gear lever knobs.

3 Remove the main gear lever and the high/low gear lever gaiters.

4 Unclip and withdraw the ashtrays from their holders, then unscrew and remove the four self-tapping screws to release the holders (Fig. 13.66).

5 Peel back the base cover in the cubby box to expose its retaining bolts. Undo the bolts and lift the box clear (Fig. 13.67).

6 Loosen the two screws retaining the console at the front end then carefully withdraw the console rearwards and upwards. Disconnect the console switch wires as it is withdrawn.

7 Remove the rear compartment heater duct (Fig. 13.68).

8 Undo the retaining nut securing the main gear lever onto its splined shaft (Fig. 13.69), note and mark their relative alignment positions, then pull the lever from the selector shaft.

9 Remove the transmission tunnel carpet and floor carpets.

10 Undo the retaining screws and remove the high/low gear lever rubber gaiter and

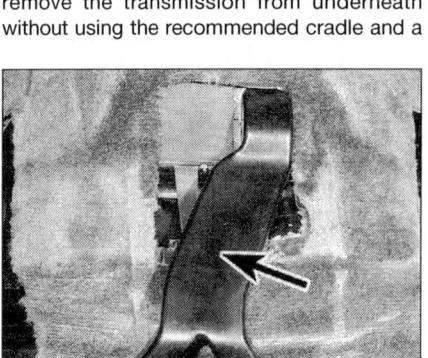

Fig. 13.67 Remove the cubby box retaining bolts (arrowed) (Sec 9B)

Fig. 13.68 Rear compartment heater duct (arrowed) (Sec 9B)

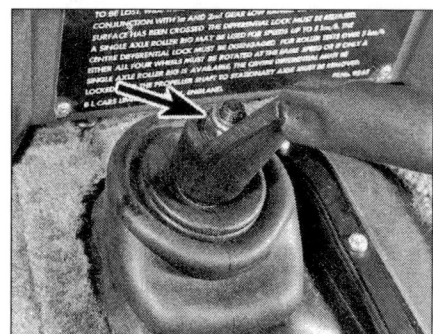

Fig. 13.69 Main gear lever retaining nut (arrowed) (Sec 9B)

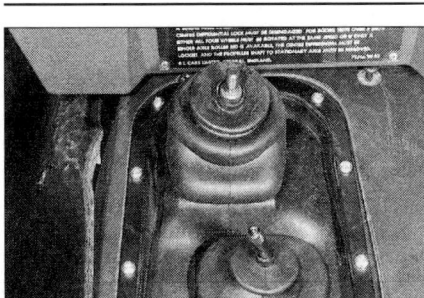

Fig. 13.70 High/low gear lever and main gear lever gaiters (Sec 9B)

Fig. 13.71 Remove the insulation cover . . . (Sec 9B)

Fig. 13.72 . . . and the aluminium top cover (Sec 9B)

retaining plate, then repeat this procedure and remove the main gear lever/top cover rubber gaiter from the top of the transmission tunnel (Fig. 13.70).

11 Lift the insulation moulding from the transmission top cover, then undo the retaining bolts and remove the aluminium top cover (Figs. 13.71 and 13.72).

12 Unbolt the front seat support frames and remove them, together with the seats. For access to the frame outer edge bolts, first detach the plastic covers which are secured by screws (Figs. 13.73, 13.74 and 13.75).

13 Undo the retaining screws and remove the handbrake lever gaiter (Fig. 13.76).

14 Remove the retaining bolts and lift clear the main gear lever housing (Fig. 13.77).

15 Unscrew the handbrake lever pivot bolt retaining nut and withdraw the bolt. Disconnect the handbrake link plate by extracting the split pin, withdrawing the clevis pin and collecting the flat washer and Thackeray washer, noting their location. Withdraw the lever and detach the handbrake warning switch leads (Figs. 13.78 and 13.79).

16 Unscrew and remove the front and rear (passenger compartment) floorpan retaining screws and bolts. Two bolts are particularly difficult to reach, these being located at the front end of the transmission cover section of the front floor section (above the bellhousing, near the bulkhead). Access to these bolts can be gained by removing the air filter unit (see

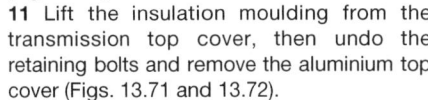

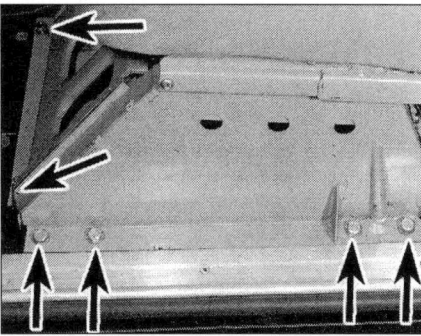

Fig. 13.73 Seat retaining bolts - leading and outer edges (arrowed) (Sec 9B)

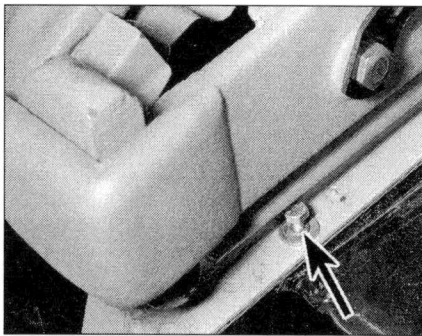

Fig. 13.74 Seat retaining bolt (arrowed) - inner edge at rear (Sec 9B)

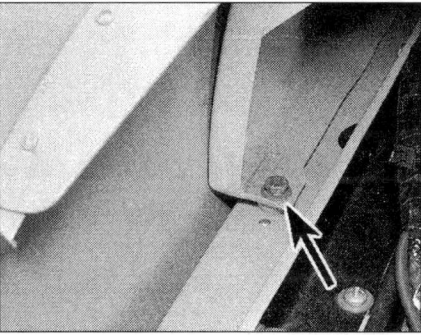

Fig. 13.75 Seat retaining bolt (arrowed) - underside (Sec 9B)

Fig. 13.76 Handbrake lever gaiter, clamp plate and retaining screws (Sec 9B)

Fig. 13.77 Removing the main gear lever housing (Sec 9B)

Fig. 13.78 Remove the handbrake lever pivot bolt and link plate clevis pin (arrowed) (Sec 9B)

Fig. 13.79 Disconnect the handbrake warning switch leads (arrowed) (Sec 9B)

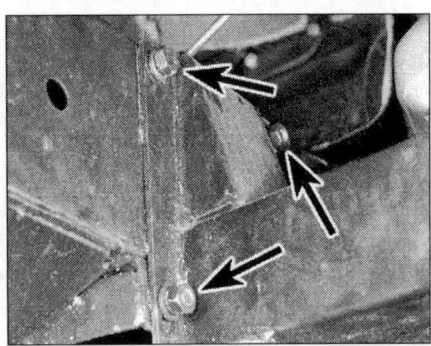

Fig. 13.80 Chassis crossmember retaining bolts (arrowed) (Sec 9B)

Fig. 13.81 Floorpan-to-chassis adjustable mounting (Sec 9B)

Fig. 13.82 Unbolt the exhaust heat shield from the floorpan (Sec 9B)

Chapter 3) and reaching down under the bulkhead from the engine compartment side. An alternative method is to remove the chassis crossmember beneath the transmission. The crossmember is secured to the chassis member each side by four bolts and nuts (Fig. 13.80). Support the crossmember, and lever or tap it downwards from the chassis, noting which way round it is fitted. With the crossmember removed, the two bolts are just accessible from underneath by reaching up between the floor panel and the transmission. Note that if the transmission is to be lowered and removed from underneath the vehicle, then the crossmember will have to be removed anyway, so try this method first.

17 Working underneath the vehicle, disconnect the floorpan rear adjustable mounting each side by extracting the split pin and withdrawing the clevis pin (Fig. 13.81). Loosen the adjuster nut to allow withdrawal of the clevis pin if necessary.

18 Unbolt and release the exhaust heat shield plate from the floorpan (Fig. 13.82).

19 Prise free and remove the floorpan from the rear passenger compartment, then repeat the procedure with the front floorpan/ transmission cover, pulling it to the rear for removal. Note that the electric fuel pump wiring is secured to the underside of the transmission cover floorpan on the left-hand side, so prise back the clip and release the leads as the pan is removed.

20 Disconnect the leads to the reverse light switch (green and green/brown) (Fig. 13.83).

21 Disconnect the leads to the differential lock switch (green and black/blue) (Fig. 13.84).

22 Undo the retaining bolts and detach the breather hoses from the main and transfer gearboxes. Refit the bolts and fibre washers to the gearboxes to avoid losing them (Fig. 13.85).

23 Disconnect the wiring and the breather hoses from their location clips on the transmission and fold them back out of the way, but note their retaining clips and locations.

24 Disconnect the speedometer cable from the transmission and fold it back out of the way (Fig. 13.86).

25 Referring to Chapter 7, unbolt and detach the front and rear propeller shafts from the drive flanges on the transfer gearbox. Tie them up out of the way.

26 Position a suitable container under the transmission and drain the oil from the main gearbox and the transfer gearbox by removing their respective drain plugs (Fig. 13.87).

27 Unbolt and detach the front exhaust pipes from the manifolds and at their single pipe connection to the silencer and steady mounting (Fig. 13.88).

28 Unbolt and detach the clutch slave cylinder from the bellhousing. Leave the hydraulic line connected to the cylinder, and position the cylinder out of the way (Fig. 13.89).

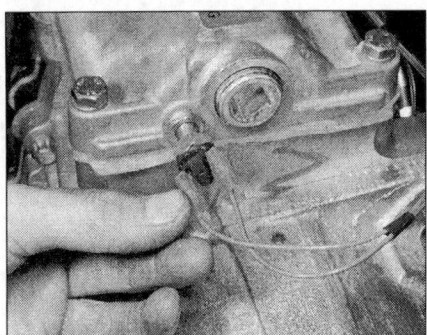

Fig. 13.83 Disconnect the reverse lamp switch leads (Sec 9B)

Fig. 13.84 Disconnect the differential lock switch leads (Sec 9B)

Fig. 13.85 Disconnect the breather hoses (main gearbox hose arrowed) (Sec 9B)

Fig. 13.86 Disconnect the speedometer cable (arrowed) (Sec 9B)

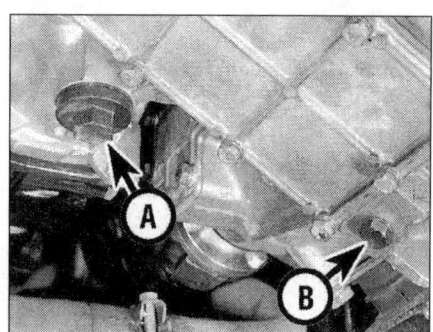

Fig. 13.87 Main gearbox (A) and transfer gearbox (B) drain plugs (Sec 9B)

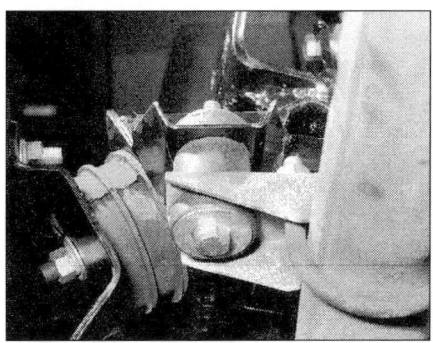
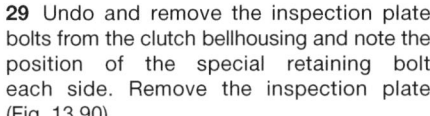

Fig. 13.88 Exhaust pipe steady mounting (Sec 9B)

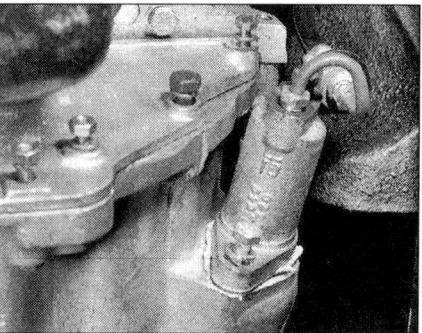

Fig. 13.89 Unbolt and remove the clutch slave cylinder from the bellhousing (Sec 9B)

Fig. 13.90 Bellhousing retaining bolts/nuts - special bolt is arrowed (Sec 9B)

29 Undo and remove the inspection plate bolts from the clutch bellhousing and note the position of the special retaining bolt each side. Remove the inspection plate (Fig. 13.90).

30 Undo and remove the clutch bellhousing-to-engine bolts and note the location of the harness locating clip.

31 The engine will now need to be supported, so position a suitable jack or safety stand under the engine and raise to support (not lift) the engine. Between the jack/stand and engine sump position a piece of wood to avoid damaging the sump.

32 The lifting sling must now be arranged around the main gearbox and the transfer gearbox so that, when lifted as a unit, the weight is equally distributed and they are kept level.

33 Wheel the gantry hoist into position over the gearbox, connect up the sling and take the weight. The hoist and sling must be as close to the transmission as possible to allow sufficient lift height clearance within the vehicle.

34 Remove the bolts from the transmission mountings on each side and detach from the chassis numbers (Fig. 13.91).

35 Unbolt and remove the upper bellhousing retaining bolts. Tilt the transmission downwards at the rear to enable the upper housing bolts to be withdrawn, but check that the engine mountings are not over-distorted.

36 Check that all of the transmission mounting and ancillary items are

disconnected, then pull the transmission rearwards to detach it from the engine. As it disengages from the clutch unit, watch out for any imbalance in the lift sling arrangement which may cause the transmission to tilt appreciably. At least one assistant should be at hand to help steady the transmission and to guide it clear of surrounding fittings when lifting it clear (Fig. 13.92). Unless the steering wheel is removed, withdraw the transmission from the passenger side.

37 If the transmission is to be lowered and removed from under the vehicle using the jack and cradle method mentioned earlier, unscrew the two bottom bolts from the rear cover of the transfer gearbox then locate the rear of the cradle into position and reinsert the bolts. Check that the cradle is securely located under the transmission, raise the back to support the assembly then withdraw the transmission rearwards and lower it once clear of the engine. Get an assistant to help steady the transmission as it is lowered and withdrawn from under the vehicle.

38 If the vehicle is to be moved whilst the transmission is out of the vehicle, locate a long bar through the clutch unit and into the flywheel pilot hole. Rest the rear of the bar on a support timber mounted transversely across and resting on top of the chassis. The engine support jack/stand can then be removed.

39 Refitting the transmission unit is a reversal of the removal sequence. In order to engage the primary pinion with the clutch splines it will probably be necessary to select a gear

and then turn the transmission brake drum whilst pushing on the rear face of the gearbox. When the splines are in alignment the gearbox will slide forwards over the shafts.

40 Smear the vertical joint face of the bellhousing cover plate with jointing compound before fitting. The cover plate and clutch slave cylinder spacing plate must also be treated with jointing compound when refitting (Loctite 290 or similar).

41 Renew all self-locking (Nyloc) nuts and split pins.

42 Do not refit the chassis crossmember until after the exhaust pipe front section and the two upper retaining bolts at the top of the transmission bellhousing (unless the air cleaner unit was removed) are in position.

43 When reconnecting the wiring to the reverse switch and differential switch, route the wires through their retaining clips so that they do not interfere with the high/low gearchange linkage assembly.

44 The same applies when reconnecting the ventilation tubes to the main gearbox and transfer gearbox. Use new fibre washers each side of the tube unions and do not overtighten the retaining bolts.

45 When refitting the clutch housing lower cover plate the special taper bolts must be correctly located in the second hole down each side. These bolts are tightened first to ensure correct positioning of the cover plate.

46 Do not fully tighten the mounting and retaining bolts until the transmission unit is fully located, then tighten them to the specified torque wrench setting.

47 When refitting the floor panels, loosely locate the retaining screws with flat washers. In some instances it may be necessary to realign the captive nuts on the underside. When all of the retaining screws and bolts are located they can be fully tightened.

48 Lubricate the handbrake linkages when reconnecting. Check that the handbrake warning switch leads are securely connected.

49 Check that the drain plugs are secured in position then top up the oil levels, referring to the Specifications in this Chapter for the lubricant types and quantities. Apply sealant

Fig. 13.91 Transmission-to-chassis mounting (Sec 9B)

Fig. 13.92 Transmission removal from within the vehicle (Sec 9B)

Fig. 13.93 Main gearbox filler/level plug (arrowed) (Sec 9B)

Fig. 13.94 Transfer gearbox filler/level plug (arrowed) (Sec 9B)

to the filler/level plugs before securing them in position (Figs. 13.93 and 13.94).

50 Before refitting the aluminium top cover, refit the gear lever housing and check the bias spring adjustment.

1986 to 1988 models

51 Disconnect the battery earth lead.
52 Refer to Section 17 and remove the centre console.
53 Remove the noise insulation pad to gain access to the gear lever gaiter.
54 Undo the four screws and drill out all the pop rivets securing the gaiter to the gearbox.
55 Disconnect the reversing light leads and pull the leads through the tunnel aperture.
56 Refer to Fig. 13.95 and undo the lower locknut from the high/low operating rod.

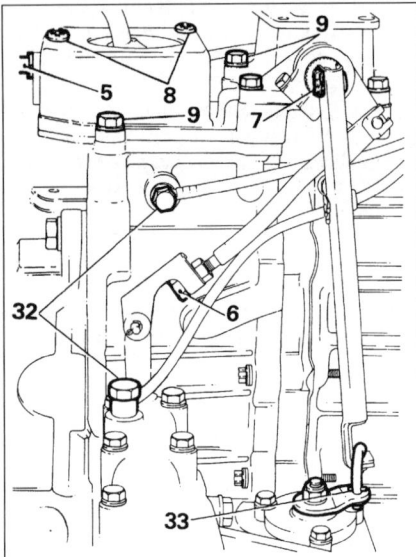

Fig. 13.95 Transmission linkage and component attachments - 1986-on models (Sec 9B)

5 *Reversing lamp leads*
6 *High/low operating rod lower locknut*
7 *Differential lock lever clevis pin spring clip*
8 *Gearchange housing top cover screws*
9 *Gearchange housing retaining bolts*
32 *Breather pipe attachments*
33 *Differential lock lever connecting link*

57 Extract the spring clip from the clevis pin securing the differential lock lever to the high/low gearchange housing.
58 Undo the two gearchange housing top cover retaining screws. Lift the cover for access and undo the gearchange housing-to-extension case retaining bolt located next to the reverse plunger assembly.
59 Undo the three remaining gearchange housing retaining bolts and remove the gearchange housing complete with transfer gear housing and gaiter.
60 Undo the nut securing the handbrake outer cable to the transmission tunnel and feed the cable assembly through its aperture to the underside of the vehicle.
61 The remainder of the procedure is basically the same as described previously for pre-1986 models and reference should be made to paragraphs 11 to 50 inclusive.

1989-on models

62 Position the vehicle over an inspection pit or jack it up and support on axle stands.
63 Disconnect the battery negative lead.
64 Remove the cooling fan blade assembly with reference to Chapter 2 noting that the screw thread is left-hand.
65 On fuel injection models disconnect the airflow meter to plenum chamber hose.
66 On carburettor models remove the air cleaner.

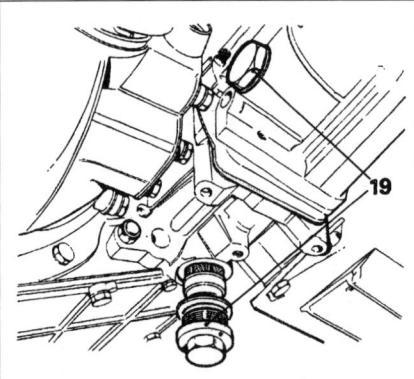

Fig. 13.96 Drain plugs (19) on the transmission extension housing and transfer box (Sec 9B)

67 Remove the main gear lever knob then select low range and remove the transfer gear lever knob.
68 Unscrew the screws and remove the glovebox liner.
69 Prise out the window lift switch panel from the front of the glovebox, then push the panel and switches back through the panel aperture and position them on the transmission tunnel.
70 Prise out the main gear lever centre panel.
71 Unscrew the screws and bolt securing the glovebox and console assembly to the transmission tunnel.
72 Remove the relay blocks from the glovebox.
73 Disconnect the wiring from the rear cigar lighter.
74 Release the handbrake then pull forward the gaiter. Extract the split pin, then remove the washer and clevis pin to release the inner cable from the handbrake lever.
75 While lifting the handbrake lever, move the glovebox to the rear away from the radio housing then remove the glovebox assembly.
76 Withdraw the sound deadening material from the top of the transmission tunnel.
77 Loosen the clamp bolt and remove the upper gear lever.
78 Unscrew the screws and remove the high/low lever and main gear lever retaining plates.
79 Working under the vehicle, position suitable containers beneath the transmission then unscrew the drain plugs from the transfer box, main gearbox and extension housing, and allow the oil to drain. Clean the filter on the extension housing. On completion refit and tighten the drain plugs using a suitable sealant on their threads before inserting them.
80 Unbolt and remove the chassis crossmember. If necessary the chassis members can be spread using a length of wood.
81 Referring to Chapter 3 remove the front exhaust downpipes and intermediate pipe together with the centre silencer.
82 Mark the drive flanges in relation to the propeller shafts then unbolt the propeller shafts and tie them to one side.
83 Loosen the clamp and disconnect the speedometer cable from the rear output housing. Unclip the cable and tie it to one side.
84 Unbolt the clutch slave cylinder from the transmission.
85 Support the weight of the transmission with a trolley jack then remove the mountings.
86 Lower the transmission until the top of the transfer box clears the rear passenger floor.
87 Remove the split pin, washer and clevis pin and disconnect the handbrake cable.
88 Unclip the handbrake cable and pass it through the support bracket, then tie the cable to one side.
89 Take the weight of the engine with a trolley jack and unscrew the bolts securing the transmission to the engine.
90 Check that all connections are released

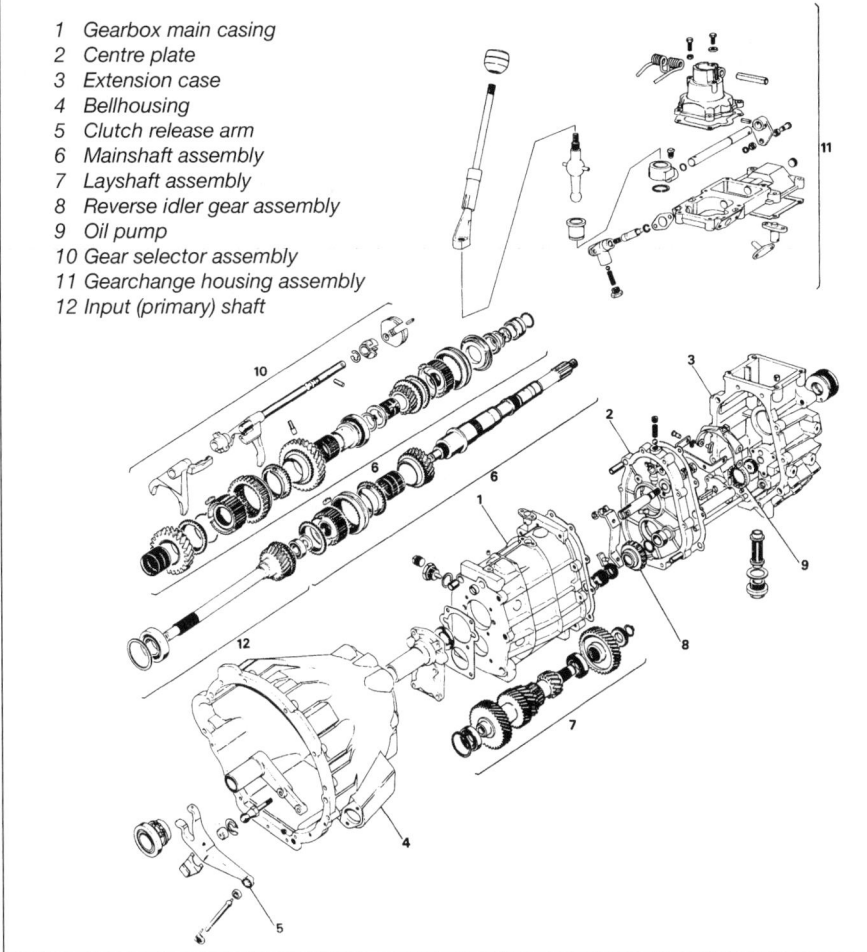

1 Gearbox main casing
2 Centre plate
3 Extension case
4 Bellhousing
5 Clutch release arm
6 Mainshaft assembly
7 Layshaft assembly
8 Reverse idler gear assembly
9 Oil pump
10 Gear selector assembly
11 Gearchange housing assembly
12 Input (primary) shaft

Fig. 13.97 Exploded view of the five-speed main gearbox (Sec 9B)

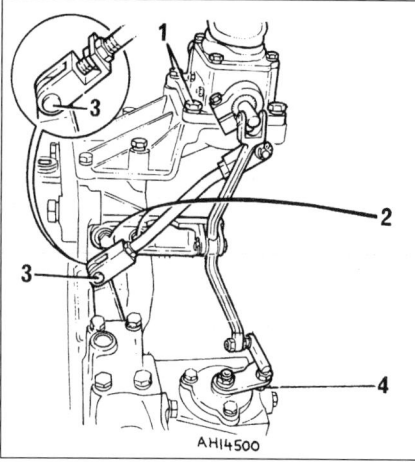

Fig. 13.98 Gearchange housing and associated connections - early models (Sec 9C)

1 Gearchange housing retaining bolts
2 Differential lock cross-shaft lever pivot bracket
3 High/low connecting rod-to-arm attachment
4 Differential lock lever assembly (early type)

PART C: TRANSFER GEARBOX - REMOVAL AND REFITTING

Pre-1989 models

1 With the main gearbox and transfer box removed and on the bench proceed as follows.

2 Extract the split pin and withdraw the clevis pin from the transmission brake link-to-handbrake link rod clevis (photo).

3 Undo the four retaining bolts and remove the handbrake lever mounting bracket from the side of the transfer gearbox (photo).

4 Unscrew and remove the two countersunk screws securing the transmission brake drum in position. Withdraw the brake drum, then undo the four bolts securing the brake unit/backplate assembly in position (photo). Withdraw the brake assembly, complete with the backplate.

from the engine then withdraw the transmission and lower it to the ground.

91 Apply sealant to the mating faces of the engine and transmission.

92 Select any gear in the main and transfer box to aid refitting and check that the clutch centre plate is centred correctly.

93 Raise the transmission and pass the handbrake cable through the aperture in the tunnel. Check that all wiring is clear of the end of the transmission.

94 Locate the transmission on the engine

then insert the bolts and tighten them to the specified torque.

95 The remaining procedure is a reversal of the removal procedure but note the following points.

(a) Tighten all nuts and bolts to the specified torque

(b) Unscrew the main gearbox and transfer box filler/level plugs and refill with the correct grade of oil until the level is to the bottom of the hole. Apply sealant to the threads of the plugs then refit and tighten them

9C.2 Handbrake link rod connection and mounting plate

9C.3 Handbrake lever mounting to the transfer gearbox

9C.4 Transmission brake drum retaining screws (arrowed)

9C.5 Undoing the transmission brake/backplate unit retaining bolts

9C.7 Tubular short cranked connecting link (as fitted to later models)

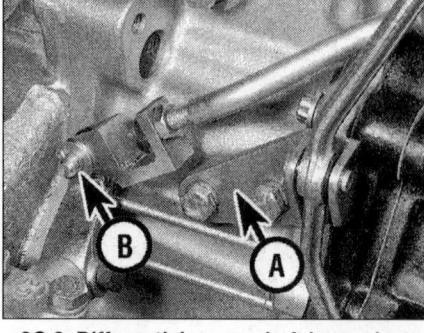

9C.8 Differential cross-shaft lever pivot bracket (A) and the high/low connecting rod-to-arm attachment (B) (later models)

5 Undo the mounting bolts and remove the right-hand mounting plate (photo).

6 On early models, detach the differential cross-shaft lever at the bottom end from the differential lock lever by undoing the self-locking nut and disconnecting the short connecting link (Fig. 13.98).

7 On later models a tubular short cranked connecting link is fitted and this can be detached by extracting the split pin and removing the flat washer (photo).

8 Unscrew the two differential cross-shaft lever pivot bracket retaining bolts (photo).

9 Extract the split pin and withdraw the clevis pin to detach the bottom end of the high/low operating arm link rod. Remove the plastic bushes.

10 Undo the four bolts retaining the gear lever housing then lift the housing clear.

11 Undo the four bolts and two nuts and remove the extension housing and main gearbox from the transfer gearbox (photo). It may be necessary to loosen the six bolts securing the high/low selector housing to allow the separation of the transfer gearbox from the extension housing.

12 Reassembly of the transfer gearbox to the main gearbox assembly is a reversal of the removal procedure, but the following points should be noted:

(a) The mating faces of the transfer gearbox and the extension housing should be cleaned of old sealant and new sealant applied (photo).

(b) Engage a gear in the main gearbox then get an assistant to lift and align the transfer gearbox with it. Carefully guide the transfer gearbox into position against the main gearbox face, taking care not to damage the oil seal. Turn the mainshaft to align it with the input gear splines in the transfer gearbox. Refit and tighten the four bolts and two nuts retaining the two assemblies together. Tighten them to the specified torque wrench setting given at the start of this Chapter.

(c) When re-assembling the handbrake and differential lock lever and linkages, smear the pivots with grease and use new split pins.

(d) Refit the high/low gearchange connecting rod, the differential lock switch and the main gear selector lever assembly, check their adjustments as described in Part E of this Section

1989-on models

13 With the main gearbox and transfer box removed, first connect a sling to the transfer box. Disconnect the high/low link from the transfer box selector lever and remove the breather pipe. Unscrew the upper and lower bolts and the two nuts and separate the transfer box from the gearbox.

14 To assemble the transfer box to the main gearbox, stand the gearbox vertically on its bellhousing on pieces of wood to prevent the primary pinion touching the bench, then lower

the transfer box into position taking care not to damage the seals. Insert the bolts and tighten to the specified torque. Refit the breather pipe and selector link.

15 The high/low link must now be adjusted. Check that the selector lever at the transfer box is in the neutral position, then position the lever at right angles to the centre line of the main gearbox and rotate the fork end of the rod until the holes align with the hole in the selector lever.

16 Refit the clevis pin and retaining clip, then select high and low to prove that the adjustment is correct.

PART D: BORG WARNER TRANSFER GEARBOX (1989-ON MODELS)

General

1 In October 1988 a new chain-driven Borg Warner transfer box and viscous coupling introduced for automatic coupling of the centre differential in slippery conditions. The new assembly replaces the previous LT230 two-speed helical gearbox introduced in 1982; it uses a Morse chain-and-sprocket drive system.

Viscous unit check

2 The viscous unit may be checked while installed on the gearbox as follows. First remove either the front or rear propeller shaft with reference to Chapter 7.

3 With the propeller shaft removed it should still be possible to drive the vehicle, proving that drive is being transferred to the propeller shaft connected to the gearbox.

4 If no drive is transferred, the viscous unit is faulty; however it is possible for the unit to partially fail. The latter will cause the engine speed to be high with little vehicle movement.

Transfer box speedometer drive pinion - renewal

5 Position the vehicle over a pit, or alternatively jack it up and support on axle stands.

6 Disconnect the battery negative lead.

9C.11 Main gearbox and extension housing separation from the transfer gearbox

9C.12 Applying sealant to the extension housing mating face

7 Unscrew the nut securing the speedometer drive clamp and withdraw the cable.

8 Prise the drive pinion assembly from the output housing.

9 Push the new drive pinion assembly into the output housing, fit the cable and secure with the clamp and nut.

Transfer box rear output shaft oil seal - renewal

10 Position the vehicle over a pit, or alternatively jack it up and support on axle stands.

11 Disconnect the battery negative lead.

12 Disconnect the rear propeller shaft from the output drive flange and tie it to one side.

13 Fully apply the handbrake, then unscrew the drive flange nut.

14 Release the handbrake, then unscrew the two screws and remove the handbrake drum.

15 Unscrew the lower bolts and remove the oil catcher from the backplate.

16 Unscrew the output shaft nut then remove the steel washer and rubber seal. Withdraw the flange.

17 Tap the dust cover from the housing and prise out the oil seal.

18 Clean the oil seal seating, then smear the new seal with a little oil and press it into position with the spring side against the circlip.

19 Fit the dust cover.

20 Where applicable release the circlip from the drive flange to allow new bolts to be fitted.

21 Check the seal contact surface on the flange. Renew the flange if the surface is corroded or if there is a deep groove.

22 Smear a little oil on the seal contact surface of the flange, then refit the flange. Renew the rubber seal if necessary, and refit the washer and a new nut. Only hand-tighten the nut at this stage.

23 Apply sealant to the oil catcher and refit it, tightening the bolts.

24 Refit the brake drum and tighten the two screws.

25 Fully apply the handbrake then tighten the flange nut to the specified torque.

26 Refit the rear propeller shaft and tighten the nuts.

Transfer box front output shaft oil seal - renewal

27 Position the vehicle over a pit, or alternatively jack it up and support on axle stands.

28 Disconnect the battery negative lead.

29 Disconnect the front propeller shaft from the flange and tie it to one side.

30 Fully apply the handbrake then unscrew the flange nut. Remove the nut, steel washer, and rubber seal. Withdraw the flange from the front of the transfer box.

31 Prise out the oil seal and clean the seating.

32 Smear the new oil seal with a little oil and press it into the housing with the spring side next to the circlip.

33 Check the seal contact surface on the flange and renew the flange if the surface is corroded or if there is a deep groove.

34 Smear a little oil on the seal contact surface of the flange, then refit the flange. Renew the rubber seal if necessary, and refit the washer and a new nut. Tighten the nut to the specified torque.

35 Refit the propeller shaft and tighten the nuts to the specified torque.

Transfer box - removal and refitting

Note: *Due to the weight of the transfer box it is important to use an adequate trolley jack fitted with a suitable cradle which will hold the transmission safely during the removal procedure.*

36 Position the vehicle over an inspection pit or alternatively jack up the vehicle and support on axle stands.

37 Disconnect the battery negative lead.

38 On fuel injection models release the airflow meter-to-plenum chamber hose.

39 On carburettor models remove the air intake ducts and withdraw the air cleaner from its location.

40 Noting that the fan blade assembly has a left-hand thread, unscrew and remove it.

41 Working inside the vehicle, unscrew the screws and remove the glovebox liner. Remove the mounting blocks from the side of the glovebox.

42 Disconnect the wiring from the rear of the cigar lighter.

43 Prise the window lift switch panel from the front of the glovebox, then move the switch panel and switches back into the glovebox and position the glovebox on the gearbox tunnel.

44 Select low range and remove the transfer lever knob.

45 Unscrew and remove the main gear lever knob.

46 Disconnect the wiring from the graphics panel on the underside of the centre panel and remove the panel.

47 Unscrew the bolts and screws securing the console assembly to the gearbox tunnel.

48 Release the handbrake and pull the rubber gaiter forwards for access to the clevis pin. Extract the split pin, and remove the

Fig. 13.99 Filler/level plug (5) and drain plug (6) on the Borg Warner transfer box (Sec 9D)

clevis pin and washer holding the handbrake cable to the handbrake lever.

49 Remove the console locating tab from the radio housing by moving the console to the rear.

50 Fully apply the handbrake, then move the glovebox to the rear away from the radio housing and remove the glovebox assembly.

51 Remove the sound deadening material from the top of the gearbox tunnel.

52 Loosen the clamp bolt and remove the upper gear lever. Unscrew the screws and remove the retaining plate securing the rubber gaiter to the top of the main gearbox.

53 Working under the vehicle, unscrew the drain plug from the bottom of the transfer box and allow the oil to drain into a suitable container. Refit the drain plug after the oil has drained, using suitable sealant on the threads.

54 On models fitted with a catalytic converter, disconnect the multi-plugs from the Lambda sensors.

55 Unbolt and remove the crossmember from below the gearbox.

56 Remove the front exhaust down pipes and intermediate pipe complete with centre silencer or catalytic converter.

57 Unbolt and remove the centre silencer heat shield.

58 Mark both drive flanges in relation to the propeller shafts for correct reassembly, then unscrew the nuts and tie the propeller shafts to one side.

59 Release the clamp and remove the speedometer cable from the rear output housing. Also unclip the cable from the side of the transfer box.

60 Using the trolley jack and cradle take the weight of the transfer box, then using a further trolley jack take the weight of the main gearbox.

61 Loosen only the right-hand transfer box mounting nut, then unscrew and remove the lower nut.

62 Unbolt and remove the transfer box to chassis right-hand outer mounting bracket, then remove the inner mounting bracket.

63 Unbolt and remove the left-hand mounting bracket.

64 Lower both the transfer box and main gearbox until the top of the transfer gearbox clears the rear passenger footwell.

65 Extract the split pin and remove the clevis pin and washer, then disconnect the handbrake cable from the brake drum.

66 Unclip the handbrake cable from the support bracket, remove it from the bracket and tie it to one side.

67 Disconnect the breather pipe from the top of the transfer box.

68 Disconnect the high/low selector rod from the transfer box lever by removing the clip and clevis pin.

69 Support the main gearbox, then unscrew the upper and lower bolts and the two nuts securing the transfer box to the main gearbox.

70 Withdraw the transfer box to the rear from the main gearbox and lower it to the ground.

71 Commence refitting by cleaning the joint faces of the transfer box and main gearbox. Apply a little oil to the lips of the input shaft oil seal.

72 Raise the transfer box and align it with the input shaft on the main gearbox. Carefully locate the transfer box over the input shaft taking care not to damage the oil seal. As the input shaft enters the transfer box it may be necessary to rotate the drive flanges in order to allow the splines to engage.

73 Refit and tighten the nuts and bolts noting that the upper left-hand bolt is the longest and locates the ring dowel.

74 Check that the selector lever at the gearbox is in neutral, then position the lever on the transfer box vertical at right angles to the centre line of the main gearbox then rotate the clevis on the end of the rod clockwise or anti-clockwise to shorten or lengthen the operating rod until the hole in the clevis aligns with the hole in the selector lever.

75 Fit the retaining clip assembly. Select high and low transfer to ensure full engagement is occurring, and repeat the above procedure if full engagement is not evident.

76 The remaining refitting procedure is a reversal of the removal procedure noting the following points:

(a) *Tighten all nuts and bolts to the specified torque*

(b) *Refill the transfer box with the correct grade of oil, then apply sealant to the threads of the plug and tighten it into position*

(c) *Check the oil level in the main gearbox and top up if necessary using the correct grade of oil*

(d) *Check the operation of the handbrake and adjust if necessary*

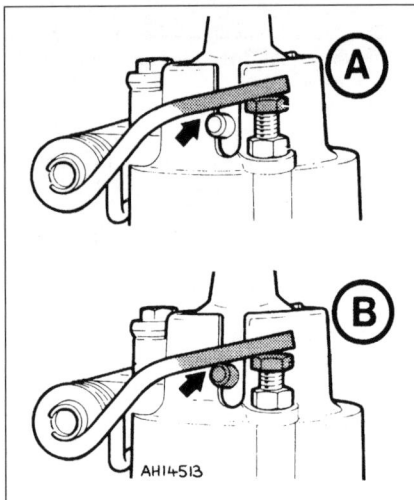

Fig. 13.100 Gear selection bias spring adjustment (Sec 9E)

A *Unscrew adjuster bolts to give clearance between the spring legs and lever cross-pin (arrowed)*

B *Tighten adjuster bolts so that spring legs just contact lever cross-pin (arrowed)*

PART E: FIVE-SPEED TRANSMISSION - SELECTOR ADJUSTMENTS

Main gearbox gear selection bias springs adjustment

Pre-1986 models

1 The gear selector bias springs are located externally on the main gear lever housing. For access, remove the main gear lever and the top covering from the transmission tunnel as described in Part B, paragraphs 1 to 6 inclusive.

2 Engage 3rd or 4th gear, loosen the two adjustment bolt locknuts and undo the bolts so that the spring leg on each side is clear of the cross pin in the lever. This should provide the gear lever with a slack radial movement (Fig. 13.100).

3 Move the gear lever to the left to take up any slack then tighten the adjustment bolt on the right-hand side to the point where the right-hand spring leg is just in contact with the gear lever cross pin on that side.

4 Move the gear lever to the right and repeat the procedure for the left-hand spring leg.

5 Now tighten each adjuster bolt progressively in equal amounts to the point where any slack radial movement of the lever is eliminated. Hold the gear lever at the lower end when making this adjustment for a more accurate assessment of the point where the slack is taken up.

6 Further tighten each adjuster bolt by two flats to set the spring tension.

7 Move the gear lever back to the neutral position, then move it backwards and forwards across the gate a few times and then release it. The lever should settle in the 3rd/4th gear selector gate position. Secure the setting by retaining the adjuster bolts in the set position and tighten the locknuts.

1986-on models

8 To gain access to the bias plate refer to Part B, paragraphs 51 onwards and carry out the operations necessary to allow removal of the housing top cover over the bias springs.

9 Slacken the four bias adjustment plate retaining bolts.

10 Select 4th gear, load the gear lever fully to the right-hand side of the gearbox and tighten the four bolts.

11 Check the gear lever operation by selecting all forward and reverse gears.

Main gearbox reverse plunger unit adjustment

Pre-1986 models

12 If the gear selection in 1st and 2nd gears still proves difficult after making the bias springs adjustment, it may be that the shim adjustment of the reverse plunger unit is incorrect. The reverse plunger also acts as a stop when these gears are selected and if

incorrectly set will cause the selector shaft to foul the reverse lever or 3rd/4th selector fork.

13 Unbolt and remove the reverse plunger unit from the selector housing. Remove the detent plunger cap, and extract the spring and ball. Extract the circlip and remove the plunger from its bore.

14 Clean the plunger housing and components thoroughly, ensuring that the threads are cleaned of Loctite sealant.

15 Smear the plunger with a light coating of oil, refit it into its bore and secure with the circlip. Do not let any oil get onto the housing threads.

16 Refit the detent ball, spring and cap. If a washer was fitted under the cap refit this also (the washer should be about 1 mm thick and was fitted to ease reverse gear selection).

17 Select 1st or 2nd gear, turning the mainshaft if necessary to obtain engagement. Insert the reverse plunger unit to the point where it is felt to contact the gear lever yoke. Apply light finger pressure to the plunger unit to maintain it in this position and measure the clearance between the plunger and selector housing mating faces using feeler gauges.

18 The shims required must equal the clearance measured plus 0.006 to 0.020 in (0.15 to 0.51 mm). Refit the reverse plunger unit ensuring that the detent cap faces upwards.

19 Move the gear lever through the 1st/2nd gate to check for satisfactory selection.

20 Remove the detent cap and smear the threads with a locking sealant, but not too much or the sealant may work its way into the housing bore when the cap is fitted.

21 Lightly screw the cap back into the plunger housing then move the gear lever through the reverse gate a minimum of ten times then connect a suitable spring balance to the gear lever directly underneath the knob. Pull on the spring balance and observe the loading required to pull the gear lever over. The correct loading should be 30 to 35 lbf (13.6 to 15.8 kgf). Tighten the housing cap until the correct loading is achieved. This should be within two full turns of the cap. Leave the cap in the set position for the time specified by the locking sealant manufacturer to allow the sealant to harden and secure the cap (about 60 minutes normally).

22 The fifth gear stop should now be adjusted as follows.

23 Check that the bias springs are correctly adjusted before making any checks or adjustments to the gear stop.

24 Unbolt and remove the 5th gear stop plate (Fig. 13.101).

25 Move the gear lever into the 5th gear engagement position turning the mainshaft if required to obtain full engagement.

26 Remove any shims from the stop unit, then refit it to the point where it is in light contact with the gear lever yoke. Hold it in this position under light finger pressure and measure the clearance between the 5th gear stop and selector housing using feeler gauges.

Fig. 13.101 Fifth gear stop plate and adjustment shims (Sec 9E)

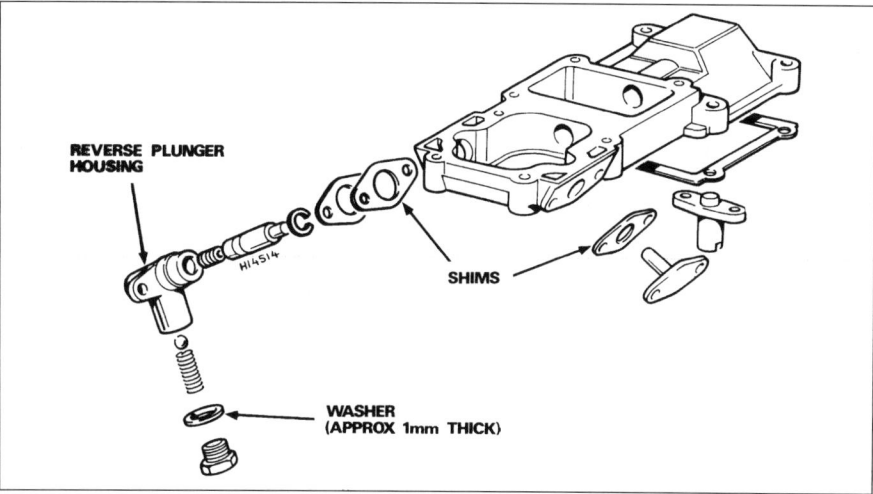

Fig. 13.102 Reverse plunger unit and adjustment shims (Sec 9E)

Also shown is the 5th gear stop and shims

27 Select shims to equal the thickness of the gap measured plus 0.012 to 0.035 in (0.3 to 0.9 mm). Refit the 5th gear stop, together with the selected shims and check the 5th gear selection. Add or subtract further shims as required to obtain a satisfactory selector action.

28 Shims for both the reverse gear stop and 5th gear stop adjustment are available in two thicknesses: 0.02 and 0.03 in (0.51 to 0.76 mm).

1986-on models

29 After carrying out the bias springs adjustment as previously described, engage 1st gear and measure the gap between the reverse plunger nose and the gear lever using feeler gauges.

30 Add or remove shims behind the plunger unit as necessary to achieve a gap of 0.024 to 0.034 in (0.60 to 0.85 mm).

High/low gearchange connecting rod adjustment

Early models

31 To check if adjustment is required, select the high, then low range gears and observe if the gear lever fouls the gate plate. If it does then adjustment is necessary.

32 Loosen the operating arm fork locknut and remove the clevis pin securing the operating arm to the high/low connecting rod (Fig. 13.104).

33 Lift the operating arm fork clear of the connecting rod and rotate the fork as required, then temporarily reconnect the fork to the rod by inserting the clevis pin only.

34 Move the gearchange lever rearwards into the high range position and the selector housing operating arm on the cross-shaft forwards into the high range position. Check that the gearchange lever does not foul the gate plate. Repeat this procedure for the low range engagement. Further adjustment of the fork may be necessary.

35 When the setting is satisfactory, move the gear lever back to the high range position, then tighten the locknut against the clevis fork. Refit the flat washer and split pin to secure the clevis pin in the connecting rod-to-operating arm connection.

36 If removal or refitting of the connecting rod-to-operating arm clevis pin is found to be difficult due to the closeness of the transfer gearbox casing an alternative adjustment method can be used.

37 Disconnect the differential lock cross-shaft lever from the gearchange cross-shaft, then unscrew the gearchange housing retaining bolts and lift the housing clear.

38 Loosen the connecting rod fork locknut and then rotate the gearchange housing to rotate the fork on the rod and adjust its length accordingly.

39 Refit the housing and check the lever adjustment as described earlier.

Later models

40 The checking and adjustment procedure is similar to that described for automatic transmission models (See Section 10, part C) except that the grommet and grommet plate are not fitted, and the gate plate housing is secured by two screws to the housing. The four main bolts are fitted *in situ* via the floor-mounted gaiter assembly.

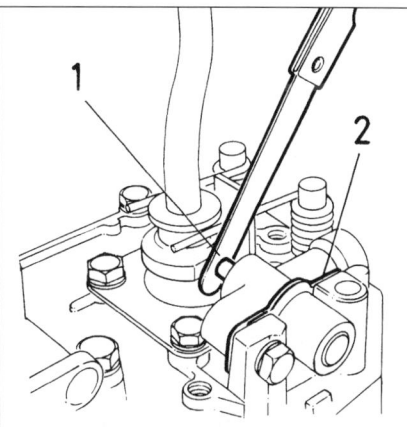

Fig. 13.103 Reverse plunger unit adjustment - 1986-on models (Sec 9E)

1 Feeler blade   2 Adjustment shims

Differential lock switch - removal, refitting and adjustment

41 Located on the front output shaft housing, the switch is removed by detaching the wires,

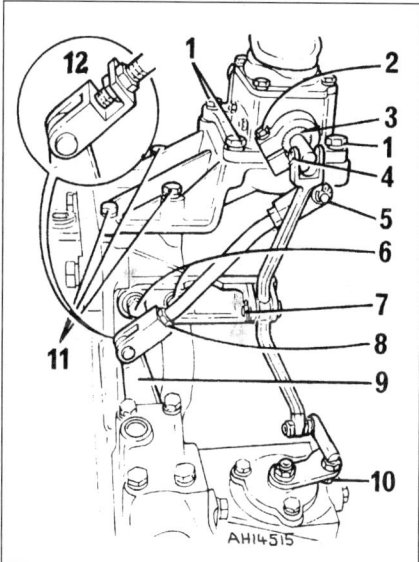

Fig. 13.104 High/low gearchange assembly (Sec 9E)

1 Gearchange housing bolts
2 Clamp bolt
3 Splined shaft and operating arm
4 Cross-shaft lever fork
5 Operating arm-to-high/low connecting rod clevis
6 Pivot bracket
7 Cross-shaft lever middle pivot
8 Operating arm fork locknut (early models)
9 High/low gearchange operating arm
10 Differential lock connecting link (short)
11 Gearchange housing (lower)-to-extension housing bolts
12 Operating arm fork (later models)

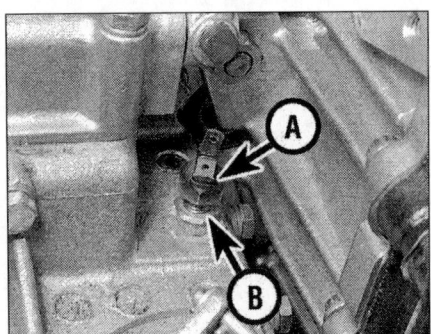

Fig. 13.105 Differential lock switch (A) and
locknut (B) (Sec 9E)

9E.44 Differential lock switch adjustment
using a multi-meter

9E.46 Reverse lamp switch location

loosening the switch locknut and unscrewing the switch unit (Fig. 13.105).

42 Correct setting is important when refitting and the following procedure should be used.

43 Move the differential lock lever to the right to select the differential lock.

44 Connect a test light or multi-meter to the switch lead terminals, then screw the switch in until the bulb lights up or a positive meter reading is given (photo). From this point tighten the switch a further half turn then retighten the locknut against the output shaft housing.

45 Detach the test equipment and return the differential lever to the left to disengage the differential lock.

Reverse light switch - removal, refitting and adjustment

46 This is located in the rear end of the gear selector housing. The removal, refitting and adjustment procedures are similar to those described for the differential lock switch, but engage reverse gear when screwing the switch unit in for adjustment (photo).

---

10 Chrysler three-speed automatic transmission

PART A: AUTOMATIC TRANSMISSION AND TRANSFER GEARBOX - DESCRIPTION, PRECAUTIONS AND MAINTENANCE

General description

1 The automatic transmission system comprises a torque converter and a fully automatic three-speed gearbox unit.

2 The torque converter enables the engine torque to be transmitted to the input shaft and thence to the gearbox multi-disc clutches. It is a sealed unit type converter and cannot be repaired.

3 The automatic gearbox unit has two multiple disc clutches, an overrun clutch, two

servos and bands, and two planetary gear sets. These give three forward and one reverse gear. An internal oil pump and valve body provide the integral hydraulic system and the gearbox is vented by a passage in the top of the oil pump. The transmission fluid is cooled by a separate oil cooler.

4 The transfer gearbox is mounted on the automatic transmission extension housing in much the same manner as that for the manual transmission. The transfer gearbox fitted is the same type as that fitted to the five-speed manual gearbox type and can be overhauled by referring to the appropriate Section in this Chapter; only the ratios differ.

5 In view of the specialised knowledge and equipment required to test and overhaul the automatic transmission, such tasks should be entrusted to your Range Rover dealer.

Special precautions

Transmission fluid

6 When topping-up the transmission fluid level or renewing the transmission fluid, use only the correct fluid specified. The use of incorrect fluid could cause irreparable transmission damage.

Engine idling

7 DO NOT allow the engine to run at idle speed with the gear selector in the P (Park) position for longer than ten minutes, or damage to the gearbox could result due to low lubricating pressure.

8 On models fitted with air conditioning equipment which is being used in high

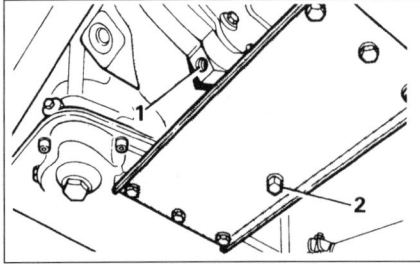

Fig. 13.106 Deep-wading drain plug
(Sec 10A)

1 Threaded torque converter drain bole
2 Plug location when not in use

ambient temperatures where extended periods of stationary idling are necessary, N (neutral) position must be selected with the handbrake fully applied.

Converter housing drain plug

9 A threaded drain hole is located in the base of the converter housing to allow any excess oil to be drained from the converter housing.

10 Where the vehicle is to be used in wading or very muddy conditions, the converter housing must be sealed by inserting the deep wading plug into the drain hole. This plug is normally located in the base of the tie plate between the engine and transmission when not required. When it is to be used, remove the plug from the tie plate and screw it into the drain hole in the converter housing. During use the plug must be periodically removed to allow any oil collected to drain from the converter housing and the plug then refitted.

Routine maintenance

Oil level - checking and topping-up

11 The automatic transmission oil level must be checked at the specified intervals. However, where the vehicle is used in deep wading conditions, the oil level must be checked daily.

12 With the vehicle standing on level ground, fully apply the footbrake and handbrake, and select N (Neutral). Start the engine and run it up to its normal operating temperature then move the gear lever through the range of gears. As each gear is selected pause

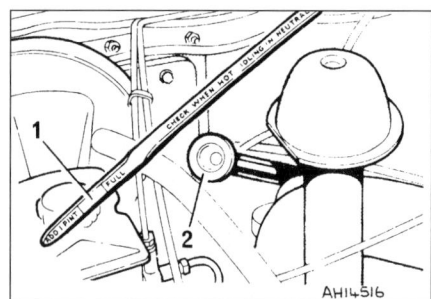

Fig. 13.107 Automatic transmission oil
level dipstick (1) and filler tube (2)
(Sec 10A)

10A.13 Checking transmission oil level on the dipstick

momentarily before selecting the next gear, and finally reselect N (Neutral).

13 With the engine still running at idle speed, withdraw the dipstick and wipe it clean using a non-fluffy cloth, then fully reinsert it and then withdraw it to check the oil level reading. The level must be maintained between the maximum (Full) mark and the minimum (Add 1 pint) mark on the dipstick (photo).

14 If required, top up the oil level with the specified lubricant through the oil filler tube (Fig. 13.107) but take care not to overfill the transmission. When refitting the dipstick ensure that it is fully located.

Oil and filter renewal

15 The automatic transmission oil and oil filter must be renewed at the specified intervals when in normal use, or on a monthly basis when the vehicle is used in arduous conditions such as severe wading.

16 The oil should be drained directly after the vehicle has been used so that the oil is warm. Park the vehicle on level ground and fully apply the handbrake. Undo the transmission drain plug and allow the oil to drain into a suitable container for disposal.

17 Undo the eight retaining bolts and remove the chassis crossmember.

18 Unbolt and remove the steady (tie) plates between the engine and transmission, and the transfer gearbox and transmission (Fig. 13.108).

19 Detach the fluid temperature sensor lead.

20 Unbolt and detach the exhaust pipe front section from the manifolds and the flange connection forward of the front silencer. Remove the U-bolt securing the front system to the left-hand transmission mountings then lower the pipe a sufficient amount to allow the transmission sump removal.

21 Undo the sump bolts then tap the sump downwards at one corner to remove it, together with its gasket.

22 Unscrew and discard the valve body filter. Fit the new filter and tighten to the specified torque.

23 Thoroughly clean the sump, refit the drain plug with a new washer then refit the sump using a new gasket. Tighten the retaining bolts to the specified torque, also the drain plug. Reconnect the sensor lead.

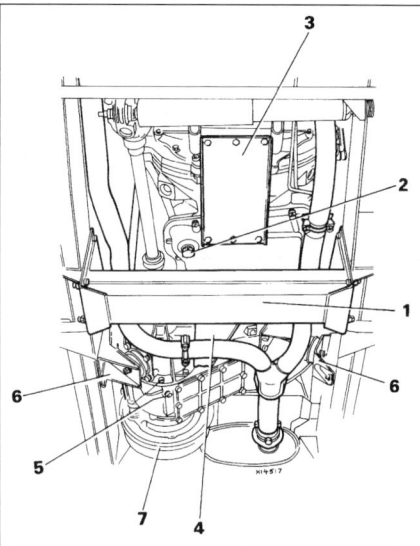

Fig. 13.108 Underside of the Chrysler automatic transmission (Sec 10A)

1 Crossmember
2 Automatic transmission drain plug in sump
3 Engine-to-gearbox steady plate
4 Gearbox-to-transfer gearbox steady plate
5 Transfer gearbox drain plug
6 Transmission mountings
7 Transmission brake

24 Refit the exhaust front section, the tie plates and the chassis crossmember. Tighten the retaining bolts to the specified torque settings.

25 Top up the transmission oil level by initially adding about one gallon (five litres) of the specified lubricant through the filler tube. Restart the engine and run it at idle speed for a minimum period of two minutes, then fully apply the footbrake and handbrake and move the selector lever through each gear position. Allow a pause as each gear is selected, then reposition in N (neutral). With the engine still running at idle speed, add further transmission fluid to bring the oil level up to the 'Add 1 pint' level mark on the dipstick.

26 Allow the engine to continue idling with the gear selector lever in neutral, then when the transmission fluid is warmed up to its normal operating temperature, recheck the level. It should be between the minimum and

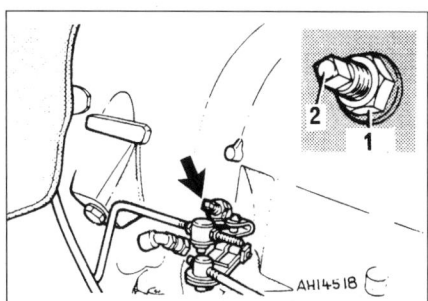

Fig. 13.110 Kickdown band adjustment screw location (2) and locknut (1) (Sec 10A)

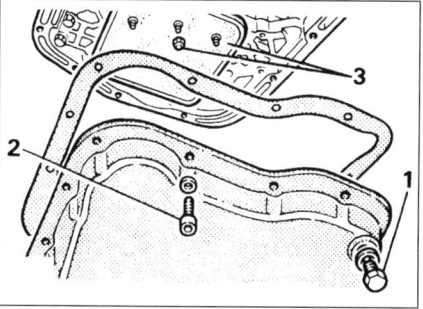

Fig. 13.109 Transmission sump drain plug and washer (1), retaining bolts (2) and filter (3) (Sec 10A)

full markings. On completion check that the dipstick is fully located.

Kickdown band adjustment

27 The kickdown band adjustment is made at regular intervals and is a task normally undertaken when renewing the transmission oil. The kickdown band adjuster screw is located on the left-hand side of the gearbox (Fig. 13.110). Loosen the adjuster screw locknut and unscrew it five full turns. The adjuster screw should now turn freely.

28 The adjustment is now made by tightening the adjuster screw to a torque wrench setting of 72 lbf in (83 kgf cm), then undo the screw from this point two and a half turns. Retain the screw in this position and tighten the locknut.

Low and reverse band adjustment

29 The low and reverse band adjustment is made at regular intervals and is a task normally undertaken during renewal of the transmission oil.

30 Drain the transmission oil and remove the sump, as described earlier. The low and reverse band adjustment screw is then accessible from within the transmission case at the lower end (Fig. 13.111).

31 The adjustment procedure now follows that described for the kickdown band.

32 On completion, refit the sump and top up the transmission oil level.

Transfer gearbox oil level - checking

33 When the vehicle is being used under severe or wading conditions, the transfer gearbox oil level should be checked daily, or

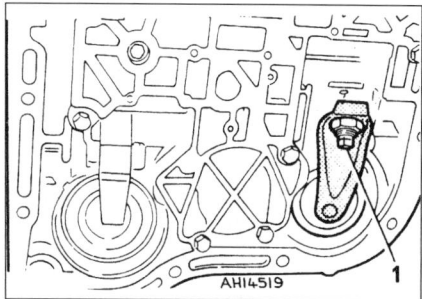

Fig. 13.111 Low and reverse band adjustment screw location (1) (Sec 10A)

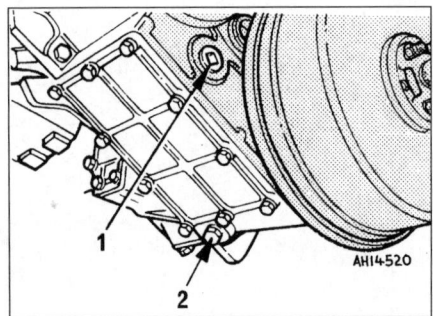

Fig. 13.112 Transfer gearbox oil level/filler plug (1) and drain plug (2) (Sec 10A)

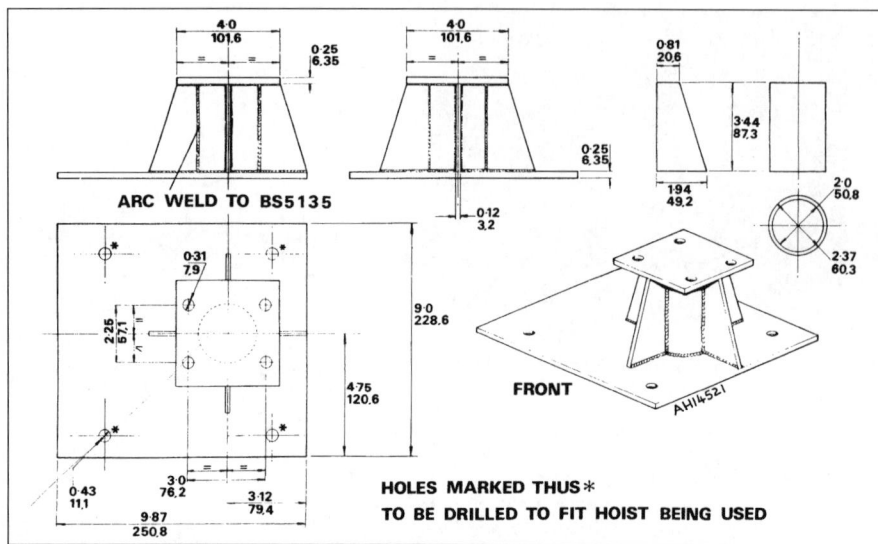

ARC WELD TO BS5135

HOLES MARKED THUS *
TO BE DRILLED TO FIT HOIST BEING USED

Fig. 13.113 Special cradle required when removing the Chrysler automatic transmission and transfer gearbox from underneath the vehicle (Sec 10B)

Dimensions in inches and millimetres

weekly, depending on the severity of conditions and usage.

34 With the vehicle parked on level ground, unscrew and remove the oil level/filler plug from the side of the transfer gearbox. The transfer gearbox oil should be level with the bottom of the level/filler plug hole. If required, top up the oil level through the level/filler plug hole using only the specified oil type. Refit the plug. If a significant amount of oil is required, or consistent topping-up is necessary, check for oil leaks and repair as necessary.

Transfer gearbox oil - renewal

35 The transfer gearbox oil must be renewed at the specified intervals under normal operating conditions, but when the vehicle is used in severe wading conditions renew the oil monthly.

36 The oil is best renewed directly after the vehicle has been used when the oil is still hot. Park the vehicle on level ground, then unscrew and remove the drain plug from the base of the transfer gearbox and drain the old oil into a suitable container for disposal.

37 When draining is complete, refit the drain plug with its washer. Undo the filler/level plug on the side of the transfer gearbox and top up the oil level through the filler plug hole with the specified oil. When the oil is level with the bottom of the filler plug hole, refit the plug.

Parking pawl engagement check

38 The automatic transmission parking pawl engagement should be checked at the specified intervals. To carry out this check the vehicle must be standing on level ground with the engine switched off.

39 Move the gear lever to the P (Park) position and release the handbrake. Try to push the vehicle forwards and rearwards. If the parking pawl does not hold consult your Range Rover dealer.

PART B: AUTOMATIC TRANSMISSION AND TRANSFER GEARBOX - REMOVAL AND REFITTING

Removal methods

1 The automatic transmission can be removed with the transfer gearbox or separately, after the removal of the transfer gearbox. Whichever method is employed, the main consideration to take into account is the considerable weight of each unit and, in addition, once freed from their mountings, they will need to be carefully supported during removal in order to overcome their imbalance.

2 The removal method described is for the transmission removal from underneath the vehicle, although it may be possible to remove them from above (within the vehicle) once they are free of their mountings and connections, in a similar manner to that described for the five-speed manual transmission (described elsewhere in this Chapter).

3 When removing the transmission from underneath you will need to make up a suitable adaptor plate with which to support the transmission during removal and refitting. It may be possible to borrow or hire this adaptor plate from your Range Rover dealer so check this first (see Fig. 13.113).

4 In addition you will need a trolley jack of sufficient capacity to support the transmission assembly during its removal and refitting.

Automatic transmission and transfer gearbox - removal and refitting

5 Disconnect the battery earth lead.

6 Remove the air cleaner unit, referring to Chapter 3.

7 Undo the mounting peg on the air cleaner left-hand side mounting and remove the coupling shaft support bracket. Detach the throttle return spring and the throttle coupling shaft (Fig. 13.114).

8 Loosen the outer two nuts which secure the cooling fan cowl. Rotate the inner cowl nuts anti-clockwise to lift the cowl so that it will not foul when the engine is lowered in subsequent operations.

9 Unclip and release the hose from the alternator mounting bracket.

10 Working inside the vehicle, remove the ashtrays and their holders from the transmission tunnel.

11 Remove the transmission tunnel carpet and insulation then undo and remove the ten screws retaining the handbrake gaiter. Withdraw the gaiter from the handbrake.

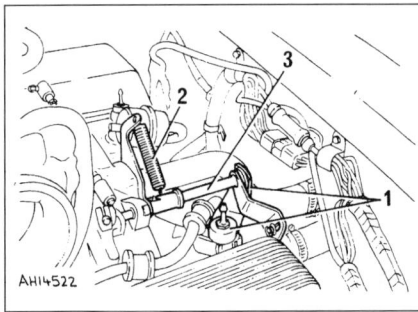

Fig. 13.114 Air cleaner left-hand mounting peg and support bracket (1), throttle return spring (2) and coupling shaft (3) (Sec 10B)

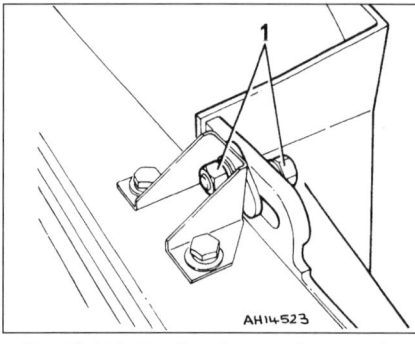

Fig. 13.115 Cooling fan cowl nuts to be loosened (1) (Sec 10B)

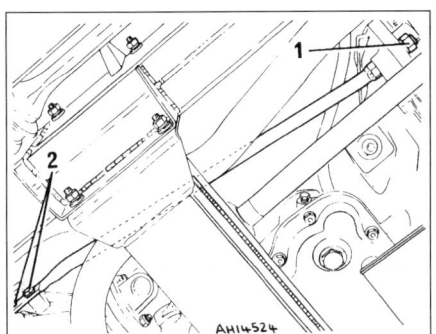

Fig. 13.116 Tie-bar-to-bellhousing (1) and - transfer gearbox (2) mountings (Sec 10B)

12 Unscrew and remove the high/low transfer gear lever knob, undo the four screws and withdraw the gaiter from the gear lever.

13 The vehicle will now need to be raised and supported on suitable safety stands to provide suitable working clearance for the transmission removal. Alternatively, if an inspection pit is available, position the vehicle over it.

14 Remove the drain plugs, and drain the gearbox and transfer gearbox oils into a suitable container for disposal. Refit the drain plugs on completion.

15 Undo the four retaining bolts and nuts each side securing the chassis crossmember. Withdraw the bolts to allow the crossmember to be removed. It should be possible to tap it down and free using a suitable mallet, but it may be necessary to use a suitable chassis spreader to free it. Support the crossmember when removing it as it is heavy.

16 Detach and remove the starter motor solenoid.

17 Referring to Chapter 3, detach and remove the front exhaust pipe system complete.

18 Remove the plate located between the gearbox and the engine.

19 Disconnect the front propeller shaft from the transfer gearbox front drive flange (having marked them for alignment). Refer to Chapter 7 for further details.

20 Disconnect the rear propeller shaft from the transmission brake (referring to Chapter 7 if necessary) and then tie the front and rear propeller shafts up out of the way.

21 Unbolt and disconnect the bellhousing-to-transfer gearbox tie-bar at each end.

22 Detach the speedometer drive cable from the transfer gearbox connection and the retaining clip.

23 Undo the nut securing the gear selector cable to the fulcrum arm and the cable from its location clamp, then position the cable to one side out of the way.

24 Disconnect the upper and lower throttle links by extracting the split pin, then undo the bellhousing nut and bolt retaining the throttle valve linkage bracket. Position the assembly to one side out of the way.

25 Position a container beneath the oil cooler pipe connections forward of the engine sump

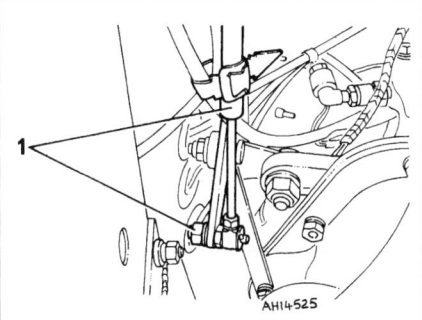

Fig. 13.117 Gear selector cable and fulcrum arm connection (1) (Sec 10B)

of the left-hand side, and undo and detach the pipes at the connectors. Loosen the retaining clamps securing the steel pipes on the left side of the engine.

26 Detach the oil cooler pipes from the transmission unions and remove the pipes. Plug the pipe ends to prevent the ingress of dirt and further leakage.

27 Unscrew the nine bellhousing cover plate retaining bolts and withdraw the cover plate.

28 Undo the four torque converter-to-driveplate retaining bolts. As the last bolt is removed, mark the relative positions of the driveplate and torque converter and bellhousing. This will ensure correct reassembly.

29 Remove the gearbox-to-transfer gearbox tie-bar.

30 The adaptor plate mentioned in paragraph 3 must now be bolted into position on the underside of the gearbox.

31 Locate the trolley jack and attach it to the adaptor plate. Raise the jack to take the weight of the transmission.

32 Unbolt and detach the transmission mounting bracket on each side.

33 Slowly lower the jack supporting the transmission just enough to allow the following items to be disconnected. As the engine will tilt with the transmission, get an assistant to keep a watchful eye on the engine ancillary items and connections to ensure that they are not damaged or distorted.

34 Disconnect the transmission selector light leads at the snap connectors, and also the

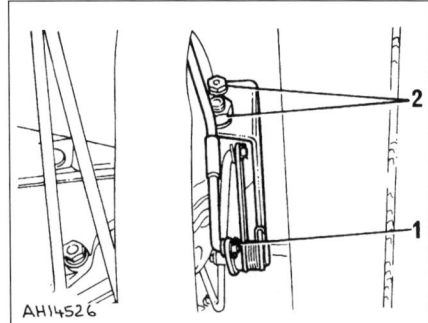

Fig. 13.118 Vertical rod to upper and lower throttle valve linkage (1) and linkage bracket to bellhousing (2) (Sec 10B)

inhibitor switch and reversing light switch leads multi-connector.

35 Unbolt and detach the breather tube banjo connector from the transfer gearbox. Refit the banjo bolt and the two washers to the transfer gearbox, and move the breather tube out of the way.

36 Detach the differential lock wiring from the clips on the transfer gearbox, also the warning light lead connectors. Note the various wiring connections then move the wires out of the way.

37 Detach the breather tube from the automatic transmission, then refit the bolt with washers. Move the breather tube out of the way.

38 Undo and remove the bellhousing bolt which retains the gearbox filler tube. Detach the filler tube from the gearbox and cover hole.

39 Position a jack under the engine and raise it to support the weight of the engine.

40 Undo and remove the three remaining bellhousing-to-engine bolts.

41 The transmission is now ready to be removed from the vehicle. Check that all connections and ancillary items are detached and positioned out of the way then carefully withdraw the transmission from the engine whilst simultaneously lowering its supporting jack under the adaptor plate. An assistant will be helpful here to help guide the unit clear from under the vehicle.

42 If the vehicle is to be moved whilst the transmission is removed, an alternative method of supporting the engine will have to be made before removing the support jack.

43 Refitting is a reversal of the removal procedure, but the following special points should be noted.

44 Do not fully tighten the respective retaining and mounting bolts until all of the

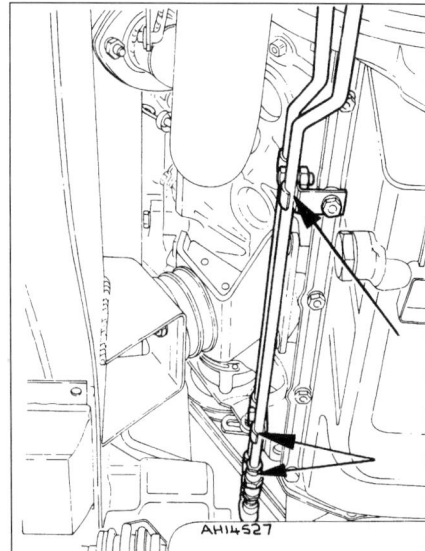

Fig. 13.119 Oil cooler pipes and connections - arrowed (Sec 10B)

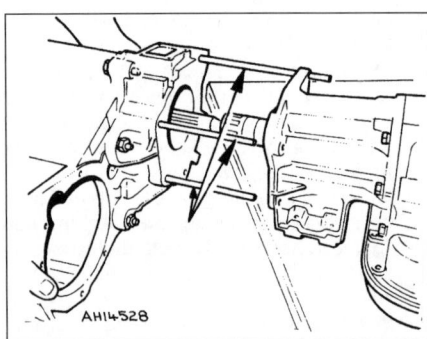

Fig. 13.120 Insert guide studs (arrowed) when reconnecting the transmission and transfer gearbox (Sec 10B)

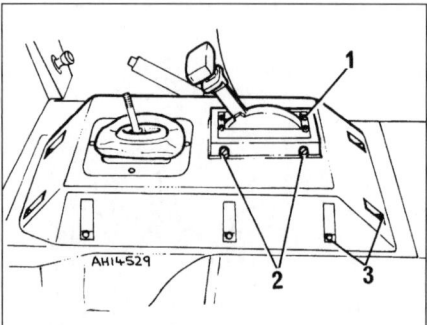

Fig. 13.121 Selector bezel retaining screws (1), selector-to-top cover screws (2) and top cover bolts (3) (Sec 10B)

bolts and fastenings of the items concerned are located, then tighten the bolts to the specified torque settings.

45 Where the old torque converter is being used, align the previously made marks of the torque converter, driveplate and bellhousing when fitting the first retaining bolt.

46 When the engine and transmission are being bolted together the bolt retaining the throttle valve linkage is fitted with its head to the rear.

47 Reconnect the wiring and breather tubes before raising the gearbox. Ensure correct connections and routing.

48 When refitting the transmission mounting bolts, fit the speedometer cable locating clip to the top front bolt on the left-hand side. The gear selector outer cable and locating clip is fitted to the left-hand mounting bracket.

49 When reconnecting the propeller shaft joint flanges, align with the marks made during removal.

50 Refit the steady plates and exhaust system before refitting the chassis crossmember.

51 On completion, remove the jacks and top up the transmission and, if applicable, the transfer gearbox oil levels with the specified lubricants.

Note: *If the old transmission fluid was badly discoloured and contaminated when drained it is advisable to flush out the oil cooler and tuber prior to reconnecting them and topping-up the transmission oil level with new fluid. Flush the old oil from the cooler by connecting a flexible pipe (hose) to the oil cooler inlet connection and then blow through the outlet connection with short sharp blasts of clean compressed air. Direct the old fluid into a container for disposal. On completing the flushing of the cooler, pump 1 pint (0.6 litre) of the specified new lubricant into the cooler before reconnecting the hoses to the transmission.*

Automatic transmission and transfer gearbox - separation and reassembly

52 Undo the five bolts securing the automatic transmission to the transfer gearbox.

53 The transfer gearbox can now be

withdrawn from the automatic transmission unit. If they prove difficult to separate, undo the six bolts securing the cover plate, withdraw the cover plate then unscrew and remove the coupling shaft bolt. The transfer gearbox, together with the extension case, can now be withdrawn from the automatic transmission unit.

54 Reassembly is a reversal of the separation procedure, but ensure that the respective mating faces are clean.

55 To ensure correct alignment of the two units and also to avoid damaging the oil seal during reassembly, fit three guide studs into position in the transfer gearbox extension case as shown (Fig. 13.120). The stud fitted to the left side will need to be longer than the other two.

56 The automatic gearbox should be set in P (Park), then the transfer gearbox aligned with the studs and slid into position. When the two units are assembled together, remove the studs and refit the retaining bolts and tighten them to the specified torque.

PART C: AUTOMATIC TRANSMISSION/TRANSFER GEARBOX SELECTOR AND ASSOCIATED COMPONENTS - REMOVAL, REFITTING AND ADJUSTMENTS

Transmission tunnel top and side covers - removal and refitting

Top cover

1 Unscrew and remove the high/low transfer differential lock lever knob.

2 Prise the ashtrays from their holders then remove the screws securing the ashtray holders.

3 Remove the cubby box base cover then undo the three screws securing the cubby box to the transmission tunnel. Remove the cubby box.

4 Remove the carpet and sound insulation covering from the transmission tunnel.

5 Undo the four screws securing the gear selector bezel. Lift away the plate and trim.

6 Undo and remove the four gear selector unit retaining bolts then push the unit downwards and detach it from the top cover. Undo the bolts and remove the top cover.

7 Refitting is a reversal of the removal procedure. When refitting the cover, check that the sealant is evenly dispersed around the aperture of the tunnel.

Side cover

8 Unfold the footwell cover on the left-hand side, then unscrew and remove the twelve retaining bolts and remove the cover.

9 Refit in the reverse order of removal. Loosely fit all the bolts before fully tightening them and ensure that the sealant is evenly dispersed around the cover aperture.

Automatic transmission gear selector unit - removal and refitting

10 Remove the transmission top cover, as described in paras 1 to 6.

11 Unscrew and remove the cable clamp-to-selector unit quadrant retaining nuts and bolts.

12 Detach the selector inner cable from the cross-shaft lever by extracting the split pin and removing the washer.

13 Disconnect the selector illumination bulb lead at the bullet connector, then withdraw the selector unit.

14 Refit in the reverse order of removal.

Automatic transmission selector rod/cable - adjustment

15 Detach and remove the transfer gear lever knob and the lever gaiter.

16 Select N (neutral) and keep it in this position throughout the adjustment.

17 Undo and remove the transmission tunnel cover retaining screws, then lift the cover just enough to allow access to the cable-to-gear selector quadrant connection.

18 Release the spring clip securing the cable trunnion to the quadrant then detach the trunnion from the quadrant.

19 Detach the transmission tunnel side cover plate (paragraph 8).

20 Check that the gear lever is still engaged

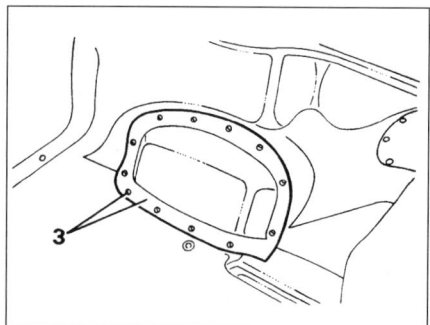

Fig. 13.122 Automatic transmission side cover (3) (Sec 10C)

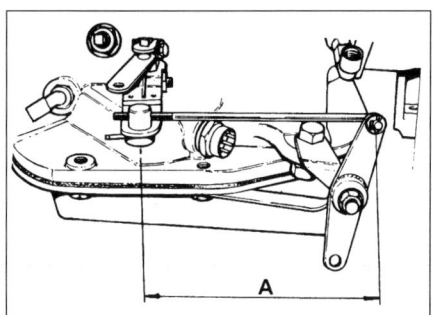

Fig. 13.123 Selector rod/cable adjustment check (Sec 10C)

A = 6.26 to 6.34 in (159 to 161 mm)

in N (Neutral) then, referring to Fig. 13.123, measure the distance A, from the centre of the selector rod to the centre of the trunnion. If the adjustment is not as specified, disconnect the selector rod from the arm (extract the split pin), then rotate the rod in the trunnion to give the correct adjustment. Reconnect the selector rod to the arm, fit the flat washer and split pin.

21 Before refitting the transmission covers check the selector cable adjustment, leaving the gear lever engaged in N (Neutral).

22 Check that the trunnion fits centrally into the corresponding gear selector quadrant hole and, if required, adjust its position on the cable thread.

23 Temporarily insert the trunnion retaining circlip and the gearbox top cover.

24 Operate the gear lever through the full range of selector positions and simultaneously check if the cable-to-link arm attachment interferes with the support bracket.

25 With the handbrake fully applied, check that the engine can be restarted when the lever is set in the P (Park) and N (Neutral) positions.

26 If the above checks are not satisfactory remove the transmission cover and make further adjustments to the selector rod and cable as necessary.

27 On completion, refit the transmission top and side covers and the transfer gear lever gaiter and knob.

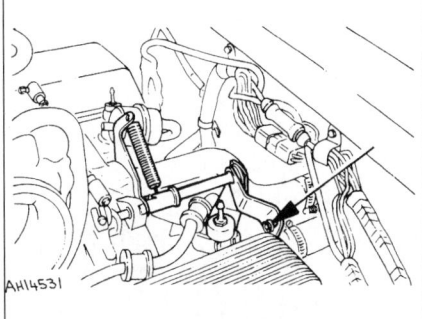

Fig. 13.125 Check the down link position at full throttle - arrowed (Sec 10C)

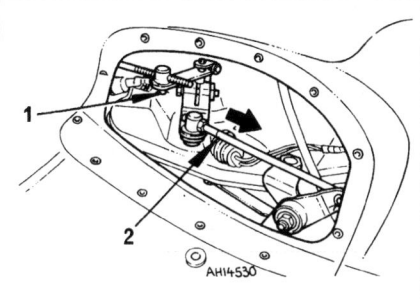

Fig. 13.124 Throttle valve lever-to-trunnion connection (1) and throttle valve lever (2) (Sec 10C)

Automatic transmission throttle valve linkage - adjustment

28 Disconnect and remove the air cleaner unit, referring to Chapter 3 for further details.

29 Remove the ashtrays and floor covering from the transmission tunnel.

30 Undo the retaining screws and withdraw the transmission tunnel side cover for access to the throttle valve linkage at the transmission.

31 Extract the split pin, remove the washers and detach the throttle valve lever from the trunnion (Fig. 13.124).

32 Get an assistant to depress the accelerator pedal to the full throttle position and then check that the down link is at the bottom of the coupling shaft lever slot (Fig. 13.125).

33 Still with the accelerator pedal in the full throttle position, move the gearbox throttle valve lever to the rear and adjust the trunnion position on the rod so that it drops into the hole in the throttle valve lever.

34 Refit the trunnion temporarily to the throttle valve lever then get the assistant to release the accelerator pedal and then fully depress it again. The adjustment is correct if the throttle valve lever remains fully rearward with no further movement to the rear possible. Repeat the adjustment if not satisfactory.

35 Release the accelerator pedal then reconnect the trunnion and fit the washer with a new split pin.

36 Refit the cover and check that it is fully sealed.

37 Refit the air cleaner unit.

38 Refit the transmission coverings.

High/low gearchange connecting rod - adjustment

39 Unbolt and remove the gearchange housing and remove the gearchange grommet plate and the lever grommet. Refit the four bolts to temporarily secure the gateplate in position.

40 Move the gear lever into high and then low range, and observe if it fouls the gateplate. If it does then adjustment is necessary.

41 Loosen the connecting rod locknuts,

move the change lever rearwards to select high range, and the selector housing operating arm forwards into high range position.

42 Retighten the locknuts and check if the lever fouls the gate plate in the high range position. Now using the same method, engage and check the lever in the low range position.

43 When adjustment is made, move the lever back to the high range position, undo the bolts securing the gate plate, refit the grommet and plate, and refit the retaining bolts.

Reverse starter switch - testing, removal and refitting

44 Remove the transmission tunnel side cover (see paragraph 8).

45 Detach the lead connector from the switch then connect up a test meter or light. If using a test light and battery, connect the earth (negative) terminal to the transmission case.

46 Connect the positive test probe to the switch centre pin, then move the selector lever to the P (Park) position and check for continuity, then move the lever to N (neutral) position and repeat the check. In each case a continuity reading should be given or, if using a test lamp, the bulb should illuminate.

47 To check the reverse light function of the switch, connect the earth lead to an outer pin on the switch and the test probe to the other pin. Select reverse and check for continuity.

48 If the switch is found to be defective it must be removed and renewed. Unscrew the switch to remove it.

49 Screw the new switch into position and connect up the lead multi-connector, but before refitting the side cover, check that the switch functions are satisfactory.

PART D: AUTOMATIC TRANSMISSION - FAULT FINDING

General

1 As has been mentioned elsewhere in this Section, no service repair work should be considered by anyone without the specialist knowledge and equipment required to undertake this work. This is also relevant to fault diagnosis. If a fault is evident, carry out the various adjustments previously described, and if the fault still exists consult the local garage or specialist.

2 Before removing the automatic transmission for repair, make sure that the repairer does not require to perform diagnostic tests with the transmission installed.

3 Most minor faults will be due to incorrect fluid level, incorrectly adjusted selector control or throttle cables and the internal brake band being out of adjustment.

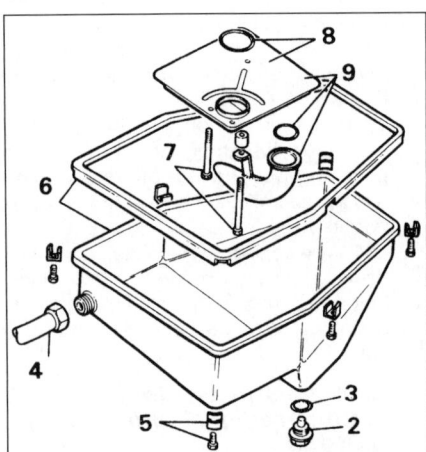

Fig. 13.126 Automatic transmission oil pan and filter screen components (Sec 11A)

2 Drain plug
3 Washer
4 Oil filler/dipstick tube
5 Retaining bolts and retaining plates
6 Oil pan and gasket
7 Filter screen retaining bolts
8 Filter screen and O-ring seal
9 Suction tube and O-ring seal

11 ZF four-speed automatic transmission

PART A: AUTOMATIC TRANSMISSION AND TRANSFER GEARBOX - DESCRIPTION, PRECAUTIONS AND MAINTENANCE

General description

1 The automatic transmission system comprises a torque converter and a fully automatic four-speed gearbox unit. The ZF transmission is fitted to all automatic transmission models from 1986 onwards in place of the Chrysler three-speed unit used previously.

2 The automatic gearbox contains a series of multiple disc clutches and planetary gear sets which provide the four forward and one reverse gears according to which of the clutches is engaged or disengaged. A lock-up clutch is used in the fourth gear range giving direct drive from the engine and eliminating power loss due to hydraulic slip in the torque converter.

3 An internal oil pump and valve body provide the integral hydraulic control system with an internally mounted fluid cooler to maintain the hydraulic fluid temperature within specified limits.

4 The transfer gearbox is mounted on the automatic transmission extension housing in much the same manner as that for the manual transmission. The transfer gearbox is the same type as that fitted to the five-speed manual gearbox and can be overhauled as described in previous Sections of this Chapter.

5 In view of the specialised knowledge and equipment required to test, repair and overhaul the automatic transmission, such tasks should be entrusted to your Range Rover dealer. Manufacturer's tools and setting gauges are required for even relatively minor operations on the ZF transmission and this severely limits the amount of work that can be undertaken by the DIY mechanic. The contents of this Section are therefore limited to maintenance tasks and general information which may be of use to the owner.

Special precautions

6 Refer to Section 10, Part A, paragraphs 6 to 10 inclusive.

Routine maintenance

Oil level - checking and topping-up

7 Refer to Section 10, Part A, paragraphs 11 to 14 inclusive.

Oil and filter screen - renewal

8 The automatic transmission oil and filter screen must be renewed at the specified intervals when in normal use or on a monthly basis when the vehicle is used in arduous conditions such as severe wading.

9 The oil should preferably be drained after the vehicle has been used so that the oil is warm.

10 Part the vehicle on level ground, fully apply the handbrake and disconnect the battery negative terminal.

11 Undo the transmission oil drain plug at the base of the oil pan (photo) and allow the oil to drain into a suitable container. Take care to avoid scalding if the oil is hot.

12 Undo the oil filler/dipstick tube from the oil pan (photo).

13 Undo the six retaining bolts (photo), and remove the retaining plates and withdraw the oil pan from the bottom of the transmission.

14 Remove the oil pan gasket.

15 Using a Torx type socket bit undo the three filter screen retaining bolts and remove the screen.

16 Separate the suction tube from the filter screen and remove the O-ring seals.

17 Thoroughly clean the oil pan and obtain a new filter screen, new O-rings, oil pan gasket and drain plug sealing ring.

18 Using the new components, refit the suction tube, filter screen and oil pan using the reversal of removal. Tighten the retaining bolts to the specified torque.

19 Refit and tighten the drain plug using the new sealing ring.

20 Reconnect the oil filler/dipstick tube and the battery negative terminal.

21 Refill the transmission with the specified lubricant through the filler tube in the engine compartment, until the level is up to the MAX mark on the dipstick.

22 Start the engine then check and top up the transmission as described in Section 10, Part A, paragraphs 11 to 14 inclusive.

Transfer gearbox oil level - checking and renewal

23 Refer to Section 10, Part A, paragraphs 33 to 37 inclusive.

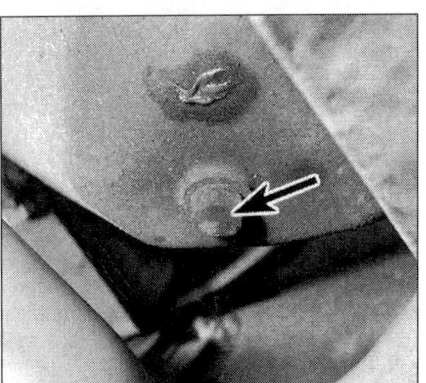

11A.11 Transmission oil drain plug (arrowed)

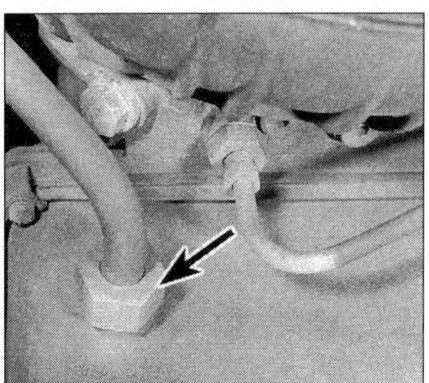

11A.12 Oil filler/dipstick tube attachment (arrowed) at the oil pan

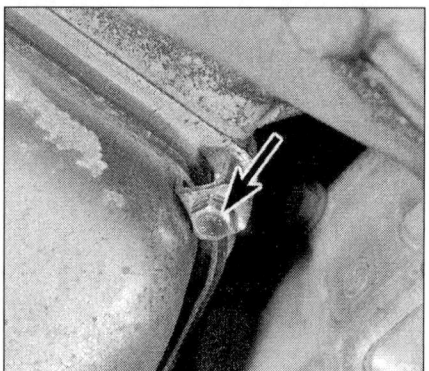

11A.13 Oil pan retaining bolt and retaining plate (arrowed)

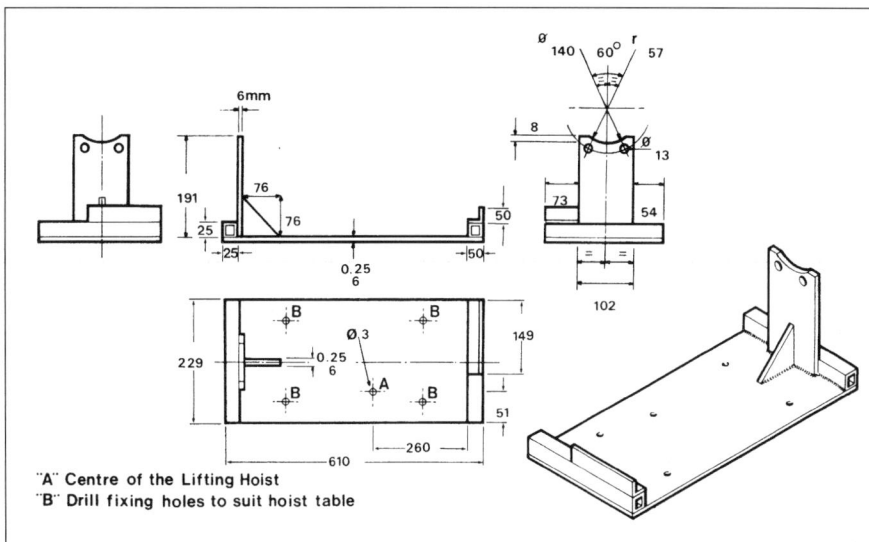

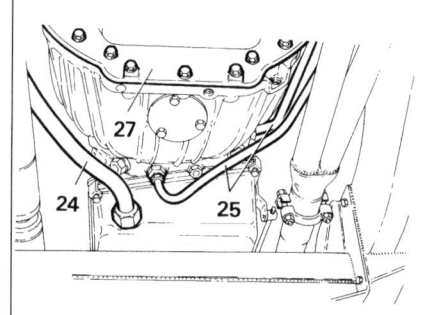

Fig. 13.128 Oil filler/dipstick tube (24), oil cooler pipes (25) and torque converter cover attachments (Sec 11B)

Fig. 13.127 Special cradle required when removing the ZF automatic transmission and transfer gearbox from underneath the vehicle (Sec 11B)

All dimensions in millimetres

"A" Centre of the Lifting Hoist
"B" Drill fixing holes to suit hoist table

PART B: AUTOMATIC TRANSMISSION AND TRANSFER GEARBOX - REMOVAL AND REFITTING

Removal methods

1 Refer to Section 10, Part B, paragraphs 1 to 4 inclusive, but note that the adaptor plate to support the ZF transmission is shown in Fig. 13.127.

Automatic transmission and transfer gearbox (pre-1989 models) - removal and refitting

2 Raise the vehicle at the front and rear, and support it on stands. Alternatively, if available, drive the vehicle onto a hydraulic ramp or over an inspection pit.
3 Disconnect the battery negative terminal.
4 Refer to Section 17 of this Chapter and remove the centre console.
5 On carburettor engine models, remove the air cleaner. On fuel injected models, remove the intake air hose between the airflow meter and plenum chamber.
6 Extract the split pin and remove the clevis pin securing the kickdown cable to the throttle linkage.
7 Remove the fan cowling from the radiator.
8 Undo the large nut securing the handbrake outer cable to the top of the gearbox tunnel. Feed the cable through the hole in the tunnel to the underside of the vehicle.
9 Undo the transmission oil pan drain plug and drain the oil into a suitable container.
10 Disconnect the speedometer cable after releasing the clamp, then detach the cable from the clips on the gearbox.
11 Disconnect the front propeller shaft from the transfer gearbox front drive flange and the

rear propeller shaft from the transmission brake. Tie the shafts up out of the way.
12 Referring to Chapter 3, if necessary, detach and remove the front exhaust pipe system complete.
13 Undo the large nut and release the oil filler/dipstick tube from the front of the oil pan.
14 Disconnect the two oil cooler pipe unions from the rear of the gearbox bellhousing.
15 Undo the retaining nuts and bolts each side securing the chassis crossmember. Withdraw the bolts to allow the crossmember

to be removed. It should be possible to tap it down and free using a suitable mallet, but it may be necessary to spread the chassis slightly using a bottle jack and blocks or similar arrangement. Support the crossmember when removing it as it is heavy.
16 Remove the torque converter cover from the front face of the bellhousing.
17 Undo the four torque converter-to-driveplate retaining bolts. As the last bolt is removed mark the relative positions of the driveplate and torque converter to ensure correct reassembly.
18 Disconnect the starter inhibitor switch wiring multi-plug on the left-hand side of the gearbox.
19 Extract the split pin and remove the washer securing the selector linkage to the lever on the left-hand side on the

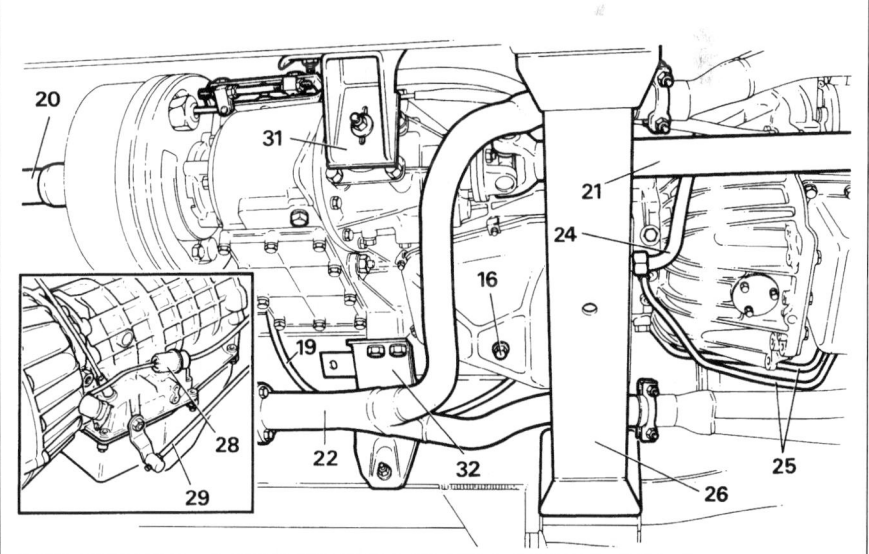

Fig. 13.129 Underside of ZF automatic transmission (Sec 11B)

16 Drain plug
19 Speedometer cable
20 Rear propeller shaft
21 Front propeller shaft

22 Front exhaust pipe system
24 Oil filler/dipstick tube
25 Oil cooler pipes
26 Chassis crossmember

28 Starter/inhibitor switch multi-plug
29 Selector linkage
31 Right-hand mounting
32 Left-hand mounting

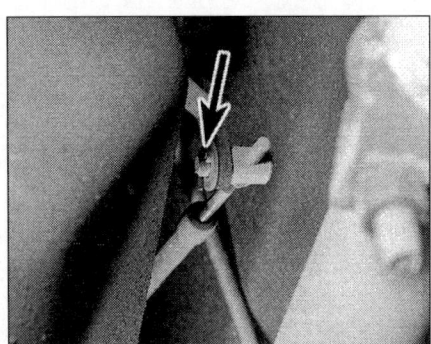

11B.19 Selector linkage-to-transmission lever retaining split pin (arrowed)

gearbox. Withdraw the linkage from the lever (photo).

20 The adaptor plate mentioned in paragraph 1 must now be bolted into position on the underside of the gearbox.

21 Locate the trolley jack and attach it to the adaptor plate. Raise the jack to just take the weight of the transmission.

22 Undo the nuts and bolts on each side securing the transmission mounting brackets to the chassis.

23 Carefully lower the jack supporting the transmission until the transmission brake drum clears the rear passenger footwell.

24 Extract the split pin and remove the washers securing the differential lock lever to the connecting rod. Disconnect the lever from the rod.

25 Disconnect the differential lock switch electrical leads.

26 Remove the transfer gearbox breather pipe.

27 Support the rear of the engine on a jack and undo all the bolts securing the bellhousing to the engine.

28 The transmission is now ready to be removed from the vehicle. Check that all connections and ancillary items are detached and positioned out of the way then carefully withdraw the transmission from the engine whilst simultaneously lowering its supporting jack under the adaptor plate. An assistant will be helpful here to help guide the unit clear from under the vehicle.

29 If the vehicle is to be moved whilst the transmission is removed, an alternative method of supporting the engine will have to be made before removing the support jack.

30 Refitting is a reversal of the removal procedure, but the following special points should be noted:

If the old transmission fluid was badly discoloured and contaminated when drained, it is advisable to flush out the oil cooler and tubes prior to reconnecting them and topping-up the transmission oil level with new fluid. Flush the old oil from the cooler by connecting a flexible pipe (hose) to the oil cooler outlet connection and then blow through the outlet connection with short sharp blasts of clean compressed air. Direct the old fluid into a container for disposal. On completing the flushing of the cooler, pump

1 pint (0.6 litre) of the specified new lubricant into the cooler before reconnecting the hoses to the transmission

Do not fully tighten the respective retaining and mounting bolts until all of the bolts and fastenings of the items concerned are located, then tighten the bolts to the specified torque settings

Where the old torque converter is being used, align the previously made marks of the torque converter, driveplate and bellhousing when fitting the first retaining bolt

31 On completion, remove the jacks and top up the transmission and, if applicable, the transfer gearbox oil levels with the specified lubricants.

Automatic transmission and transfer gearbox (1989-on models) - removal and refitting

32 Position the vehicle over an inspection pit or alternatively jack it up and support on axle stands.

33 Disconnect the battery negative lead.

34 Remove the viscous cooling fan assembly with reference to Chapter 2.

35 On fuel injection models release the clamp and remove the air intake hose from the plenum chamber with reference to Chapter 3.

36 On carburettor models remove the air cleaner and air ducts with reference to Chapter 3.

37 Disconnect the throttle cable from the linkage.

38 Unclip the gearbox breather pipes from the rear of the right-hand cylinder head.

39 Pull out the gearbox fluid level dipstick.

40 Working inside the vehicle select low range, then unscrew and remove the transfer gearbox selector knob.

41 Release the main gearbox top cover and remove the circlip, then withdraw the detent button. Extract the circlip above the selector knob holding nut, unscrew the nut and remove the washer, then remove the selector knob.

42 Prise the inset panel out of the floor mounted console together with the gear selector illumination panel and ashtray. Disconnect the graphics panel wiring and remove the inset panel.

43 Unscrew the screws and remove the glovebox liner.

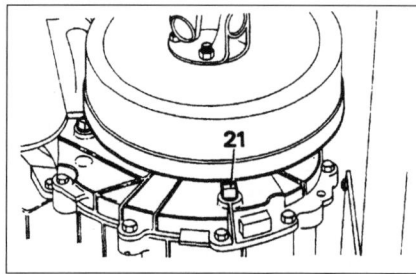

Fig. 13.130 Automatic transmission drain plug (21) (Sec 11B)

44 Prise the electric window switch panel from the front of the glovebox, then push the panel complete with the switches through the panel opening and position it on the gearbox tunnel.

45 Unscrew the bolts and screws holding the glovebox and console assembly to the gearbox tunnel.

46 Remove the two relays from the inner side of the glovebox.

47 Disconnect the wiring from the cigar lighter.

48 Disconnect the handbrake cable from the handbrake lever, then lift up the lever and at the same time disconnect the glovebox and console assembly from the lower facia. Remove the assembly from inside the vehicle.

49 Release the clip and pull the handbrake adjustment thumb wheel from the outer sleeve. Push the sleeve through under the vehicle.

50 Remove the sound deadening trim from the top of the gearbox tunnel.

51 Unscrew the screws and remove the retaining plate from around the transfer gearbox lever.

52 Working under the vehicle, position suitable containers beneath the main transmission and transfer box, then unscrew the drain plugs and drain the oil. To help the oil to drain faster remove the filler/level plugs. Clean, refit and tighten the plugs after draining the oil, and apply suitable sealant to the threads of the plugs before inserting them.

53 On models fitted with a catalytic converter disconnect the multiplugs from the Lambda sensors.

54 Have an assistant support the exhaust system, then unscrew the bolts securing the cross member to the underbody.

55 Remove the front exhaust downpipes and the intermediate pipe complete with centre silencer or catalytic converter as applicable.

56 Release the two clamps securing the gearbox oil cooler feed and return pipes to the side of the engine sump.

57 Position a suitable container beneath the gearbox then disconnect the oil cooler feed and return pipes from the bottom and side of the gearbox. Plug the ends and apertures to prevent the ingress of foreign matter.

58 Unscrew the union nut and detach the dipstick tube from the front of the gearbox oil pan.

59 Mark the propeller shaft and transfer box drive flanges in relation to each other to ensure correct reassembly. Unscrew the bolts, then disconnect the shafts and tie them to one side.

60 Unscrew the nut and remove the speedometer cable from the rear output housing, then tie the cable to one side.

61 Disconnect the main gearbox selector cable and rod from the left-hand side of the gearbox, and position the cable to one side.

62 Disconnect the wiring from the main gearbox inhibitor switch.

63 Where applicable disconnect the wiring from the speed transducer.

64 Unbolt the cover plate from the transmission bellhousing, then rotate the engine using a spanner on the crankshaft pulley bolt until two of the four bolts securing the driveplate to the torque converter are visible.

65 Using a wide-bladed screwdriver hold the driveplate stationary, then unscrew the two bolts. Mark one of the bolt holes and driveplate to ensure correct reassembly.

66 Turn the engine half a turn and remove the two remaining bolts.

67 Using a trolley jack beneath the rear output housing or brake drum, support the weight of the transmission assembly.

68 Unscrew the bolts securing the transfer box mountings to the underbody.

69 Using the adaptor plate and trolley jack, support the transmission, then remove the trolley jack from the rear of the transfer box.

70 Lower the transmission until the top of the transfer box clears the rear passenger footwell.

71 Using a trolley jack, support the weight of the engine.

72 Unscrew and remove the bolts securing the transmission to the engine noting that one of the bolts holds the fluid level dipstick tube.

73 Carefully withdraw the transmission from the engine making sure that the torque converter remains fully inserted in the transmission to prevent fluid escaping. Lower the transmission to the ground and remove from under the vehicle.

74 If the vehicle is to be moved whilst the transmission is removed, an alternative method of supporting the engine will have to be made before removing the support jack.

75 Refitting is a reversal of the removal procedure but refer also to paragraphs 30 and 31 of Part B, and note the following additional points:

(a) *Apply locking fluid to the threads of the bolts securing the driveplate to the torque converter before inserting them and tightening to the specified torque*

(b) *Renew the exhaust downpipe gaskets and refit the exhaust system with reference to Chapter 3*

Transfer gearbox (pre-1989 models) - removal and refitting

76 Refer to Section 9, Part B, paragraphs 53 to 57.

Transfer gearbox (1989-on models) - general

77 The procedures described in Section 9, Part I apply equally to automatic transmission models. However, when removing and refitting the transfer box, the following additional work is necessary:

(a) *After paragraph 44, unclip the top cover from the selector lever and remove the circlip. Withdraw the detent button. Remove the circlip above the selector*

knob nut then remove the nut and washer and withdraw the selector knob

(b) *After paragraph 45 prise the centre panel out of the floor mounted console*

(c) *After paragraph 59, unbolt the tie-bar from the transmission*

PART C: AUTOMATIC TRANSMISSION - FAULT FINDING

General

1 Refer to Section 10, Part D, but note that all repairs and adjustments should be entrusted to a suitably equipped dealer or transmission specialist due to the necessary use of manufacturer's special tools.

12 Propeller shafts

Propeller shaft (models fitted with a catalytic converter) - description

1 On models fitted with a catalytic converter in the exhaust system, the front propeller shaft is of a solid bar type (photo). The rear shaft on these models is of a standard tubular type.

Propeller shaft (models fitted with a catalytic converter) - removal and refitting

2 The front propeller shaft must be fitted with the splined sleeve towards the front end of the transfer box. This is the opposite way round to the information given in Chapter 7, which applies only to non-catalyst models.

3 The rear propeller shaft is fitted as described in Chapter 7 with the sleeve adjacent to the transmission brake.

12.1 Solid bar front propeller shaft and joint fitted to models fitted with a catalytic converter

13 Front and rear axles

Axle breathers - general

1 To prevent the possibility of oil leakage past the axle seals caused by pressure within the casing, later models have axle breathers fitted.

2 The location and layout of the breathers and tubes are shown in Figs. 13.131 and 13.132.

3 If the breathers and tubes are removed at any time it is essential when refitting them to check that they are correctly relocated, and that they are not blocked by excessive bending or damage.

General description (models with ABS)

4 On models fitted with ABS, the front driveshaft and rear half shaft are splined at their outer ends to a drive member bolted to the hub. On the rear axle, a sensor ring with

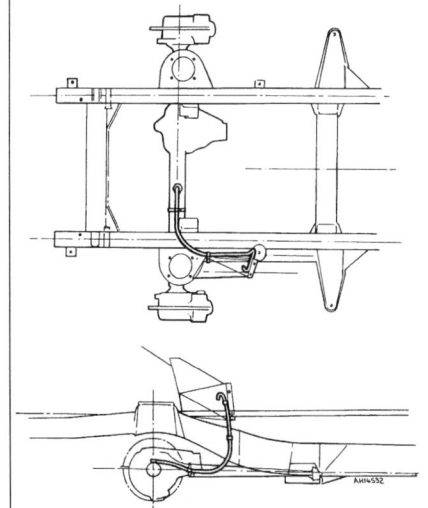

Fig. 13.131 Front axle breather location - later models (Sec 13)

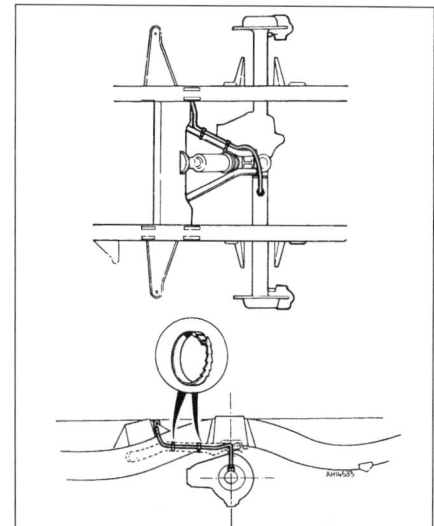

Fig. 13.132 Rear axle breather location - later models (Sec 13)

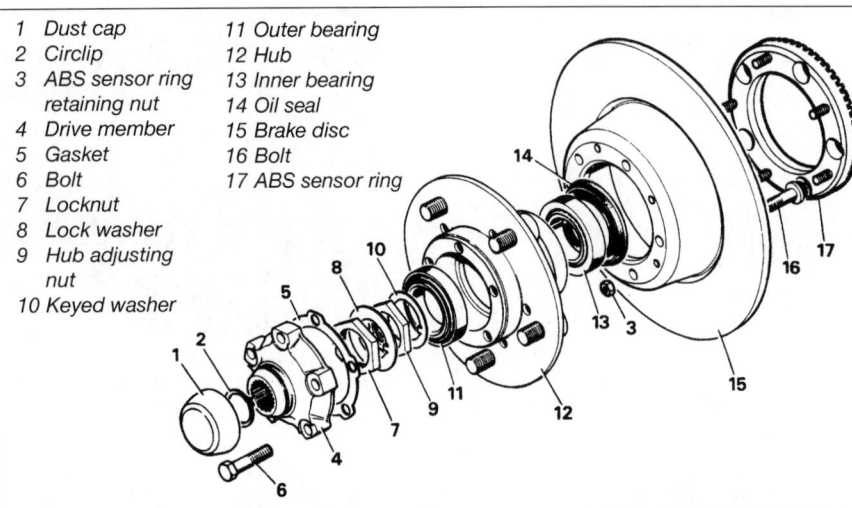

1 Dust cap	11 Outer bearing
2 Circlip	12 Hub
3 ABS sensor ring retaining nut	13 Inner bearing
4 Drive member	14 Oil seal
5 Gasket	15 Brake disc
6 Bolt	16 Bolt
7 Locknut	17 ABS sensor ring
8 Lock washer	
9 Hub adjusting nut	
10 Keyed washer	

Fig. 13.133 Rear hub components on models fitted with ABS (Sec 13)

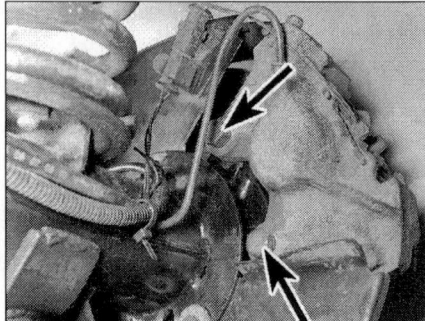

13.17A Rear brake caliper mounting bolts (arrowed)

13.17B Carefully withdraw the brake caliper from the brake disc and tie it to one side

vertical teeth is bolted through the brake disc to the hub from the inside. On the front axle the sensor teeth are incorporated in the constant velocity joint yoke.

Rear axle half shaft (models with ABS) - removal and refitting

5 Loosen the rear wheel nuts, then jack up the rear of the vehicle and support on axle stands. Remove the roadwheel.
6 Using a screwdriver, prise off the hub dust cover.
7 Unscrew the bolts securing the driving member to the hub assembly, then withdraw the member together with the half shaft from the rear axle. Remove the gasket.
8 Using circlip pliers remove the circlip from the outer end of the half shaft and pull off the driving member.
9 If there has been any loss of oil from the rear hub, the oil seals should be renewed and this will require the removal of the rear hub and stub axle as described later in this Section.
10 if the oil seals are in good condition first clean the driving member and the hub.
11 Insert the half shaft into the rear axle casing until it is engaged with the differential side gear. Take care not to damage the oil

seal as the half shaft moves through it.
12 Refit the driving member together with a new gasket, and tighten the bolts progressively to the specified torque.
13 Fit the circlip to the rear half shaft making sure that it locates in the groove correctly.
14 Tap the dust cap onto the hub.

Rear axle (models with ABS) - removal and refitting

15 The procedure is basically as described in Chapter 8, although it will be necessary to disconnect the ABS sensor wiring.

Rear wheel hub and bearings (models with ABS) - removal, overhaul and refitting

16 Loosen the rear wheel nuts, then jack up the rear of the vehicle and support on axle stands. Remove the roadwheel.
17 Taking care not to damage or bend the hydraulic brake pipe, detach the brake pipe from the rear axle and casing clips, then unscrew and remove the rear brake caliper mounting bolts and tie the caliper and brake pipe to one side (photos).
18 Using a screwdriver, prise off the hub dust cover.
19 Using circlip pliers remove the circlip from

the outer end of the rear half shaft.
20 Unscrew the bolts and withdraw the driving member from the hub assembly. Remove the gasket.
21 Bend back the tab washer then unscrew and remove the locknut followed by the tab washer.
22 Unscrew and remove the hub adjusting nut followed by the keyed washer (photo).
23 Withdraw the hub and brake disc assembly from the rear axle (photo).
24 Remove the outer bearing from the hub.
25 Mark the ABS sensor ring and brake disc in relation to the hub.
26 Unscrew the nylon nuts and withdraw the ABS sensor ring from the inside of the brake disc (photos).
27 Unbolt the brake disc from the hub.

13.22 Keyed washer (arrowed) on the rear hub stub axle

13.23 Removing the rear hub and brake disc assembly

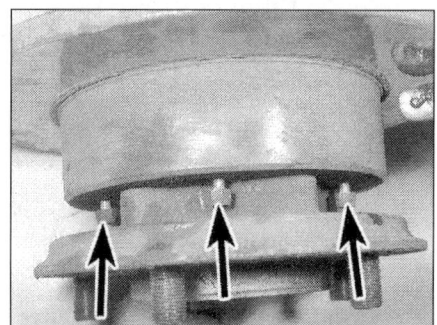

13.26A Unscrew the nylon nuts (arrowed) . . .

13.26B . . . and withdraw the ABS sensor ring from the brake disc

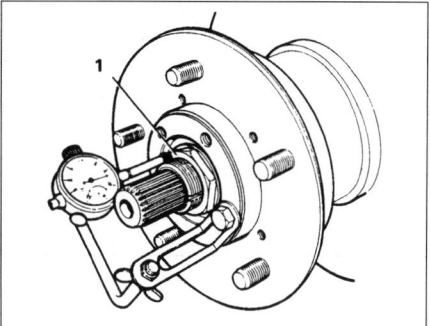

Fig. 13.134 Checking the endfloat of the rear hub with a dial gauge (Sec 13)

1 Adjusting nut

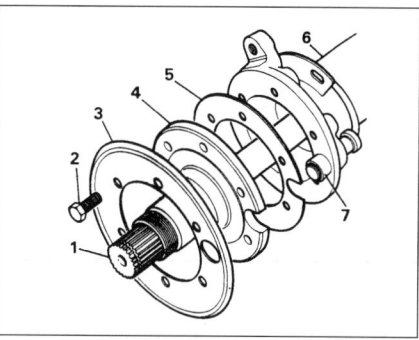

Fig. 13.135 Rear stub axle components (Sec 13)

1 Half shaft	5 Gasket
2 Bolt	6 Rear axle
3 Mudshield	7 ABS sensor bush
4 Stub axle	sleeve

28 Using a soft metal drift, drive out the inner bearing and oil seal. Discard the oil seal.

29 Drive out both bearing outer tracks from inside the hub.

30 Clean the hub and examine it thoroughly for wear and damage. If any of the roadwheel studs are damaged they may be pressed out and new ones inserted. Note that the manufacturers stipulate it is only permissible to renew a maximum of two studs after which the complete hub should be renewed. If there is any doubt how many of the studs have been renewed, renew the complete hub as a safety precaution.

31 Examine the bearing rollers and tracks for signs of pitting and wear, and if necessary renew them.

32 Examine the sensor ring studs for damage and if necessary renew them. Apply a little locking fluid to the threads of the studs before inserting them and tightening them.

33 Using a soft metal drift, drive the outer tracks into the hub squarely until they abut the shoulder.

34 Pack the inner bearing with grease then locate it in the hub; press a new oil seal into position using a block of wood. The oil seal must be fitted with its closed side facing outwards, and it must be flush with the inner end of the hub.

35 Apply a little grease between the lips of the oil seal.

36 Fit the brake disc to the hub making sure that the previously made marks are aligned. Apply a little locking fluid to the threads of the

bolts, then insert them in the holes and tighten them progressively to the specified torque.

37 Fit the sensor ring together with new nylon nuts and tighten them progressively. Check that there is minimal runout of the ring.

38 Pack the outer bearing with grease then locate it in the outer track.

39 Clean the rear axle and half shaft. Withdraw the ABS sensor slightly from the mounting sleeve while the hub is being fitted.

40 Locate the hub assembly on the rear axle and fit the keyed washer.

41 Fit the hub adjusting nut and tighten by hand whilst rotating the hub until all endplay is eliminated.

42 If a dial gauge is available back off the adjusting nut until the endfloat is between 0.013 and 0.05 mm (0.0005 and 0.002 in). If a dial gauge is not available back off the nut until it is just possible to detect a small endfloat.

43 Fit a new keyed locktab washer, then fit and tighten the hub nut. Recheck the endfloat then bend over the locktab washer.

44 Refit the driving member together with a new gasket and tighten the bolts progressively to the specified torque.

45 Fit the circlip to the rear half shaft making sure that it locates in the groove correctly.

46 Tap the dust cap onto the hub.

47 Refit the brake caliper and tighten the bolts to the specified torque. Attach the hydraulic brake pipes to the axle casing.

48 Push the ABS sensor into its holder until it

touches the sensor ring. The sensor will be set to its correct position when the hub is rotated.

49 Refit the roadwheel and tighten the nuts. Lower the vehicle to the ground.

50 Depress the footbrake pedal several times to set the brake pads in their normal position.

Rear stub axle (models with ABS) - removal and refitting

51 Remove the hub complete as described earlier in this Section.

52 Unscrew and remove the six bolts retaining the stub axle to the rear axle casing.

53 Withdraw the mudshield followed by the stub axle and gasket.

54 Pull the half shaft from the rear axle casing.

55 Clean the components and the rear axle casing.

56 Examine the oil seal in the stub axle and if necessary hook it out with a screwdriver (photo), clean the seating and drive in a new oil seal making sure that its closed side is fitted flush with the inner end of the stub axle. Apply a little oil to the lips of the oil seal.

57 Commence refitting by locating the stub axle together with a new gasket on the end of the rear axle casing. Locate the mudshield with the bolt holes correctly aligned. Insert the

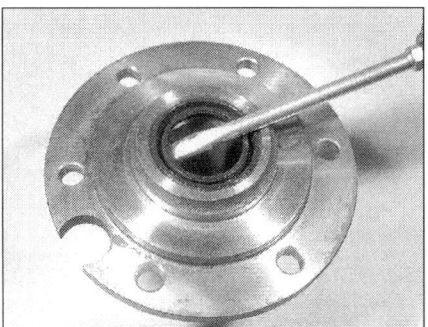

13.56 Removing the oil seal from the stub axle

13.57A Locate the stub axle on the rear axle casing . . .

13.57B . . . refit the mudshield . . .

13.57C . . . and tighten the bolts

13.61A Removing the driveshaft assembly from the front axle casing

13.58 Inserting the half shaft in the rear axle casing

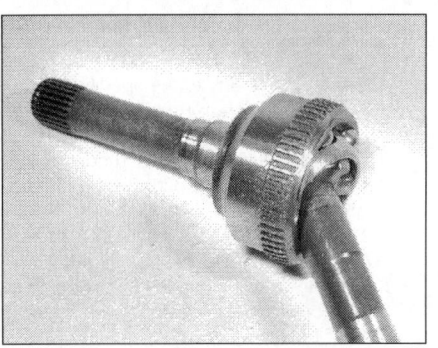

13.61B View of the constant velocity joint on the bench

bolts and tighten them to the specified torque progressively (photos).

58 Insert the half shaft into the rear axle casing until it is engaged with the differential side gear. Take care not to damage the oil seal as the half shaft moves through it (photo).

59 Refit the hub assembly as described earlier in this Section.

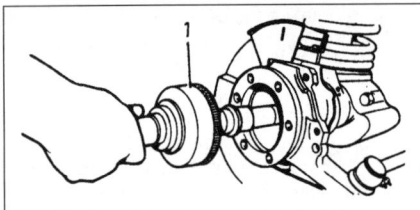

Fig. 13.136 Removing the front drive-shaft (1) from the front axle casing (Sec 13)

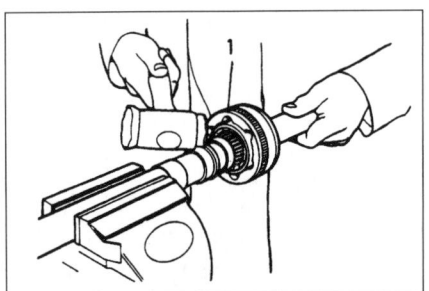

Fig. 13.137 Removing the constant velocity joint (1) from the driveshaft (Sec 13)

Front axle driveshaft and constant velocity joint (models with ABS) - removal, overhaul and refitting

60 Remove the front stub axle as described later in this Section.

61 Withdraw the driveshaft and constant velocity joint from the front axle casing (photos).

62 Mount the driveshaft in a soft-jawed vice, then drive the constant velocity joint from the driveshaft using a soft-faced mallet.

63 Remove the circlip and collar from the driveshaft.

64 Mark the joint inner and outer races and the cage in relation to each other, then tilt the cage and inner race to remove the balls.

65 Turn the cage so that it lines up with the axis of the joint, with two opposite windows in line with the two lands of the housing. Withdraw the cage.

66 Turn the inner track at right angles to the cage with the lands and openings in line with each other, then remove the inner race.

67 Clean all of the components and examine them for wear and damage.

68 Reassembly is a reversal of the dismantling procedure but lubricate the joint with the recommended oil.

69 With the joint assembled check that the endfloat does not exceed 0.64 mm (0.025 in).

70 Fit the collar and a new circlip to the driveshaft.

71 Locate the constant velocity joint on the driveshaft splines, then use a soft-faced mallet to drive the joint onto the driveshaft.

72 Insert the driveshaft and constant velocity joint into the front axle casing and, when engaged with the differential side gears, push it fully home. When inserting the driveshaft take care not to damage the oil seal.

73 Refit the front stub axle as described later in this Section.

Front axle (models with ABS) - removal and refitting

74 The procedure is as described in Chapter 8 although it will be necessary to disconnect the wiring for the ABS sensors.

Front wheel hub and bearings (models with ABS) - removal, overhaul and refitting

75 Loosen the front wheel nuts, then jack up the front of the vehicle and support on axle stands. Remove the roadwheel.

76 Remove the front brake caliper with reference to Chapter 8.

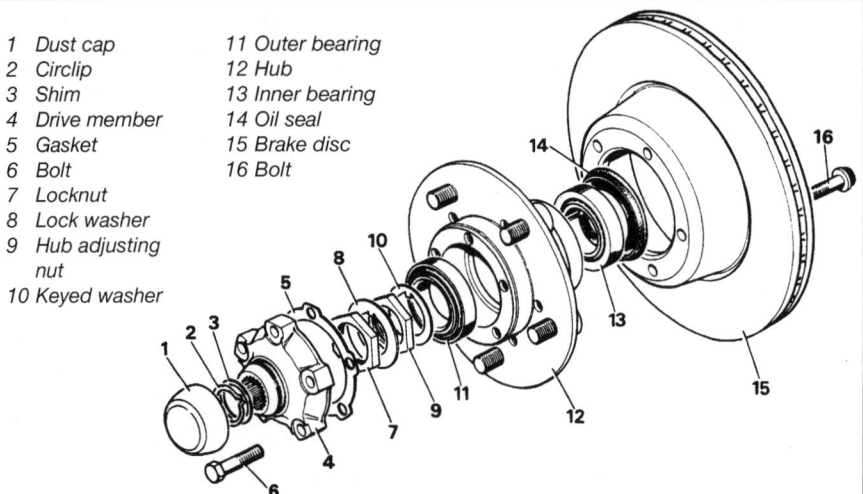

1 Dust cap	11 Outer bearing
2 Circlip	12 Hub
3 Shim	13 Inner bearing
4 Drive member	14 Oil seal
5 Gasket	15 Brake disc
6 Bolt	16 Bolt
7 Locknut	
8 Lock washer	
9 Hub adjusting nut	
10 Keyed washer	

Fig. 13.138 Front hub components on models fitted with ABS (Sec 13)

13.77 Removing the hub dust cover

13.78A Remove the circlip . . .

13.78B . . . and shim

77 Using a screwdriver, prise off the hub dust cover (photo).

78 Using circlip pliers remove the circlip from the outer end of the front driveshaft, then remove the driveshaft shim (photos). Keep the shim in a safe place as it determines the amount of driveshaft endplay.

79 Unscrew the bolts and withdraw the driving member from the hub assembly. Remove the gasket (photo).

80 Bend back the tab washer, then unscrew and remove the locknut followed by the tab washer (photo).

81 Unscrew and remove the hub adjusting nut followed by the keyed washer (photos).

82 Withdraw the hub and brake disc assembly from the front stub axle (photo).

83 Remove the outer bearing from the hub (photo).

84 Mark the hub and brake disc in relation to each other.

85 Unbolt the brake disc from the hub (photo).

86 Using a soft metal drift, drive out the inner bearing and oil seal. Discard the oil seal.

87 Drive out both bearing outer tracks from inside the hub.

88 Clean the hub and examine it thoroughly for wear and damage. If any of the roadwheel studs are damaged they may be pressed out and new ones inserted. Note that the manufacturers stipulate it is only permissible to renew a maximum of two studs after which

13.79 Removing the driving member and gasket

13.80 Removing the locknut and tab washer

13.81A Removing the hub adjusting nut . . .

13.81B . . . and keyed washer

13.82 Removing the hub and brake disc assembly

13.83 Removing the outer bearing

13.85 Unbolting the brake disc from the hub

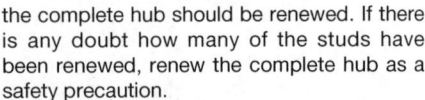
13.98 Adjusting the front hub endplay using a dial gauge

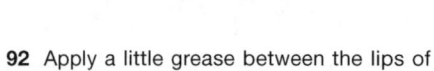
13.99A Tightening the hub nut

13.99B Bending over the locktab washer

the complete hub should be renewed. If there is any doubt how many of the studs have been renewed, renew the complete hub as a safety precaution.

89 Examine the bearing rollers and tracks for signs of pitting and wear, and if necessary renew them.

90 Using a soft metal drift, drive the outer tracks into the hub squarely until they abut the shoulder.

91 Pack the inner bearing with grease then locate it in the hub; press a new oil seal into position using a block of wood. The oil seal must be fitted with its closed side facing outwards, and it must be flush with the inner end of the hub.

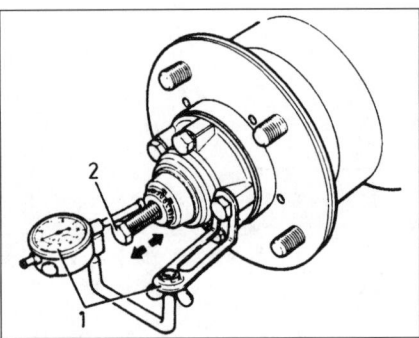

Fig. 13.139 Checking the endfloat of the driveshaft with a dial gauge (Sec 13)

1 Dial gauge and support bracket
2 Bolt screwed into the end of the driveshaft

92 Apply a little grease between the lips of the oil seal.

93 Fit the brake disc to the hub making sure that the previously made marks are aligned. Apply a little locking fluid to the threads of the bolts then insert them in the holes and tighten them progressively to the specified torque.

94 Pack the outer bearing with grease then locate it in the outer track.

95 Clean the front stub axle and driveshaft.

96 Locate the hub assembly on the stub axle and fit the keyed washer.

97 Fit the hub adjusting nut and tighten by hand whilst rotating the hub until all endplay is eliminated.

98 If a dial gauge is available back off the adjusting nut until the endfloat is between 0.013 and 0.05 mm (0.0005 and 0.002 in) (photo). If a dial gauge is not available back off the nut until it is just possible to detect a small endfloat.

99 Fit a new keyed locktab washer, then fit and tighten the hub nut. Recheck the endfloat then bend over the locktab washer (photos).

100 Refit the driving member together with a new gasket and tighten the bolts progressively to the specified torque.

101 Fit the shim and circlip to the driveshaft making sure that the shim locates in the groove correctly.

102 The endplay of the driveshaft must now be checked using a dial gauge in contact with the outer end of the driveshaft. Fit a suitable bolt to the end of the driveshaft, and move the

driveshaft out and in while noting the reading on the dial gauge. The endplay should be between 0.08 and 0.25 mm (0.003 to 0.010 in). If the endplay requires adjustment, measure the thickness of the existing shim and renew it with one which will give the correct endplay (photo).

103 Tap the dust cap onto the hub.

104 Refit the brake caliper with reference to Chapter 8, then bleed the brake hydraulic system with reference to Section 14 of this Supplement.

105 Refit the roadwheel and tighten the nuts. Lower the vehicle to the ground.

106 Depress the footbrake pedal several times to set the brake pads in their normal position.

Front stub axle (models with ABS) - removal, overhaul and refitting

107 Remove the front hub as described earlier in this Section.

108 Unscrew the drain plug and drain the oil from the swivel pin housing into a suitable container. On completion refit and tighten the drain plug.

109 Unscrew the bolts retaining the stub axle to the swivel pin housing (photos).

110 Withdraw the mud shield followed by the stub axle (photo). Remove the gasket.

111 Drill and chisel off the thrust ring from the inner end of the stub axle taking care not to cause any damage (photo).

13.102 Checking the endplay of the front driveshaft using a dial gauge

13.109A Unscrew the bolts . . .

13.109B . . . and remove them from the stub axle

13.110 Removing the front stub axle

13.111 Thrust ring (arrowed) located on the inner end of the stub axle

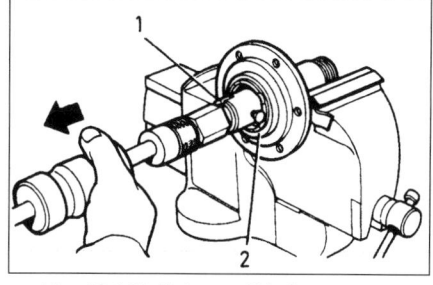

Fig. 13.140 Using a slide hammer to remove the bearing and seal from the stub axle (Sec 13)

1 Slide hammer adaptor
2 Bearing and seal

112 Using a soft metal drift, drive the bearing and oil seal out of the stub axle. Alternatively, use a slide hammer to remove the bearing and seal.

113 Clean the stub axle and swivel pin housing, and examine all of the components for wear and damage. Spin the bearings by hand and check for roughness and tight spots.

114 Apply some EP 90 oil to the new oil seal, then press it into the stub axle using a metal tube to keep it square. Make sure that the closed end of the seal is towards the outer end of the stub axle.

115 Press the bearing into the stub axle with its part number visible. Use a metal tube on the outer track only and press the bearing into the stub axle until flush with the inner face of the stub axle.

116 Press a new thrust ring onto the stub axle.

117 Refit the stub axle together with a new gasket followed by the mud shield. Apply locking fluid to the threads of the bolts then insert and tighten them to the specified torque.

118 Refit the front hub as described earlier in this Section.

119 Remove the filler and level plugs from the swivel pin housing.

120 Inject approximately 0.35 litre (0.6 pint) of the recommended oil into the swivel pin

housing until it reaches the bottom of the level plug hole (photo). Fit and tighten the filler and level plugs, and wipe away any surplus oil.

Front swivel pin housing - removal, overhaul and refitting

121 Remove the front hub, stub axle and driveshaft as described earlier in this Section.
122 Unscrew the two nuts and bolt, and remove the brake disc backplate.

123 Unscrew the nut and disconnect the steering track rod end from the housing.
124 Unscrew the nut and disconnect the steering box drop arm balljoint.
125 Disconnect the hydraulic brake hoses from the bracket.
126 Remove the ABS sensor.
127 Unbolt the retaining plate from the housing, and prise out the oil seal.
128 Remove the countersunk screws, and remove the damper and shield bracket and

13.120 Topping-up the front swivel pin housing

1 Adding oil through a plastic filler tube
2 Oil level plug hole
3 Drain plug

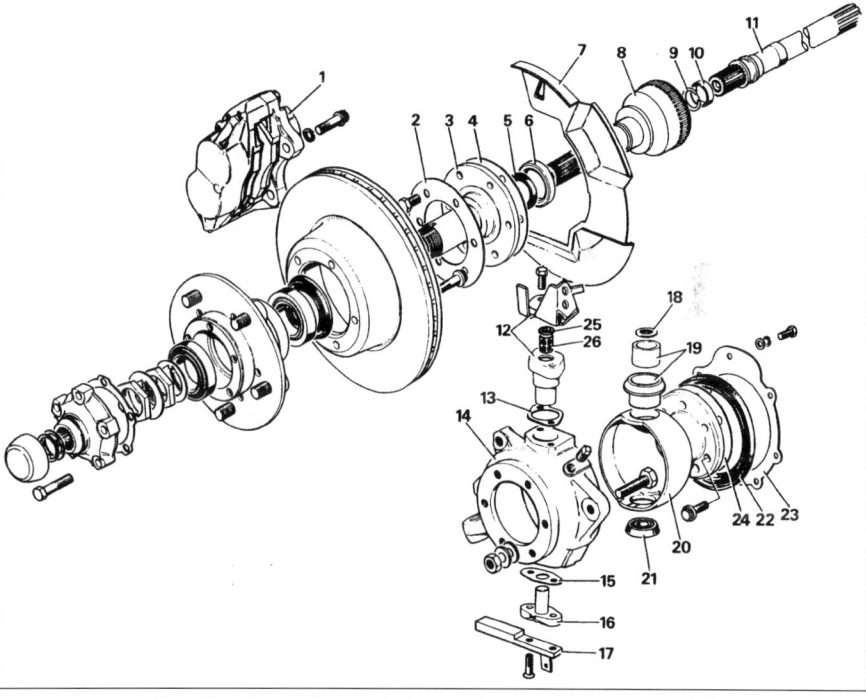

Fig. 13.141 Front swivel pin housing components (Sec 13)

1 Brake caliper	10 Bush	18 Thrustwasher
2 Mud shield	11 Inner section of driveshaft	19 Bush and housing
3 Stub axle	12 Upper swivel pin and brake	20 Swivel pin bearing housing
4 Gasket	hose bracket	21 Lower swivel pin bearing
5 Oil seal	13 Shim	22 Oil seal
6 Bearing	14 Swivel pin housing	23 Oil seal retaining plate
7 Brake disc backplate	15 Gasket	24 Gasket
8 Constant velocity joint	16 Lower swivel pin	25 Oil seal
9 Circlip	17 Damper and shield bracket	26 ABS sensor bush

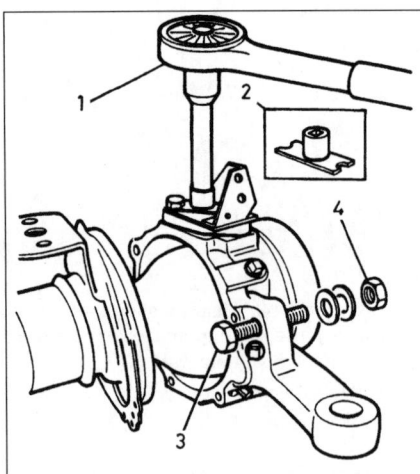

Fig. 13.142 Using a torque wrench to check the preload of the bearings in the swivel pin housing (Sec 13)

1 Torque wrench
2 Tool for checking the bearing preload at swivel pin axis
3 Steering lock stop bolt
4 Nut

the lower swivel pin. Tap out the lower swivel pin by tapping it on the small lug. Remove the gasket.

129 Unbolt the top swivel pin and hydraulic brake hose bracket. Note the number of shims fitted.

130 Withdraw the swivel pin housing, and at the same time recover the lower taper bearing.

131 If the housing is to be renewed unscrew the drain, level and filler plugs and drain the oil into a suitable container. Also remove the lock-stop bolt.

132 Unbolt the swivel pin bearing housing from the axle case.

133 Prise out the oil seal and remove the gasket.

134 Using a soft metal drift, drive out the lower swivel pin bearing outer track.

135 Press or drive out the upper swivel pin bush housing assembly. Remove the thrust washer.

136 Clean all the components, and examine them for wear and damage. Obtain new bushes and bearings as necessary.

137 Press in the lower swivel pin bearing track, followed by the bush and bush housing. The lip of the bush should face the rear oil seal.

138 Press in the driveshaft oil seal making sure that the lips face the rear of the housing. The seal should be flush with the rear of the housing. Apply a little grease to the lips of the seal.

139 Locate the thrustwasher in the top swivel pin bush with the black coating uppermost.

140 Temporarily hang the oil seal and retainer plate over the back of the swivel pin bearing housing, making sure that they are in the correct order.

141 Refit the swivel pin housing to the front axle and tighten the bolts progressively to the specified torque starting with the top fixing dowel bolt.

142 Grease the lower swivel pin bearing and fit it to the bearing housing.

143 Locate the swivel pin housing over the bearing housing.

144 Fit the lower swivel pin together with a new gasket making sure that the lip is on the outside. Do not fit the screws at this stage.

145 Fit the sensor bush and oil seal with the lip side facing to the top swivel pin.

146 Apply oil to the top swivel pin and fit it together with the existing shims.

147 Apply locking fluid to the threads of the bolts, then refit the brake hose bracket and hand-tighten the top swivel pin bolts.

148 Apply locking fluid to the threads of the bolts, then refit the damper and shield bracket; tighten the bolts to the specified torque.

149 Now tighten the top brake hose bracket bolts.

150 The preload on the bearings must now be checked. The preload should be between 0.2 and 0.25 mm (0.008 and 0.010 in) without the swivel housing oil seal and axle being fitted. The torque required to turn the swivel housing from lock to lock should be 5.1 to 7.3 Nm (45 to 65 lbf in). If adjustment is necessary, shims should be added to, or removed from, the top swivel pin. To make the check a tool may be made to locate between the top bolts as shown in Fig. 13.142.

151 Apply grease between the lips of the swivel housing oil seal, then secure the oil seal and retaining plate by tightening the bolts to the specified torque.

152 Fit the track rod end and drop arm together with new split pins.

153 Fit the lock-stop bolt loosely for adjustment later.

154 Refit the driveshaft, stub axle and back plate, and tighten the bolts to the specified torque.

155 Refit the hydraulic brake hoses to the bracket.

156 Refit the hub as described earlier in this Section.

157 Make sure that the swivel pin housing drain plug is tightened then remove the filler and level plugs.

158 Inject approximately 0.35 litre (0.6 pint) of the recommended oil into the filler plug hole until the level is up to the bottom of the level plug hole. Refit and tighten the filler and level plugs, and wipe away any surplus oil.

159 Adjust the steering lock-stop bolt to provide a clearance of 20 mm (0.787 in) between the tyre wall and the radius arm. Tighten the locknut noting that it also secures the brake disc backplate.

160 Refit the ABS sensor as described in Section 14.

14 Braking system

Warning: Hydraulic fluid is poisonous; wash off immediately and thoroughly in the case of skin contact, and seek immediate medical advice if any fluid is swallowed or gets into the eyes. Certain types of hydraulic fluid are inflammable, and may ignite when allowed into contact with hot components; when servicing any hydraulic system, it is safest to assume that the fluid IS inflammable, and to take precautions against the risk of fire as when handling petrol. Hydraulic fluid is also an effective paint stripper, and will attack certain plastics; if any is spilt, it should be washed off immediately using copious quantities of fresh water. Finally, it is hygroscopic (it absorbs moisture from the air) old fluid may be contaminated and unfit for further use. When topping-up or renewing the fluid, always use the recommended type, and ensure that it comes from a freshly-opened sealed container.

Warning: Renew both sets of front brake pads at the same time - never renew the pads on only one wheel, as uneven braking may result note that the dust created by wear of the pads may contain asbestos, which is a health hazard. Never blow it out with compressed air, and do not inhale it. A suitable filtering mask should be worn when working on the brakes. DO NOT use petroleum-based solvents to clean brake parts - use brake cleaner or methylated spirit only. Similar instructions apply when renewing the brake shoes in that they should only be renewed as sets.

Brake pad and lining renewal

1 Whenever new brake pads and linings have been fitted a suitable running-in period should be observed, when heavy braking should be avoided wherever possible. The running-in period allows the new brake pads, linings, discs or drums to wear themselves in so that a full friction surface contact is achieved. The suggested running-in period by the manufacturers is 350 miles (600 km).

2 On later models brake pad wear sensors are incorporated into the front right-hand and rear left-hand inboard brake pads. The sensors illuminate a warning light in the instrument panel when the lining thickness has worn down to approximately 0.12 in (3.0 mm). When renewing the pads the sensor wiring must be disconnected at the wiring multi-plug.

Brake hydraulic system components - modifications

3 In order to comply with EEC brake regulations, the brake pipes and connections

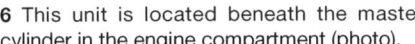

14.3 Later-type brake master cylinder showing the PDWA (A) and warning switch (B)

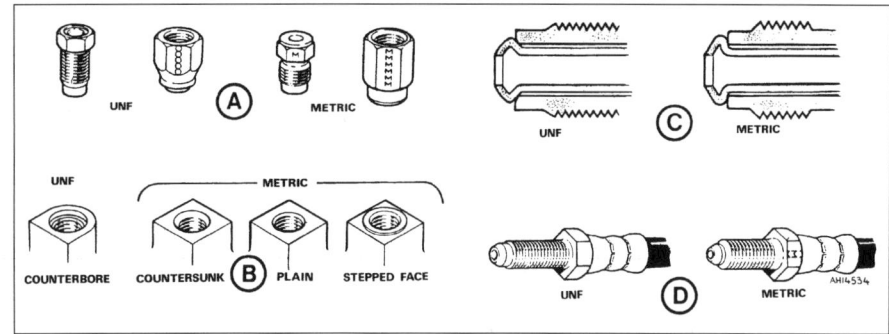

Fig. 13.143 Brake hydraulic system component fittings identification (Sec 14)

A Tube nut types   B Port types   C Flare types   D Hose types

were changed from non-metric (UNF) to metric connections. At the same time the master cylinder was fitted with an integral pressure differential warning actuator (photo).

4 The metric brake line system can be identified by a yellow label attached to the brake servo hose. The pressure differential warning actuator (PDWA) can be seen in the end of the master cylinder.

5 It is important when renewing any part of the brake system not to mix non-metric with metric components. The threads and fitting can be identified by external markings, and also by hose and colour codes (Fig. 13.143). Note that, unlike non-metric thread hoses, the metric thread hoses do not use sealing washers.

Brake pressure reducing valve - removal and refitting

6 This unit is located beneath the master cylinder in the engine compartment (photo).

7 To remove the unit, first place a film of clean polythene over the filler neck of the brake fluid reservoir and refit the cap. This will reduce fluid loss when the brake pipes are disconnected from the valve unit.

8 Clean the brake pipe connections at the pressure reducing valve, then loosen and detach the inlet and outlet pipe connections at the valve. Plug the pipes and the valve ports to prevent fluid leakage and the ingress of dirt.

9 Unscrew and remove the valve unit retaining bolt, and remove the valve.

14.6 Brake pressure-reducing valve

10 Refit in the reverse order of removal.

11 Ensure that the brake line connections are clean when reconnecting them. Bleed the brakes on completion in accordance with the instructions given in Section 2 of Chapter 9 and paragraph 15 in this Section.

Master cylinder and brake pressure warning switch - later models

12 On later models the brake master cylinder differs to that fitted to earlier variants in having the brake pressure warning switch and the pressure differential warning actuator fitted as an integral part of the cylinders.

13 The master cylinder removal and overhaul procedure remains the same as that described in Section 10 of Chapter 9, except that the leads to the brake pressure warning switch will need to be disconnected and the switch removed by unscrewing it from the master cylinder body.

14 When refitting the brake pressure warning switch, tighten it to the specified torque given at the start of this Chapter.

Brake hydraulic system - bleeding

15 When bleeding the brake hydraulic system on later models with the brake pressure warning switch fitted in the side of the master cylinder, disconnect the switch leads then unscrew the switch four complete turns. The procedure is then as described in Section 2 of Chapter 9.

16 On completion retighten the switch to the specified torque and reconnect the leads.

Master cylinder - description

17 As from 1987 a revised master cylinder is fitted. The procedures are similar to those described in Chapter 9 although the internal components are as shown in Fig. 13.144.

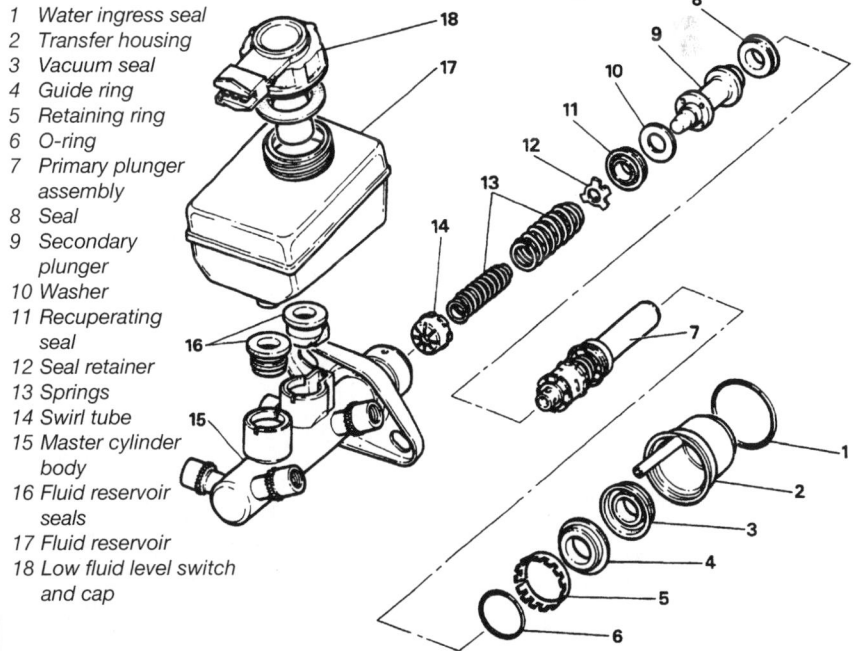

1 Water ingress seal
2 Transfer housing
3 Vacuum seal
4 Guide ring
5 Retaining ring
6 O-ring
7 Primary plunger assembly
8 Seal
9 Secondary plunger
10 Washer
11 Recuperating seal
12 Seal retainer
13 Springs
14 Swirl tube
15 Master cylinder body
16 Fluid reservoir seals
17 Fluid reservoir
18 Low fluid level switch and cap

Fig. 13.144 Exploded view of the brake master cylinder fitted to 1987-on models (Sec 14)

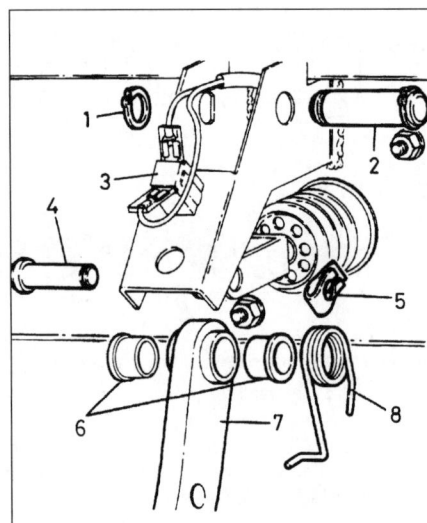

Fig. 13.145 Brake pedal components for 1987-on models (Sec 14)

1 *Circlip*	5 *Spring clip*
2 *Pivot bolt*	6 *Bushes*
3 *Stop-lamp switch*	7 *Pedal*
4 *Clevis pin*	8 *Return spring*

Brake pedal (1987-on models) - removal and refitting

18 The brake pedal is attached to the vacuum servo pushrod by a clevis and spring clip instead of a pivot bolt.

Vacuum servo unit (1987-on models) - removal and refitting

19 The procedure is similar to that described in Chapter 9, but it will be necessary to remove the lower facia panel from inside the vehicle. A spacer is fitted between the servo unit and the bulkhead, and this must always be refitted. Where a new servo unit is being fitted, the spacer must be transferred to the new unit.

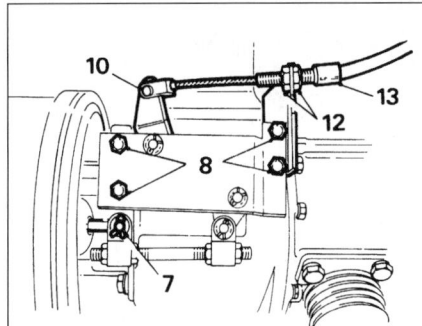

Fig. 13.148 Handbrake cable and linkage - 1986 models (Sec 14)

7 *Adjustment link clevis pin*
8 *Linkage and bracket assembly retaining bolts*
10 *Inner cable-to-linkage attachment*
12 *Adjusting locknuts*
13 *Threaded portion of outer cable*

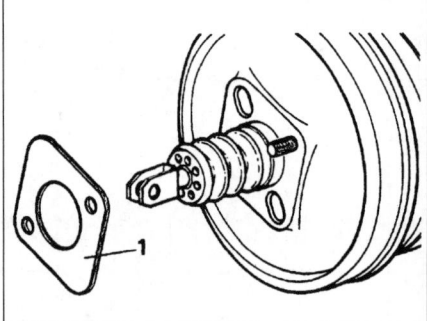

Fig. 13.146 Spacer (1) fitted to the vacuum servo unit on 1987-on models (Sec 14)

Transmission brake (handbrake) cable (1986 models) - removal, refitting and adjustment

Removal and refitting

20 A cable is used to connect the handbrake lever to the transmission brake linkage in place of the rod and lever system used on earlier modes. removal and refitting of the cable is as follows.
21 With the vehicle parked on level ground, chock the wheels and release the handbrake.
22 Disconnect the battery negative terminal.
23 Open the centre console stowage box lid, undo the two screws and lift out the liner.
24 Extract the split pin and remove the clevis pin securing the cable to the handbrake lever.
25 Undo the nut securing the outer cable to the top of the transmission tunnel. Remove the nut and push the cable assembly through the tunnel to the underside of the vehicle.
26 From below, extract the split pin and remove the washers and clevis pin securing the adjustment link to the brake drum actuating lever.
27 Undo the four bolts and withdraw the linkage and bracket assembly from the side of the transfer gearbox.
28 Remove the linkage and handbrake cable from under the vehicle.
29 Extract the split pin and remove the washers and clevis pin securing the inner cable to the linkage. Undo the two locknuts securing the outer cable to the retaining bracket and remove the cable.

14.31A Transmission brake adjuster - later models

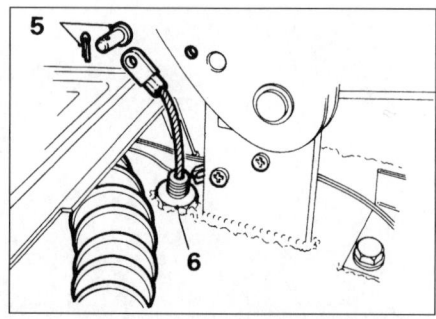

Fig. 13.147 Handbrake cable split pin and clevis pin (5) and cable securing nut (6) - 1986 models (Sec 14)

30 Refitting is the reversal of removal. When fitting the outer cable to the retaining bracket, position the adjusting locknuts centrally on the threaded portion of the cable initially.

Adjustment

31 An external adjuster is fitted, being located on the forward side of the brake backplate. Access to the adjuster is from underneath the vehicle on the left-hand side (photos). Adjust the handbrake as follows.
32 Fully release the handbrake.
33 Turn the adjuster in a clockwise direction until the brake shoes are in contact with the drum. At each quarter-turn of the adjuster, a click will be heard and felt.
34 Turn the adjuster anti-clockwise half a turn (two clicks), then fully apply the handbrake to centralise the shoes.
35 Remove the roadwheel chocks then release and fully apply the handbrake to check that the handbrake lever fully operates the brake shoes on the third or fourth click of the ratchet. It may be necessary to reposition the adjustment link locknuts if there is insufficient thread on the handbrake cable end to achieve the correct setting.

Transmission brake (handbrake) cable (1987/1988 models) - removal, refitting and adjustment

Removal and refitting

36 With the vehicle on level ground, chock the roadwheels and select P.

14.31B General view of the transmission brake - later models

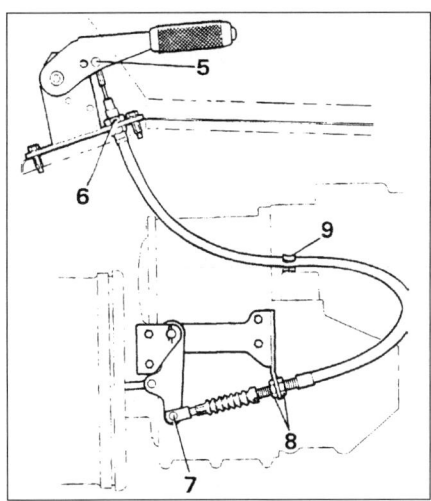

Fig. 13.149 Handbrake cable and linkage - 1987 and 1988 models (Sec 14)

5 Clevis pin and split pin
6 Outer cable upper mounting nut
7 Clevis pin and split pin
8 Adjusting locknuts
9 Retaining clip

37 Disconnect the battery negative lead and fully release the handbrake.
38 Working inside the vehicle, unscrew the glovebox liner mounting screws and remove the liner in order to gain access to the bottom of the handbrake pivot bracket.
39 Extract the split pin and pull out the clevis pin from the handbrake lever.
40 Unscrew the nut securing the top of the handbrake outer cable to the bracket, then slide the nut off the cable and push the inner and outer cables down through the floor.
41 Working under the vehicle, extract the split pin and remove the washer and clevis pin securing the adjustment link to the brake drum actuating lever.
42 Unscrew the locknuts and release the handbrake outer cable from its bracket.
43 Release the outer cable from the clip on the side of the transfer box and withdraw the cable assembly from under the vehicle.
44 Commence refitting by inserting the top of the outer cable through the floor and fitting the nut.
45 Connect the inner cable to the handbrake lever and fit the clevis pin and new split pin.
46 Press the outer cable into the clip on the side of the transfer box.
47 Insert the lower end of the cable through the bracket and loosely screw on the locknuts.
48 Connect the cable to the brake drum actuating lever and fit the clevis pin together with a washer and new split pin.

Adjustment

49 Turn the adjuster clockwise until the brake shoes are locked against the drum.
50 Finger-tighten then fully tighten the locknuts securing the outer cable to the bracket.

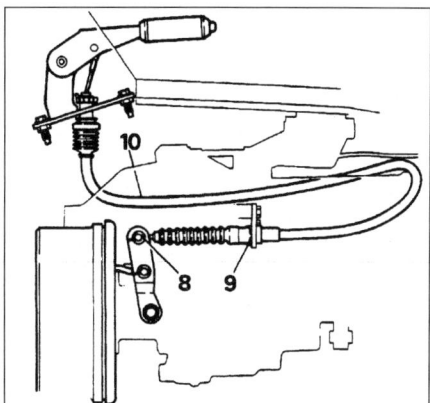

Fig. 13.150 Handbrake cable and linkage - 1989 models (Sec 14)

8 Clevis pin   10 Outer cable
9 Circlip

51 Apply the handbrake then loosen the adjuster until the handbrake lever locks the brake drum on the second or third notch of the ratchet.
52 Refit the glovebox liner.
53 Reconnect the battery negative lead, then apply the handbrake and lower the vehicle to the ground.

Transmission brake (handbrake) cable (1989-on models) - removal, refitting and adjustment

Removal and refitting

54 The cable was modified in 1989, and the outer cable lower end is now secured with a circlip instead of locknuts. The upper end is secured with an adjustment thumbwheel and a circlip.

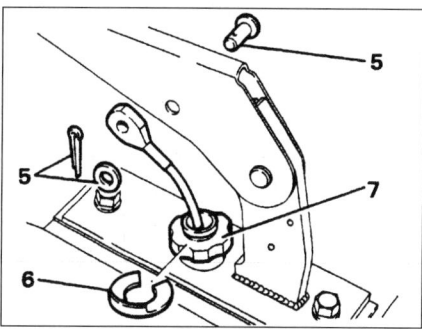

Fig. 13.151 Handbrake cable upper mounting - 1989 models (Sec 14)

5 Clevis pin and split pin   7 Thumbwheel
6 Clip

55 The removal and refitting of the cable is similar to that described in the previous paragraphs for earlier models but noting the new attachment of the outer cable; the adjustment procedure is different, as follows.

Adjustment

56 Chock the roadwheels, then fully release the handbrake.
57 Working under the vehicle, turn the adjuster clockwise until the shoes are locked against the brake drum, then back off the adjustment until the drum is free to rotate.
58 Adjust the thumbwheel below the handbrake lever until the handbrake is fully applied at the third notch.
59 Note that it is important to adjust the brake drum first before adjusting the thumbwheel. The thumbwheel adjustment must not be used to compensate for incorrect adjustment at the brake drum.
60 Fully apply the handbrake several times, then check that the adjustment is still correct.

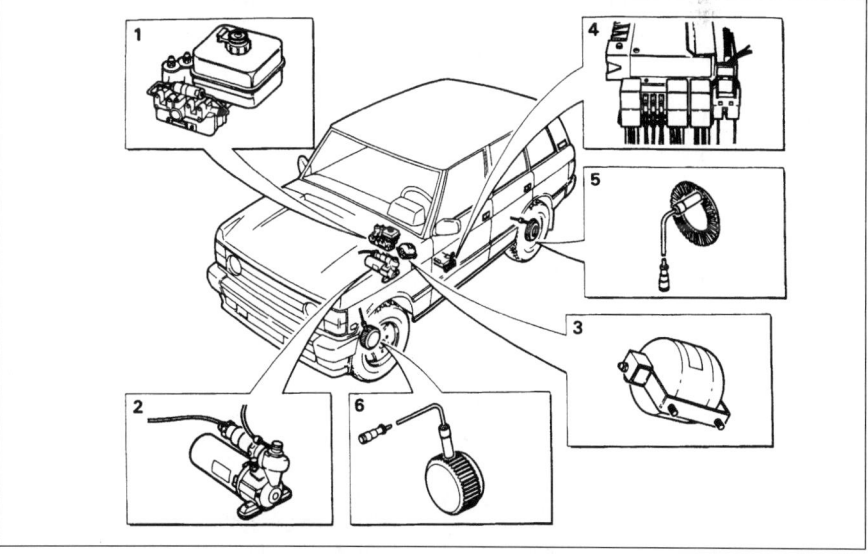

Fig. 13.152 ABS components (Sec 14)

1 Hydraulic booster unit   4 Electronic control unit
2 Power unit hydraulic pump   (ECU), relays and fuses
3 Accumulator

5 Rear sensors/exciter rings
6 Front sensors/exciter rings

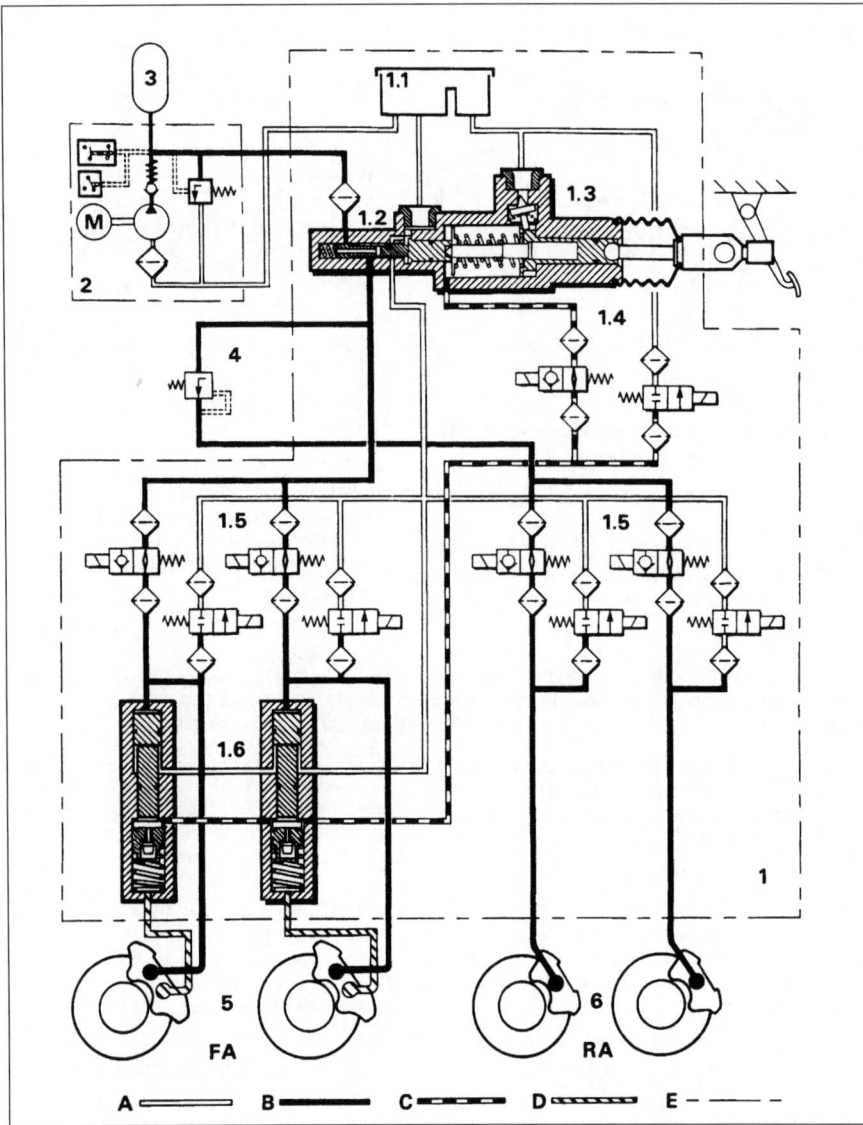

Fig. 13.153 Diagram of the ABS system (Sec 14)

1 Hydraulic booster unit	2 Hydraulic power unit	A Fluid feed/return
1.1 Fluid reservoir	3 Accumulator	B Power circuit
1.2 Power valve	4 Pressure-conscious	C Hydrostatic (master
1.3 Master cylinder	reducing valve (PCRV)	cylinder) circuit
1.4 Isolating valve	5 Front brake caliper	D Combined
1.5 Solenoid control valves	6 Rear brake caliper	hydrostatic/power circuit
1.6 Servo cylinders		E Component enclosure

Anti-lock brake system - general description and precautions

61 The anti-lock brake system (ABS) prevents the wheels locking during brake application, so improving steerability and stability especially under emergency conditions. The ABS system may be fitted as an option to models other than the EFiSE from October 1989, but is fitted as standard to the EFiSE. It is an advanced Clayton Dewandre-Wabco four-channel system incorporating separate circuits for each rear wheel whereas most ABS systems only have one circuit to the rear wheels. It uses an electrically

powered hydraulic booster pump for the servo effect.

62 The hydraulic system consists of two completely independent circuits. The front upper pistons and both of the rear calipers form the power circuit, and the front lower pistons form the power and hydrostatic circuit.

Anti-lock brake system - depressurising

63 The ABS accumulator must be depressurised before bleeding the circuit or working on any of the components. To do this first switch off the ignition.

14.71 Pressure bleeding kit fitted to the brake fluid reservoir

64 Depress the footbrake pedal 30 times and note that the pedal travel will increase and there will be reduced resistance felt on the pedal.

65 Wait for approximately 60 seconds, then depress the footbrake pedal four more times. This procedure will ensure that all pressure is released from the brake hydraulic circuit.

Brake hydraulic system (anti-lock brake system) - bleeding

Note: From experience it has been found that the best way to bleed the ABS system is to use a pressure bleeder. Using only the brake pedal method to bleed the system will invariably result in air still being left in the circuit and under hard braking this may well cause the brakes to pull to one side. One suitable pressure bleeding kit obtainable from motor accessory shops uses air pressure from the spare wheel to provide pressure to the brake fluid reservoir

66 Refer to Chapter 9 and obtain either a brake bleeding kit or a clean jar and length of clear plastic tubing.

67 Clean all of the bleed screws and the hydraulic fluid filler cap.

68 During the bleeding procedure make sure that the fluid level never drops below the 'MIN' level. If the pressure bleeding kit recommended is used then the fluid level will be maintained at the correct level automatically.

69 Depressurise the ABS system as described earlier. Do not switch on the ignition until instructed in the following paragraphs.

70 Top up the fluid level to the 'MAX' mark.

71 Connect the pressure bleeding kit to the fluid reservoir in accordance with the manufacturer's instructions so that pressure is applied to the fluid (photo).

72 Fully depress the brake pedal slowly five times releasing the pedal for 5 to 10 seconds after each stroke. Repeat this procedure until resistance is felt. If no resistance is felt check that the clevis pin is connected to the upper hole in the brake pedal.

73 Bleed the lower bleed screws (hydrostatic circuit) in the front brake calipers first, starting

14.74 Bleeding the ABS pump

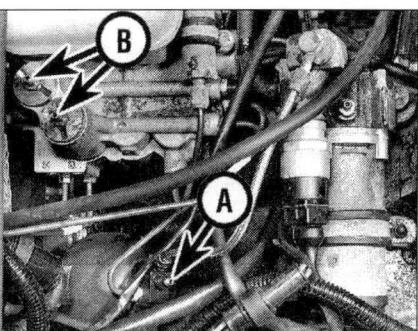

14.75 Bleed screws on the accumulator (A) and hydraulic booster (B)

with the outer screw on the driver's side, then the outer screw on the passenger's side, followed by the inner screw on the passenger's side and finally the inner screw on the driver's side. Fit the bleed tube, then open the bleed screw by half a turn and allow the fluid to escape until there is no sign of air bubbles in the fluid. Tighten the bleed screw and remove the bleed tube. Repeat the procedure on the remaining bleed screws in the hydrostatic circuit.

74 Next bleed the screw located on top of the pump, in front of the ABS unit (photo). Open the screw and allow the fluid to flow until it is clear of air bubbles then tighten the screw.

75 Bleed the accumulator next to the ABS unit as follows (photo). First attach the bleed tube to the bleed screw. Open the bleed screw, then switch on the ignition and run the pump for 3 to 4 seconds and switch off again. Repeat this procedure until no further air bubbles emerge, then tighten the screw and disconnect the bleed tube.

76 Connect the bleed tube to one of the two hydraulic booster bleed screws. Open the screw and have an assistant depress the brake pedal, then switch on the ignition and run the pump until no further air bubbles emerge. Tighten the screw, switch off the ignition and release the brake pedal. Bleed the remaining hydraulic booster bleed screw in the same manner.

77 The remaining bleed screws on all four calipers must now be bled (power circuit).

First connect the bleed tube to one of the upper front bleed screws (photo), have an assistant depress the brake pedal, open the bleed screw, then switch on the ignition and run the pump for 3 to 4 seconds repeating the procedure until no further air bubbles emerge. Switch off the ignition, tighten the bleed screw and release the brake pedal.

78 Bleed the remaining upper front bleed screw and the two rear bleed screws in the same way (photo).

79 Bleed the master cylinder by switching on the ignition. The system pressure will increase and the pump will cut out. If the pump does not cut out after running for 45 seconds, check the system for leaks.

80 Bleed the lower front (hydrostatic) circuit again by connecting the bleed tube to one lower front bleed screw. Depress the brake pedal several times using only the lower two thirds of pedal travel, until no further air bubbles emerge. If the fluid warning light comes on during the procedure, stop depressing the pedal and allow the pressure to build up before continuing. Tighten the bleed screw and release the pedal. Repeat the procedure on the remaining front lower bleed screws.

81 Disconnect the pressure bleeding kit and make sure that the fluid is at the correct level in the fluid reservoir.

82 Wipe clean any surplus hydraulic fluid, then check the circuit for leaks by switching on the ignition and depressing the brake pedal. If two full brake pedal applications

switch on the pump from the fully charged condition, then it will be necessary to repeat the bleeding procedure.

Brake calipers (anti-lock brake system) - removal and refitting

83 The procedure is similar to that described in Chapter 9, however a brake hose clamp should be used on the adjacent hydraulic hose instead of the polythene film. Provided that the fluid level in the reservoir has not dropped below the 'MIN' level mark while the caliper has been removed, then it is sufficient to bleed only the bleed screws on the caliper. However if there has been excessive loss of fluid, then it will be necessary to bleed the complete system as described earlier.

Hydraulic booster unit (anti-lock brake system) - removal and refitting

84 Disconnect the battery negative lead and depressurise the hydraulic system as described earlier.

85 Clean the area around the hydraulic booster unit, then disconnect the booster multi-plug and the wiring from the low fluid warning switch on the reservoir filler cap. Disconnect the booster earth strap.

86 Unscrew the union nuts securing the brake pipes to the booster unit, accumulator and hydraulic power unit. The pipes and corresponding location should be marked to ensure correct refitting. Seal the ends of the pipes and the component apertures with suitable plugs to prevent the ingress of dirt.

87 Working inside the vehicle, remove the lower facia trim panel with reference to Chapter 12.

88 Pull the spring clip from the clevis pin securing the booster push rod to the brake pedal and pull out the clevis pin.

89 Unscrew and remove the booster unit mounting nuts and washers, and withdraw the unit from the bulkhead in the engine compartment.

90 If a new booster unit is being fitted note that it should remain in its sealed packing until just prior to fitting it. Note also that a use by date is given on the packing, and this should be strictly adhered to. Do not fit a booster unit if the date has elapsed.

91 Refitting is a reversal of the removal procedure, but note the following additional points:

(a) *Make sure that clevis pin is fitted to the TOP hole In the brake pedal*

(b) *Adjust the stop-light switch by pulling out the black plunger then pulling the brake pedal back fully to reset the switch*

(c) *Bleed the complete system as described earlier*

Brake fluid reservoir seals - renewal

92 Remove the booster unit as described earlier, unscrew the filler cap and drain the fluid into a suitable container.

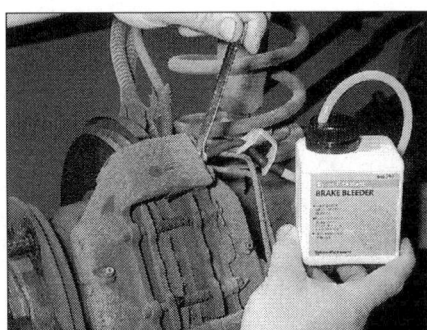

14.77 Bleeding the front power circuit

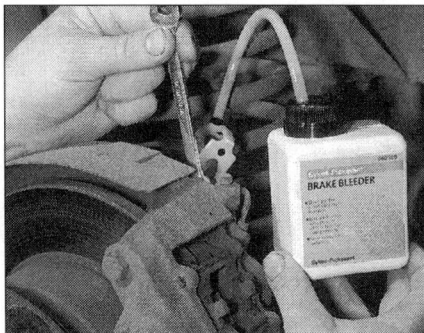

14.78 Bleeding the rear power circuit

93 Thoroughly clean the fluid reservoir.

94 Unscrew the bolt adjacent to the low pressure suction hose outlet and carefully ease out the reservoir from the booster unit.

95 Carefully prise out the two seals from the top of the booster unit taking care not to allow any particles of rubber to enter the unit.

96 Fit the new seals, followed by the reservoir and tighten the mounting bolt to the specified torque.

97 Refit the booster unit as described earlier.

Hydraulic power unit pump (anti-lock brake system) - removal and refitting

98 Disconnect the battery negative lead.

99 Depressurise the system as described earlier.

100 Unscrew the union nut and disconnect the accumulator braided hose from the pump. Attach a hose clamp to the low pressure suction hose from the fluid reservoir, then disconnect the hose and plug its end to prevent the ingress of foreign matter.

101 Disconnect the multi-plug from the pressure switch.

102 Separate the wiring connector for the power unit.

103 Unscrew and remove the mounting nuts and washers from underneath the hydraulic power unit pump, and withdraw the unit together with the mountings.

104 Refitting is a reversal of the removal procedure, but note the following additional points:

(a) Check the condition of the sealing washers on the high pressure hose and fit new ones if necessary

(b) Bleed the system as described earlier in this Section and finally top up the level of fluid in the reservoir

Accumulator (anti-lock brake system) - removal and refitting

Note: *The accumulator is charged with nitrogen and must be handled with extreme care. Do not puncture or burn the accumulator.*

105 Disconnect the battery negative lead.

106 Depressurise the system as described earlier in this Section.

107 Unscrew the union nuts and disconnect the fluid inlet and outlet pipes from the accumulator.

108 Working under the vehicle, remove the wheelarch inner liner and unscrew the two nuts and washers securing the accumulator.

109 Remove the accumulator from the engine compartment.

110 Refitting is a reversal of the removal procedure, but note the following additional points:

(a) Check the condition of the sealing washers on the high pressure hose and fit new ones if necessary

(b) Bleed the hydraulic system as described earlier in this Section

Electronic control unit (anti-lock brake system) - removal and refitting

111 From the left-hand front seat, remove the front and side trim.

112 Move the seat fully to the rear and raise the seat cushion height to allow access to the ECU.

113 Disconnect the battery negative lead.

114 Press the clip retaining the ECU plug.

115 Swivel out the multi-plug from the retaining clip and unhook it from the other end.

116 Unscrew the two screws from the mounting bracket and withdraw the ECU from the clip.

117 Refitting is a reversal of the removal procedure, but ensure that the ECU multi-plug is refitted so that it is held by the spring clip.

Front sensor (anti-lock brake system) - removal and refitting

Note: *If a sensor is removed, a new sensor bush and seal must be fitted.*

118 Disconnect the battery negative lead.

119 Jack up the front of the vehicle and support on axle stands.

120 Disconnect the wiring connector located on the inner wing panel next to the bulkhead cover panel.

121 Remove the sensor lead and pad wear harness plug from the clips.

122 Clean the area around the sensor to prevent the ingress of foreign matter.

123 Using a suitable lever, prise the sensor from its mounting bush.

124 Release the cable ties and remove the sensor lead from the vehicle.

125 Unscrew and remove the top swivel retaining bolts together with the hydraulic brake hose bracket.

126 Remove the sensor seal and bush.

127 Clean the components and examine them for wear and damage.

128 Commence refitting by inserting the sensor bush and seal.

129 Apply locking fluid to the threads of the bolts then refit the top swivel bolts and bracket, and tighten the bolts to the specified torque.

130 Smear the sensor with EP 90 oil, then push the sensor through the bush until it contacts the exciter ring.

131 Rotate the wheel and at the same time turn the steering from lock to lock to set the sensor air gap.

132 Refit the wiring lead and connectors, making sure that they follow the original routing.

133 It is now necessary to clear the error code from the ECU as described later in this Section.

134 Finally drive the vehicle and check that the ABS warning light is extinguished.

Rear sensor (anti-lock brake system) - removal and refitting

Note: *If a sensor is removed, a new sensor bush must be fitted.*

135 Disconnect the battery negative lead.

136 Disconnect the sensor wiring lead located above the rear axle.

137 Release the sensor from its location clip.

138 Unscrew the mudshield mounting bolts.

139 Prise the sensor from its mounting bush using a suitable lever.

140 Release the cable ties and remove the sensor lead from the vehicle. Note that the two rear sensor leads are integral with the pad wear harness and, if the sensor is faulty, the complete harness must be changed.

141 Remove the sensor bush.

142 Clean the components and examine them for wear and damage.

143 Fit the sensor bush.

144 Apply a little silicone grease to the sensor, then push the sensor through the bush until it touches the exciter ring. The sensor will be set to its correct position when the vehicle is driven.

145 Reconnect the wiring making sure that the routing is the same as the original.

146 It is now necessary to clear the error code from the ECU as described later in this Section.

147 Finally drive the vehicle and check that the ABS warning light is extinguished.

Stop-light switch (anti-lock brake system) - removal and refitting

148 Switch off the ignition and disconnect the battery negative lead.

149 Working inside the vehicle remove the lower facia trim panel.

150 Disconnect the wiring from the switch.

151 Depressurise the hydraulic system as described earlier in this Section.

152 Depress the brake pedal, then pull the red sleeve and the black switch plunger fully forward.

153 Making sure that the red sleeve is fully forwards, release the switch retaining clips and withdraw the switch.

154 To refit the switch, pull the red sleeve and the black plunger fully forward. Depress the brake pedal and fit the switch making sure that the retaining clips are fully located.

155 Hold the switch firmly in place, and pull the brake pedal back fully to set the switch.

156 Reconnect the wiring to the switch and refit the lower facia trim panel, then reconnect the battery negative lead.

Sensor exciter rings (anti-lock brake system) - removal and refitting

157 The exciter rings on the rear wheels are located inboard of the brake discs, and their removal and refitting is covered in Section 13.

158 On the front, the exciter teeth are located on the perimeter of the constant velocity joint yoke, and the removal and refitting of the driveshaft is described in Section 13. The teeth cannot be removed from the driveshaft.

Brake testing on a rolling road - special precautions

159 When the efficiency of the front or rear roadwheel brakes is to be tested using a two-wheel self-powered rolling road (such as for the MOT certificate) it is essential that the following conditions are met:

(a) Disengage the centre differential
(b) The transfer gearbox must be in neutral
(c) The axle speed must not exceed 3 mph (5 kph)

160 The following conditions must be met where a self-powered four-wheel rolling road is to be used:

(a) All rollers must turn at the same speed
(b) Disengage the centre differential

161 If the vehicle is to be checked on a free-running four-wheel rolling road then the centre differential must be engaged. For high speed testing consult your Range Rover dealer as special tyres may need to be fitted to suit the rolling road type.

162 If the vehicle is to be checked on a free-running two-wheel rolling road under high speed conditions then the propeller shaft to the stationary axle must be detached. the stationary wheels chocked and the centre differential engaged.

163 The tyres may also need to be changed according to the rolling road type consult your

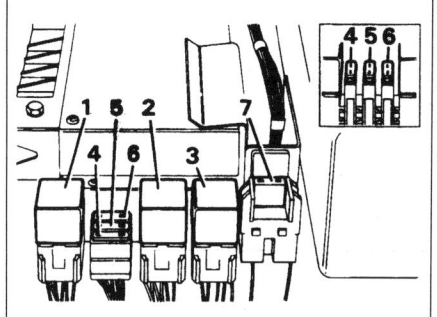

Fig. 13.154 ABS relays and fuses (Sec 14)

1 ABS warning lamp relay, green base - AB12
2 Valve relay, black base - AB14
3 Hydraulic pump relay, black base - AB2
4 Hydraulic pump relay fuse, 5 amp tan - AB10
5 Stop-lamp switch, diagnostic plug, ECU pin 9 fuse, 5 amp tan - AB11
6 Valve relay fuse, 25 amp white - AB13
7 Hydraulic pump relay fuse 30 amp green MAXI type fuse - AB1

Inset shows fuse position on early 1990 models

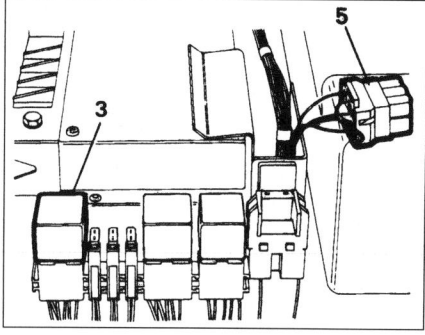

Fig. 13.155 ABS warning lamp relay (3) and diagnostic plug (5) (Sec 14)

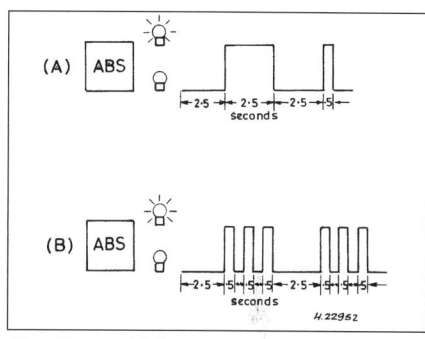

Fig. 13.156 ABS fault diagnosis blink code sequence (Sec 14)

A Start phase
B First part of fault code number

dealer to check this point. Do not make extended high speed tests on a rolling road unless provision has been made for the vehicle to be adequately cooled.

Anti-lock brake system - fault finding

The ABS ECU includes a fault diagnosis memory function to enable a fault to be located and rectified quickly. Whenever a fault occurs, the ABS warning lamp on the instrument panel will be illuminated.

Before commencing the main fault finding procedure, carry out the following:

(a) Examine all wiring for signs of damage
(b) Check all earth wires from the ABS components
(c) Check that the battery is in a good state of charge
(d) Check the fluid level in the reservoir
(e) Check all ABS fuses and electrical wiring
(f) Check that the rear hub endfloat is correct

Because of reasons of safety it is recommended that the vehicle be taken to a Rover dealer if a fault remains after making the latter checks; however, for those who are proficient at making electrical checks, the

following procedure will help to isolate the area of the fault.

The manufacturer's use a dedicated tester to check the ABS, although the following procedure will locate the general area of any faults. A female plug will be required to fit on the diagnostic plug located under the seat, and it must be wired to connect the ECU pin 14 to earth by bridging the black/pink and black diagnostic plug wires.

Switch off the ignition, then remove the seat side trim for access to the ECU and relays, and, on early models, the diagnostic plug also. Remove the access plate from the seat base front trim panel, and pull the blue diagnostic plug from its clip through the opening.

Unplug the ABS warning light relay.

Turn on the ignition and note that the ABS warning light comes on.

Connect the female plug to the diagnostic plug. After five seconds the ABS warning light

will go out as the blink code cycle commences. The start phase consists of a pause, a flash, a pause and a flash as shown in Fig. 13.156. Next there will be a pause of 2.5 seconds followed by a series of flashes which form the first part of the fault code number. There will then be a further pause of 2.5 seconds followed by the second part of the fault code number. The code phase will repeat itself until the plug is disconnected, but note that the code will be cleared from the memory when the plug is disconnected so it is important to know what the particular fault code is.

The memory can store more than one fault code, so the plugs should be reconnected to check for any other codes.

Make sure that the relay is reconnected after completing the fault code test.

The following code causes are not comprehensive, and a Range Rover dealer should be contacted if necessary:

Fault code	Reason	Remedy
2-12 front right 2-13 rear left 2-14 front left 2-15 rear right	Too large an air gap, or sensor has been forced out by exciter ring	Check sensor setting and for damage to exciter ring. Check rear bearing endfloat

Continued overleaf

Fault code	Reason	Remedy
5-12 front right 5-13 rear left 5-14 front left 5-15 rear right	Sensor or wiring has intermittent fault	Check wiring
6-12 front right 6-13 rear left 6-14 front left 6-15 rear right	No output from sensor. Sensor may have too large an air gap	Check sensor setting. Fit new sensor bush if necessary
4-12 front right 4-13 rear left 4-14 front left 4-15 rear right	Wiring to sensor broken or sensor resistance too high	Check wiring or fit new sensor
2-6 stop-light switch	Faulty switch or wiring. Fuse A5 blown or not fitted	Check that pedal returns fully to stop. Slowly operate pedal by hand and check that two clicks are heard from switch; stop-lights come on at first click. Otherwise check wiring and fuse
2-7	Continuous supply to ECU with ignition off. Faulty valve relay or wiring	Check wiring and valve
2-8	No voltage to ABS solenoid valves. Faulty valve relay or wiring	Check wiring
3-0 to 3-9	Open circuit in connection from ECU to solenoid valve in booster, or in ECU.	Check wiring and connectors. Renew ECU if wiring correct
4-0 to 4-9	Short circuit to earth in connection from ECU to solenoid valve in booster	Check wiring and connectors. Renew ECU if wiring correct
5-0 to 5-9	Short circuit to 12 volt in connection from ECU to solenoid valve in booster. Possible earth fault	Check wiring and connectors. Renew ECU if wiring correct
6-0 to 6-9	Short circuit between two connections from ECU to solenoid valve in booster	Check wiring, connectors and booster. Renew ECU if no fault found

15 Electrical system

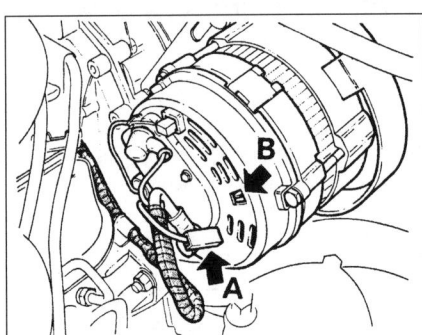

Fig. 13.157 Alternator wiring harness showing the spare brown lead (A) and the spare Lucar connection (B) (Sec 15)

Do not connect A and B together

Lucas 25 ACR alternator

1 On later models the wiring connections to the 25 ACR alternator differ in that they are attached by stud and nut fixings instead of the moulded multi-connector previously used.

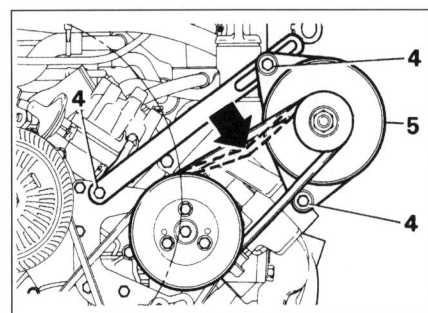

Fig. 13.158 Alternator drivebelt adjustment - later models (Sec 15)

4 *Adjustment and mounting bolts*
5 *Alternator*
Arrow indicates tension checking point

2 Whilst the later type alternator is directly replaceable with the earlier type, the wiring connections will have to be changed to suit.

Alternator wiring harness

3 The alternator wiring harness has a spare brown lead taped to the cable assembly. This lead is for use with a split charge system or battery-sensed alternator system only. Care must be taken never to allow this lead to be attached to the spare Lucar connection on current machine-sensed alternators.

Alternator drivebelt - adjustment

4 On later models equipped with power-assisted steering and air conditioning, the alternator is driven by a short belt directly off the power steering pump pulley. This, in turn, is belt driven from the crankshaft pulley.
5 Removal, refitting and adjustment procedures are essentially the same as described in Chapter 10, Section 78, but if the drivebelt is to be removed, the water pump drivebelt and power steering pump drivebelt

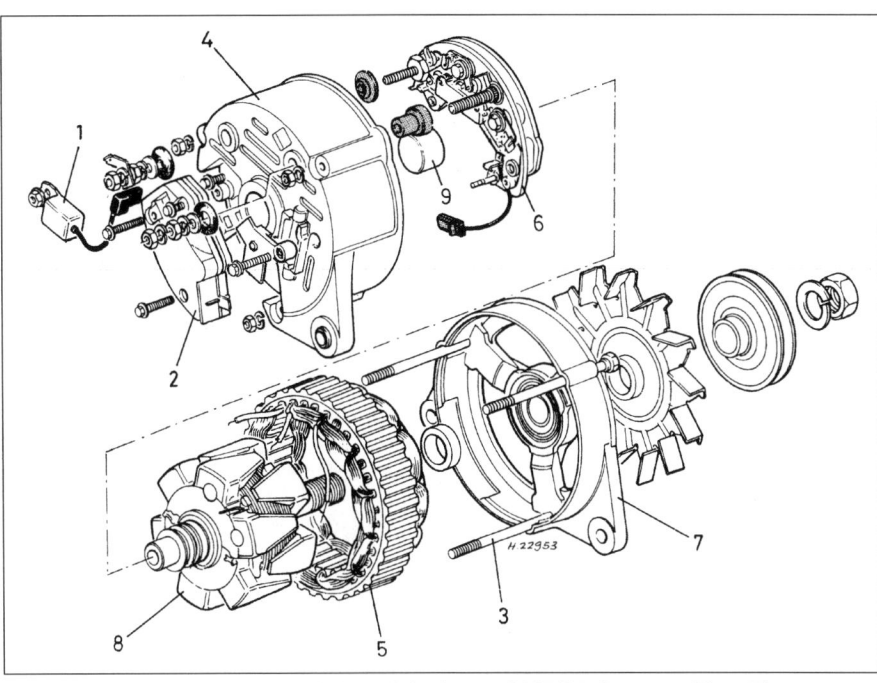

Fig. 13.159 Exploded view of the Lucas A127/65 alternator (Sec 15)

1 Suppression capacitors
2 Regulator/brushbox assembly
3 Bolts
4 Slip ring end bracket
5 Stator
6 Rectifier
7 Drive end bracket/bearing assembly
8 Rotor
9 Slip ring end bearing

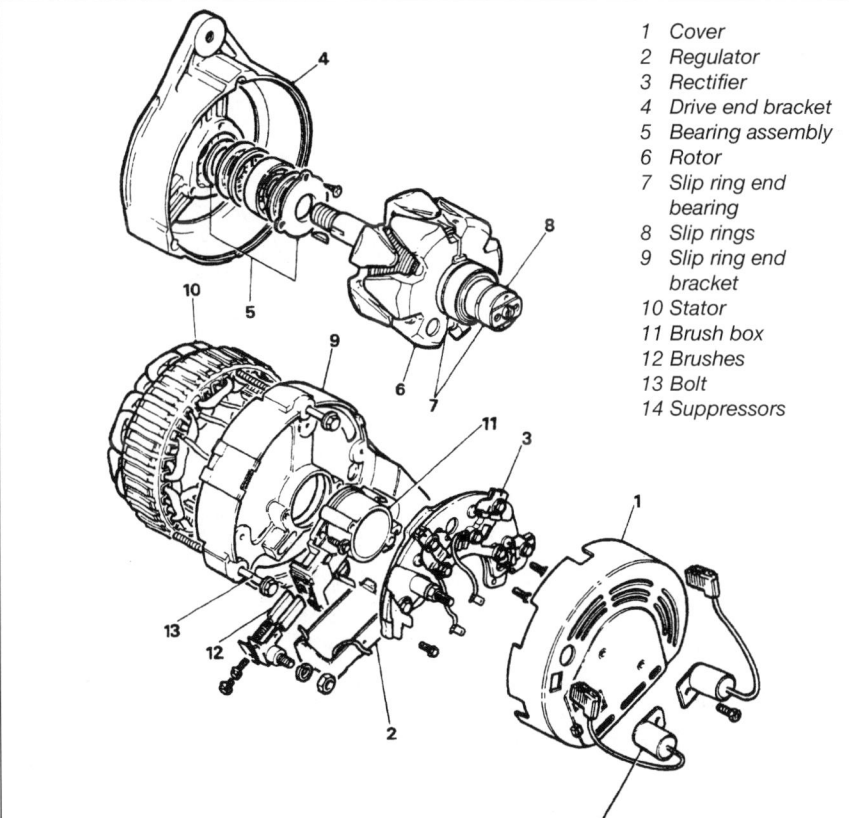

1 Cover
2 Regulator
3 Rectifier
4 Drive end bracket
5 Bearing assembly
6 Rotor
7 Slip ring end bearing
8 Slip rings
9 Slip ring end bracket
10 Stator
11 Brush box
12 Brushes
13 Bolt
14 Suppressors

Fig. 13.160 Exploded view of the Lucas A133/80 alternator (Sec 15)

will have to be removed first. These operations are described elsewhere in this Chapter.

Lucas A127/65 alternator (1987-on models) - removal, refitting and brush renewal

6 The removal and refitting procedure is the same as that described in Chapter 10.

7 To remove the combined brush and regulator unit, unscrew the screws and disconnect the lead, then withdraw the unit from the rear of the alternator.

8 Measure the length of the brushes from the moulding. if they are less than the minimum amount given in the Specifications, renew the unit.

9 Clean the brush holder and check that the brushes move freely against the tension of the springs. Also clean the alternator slip rings with a fuelmoistened cloth or, if they are very dirty, with fine emery cloth.

10 Refit the brush and regulator unit to the alternator and tighten the screws. Take care not to damage the brushes as the unit is located in position. Reconnect the lead.

Lucas A 133/80 alternator (1988-on models) - removal, refitting and brush renewal

11 The removal and refitting procedure is the same as that described in Chapter 10, but the drivebelt tension is as given in the Specifications.

12 Brush renewal is similar to that described in Chapter 10, but refer to the exploded diagram in Fig. 13.160.

Alternator heat shield (1990-on models) - removal and refitting

13 Disconnect the battery negative lead.

14 Unscrew the mounting screw securing the heat shield to the rocker cover.

15 Unscrew the nut and remove the heat shield from the rear of the alternator.

16 Refitting is a reversal of the removal procedure.

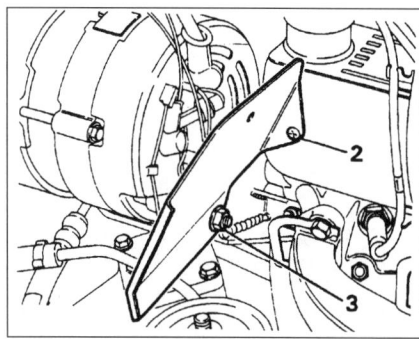

Fig. 13.161 Alternator heat shield fitted to 1990-on models (Sec 15)

2 Mounting screw   3 Mounting nut

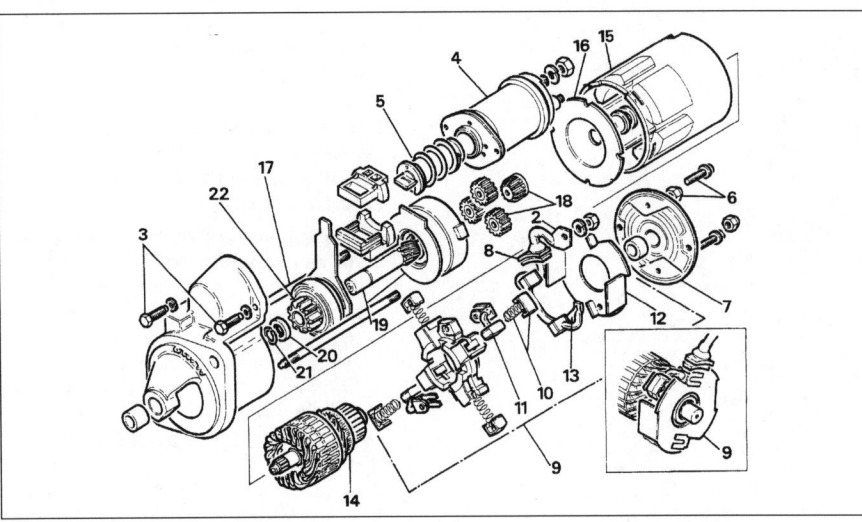

Fig. 13.162 Exploded view of the M78R starter motor (Sec 15)

2   Solenoid to motor cable
3   Solenoid mounting bolts
4   Solenoid
5   Solenoid plunger
6   Bolts and nuts
7   Commutator end bracket
8   Rubber grommet
9   Brushbox assembly

10 Brush springs
11 Earth brushes
12 Insulating plate
13 Bus bar and brushes
14 Armature
15 Yoke
16 Intermediate bracket

17 Through bolts
18 Sun and planet gears
19 Drive shaft sprocket
    assembly
20 Thrust collar
21 Jump ring
22 Drive assembly

Lucas M78R starter motor - overhaul

17 Disconnect the braid between the starter motor and the solenoid terminal.
18 Unscrew the solenoid mounting screws and withdraw the solenoid.

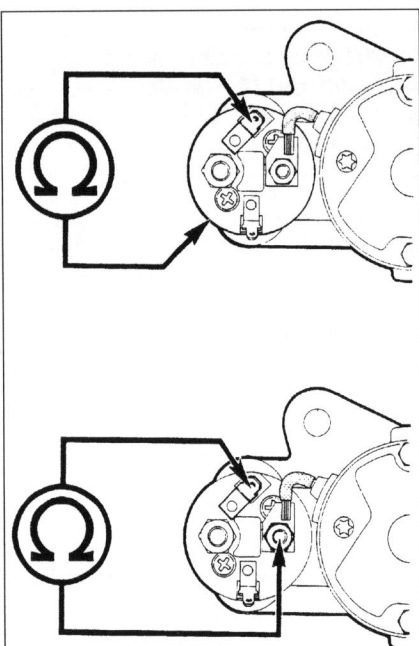

Fig. 13.163 Checking the resistance of the solenoid windings on the M78R starter motor (Sec 15)

19 Lift up and remove the solenoid plunger.
20 Unscrew the nuts and screws, and remove the commutator end bracket.
21 Prise the grommet from the yoke.
22 Remove the brushbox from the armature then remove the brush springs.
23 Release the earth brushes from the clips.
24 Remove the insulating plate, then withdraw the brushes and bus bar.
25 Remove the armature followed by the yoke and intermediate bracket.
26 Unscrew and remove the through bolts from the drive end bracket.
27 Remove the sun and planet gears, and push the driveshaft sprocket assembly from the drive end bracket.
28 Drive the thrust collar over the jump ring, then prise the jump ring from its locating groove.
29 Withdraw the drive assembly from the driveshaft.
30 To test the solenoid windings, connect an ohmmeter between the solenoid trigger

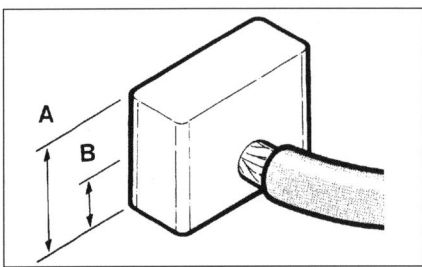

Fig. 13.164 Length of brushes on the M78R starter motor (Sec 15)

A 9 mm (new)   B 3.5 mm (minimum)

terminal and earth. The resistance should be 1.074 ± 0.035 ohms. Now connect the ohmmeter between the terminal and the motor input terminal. The resistance should now be 0.298 ± 0.015 ohms. Renew the solenoid if the readings are incorrect.
31 Connect the ohmmeter between the motor input terminal and the battery connection terminal. With the solenoid removed the resistance should be infinity, but with the solenoid plunger operated by hand the resistance should be zero.
32 Check the plunger return spring at the same time.
33 Check that the brush springs are in good condition and that the brushes move freely in their holders. Clean away any carbon dust from the brushes with a fuel dampened cloth. Check that the minimum length of the brushes is 3.5 mm (0.138 in), and renew them if it is less than this.
34 Ideally the armature insulation should be checked using a 110 volt supply and test bulb between each segment and the central shaft. Using an ohmmeter in the same manner will check if there are any short-circuits to earth.
35 Clean the armature surface using fine emery cloth. If necessary the armature maybe machined to a minimum diameter of 28.8 mm (1.13 in), but otherwise the armature should be renewed. Do not undercut the armature segments.
36 Check that the one-way clutch only allows the pinion to rotate in one direction.
37 Check the bearings and bushes for excessive wear and damage. New bushes may be fitted if necessary but they should be soaked in engine oil for 30 minutes before fitting.
38 Refitting is a reversal of the removal procedure but lubricate all moving parts as they are assembled.

Headlamp unit (1987-on models) - removal and refitting

39 Disconnect the battery negative lead.

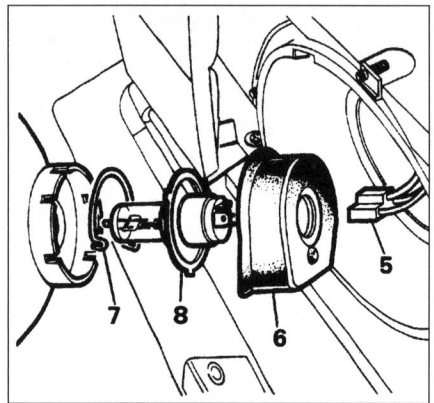

Fig. 13.165 Headlamp bulb components on 1988-on models (Sec 15)

5   Wiring plug
6   Rubber dust cover
7   Spring clip
8   Bulb

15.41A Unscrew the screws . . .

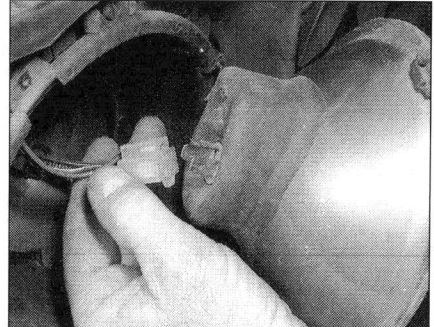

15.41B . . . and remove the headlamp retaining ring

15.42 Disconnecting the wiring from the back of the headlamp

40 Remove the radiator grille as described in Section 17.
41 Support the headlamp unit, then unscrew the screws and remove the retaining ring (photos). Do not unscrew the headlamp beam adjusting screws.
42 Withdraw the headlamp sealed beam unit and disconnect the wiring plug from the rear (photo).
43 Unscrew the screws then prise away the grommet and remove the headlamp bowl.
44 Refitting is a reversal of the removal procedure but have the beam alignment adjusted as soon as possible.

Headlamp bulb (1988-on models) - renewal

45 The sealed beam headlamp is now replaced by a conventional headlamp incorporating a normal bulb. First disconnect the battery negative lead.
46 Remove the radiator grille as described in Chapter 12.
47 Support the headlamp, then unscrew the three screws and remove the retaining ring. Do not disturb the beam adjustment screws.
48 Withdraw the headlamp unit and disconnect the wiring from the bulb terminals.
49 Pull off the rubber dust cover, then release the spring clip and remove the bulb (photos).
50 If necessary, unscrew the screws and withdraw the headlamp bowl.
51 Refitting is a reversal of the removal procedure

Front side and flasher lamp (1987-on models) - removal and refitting

52 Disconnect the battery negative lead.
53 Unscrew and remove the two screws and washers from the top of the lamp unit, then lift the lens assembly to gain access to the rear of the lamp (photos).
54 Remove the waterproof cover then depress the clips and withdraw the bulb holder (photo).
55 To remove a bulb, depress and twist it. The direction indicator bulb is located at the top and the side lamp bulb is at the bottom.
56 To remove the complete assembly, disconnect the multi-plug (photo).

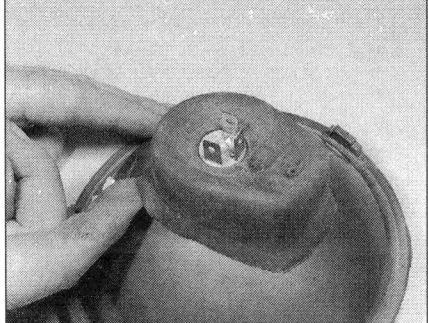

15.49A Pull off the rubber dust cover . . .

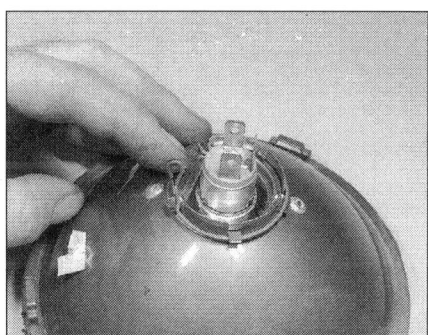

15.49B . . . release the spring clip . . .

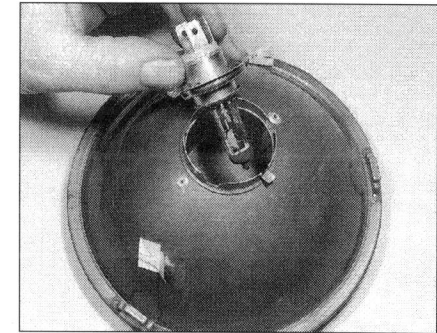

15.49C . . . and remove the bulb

15.53A Unscrew the upper screws . . .

15.53B . . . and lift the lens assembly from the lower mounting pegs

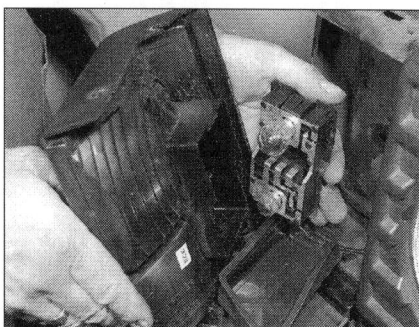

15.54 Withdrawing the front side and flasher lamp bulbholder

15.56 Front side and flasher lamp wiring connector

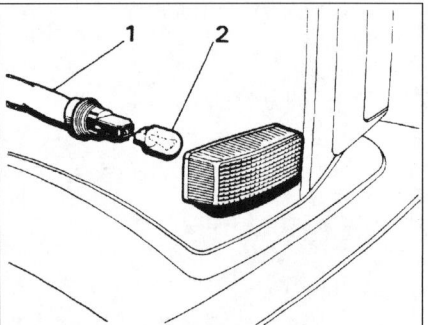

Fig. 13.166 Side repeater lamp fitted from 1987 onwards (Sec 15)

1 Bulbholder and wiring harness   2 Bulb

15.58 Removing the side repeater lamp bulbholder

57 Refitting is a reversal of the removal procedure.

Side repeater lamp bulb (1987-on models) - renewal

58 Reach up through the wheelarch to the rear of the side repeater lamp. Twist the bulbholder anti-clockwise to release it from the lamp (photo).
59 Pull the wedge type bulb from the bulbholder.
60 Fit the new bulb using a reversal of the removal procedure.

Differential lock warning lamp bulb (1987-on models) - renewal

61 Using a screwdriver prise the warning lamp out of the radio console.
62 Disconnect the wiring and withdraw the lamp.
63 Depress the sides and slide the lens back off the body.
64 Remove the amber lens, then depress and twist the bulb to remove it.
65 Refitting is a reversal of the removal procedure.

Number plate lamp (later models) - general

66 Although different in design to early models, the rear number plate lamp unit and its bulb can be removed and refitted in the same manner as that of the earlier type (photo).

Fuses

67 On later models the main fusebox is accessible from within the vehicle, being located next to the heater/ventilation control panel on the lower facia.
68 Prise free and unclip the cover for access to the fuses.
69 It will be noted that the cover inner face retains spare 10 amp and 20 amp fuses and also has a label for fuse identification and value for the various circuits. Whenever a spare fuse is used it should be replaced with an 'Autofuse' of the correct value (photo).
70 To remove the fusebox unit, disconnect the battery earth lead then undo the two retaining screws and release the fuse holder unit from the facia (photo). The wiring to the rear of the fuse holder can then be inspected and detached as required.

Relays (pre-1988 models) - general

71 On later models, further circuit relays have been added and these are located under the

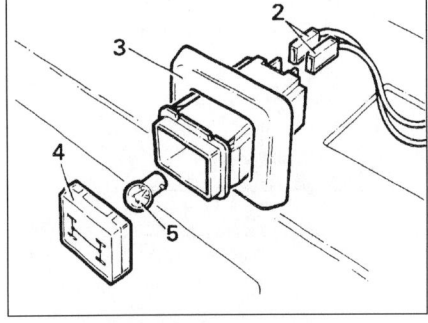

Fig. 13.167 Differential lock warning lamp (Sec 15)

2 Wiring connectors   4 Amber lens
3 Lamp body   5 Bulb

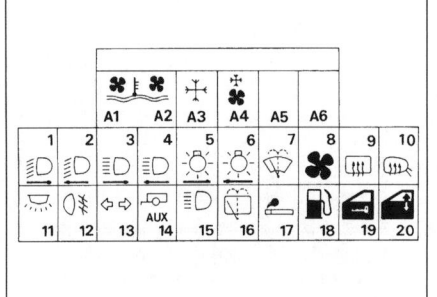

Fig. 13.168 Fuse circuits identification label (Sec 15)

Refer to Specifications for circuits protected and fuse ratings

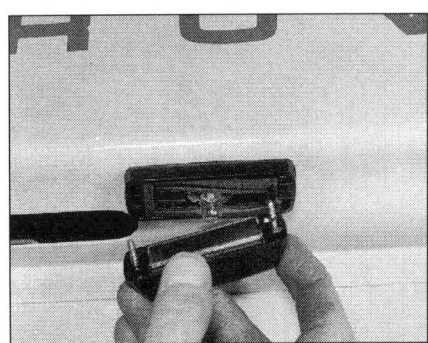

15.66 Number plate lamp lens and cover removal

15.69 Fusebox cover showing fuse identification, spare fuses and fuse removal tool - later models

15.70 Removing a fusebox retaining screw

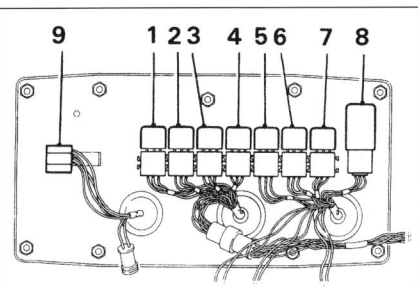

Fig. 13.169 Relay locations on engine compartment closure panel (Sec 15)

1   *Air conditioning fan relay*
2   *Air conditioning relay*
3   *Compressor clutch relay*
4   *Fan relay*
5   *Starter solenoid relay*
6   *Heater rear window relay*
7   *Brake failure warning check relay*
8   *Headlamp wash timer unit*
9   *Ignition pick-up point*

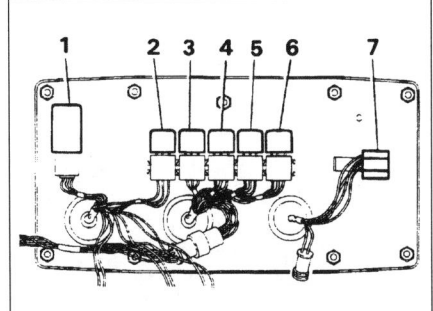

Fig. 13.171 Relay locations viewed from the engine compartment (1988-on models) (Sec 15)

1   *Headlamp wash timer unit*
2   *Heated rear window*
3   *Starter solenoid relay*
4   *Compressor clutch*
5   *Condenser fan*
6   *Air conditioning/heater*
7   *Stowage position*

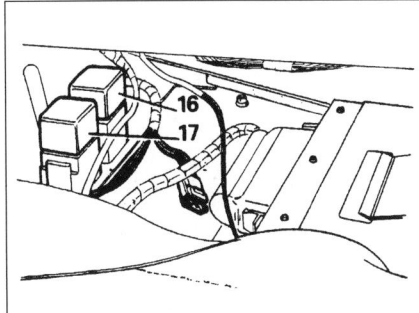

Fig. 13.173 Relays mounted beneath the right-hand front seat (1988-on models) (Sec 15)

16 *Main EFI relay*
17 *Fuel pump relay*

15.71 Relay panel unit location under facia - later models (pre-1990)

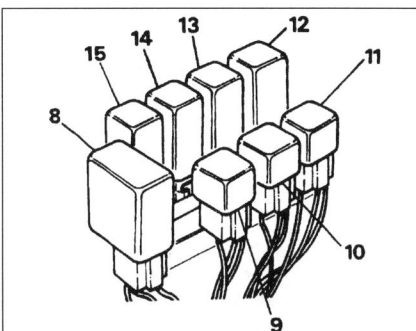

Fig. 13.172 Steering column-mounted relays (1988-on models) (Sec 15)

8   *Rear wiper relay*
9   *Ignition load relay*
10 *Window lift relay*
11 *Auxiliary lamp relay*
12 *Front wiper relay*
13 *Voltage-sensitive switch*
14 *Interior lamp delay*
15 *Flasher/hazard unit*

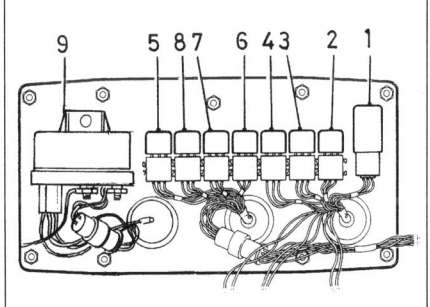

Fig. 13.174 Relay locations viewed from the engine compartment (1989-on models) (Sec 15)

1   *Headlamp wash timer unit*
2   *Heated rear window relay*
3   *Starter solenoid relay*
4   *Brake check relay*
5   *Fresh air solenoid relay*
6   *Compressor clutch relay*
7   *Condenser fan relay*
8   *Air conditioning/heater*
9   *Glow plug timer unit*

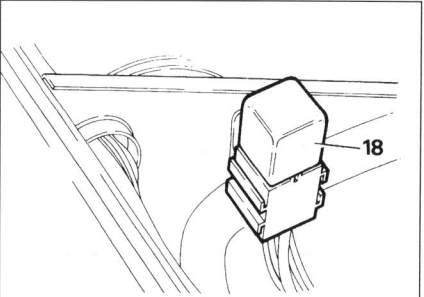

Fig. 13.170 Fuel cut-off relay (18) located in the engine compartment - carburettor models (Sec 15)

lower facia panel on the driver's side (photo), or in the engine compartment attached to the closure panel (Fig. 13.169).

72 Access to the relays is gained after removing the lower facia panel or closure panel. The relays are a push-fit in their holders.

Relays (1988-on models) - general

73 The relay locations are shown in Figs. 13.169 and 13.173 inclusive.

Relays (1989-on models and March 1988-on Vogue models) - general

74 The relay locations are shown in Figs. 13.174 to 13.179 inclusive. The seat adjustment relay is located beneath the left-hand front seat next to the fusebox. The main EFI (black terminal block) and fuel pump (blue terminal block) relays are mounted beneath the right-hand front seat. The sunroof relay is located on the side of the steering column

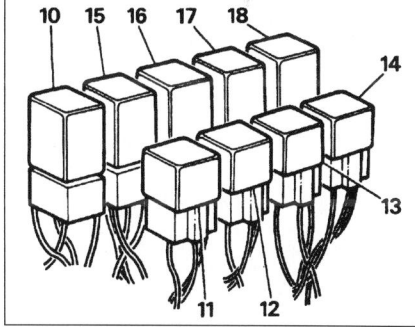

Fig. 13.175 Steering column relays (1989-on models) (Sec 15)

10 *Rear wiper delay*
11 *Auxiliary lamp relay (where fitted)*
12 *Ignition load relay*
13 *Headlamp relay*
14 *Heater/air conditioning relay*
15 *Interior lamp delay*
16 *Flasher/hazard unit*
17 *Voltage-sensitive switch (air conditioning)*
18 *Front wiper delay*

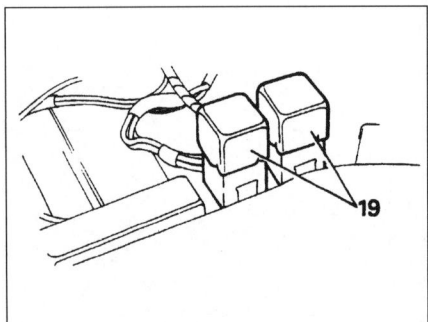

Fig. 13.176 Seat adjustment relay (19) located beneath the left-hand front seat (1989-on models) (Sec 15)

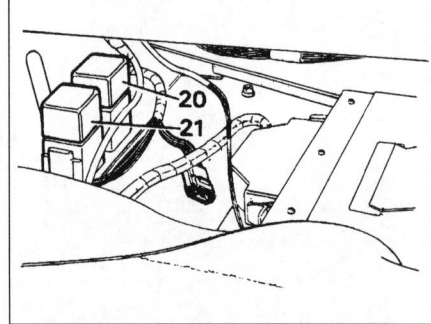

Fig. 13.177 Relays located beneath the right-hand front seat (1989-on models) (Sec 15)

20 Main EFI relay   21 Fuel pump relay

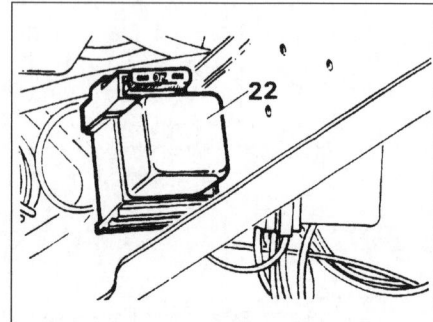

Fig. 13.178 Electric sunroof relay (22) located on the steering column support bracket (1989-on models) (Sec 15)

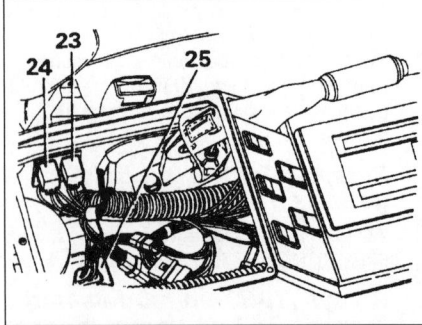

Fig. 13.179 Relays located behind the glovebox (1989-on models) (Sec 15)

23 Electric window relay (blue terminal)
24 Electric window relay (black terminal)
25 Window lift one touch control unit

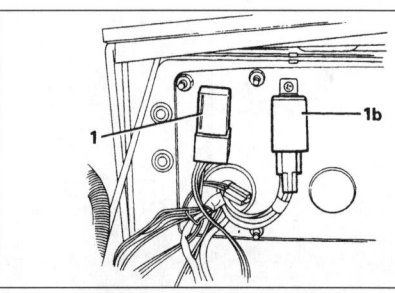

Fig. 13.180 Relays located on the bulkhead (1990-on models) (Sec 15)

1 Headlamp wash timer unit
1b Glow plug timer unit (Diesel models)

15.75A Relays located behind the left-hand footwell trim panel

15.75B Relays located behind the right-hand footwell trim panel

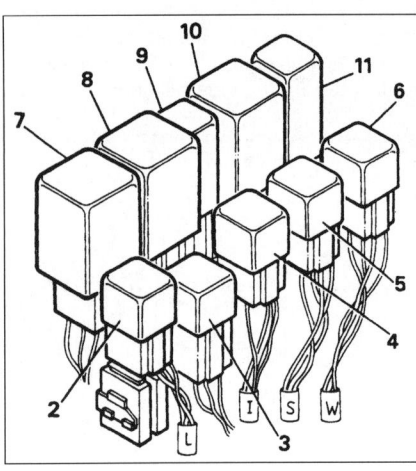

Fig. 13.181 Relays located on the steering column (1990-on models) (Sec 15)

2 Headlamp relay
3 Heated front screen relay
4 Ignition load relay
5 Starter solenoid relay
6 Heated rear window relay
7 Rear wiper delay
8 Interior lamp delay/timer
9 Heated front screen timer unit
10 Voltage-sensitive switch
11 Front wiper delay

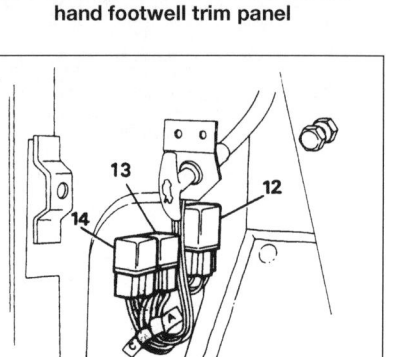

Fig. 13.182 Left-hand footwell mounted relays (1990-on models) (Sec 15)

12 Flasher/hazard unit
13 Auxiliary lamp relay
14 Sunroof auxiliary relay
Left-hand-drive model shown

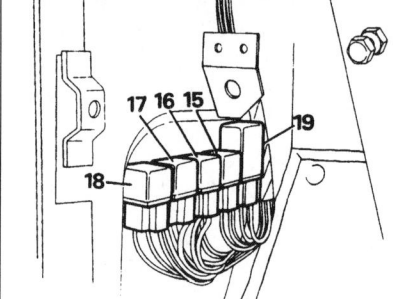

Fig. 13.183 Right-hand footwell mounted relays (1990-on models) (Sec 15)

15 Air conditioning/heater relay
16 Compressor clutch relay
17 Heater/air conditioning load relay
18 Condenser fan relay
19 Air conditioning diode pack

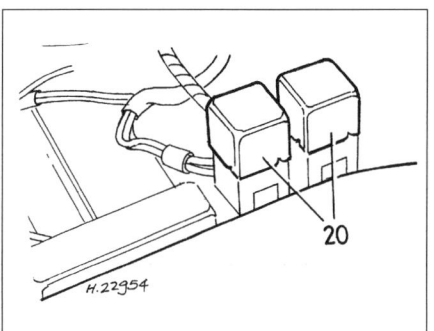

Fig. 13.184 Seat adjustment relays (20)
(1990-on models) (Sec 15)

support bracket behind the lower facia panel.
The electric window relays are located behind
the glovebox liner.

Relays (1990-on models) - general

75 The relay positions are shown in Figs.
13.180 and 13.187 inclusive (photos).

Column-mounted switches - later models

76 Whilst the individual functions and
removal procedures of the column-mounted
stalk switches are similar to the earlier
models, their positions have been changed
and are as follows:

(a) **Main lighting switch:** *This is located on
the left-hand side of the steering column
and is the front stalk switch*

(b) **Combination dipswitch, direction
indicator horn and flasher switch:** *This
is located on the left-hand side of the
steering column and is the rear stalk
switch*

(c) **Rear screen wiper/washer switch:** *This
is located on the right-hand side of the
steering column and is the front stalk
switch*

(d) **Windscreen wiper/washer switch:** *This
is located on the right-hand side of the
steering column and is the rear stalk
switch*

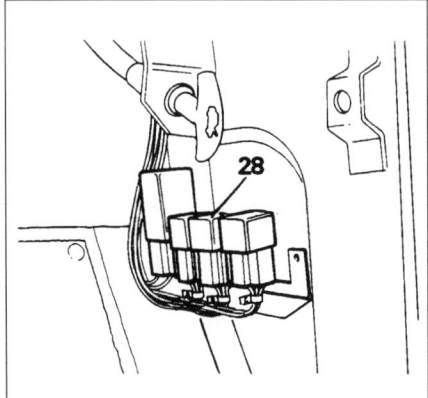

Fig. 13.187 Brake check relay (28) (1990-
on models) (Sec 15)

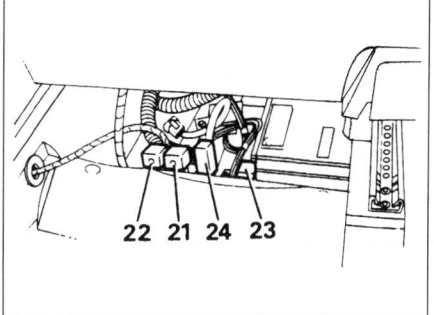

Fig. 13.185 Relays mounted beneath the
right-hand front seat (1990-on models)
(Sec 15)

21 Main EFI relay
22 Fuel pump relay
23 Cruise control relay
24 Condenser fan timer unit

(e) **The rear foglamp switch:** *This is located
on the auxiliary switch panel*

(f) **The rear screen wiper/washer switch:**
*This is connected to the mounting bracket
attached to the lower shroud by retaining
bolts. Undo the bolts to remove the
switch from the mounting bracket (photo)*

77 On 1987 models, an entirely new design
of column-mounted switch is used, and the
removal and refitting procedures are as
follows.

78 Disconnect the battery negative terminal.

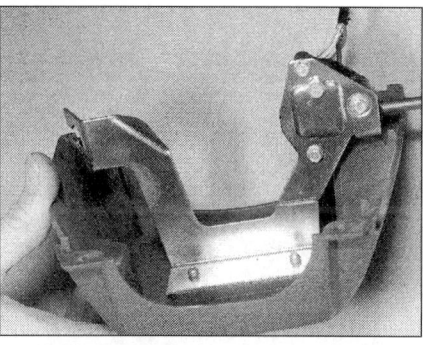

15.76 Steering column lower shroud
showing rear screen wiper/washer switch
attachment, and main lighting switch
bracket on left

15.80B Separating the two column shroud
halves

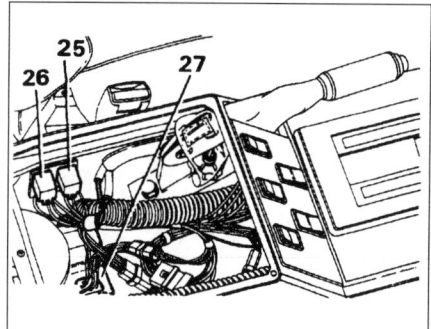

Fig. 13.186 Relays mounted beneath the
glovebox (1990-on models) (Sec 15)

25 Rear window lift relay
26 Front window lift relay
27 Window lift one-touch unit

79 Remove the steering wheel as described
in the next Section.

80 Undo the screws securing the two
steering column shrouds to the column and
remove both shrouds (photos).

81 Disconnect the wiring multi-plug at the
rear of the switch by depressing the two
catches and pulling (photo).

82 Depress the two tags at the top and
bottom of the switch then pull the switch out
of the steering column boss (photos).

83 To remove the steering column boss from
the column, carefully lift up the retaining clips

15.80A Column shroud retaining screw
locations (arrowed)

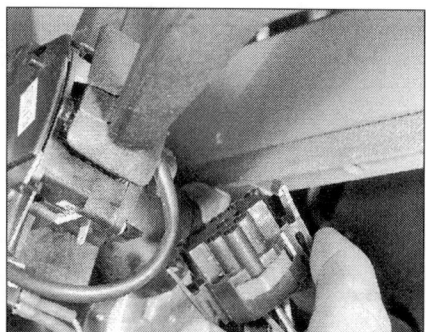

15.81 Disconnecting column switch wiring
multi-plug

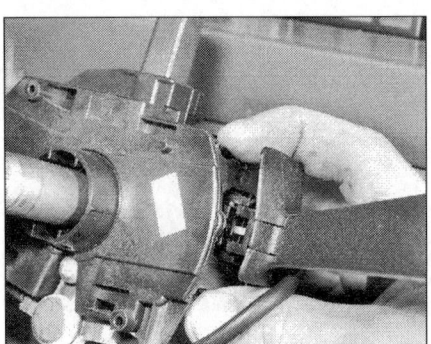

15.82A Depress the tags at the top and bottom . . .

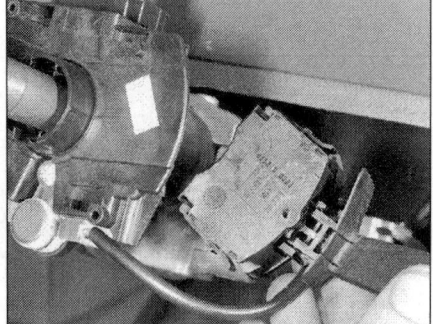

15.82B . . . to release the switch from the column boss

15.83 Fibre-optic guide attachment at bulb housing (arrowed)

and slip the fibre optic guides out of the bulb housing (photo).

84 Slacken the clamping screw and withdraw the boss from the steering column.

85 To remove the rear screen wiper/washer switch from the right-hand column shroud, carefully prise the switch from its location and disconnect the wiring connectors (photo).

86 Refitting the steering column boss and the column switches is the reversal of removal.

Auxiliary switch panel (later models) - removal and refitting

87 The auxiliary switch panel can be prised free from the lower facia and partially withdrawn to allow the switches or their warning bulbs (where applicable) to be removed.

88 With the panel withdrawn from the facia, unclip and release the switch lead connector, pull free the switch symbol fibre optic leads (at the top), and, where applicable, withdraw the warning lamp bulb holder. The switch can then be unclipped and removed from the panel.

89 Refit in reverse order and check the switch concerned for satisfactory operation.

Centre console switches - removal and refitting

90 On models equipped with electrically-operated windows the control switches are arranged on a panel at the rear of the centre console.

91 The switches can be removed by carefully prising them from their location and disconnecting the wiring multi-plug (photo).

92 On later models auxiliary switches are situated in a group at the front of the centre console and these are also removed as just described (photo).

93 All switches are refitted using the reverse sequence to removal.

Choke cable warning lamp switch - removal and refitting

94 The choke cable warning lamp switch is located on the underside of the choke cable knob attachment to the facia panel. For access, undo the retaining screws and withdraw the lower facia panel on the right-hand side (photo).

95 Disconnect the wiring connections from the switch (photo), then loosen the locknut and unscrew the switch retaining strap bolt. Remove the switch.

96 Refit in the reverse order of removal and check operation before refitting the lower facia panel.

Exterior mirror control switch (1987-on models) - removal and refitting

97 Disconnect the battery negative lead.

98 Using a screwdriver prise the four air vents out of the facia, then unscrew the screws and withdraw the facia sufficient to gain access to the rear of the switches.

99 Disconnect the wiring plug from the rear of the mirror control switch.

100 Using a small screwdriver, prise the rocker button from the outside of the switch.

15.85 Rear screen wiper/washer switch removal

15.91 Centre console switch removal

15.92 Auxiliary switch removal

15.94 Remove the lower facia panel on the right-hand side . . .

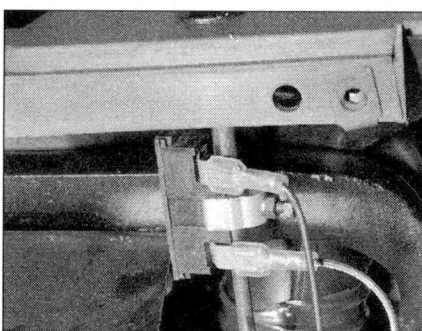

15.95 . . . for access to the choke control and warning lamp unit

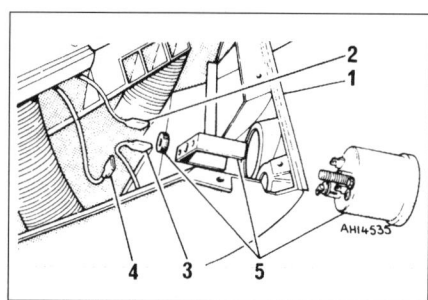

Fig. 13.188 Exterior mirror control switch (1987-on models) (Sec 15)

6 *Multi-plug*
7 *Button*
8 *Retaining collar*
9 *Switch*
10 *Multi-plug*
11 *Switch housing*

101 Unscrew the plastic collar and remove the switch from the rear of the facia.
102 Disconnect the multi-plug at the rear of the selector switch.
103 Press the rear of the switch housing and remove it from the facia.
104 Refitting is a reversal of the removal procedure.

Clock (early models) - removal and refitting

105 Disconnect the battery earth lead.
106 Undo the heater control knob grub screws and pull the knobs free.
107 Undo the two heater escutcheon plate retaining screws and then withdraw the plate.
108 Unscrew and remove the heater console-

to-facia panel retaining screws (four at the top edge).
109 Remove the central louvre.
110 Open the glovebox lid on the passenger side then remove the heater console bottom retaining screw.
111 The console can now be eased away to allow access to the clock. Detach the connecting wires, noting respective connections. Unscrew the knurled retaining nut and remove the clock retaining bracket. Withdraw the clock.
112 The bulb and holder can be pulled from the clock and the bulb extracted for renewal.
113 Refit in the reverse order of removal and reset the clock.

Clock (later models) - removal and refitting

114 Disconnect the battery earth lead.
115 The clock is secured in its aperture in the facia by spring clips, and it may be possible to carefully prise it free from its aperture. Failing this, remove the face level vent on one or both sides of the clock and, reaching through the vent aperture, push the clock out of the facia from the rear (photo).
116 Disconnect the wiring and pull free the bulb holder to remove the clock completely.
117 Refit in the reverse order of removal, then reset the clock.

Instrument panel (later models) - removal and refitting

118 The removal and refitting of the instrument panel unit and its associated

Fig. 13.189 Clock removal - early models (Sec 15)

1 *Console*
2 *Feed (+) wire*
3 *Earth (–) wire*
4 *Clock illumination wire*
5 *Nut and bracket*

fittings on later models is similar to that for early models, but the layout differs slightly (photo).

Instrument panel (1990-on models) - removal and refitting

119 An electronic speedometer is fitted to the instrument panel, so the previous requirement to disconnect the speedometer cable no longer applies.
120 Disconnect the battery negative lead.
121 Remove the lower facia panel by first removing the side vent and surround for access to the facia screws. With the lower facia panel removed, unscrew and remove the instrument panel lower mounting nuts together with spring and plain washers (photos).

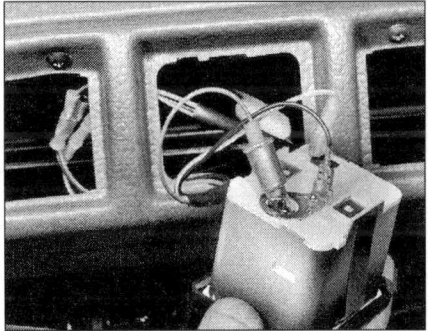

15.115 Clock removal - later models

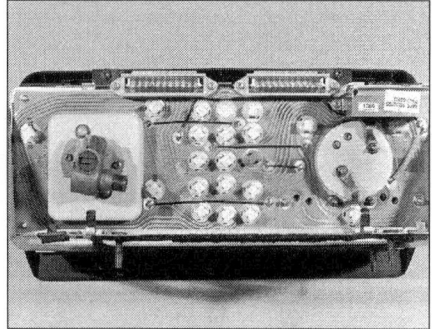

15.118 Instrument panel rear face layout - later models

15.121A Remove the side vent . . .

15.121B . . . then remove the surround screws and surround . . .

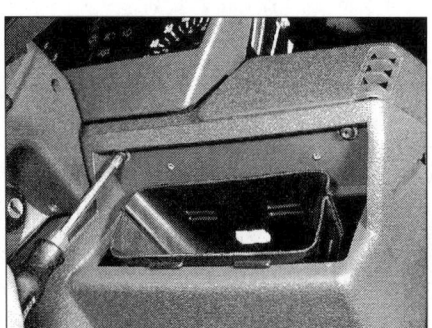

15.121C . . . for access to the lower facia mounting screws

15.121D Instrument panel lower mounting nut

15.122 Disconnecting the multi-plugs from the rear of the instrument panel

122 Unclip the cowl from the rear, then disconnect the multi-plugs and the single plug from the printed circuit connectors (photo).
123 Withdraw the instrument panel from the facia.
124 Refitting is a reversal of the removal procedure.

Instruments (1990-on models) - removal and refitting

125 With the instrument panel removed, unscrew the mounting screws and remove the mounting bracket (photo).
126 Unscrew the two upper screws and remove the bezel from the front of the instrument panel.
127 Remove the curved lens by depressing the tabs and easing the top of the lens followed by the bottom edge.
128 Release the upper and lower tabs and remove the instrument case.

Tachometer, fuel and temperature gauges

129 Remove the two illumination bulb holders, then unscrew the three large screws. Note the position of the black and white leads on the screws.
130 Remove the unit from the front of the instrument panel.

Speedometer

131 Remove the two illumination bulb holders, then unscrew the three large screws

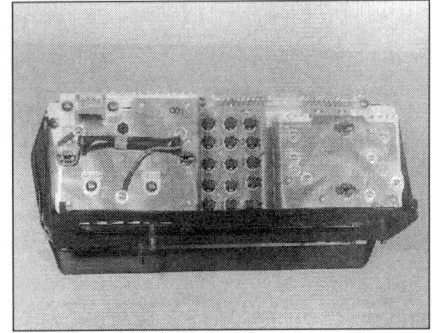

15.125 Rear view of the instrument panel

1 Tachometer, fuel and temperature gauges
2 Ignition warning bulb and holder
3 Illumination bulb and holder
4 Warning lamp bulb and holder
5 Printed circuit input tags
6 Printed circuit
7 Warning lamp panel
8 Instrument case
9 Curved lens
10 Housing
11 Speedometer

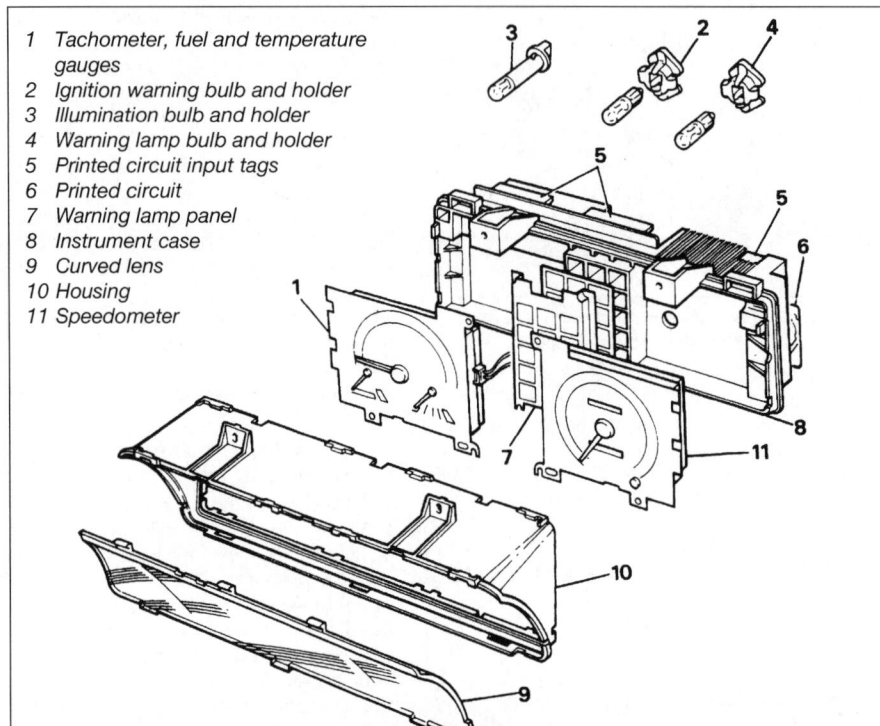

Fig. 13.190 Instrument panel components (1990-on models) (Sec 15)

and withdraw the speedometer from the front of the instrument panel.

Printed circuit

132 Remove the tachometer and speedometer as previously described.
133 Note the position of the warning light bulbs and remove them from the printed circuit.

134 Unscrew the screws and remove the wiring connectors to release the printed circuit tags and the input plug.

135 Unscrew the screws and remove the printed circuit taking care to release it from the locating pegs.

136 Refitting is a reversal of the removal procedure.

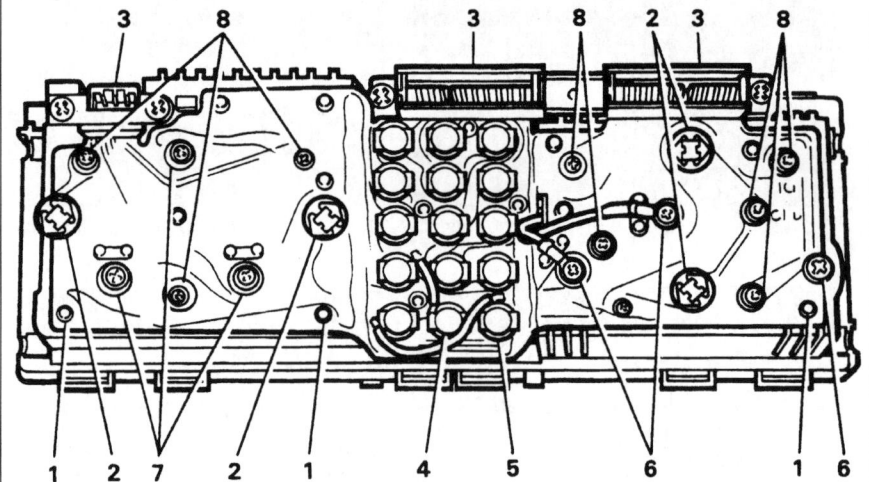

Fig. 13.191 Rear view of instrument panel (1990-on models) (Sec 15)

1 Printed circuit location pegs
2 Illumination bulbs
3 Wiring harness connectors
4 Warning lamp bulbs
5 No-charge warning lamp bulb
6 Tachometer/fuel/ temperature gauge securing screws
7 Speedometer securing screws
8 Printed circuit securing screws

15.139 Removing the tailgate wiper arm

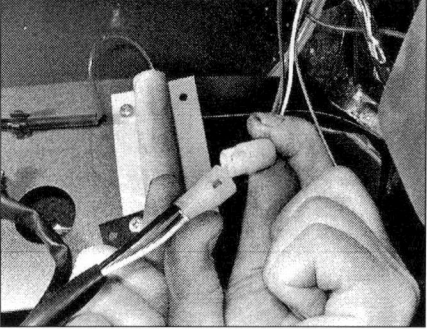

15.145A Disconnecting the tailgate wiper motor multi-plug

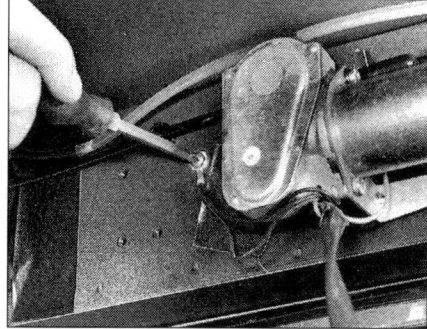

15.145B Removing the earth wire screw

Tailgate wiper arm (1987-on models) - removal and refitting

137 If necessary operate the wipers until they stop at their rest position.

138 Pull up the end cap from the base of the wiper arm for access to the wiper arm spindle.

139 Note the position of the wiper arm on the spindle, then unscrew the nut and withdraw the arm from the spindle (photo).

140 Refitting is a reversal of the removal procedure but make sure that the wiper blade is located at its rest position just clear of the windscreen surround.

Tailgate wiper motor (1987-on models) - removal and refitting

141 Disconnect the battery negative lead.

142 Remove the headlining rear section for access to the tailgate wiper motor assembly.

143 Remove the wiper arm and blade as described previously in this Section.

144 Loosen only the nut securing the wiper motor to the body. Do not remove it at this stage.

145 Disconnect the wiring at the multi-plug, and unscrew the earth wire screw (photos).

146 Unscrew and remove the two mounting screws (photo).

147 Support the wiper motor, then completely unscrew the nut and remove the cover from the spindle. Remove the washer and seal (photos).

148 Withdraw the wiper motor from the body (photo).

149 Refitting is a reversal of the removal procedure but make sure that the spacer is fitted correctly.

Heated windscreen washer jets and thermostat (1989-on models) - removal and refitting

150 The windscreen washer jets are heated electrically when the temperature drops to 4°C or less, and the heating is switched off when the temperature rises to 10°C or higher. A thermostat is located by the side of the right-hand headlight.

15.146 Unscrewing the tailgate wiper motor mounting screws

15.147A Remove the cover . . .

15.147B . . . followed by the nut . . .

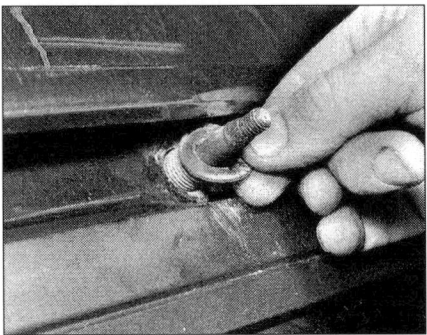

15.147C . . . washer and seal

15.148 Removing the tailgate wiper motor

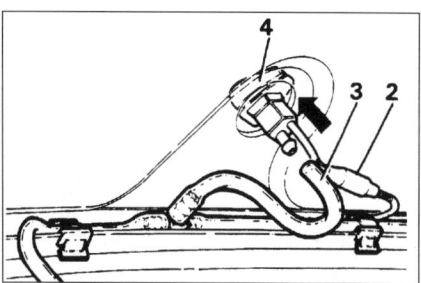

Fig. 13.192 Heated windscreen washer jet removal (1989-on models) (Sec 15)

2 Wiring connector   4 Jet assembly
3 Washer tube

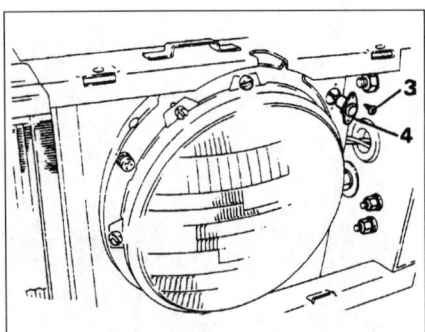

Fig. 13.193 Thermostat for the heated windscreen washer jet (1989-on models) (Sec 15)

3 Screw   4 Thermostat

151 To remove a jet, first disconnect the battery negative lead, then disconnect the wiring plug near the jet. Disconnect the washer tube and push up the jet from its mounting. If necessary, remove the washer jet mounting from the bonnet.

152 To remove the thermostat, disconnect the battery negative lead, then remove the radiator grille. Unscrew the screws and withdraw the thermostat from the right-hand headlight mounting panel, then disconnect the wiring.

153 Refitting of both the jet and thermostat are a reversal of the removal procedure.

Dim-dip headlamps control unit (1987-on models) - removal and refitting

154 As from 1st October 1986 a dim-dip headlamp control unit is fitted in order to prevent the vehicle being driven with only the side-lamps being switched on. The control unit supplies a low voltage to the dipped headlamps when the sidelamps are switched on with the ignition also switched on. When the headlamps are switched on, full voltage is supplied to the headlamps.

155 Disconnect the battery negative lead.

156 Remove the lower facia panel.

157 Unscrew the mounting screws and recover the spacer, then disconnect the wiring and withdraw the control unit.

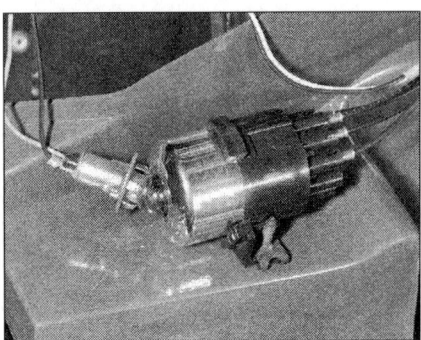

15.161 Bulb and holder removal from the fibre-optic unit

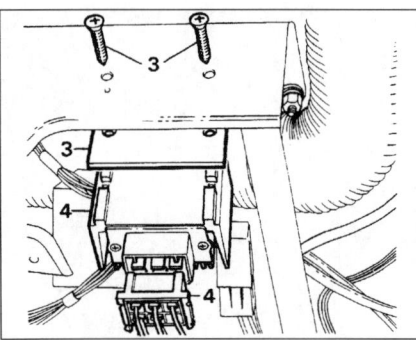

Fig. 13.194 Dim-dip headlamp control unit (1987-on models) (Sec 15)

3 Mounting screws and spacer
4 Electronic control unit

158 Refitting is a reversal of the removal procedure.

Fibre optic lamp unit - general

159 This unit is attached to the lower facia panel directly beneath the auxiliary switch panel unit. The fibre optic leads from the unit to illuminate the auxiliary switched, but not their warning lamps (where applicable).

160 Detach and withdraw the lower facia panel so that access can be gained to the switch (photo). Leave the switch leads attached.

161 Pull free the bulb holder from the base of the lamp unit then withdraw the bulb from its holder for renewal (photo).

162 To remove the unit, pull free the fibre optic leads, remove the bulb holder then undo the two retaining screws and remove the unit from the panel.

163 Refit in the reverse order of removal.

Radio (later models) - removal and refitting

164 On later models the radio is located in a housing above the centre console. Removal and refitting procedures are as follows.

165 Disconnect the battery negative terminal.

166 Carefully prise the outer surround away from the radio.

167 Slide the retaining clip on the lower edge

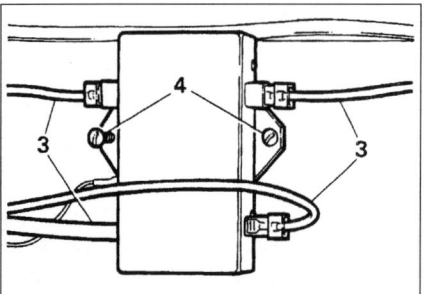

Fig. 13.195 Radio aerial amplifier (1987-on models) (Sec 15)

3 Wiring and aerial   4 Mounting screws

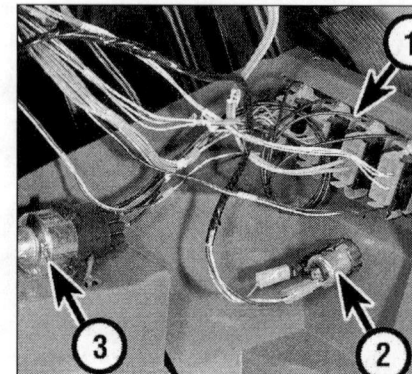

15.160 Underside view of the lower facia panel

1 Auxiliary switches   3 Fibre-optic unit
2 Cigar lighter

of the radio faceplate to the left and withdraw the radio from the housing.

168 Disconnect the aerial, speaker and electrical connections at the rear of the radio and remove the radio.

169 Refitting is the reversal of removal.

Radio aerial amplifier (1987-on models) - removal and refitting

170 The radio aerial is incorporated in the rear window heater element, and an amplifier is located next to the tailgate wiper motor. First disconnect the battery negative lead.

171 Remove or lower the rear headlining.

172 Disconnect the wiring and the aerial from the amplifier noting the locations for correct refitting.

173 Unscrew the mounting screws and remove the amplifier.

174 Refitting is a reversal of the removal procedure.

Heated front windscreen (1990-on models) - general

175 The heated front windscreen will function when the switch is operated with the ignition switched on. The circuit incorporates a timer which turns the heating off after

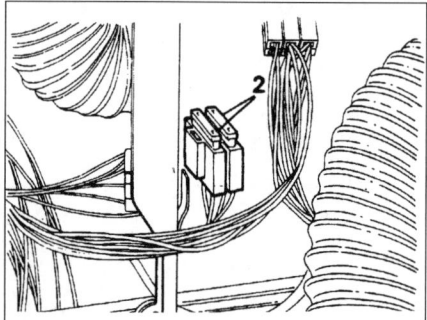

Fig. 13.196 Heated front windscreen fuses (2) (1990-on models) (Sec 15)

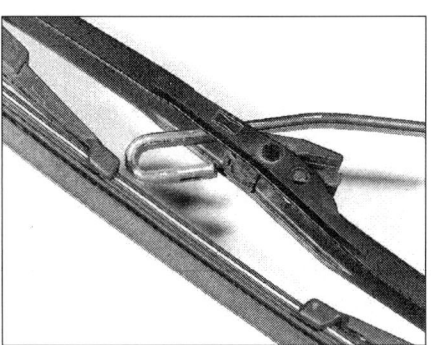

15.177 Removing the wiper arm off the blade

15.180A Using a small screwdriver inserted on the edge of the lens . . .

15.180B . . . to remove the lens

approximately 7.5 minutes. The circuit will also be switched off if the ignition switch is turned off or if the heated front switch is operated again during the cycle.

176 The circuit is protected by two plug-in type 25 amp fuses located next to the relays on the steering column.

Windscreen wiper blade (later models) - removal and refitting

177 Swivel the arm away from the windscreen, then depress the clip and slide the blade down the arm away from the hooked end. Withdraw the blade over the arm (photo).

178 Refitting is a reversal of the removal procedure.

Front door courtesy lamp bulbs - renewal

179 On later models there are two courtesy lamps on the front doors, one on the rear edge of the door and the other on the bottom edge of the door.

180 Open the door and use a small screwdriver to prise out the lens (photos).

181 Ease the lamp bulbholder out of the door and pull the bulb from the wedge type fitting (photos).

182 Refitting is a reversal of the removal procedure.

15.181A Ease the lamp bulbholder out of the door . . .

16 Suspension and steering

Front and rear anti-roll bars - removal and refitting

1 As from September 1990, anti-roll bars are fitted to both the front and rear; at the time of writing no information was available on the removal and refitting procedures.

Rear shock absorber - removal, refitting and overhaul

2 The removal and refitting procedure is similar to that described in Chapter 11, but there is a self-locking nut fitted to the upper

15.181B . . . and pull out the bulb

mounting, and the upper rubber bush is in one piece instead of two (photo).

3 To renew the upper bush, remove the shock absorber and mount it in a vice. Either use two screwdrivers to force out the bushes, or alternatively use metal tubing and spacers to remove it (photo).

4 Dip the new bush in soapy water before pressing it into position in the vice.

Steering box drop arm balljoint - renewal

5 On pre-1983 models the balljoint on the steering box drop arm is integral with the drop arm and cannot be renewed separately, on later models the balljoint is separate and may be renewed without renewal of the drop arm (photo).

16.2 Unscrewing the self-locking nut from the rear shock absorber upper mounting

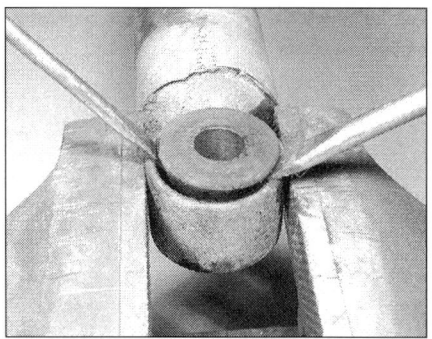

16.3 Using two screwdrivers to remove the rear shock absorber upper mounting rubber

16.4 Pressing in the new rear shock absorber upper mounting rubber

16.9 Circlip retaining the steering box drop arm balljoint on later models

6 Where an early integral balljoint or drop arm is to be renewed, it will be necessary to obtain both the later balljoint components and the later drop arm.

7 The balljoint is available as a repair kit for the later type of drop arm. To renew the balljoint, first remove the drop arm with reference to Chapter 11 and clean its exterior surface.

8 Prise off the spring ring retainers and

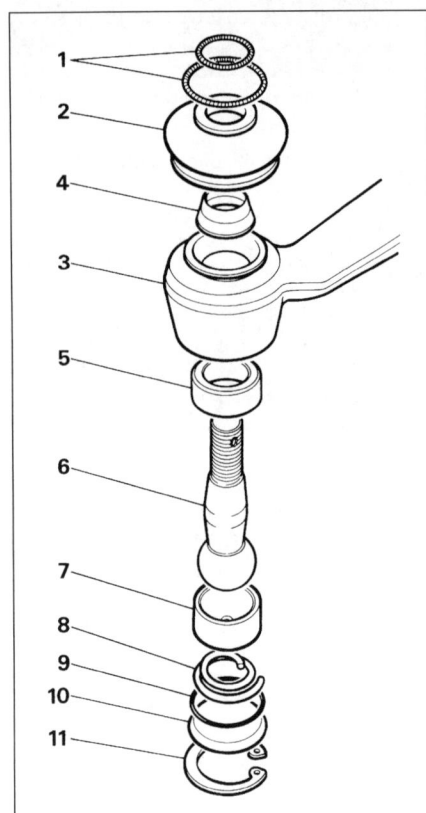

Fig. 13.199 Exploded view of the drop arm balljoint (Sec 16)

1 Spring rings	7 Top socket
2 Rubber dust cover	8 Spring
3 Drop arm	9 O-ring
4 Retainer	10 Cover plate
5 Bottom socket	11 Circlip
6 Ballpin	

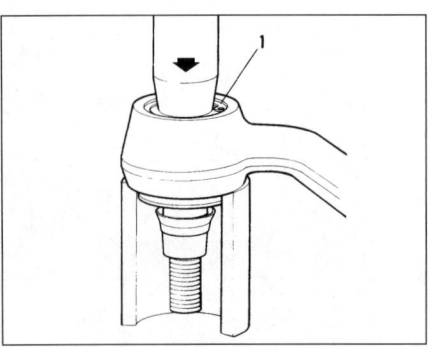

Fig. 13.197 Depressing the cover plate to remove the circlip (Sec 16)

remove the rubber dust cover from the threaded end of the balljoint.

9 The circlip must now be removed from the other end of the balljoint (photo). To do this it is important to relieve the pressure from the circlip otherwise it will spring out of its groove with considerable force and could cause personal injury. A press is ideal for this although a similar arrangement can be made using a large vice and length of metal tube. Refer to Fig.13.197 and support the drop arm on the metal tube then, using a metal bar, press down on the cover plate to relieve pressure on the circlip. The circlip may now be removed using circlip pliers.

10 Remove the cover plate, O-ring, spring, and top socket.

11 At this stage it will not be possible to pull out the ball-pin as it will be held by the retainer. To free it from the retainer, hold the drop arm with the ball-pin uppermost and use a soft faced mallet to drive out the ballpin. Both items can then be removed from the drop arm.

12 To remove the bottom socket, use a narrow drift to drive it out from the drop arm. If necessary apply a little heat with a blow lamp or heat source.

13 Thoroughly clean the seating in the drop arm.

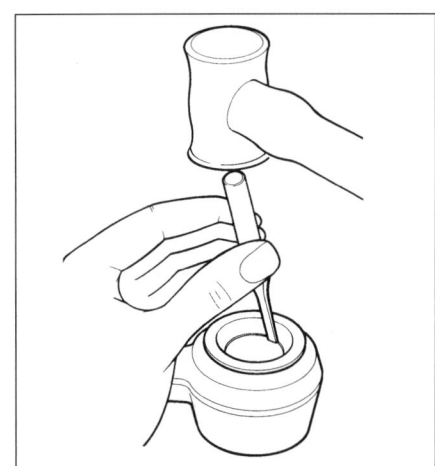

Fig. 13.200 Driving out the bottom socket (Sec 16)

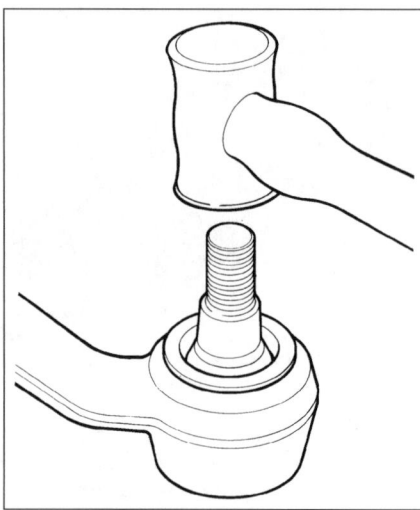

Fig. 13.198 Driving out the ballpin (Sec 16)

14 Press the bottom socket into the drop arm until it contacts the shoulder.

15 Dip the ball-pin in suitable grease and locate it in the drop arm. Pack the seating area in the drop arm with grease.

16 Fit the top socket (the one with a hole in its centre), followed by the spring with its small diameter towards the ball-pin.

17 Fit the O-ring and cover plate, then depress the cover and fit the circlip making sure that it is located correctly in the groove.

18 Press the retainer onto the ball pin until the top edge is level with the edge of the taper.

19 Fit the rubber dust cover and retain with the two spring rings.

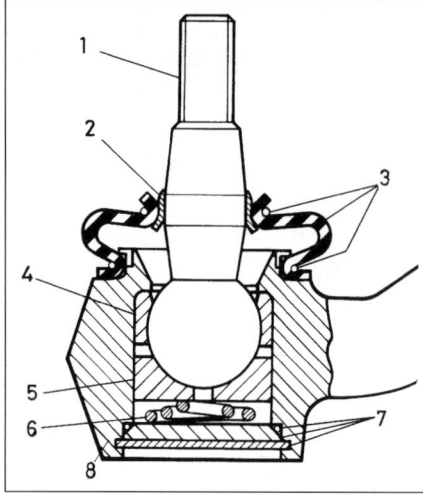

Fig. 13.201 Cross-section of the drop arm balljoint (Sec 16)

1 Ballpin	5 Top socket
2 Retainer	6 Spring
3 Rubber dust cover and retaining springs	7 Cover plate and O-ring
4 Bottom socket	8 Body

16.21 Steering wheel centre safety pad push-fit lugs

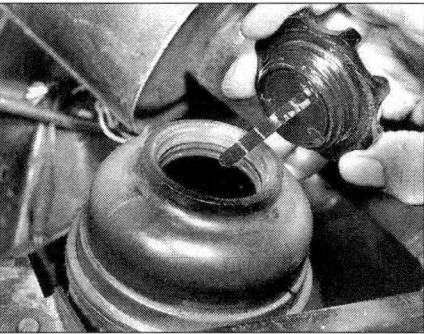

16.23 Checking the fluid level on reservoir filler cap fitted with dipstick

16.24 Checking the fluid level in the non-dipstick type power steering reservoir. Check the cap seal (arrowed)

Steering lock stop - checking and adjustment

20 When checking and adjusting the steering lock stop, as described in Section 33 of Chapter 11, it is important that the prescribed setting adjustment is adhered to. Any attempt to improve the steering lock by altering the setting beyond that specified will cause the steering rocker arm to foul with the steering box lock stops and place excessive loading on the rocker arm when under full lock. Any deviation from the specified setting is not permissible.

Steering wheel (1987-on models) - removal and refitting

21 The procedure is the same as described in Chapter 11, Section 25 except that the central safety pad is retained by four push-fit lugs (photo). To remove the pad, carefully lever it off the steering wheel boss using a suitable flat bladed tool. In most cases this can be done using the fingers.
22 To refit the pad simply push it firmly into place.

Power steering pump reservoir- fluid level checking

23 The power steering system fluid reservoir filler cap on some models incorporates a dipstick. When checking the fluid level on such

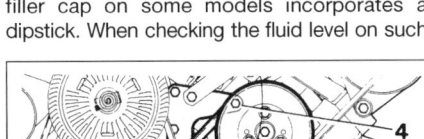

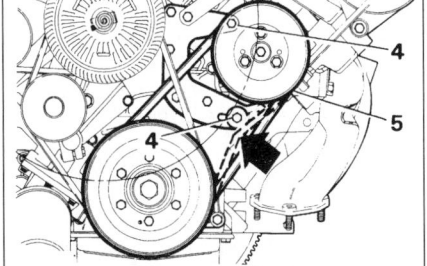

Fig. 13.202 Power steering pump drivebelt adjustment - later models (Sec 16)

4 Mounting and adjustment bolts
5 Power steering pump
Arrow indicates tension checking point

models ensure that the filler cap and the dipstick are cleaned, then refitted and fully tightened down before removal to check the fluid level (photo). If the cap is not fully tightened a false reading will be given and the reservoir will then be overfilled as a consequence.
24 When the filler cap is removed (either type), also check that the cap seal is in good condition. Renew the seal if necessary (photo).

Power steering pump drivebelt (later models) - removal refitting and adjustment

25 Remove the fanbelt with reference to Section 5 of this Chapter.
26 Loosen the alternator mounting bolts and swivel the alternator in towards the engine. Remove the drivebelt from the alternator and steering pump pulleys.
27 Follow the procedure described in Chapter 11, Section 29.
28 Refer to Section 15 when refitting the alternator and to Section 5 when refitting the fanbelt.

Alloy roadwheels - general

29 On later models, optional alloy roadwheels became available in place of the standard pressed-steel type normally fitted. At the same time the roadwheel hubs and fixing studs were modified to suit, the studs being identified by a slot or triangle stamped into the outer endface.

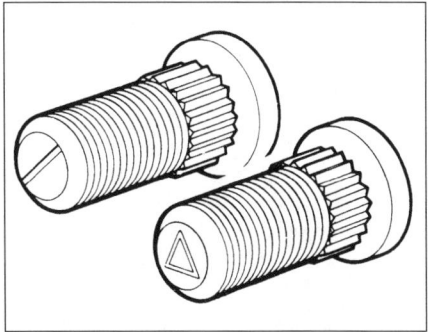

Fig. 13.203 Alloy roadwheel studs showing identification slot or triangle (Sec 16)

30 It is important to note that alloy roadwheels must not be fitted to earlier models unless they have had the later hub/stud assemblies changed to suit. Consult your Range Rover dealer before fitting the alloy roadwheels to earlier models to check for suitability.
31 Whenever an alloy roadwheel is removed, it is advisable to spray the wheel location face with an anti-seize compound. The manufacturers suggest Rocol or an equivalent compound. Do not allow the compound to be sprayed on the brake discs or wheel studs.
32 With regard to maintenance, alloy roadwheels should be checked regularly for signs of damage and for corrosion. If a wheel is damaged, it must be renewed. Regular cleaning with a proprietary wheel cleaner and an annual protective coating of a suitable compound will prevent severe corrosion and keep them looking smart. If the wheels are allowed to become severely corroded have them checked by your Range Rover dealer for advice on their safety and possible renovation.
33 Special roadwheel nuts are fitted with alloy wheels. These nuts have a rotating washer located under the bolt head. Although the washer is staked to prevent it from being separated from the nut it is advisable, whenever they are removed, to check that the washer is in position on each nut and that it is free to rotate, but not loose enough to be separated from the nut. If any nuts are found to be defective, renew as necessary.

Under-ride protection bar- general

34 An under-ride protection bar becomes available as an optional fitting to the new models from 1982 but, where required, it can be fitted to earlier models. The protection bar is mounted transversely under the chassis at the front and provides protection to the steering gear and associated components against damage when travelling over rough terrain.

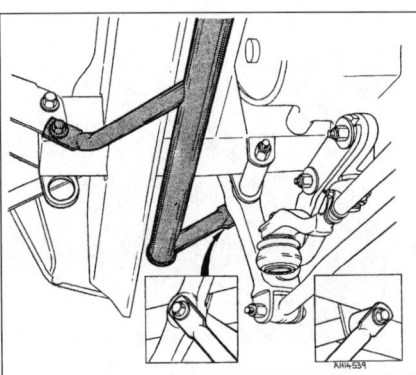

Fig. 13.204 Under-ride protection bar (Sec 16)

17 Bodywork and fittings

PART A: GENERAL

Decker panel - removal and refitting

1 The decker panel is located at the rear of the bonnet.

2 Unbolt and remove the bonnet (Section 7 in Chapter 12, or later in this Section for 1987-on models).

3 On carburettor models remove the air cleaner unit (Section 3 in Chapter 3).

4 Remove the windscreen wiper arms and blades, as described in Chapter 10, Section 33.

5 Unscrew and remove the decker panel retaining screws along the top leading edge (refer to Fig. 12.1).

6 Unscrew and remove the retaining screw each side at the top rear edge (open the doors for access).

7 Unscrew and remove the two side bolts from within the cavity.

8 Withdraw the decker panel forwards from under the windscreen lower rubber moulding and remove it. On some models it will also be necessary to disconnect the engine

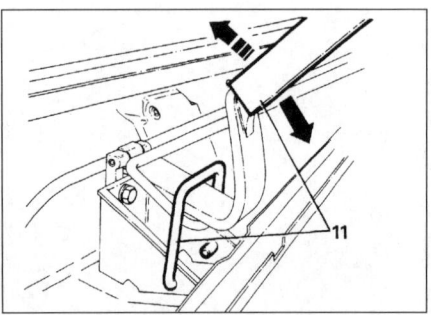

Fig. 13.205 Assisted bonnet lift removal (Sec 17A)

11 Extension tube and stop bracket

compartment light switch lead and, where applicable, the radio aerial.

9 Refit in the reverse order of removal. Slide the panel under the windscreen lower rubber moulding and locate all of the retaining screws and bolts prior to fully tightening them.

Bonnet (1987-on models) - removal and refitting

10 The procedure is the same as described in Section 7 of Chapter 12 except that the bonnet now pivots on concealed hinges that no longer protrude above the body line.

11 The bonnet-to-hinge retaining bolt locations are shown in the accompanying photo (photo).

Assisted bonnet lift (1987-on models) - removal and refitting

12 Remove the windscreen wiper arms, then raise the bonnet and support in the open position (photo).

13 Disconnect the battery negative lead.

14 Disconnect the wiring for the bonnet illumination lamp.

15 Disconnect the washer fluid feed pipe at the T-joint, and release it from the clip.

16 With the aid of an assistant, support the bonnet then unscrew the bolts securing the bonnet to the hinges. Note that the front bolt of the left-hand hinge is used to secure an engine earthing cable.

17 Lift off the bonnet and place it in a safe place.

17A.11 Later type concealed bonnet hinge attachments to bonnet

18 Unscrew both wiper box wheel nuts and remove the rubber spacers.

19 Unscrew the decker panel mounting bolts. Note that access to the rear bolts is gained by opening the doors. Recover the nylon washers.

20 Remove the screws from the front of the decker panel water channel.

21 Locate extension tubes over both of the hinge arms, then pull down the hinges and withdraw the decker panel from the wiper arm spigot bosses and along the tubes until the panel is clear of the vehicle. Position the decker panel to one side. When clear of the vehicle, carefully allow the torsion bar tension to return the hinges to their normal position.

22 Using an extension tube, lower one of the hinges until the stop bracket can be removed, then remove the bracket and allow the hinge to return to its upright position (photo).

23 Remove the torsion bar from the retaining clip (photo).

24 Remove the torsion bar from the remaining hinge and bracket, then unbolt the hinge from its mounting.

25 Refitting is a reversal of the removal procedure, but on completion lift the bottom lip of the windscreen rubber up and onto the decker panel.

Facia panels (pre-1986 models) - removal and refitting

26 Before carrying out any of the following, disconnect the battery negative lead.

17A.12 Removing the windscreen wiper arms

17A.22 Assisted bonnet lift hinge and springs

17A.23 Inner clips retaining the torsion bars

17A.30 Rheostat (dimmer) switch and retaining screws on the steering column lower facia panel

Lower facia panel driver's side

27 Undo and remove the five retaining screws and withdraw the lower facia panel, together with the driver's side glovebox. Note the spacer fitted on the right-hand end between the facia panels (upper and lower).
28 Refit in the reverse order to removal.

Steering column lower facia panel

29 Remove the eight retaining screws, lower the panel sufficiently far to allow the rheostat wiring connections to be detached, then remove the panel.
30 To remove the rheostat switch, undo the two retaining screws and withdraw the unit from the panel (photo). 31 Refit in the reverse order to removal.

Lower centre facia panel

32 Undo the retaining screws and pull free the heater/ventilation control knobs (photo).
33 Undo the two heater/ventilation control panel retaining screws then remove the panel (photo).
34 Undo and remove three retaining screws from the lower edge of the panel and two screws each side (facing). Partially withdraw the panel so that the auxiliary switch panel and cigar lighter can be disconnected or removed from the heater/ventilation panel. Pull free the heater control illumination bulb holders (photo) and withdraw the panel.
35 Refit in the reverse order of removal.

Glovebox - passenger's side

36 This is secured by screws at the side and

17A.32 Undoing the control knob retaining screw

rear, the rear screws being shown in the photo (photo).

Clock/vent facia panel

37 Remove the glovebox and the lower centre facia panel as described previously.
38 Remove the clock and the fresh air louvre vents each side.
39 Undo the retaining screw and remove the side trim piece (photo). 40 Undo and remove the four screws at the front via the vent apertures.
41 Unscrew and remove the nearside retaining screw (photo).
42 Undo and remove the single screw from the underside on the left. 43 Undo the two screws from the underside near the grab handle.
44 The panel can then be withdrawn.

17A.34 Heater/ventilation control illumination bulb and holder

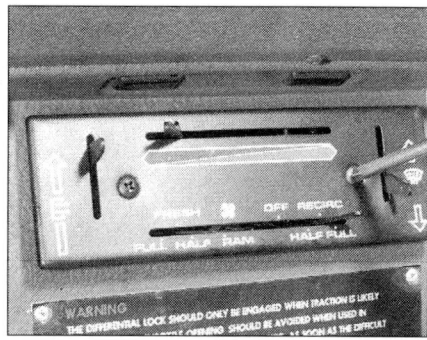

17A.33 Undoing the heater/ventilation panel retaining screws

45 If required, the grab handle can be removed by undoing the three nuts and washers from the underside of the upper facia panel.
46 Refit the clock/centre vents facia panel by reversing the removal procedure.

Facia panels (1986-on models) - removal and refitting

47 Before carrying out any of the following, disconnect the battery negative lead.

Lower facia panel - driver's side

48 On models equipped with air conditioning carefully prise out the louvred vent panel nearest to the door.
49 Undo the two screws from the bottom of the panel above the pedals (photo).

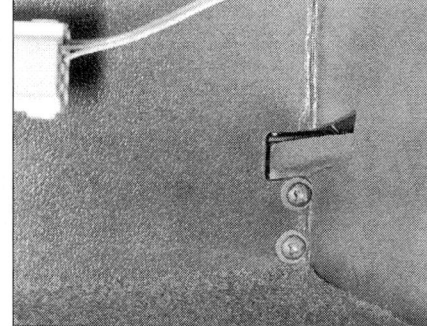

17A.36 Glovebox inner retaining screws

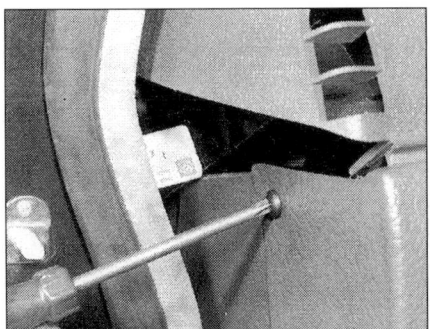

17A.39 Remove the side trim retaining screw

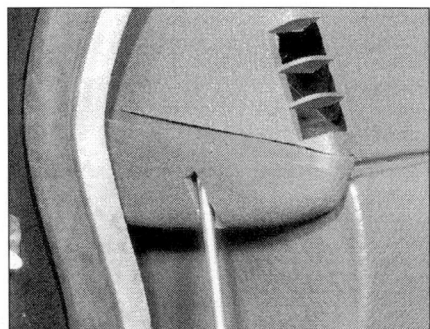

17A.41 Lower facia side retaining screw removal

17A.49 Undo the two screws from the bottom of the facia. Right-hand screw arrowed

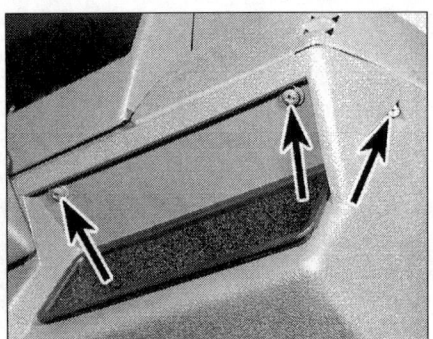

17A.50 Facia panel upper and side retaining screws (arrowed)

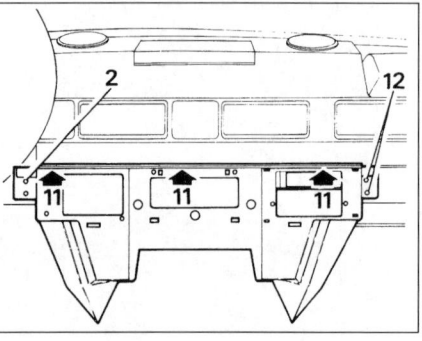

Fig. 13.206 Centre facia panel removal - 1986-on models (Sec 17A)

2 Retaining screw location (driver's side)
11 Centre retaining screw locations
12 Retaining screw locations (passenger's side)
Left-hand-drive model shown

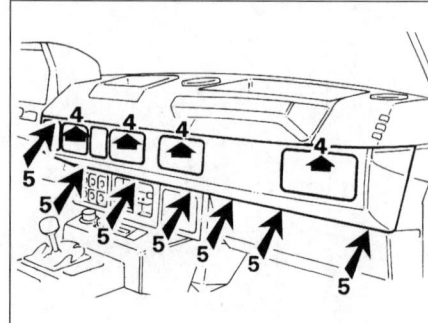

Fig. 13.207 Facia louvre panel removal - 1986-on models (Sec 17A)

4 Securing screw locations behind louvred grilles on air-conditioned models
5 Remaining screw locations
Left-hand-drive model shown

50 Undo the single screw on the extreme right-hand side of the panel and the two screws above the louvred vent panel or oddments box aperture (photo).
51 Undo the single screw to the left of the steering column, lower the panel and disconnect the switch wiring (where applicable). Remove the panel from the vehicle.
52 Refitting is the reversal of removal.

Radio housing

53 Remove the radio as described in Section 15 and the centre console as described later in this Section.
54 Undo the single screw securing the housing to the transmission tunnel.
55 Tilt the front of the housing upwards and manoeuvre it away from the facia to the limits of the cigar lighter electrical leads.
56 Disconnect the cigar lighter electrical leads and remove the radio housing.
57 Refitting is a reversal of removal.

Centre facia panel

58 Remove the lower facia panel and the radio housing as previously described.
59 Detach the fusebox cover and undo the three main and auxiliary fusebox retaining screws.
60 Pull the four heater control knobs off their levers.
61 Undo the two screws securing the top of the heater graphics panel, pull the panel away and disconnect the illumination bulbs. Remove the graphics panel.
62 Carefully prise out the auxiliary switch panel from its location. Label each switch multi-plug for identification then disconnect them from the switches.
63 Undo the three screws securing the centre facia panel to facia louvre panel.
64 Undo the two screws on the right and single screw on the left at the side of the centre facia panel.
65 Manoeuvre the panel from its location and remove it from the vehicle.
66 Refitting is a reversal of removal.

Facia louvre panel

67 Carefully prise the clock out of its location, disconnect the wiring and remove the clock.

68 Undo the single screw adjacent to the passenger courtesy light switch securing the end of the louvre panel in position.
69 On models equipped with air conditioning ease out the four louvred grilles. Undo the eight screws at the top of the louvre apertures and the additional screw above the air conditioning control panel.
70 On models without air conditioning undo the five parcel shelf securing screws and withdraw the shelf. Now undo the four nuts and bolts located behind the panel and securing it to the top rail. Prise out the two centre louvre grilles and undo the four screws in the louvre apertures.
71 On all models undo the three screws securing the facia louvre panel to the centre facia panel.
72 On air conditioned models undo the remaining three screws above the blower motor trim panel.
73 Ease the facia louvre panel forward and disconnect the switch electrical wiring (where applicable). Withdraw the panel from the vehicle.
74 Refitting is the reversal of removal.

Facia top rail

75 Remove the steering wheel as described in Section 16.
76 Remove the lower facia panel, radio

17A.82 Prise out the window lift switch panel from the centre console

housing, centre facia panel and facia louvre panel as previously described.
77 Remove the instrument panel housing as described in Section 28 of Chapter 10.
78 Lift up the passenger map tray rubber mat and undo the five screws, nuts and washers securing the grab handle and facia top rail to the bulkhead.
79 Disconnect the air vent hoses from the heater and remove the top rail from the vehicle.
80 Refitting is a reversal of removal.

Centre console (later models) - removal and refitting

81 Disconnect the battery negative lead.
82 Carefully prise out the window lift switch panel, label and disconnect the switch wiring then remove the panel (photo).
83 Undo the four screws and remove the cubby box liner (photo).
84 From inside the cubby box aperture disconnect the leads to the rear passenger cigar lighter (photo).
85 Chock the wheels and release the handbrake. From inside the cubby box aperture disconnect the handbrake cable from the handbrake lever. Now raise the lever fully.
86 Remove the transfer gear lever knob and,

17A.83 Undo the screws (arrowed) and remove the cubby box liner

17A.84 Disconnect the cigar lighter leads

17A.87A On automatic transmission models, prise up the selector lever top cover . . .

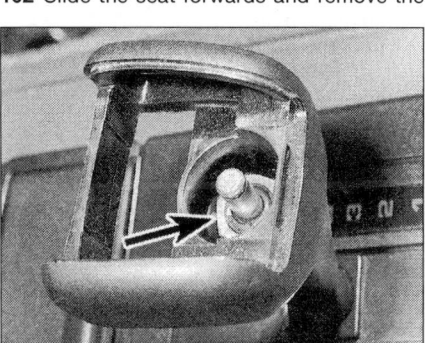

17A.87B . . . and extract the circlip (arrowed)

on manual transmission models, the main gear lever knob.

87 On automatic transmission models carefully prise up the selector lever top cover and extract the lever detent retaining circlip (photos).

88 Remove the lever detent and unscrew the lever handle retaining nut (photo). Withdraw the handle from the lever.

89 Carefully prise the inset panel around the gear levers away from the outer surround, then remove it from the console. On automatic transmission models, disconnect the selector illumination bulb holders as the panel is removed (photos).

90 Undo the two bolts at the rear and two screws at the front securing the console to the transmission tunnel (photo).

91 Move the console to the rear to detach the location tab from the bottom of the radio housing then manoeuvre the console out of the vehicle.

92 Refitting is the reversal of removal.

Front seat (later two-door models) - removal and refitting

93 Undo the nut and bolt at the front of each seat side.

94 Undo the six screws securing the outer seat base trim panel and remove the panel.

95 At the outer rear of the seat base undo the two screws and remove the plate.

96 Undo the rear retention bar upper bolt and push the bar downwards.

97 Disconnect the retaining spring below the seat squab.

98 Withdraw the seat from the vehicle.

99 Refitting is the reversal of removal.

Front seat (later four-door models) - removal and refitting

100 Undo the four screws securing the outer seat base trim panel and remove the panel.

101 Slide the seat rearwards and undo the two socket-headed bolts, one located in each seat runner (photo).

102 Slide the seat forwards and remove the

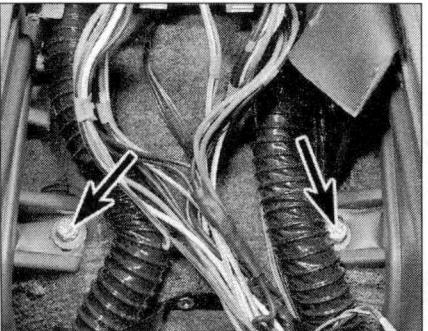

17A.88 Unscrew the lever handle retaining nut (arrowed)

remaining two bolts in a similar fashion then remove the seat from the vehicle.

103 Refitting is the reversal of removal.

Electrically operated front seat (Vogue SE models, March 1988-on) - removal and refitting

104 Unscrew the screws and withdraw the seat side trim panel, then unscrew the bolt securing the seat belt to the side of the seat.

105 Position the seat fully to the rear, and unscrew the front mounting bolts from the slide channels.

106 Position the seat fully to the front, and unscrew the rear mounting bolts from the slide channels.

107 Disconnect the battery negative lead.

17A.89A Prise up the inset panel . . .

17A.89B . . . and, where fitted, disconnect the illumination bulb holders (arrowed)

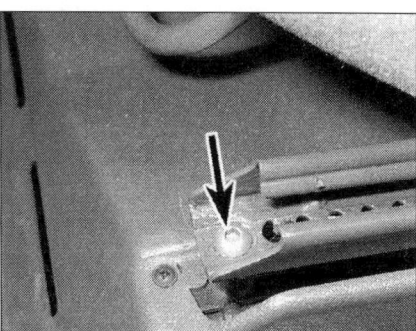

17A.90 Centre console rear retaining bolts (arrowed)

17A.101 Front seat runner retaining bolt location (arrowed)

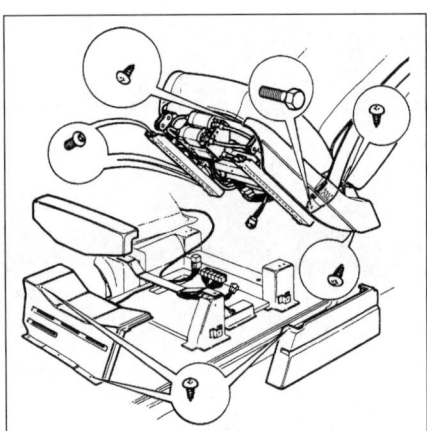

Fig. 13.208 Electrically-operated front seat removal (Sec 17A)

108 Disconnect the wiring plugs from the seat motors and seat control switch. Where necessary also disconnect the seat belt warning system wiring.

109 Withdraw the seat from inside the vehicle.

110 Refitting is a reversal of the removal procedure but make sure that the wiring is located so that it is not damaged by the movement of the seat.

Electrically operated front seat motors (Vogue SE models, March 1988-on) - removal and refitting

111 Four electric motors are mounted beneath the front seats to control fore-and-aft

17A.114A Removing the lower motor from its bracket

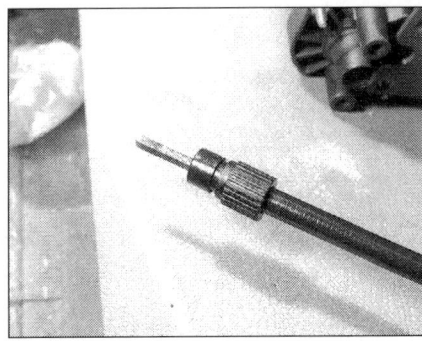

17A.114B End of a drive cable

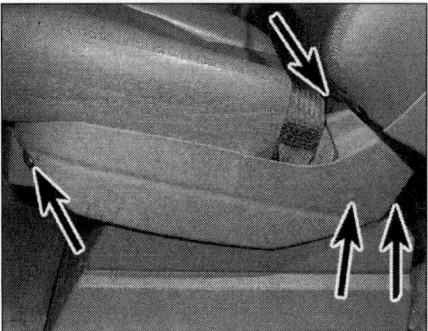

17A.113A Seat base trim securing screws

and height positioning of the seat. The motors operate with the ignition on or with the front door open.

112 Move the seat so that the motors are accessible, then disconnect the battery negative lead.

113 Remove the seat base trim then unscrew the screws from each side of the motor (photos).

114 Withdraw the motor from its mounting and disconnect the drive cables by unscrewing the ferrules (photos).

115 Disconnect the wiring plugs and remove the motor.

116 Refitting is a reversal of the removal procedure.

Split rear seat locking mechanism (1989-on models) - removal and refitting

117 The rear seat locking mechanism incorporates a pushbutton release instead of the finger lift button. First depress the button and fold the seat forwards.

118 Unscrew and remove the button.

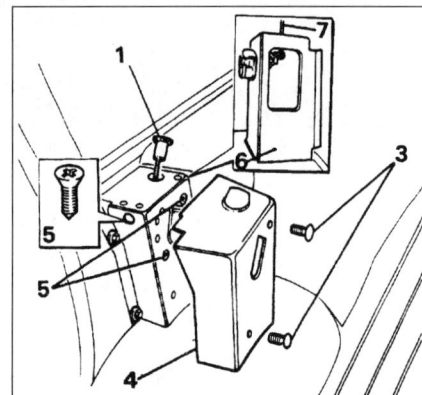

Fig. 13.209 Split rear seat locking mechanism components for 1989-on models (Sec 17A)

1 Seat release	5 Screws
button	6 Latch
3 Retaining buttons	7 Control rod
4 Trim covering	

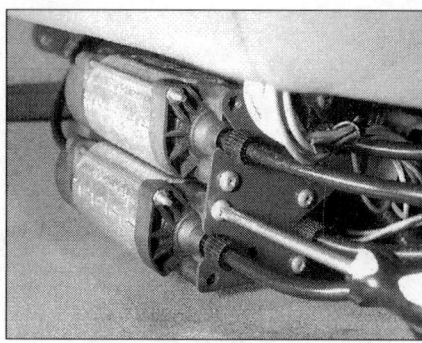

17A.113B Removing the seat motor side screws

119 Prise out the two trim buttons holding the trim to the latch tower and remove the trim.

120 Unscrew the screws and remove the latch from the tower. Note that access to the single screw is through the hole in the front of the tower.

121 Recover the latch from the opening at the rear of the tower; also recover the single screw.

122 Release the control rod from the latch at the plastic clip.

123 Refitting is a reversal of the removal procedure, but when screwing the button onto the control rod there must be a gap of 5 to 8 mm (0.196 to 0.312 in) between the button head and the lip of the trim covering after the button has been depressed.

Exterior rear view mirror (later models) - glass renewal

124 Push the inner (wider) end of the mirror glass inward to its full extent.

125 Place your fingers behind the outer (narrower) end of the glass and pull outwards to release the four retaining clips.

126 On electrically-operate versions disconnect the wiring then remove the glass from the mirror body.

127 Refitting is the reversal of removal.

Exterior rear view mirror (later models) - removal and refitting

128 Disconnect the battery negative terminal.

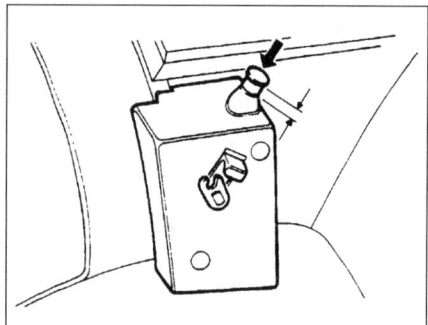

Fig. 13.210 Split rear seat release button adjustment dimension (Sec 17A)

17A.129 Removing the interior trim plate

17A.130 Exterior mirror wiring plug and mounting screws

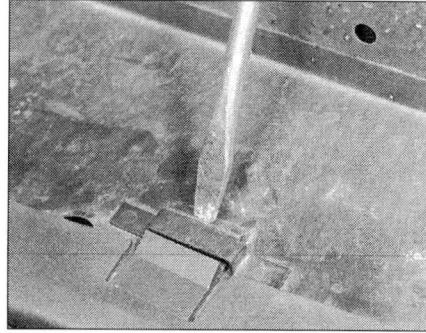

17A.134A Depress the grille retaining tag ends . . .

129 Prise off the interior trim plate and disconnect the two wiring multi-plugs (where applicable) (photo).
130 Support the mirror and undo the three retaining screws (photo).
131 Pull the inner mounting plate, complete with the two retaining clips, away from the door frame then detach the mirror assembly and rubber seal from the outer door frame.
132 Refitting is the reversal of removal.

Horizontal bar radiator grille (1987-on models) - removal and refitting

133 Raise the bonnet and support it in the open position.
134 Using a screwdriver or similar, depress the end of the grille upper retaining tags and push them through their retainers (photos).
135 Disengage the lower locating lugs and remove the grille from the vehicle (photo).
136 Refitting is the reversal of removal.

Electric sunroof (1987-on models) - general

137 It is recommended that any work necessary on the electric sunroof should be left to a specialist, an exploded view is shown in Fig. 13.211 for those who have the expertise to dismantle the sunroof.
138 The stepper relay for the sunroof is located on a bracket behind the interior light mounting bracket.

Heater unit (1990-on models) - removal and refitting

139 The procedure is similar to that described in Chapter 12, but there are additional wiring connectors to the electric thermostat at the rear of the evaporator housing, and to the vent lever microswitch.

Fresh air solenoid switch vacuum unit (1990-on models) - removal and refitting

140 Disconnect the battery negative lead.
141 Working inside the vehicle remove the transmission lever surround and the radio mounting console, then remove the centre facia unit and the lower facia panel.

17A.134B . . . and push the tags through the retainers

17A.135 Radiator grille lower locating lugs (arrowed)

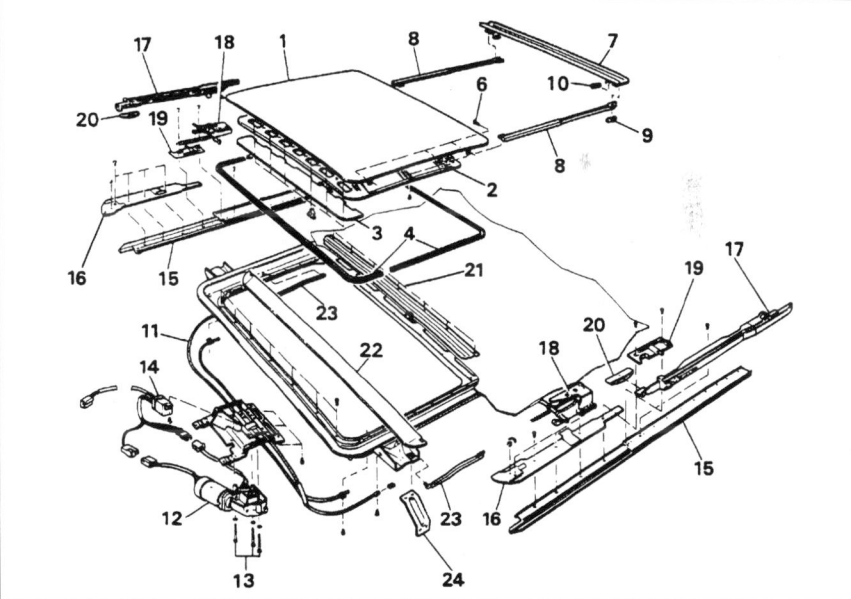

Fig. 13.211 Exploded view of the electric sunroof (Sec 17A)

1 Roof panel	9 Support bracket	17 Slide mechanism
2 Blind	10 Slide shoe	18 Rear guide
3 Insulation	11 Motor bracket/guide tube	19 Pivot bracket
4 Front and rear roof seals	assembly	20 Slide shoe
5 Blind retaining screws	12 Operating motor	21 Rear edge trim finisher
6 Roof panel retaining	13 Motor mounting screws	22 Wind deflector assembly
screws	14 Relay	23 Wind deflector operating
7 Water channel	15 Lower guide rails	arms
8 Connectors	16 Front guide rails	24 Support bracket

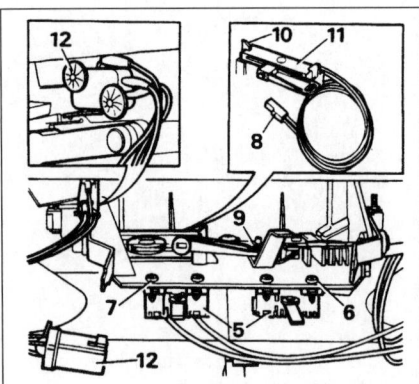

Fig. 13.212 Heater and air conditioning controls for 1990-on models (Sec 17A)

5 Wiring connectors
6 Fan speed switch mounting screws
7 Air conditioning/fresh air/recirculating switch mounting screws
8 Potentiometer wiring connector
9 Wiring connector on the heat control lever
10 Potentiometer mounting
11 Potentiometer
12 Microswitch and retaining clips

142 To remove the solenoid switch, first disconnect the wiring from the solenoid and disconnect the two vacuum hoses. Unscrew the screws and withdraw the solenoid.

143 To remove the vacuum unit, disconnect the vacuum hose and remove the actuating rod securing clip. Unscrew the mounting screws and remove the vacuum unit.

144 Refitting is a reversal of the removal procedure.

Heater and air conditioning controls (1990-on models) - removal and refitting

145 Disconnect the battery negative lead.

146 Working inside the vehicle remove the transmission lever surround and radio housing.

147 Remove the lower facia panel followed by the centre console.

148 Disconnect the wiring plugs from the fan speed and recirculating/fresh air switches.

149 To remove the fan speed switch, unscrew the screws and remove the switch.

150 Unscrew the screws and remove the air conditioning/fresh air/recirculating switch.

151 To remove the potentiometer, disconnect the wiring from the electronic thermostat behind the evaporator housing, and prise the cable connection from the heat control lever. Withdraw the potentiometer together with the connecting arm to the heat control lever. Pull the wiring through the rubber grommet.

152 To remove the microswitch, disconnect the wiring multi-plug, lift the vent lever, remove the two retaining clips and withdraw the microswitch.

153 Refitting is a reversal of the removal procedure. Make sure that the controls work

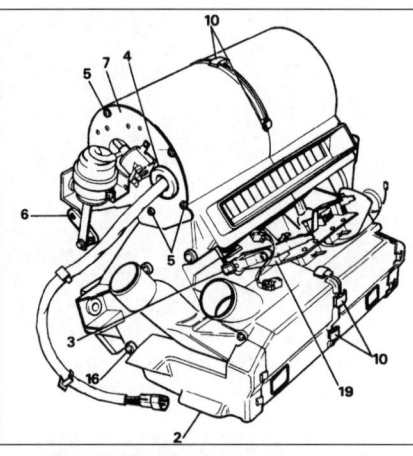

Fig. 13.213 Heater fan motor unit components (Sec 17A)

2 Left-hand air duct to footwell outlet
3 Vent control rod
4 Grommet
5 Screws
6 Vacuum unit-to-air flap linkage
7 Side cover
10 Spring clips
16 Air flap pivot
19 Heater control panel

correctly before refitting the facia and trim panels.

Heater fan motor, rotor and resistance unit (1990-on models) - removal and refitting

154 Remove the heater assembly as described previously. 155 Remove the left-hand air duct to footwell outlet.

156 Note the position of the vent control rod, then disconnect the rod by prising open the plastic clip.

157 Remove the rubber grommet from the side cover.

158 Unscrew the side cover retaining screws, and remove the linkage between the vacuum unit and air flap.

159 Remove the side cover sufficient to expose the fan motor and resistance unit.

160 Push back the mounting straps and remove the resistance unit.

161 Fully remove the side cover and feed the wiring through the hole.

162 Release the spring clips, circlips and screws securing the heater casing halves together, making sure that all of the fittings and foam gaskets are also removed.

163 Remove the air flap by sliding its lower edge through the gap between the motor housing and the outer case, at the same time separating the heater casing halves.

164 Note the position of the air flaps for correct reassembly.

165 Prise the plastic tabs away from the motor and remove the motor assembly. Note the position of the wiring to ensure correct reassembly.

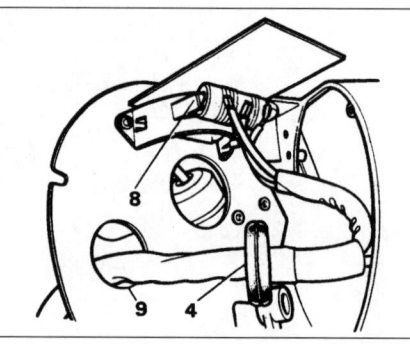

Fig. 13.214 Inner view of the heater fan motor cover (Sec 17A)

4 Grommet
8 Resistance unit
9 Hole in cover for grommet

166 Refitting is a reversal of the removal procedure. If necessary renew the foam gaskets.

Heater radiator (1990-on models) - removal and refitting

167 Remove the heater assembly as described previously.

168 Remove the left-hand air duct to footwell outlet.

169 Note the position of the vent control rod for correct reassembly, then disconnect the rod by prising open the plastic clip.

170 Remove the spring clips, circlips, and screws and separate the two halves of the heater casing making sure that all of the fittings and foam gaskets are also removed.

171 Remove the pad from the coolant hose connections.

172 Remove the air flap by sliding its lower edge through the gap between the motor housing and the outer case, at the same time separating the heater casing halves.

173 Note the position of the air flaps for correct reassembly.

174 Remove the separate panel, then remove the heater radiator together with the foam packing.

175 Refitting is a reversal of the removal procedure. If necessary renew the foam gaskets.

Air conditioning system-precautions

Where fitted, the following special precautions should be noted concerning the air conditioning system.

176 Never: disconnect any part of the air conditioning refrigeration circuit unless the system has first been discharged by your dealer or a qualified refrigeration engineer.

177 Where the compressor or condenser obstruct other mechanical operations such as engine removal, then it is permissible to unbolt their mountings and move them to the limit of their flexible hose deflection, but not to disconnect the hoses. If there is still

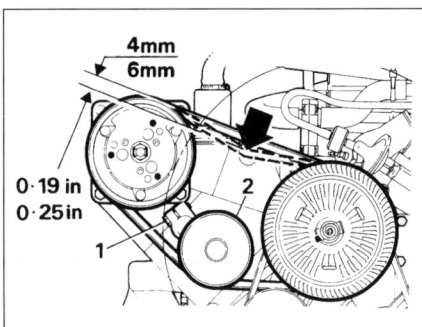

Fig. 13.215 Air conditioning compressor drivebelt adjustment (Sec 17A)

1 Jockey wheel clamp bolt
2 Jockey wheel
Arrow indicates tension checking point

insufficient room to carry out the required work then the system must be discharged before disconnecting and removing the assemblies. The system will, of course, have to be recharged on completion.

178 Regularly check the condenser for clogging with flies or dirt. Hose clean with water or compressed air.

179 If any part of the wiring harness is to be disconnected or disturbed, ensure that the connectors are suitably marked to avoid confusion when refitting. Also ensure that all wiring is reconnected securely and kept well clear of the exhaust manifolds.

Air conditioning system compressor drivebelt - removal, refitting and adjustment

180 To remove the compressor drivebelt first remove the alternator drivebelt or fanbelt according to the belt configuration of the vehicle being worked on.

181 On early models slacken the compressor pivot and adjuster bolts, move the compressor towards the engine and slip the belt off the pulleys. On later models slacken the jockey wheel clamp bolt, move the jockey wheel to relieve the tension on the belt and remove the belt.

182 Slip the new belt over the pulleys and adjust as follows.

183 On early models move the compressor outward to tension the belt until the belt deflection is 0.2 in (5.0 mm) at the centre point between the idler pulley and compressor pulley. Hold the compressor in this position and tighten the pivot and adjuster bolts.

184 On later models tension the belt by moving the jockey wheel until the belt deflection is 0.19 to 0.25 in (4.0 to 6.0 mm) between the compressor pulley and water pump pulley. Hold the jockey wheel in this position and tighten the clamp bolt.

185 On all models refit the alternator drivebelt or fanbelt as applicable using the procedures described elsewhere in this Chapter.

PART B: DOORS AND TAILGATE

Door trim panels - removal and refitting

Front door - 1986-on models

1 Prise out the trim button over the interior handle trim surround and unscrew the trim retaining screw. Remove the trim surround from the handle (photos).

2 Prise the veneer trim from the armrest/door pull, undo the two retaining screws and remove the door pull (photos).

3 Where fitted undo the retaining screws and remove the stowage bin from the door (photo).

4 Using a flat-bladed tool prise the lower part of the panel away from the door to release the retaining pegs (photo). Ease the panel out at

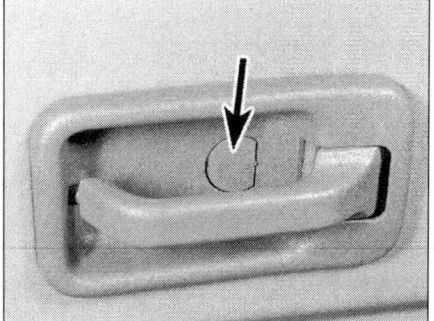

17B.1A Prise out the trim button (arrowed) . . .

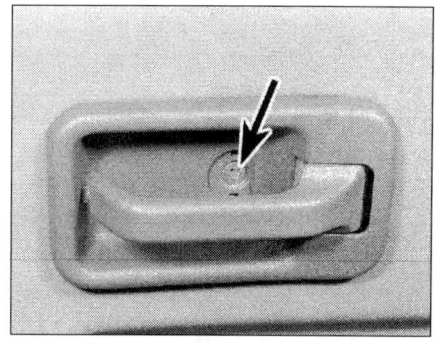

17B.1B . . . undo the retaining screw . . .

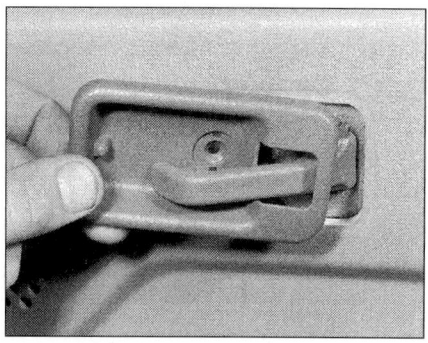

17B.1C . . . and remove the trim surround

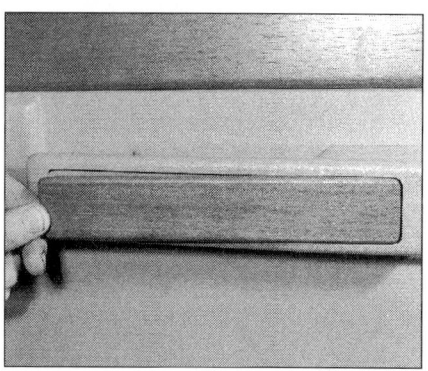

17B.2A Prise the veneer trim from the armrest/door pull . . .

17B.2B . . . undo the two screws and remove the door pull

17B.3 Undo the stowage bin retaining screws (where fitted)

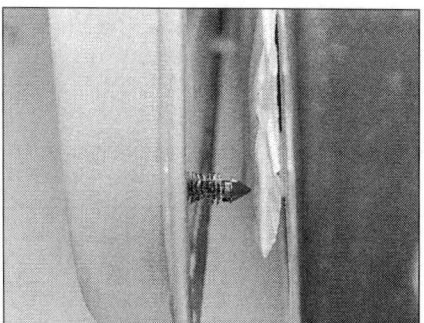

17B.4 Ease away the door panel to release the retaining pegs

17B.5 Disconnect the speaker wiring

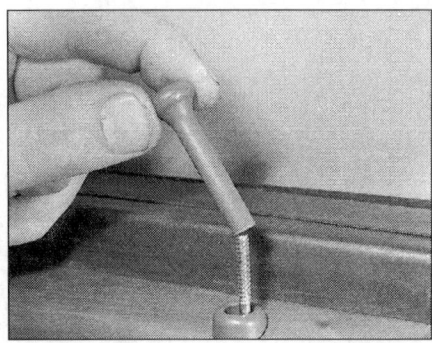

17B.6 Unscrew the interior lock button

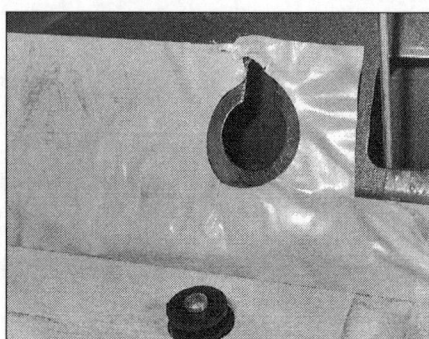

17B.7 Trim capping retaining studs and location holes in door panel

17B.9A Unscrew the screw . . .

17B.9B . . . and remove the inner door handle surround

the bottom and pull down to release the upper edge from the trim capping.

5 Disconnect the speaker wiring and remove the trim panel (photo).

6 To remove the trim capping unscrew the interior lock button (photo) then push the capping down and pull outwards.

7 Refitting is the reversal of removal. When fitting the trim capping enter the retaining studs into their holes, then push the capping upwards (photo). Ensure that the trim capping is in place before refitting the trim panel.

Front door (four-door models) - 1989-on

8 Disconnect the battery negative lead.

9 Unscrew the screw and remove the inner door handle surround (photos).

10 Prise the locking button surround from the top of the trim panel (photo).

11 Prise the two plugs from the bottom of the door-pull pocket then unscrew the screws and remove the pocket (photos).

12 Using a wide-bladed screwdriver prise the trim panel away from the door, then disconnect the speaker wiring and electric window wiring. If it is required to remove the plastic membrane from the inside of the door, unscrew and remove the bracket and speaker, prise out the plastic sockets and carefully pull off the membrane (photos).

13 If necessary, remove the screws from the rear of the panel and remove the stowage bin front panel.

17B.10 Removing the locking button surround

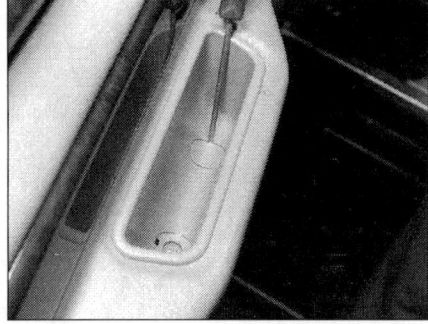

17B.11A Prise out the plugs . . .

17B.11B . . . and remove the screws and pocket

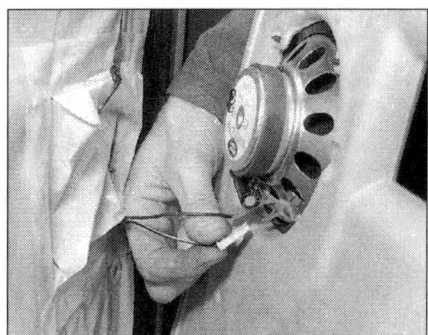

17B.12A Disconnecting the speaker wiring from the inside of the trim panel

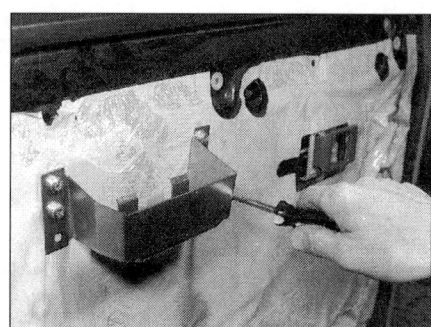

17B.12B Removing the bracket

17B.12C Speaker and bracket

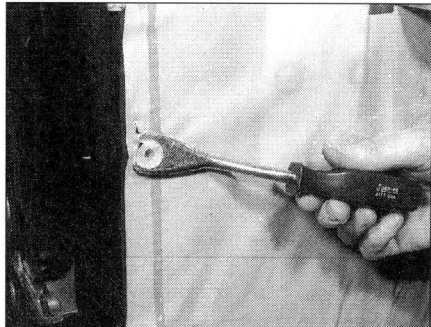

17B.12D Prising out the plastic sockets

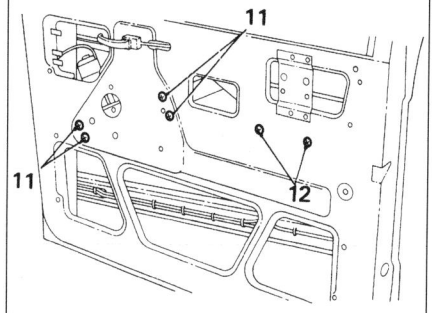

Fig. 13.216 Electrically-operated front door glass regulator retaining screws (11) and lower window lift channel retaining screws (12) (Sec 17B)

14 Refitting is a reversal of the removal procedure.

Rear door pre-1988 models

15 Unscrew the interior lock button.
16 On models equipped with manually-operated windows, undo the retaining screw and withdraw the window regulator handle.
17 Undo the two armrest securing screws and remove the armrest.
18 Prise free the interior handle trim surround which comprises an upper and lower section.
19 The trim panel can now be removed by using a flat-bladed tool to prise it away from the door and release the plastic retaining pegs.
20 Refitting is the reversal of removal.

Rear door - 1986-on models

21 This is essentially the same as for the front door trim panel as previously described.

Rear door (four-door models) 1989-on

22 Disconnect the battery negative lead.
23 Unscrew the screw and remove the inner door handle surround.
24 Prise out the lock button surround from the trim panel.
25 Prise out the covers and unscrew the two screws from the bottom of the door pull pocket. Remove the pocket.
26 Using a wide-bladed screwdriver, prise the trim panel away from the door.
27 Disconnect the wiring from the electric window switch.
28 Push out the window lift switch from behind the panel.

Rear door glass (four-door models) - removal and refitting 𝄭𝄭𝄭

29 Remove the rear door trim panel as previously described.
30 Temporarily refit the window regulator handle (where applicable) and adjust the window so that the lift arm stud is visible in the glass lifting channel. Support the glass in this position with a block of wood.
31 Unscrew and remove the four bolts securing the window regulator to the door inner panel, then disconnect the lift arm stud from the glass channel and withdraw the

regulator through the aperture in the inner door panel.
32 Detach the control rod from the door release handle by pulling it free from the plastic connector.
33 Raise the glass to the closed position and tape it to the door frame at the top for support. Remove the wooden support block.
34 Unscrew and remove the bolt (with the spring and flat washer) retaining the short rear glass run channel at the boot.
35 Undo the two screws (with the shakeproof and flat washers) retaining the front door frame at the hinge face of the door.
36 Undo the two screws (with the shakeproof and flat washers) retaining the rear door frame at the trailing (lock) end of the door.
37 Detach and remove the waist rail finisher which is secured in position by two self-tapping screws or pop rivets. If pop rivets are used they will have to be drilled through to release them.
38 Unclip and remove the weather strip from the outer door panel.
39 Unclip and remove the inner seals from the inner door panel.
40 The door frame and glass can now be lifted from the door. Untape and remove the glass from the frame.
41 Refitting is a reversal of the removal procedure.

Front door glass and regulator (electrically-operated windows) - removal and refitting 𝄭𝄭𝄭

42 Ensure that the window glass is fully closed and secure it in this position with tape to prevent it dropping.
43 Disconnect the battery negative terminal.
44 Remove the door trim panel and capping as described previously.
45 Carefully peel back the plastic weatherstrip for access to the door components.
46 Release the window lift motor wiring harness from the three clips on the edge of the door panel aperture.
47 Undo the three motor retaining bolts (photo) and withdraw the motor through the door panel aperture.

48 Disconnect the wiring harness connectors and remove the motor.
49 Undo the four screws securing the regulator to the door panel.
50 Undo the two screws securing the lower window lift channel then slide the channel off the lifting arm stud.
51 Disengage the lifting arm stud from the upper lifting channel and remove the regulator by manoeuvring it out of the lower door panel aperture.
52 Remove the exterior rear view mirror as described earlier in this Section.
53 Remove the waist rail seal from the top of the door aperture.
54 From the forward facing edge of the door undo the two front door frame retaining bolts.
55 From the rearward facing edge of the door undo the single rear door frame retaining bolt.
56 Undo the bolt located in the recessed hole in the front of the inner panel below the exterior mirror mounting plate.
57 From inside the door undo the screw securing the bottom rear glass channel.
58 Carefully lift the door glass frame complete with glass out of the door panel and place the frame on the bench.
59 Release the adhesive tap securing the glass to the frame and slide the glass out of the door frame channel.
60 Refitting is the reversal of removal.

17B.47 Door window motor retaining bolts (arrowed)

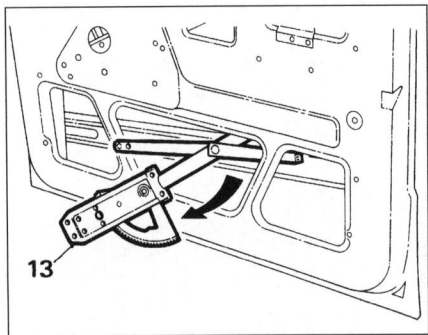

Fig. 13.217 Electrically-operated door glass regulator (13) removal from front door (Sec 17B)

Rear door glass and regulator (electrically-operated windows) - removal and refitting

61 Proceed as described for the front door glass and regulator in paragraphs 42 to 49 inclusive.

62 Carefully disengage the lifting arm stud from the glass lifting channel and extract the regulator from the lower aperture in the door panel.

63 Remove the waist rail seal from the top of the door aperture.

64 From inside the door undo the bolt securing the bottom of the shaft rear glass run channel.

65 From the forward facing edge of the door undo the two front door frame retaining bolts.

66 From the rearward facing edge of the door undo the two rear door frame retaining bolts.

67 Carefully lift the door glass frame complete with glass out of the door panel and place the frame on the bench.

68 Release the adhesive tape securing the glass to the frame and slide the glass out of the door frame channel.

69 Refitting is the reversal of removal.

Front door (four-door models) pre-1989 - removal and refitting

70 Remove the front door trim panel as described in Section 15 of Chapter 12, or earlier in this Section for later models.

17B.82 Removing the door lock actuator

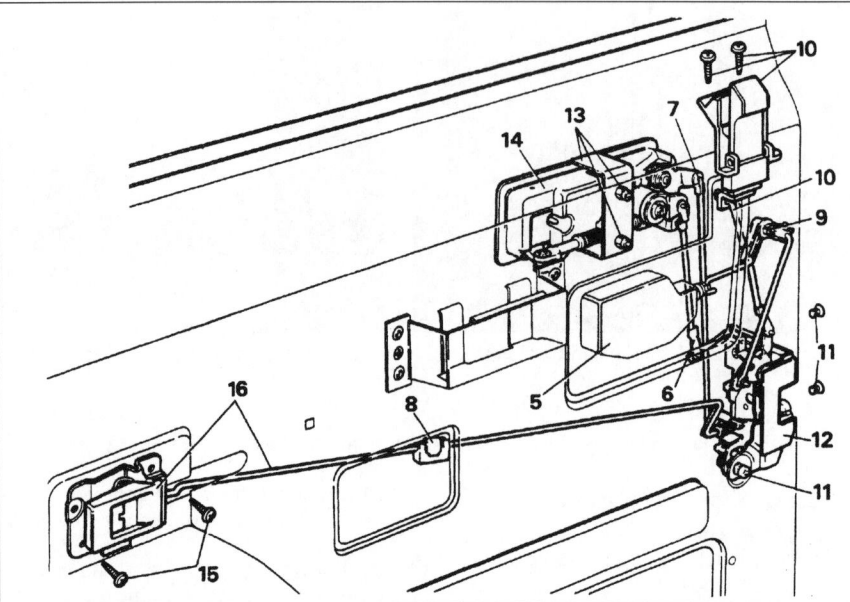

Fig. 13.218 Front door lock components for 1989-on models (Sec 17B)

5 Door lock actuator
6 Private lock control rod
7 Exterior handle control rod
8 Control rod connector
9 Quadrant
10 Locking knob

11 Door lock mounting screws
12 Door lock
13 Exterior door handle mounting screws and bracket

14 Exterior door handle
15 Remote inner door handle mounting screws
16 Remote inner door handle and control rod

71 Peel back the insulation sheet from the inner door panel.

72 Remove the door glass, referring to Section 15 in Chapter 12, or earlier in this Section for later models.

73 Detach the control rod from the key lock by releasing the metal securing clip.

74 Pull free the control rod from the door outer release handle, then detach the control rod from the inner door release handle by pulling it from the plastic connector block. Note that the control rod is also located in a guide bracket on the outboard side of the inner panel (within the cavity).

75 Undo and remove the two countersunk screws retaining the lock unit on the outside, and the single screw with its shakeproof washer on the inside, and then withdraw the lock unit from the door.

76 The door inner and outer release handles can be removed in the same manner as that described for the rear door handles (described in the following sub-section).

77 Refit in the reverse order of removal.

Front door lock, interior and exterior handles (four-door models) 1989-on - removal and refitting

78 Remove the trim panel as described in the previous paragraphs.

79 Pull the plastic membrane from the door inner panel.

80 Remove the electric window lift motor.

81 Remove the door window glass and regulator.

82 Remove the door lock actuator (photo).

83 Unclip the bottom of the exterior door handle control rod from the private key operated lock.

84 Pull the exterior door handle control rod from the plastic ferrule on the handle (photo).

85 Working through the aperture in the door panel, unclip the inner door handle remote control rod and pull it out of the plastic connector.

86 Push out the pin securing the quadrant to the door panel, then push out the quadrant.

87 Unscrew the two screws securing the lock button to the door, then disconnect the button from the control rod.

88 Unscrew the mounting screws securing the lock to the door and withdraw the lock through the lower rear aperture on the inner panel. The lock has two countersunk screws

17B.84 View of the exterior door handle from the inside of the door

17B.88 Front door lock mounting screws

and one single screw with a shakeproof washer (photo).

89 To remove the exterior door handle, unscrew the two mounting nuts, gaining access through the upper rear aperture.

90 To remove the inner door handle, unscrew the two mounting screws and withdraw the handle together with half of the control rod (photo).

91 Refitting is a reversal of the removal procedure.

Front door lock and handle assembly (four-door models) 1989-on - adjustment

92 With the inner door handle surround refitted, allow the handle to set to its normal operating position.

93 Turn the nylon nut at the door lock clockwise or anti-clockwise to shorten or lengthen the rod.

94 Disconnect the control rod at the rear of the exterior door handle by pulling the rod from the plastic ferrule, then turn the rod clockwise or anti-clockwise to shorten or lengthen it. Refit the rod to the plastic ferrule.

95 Check that the exterior handle opens the door before it reaches the end of its movement, so that there is a slight reserve of movement.

Rear door lock (four-door models) pre-1989 - removal and refitting

96 Remove the rear door trim panel as described previously.

97 Detach the control knob from the connector block within the door.

98 Release the metal retaining clip and release the manual lock control rod from the door lock.

99 Pull free and detach the control rod from the plastic ferrule of the outer door release handle.

100 Unscrew and remove the two countersunk screws securing the lock unit to the outer face, and the single screw with shakeproof washers securing on the inside. Withdraw the lock unit, complete with the control rods.

101 If required, the inner door release handle can be removed by undoing the four retaining screws and flat washers.

17B.90 Inner door handle and mounting screws

102 The outer door release handle is secured by two nuts and shakeproof washers on the inside.

103 To remove the manual (sill) lock quadrant, insert a rod or screwdriver of suitable diameter into the square insert and press the plastic lock pin through to release it. When loosened the insert can be pushed into the door and the quadrant unit withdrawn, with its control rods, from the lower aperture in the inner door panel.

104 Refitting is a reversal of the removal procedure.

105 When refitting the lock quadrant, push the lock pin into the square insert from the outside until it is a flush fit.

106 When refitting the inner door handle, the front centre screw must be fitted first.

107 Although adjustment to the door lock release mechanism should not normally be necessary, the outer door handle connecting rod length can be varied to suit, and the inner handle position can be adjusted by

loosening its retaining screws. When the position is adjusted retighten the front centre screw first.

108 On completion check that the door lock releases before the total handle movement is used up to allow for a minimal amount of overthrow movement.

Rear door lock, interior and exterior handles (four-door models) 1989-on - removal and refitting

109 With the window fully closed, disconnect the battery negative lead.

110 Remove the trim panel as described in the previous paragraphs.

111 Disconnect the control rod from the inner handle by pulling the rod out of its location at the door lock.

112 Release the metal clip and disconnect the locking control rod from the door lock.

113 Disconnect the control rod from the exterior handle by pulling it out of the plastic ferrule.

114 Unscrew the lock mounting screws (two countersunk screws on the door edge, and one single screw and shakeproof washer on the inside of the door) and withdraw the lock through the upper rear aperture in the inner door. Note the location of any spacers between the lock and the door panel.

115 To remove the outer door handle, unscrew the two mounting nuts and remove the retaining bracket. Detach the exterior door handle from the outer door panel.

116 Unscrew the two screws and withdraw the inner door handle together with the control rod.

117 Unscrew the two screws and detach the locking button from the quadrant.

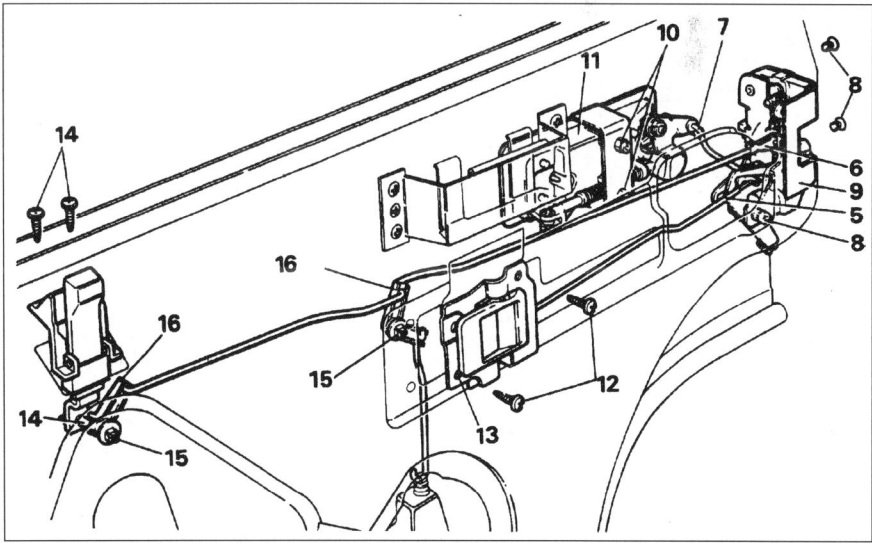

Fig. 13.219 Rear door lock components for 1989-on models (Sec 17B)

5 Control rod	10 Exterior handle mounting nuts and bracket	13 Remote inner door handle
6 Locking knob control rod		14 Locking knob mounting screws
7 Exterior handle control rod	11 Exterior handle	
8 Door lock mounting screws	12 Remote inner door handle mounting screws	15 Plastic locking pins
9 Door lock		16 Quadrants

118 Using a small screwdriver or similar tool, press the plastic pins through the square inserts in the inner door panel until they can be recovered from inside the door.

119 Disconnect the quadrants from the inner door panel and release the control rods.

120 Remove the quadrant from the inner door panel.

121 Refitting is a reversal of the removal procedure. When refitting the quadrants, enter the locking pins in the square insert from the outside and press them in flush.

Rear door lock and handle assembly (four-door models) 1989-on - adjustment

122 Detach the short offset control rod at the rear of the door outer
release handle, then turn the rod clockwise or anti-clockwise to shorten or lengthen it.

123 Check that the exterior handle opens the door before it reaches the end of its movement, so that there is a slight reserve of movement.

Front door (four-door models) March 1989-on - removal and refitting

124 Disconnect the battery negative lead.

125 Open the door, then lever off the trim panel from the side of the footwell and remove the two plastic clips.

126 Disconnect the wiring plugs for the door services, then prise out the rubber grommet and feed the wiring out through the hole.

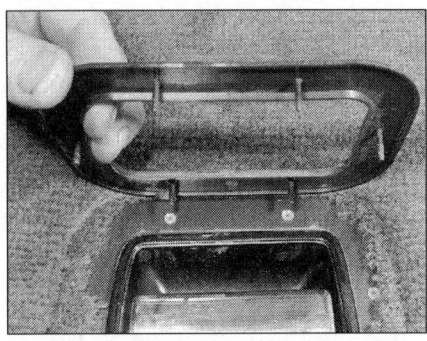

17B.146 Prise up the tailgate interior release handle surround

127 Using a small drift, drive out the door check pin.

128 Pull the clips from the upper grooves in the hinge pins.

129 With the help of an assistant, lift the door upwards off the hinge pins.

130 Refitting is a reversal of the removal procedure but adjust the door centrally within the door aperture as follows. To adjust the door forwards or backwards, either add or take away shims from between the hinge and door. Up-and-down or in-and-out adjustment is made by loosening the Torx screws securing the hinges to the door. Any adjustment of the door position will necessitate adjustment of the striker so that it enters the lock centrally. Shims may also be added to, or removed from, between the striker and the B-post.

Rear door (four-door models) pre-March 1989 - removal and refitting

131 Disconnect the battery negative terminal.

132 Open the door concerned and then unscrew the locking knob.

133 Fully close the door window, then undo the retaining screw and withdraw the window regulator handle.

134 Undo the two armrest securing screws and remove the armrest.

135 Prise free the door release handle bezel which comprises an upper and lower section.

136 The door trim pad can now be removed by carefully prising it away from the door using a flat implement inserted around the periphery of the trim. The trim is secured by eighteen plastic clips which should pop free as leverage is applied. With the trim panel removed, peel back and remove the plastic insulation sheet.

137 Extract the circlip from the check strap clevis pin then withdraw the pin with its spacers.

138 Get an assistant to support the door during its removal and mark an outline around the door hinges to provide an alignment guide when refitting. Undo the lower hinge bolts, then the upper hinge bolts and remove the door. Note any adjustment shims which may be fitted between the hinge and door pillar.

139 Refit in the reverse order of removal, if adjustment is required adjust the door in the same manner as that described for the front doors in Chapter 12.

Rear door (four-door models) March 1989-on - removal and refitting

140 Disconnect the battery negative lead.

141 Prise out the rubber grommet from the B-post, pull out the wiring and disconnect the plugs.

142 Unbolt the door check strap from the B-post.

143 Pull the clips from the upper grooves in the hinge pins.

144 With the help of an assistant, lift the door upwards off the hinge pins.

145 Refitting is a reversal of the removal procedure but adjust the door centrally within the door aperture as follows. To adjust the door forwards or backwards, either add or take away shims from between the hinge and door. Up-and-down or in- and-out adjustment is made by loosening the Torx screws securing the hinges to the door. Any adjustment of the door position will necessitate adjustment of the striker so that it enters the lock centrally. Shims may also be added to, or removed from, between the striker and the B-post.

Tailgate lock (1987-on models) - removal and refitting

146 Open the lower tailgate and carefully prise up the surround over the interior release handle (photo).

147 Undo the screws securing the trim panel to the inner face of the tailgate (photo). Note that close inspection is needed to find these screws as they are deeply embedded in the pile of the panel material. Note also that they are of different lengths so record their locations.

148 Undo the screws securing the linkage access panel and interior release handle to the tailgate and remove the panel (photo). If required the release handle can be removed from the panel by undoing the two nuts on the reverse side (photos).

17B.147 Undo the trim panel retaining screws

17B.148A Undo the linkage access panel retaining screws

17B.148B Interior release handle to access panel retaining nuts (arrowed)

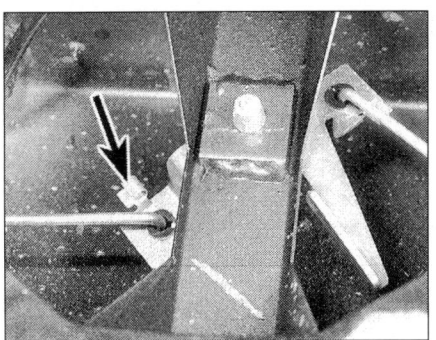

17B.149 Release the operating rod retaining clips (arrowed)

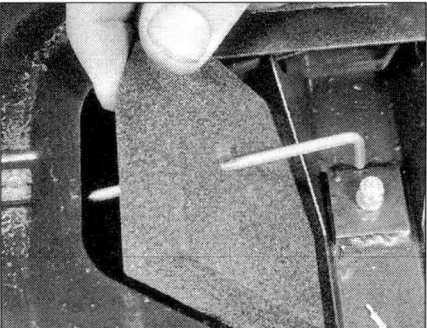

17B.150 Slide off the foam anti-rattle pad

17B.151A Undo the lock retaining screws . . .

149 Release the retaining clips as required securing the left-hand and right-hand lock operating rods to the bellcrank (photo). Slip the rod out of its nylon bush in the bellcrank.

150 Slide the foam anti-rattle pad off the end of the operating rod (photo).

151 From the side of the tailgate undo the two screws and withdraw the lock mechanism, spacing pad and operating rod (photos).

152 If necessary remove the operating rod from the lock mechanism by releasing it from its retaining lug (photo).

153 Refitting is the reversal of removal. Should adjustment be necessary this is achieved by carefully bending the operating rods to increase or decrease their length as required.

Central door locking system - general

154 This system is fitted to four-door models only. The four doors (but not the tailgate) are locked automatically by means of the external door key or by the internal lock button.

155 The system is operated electrically and comprises a control unit fitted to the steering column support bracket under the lower facia panel, and a lock actuator unit in each door.

Central door locking system control unit (pre-1990 models) - removal and refitting

156 Disconnect the battery earth lead.

157 Undo the five retaining screws and remove the lower facia panel.

158 Detach the wiring multi-plug connector from the base of the control unit.

159 Unscrew and remove the two screws securing the control unit to the steering column support bracket and remove the unit. The unit is not repairable and if defective must be renewed.

160 Refit in the reverse order of removal.

Central door locking system actuator unit - removal and refitting

161 Remove the door trim panel as described in Section 15 of Chapter 12, or earlier in this Section for later models.

162 Peel back the insulation sheet at the top rear corner to gain access to the actuator unit within the door.

163 On front doors, undo the four actuator unit mounting plate retaining screws (photo).

On rear doors undo the two actuator unit-to-door mounting screws.

164 Disconnect the wiring connection to the actuator unit by releasing the securing clip. On rear doors the wiring and connector plug are secured to the door inner panel by two spring clips, access to which is gained through the aperture in the inner panel.

165 Withdraw the actuator unit, manoeuvring it so that the operating rod can be detached from the actuator link of the door lock (photo).

166 When the actuator unit is withdrawn, the wiring connectors will be exposed as they are pulled from their channel and can be disconnected and the actuator fully removed.

167 The actuator units are not repairable and, if defective, must be renewed. Disconnect the front door actuator unit from its mounting plate by undoing the two rubber mounted screws (photo).

17B.151B . . . and remove the lock and operating rod

17B.152 Lock mechanism operating rod retaining clip (arrowed)

17B.163 Removing the central door locking actuator retaining plate screws

17B.165 Detach the operating rod . . .

17B.167 . . . and undo the actuator-to-retaining plate screws

168 Refit the actuator unit in the reverse order of removal.

169 When attaching the actuator mounting plate to the inner door panel (front door units), adjust the mounting plate so that it is in the centre of the slotted holes.

170 Do not refit the door trim panel until the locking action is checked as follows.

171 Check the lock actuation manually and electrically to ensure that the actuator operating rod does not restrict the operation of either locking method. If necessary adjust the mounting position of the actuator to suit.

172 On the front doors, move the manual lock to the halfway position of its total movement then hold it in this position and check that the door locks electrically. Further adjustment of the mounting plate may be necessary to achieve this.

Central door locking system control unit (1990-on models) - removal and refitting

173 The central door locking system is now activated from both driver's and passenger's doors, and an activator is located in both front doors. The electronic control unit is located on the steering column support bracket.

174 Disconnect the battery negative lead.

175 Remove the lower facia panel.

176 Disconnect the wiring multi-plug.

177 Unscrew the mounting screws and remove the control unit from the steering column support bracket.

178 Refitting is a reversal of the removal procedure.

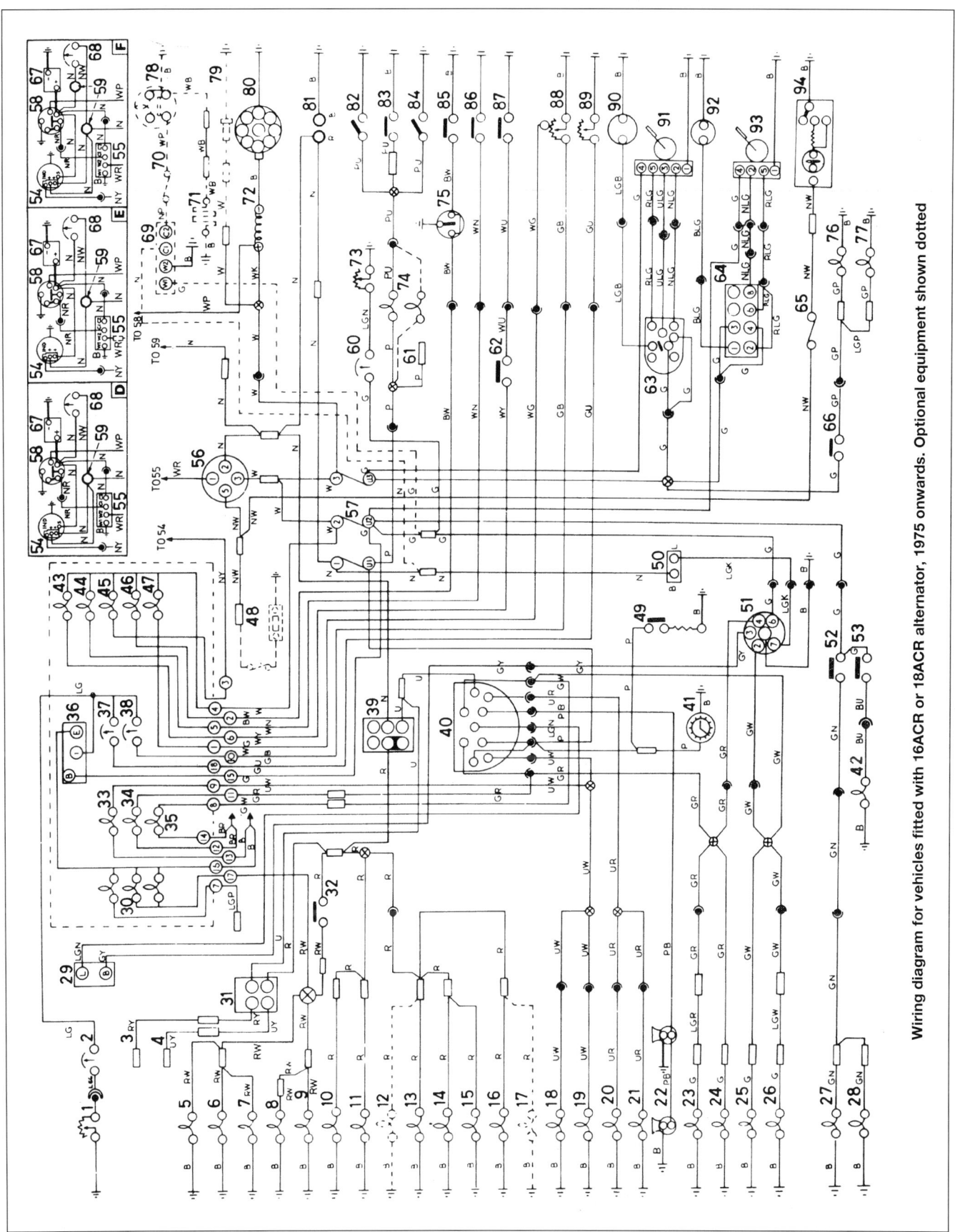

Wiring diagram for vehicles fitted with 16ACR or 18ACR alternator, 1975 onwards. Optional equipment shown dotted

Key to wiring diagram for vehicles fitted with 16ACR or 18ACR alternator, 1975 onwards, and for vehicles fitted with voltmeter instead of ammeter

1	Oil temperature transmitter	31	Auxiliary driving lamps switch	64	Rear wiper and washer switch
2	Oil temperature gauge	32	Panel lights switch	65	In-line fuse for heater
3	Pick-up point for auxiliary driving lamps	33	Warning light, headlamp main beam	66	Stop-lamps switch
4	Pick-up point for auxiliary driving lamps	34	Warning light, indicator, LH	67	Battery
5	Ammeter (or battery voltmeter) illumination	35	Warning light, indicator, RH	68	Ammeter (or battery voltmeter)
		36	Voltage stabiliser	69	Relay for heated rearscreen
6	Oil temperature gauge illumination	37	Water temperature gauge	70	In-line fuse for heated rear screen
7	Cigar lighter illumination	38	Fuel gauge	71	Heated rear screen
8	Oil pressure gauge illumination	39	Main light switch	72	Ignition coil
9	Clock illumination	40	Headlamps, direction indicators and horn switch	73	Oil pressure transmitter
10	Sidelamp, LH			74	Interior light
11	Sidelamp, RH	41	Clock	75	Shuttle valve for brake switch
12	Side marker lamp, tail, LH, as applicable	42	Warning light, differential lock switch	76	Stop-lamp, LH
		43	Warning light, choke	77	Stop-lamp, RH
13	Tail lamp, LH	44	Warning light, oil pressure	78	Heated rear screen switch
14	Number plate illumination	45	Warning light, ignition	79	Fuel pump
15	Number plate illumination	46	Warning light, brake	80	Distributor
16	Tail lamp, RH	47	Warning light, fuel level	81	Inspection light sockets
17	Side marker lamp, tail, RH, as applicable	48	Pick-up point for radio	82	Courtesy light switch
		49	Cigar lighter	83	Interior light switch
18	Headlamp main beam, RH	50	Hazard warning unit	84	Courtesy light switch
19	Headlamp main beam, LH	51	Hazard warning switch	85	Handbrake switch
20	Headlamp dip, RH	52	Reversing lights switch	86	Oil pressure switch
21	Headlamp dip, LH	53	Differential lock switch	87	Choke control pick-up point switch
22	Horns	54	Alternator	88	Fuel gauge, tank unit
23	Indicator lamp, rear LH	55	Relay for starter motor	89	Water temperature transmitter
24	Indicator lamp, front LH	56	Ignition/starter switch	90	Windscreen washer motor
25	Indicator lamp, front RH	57	Fuses	91	Windscreen wiper motor
26	Indicator lamp, rear RH	58	Starter motor	92	Rear screen washer motor
27	Reversing lamp	59	Terminal post	93	Rear screen wiper motor
28	Reversing lamp	60	Oil pressure gauge	94	Heater motor
29	Indicator unit	61	Pick-up point for seven-pin trailer socket		
30	Trailer illumination	62	Choke switch		
		63	Front wiper and washer switch		

Later vehicles may be fitted with air cord 12 volt oil pressure gauges not wired via the voltage stabiliser or 10 volt gauges in circuit with it

Cable colour code

B Black	L Light	P Purple	U Blue
G Green	N Brown	R Red	W White
K Pink	O Orange	S Slate	Y Yellow

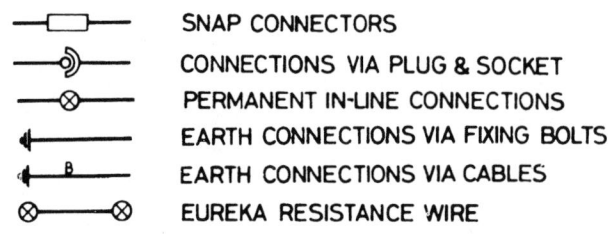

SNAP CONNECTORS

CONNECTIONS VIA PLUG & SOCKET

PERMANENT IN-LINE CONNECTIONS

EARTH CONNECTIONS VIA FIXING BOLTS

EARTH CONNECTIONS VIA CABLES

EUREKA RESISTANCE WIRE

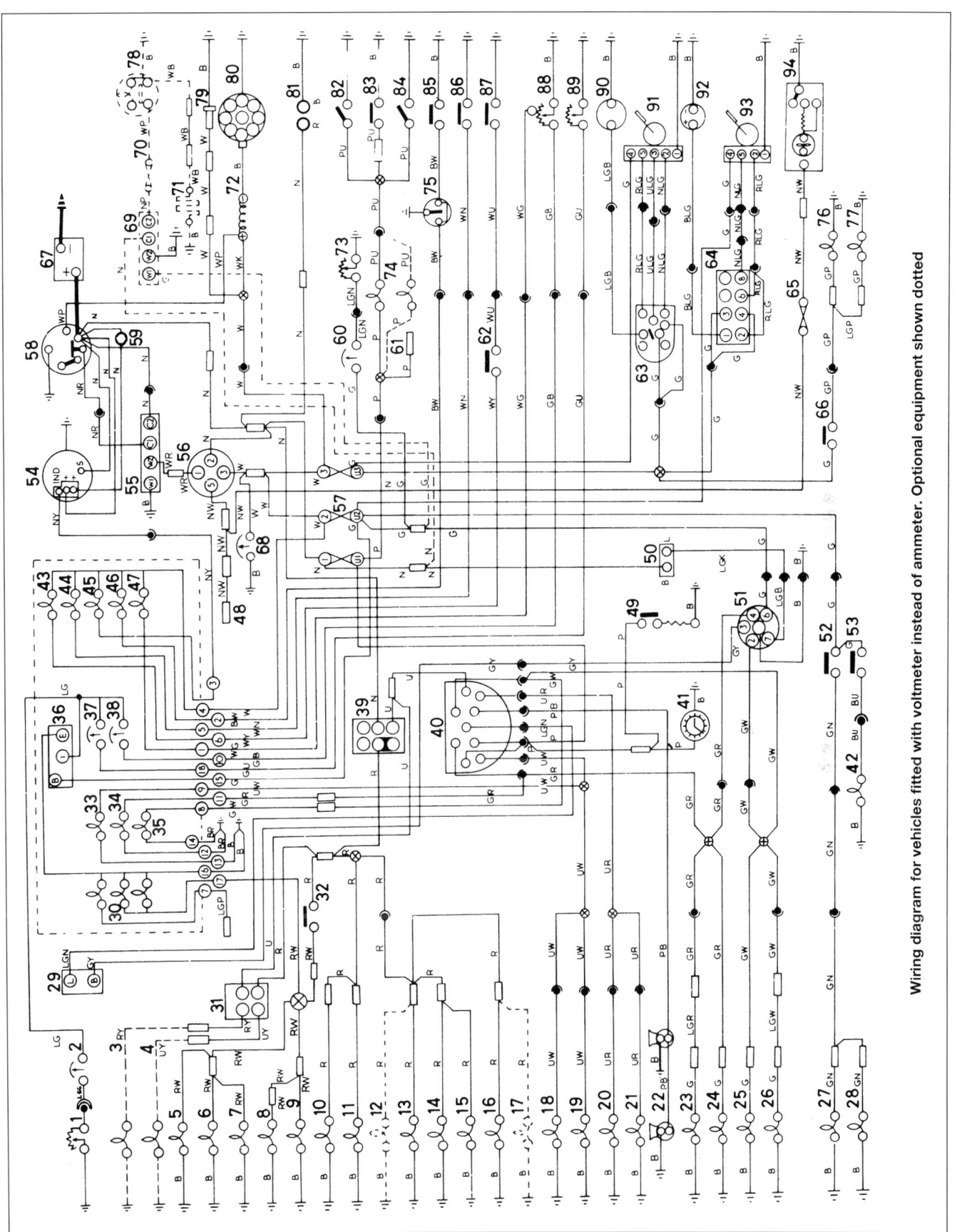

Wiring diagram for vehicles fitted with voltmeter instead of ammeter. Optional equipment shown dotted

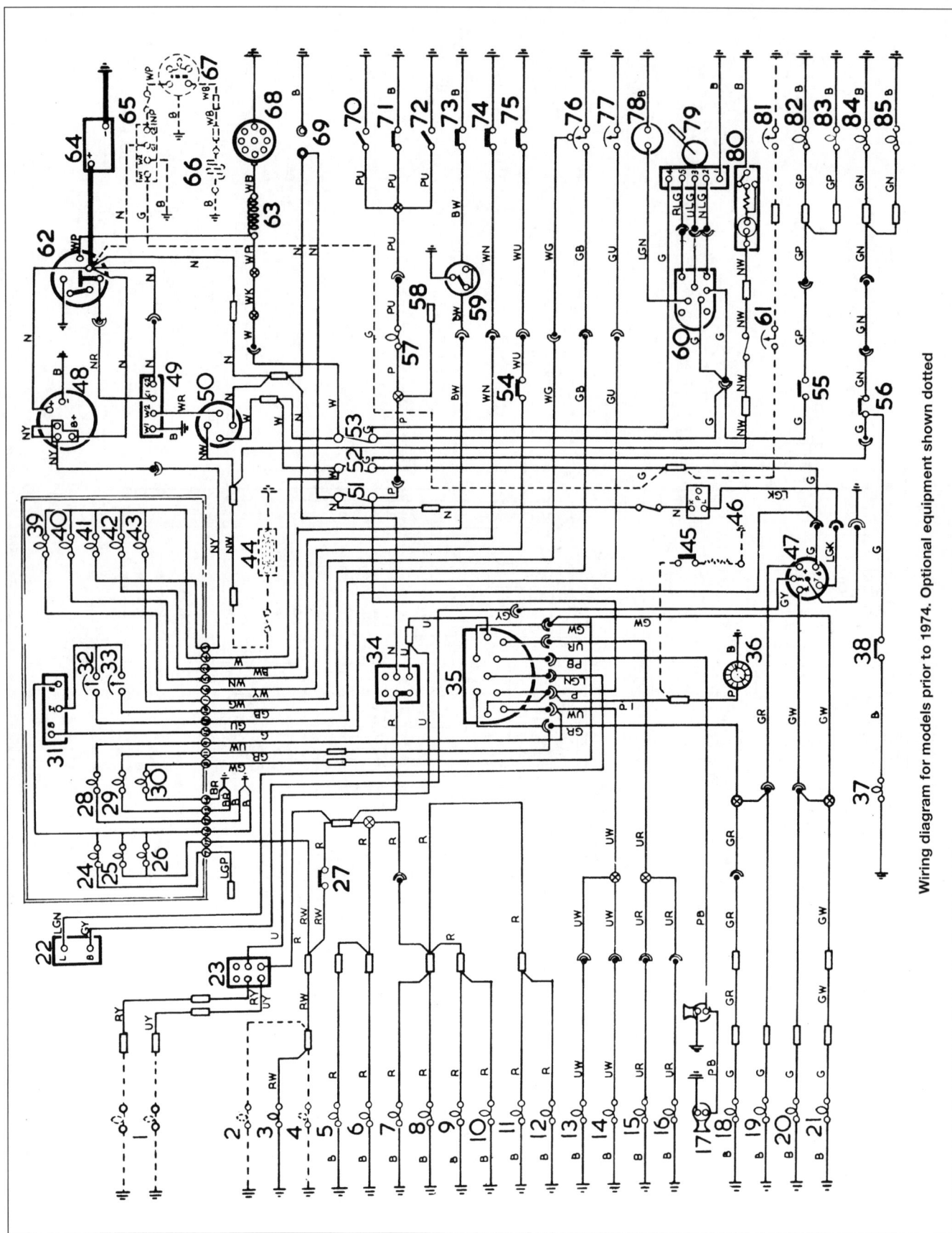

Wiring diagram for models prior to 1974. Optional equipment shown dotted

Key to wiring diagram for Models prior to 1974

1	Auxiliary driving lamps	30	RH indicator warning light	58	Trailer socket connection
2	Cigar lighter illumination	31	Voltage stabiliser	59	Shuttle valve (brake warning)
3	Clock illumination	32	Water temperature gauge	60	Windscreen wiper and washer switch
4	Auxiliary instrument illumination feed	33	Fuel gauge	61	Oil pressure gauge
5	LH front side lamp	34	Lighting switch	62	Pre-engaged starter
6	RH front side lamp	35	Indicator, headlamp dip and horn switch	63	Coil
7	LH rear marker lamp (NADA only)			64	Battery
8	LH rear tail lamp	36	Clock	65	Relay
9	Number plate illumination lamp	37	Differential lock warning light	66	Heated rear screen
10	Number plate illumination lamp	38	Differential lock warning light switch	67	Heated rear screen switch
11	RH rear tail lamp	39	Choke warning light switch	68	Distributor
12	RH rear marker lamp (NADA only)	40	Oil pressure warning light	69	Inspection sockets
13	RH headlamp, main	41	Ignition warning light	70	Courtesy light switch
14	LH headlamp, main	42	Brake warning light	71	Interior light switch
15	RH headlamp, dip	43	Fuel level warning light	72	Courtesy light switch
16	LH headlamp, dip	44	Radio	73	Handbrake switch
17	Horns	45	Cigar lighter	74	Oil pressure switch
18	LH rear indicator	46	Hazard warning unit	75	Choke thermostat
19	LH front indicator	47	Hazard warning switch	76	Fuel gauge unit
20	RH front indicator	48	Alternator	77	Water temperature transmitter
21	RH rear indicator	49	Starting relay	78	Screen washer motor
22	Indicator unit	50	Ignition switch and steering lock	79	Windscreen wiper motor
23	Auxiliary driving lamp switch	51	Fuse (1)	80	Heater motor
24	Trailer warning light	52	Fuse (2)	81	Oil pressure transmitter
25	Instrument illumination	53	Fuse (3)	82	Stop-light, RH
26	Instrument illumination	54	Choke switch	83	Stop-light, LH
27	Panel light switch	55	Stop-lamp switch	84	Reversing light RH
28	Main beam warning light	56	Reversing light switch	85	Reversing light LH
29	LH indicator warning light	57	Interior light		

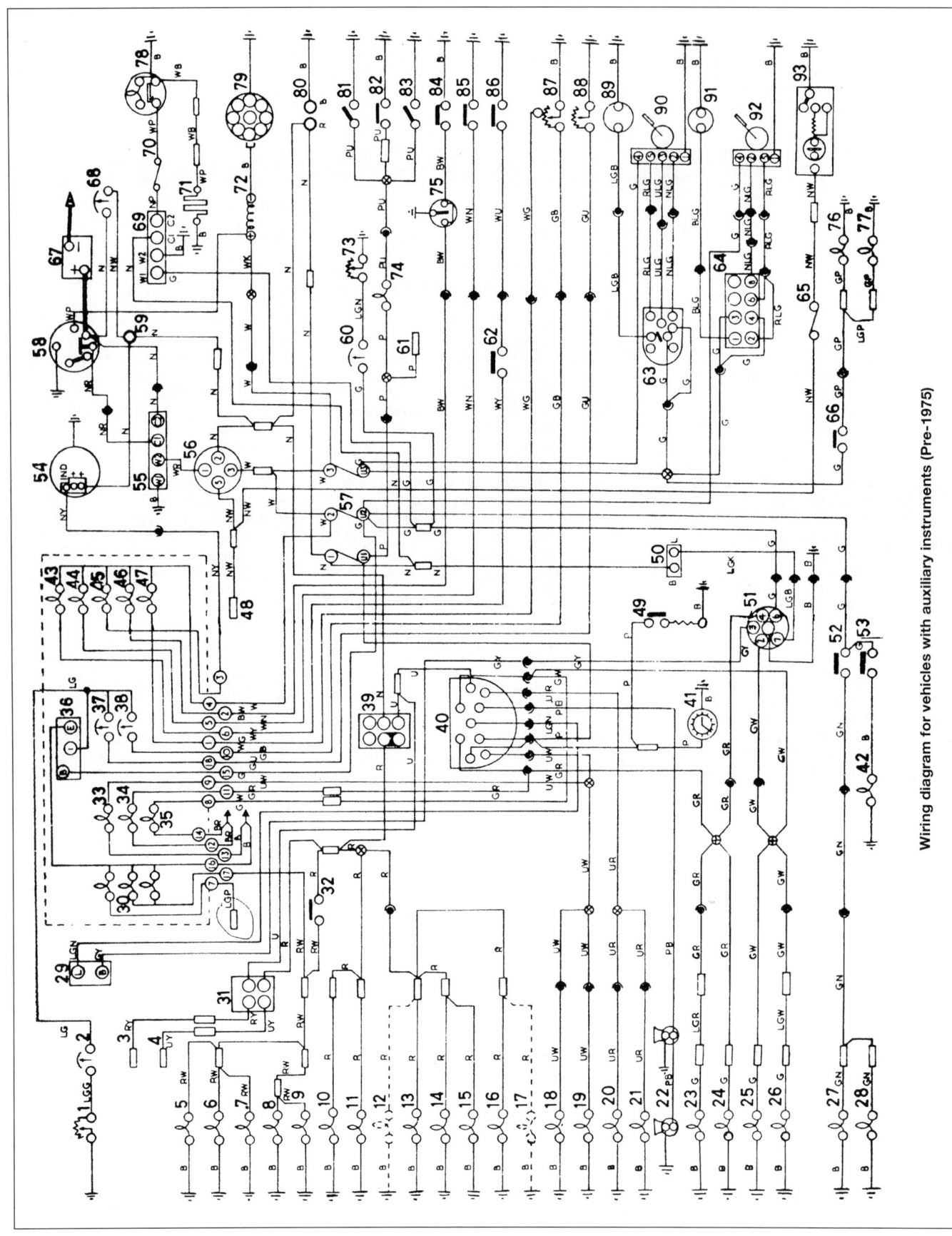

Wiring diagram for vehicles with auxiliary instruments (Pre-1975)

Key to wiring diagram for vehicles with auxiliary instruments (Pre-1975)

1	Oil temperature transmitter	31	Auxiliary driving lamps switch	62	Choke switch
2	Oil temperature gauge	32	Panel lights switch	63	Front wiper and washer switch
3	Pick-up point for auxiliary driving lamps	33	Warning light. headlamp main beam	64	Rear wiper and washer switch
4	Pick-up point for auxiliary driving lamps	34	Warning light, indicator, LH	65	In-line fuse for heater
5	Ammeter illumination	35	Warning light, indicator, RH	66	Stop-lamps switch
6	Oil temperature gauge illumination	36	Voltage stabiliser	67	Battery
7	Cigar lighter illumination	37	Water temperature gauge	68	Ammeter
8	Oil pressure gauge illumination	38	Fuel gauge	69	Relay for heated rear screen
9	Clock illumination	39	Main light switch	70	In-line fuse for heated rear screen
10	Sidelamp, LH	40	Headlamps, direction indicators and horn switch	71	Heated rear screen
11	Sidelamp, RH	41	Clock	72	Ignition coil
12	Side marker lamp, tail, LH, as applicable	42	Warning light. differential lock switch	73	Oil pressure transmitter
13	Tail lamp, LH	43	Warning light, choke	74	Interior light
14	Number plate illumination	44	Warning light, oil pressure	75	Shuttle valve for brake switch
15	Number plate illumination	45	Warning light, ignition	76	Stop-lamp, LH
16	Tail lamp, RH	46	Warning light, brake	77	Stop-lamp, RH
17	Side marker lamp ,tail, RH, as applicable	47	Warning light, fuel level	78	Heated rear screen switch
18	Headlamp main beam, RH	48	Pick-up point for radio	79	Distributor
19	Headlamp main beam, LH	49	Cigar lighter	80	Inspection light sockets
20	Headlamp dip, RH	50	Hazard warning unit	81	Courtesy light switch
21	Headlamp dip, LH	51	Hazard warning switch	82	Interior light switch
22	Horns	52	Reversing lights switch	83	Courtesy light switch
23	Indicator lamp, rear LH	53	Differential lock switch	84	Handbrake switch
24	Indicator lamp, front LH	54	Alternator	85	Oil pressure switch
25	Indicator lamp, front RH	55	Relay for starter motor	86	Choke control pick-up point switch
26	Indicator lamp, rear RH	56	Ignition/starter switch	87	Fuel gauge, tank unit
27	Reversing lamp	57	Fuses	88	Water temperature transmitter
28	Reversing lamp	58	Starter motor	89	Windscreen washer motor
29	Indicator unit	59	Terminal post	90	Windscreen wiper motor
30	Trailer illumination	60	Oil pressure gauge	91	Rear screen washer motor
		61	Pick-up point for seven-pin trailer socket	92	Rear screen wiper motor
				93	Heater motor

Wiring diagram for trailer lighting circuit

1 Replacement flasher unit
2 Side marker lamp, LH
3 Tail lamp, LH
4 Indicator lamp, LH
5 Indicator lamp, RH
6 Stop-lamp, LH
7 Stop-lamp, RH
8 Instrument binnacle
9 From indicator switch
10 From hazard warning switch

11 To number plate illumination
12 Feed from fuse A2
13 Seven-pin vehicle socket
14 Dotted lines indicate vehicle wiring
15 Chain dotted lines indicate vehicle wiring repositioned
16 Unbroken lines indicate the conversion harness

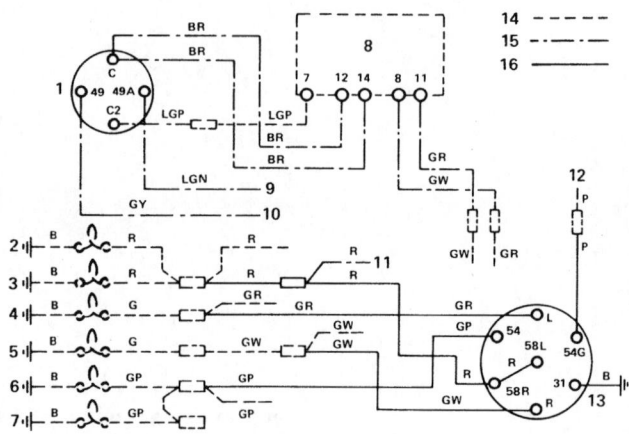

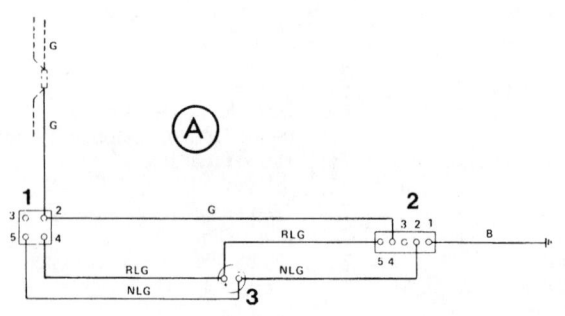

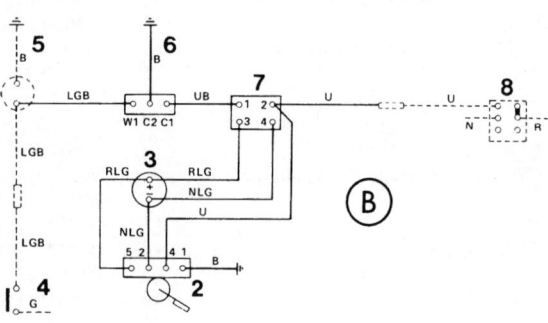

Circuit diagram for headlamp wipers and washers

1 Headlamp wiper washer switch
2 Headlamp wiper motor
3 Headlamp washer pump
4 Windscreen washer switch
5 Windscreen washer pump
6 Headlamp wiper relay
7 Headlamp wiper relay unit
8 Vehicle lighting switch
A Earlier vehicles
B Later vehicles

Circuit diagram for split charging facility

1 Lighting switch
2 Connection to starter relay
3 Steering lock and ignition switch
4 Voltmeter
5 Vehicle battery
6 Inspection lamp sockets
7 Starter motor
8 Split charge diode

9 Fuse unit
10 Terminal bracket for second battery
11 Second bracket
12 Alternator

Circuits shown dotted are existing and contained in the basic vehicle. Circuits shown in full are additional

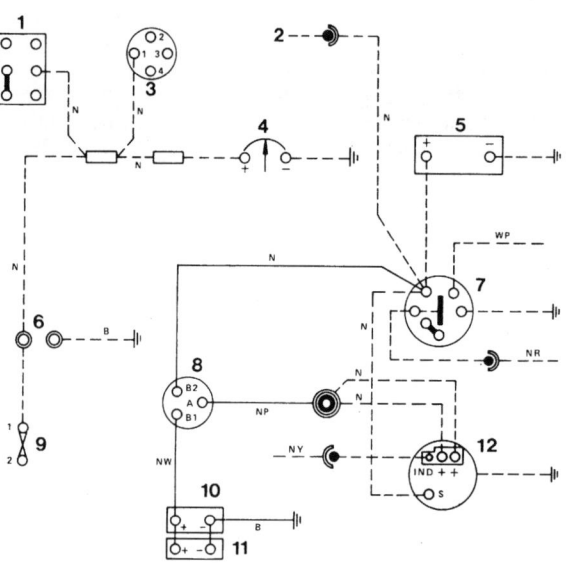

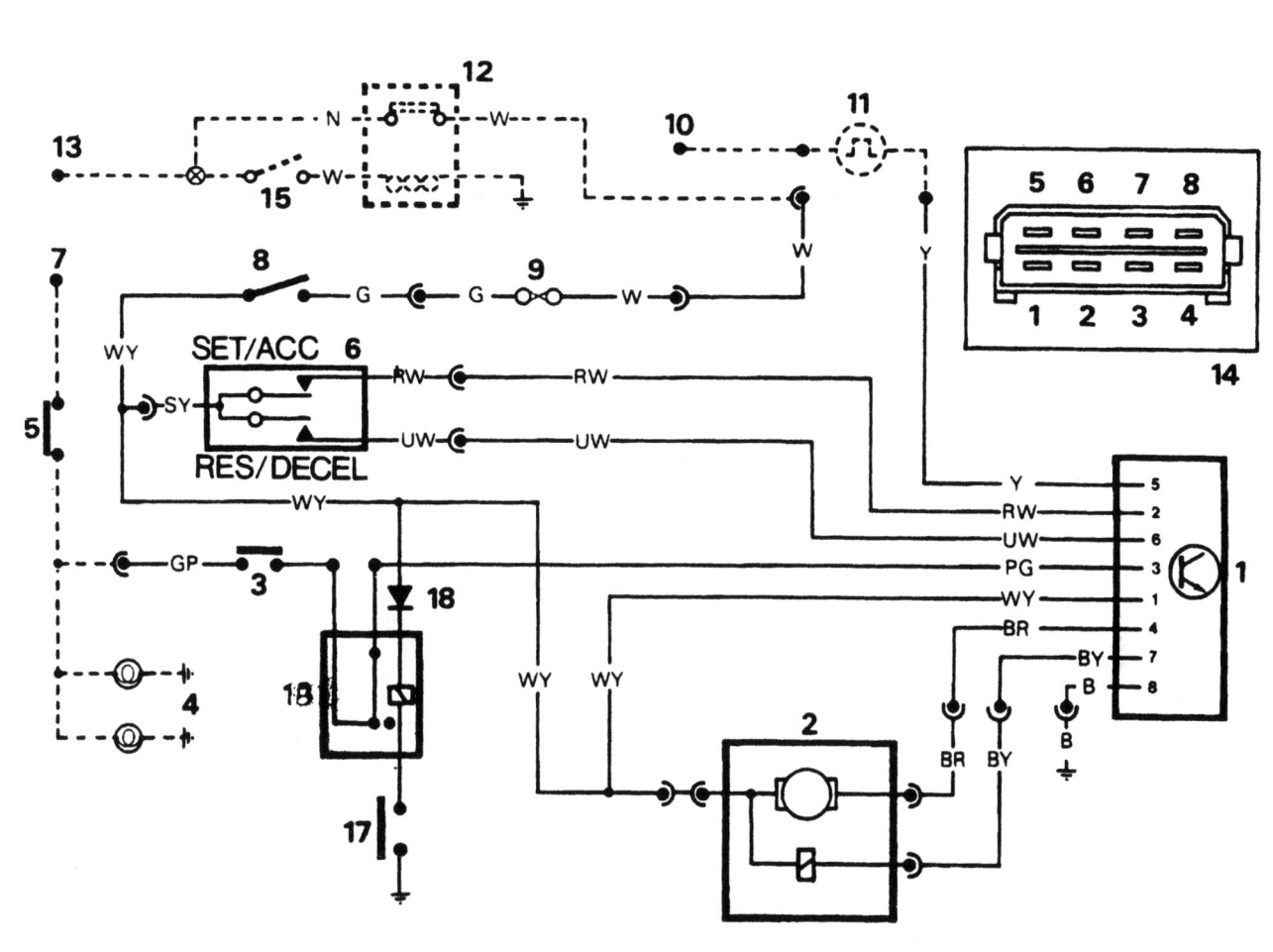

Wiring diagram for cruise control system

1	Cruise control ECU	14	Cruise control multi-plug
2	Vacuum pump	1	Power supply from marker switch
3	Brake switch/vent valve	2	SET switch connection
4	Stop-lamps	3	Earth connection
5	Brake switch	4	Vacuum pump motor connection
6	SET/RESUME switches	5	Speed transducer connection
7	Stop-lamp supply connection	6	RESUME switch connection
8	Cruise control switch	7	Vacuum pump solenoid valve connection
9	Fuse C5 (auxiliary fuse panel)	8	ECU earth
10	Speed transducer supply (12V+)		
11	Speed transducer	15	Ignition switch (item 8 in main wiring diagram)
12	Ignition load relay (item 1 in main wiring diagram)	16	Neutral lockout relay
13	Battery feed (12V+)	17	Start inhibit switch
		18	Diode

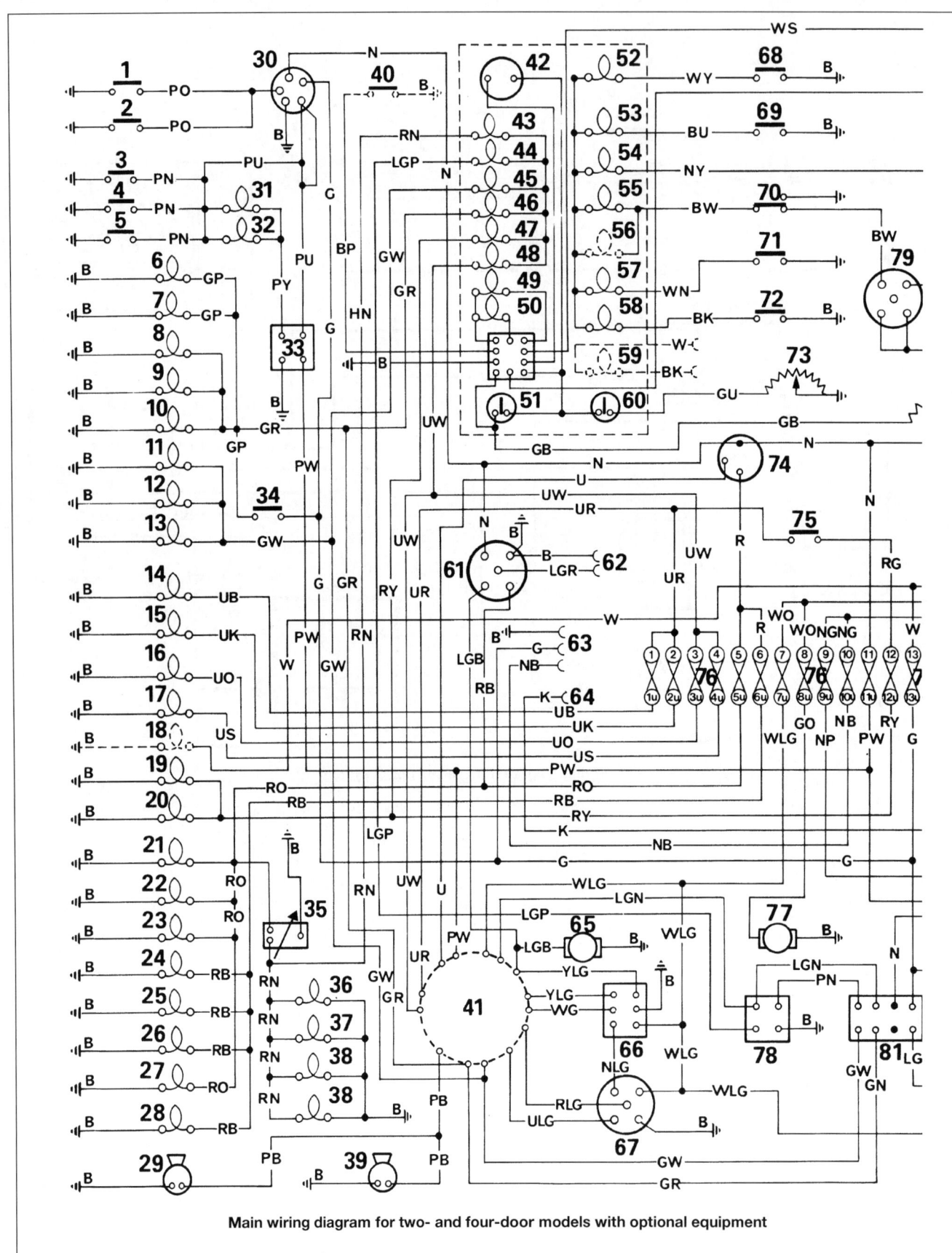

Main wiring diagram for two- and four-door models with optional equipment

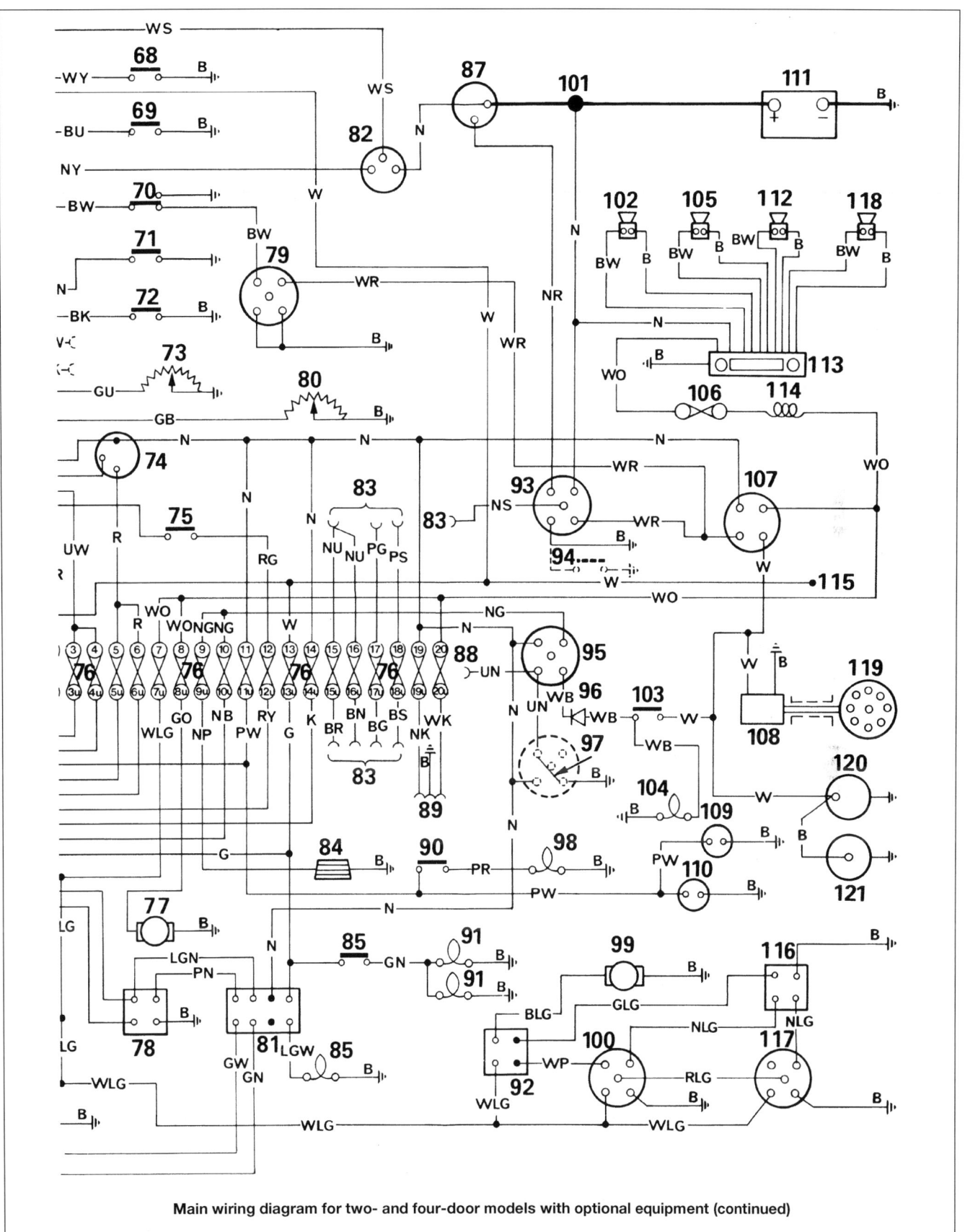

Main wiring diagram for two- and four-door models with optional equipment (continued)

Key to main wiring diagram for two- and four-door models with optional equipment

1	Front door switch (left-hand)	41	Steering column switches	82	Alternator
2	Front door switch (right-hand)	42	Tachometer	83	Air conditioning (option)
3	Tailgate switch	43	Instrument illumination	84	Heated rear screen
4	Rear door switch (left-hand)	44	Trailer warning light	85	Reverse lamp switch
5	Rear door switch (right-hand)	45	Right-hand indicator	86	Hazard warning lamp
6	Stop lamp (right-hand)	46	Left-hand indicator	87	Starter solenoid
7	Stop lamp (left-hand)	47	Rear fog warning light	88	Split charge relay (option)
8	Left-hand front indicator lamp	48	Headlamp warning light	89	Electric windows and central door
9	Left-hand rear indicator lamp	49	Oil cooler temperature warning light		locking (options)
10	Left-hand side repeater lamp	50	Low fuel warning light	90	Engine compartment (bonnet) light
11	Right-hand front indicator lamp	51	Fuel indicator warning light		switch
12	Right-hand rear indicator lamp	52	Cold start warning light	91	Reverse lamps
13	Right-hand side repeater lamp	53	Differential lock warning light	92	Rear wipe/wash switch
14	Right-hand headlamp dip	54	Ignition warning light	93	Starter solenoid relay
15	Left-hand headlamp dip	55	Brake failure warning light	94	Start inhibitor switch (automatic)
16	Right-hand headlamp main	56	Brake failure warning light (Australia)	95	Heated rear window relay
17	Left-hand headlamp main	57	Oil pressure warning light	96	Diode
18	Automatic gear selector graphics	58	Park brake warning light	97	Voltage switch (option)
	illumination	59	Park brake warning light (Australia)	98	Bonnet lamp
19	Right-hand rear foglamp	60	Water temperature gauge	99	Rear screen wash motor
20	Left-hand rear foglamp	61	Headlamp wash timer (option)	100	Rear wiper relay
21	Right-hand number plate lamp	62	Headlamp wash pump (option)	101	Terminal post
22	Right-hand side lamp	63	Heated electric mirrors (option)	102	Left-hand rear speaker (option)
23	Right-hand tail lamp	64	Trailer socket (option)	103	Heated rear window switch
24	Left-hand number plate lamp	65	Front screen wash	104	Heated rear window warning lamp
25	Left-hand side lamp	66	Wiper delay	105	Right-hand rear speaker (option)
26	Left-hand tail lamp	67	Wiper motor	106	Radio fuse
27	Radio illumination	68	Cold start warning lamp switch	107	Ignition switch
28	Switch illumination	69	Differential lock switch	108	Constant energy ignition unit
29	Right-hand horn	70	Brake failure switch	109	Cigar lighter
30	Interior lamp delay	71	Oil pressure switch	110	Clock
31	Front interior lamp	72	Park brake switch	111	Battery
32	Rear interior lamp	73	Water temperature transducer	112	Left-hand front speaker
33	Interior lamp switch	74	Light switch	113	Radio (option)
34	Stop lamp switch	75	Rear foglamp switch	114	Radio choke
35	Rheostat	76	Fuses	115	Split charge relay (option)
36	Cigar lighter illumination	77	Heater motor switch	116	Rear wiper delay
37	Clock illumination	78	Flasher unit	117	Rear wiper motor
38	Heater illumination	79	Brake failure warning lamp check	118	Right-hand front speaker
39	Left-hand horn		relay	119	Distributor
40	Automatic transmission oil cooler	80	Fuel tank unit	120	Fuel pump
	temperature switch	81	Hazard switch	121	Fuel pump capacitor

Key to main wiring diagram for manual transmission models

1	Oil temperature transmitter	37	Main beam warning light	71	Starter motor
2	Front foglamp pick-up point	38	LH indicator warning light	72	Resistive wire
3	Front foglamp pick-up point	39	RH indicator warning light	73	Oil pressure transmitter
4	Battery voltmeter illumination	40	Voltage stabiliser	74	Courtesy lighting delay unit
5	Oil temperature gauge illumination	41	Water temperature gauge	75	Heated rear screen switch
6	Cigar lighter illumination	42	Fuel gauge	76	Front wiper washer switch
7	Oil pressure gauge	43	Rear fog lighting switch	77	Rear wiper washer switch
8	Clock illumination	44	Differential lock switch	78	Heater motor
9	LH Front side lamp	45	Rear fog warning light	79	Coil
10	RH Front side lamp	46	Sidelight warning light	80	Fuse
11	Number plate illumination	47	Lighting switch	81	Battery
12	Number plate illumination	48	Indicator, headlamps, dipped beam	82	Electric fuel pump
13	LH Rear tail lamp		and horn switch	83	Distributor
14	RH Rear tail lamp	49	Clock	84	Inspection sockets
15	Underbonnet illumination	50	Reverse lamp switch	85	Courtesy lighting switches
16	Direction indicator side repeater	51	Choke warning lamp	86	Interior lighting switch
17	LH Front indicator lamp	52	Oil warning lamp	87	Courtesy lighting switches
18	Horns	53	Ignition warning lamp	88	Brake circuit check relay
19	RH Headlamp main beam	54	Brake warning lamp	89	Oil pressure switch
20	LH Headlamp main beam	55	Fuel warning lamp	90	Choke thermocoupling switch
21	RH Headlamp dipped beam	56	Cigar lighter	91	Park brake warning light (optional)
22	LH Headlamp dipped beam	57	Hazard warning switch	92	Fuel gauge unit
23	LH Rear indicator	58	Radio speakers	93	Water temperature transmitter
24	Direction indicator side repeater	59	Fuse unit	94	Relay (heated rear screen)
25	RH Front indicator lamp	60	Hazard unit	95	Heated rear screen
26	RH Rear indicator lamp	61	Ignition switch	96	Front screen washer motor
27	Reverse lamp LH	62	Battery voltmeter	97	Two speed front wiper motor
28	Reverse lamp LH	63	Brake fluid pressure switch	98	Rear screen washer motor
29	Oil temperature gauge	64	Choke switch	99	Single speed rear wiper motor
30	Underbonnet lamps	65	Alternator	100	LH stop lamp
31	Direction indicator switch	66	Starter relay	101	RH stop lamp
32	Trailer warning light	67	Interior lights	102	LH rear foglamp
33	Panel illumination	68	Heater fuse	103	RH rear foglamp
34	Panel illumination	69	Stop lamp switch	104	Trailer socket connection
35	Panel lighting switch	70	Oil pressure gauge	105	Programmed wash/wipe unit
36	Differential lock warning light				

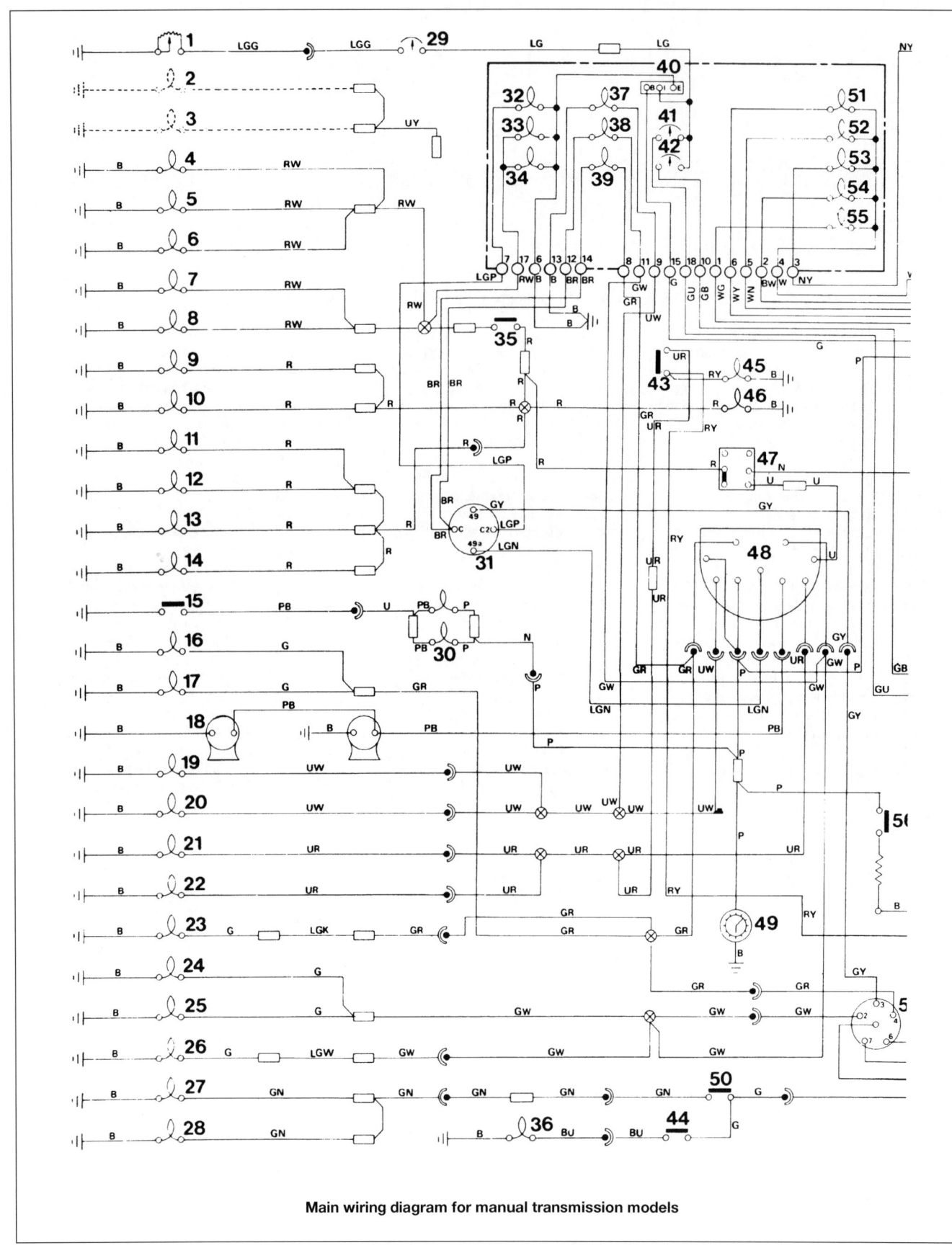

Main wiring diagram for manual transmission models

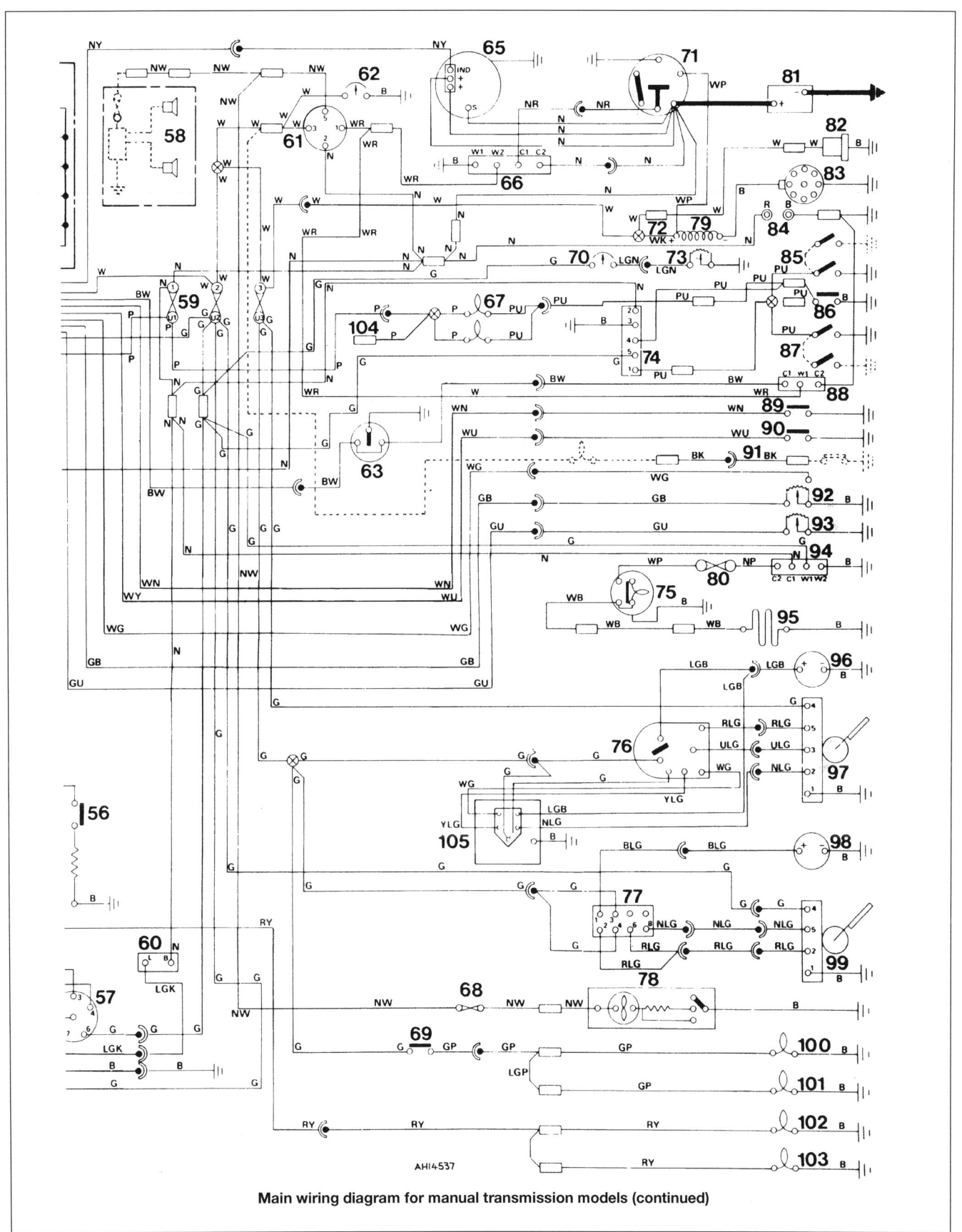

Main wiring diagram for manual transmission models (continued)

AHI4537

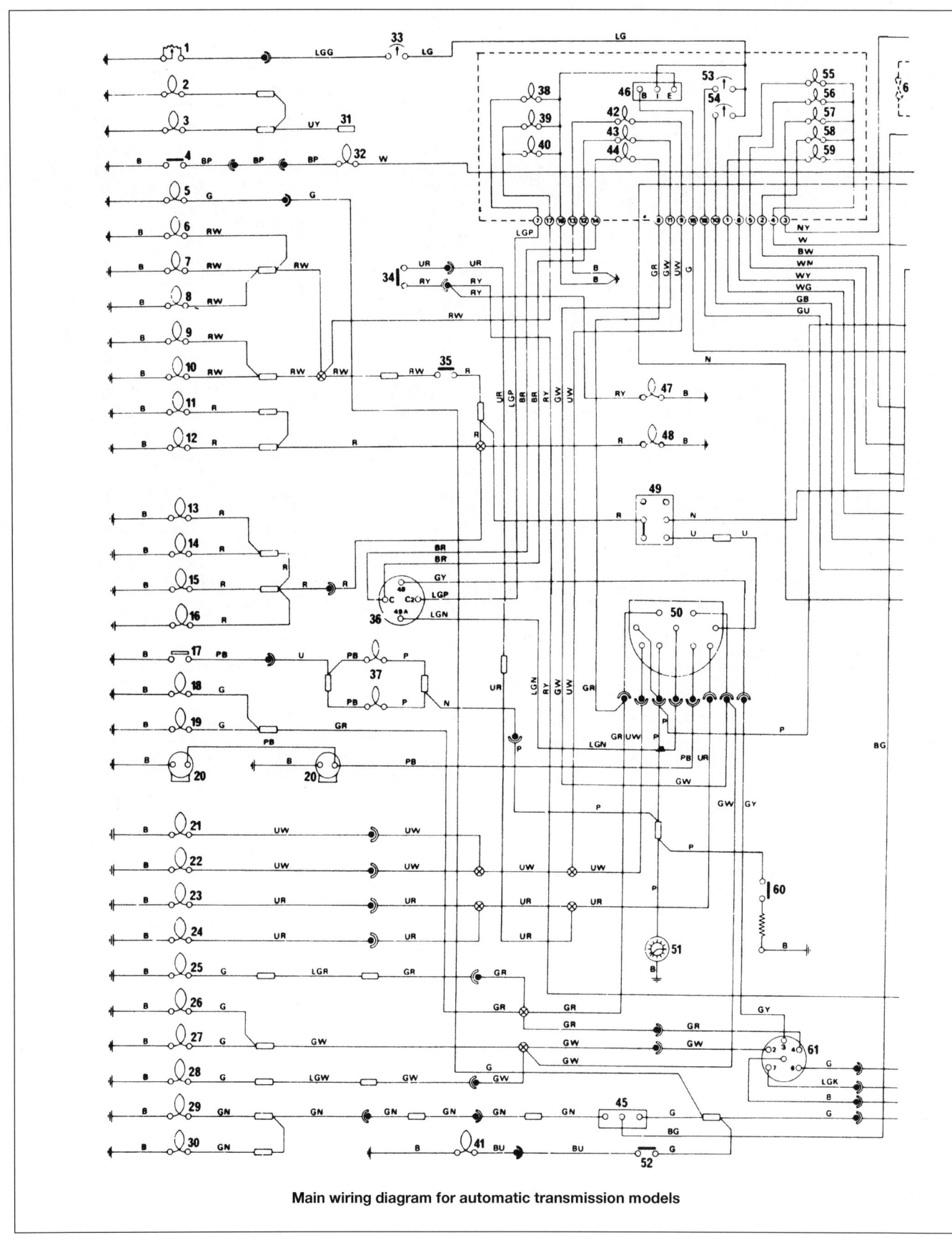

Main wiring diagram for automatic transmission models

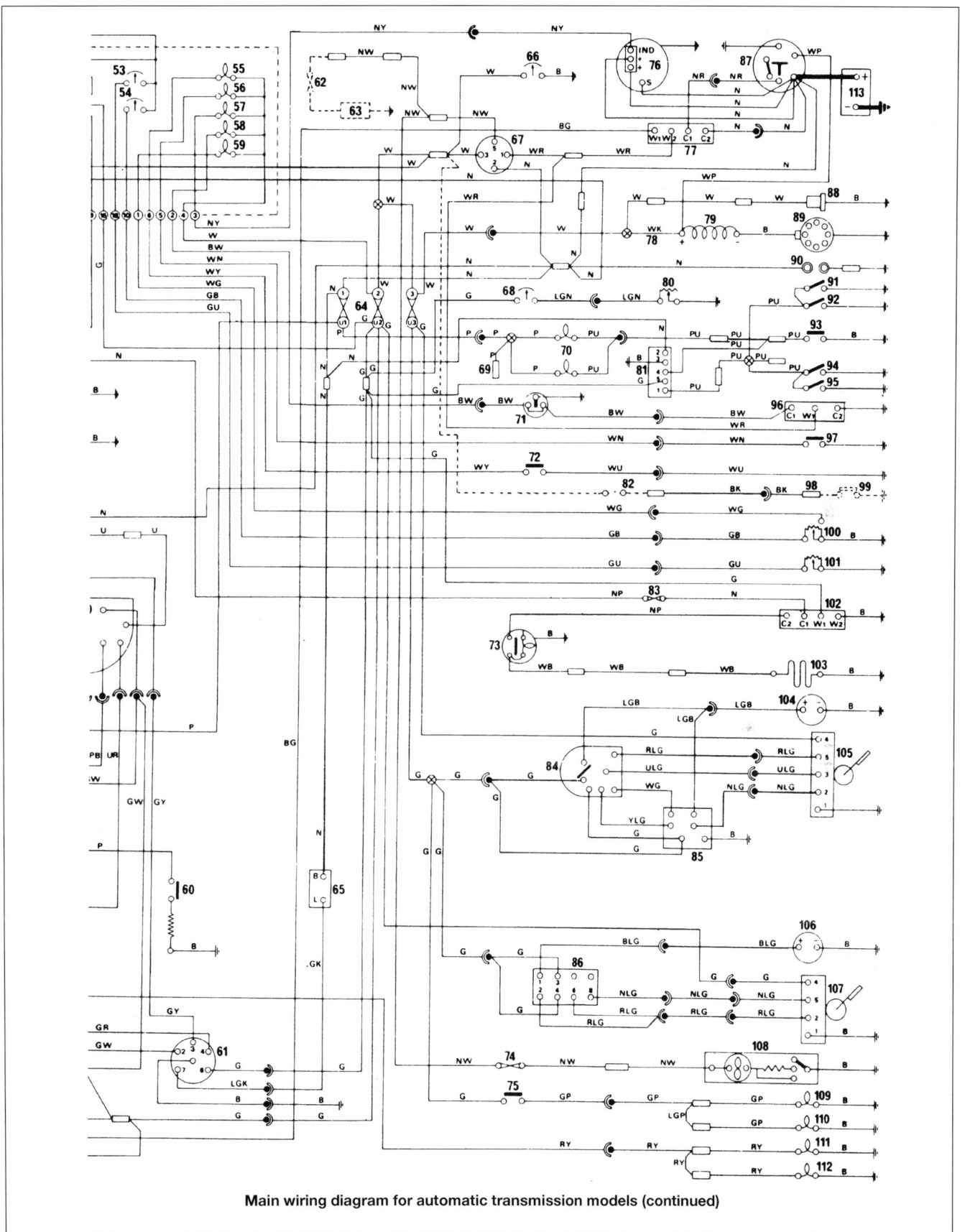

Main wiring diagram for automatic transmission models (continued)

Key to main wiring diagram for automatic transmission models

1	Oil temperature transmitter	37	Underbonnet lamps (one lamp or two according to specification)	74	Heater fuse
2	LH Front foglamp			75	Stop lamp switch
3	RH front foglamp	38	Trailer warning light	76	Alternator
4	Automatic gearbox oil cooler temperature switch	39	Panel illumination	77	Starter relay
		40	Panel illumination	78	Resistive wire
5	Automatic gearbox graphics illumination	41	Differential lock warning light	79	Coil
		42	Main beam warning light	80	Oil pressure transmitter
6	Battery voltmeter illumination	43	LH indicator warning light	81	Courtesy light delay unit (when fitted)
7	Oil temperature gauge illumination	44	RH indicator warning light	82	Park brake warning light (when fitted)
8	Cigar lighter illumination	45	Neutral, Start & Reverse lighting switch	83	Rear screen fuse
9	Clock illumination			84	Front wash/wiper switch
10	Oil pressure indicator	46	Voltage stabiliser	85	Programmed wash/wipe control unit
11	LH Front sidelamp	47	Rear fog warning light	86	Rear wash/wipe switch/control unit
12	RH Front sidelamp	48	Sidelamps warning light	87	Starter motor
13	Number plate illumination	49	Lighting switch	88	Electric fuel pump
14	Number plate illumination	50	Indicator, headlamp dip and horn switch	89	Distributor
15	LH Rear tail lamp			90	Inspection sockets
16	RH Rear tail lamp	51	Clock	91	Courtesy light switch (4-door only)
17	Underbonnet illumination (where fitted)	52	Differential lock warning light switch	92	Courtesy light switch
		53	Water indicator	93	Interior light switch
18	LH Direction indicator side repeater	54	Fuel indicator	94	Courtesy light switch
19	LH Front indicator lamp	55	Choke warning light	95	Courtesy light switch (4-door only)
20	Horns	56	Oil warning light	96	Brake circuit check relay
21	RH Headlamp main beam	57	Ignition warning light	97	Oil pressure switch
22	LH Headlamp main beam	58	Brake warning light	98	Park brake pick-up point
23	RH Headlamp dipped beam	59	Fuel warning light	99	Park brake switch (if fitted)
24	LH Headlamp dipped beam	50	Cigar lighter	100	Fuel gauge transmitter
25	LH Rear indicator lamp	61	Hazard warning switch	101	Water temperature transmitter
26	RH Direction indicator side repeater	62	Radio fuse (when fitted)	102	Heated rear screen relay
27	RH Front indicator lamp	63	Radio (when fitted)	103	Heated rear screen element
28	RH Rear indicator lamp	64	Fuse unit	104	Front screen washer motor
29	LH Reverse lamp	65	Hazard unit	105	Front screen wiper motor
30	RH Reverse lamp	66	Battery voltmeter	106	Rear screen washer motor
31	Front foglamps pick-up point	67	Ignition switch	107	Rear screen wiper motor
32	Oil cooler temperature warning light	68	Oil pressure indicator	108	Heater motor
		69	Trailer socket connection	109	LH Stop lamp
33	Oil temperature gauge	70	Interior lights	110	RH Stop lamp
34	Rear foglamp switch	71	Brake fluid check switch	111	LH Rear foglamp
35	Panel lighting switch	72	Choke switch	112	RH Rear foglamp
36	Direction indicator switch	73	Heater rear screen switch	113	Battery

Key to main wiring diagram for all models - 1986-on

1	Front interior lamp	51	LH horn	98	Hazard warning lamp
2	Rear interior lamp	52	RH horn	99	Reversing lamp switch
3	LH front door switch	53	Tachometer	100	Heated rear screen
4	RH front door switch	54	Instrument illumination (6 bulbs)	101	Starter solenoid
5	Tailgate switch	55	Trailer warning	102	Alternator
6	LH rear door switch	56	RH indicator warning light	103	Brake failure warning lamp check
7	RH rear door switch	57	LH indicator warning light		relay
8	RH stop lamp	58	Rear fog warning light	104	Fuel tank unit
9	LH stop lamp	59	Headlamp warning light	105	Air conditioning (option)
10	LH front indicator lamp	60	High transfer oil temperature warning	106	Split charge relay (option)
11	LH rear indicator lamp		light	107	Electric windows and central door
12	LH side repeater lamp	61	Low fuel warning light		locking (option)
13	RH front indicator lamp	62	Multi-function unit in binnacle	108	Under bonnet illumination switch
14	RH rear indicator lamp	63	Fuel indicator gauge	109	Reverse lamps
15	RH side repeater lamp	64	Cold start warning light (carburettor	110	Fuel pump
16	RH auxiliary driving lamp		versions only)	111	Pick-up point for petrol ignition wiring
17	LH auxiliary driving lamp	65	Differential lock warning light	112	Terminal post
18	Auxiliary driving lamp switch	66	Ignition warning light	113	Battery
19	RH headlamp dip	67	Brake failure warning light	114	LH rear speaker (option)
20	LH headlamp dip	68	Brake pad wear warning light	115	RH rear speaker (option)
21	RH headlamp main	69	Oil pressure warning light	116	LH front speaker
22	LH headlamp main	70	Park brake warning light	117	RH front speaker
23	RH rear foglamp	71	Park brake warning light (Australia)	118	Radio (option)
24	LH foglamp	72	Water temperature gauge	119	Radio fuse
25	RH number plate lamp	73	Headlamp wash timer (option)	120	Radio choke
26	RH sidelamp	74	Headlamp wash pump (option)	121	Fuel shut-off relay (carburettor
27	RH tail lamp	75	Head electric mirrors (option)		models only)
28	LH number plate lamp	76	Trailer socket (option)	122	Starter solenoid relay
29	LH sidelamp	77	Front screen wash	123	Ignition start switch
30	LH tail lamp	78	Front wiper delay	124	Start inhibitor switch (Automatic)
31	Radio illumination	79	Wiper motor	125	Split charge relay (option)
32	Switch illumination	80	Steering column switches	126	Heater rear window relay
33	Switch illumination	81	Cold start warning lamp switch	127	Diode
34	Automatic selector illumination		(carburettor only)	128	Heater rear window switch
35	Automatic selector illumination	82	Differential lock switch	129	Voltage switch (option)
36	LH door lamps	83	Brake failure switch	130	Heated rear window warning lamp
37	RH door lamps	84	Diode	131	Bonnet lamp
38	Inter lamp delay	85	Front brake pad wear	132	Cigar lighter (dash)
39	Automatic transfer oil temperature	86	Rear brake pad wear	133	Cigar lighter (cubby box)
	switch	87	Diode	134	Clock
40	Diode	88	Oil pressure switch	135	Rear screen washer motor
41	Interior lamp switch	89	Park brake switch	136	Rear wiper delay
42	Stop lamp switch	90	Pick-up point for park brake warning	137	Rear wash wipe switch
43	Auxiliary lamps delay		light (Australia)	138	Rear wiper relay
44	Rheostat	91	Water temperature transducer	139	Rear wiper motor
45	Front cigar lighter illumination	92	Light switch	140	Constant energy unit
46	Clock illumination	93	Rear foglamp switch	141	Distributor
47	Heater illumination	94	Main fusebox	142	Ignition pick-up point (petrol injection
48	Heater illumination	95	Heater motor and switch unit		only)
49	Heater illumination	96	Flasher unit	143	Not used
50	Heater illumination	97	Hazard switch		

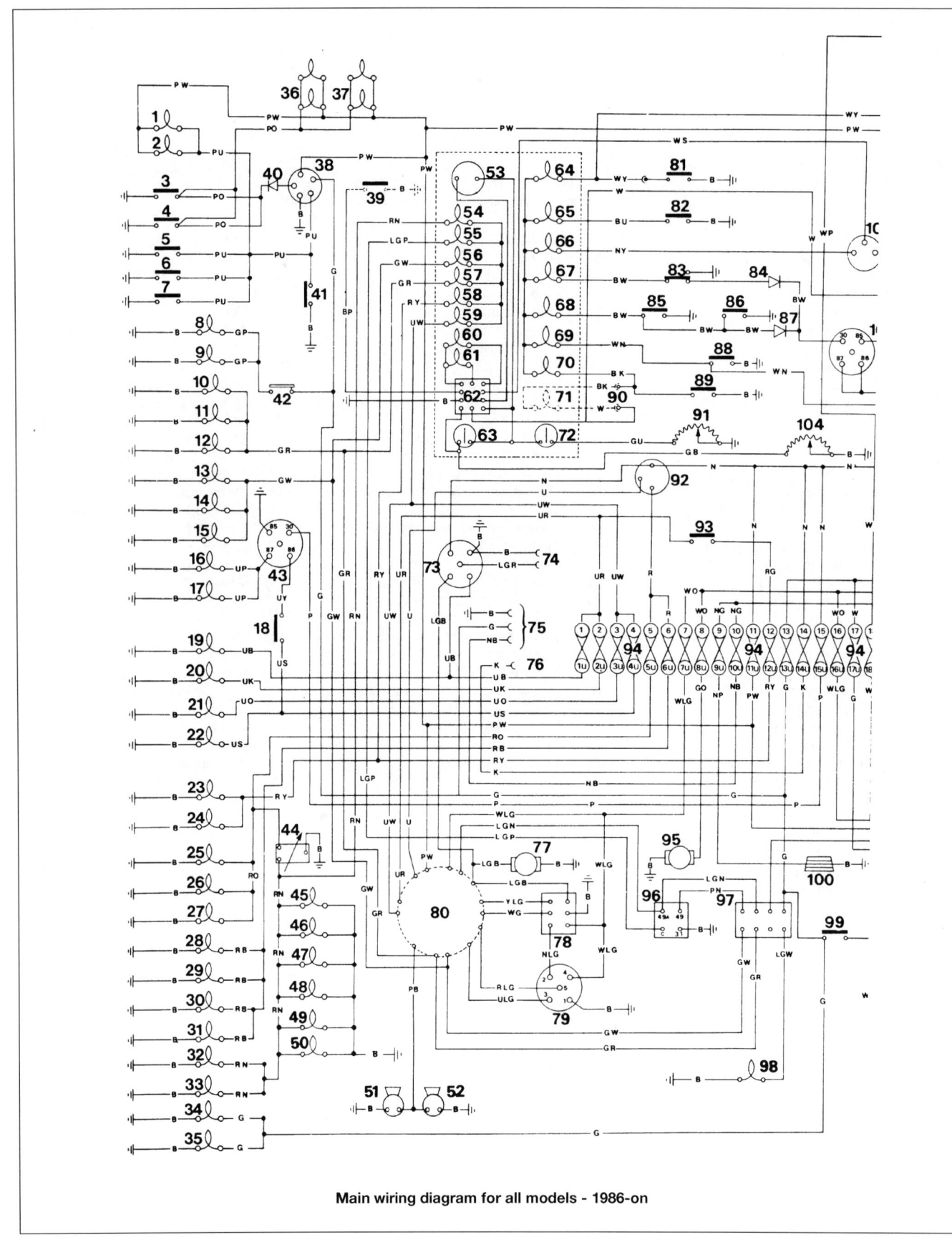

Main wiring diagram for all models - 1986-on

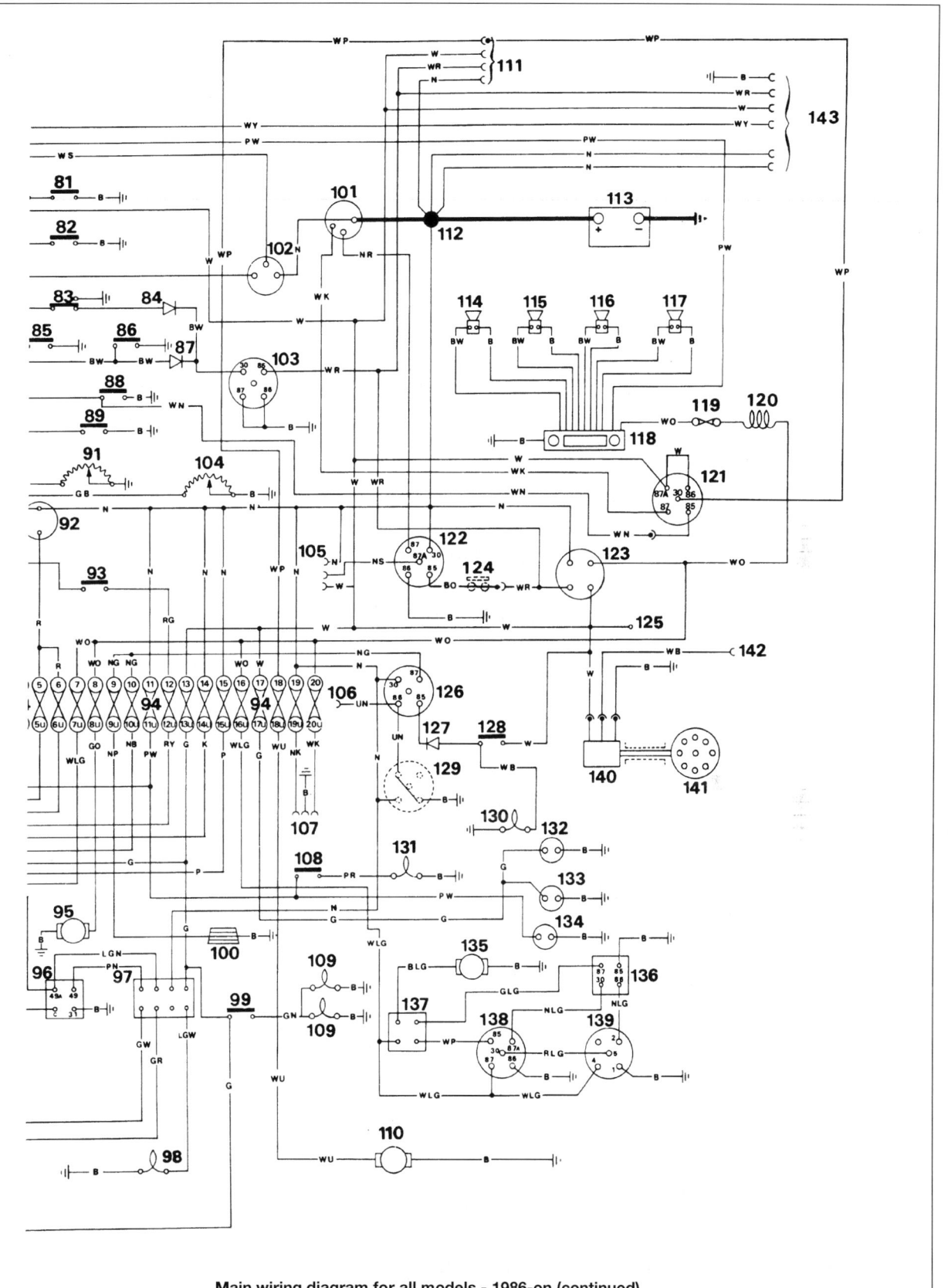

Main wiring diagram for all models - 1986-on (continued)

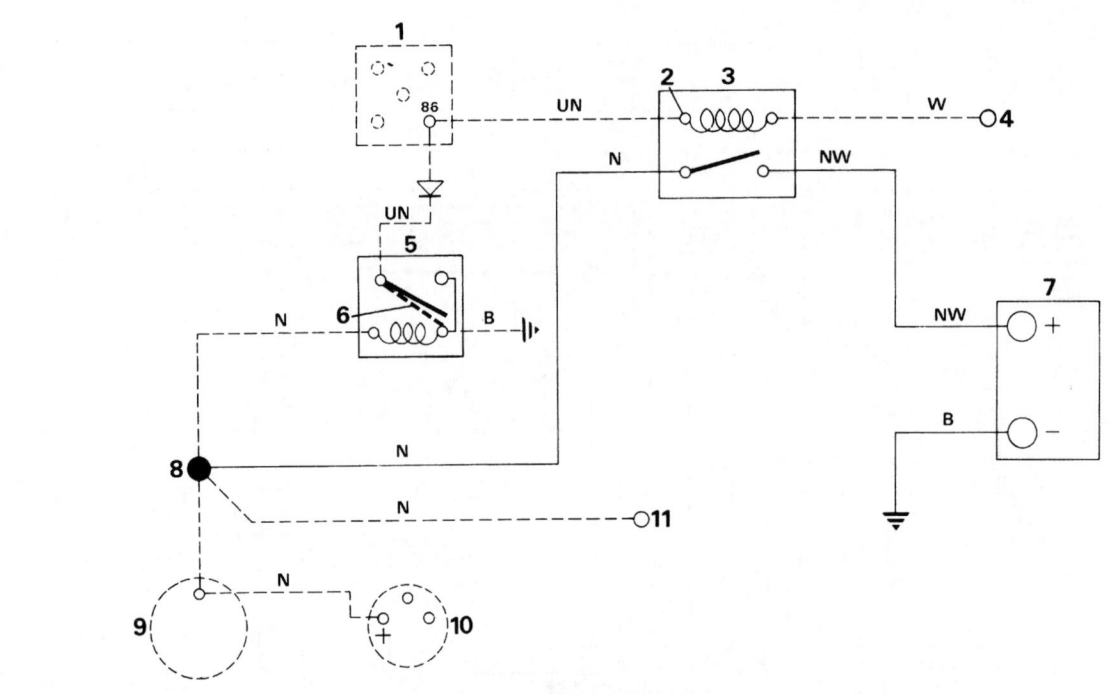

Wiring diagram for split charging circuits - 1986-on

1   Heated rear window relay
2   Pick-up point for split charge relay (items 106 and 125 on main wiring diagram)
3   Split charge relay
4   Fusebox

5   Voltage sensitive switch
6   Link wire (removed from plug when voltage sensitive switch is fitted)
7   Terminal box auxiliary battery
8   Terminal post
9   Starter motor

10 Alternator
11 Vehicle battery

Note: *Chain dotted lines indicate existing parts*

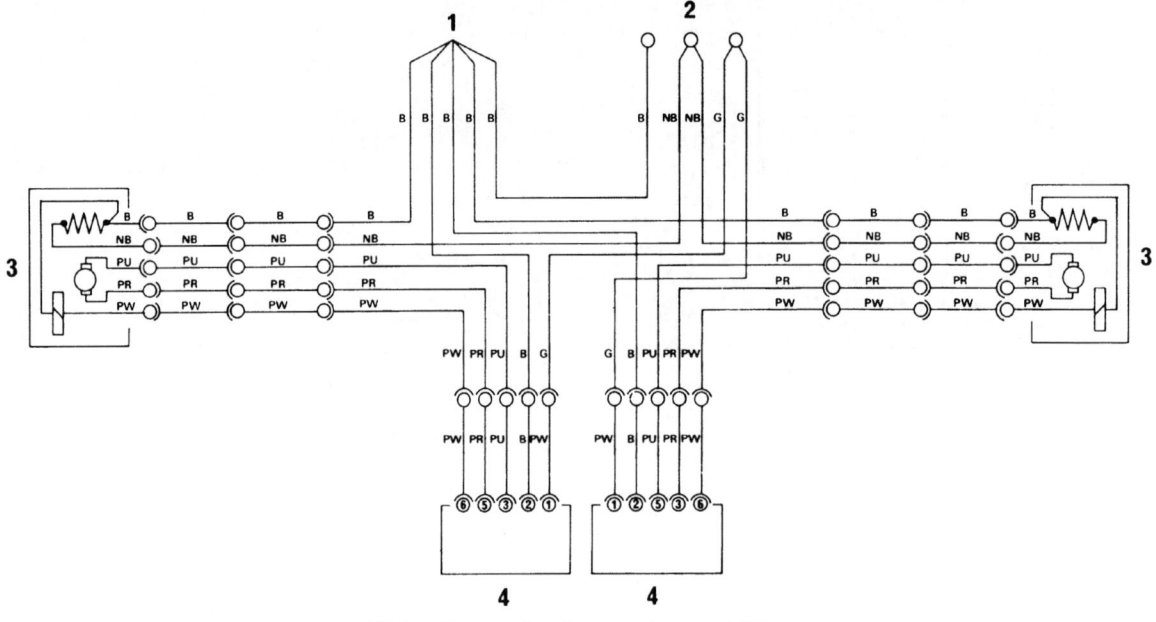

Wiring diagram for electric mirrors - 1986-on

1   Clinch
2   Main cable connections (item 75 on main wiring diagram)

3   Mirrors
4   Mirror switches

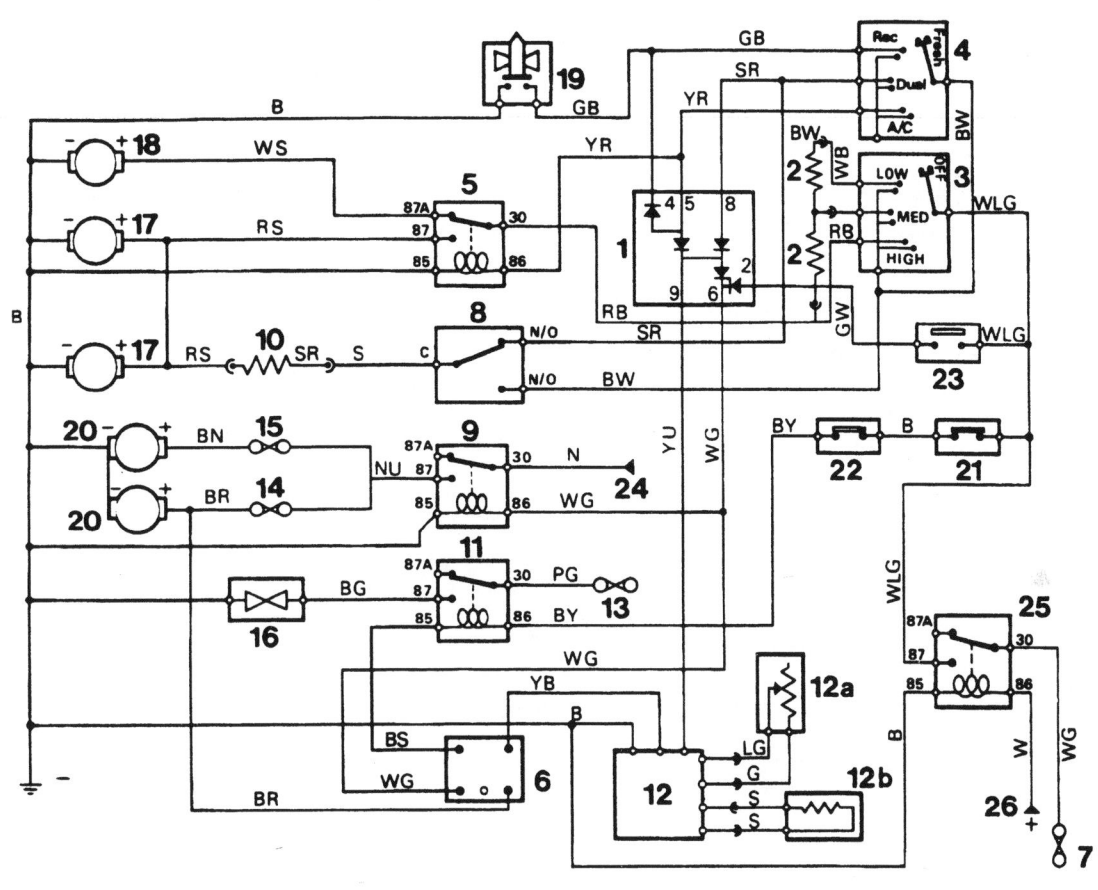

Wiring diagram for typical air conditioning system

1	Diode pack	10	Two-level resistor	18	Heater motor
2	Resistors	11	Compressor clutch relay	19	Fresh air solenoid
3	Fan speed switch	12	Thermostat	20	Condenser fan motors
4	Air conditioning/re-circ/fresh air switch	12a	Temperature control potentiometer	21	High-pressure switch
		12b	Evaporator temperature sensor	22	Low-pressure switch
5	Heater/air conditioning relay	13	Fuse B7	23	Engine coolant temperature switch
6	Cable connection to ECU	14	Fuse B8	24	12V supply
7	Fuse C9 - main fuse panel	15	Fuse B9	25	Heater/air conditioning load relay
8	Face vent switch	16	Compressor clutch	26	12V supply from ignition load relay
9	Condenser fan relay	17	Air conditioning motors		

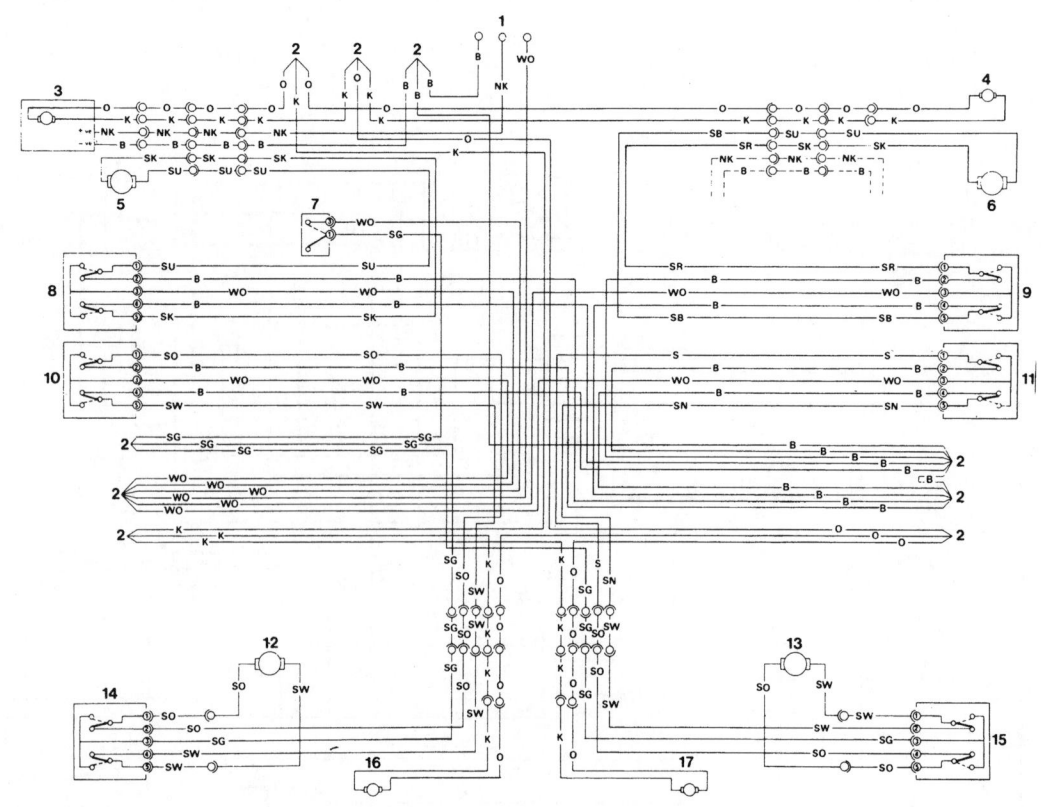

Wiring diagram for electric windows and central locking - 1986-on

1	Main cable connections (item 107 on main wiring diagram)	6	Window lift motor right-hand front	14	Window lift switch left-hand rear door
2	Clinches	7	Isolator switch	15	Window lift switch right-hand rear door
3	Switch unit central door locking (driver's door)	8	Window lift switch left-hand front	16	Lock unit central door locking left-hand rear
		9	Window lift switch right-hand front		
4	Lock unit central door locking (front passenger door)	10	Window lift switch left-hand rear	17	Lock unit central door locking right-hand rear
		11	Window lift switch right-hand rear		
		12	Window lift motor left-hand rear		
5	Window lift motor left-hand front	13	Window lift motor right-hand rear		

Key to wiring diagram for window lifts and door locks - 1988 models

1	Main cable connections NK Battery feed (12V+) WO Ignition key position 1 B Earth	5	Central locking lock unit - front passenger's door	13	Window lift motor - left-hand rear
		6	Window lift motor - left-hand front	14	Window lift motor - right-hand rear
		7	Window lift motor - right-hand front	15	Window lift switch - left-hand rear
2	Clinches	8	Isolation switch	16	Window lift switch - right-hand rear
3	Central locking switch unit - driver's door	9	Window lift switch - left-hand front	17	Central locking lock unit - left-hand rear
		10	Window lift switch - right-hand front	18	Central locking lock unit - right-hand rear
4	Fuel flap actuator	11	Window lift switch - left-hand rear	19	Rocker switch operating levers
		12	Window lift switch - right-hand rear		

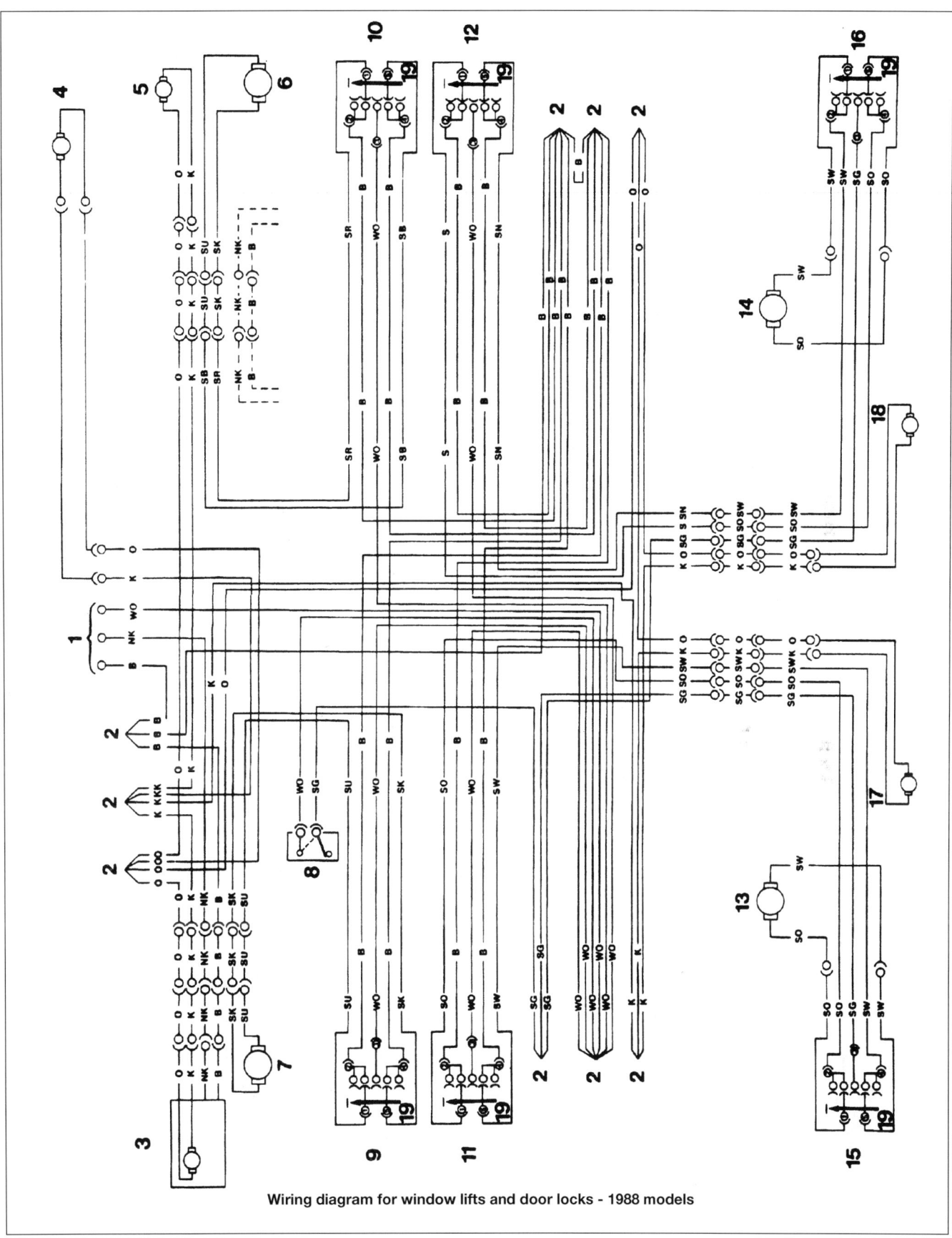

Wiring diagram for window lifts and door locks - 1988 models

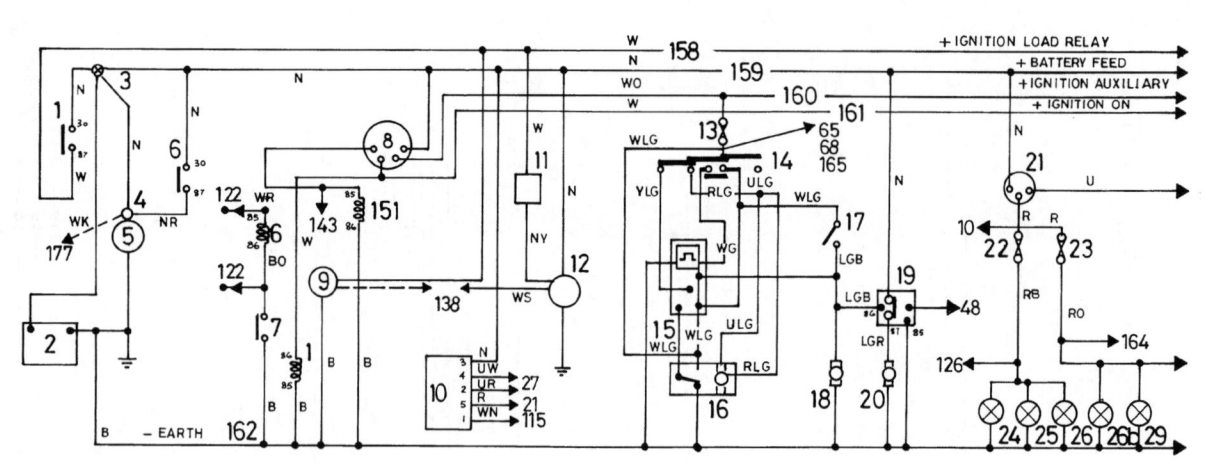

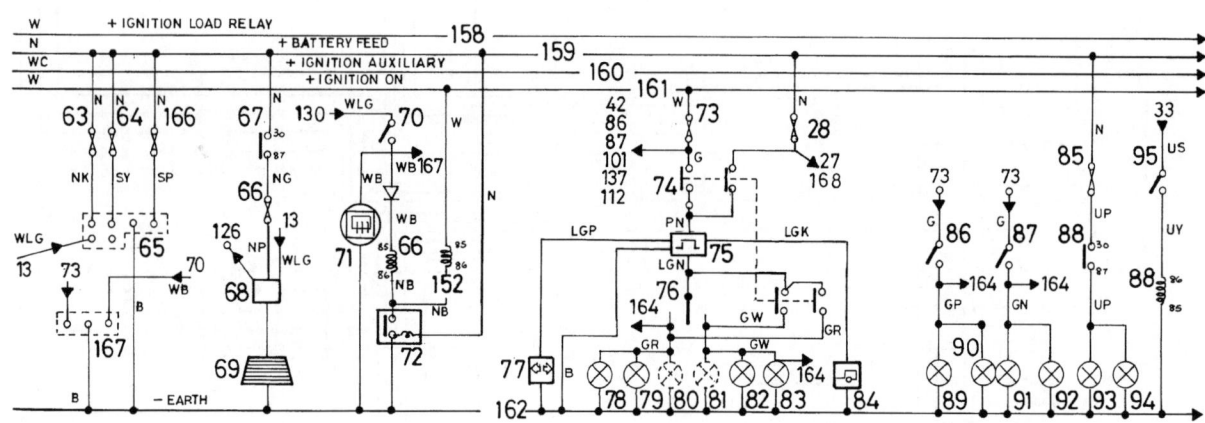

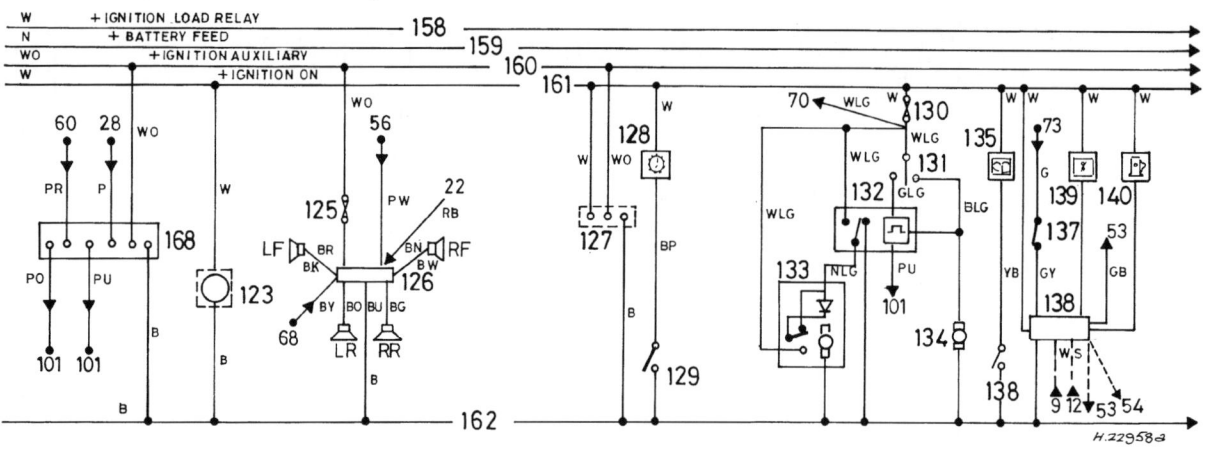

Main wiring diagram - 1989 models

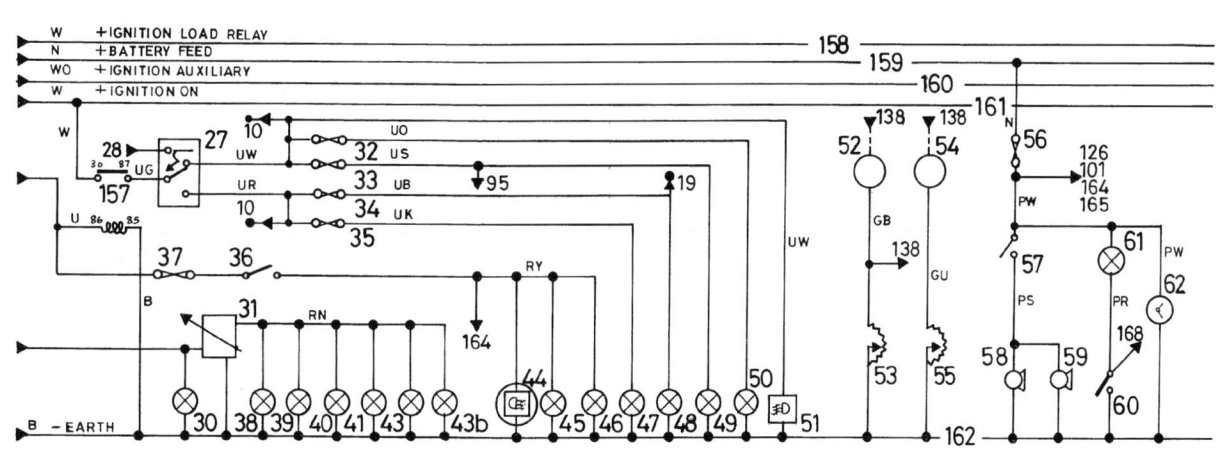

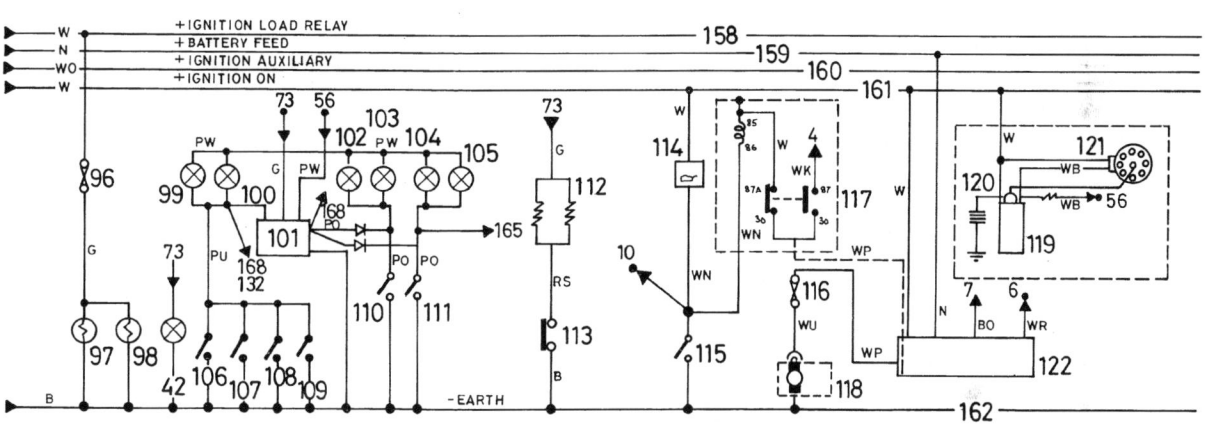

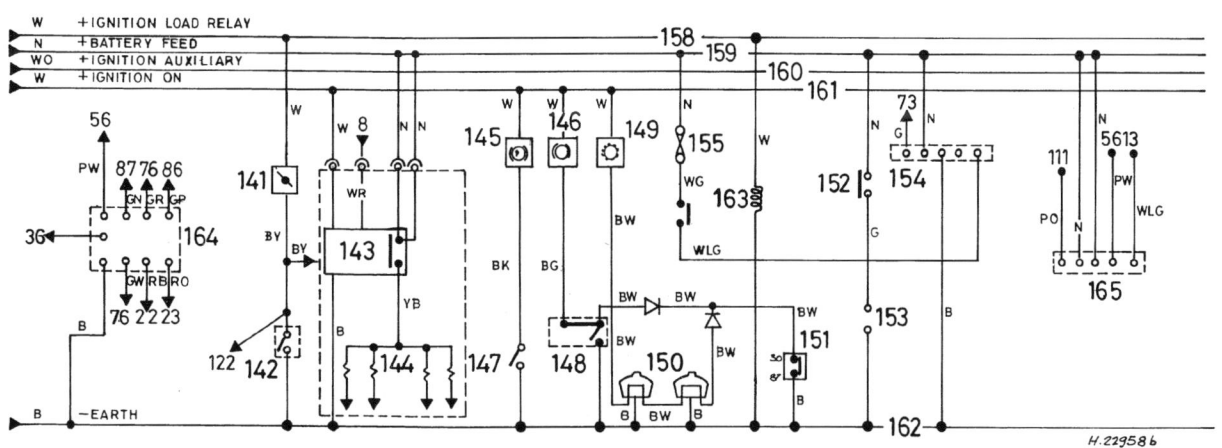

Main wiring diagram - 1989 models (continued)

H.22958b

Key to main wiring diagram - 1989 models

1	Ignition load relay	30	RH tail lamp	58	RH horn
2	Battery	31	Rheostat	59	LH horn
3	Terminal post	32	Fuse 3	60	Underbonnet light switch
4	Starter solenoid	33	Fuse 4	61	Underbonnet light
5	Starter motor	34	Fuse 1	62	Clock
6	Starter relay	35	Fuse 2	63	Fuse 19
7	Starter inhibit switch (Automatic)	36	Rear foglamp switch	64	Fuse 20
8	Ignition switch	37	Fuse 12	65	Pick-up point central locking/window lift (option)
9	Tachometer	38	Switch illumination (2 off)		
10	Voltage transformer (dim/dip)	39	Cigar lighter illumination (2 off)	66	Heated rear window relay
11	Ignition warning lamp	40	Heater illumination (4 off)	67	Fuse 9
12	Alternator	41	Clock illumination	68	Radio aerial amplifier
13	Fuse 7	42	Automatic gear selector illumination (2 off)	69	Heated rear screen
14	Front wipe/wash switch			70	Heated rear screen switch
15	Front wipe delay unit	43	Instrument illumination (6 off)	71	Heated rear screen warning lamp
16	Front wiper motor	43b	Column switch illumination	72	Voltage sensitive switch
17	Front wash switch	44	Rear fog warning lamp	73	Fuse 13
18	Front wash pump	45	LH rear fog	74	Hazard switch
19	Headlamp wash timer unit (option)	46	RH rear fog	75	Hazard switch
20	Headlamp wash pump (option)	47	LH dip beam	76	Direction indicator switch
21	Main lighting switch	48	RH dip beam	77	Hazard/indicator warning lamp
22	Fuse 6	49	LH main beam	78	LH rear indicator lamp
23	Fuse 5	50	RH main beam	79	LH front indicator lamp
24	LH side lamp	51	Main beam warning lamp	80	LH side repeater lamp
25	LH tail lamp	52	Fuel gauge	81	RH side repeater lamp
26	LH number plate lamp	53	Fuel gauge sender unit	82	RH front indicator lamp
26b	RH number plate lamp	54	Water temperature gauge	83	RH rear indicator lamp
27	Main beam dip/flash switch	55	Water temperature sender unit	84	Trailer warning lamp
28	Fuse 14	56	Fuse 11	85	Fuse 15
29	RH side lamp	57	Horn switch	86	Stop lamp switch

Key to main wiring diagram - 1989 models (continued)

87	Reverse lamp switch	118	Fuel pump (petrol models)	141	Cold start/diesel glow plug warning lamp
88	Auxiliary lamp relay (option)	119	Ignition coil (petrol models)	142	Cold start switch (carburettor)
89	LH stop lamp	120	Capacitor (petrol models)	143	Glow plug timer (diesel)
90	RH stop lamp	121	Distributor (petrol models)	144	Glow plugs (diesel)
91	LH reverse lamp	122	EFI harness plug	145	Handbrake warning lamp
92	RH reverse lamp	123	Fuel shut-off solenoid (Diesel)	146	Brake fail warning lamp
93	LH auxiliary lamp (option)	124	Not used	147	Handbrake warning switch
94	RH auxiliary lamp (option)	125	Radio fuse	148	Brake fluid level warning switch
95	Auxiliary lamp switch (option)	126	Radio and four speakers	149	Brake pad wear warning lamp
96	Fuse 17		LF-left hand front speaker	150	Brake pad wear sensors
97	Dash cigar lighter		LR-left hand rear speaker	151	Brake check relay
98	Cubby box cigar lighter		RF-right hand front speaker	152	Split charge relay (option)
99	Front interior lamp		RR-right hand rear speaker	153	Split charge terminal post (option)
100	Rear interior lamp	127	Sun roof pick-up point (option)	154	Heater/air conditioning connections
101	Interior lamp delay unit	128	Automatic transmission oil temperature warning lamp	155	Fuse 8
102	LH door edge lamp			156	Coil negative (engine RPM input to ECU)
103	LH puddle lamp	129	Automatic transmission oil temperature switch		
104	RH door edge lamp			157	Headlamp relay
105	RH puddle lamp	130	Fuse 16	158	Ignition load relay (+)
106	Interior lamp switch	131	Rear wash wipe switch	159	Battery feed (+)
107	LH rear door switch	132	Rear wipe delay unit	160	Ignition auxiliary (+)
108	RH rear door switch	133	Rear wiper motor	161	Ignition on (+)
109	Tailgate switch	134	Rear screen wash pump	162	Earth (–)
110	LH front door switch	135	Low screen wash fluid level warning lamp	163	Heater/air conditioning relay
111	RH front door switch			164	Trailer pick-up point
112	Heated jets	136	Low screen wash switch	165	Electric seats pick-up point (option)
113	Thermostat heated jets	137	Low coolant switch	166	Fuse 10
114	Oil pressure warning lamp	138	Multi-function unit in binnacle	167	Electric mirrors pick-up point (option)
115	Oil pressure switch	139	Low coolant level warning lamp	168	Alarm connection (dealer fit)
116	Fuse 18	140	Low fuel level warning lamp		
117	Fuel cut off relay (carburettor models)				

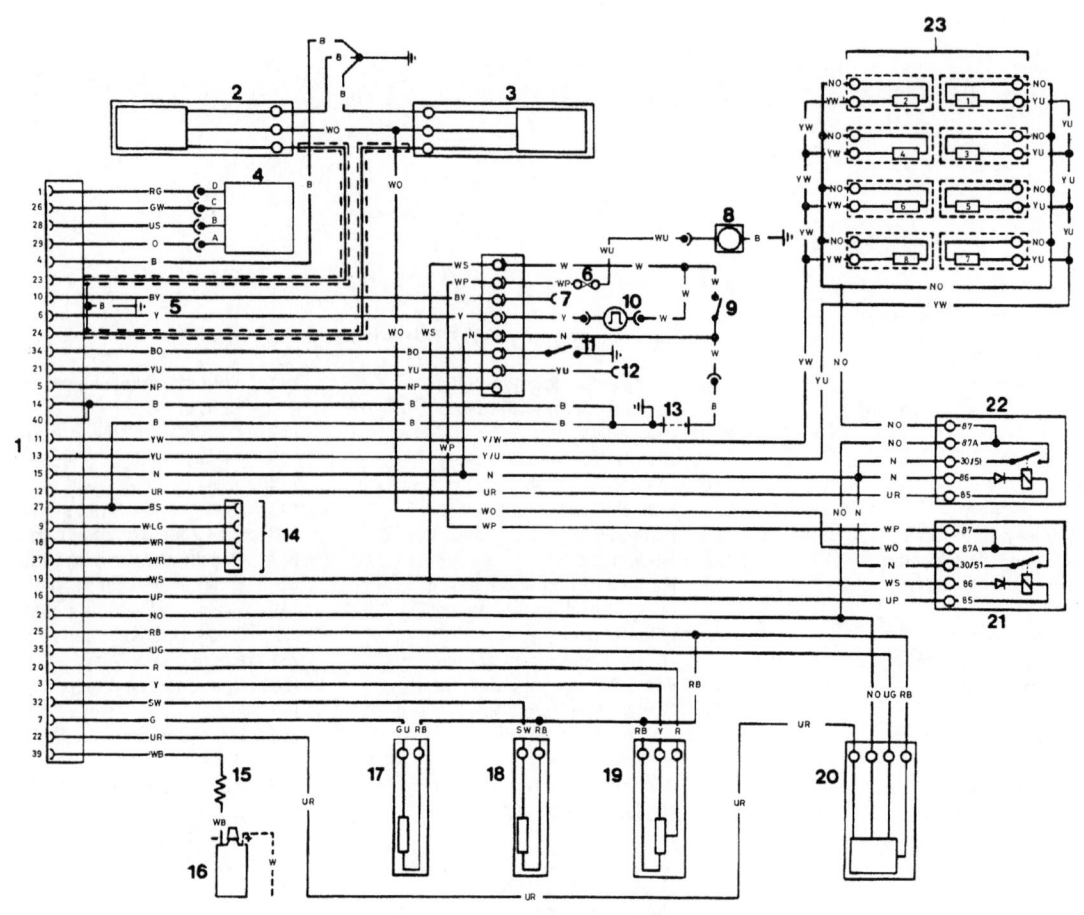

Wiring diagram for 1988/1989 Lucas Hot-wire fuel injection system

1	ECU connector	8	Fuel pump	15	In-line resistor
2	Lambda sensor (A-left side)	9	Ignition switch	16	ignition coil (-ve)
3	Lambda sensor (B-right side)	10	Road speed transducer	17	Coolant temperate sensor
4	Bypass air valve (stepper motor) - fast idle	11	Automatic transmission neutral switch	18	Fuel temperature sensor
5	Lambda sensor screened earth	12	Air conditioning circuit pick-up point	19	Throttle potentiometer
6	Fuse 18	13	Battery	20	Airflow sensor
7	EFI warning symbol pick-up point	14	Diagnostic plug	21	Fuel pump relay
				22	Injectors

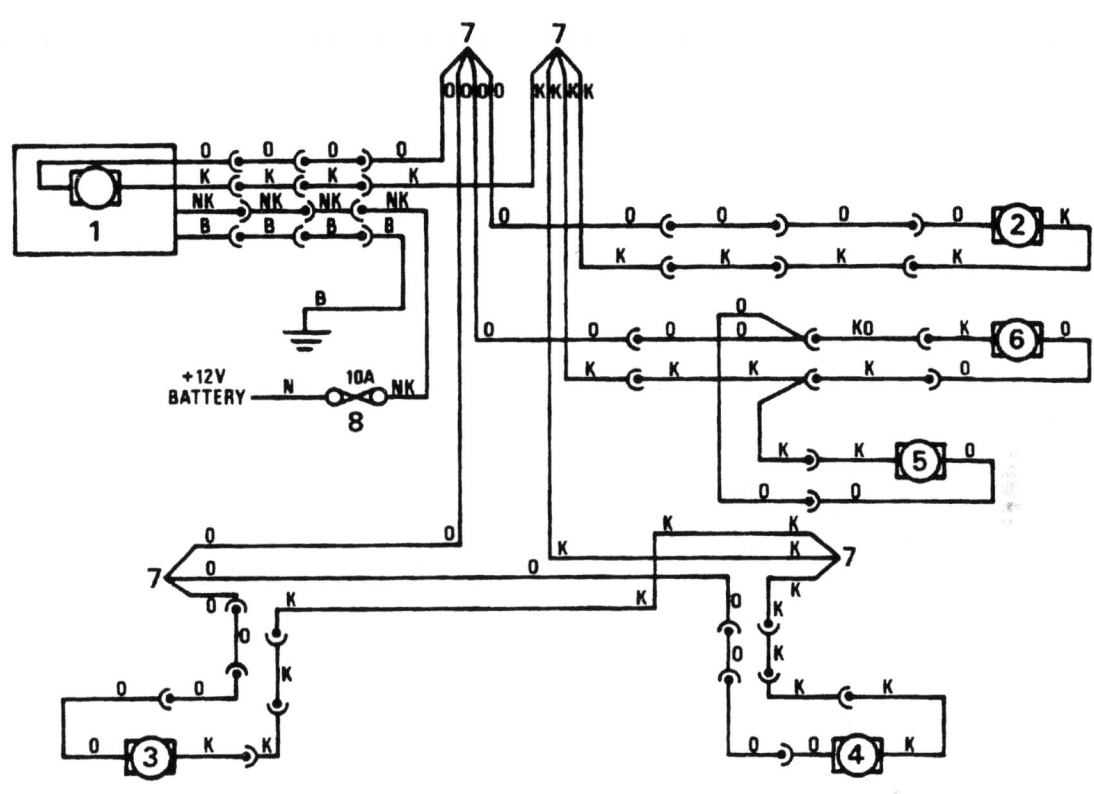

Wiring diagram for central locking - 1989 models

1	Switch/lock unit, driver's door	4	Lock unit, right-hand rear door	6	Clinches
2	Lock unit, front passenger's door	5	Lock unit, tailgate	7	Fuse 19
3	Lock unit, left-hand rear door				

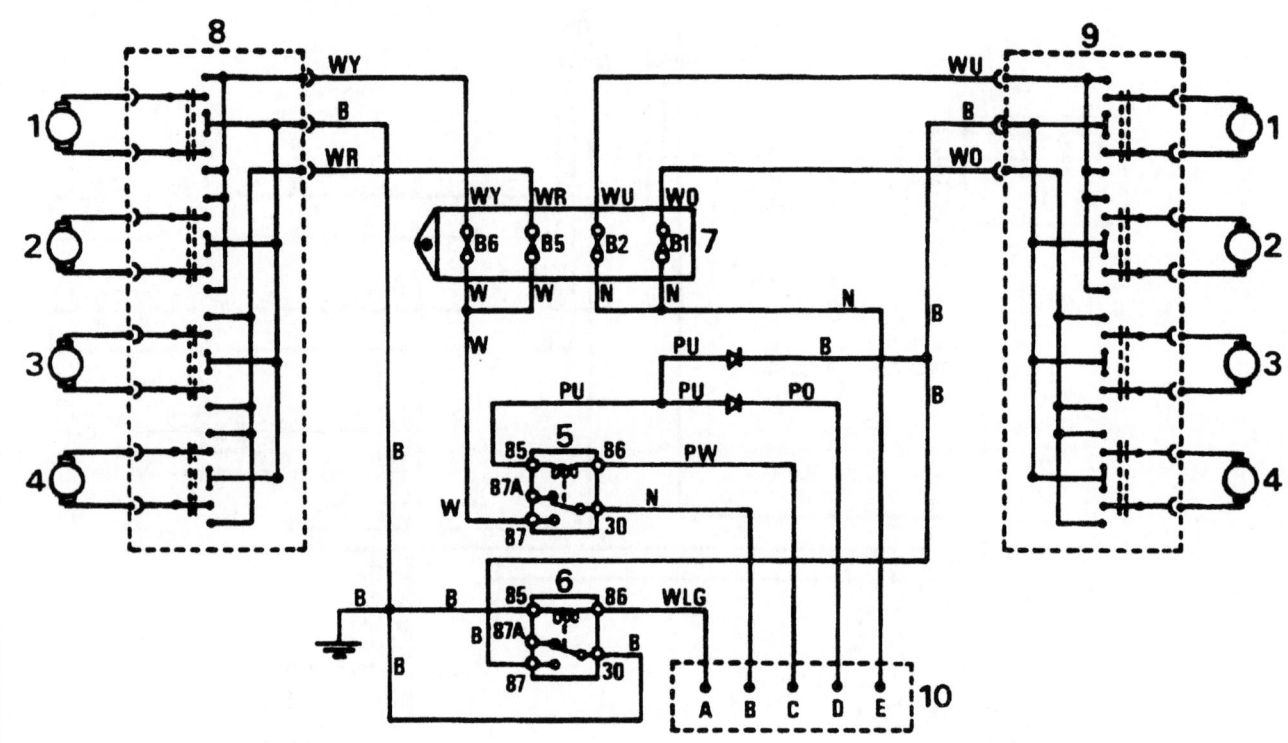

Wiring diagram for electric seat adjustment - 1989 models

1	Seat recline motor	6	Load relay, fused auxiliary feed	11	A	Fused auxiliary feed
2	Seat height (rear) motor	7	Auxiliary fusebox (B)		B	Battery feed (12V+)
3	Seat base motor	8	Driver's seat control		C	Fused 12V feed
4	Seat height (front) motor	9	Passenger's seat control		D	Courtesy switch earth
5	Load relay, from driver's door courtesy switch	10	Main cable connections		E	Battery feed (12V+)

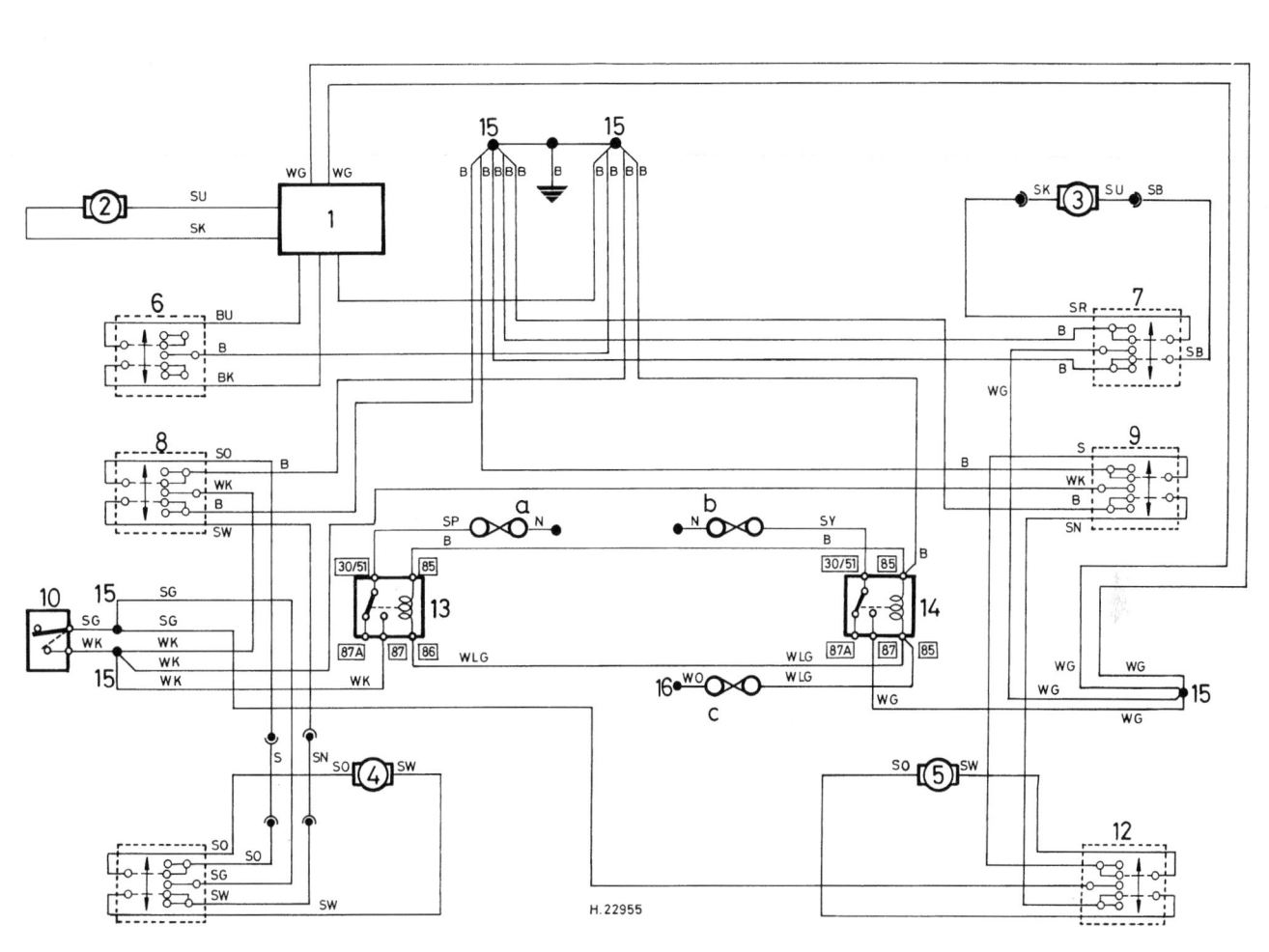

Wiring diagram for electric window lifts - 1989 models

1	Control unit, driver's door	8	Lift switch, left-hand rear door	14	Front windows relay
2	Lift motor, driver's window	9	Lift switch, right-hand rear door	15	Clinches
3	Lift motor, front passenger's door	10	Isolator switch	16	Main cable fuses
4	Lift motor, left-hand rear	11	Lift switch - in left-hand rear door		a Fuse 10
5	Lift motor, right-hand rear	12	Lift switch - in right-hand rear door		b Fuse 20
6	Lift switch, driver's window	13	Rear windows relay		c Fuse 7
7	lift switch, front passenger's window				

H.22955

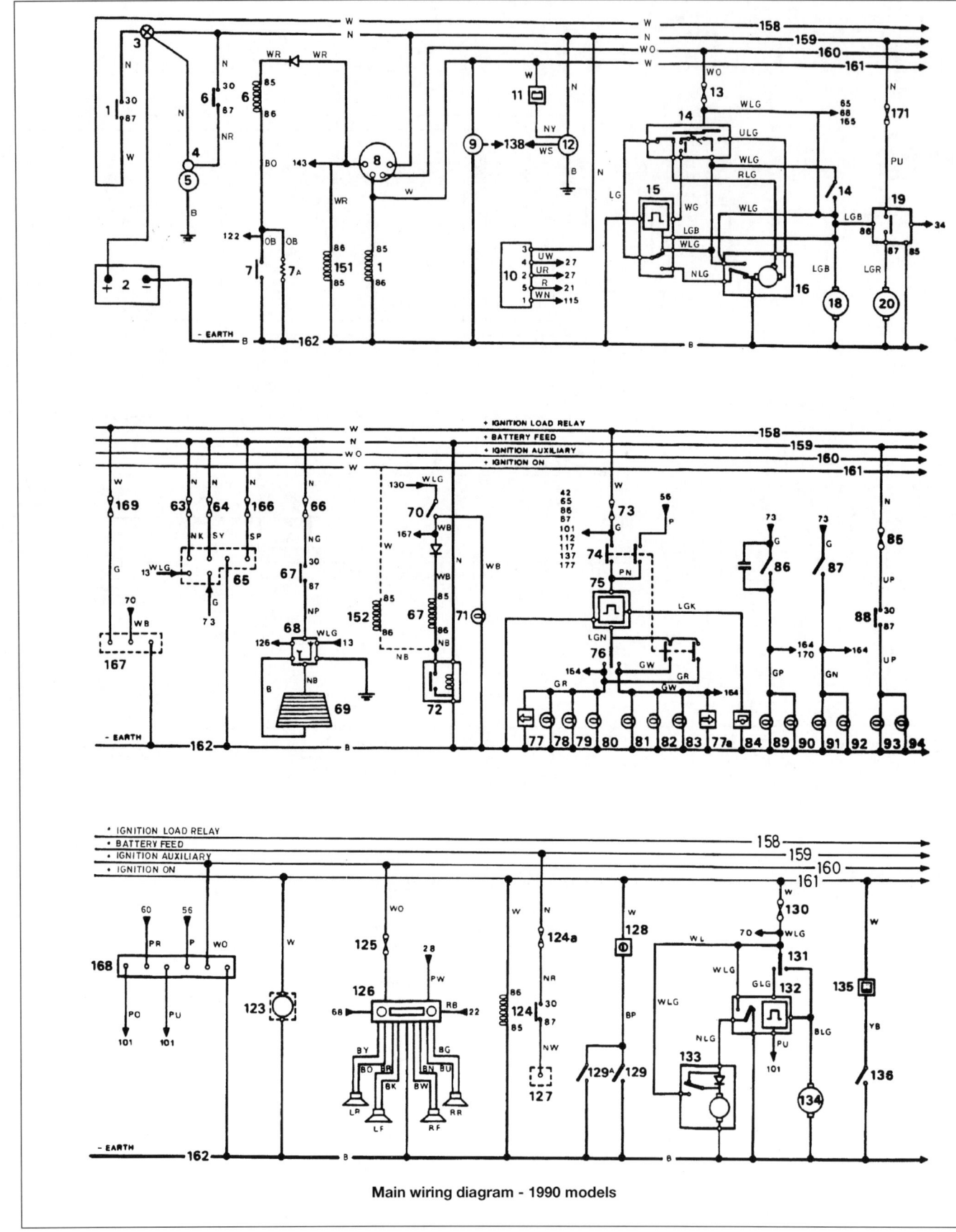

Main wiring diagram - 1990 models

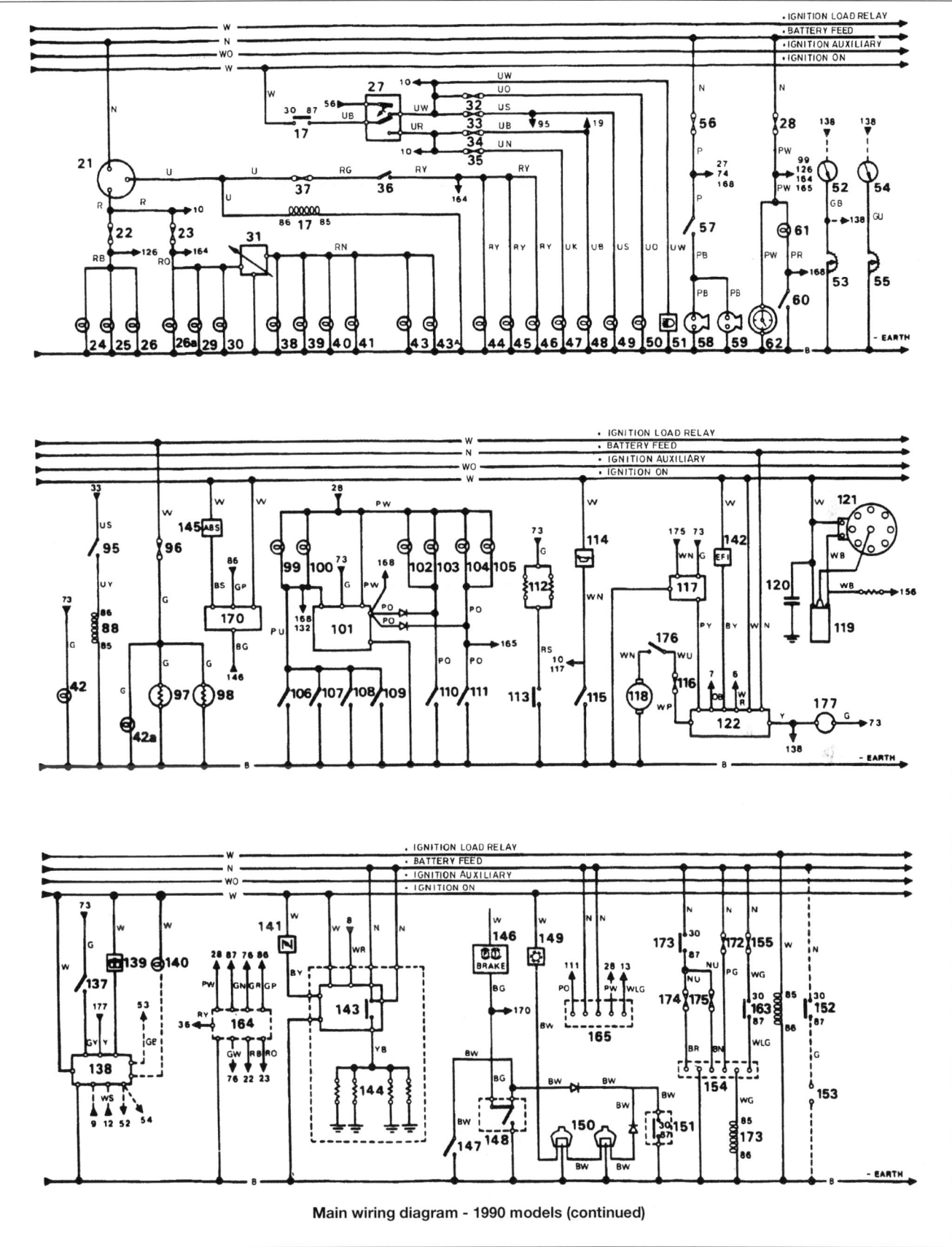

Main wiring diagram - 1990 models (continued)

Key to main wiring diagram - 1990 models

1	Ignition load relay	32	Fuse A8	61	Underbonnet light
2	Battery	33	Fuse A2	62	Clock
3	Terminal post	34	Fuse A9	63	Fuse C7
4	Starter solenoid	35	Fuse A1	64	Fuse C8
5	Starter motor	36	Rear fog switch	65	Pick-up point central locking/window lift
6	Starter relay	37	Fuse A4		
7	Starter inhibit switch	38	Switch illumination (2 off)	66	Fuse C1
7a	Resistor (manual)	39	Cigar lighter illumination (2 off)	67	Heated rear screen relay
8	Ignition switch	40	Heater illumination (4 off)	68	Radio aerial amplifier
9	Tachometer	41	Clock illumination	69	Heated rear screen
10	Voltage transformer (dim/dip)	42	Automatic gear selector illumination (2 off) - post April 1990	70	Heated rear screen switch
11	Ignition warning lamp			71	Heated rear screen warning lamp
12	Alternator	42a	Auto gear selector illumination (2 off) - pre April 1990	72	Voltage sensitive switch
13	Fuse B1			73	Fuse A5
14	Front wipe/wash switch	43	Instrument illumination (4 off)	74	Hazard switch
15	Front wipe delay unit	43a	Column switch illumination	75	Flasher unit
16	Front wiper motor	44	Rear fog warning lamp	76	Direction indicator switch
17	Headlamp relay	45	LH rear fog lamp	77	LH indicator warning lamp
18	Front wash pump	46	RH rear fog lamp	77a	RH indicator warning lamp
19	Headlamp wash timer unit	47	LH dip beam	78	LH rear indicator warning lamp
20	Headlamp wash pump	48	RH dip beam	79	LH front indicator lamp
21	Main lighting switch	49	LH high beam	80	LH side repeater lamp
22	Fuse A3	50	RH high beam	81	RH side repeater lamp
23	Fuse A7	51	Main beam warning lamp	82	RH front indicator lamp
24	LH side lamp	52	Fuel gauge	83	RH rear indicator lamp
25	LH tail lamp	53	Fuel gauge sender unit	84	Trailer warning lamp
26	LH number plate lamp	54	Water temperature gauge	85	Fuse A6
26a	RH number plate lamp	55	Water temperature sender unit	86	Stop lamp switch
27	High beam dip/flash switch	56	Fuse B3	87	Reverse lamp switch
28	Fuse B2	57	Horn switch	88	Front auxiliary lamp relay
29	RH side lamp	58	RH horn	89	LH stop lamp
30	RH tail lamp	59	LH horn	90	RH stop lamp
31	Rheostat	60	Underbonnet illumination switch	91	LH reverse lamp

Key to main wiring diagram - 1990 models (continued)

92	RH reverse lamp	124a	Fuse B5	147	Handbrake warning switch
93	LH front auxiliary lamp	125	Radio fuse	148	Brake fluid level warning switch
94	RH front auxiliary lamp	126	Radio and four speakers	149	Brake pad wear warning lamp
95	Front auxiliary lamp switch		LF-left hand front speaker	150	Brake pad wear sensors
96	Fuse B4		LR-left hand rear speaker	151	Brake check relay
97	Dash cigar lighter		RF-right hand front speaker	152	Split charge relay (option)
98	Glovebox cigar lighter		RR-right hand rear speaker	153	Split charge terminal post (option)
99	Front interior lamp	127	Sun roof pick-up point	154	Heater/air conditioning connections
100	Rear interior lamp	128	Auto transmission and transfer box	155	Fuse C9
101	Interior lamp delay unit		oil temperature warning lamp	156	Coil negative (engine RPM input to
102	LH door edge lamp	129	Auto transmission oil temperature		ECU)
103	LH puddle lamp		switch	157	Not used
104	RH door edge lamp	129a	Transfer box oil temperature switch	158	Ignition load relay (+)
105	RH puddle lamp	130	Fuse C3	159	Battery feed (+)
106	Interior lamp switch	131	Rear wash/wipe switch	160	Ignition auxiliary (+)
107	LH rear door switch	132	Rear wipe delay unit	161	Ignition on (+)
108	RH rear door switch	133	Rear wiper motor	162	Earth (–)
109	Tailgate switch	134	Rear screen wash pump	163	Heater/air conditioning relay
110	LH front door switch	135	Low screen wash fluid level warning	164	Trailer pick-up point
111	RH front door switch		lamp	165	Electric seats pick-up point (option)
112	Heated washer jets (front screen)	136	Low screen wash switch	166	Fuse C2
113	Thermostat heated jets	137	Low coolant switch	167	Electric mirrors pick-up point
114	Oil pressure warning lamp	138	Electronic speedometer and	168	Alarm pick-up point
115	Oil pressure switch		instrument controls	169	Fuse C5
116	Fuse C4	139	Low coolant level warning lamp	170	ABS pick-up point
117	Heated front screen connections	140	Low fuel level warning lamp	171	Fuse B6
118	Fuel pump (petrol models)	141	Glow plug warning lamp (Diesel)	172	Fuse B7
119	Ignition coil	142	EFI warning lamp	173	Condenser fan relay
120	Capacitor	143	Glow plug timer unit	174	Fuse B8
121	Distributor	144	Glow plugs (diesel)	175	Fuse B9
122	EFI Harness plug	145	ABS warning lamp	176	Inertia switch
123	Fuel shut-off solenoid (Diesel)	146	Handbrake/brake level/pressure	177	Speed transducer
124	Sun roof relay		warning lamp		

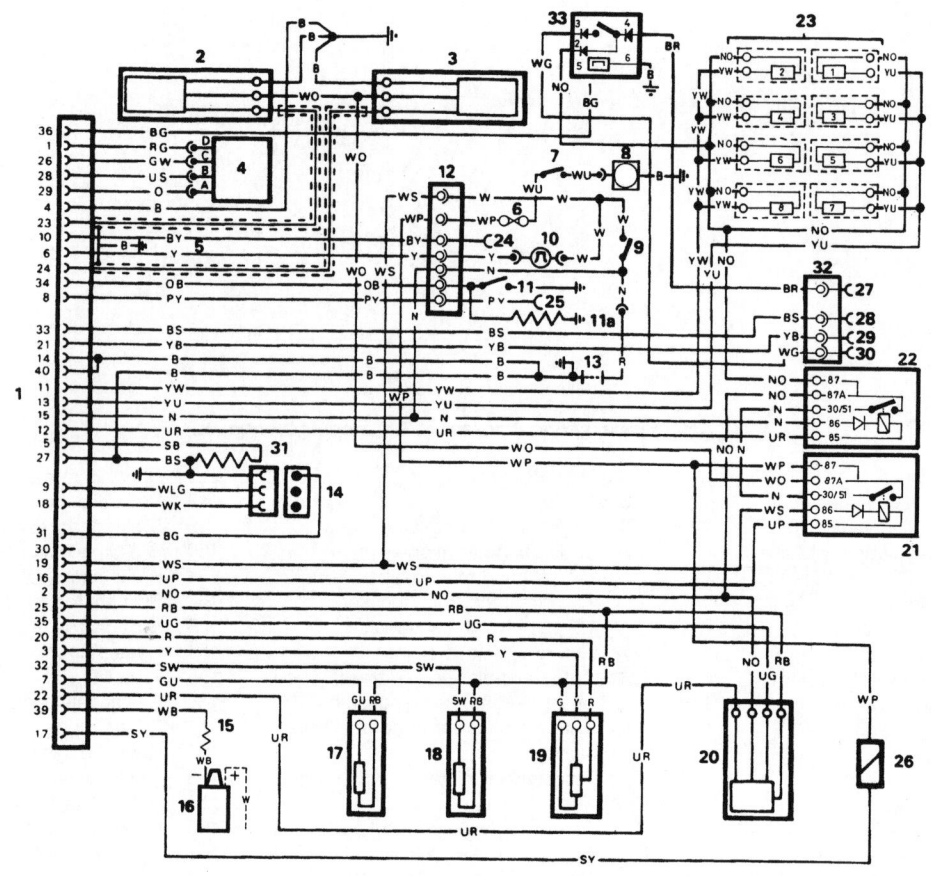

Wiring diagram for 1990 Lucas Hot-wire fuel injection system

1	ECU connector	11a	Resistor - 510 ohms (manual gearbox)	22	Main relay
2	Lambda sensor (A - left side)			23	Injectors
3	Lambda sensor (B - right side)	12	Main cable connector	24	EFI warning symbol pick-up point
4	Bypass air valve (stepper motor) - fast idle	13	Battery	25	Heater front screen sensor
		14	Diagnostic plug	26	Purge control valve (where fitted)
5	Lambda sensor screened earth	15	In-line resistor	27	12V+ from fan relay
6	Fuse 18	16	Ignition coil (-ve)	28	Air conditioning output control
7		17	Coolant temperature sensor	29	Air conditioning load input
8	Fuel pump	18	Fuel temperature sensor	30	Fan relay feed
9	Ignition switch	19	Throttle potentiometer	31	Tune select resistor
10	Road speed transducer	20	Airflow sensor	32	Heater/air conditioning
11	Automatic transmission neutral switch	21	Fuel pump relay	33	Condenser fan liner control

Wiring diagram for central locking - 1990 models

1	Switch/lock unit, driver's door	5	Fuel flap actuator
2	Switch/lock unit, front passenger's door	6	Lock unit tailgate
3	Lock unit, left-hand rear door relay	7	Suppressor
4	Lock unit, right-hand rear door relay	8	Fuse A5
9	Feed from ignition load relay		
10	Fuse C7		
11	Battery feed (12V+)		
12	Control unit		

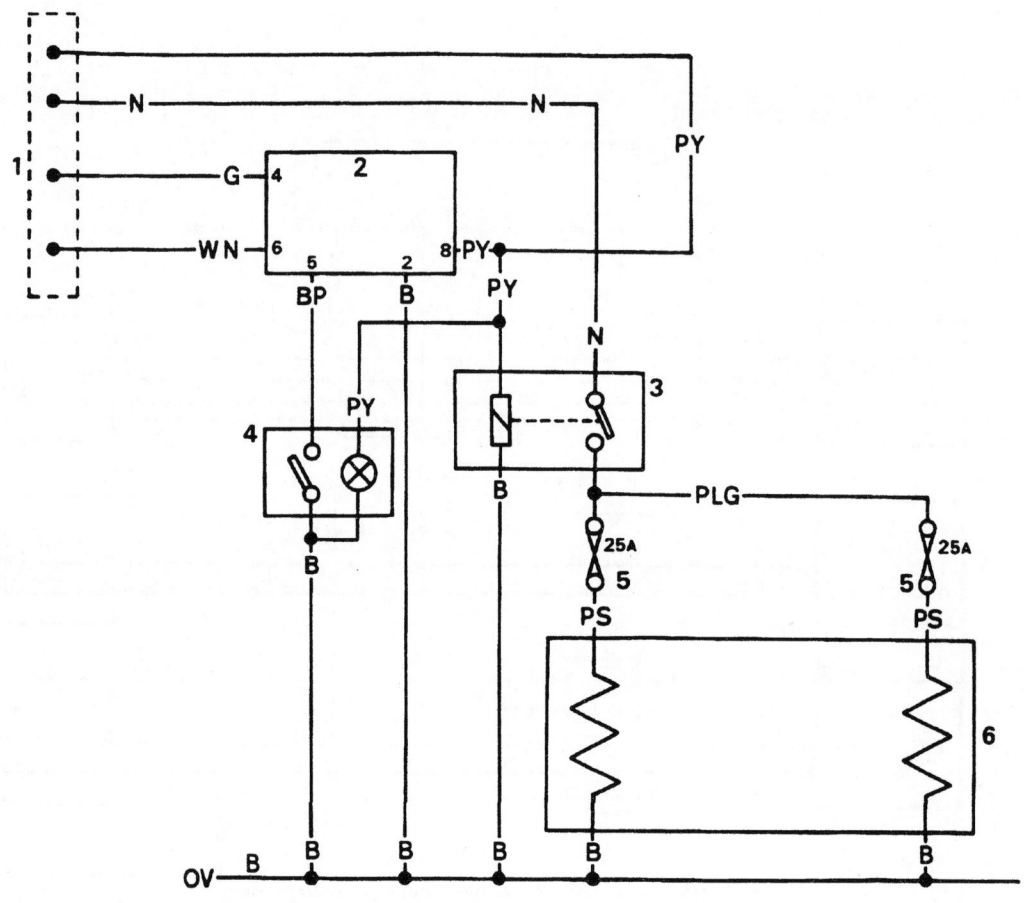

Wiring diagram for heated front screen - 1990 models

1	Main harness connections	2	Timer
N	Battery feed (12V+)	3	Load relay
G	Ignition feed (12V+)	4	Switch/warning lamp
P/Y	EFI harness plug	5	In-line fuses - 25A
W/N	Oil pressure switch	6	Heated screen
B	Earth		

This is a guide to getting your vehicle through the MOT test. Obviously it will not be possible to examine the vehicle to the same standard as the professional MOT tester. However, working through the following checks will enable you to identify any problem areas before submitting the vehicle for the test.

Where a testable component is in borderline condition, the tester has discretion in deciding whether to pass or fail it. The basis of such discretion is whether the tester would be happy for a close relative or friend to use the vehicle with the component in that condition. If the vehicle presented is clean and evidently well cared for, the tester may be more inclined to pass a borderline component than if the vehicle is scruffy and apparently neglected.

It has only been possible to summarise the test requirements here, based on the regulations in force at the time of printing. Test standards are becoming increasingly stringent, although there are some exemptions for older vehicles.

An assistant will be needed to help carry out some of these checks.

The checks have been sub-divided into four categories, as follows:

1 Checks carried out **FROM THE DRIVER'S SEAT**

2 Checks carried out **WITH THE VEHICLE ON THE GROUND**

3 Checks carried out **WITH THE VEHICLE RAISED AND THE WHEELS FREE TO TURN**

4 Checks carried out on **YOUR VEHICLE'S EXHAUST EMISSION SYSTEM**

---

1 Checks carried out **FROM THE DRIVER'S SEAT**

Handbrake

☐ Test the operation of the handbrake. Excessive travel (too many clicks) indicates incorrect brake or cable adjustment.

☐ Check that the handbrake cannot be released by tapping the lever sideways. Check the security of the lever mountings.

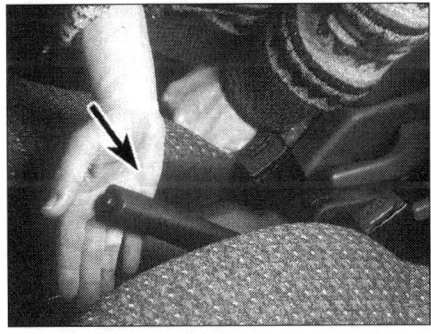

Footbrake

☐ Depress the brake pedal and check that it does not creep down to the floor, indicating a master cylinder fault. Release the pedal, wait a few seconds, then depress it again. If the pedal travels nearly to the floor before firm resistance is felt, brake adjustment or repair is necessary. If the pedal feels spongy, there is air in the hydraulic system which must be removed by bleeding.

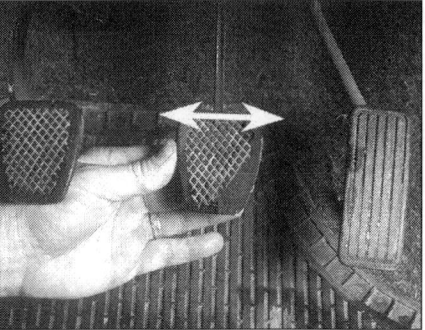

☐ Check that the brake pedal is secure and in good condition. Check also for signs of fluid leaks on the pedal, floor or carpets, which would indicate failed seals in the brake master cylinder.

☐ Check the servo unit (when applicable) by operating the brake pedal several times, then keeping the pedal depressed and starting the engine. As the engine starts, the pedal will move down slightly. If not, the vacuum hose or the servo itself may be faulty.

Steering wheel and column

☐ Examine the steering wheel for fractures or looseness of the hub, spokes or rim.

☐ Move the steering wheel from side to side and then up and down. Check that the steering wheel is not loose on the column, indicating wear or a loose retaining nut. Continue moving the steering wheel as before, but also turn it slightly from left to right.

☐ Check that the steering wheel is not loose on the column, and that there is no abnormal

movement of the steering wheel, indicating wear in the column support bearings or couplings.

Windscreen, mirrors and sunvisor

☐ The windscreen must be free of cracks or other significant damage within the driver's field of view. (Small stone chips are acceptable.) Rear view mirrors must be secure, intact, and capable of being adjusted.

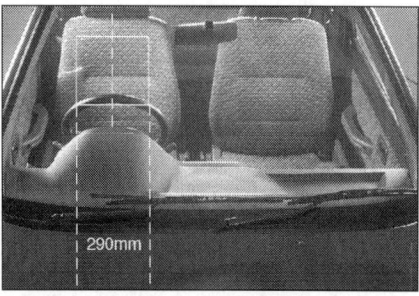

290mm

☐ The driver's sunvisor must be capable of being stored in the "up" position.

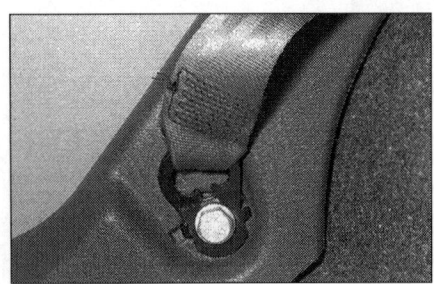

Seat belts and seats

Note: *The following checks are applicable to all seat belts, front and rear.*

☐ Examine the webbing of all the belts (including rear belts if fitted) for cuts, serious fraying or deterioration. Fasten and unfasten each belt to check the buckles. If applicable, check the retracting mechanism. Check the security of all seat belt mountings accessible from inside the vehicle.

☐ Seat belts with pre-tensioners, once activated, have a "flag" or similar showing on the seat belt stalk. This, in itself, is not a reason for test failure.

☐ The front seats themselves must be securely attached and the backrests must lock in the upright position.

Doors

☐ Both front doors must be able to be opened and closed from outside and inside, and must latch securely when closed.

2 Checks carried out **WITH THE VEHICLE ON THE GROUND**

Vehicle identification

☐ Number plates must be in good condition, secure and legible, with letters and numbers correctly spaced – spacing at (A) should be at least twice that at (B).

☐ The VIN plate and/or homologation plate must be legible.

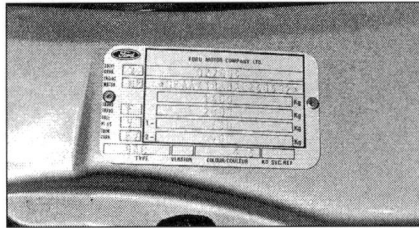

Electrical equipment

☐ Switch on the ignition and check the operation of the horn.

☐ Check the windscreen washers and wipers, examining the wiper blades; renew damaged or perished blades. Also check the operation of the stop-lights.

☐ Check the operation of the sidelights and number plate lights. The lenses and reflectors must be secure, clean and undamaged.

☐ Check the operation and alignment of the headlights. The headlight reflectors must not be tarnished and the lenses must be undamaged.

☐ Switch on the ignition and check the operation of the direction indicators (including the instrument panel tell-tale) and the hazard warning lights. Operation of the sidelights and stop-lights must not affect the indicators - if it does, the cause is usually a bad earth at the rear light cluster.

☐ Check the operation of the rear foglight(s), including the warning light on the instrument panel or in the switch.

☐ The ABS warning light must illuminate in accordance with the manufacturers' design. For most vehicles, the ABS warning light should illuminate when the ignition is switched on, and (if the system is operating properly) extinguish after a few seconds. Refer to the owner's handbook.

Footbrake

☐ Examine the master cylinder, brake pipes and servo unit for leaks, loose mountings, corrosion or other damage.

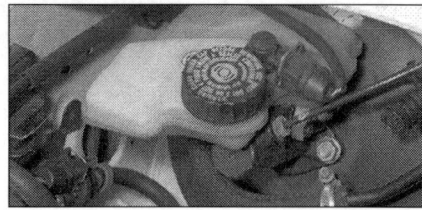

☐ The fluid reservoir must be secure and the fluid level must be between the upper (**A**) and lower (**B**) markings.

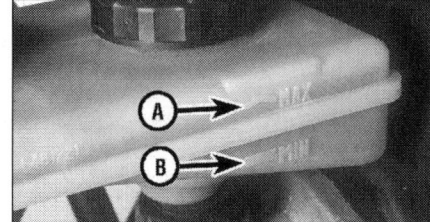

☐ Inspect both front brake flexible hoses for cracks or deterioration of the rubber. Turn the steering from lock to lock, and ensure that the hoses do not contact the wheel, tyre, or any part of the steering or suspension mechanism. With the brake pedal firmly depressed, check the hoses for bulges or leaks under pressure.

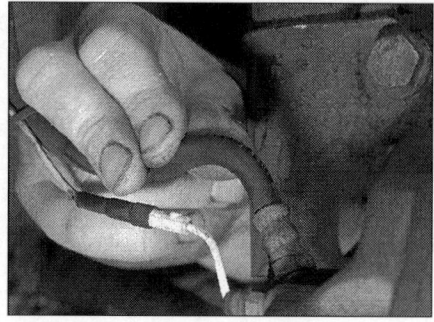

Steering and suspension

☐ Have your assistant turn the steering wheel from side to side slightly, up to the point where the steering gear just begins to transmit this movement to the roadwheels. Check for excessive free play between the steering wheel and the steering gear, indicating wear or insecurity of the steering column joints, the column-to-steering gear coupling, or the steering gear itself.

☐ Have your assistant turn the steering wheel more vigorously in each direction, so that the roadwheels just begin to turn. As this is done, examine all the steering joints, linkages, fittings and attachments. Renew any component that shows signs of wear or damage. On vehicles with power steering, check the security and condition of the steering pump, drivebelt and hoses.

☐ Check that the vehicle is standing level, and at approximately the correct ride height.

Shock absorbers

☐ Depress each corner of the vehicle in turn, then release it. The vehicle should rise and then settle in its normal position. If the vehicle continues to rise and fall, the shock absorber is defective. A shock absorber which has seized will also cause the vehicle to fail.

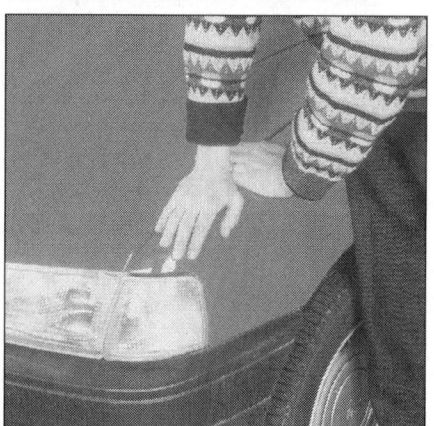

Exhaust system

☐ Start the engine. With your assistant holding a rag over the tailpipe, check the entire system for leaks. Repair or renew leaking sections.

3 Checks carried out
WITH THE VEHICLE RAISED AND THE WHEELS FREE TO TURN

Jack up the front and rear of the vehicle, and securely support it on axle stands. Position the stands clear of the suspension assemblies. Ensure that the wheels are clear of the ground and that the steering can be turned from lock to lock.

Steering mechanism

☐ Have your assistant turn the steering from lock to lock. Check that the steering turns smoothly, and that no part of the steering mechanism, including a wheel or tyre, fouls any brake hose or pipe or any part of the body structure.

☐ Examine the steering rack rubber gaiters for damage or insecurity of the retaining clips. If power steering is fitted, check for signs of damage or leakage of the fluid hoses, pipes or connections. Also check for excessive stiffness or binding of the steering, a missing split pin or locking device, or severe corrosion of the body structure within 30 cm of any steering component attachment point.

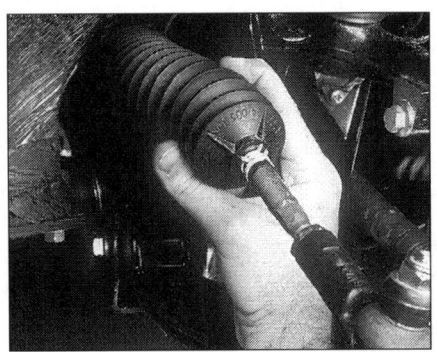

Front and rear suspension and wheel bearings

☐ Starting at the front right-hand side, grasp the roadwheel at the 3 o'clock and 9 o'clock positions and rock gently but firmly. Check for free play or insecurity at the wheel bearings, suspension balljoints, or suspension mountings, pivots and attachments.

☐ Now grasp the wheel at the 12 o'clock and 6 o'clock positions and repeat the previous inspection. Spin the wheel, and check for roughness or tightness of the front wheel bearing.

☐ If excess free play is suspected at a component pivot point, this can be confirmed by using a large screwdriver or similar tool and levering between the mounting and the component attachment. This will confirm whether the wear is in the pivot bush, its retaining bolt, or in the mounting itself (the bolt holes can often become elongated).

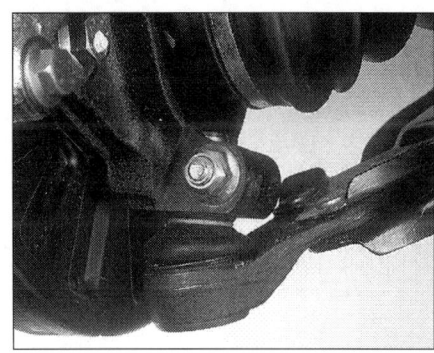

☐ Carry out all the above checks at the other front wheel, and then at both rear wheels.

Springs and shock absorbers

☐ Examine the suspension struts (when applicable) for serious fluid leakage, corrosion, or damage to the casing. Also check the security of the mounting points.

☐ If coil springs are fitted, check that the spring ends locate in their seats, and that the spring is not corroded, cracked or broken.

☐ If leaf springs are fitted, check that all leaves are intact, that the axle is securely attached to each spring, and that there is no deterioration of the spring eye mountings, bushes, and shackles.

☐ The same general checks apply to vehicles fitted with other suspension types, such as torsion bars, hydraulic displacer units, etc. Ensure that all mountings and attachments are secure, that there are no signs of excessive wear, corrosion or damage, and (on hydraulic types) that there are no fluid leaks or damaged pipes.

☐ Inspect the shock absorbers for signs of serious fluid leakage. Check for wear of the mounting bushes or attachments, or damage to the body of the unit.

Driveshafts
(fwd vehicles only)

☐ Rotate each front wheel in turn and inspect the constant velocity joint gaiters for splits or damage. Also check that each driveshaft is straight and undamaged.

Braking system

☐ If possible without dismantling, check brake pad wear and disc condition. Ensure that the friction lining material has not worn excessively, (A) and that the discs are not fractured, pitted, scored or badly worn (B).

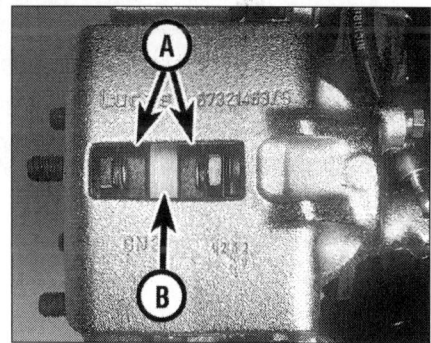

☐ Examine all the rigid brake pipes underneath the vehicle, and the flexible hose(s) at the rear. Look for corrosion, chafing or insecurity of the pipes, and for signs of bulging under pressure, chafing, splits or deterioration of the flexible hoses.

☐ Look for signs of fluid leaks at the brake calipers or on the brake backplates. Repair or renew leaking components.

☐ Slowly spin each wheel, while your assistant depresses and releases the footbrake. Ensure that each brake is operating and does not bind when the pedal is released.

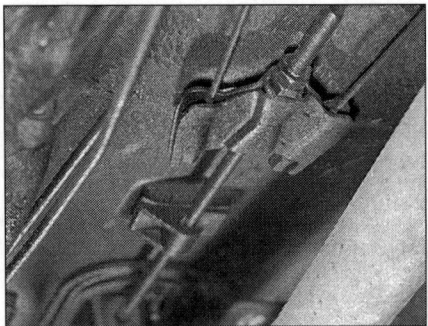

□ Examine the handbrake mechanism, checking for frayed or broken cables, excessive corrosion, or wear or insecurity of the linkage. Check that the mechanism works on each relevant wheel, and releases fully, without binding.

□ It is not possible to test brake efficiency without special equipment, but a road test can be carried out later to check that the vehicle pulls up in a straight line.

Fuel and exhaust systems

□ Inspect the fuel tank (including the filler cap), fuel pipes, hoses and unions. All components must be secure and free from leaks.

□ Examine the exhaust system over its entire length, checking for any damaged, broken or missing mountings, security of the retaining clamps and rust or corrosion.

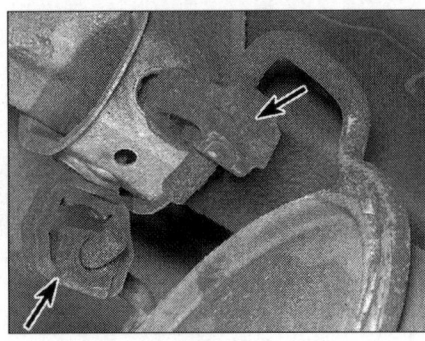

Wheels and tyres

□ Examine the sidewalls and tread area of each tyre in turn. Check for cuts, tears, lumps, bulges, separation of the tread, and exposure of the ply or cord due to wear or damage. Check that the tyre bead is correctly seated on the wheel rim, that the valve is sound and properly seated, and that the wheel is not distorted or damaged.

□ Check that the tyres are of the correct size for the vehicle, that they are of the same size and type on each axle, and that the pressures are correct.

□ Check the tyre tread depth. The legal minimum at the time of writing is 1.6 mm over at least three-quarters of the tread width. Abnormal tread wear may indicate incorrect front wheel alignment.

Body corrosion

□ Check the condition of the entire vehicle structure for signs of corrosion in load-bearing areas. (These include chassis box sections, side sills, cross-members, pillars, and all suspension, steering, braking system and seat belt mountings and anchorages.) Any corrosion which has seriously reduced the thickness of a load-bearing area is likely to cause the vehicle to fail. In this case professional repairs are likely to be needed.

□ Damage or corrosion which causes sharp or otherwise dangerous edges to be exposed will also cause the vehicle to fail.

4 Checks carried out on YOUR VEHICLE'S EXHAUST EMISSION SYSTEM

Petrol models

□ Have the engine at normal operating temperature, and make sure that it is in good tune (ignition system in good order, air filter element clean, etc).

□ Before any measurements are carried out, raise the engine speed to around 2500 rpm, and hold it at this speed for 20 seconds. Allow the engine speed to return to idle, and watch for smoke emissions from the exhaust tailpipe. If the idle speed is obviously much too high, or if dense blue or clearly-visible black smoke comes from the tailpipe for more than 5 seconds, the vehicle will fail. As a rule of thumb, blue smoke signifies oil being burnt (engine wear) while black smoke signifies unburnt fuel (dirty air cleaner element, or other carburettor or fuel system fault).

□ An exhaust gas analyser capable of measuring carbon monoxide (CO) and hydrocarbons (HC) is now needed. If such an instrument cannot be hired or borrowed, a local garage may agree to perform the check for a small fee.

CO emissions (mixture)

□ At the time of writing, for vehicles first used between 1st August 1975 and 31st July 1986 (P to C registration), the CO level must not exceed 4.5% by volume. For vehicles first used between 1st August 1986 and 31st July 1992 (D to J registration), the CO level must not exceed 3.5% by volume. Vehicles first

used after 1st August 1992 (K registration) must conform to the manufacturer's specification. The MOT tester has access to a DOT database or emissions handbook, which lists the CO and HC limits for each make and model of vehicle. The CO level is measured with the engine at idle speed, and at "fast idle". The following limits are given as a general guide:

At idle speed -
  CO level no more than 0.5%
At "fast idle" (2500 to 3000 rpm) -
  CO level no more than 0.3%
  (Minimum oil temperature 60°C)

□ If the CO level cannot be reduced far enough to pass the test (and the fuel and ignition systems are otherwise in good condition) then the carburettor is badly worn, or there is some problem in the fuel injection system or catalytic converter (as applicable).

HC emissions

□ With the CO within limits, HC emissions for vehicles first used between 1st August 1975 and 31st July 1992 (P to J registration) must not exceed 1200 ppm. Vehicles first used after 1st August 1992 (K registration) must conform to the manufacturer's specification. The MOT tester has access to a DOT database or emissions handbook, which lists the CO and HC limits for each make and model of vehicle. The HC level is measured with the engine at "fast idle". The following is given as a general guide:

At "fast idle" (2500 to 3000 rpm) -
  HC level no more than 200 ppm
  (Minimum oil temperature 60°C)

□ Excessive HC emissions are caused by incomplete combustion, the causes of which can include oil being burnt, mechanical wear and ignition/fuel system malfunction.

Diesel models

□ The only emission test applicable to Diesel engines is the measuring of exhaust smoke density. The test involves accelerating the engine several times to its maximum unloaded speed.

Note: *It is of the utmost importance that the engine timing belt is in good condition before the test is carried out.*

□ The limits for Diesel engine exhaust smoke, introduced in September 1995 are:
Vehicles first used before 1st August 1979:
  Exempt from metered smoke testing, but must not emit "dense blue or clearly visible black smoke for a period of more than 5 seconds at idle" or "dense blue or clearly visible black smoke during acceleration which would obscure the view of other road users".
Non-turbocharged vehicles first used after 1st August 1979: 2.5m-1
Turbocharged vehicles first used after 1st August 1979: 3.0m-1

□ Excessive smoke can be caused by a dirty air cleaner element. Otherwise, professional advice may be needed to find the cause.

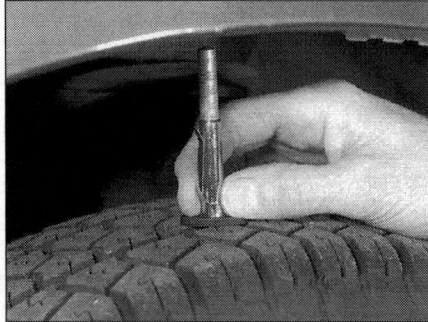

Introduction

A selection of good tools is a fundamental requirement for anyone contemplating the maintenance and repair of a motor vehicle. For the owner who does not possess any, their purchase will prove a considerable expense, offsetting some of the savings made by doing-it-yourself. However, provided that the tools purchased meet the relevant national safety standards and are of good quality, they will last for many years and prove an extremely worthwhile investment.

To help the average owner to decide which tools are needed to carry out the various tasks detailed in this manual, we have compiled three lists of tools under the following headings: *Maintenance and minor repair*, *Repair and overhaul*, and *Special*. Newcomers to practical mechanics should start off with the *Maintenance and minor repair* tool kit, and confine themselves to the simpler jobs around the vehicle. Then, as confidence and experience grow, more difficult tasks can be undertaken, with extra tools being purchased as, and when, they are needed. In this way, a *Maintenance and minor repair* tool kit can be built up into a *Repair and overhaul* tool kit over a considerable period of time, without any major cash outlays. The experienced do-it-yourselfer will have a tool kit good enough for most repair and overhaul procedures, and will add tools from the *Special* category when it is felt that the expense is justified by the amount of use to which these tools will be put.

Maintenance and minor repair tool kit

The tools given in this list should be considered as a minimum requirement if routine maintenance, servicing and minor repair operations are to be undertaken. We recommend the purchase of combination spanners (ring one end, open-ended the other); although more expensive than open-ended ones, they do give the advantages of both types of spanner.

☐ *Combination spanners:*
  Metric - 8 to 19 mm inclusive
☐ *Adjustable spanner - 35 mm jaw (approx.)*
☐ *Spark plug spanner (with rubber insert) - petrol models*
☐ *Spark plug gap adjustment tool - petrol models*
☐ *Set of feeler gauges*
☐ *Brake bleed nipple spanner*
☐ *Screwdrivers:*
  Flat blade - 100 mm long x 6 mm dia
  Cross blade - 100 mm long x 6 mm dia
  Torx - various sizes (not all vehicles)
☐ *Combination pliers*
☐ *Hacksaw (junior)*
☐ *Tyre pump*
☐ *Tyre pressure gauge*
☐ *Oil can*
☐ *Oil filter removal tool*
☐ *Fine emery cloth*
☐ *Wire brush (small)*
☐ *Funnel (medium size)*
☐ *Sump drain plug key (not all vehicles)*

Repair and overhaul tool kit

These tools are virtually essential for anyone undertaking any major repairs to a motor vehicle, and are additional to those given in the *Maintenance and minor repair* list. Included in this list is a comprehensive set of sockets. Although these are expensive, they will be found invaluable as they are so versatile - particularly if various drives are included in the set. We recommend the half-inch square-drive type, as this can be used with most proprietary torque wrenches.

The tools in this list will sometimes need to be supplemented by tools from the *Special* list:

☐ *Sockets (or box spanners) to cover range in previous list (including Torx sockets)*
☐ *Reversible ratchet drive (for use with sockets)*
☐ *Extension piece, 250 mm (for use with sockets)*
☐ *Universal joint (for use with sockets)*
☐ *Flexible handle or sliding T "breaker bar" (for use with sockets)*
☐ *Torque wrench (for use with sockets)*
☐ *Self-locking grips*
☐ *Ball pein hammer*
☐ *Soft-faced mallet (plastic or rubber)*
☐ *Screwdrivers:*
  Flat blade - long & sturdy, short (chubby), and narrow (electrician's) types
  Cross blade – long & sturdy, and short (chubby) types
☐ *Pliers:*
  Long-nosed
  Side cutters (electrician's)
  Circlip (internal and external)
☐ *Cold chisel - 25 mm*
☐ *Scriber*
☐ *Scraper*
☐ *Centre-punch*
☐ *Pin punch*
☐ *Hacksaw*
☐ *Brake hose clamp*
☐ *Brake/clutch bleeding kit*
☐ *Selection of twist drills*
☐ *Steel rule/straight-edge*
☐ *Allen keys (inc. splined/Torx type)*
☐ *Selection of files*
☐ *Wire brush*
☐ *Axle stands*
☐ *Jack (strong trolley or hydraulic type)*
☐ *Light with extension lead*
☐ *Universal electrical multi-meter*

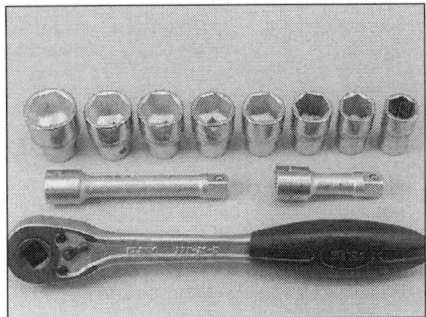
Sockets and reversible ratchet drive

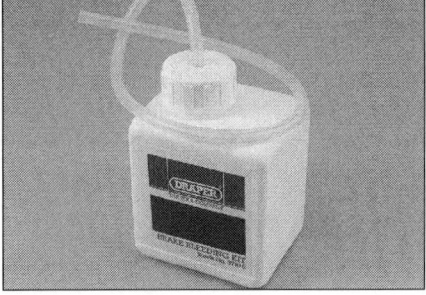
Brake bleeding kit

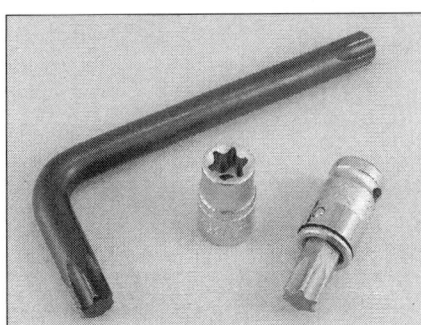
Torx key, socket and bit

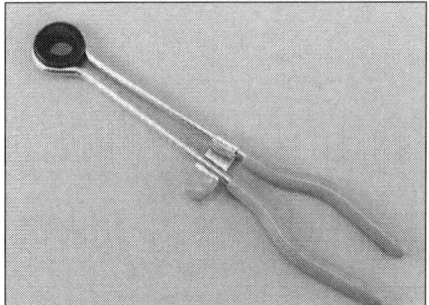
Hose clamp

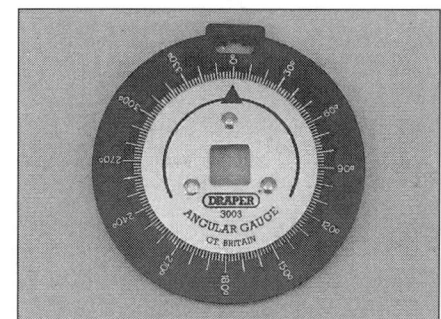
Angular-tightening gauge

Special tools

The tools in this list are those which are not used regularly, are expensive to buy, or which need to be used in accordance with their manufacturers' instructions. Unless relatively difficult mechanical jobs are undertaken frequently, it will not be economic to buy many of these tools. Where this is the case, you could consider clubbing together with friends (or joining a motorists' club) to make a joint purchase, or borrowing the tools against a deposit from a local garage or tool hire specialist. It is worth noting that many of the larger DIY superstores now carry a large range of special tools for hire at modest rates.

The following list contains only those tools and instruments freely available to the public, and not those special tools produced by the vehicle manufacturer specifically for its dealer network. You will find occasional references to these manufacturers' special tools in the text of this manual. Generally, an alternative method of doing the job without the vehicle manufacturers' special tool is given. However, sometimes there is no alternative to using them. Where this is the case and the relevant tool cannot be bought or borrowed, you will have to entrust the work to a dealer.

- [ ] *Angular-tightening gauge*
- [ ] *Valve spring compressor*
- [ ] *Valve grinding tool*
- [ ] *Piston ring compressor*
- [ ] *Piston ring removal/installation tool*
- [ ] *Cylinder bore hone*
- [ ] *Balljoint separator*
- [ ] *Coil spring compressors (where applicable)*
- [ ] *Two/three-legged hub and bearing puller*
- [ ] *Impact screwdriver*
- [ ] *Micrometer and/or vernier calipers*
- [ ] *Dial gauge*
- [ ] *Stroboscopic timing light*
- [ ] *Dwell angle meter/tachometer*
- [ ] *Fault code reader*
- [ ] *Cylinder compression gauge*
- [ ] *Hand-operated vacuum pump and gauge*
- [ ] *Clutch plate alignment set*
- [ ] *Brake shoe steady spring cup removal tool*
- [ ] *Bush and bearing removal/installation set*
- [ ] *Stud extractors*
- [ ] *Tap and die set*
- [ ] *Lifting tackle*
- [ ] *Trolley jack*

Buying tools

Reputable motor accessory shops and superstores often offer excellent quality tools at discount prices, so it pays to shop around.

Remember, you don't have to buy the most expensive items on the shelf, but it is always advisable to steer clear of the very cheap tools. Beware of 'bargains' offered on market stalls or at car boot sales. There are plenty of good tools around at reasonable prices, but always aim to purchase items which meet the relevant national safety standards. If in doubt, ask the proprietor or manager of the shop for advice before making a purchase.

Care and maintenance of tools

Having purchased a reasonable tool kit, it is necessary to keep the tools in a clean and serviceable condition. After use, always wipe off any dirt, grease and metal particles using a clean, dry cloth, before putting the tools away. Never leave them lying around after they have been used. A simple tool rack on the garage or workshop wall for items such as screwdrivers and pliers is a good idea. Store all normal spanners and sockets in a metal box. Any measuring instruments, gauges, meters, etc, must be carefully stored where they cannot be damaged or become rusty.

Take a little care when tools are used. Hammer heads inevitably become marked, and screwdrivers lose the keen edge on their blades from time to time. A little timely attention with emery cloth or a file will soon restore items like this to a good finish.

Working facilities

Not to be forgotten when discussing tools is the workshop itself. If anything more than routine maintenance is to be carried out, a suitable working area becomes essential.

It is appreciated that many an owner-mechanic is forced by circumstances to remove an engine or similar item without the benefit of a garage or workshop. Having done this, any repairs should always be done under the cover of a roof.

Wherever possible, any dismantling should be done on a clean, flat workbench or table at a suitable working height.

Any workbench needs a vice; one with a jaw opening of 100 mm is suitable for most jobs. As mentioned previously, some clean dry storage space is also required for tools, as well as for any lubricants, cleaning fluids, touch-up paints etc, which become necessary.

Another item which may be required, and which has a much more general usage, is an electric drill with a chuck capacity of at least 8 mm. This, together with a good range of twist drills, is virtually essential for fitting accessories.

Last, but not least, always keep a supply of old newspapers and clean, lint-free rags available, and try to keep any working area as clean as possible.

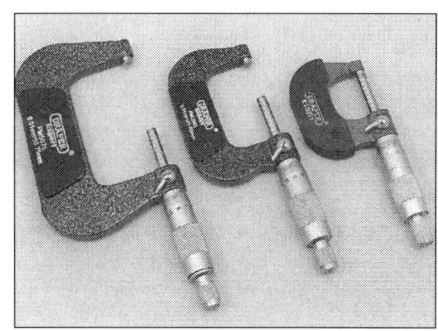

Micrometers

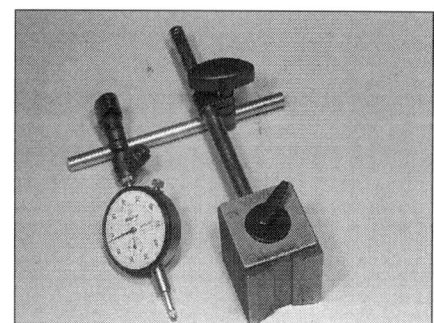

Dial test indicator ("dial gauge")

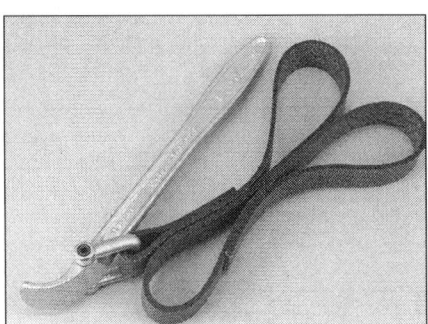

Strap wrench

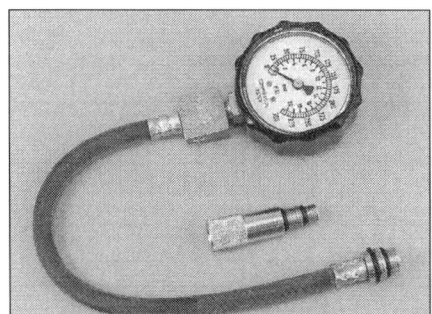

Compression tester

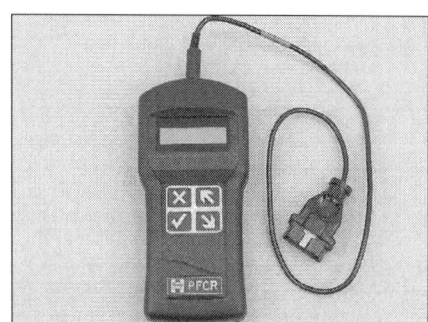

Fault code reader

Whenever servicing, repair or overhaul work is carried out on the car or its components, observe the following procedures and instructions. This will assist in carrying out the operation efficiently and to a professional standard of workmanship.

Joint mating faces and gaskets

When separating components at their mating faces, never insert screwdrivers or similar implements into the joint between the faces in order to prise them apart. This can cause severe damage which results in oil leaks, coolant leaks, etc upon reassembly. Separation is usually achieved by tapping along the joint with a soft-faced hammer in order to break the seal. However, note that this method may not be suitable where dowels are used for component location.

Where a gasket is used between the mating faces of two components, a new one must be fitted on reassembly; fit it dry unless otherwise stated in the repair procedure. Make sure that the mating faces are clean and dry, with all traces of old gasket removed. When cleaning a joint face, use a tool which is unlikely to score or damage the face, and remove any burrs or nicks with an oilstone or fine file.

Make sure that tapped holes are cleaned with a pipe cleaner, and keep them free of jointing compound, if this is being used, unless specifically instructed otherwise.

Ensure that all orifices, channels or pipes are clear, and blow through them, preferably using compressed air.

Oil seals

Oil seals can be removed by levering them out with a wide flat-bladed screwdriver or similar implement. Alternatively, a number of self-tapping screws may be screwed into the seal, and these used as a purchase for pliers or some similar device in order to pull the seal free.

Whenever an oil seal is removed from its working location, either individually or as part of an assembly, it should be renewed.

The very fine sealing lip of the seal is easily damaged, and will not seal if the surface it contacts is not completely clean and free from scratches, nicks or grooves. If the original sealing surface of the component cannot be restored, and the manufacturer has not made provision for slight relocation of the seal relative to the sealing surface, the component should be renewed.

Protect the lips of the seal from any surface which may damage them in the course of fitting. Use tape or a conical sleeve where possible. Lubricate the seal lips with oil before fitting and, on dual-lipped seals, fill the space between the lips with grease.

Unless otherwise stated, oil seals must be fitted with their sealing lips toward the lubricant to be sealed.

Use a tubular drift or block of wood of the appropriate size to install the seal and, if the seal housing is shouldered, drive the seal down to the shoulder. If the seal housing is unshouldered, the seal should be fitted with its face flush with the housing top face (unless otherwise instructed).

Screw threads and fastenings

Seized nuts, bolts and screws are quite a common occurrence where corrosion has set in, and the use of penetrating oil or releasing fluid will often overcome this problem if the offending item is soaked for a while before attempting to release it. The use of an impact driver may also provide a means of releasing such stubborn fastening devices, when used in conjunction with the appropriate screwdriver bit or socket. If none of these methods works, it may be necessary to resort to the careful application of heat, or the use of a hacksaw or nut splitter device.

Studs are usually removed by locking two nuts together on the threaded part, and then using a spanner on the lower nut to unscrew the stud. Studs or bolts which have broken off below the surface of the component in which they are mounted can sometimes be removed using a stud extractor. Always ensure that a blind tapped hole is completely free from oil, grease, water or other fluid before installing the bolt or stud. Failure to do this could cause the housing to crack due to the hydraulic action of the bolt or stud as it is screwed in.

When tightening a castellated nut to accept a split pin, tighten the nut to the specified torque, where applicable, and then tighten further to the next split pin hole. Never slacken the nut to align the split pin hole, unless stated in the repair procedure.

When checking or retightening a nut or bolt to a specified torque setting, slacken the nut or bolt by a quarter of a turn, and then retighten to the specified setting. However, this should not be attempted where angular tightening has been used.

For some screw fastenings, notably cylinder head bolts or nuts, torque wrench settings are no longer specified for the latter stages of tightening, "angle-tightening" being called up instead. Typically, a fairly low torque wrench setting will be applied to the bolts/nuts in the correct sequence, followed by one or more stages of tightening through specified angles.

Locknuts, locktabs and washers

Any fastening which will rotate against a component or housing during tightening should always have a washer between it and the relevant component or housing.

Spring or split washers should always be renewed when they are used to lock a critical component such as a big-end bearing retaining bolt or nut. Locktabs which are folded over to retain a nut or bolt should always be renewed.

Self-locking nuts can be re-used in non-critical areas, providing resistance can be felt when the locking portion passes over the bolt or stud thread. However, it should be noted that self-locking stiffnuts tend to lose their effectiveness after long periods of use, and should then be renewed as a matter of course.

Split pins must always be replaced with new ones of the correct size for the hole.

When thread-locking compound is found on the threads of a fastener which is to be re-used, it should be cleaned off with a wire brush and solvent, and fresh compound applied on reassembly.

Special tools

Some repair procedures in this manual entail the use of special tools such as a press, two or three-legged pullers, spring compressors, etc. Wherever possible, suitable readily-available alternatives to the manufacturer's special tools are described, and are shown in use. In some instances, where no alternative is possible, it has been necessary to resort to the use of a manufacturer's tool, and this has been done for reasons of safety as well as the efficient completion of the repair operation. Unless you are highly-skilled and have a thorough understanding of the procedures described, never attempt to bypass the use of any special tool when the procedure described specifies its use. Not only is there a very great risk of personal injury, but expensive damage could be caused to the components involved.

Environmental considerations

When disposing of used engine oil, brake fluid, antifreeze, etc, give due consideration to any detrimental environmental effects. Do not, for instance, pour any of the above liquids down drains into the general sewage system, or onto the ground to soak away. Many local council refuse tips provide a facility for waste oil disposal, as do some garages. If none of these facilities are available, consult your local Environmental Health Department, or the National Rivers Authority, for further advice.

With the universal tightening-up of legislation regarding the emission of environmentally-harmful substances from motor vehicles, most vehicles have tamperproof devices fitted to the main adjustment points of the fuel system. These devices are primarily designed to prevent unqualified persons from adjusting the fuel/air mixture, with the chance of a consequent increase in toxic emissions. If such devices are found during servicing or overhaul, they should, wherever possible, be renewed or refitted in accordance with the manufacturer's requirements or current legislation.

OIL CARE

FOLLOW THE CODE

OIL BANK LINE
0800 66 33 66
www.oilbankline.org.uk

Note: It is antisocial and illegal to dump oil down the drain. To find the location of your local oil recycling bank, call this number free.

Buying spare parts

Spare parts are available from many sources, for example: Range Rover garages, other garages and accessory shops, and motor factors. Our advice regarding spare part source is as follows:

Officially appointed Range Rover garages – This is the best source of parts which are peculiar to your vehicle and are otherwise not generally available (eg complete cylinder heads, internal gearbox components, badges, interior trim, etc). It is also the only place at which you should buy parts if your vehicle is still under warranty – non-Range Rover components may invalidate the warranty. To be sure of obtaining the correct parts it will always be necessary to give the storeman your vehicle's engine and chassis number, and if possible, to take the old part along for positive identification. Remember that many parts are available on a factory exchange scheme – any parts returned should always be clean! It obviously makes good sense to go straight to the specialists on your vehicle for this type of part, for they are best equipped to supply you.

Other garages and accessory shops – These are often very good places to buy materials and components needed for the maintenance of your vehicle (eg oil filters, bulbs, fan belts, oil and greases, touch-up paint, filler paste, etc). They also sell general accessories, usually have convenient opening hours, charge lower prices and can often be found not far from home.

Motor factors – Good factors will stock all of the more important components which wear out relatively quickly (eg clutch components, pistons, valves, exhaust systems, brake cylinders/pipes/hoses/seals/pads, etc). Motor factors will often provide new or reconditioned components on a part exchange basis – this can save a considerable amount of money.

Vehicle identification numbers

The chassis number will be found on a plate attached to the front body crossmember above the radiator grille (photo).

The engine number is stamped on the cylinder block on the left-hand top face in the centre (photo).

The gearbox number is stamped on the front of the gearbox in early models (photo) and on the lower rear face of the transfer box in later models.

The front axle number is stamped on the front of the axle casing on the left-hand side (photo) and the rear axle number is on the rear of the axle casing, also on the left-hand side.

Chassis number plate

Engine number location between the manifold branches

Gearbox number (arrowed) – early models

Front axle number (arrowed)

Introduction

The vehicle owner who does his or her own maintenance according to the recommended schedules should not have to use this section of the manual very often. Modern component reliability is such that, provided those items subject to wear or deterioration are inspected or renewed at the specified intervals, sudden failure is comparatively rare. Faults do not usually just happen as a result of sudden failure, but develop over a period of time. Major mechanical failures in particular are usually preceded by characteristic symptoms over hundreds or even thousands of miles. Those components which do occasionally fail without warning are often small and easily carried in the vehicle.

With any fault finding, the first step is to decide where to begin investigations. Sometimes this is obvious, but on other occasions a little detective work will be necessary. The owner who makes half a dozen haphazard adjustments or replacements may be successful in curing a fault (or its symptoms), but he will be none the wiser if the fault recurs and he may well have spent more time and money than was necessary. A calm and logical approach will be found to be more satisfactory in the long run. Always take into account any warning signs or abnormalities that may have been noticed in the period preceding the fault – power loss, high or low gauge readings, unusual noises or smells, etc – and remember that failure of components such as fuses or spark plugs may only be pointers to some underlying fault.

The pages which follow here are intended to help in cases of failure to start or breakdown on the road. There is also a Fault Diagnosis Section at the end of each Chapter which should be consulted if the preliminary checks prove unfruitful. Whatever the fault, certain basic principles apply. These are as follows:

Verify the fault. This is simply a matter of being sure that you know what the symptoms are before starting work. This is particularly important if you are investigating a fault for someone else who may not have described it very accurately.

Don't overlook the obvious. For example, if the vehicle won't start, is there petrol in the tank? (Don't take anyone else's word on this particular point, and don't trust the fuel gauge either!) If an electrical fault is indicated, look for loose or broken wires before digging out the test gear.

Cure the disease, not the symptom. Substituting a flat battery with a fully charged one will get you off the hard shoulder, but if the underlying cause is not attended to,the new battery will go the same way. Similarly, changing oil-fouled spark plugs for a new set will get you moving again, but remember that the reason for the fouling (if it wasn't simply an incorrect grade of plug) will have to be established and corrected.

Don't take anything for granted. Particularly, don't forget that a 'new' component may itself be defective (especially if it's been rattling round in the boot for months), and don't leave components out of a fault diagnosis sequence just because they are new or recently fitted. When you do finally diagnose a difficult fault, you'll probably realise that all the evidence was there from the start.

Electrical faults

Electrical faults can be more puzzling than straightforward mechanical failures, but they are no less susceptible to logical analysis if the basic principles of operation are understood. Vehicle electrical wiring exists in extremely unfavourable conditions – heat, vibration and chemical attack and the first things to look for are loose or corroded connections and broken or chafed wires, especially where the wires pass through holes in the bodywork or are subject to vibration.

All metal-bodied vehicles in current production have one pole of the battery 'earthed', ie connected to the vehicle bodywork, and in nearly all modern vehicles it is the negative (–) terminal. The various electrical components – motors, bulb holders, etc – are also connected to earth, either by means of a lead or directly by their mountings. Electric current flows through the component and then back to the battery via the bodywork. If the component mounting is loose or corroded, or if a good path back to the battery is not available, the circuit will be incomplete and malfunction will result. The engine and/or gearbox are also earthed by means of flexible metal straps to the body or subframe; if these straps are loose or missing, starter motor, generator and ignition trouble may result.

Assuming the earth return to be satisfactory, electrical faults will be due either to component malfunction or to defects in the current supply. Individual components are dealt with in Chapter 10. If supply wires are broken or cracked internally this results in an open-circuit, and the easiest way to check for this is to bypass the suspect wire temporarily with a length of wire having a crocodile clip or suitable connector at each end. Alternatively, a 12V test lamp can be used to verify the presence of supply voltage at various points along the wire and the break can be thus isolated.

If a bare portion of a live wire touches the bodywork or other earthed metal part, the electricity will take the low-resistance path thus formed back to the battery: this is known as a short-circuit. Hopefully a short-circuit will blow a fuse, but otherwise it may cause burning of the insulation (and possibly further short-circuits) or even a fire. This is why it is inadvisable to bypass persistently blowing fuses with silver foil or wire.

Spares and tool kit

Most vehicles are supplied only with sufficient tools for wheel changing; the *Maintenance and minor repair* tool kit detailed in *Tools and working facilities*, with the addition of a hammer, is probably sufficient for those repairs that most motorists would consider attempting at the roadside. In addition a few items which can be fitted without too much trouble in the event of a breakdown should be carried. Experience and available space will modify the list below, but the following may save having to call on professional assistance:

- [ ] *Spark plugs, clean and correctly gapped*
- [ ] *HT lead and plug cap – long enough to reach the plug furthest from the distributor*
- [ ] *Distributor rotor, condenser and contact breaker bpoints*
- [ ] *Drivebelt(s) — emergency type may suffice*
- [ ] *Spare fuses*
- [ ] *Set of principal light bulbs*
- [ ] *Tin of radiator sealer and hose bandage*
- [ ] *Exhaust bandage*
- [ ] *Roll of insulating tape*
- [ ] *Length of soft iron wire*
- [ ] *Length of electrical flex*
- [ ] *Torch or inspection lamp (can double as test lamp)*

- [ ] *Battery jump leads*
- [ ] *Tow-rope*
- [ ] *Ignition waterproofing aerosol*
- [ ] *Litre of engine oil*
- [ ] *Sealed can of hydraulic fluid*
- [ ] *Emergency windscreen*
- [ ] *Wormdrive clips*
- [ ] *Tube of filler paste*

If spare fuel is carried, a can designed for the purpose should be used to minimise risks of leakage and collision damage. A first aid kit and a warning triangle, whilst not at present compulsory in the UK, are obviously sensible items to carry in addition to the above. When touring abroad it may be advisable to carry additional spares which, even if you cannot fit them yourself, could save having to wait while parts are obtained. The items below may be worth considering:

- [ ] *Throttle cable*
- [ ] *Cylinder head gasket*
- [ ] *Alternator brushes*

One of the motoring organisations will be able to advise on availability of fuel, etc, in foreign countries.

Engine will not start

Engine fails to turn when starter operated

- [ ] Flat battery (recharge use jump leads or push start)
- [ ] Battery terminals loose or corroded
- [ ] Battery earth to body defective
- [ ] Engine earth strap loose or broken
- [ ] Starter motor (or solenoid) wiring loose or broken
- [ ] Ignition/starter switch faulty
- [ ] Major mechanical failure (seizure)
- [ ] Starter or solenoid internal fault (see Chapter 10)

Starter motor turns engine slowly

- [ ] Partially discharged battery (recharge, use jump leads, or push start)
- [ ] Battery terminals loose or corroded

- [ ] Battery earth to body defective
- [ ] Engine earth strap loose
- [ ] Starter motor (or solenoid) wiring loose
- [ ] Starter motor internal fault (see Chapter 10)

Starter motor spins without turning engine

- [ ] Flywheel gear teeth damaged or worn
- [ ] Starter motor mounting bolts loose

Engine turns normally but fails to start

- [ ] Damp or dirty HT leads and distributor cap (crank engine and check for spark)
- [ ] No fuel in tank (check for delivery)
- [ ] Fouled or incorrectly gapped spark plugs (remove, clean and regap)
- [ ] Other ignition system fault (see Chapter 4)
- [ ] Other fuel system fault (see Chapter 3)

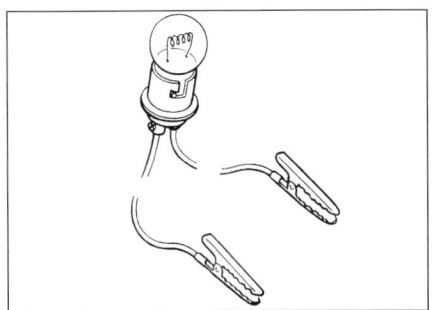

A simple test lamp is useful for checking electrical faults

Carrying a few spares may save you a long walk!

- [ ] Poor compression (see Chapter 1)
- [ ] Major mechanical failure (eg camshaft drive)

Engine fires but will not run

- [ ] Air leaks at carburettor or inlet manifold
- [ ] Fuel starvation (see Chapter 3)
- [ ] Ignition fault (see Chapter 4)

Engine cuts out and will not restart

Engine cuts out suddenly – ignition fault

- [ ] Loose or disconnected LT wires
- [ ] Wet HT leads or distributor cap (after traversing water splash)
- [ ] Coil failure (check for spark)
- [ ] Other ignition fault (see Chapter 4)

Engine misfires before cutting out – fuel fault

- [ ] Fuel tank empty
- [ ] Fuel pump defective or filter blocked (check for delivery)

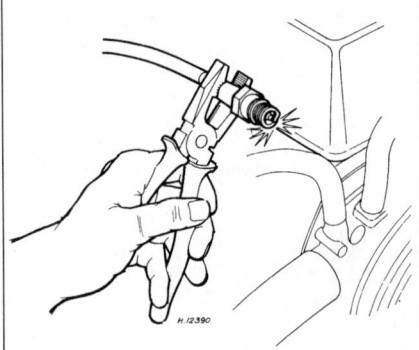

Crank engine and check for spark. Note use of insulated tool

- [ ] Fuel tank filler vent blocked (suction will be evident on releasing cap)
- [ ] Carburettor needle valve sticking
- [ ] Carburettor jets blocked (fuel contaminated)
- [ ] Other fuel system fault (see Chapter 3)

Engine cuts out – other causes

- [ ] Serious overheating
- [ ] Major mechanical failure (eg camshaft drive)

Engine overheats

Ignition (no-charge) light illuminated

- [ ] Slack or broken drivebelt – re-tension or renew (Chapter 2)

Ignition warning light not illuminated

- [ ] Coolant loss due to internal or external leakage (see Chapter 2)
- [ ] Thermostat defective
- [ ] Low oil level
- [ ] Brakes binding
- [ ] Radiator clogged externally or internally
- [ ] Engine waterways clogged
- [ ] Ignition timing incorrect or automatic advance malfunctioning
- [ ] Mixture too weak

Note: *Do not add cold water to an overheated engine or damage may result*

Low engine oil pressure

Note: *Low oil pressure in a high-mileage engine at tickover is not necessarily a cause for concern. Sudden pressure loss at speed is far more significant. In any event check the gauge or warning light sender before condemning the engine.*

Gauge reads low or warning light illuminated with engine running

- [ ] Oil level low or incorrect grade
- [ ] Defective gauge or sender unit
- [ ] Wire to sender unit earthed
- [ ] Engine overheating
- [ ] Oil filter clogged or bypass valve defective
- [ ] Oil pressure relief valve defective
- [ ] Oil pick-up strainer clogged
- [ ] Oil pump worn or mountings loose
- [ ] Worn main or big-end bearings

Engine noises

Pre-ignition (pinking) on acceleration

- [ ] Incorrect grade of fuel
- [ ] Ignition timing incorrect
- [ ] Distributor faulty or worn
- [ ] Worn or maladjusted carburettor
- [ ] Excessive carbon build-up in engine

Whistling or wheezing noises

- [ ] Leaking vacuum hose
- [ ] Leaking carburettor or manifold gasket
- [ ] Blowing head gasket

Tapping or rattling

- [ ] Worn valve gear
- [ ] Worn timing chain or belt
- [ ] Broken piston ring (ticking noise)

Knocking or thumping

- [ ] Unintentional mechanical contact (eg fan blades)
- [ ] Worn drivebelt
- [ ] Peripheral component fault (generator, water pump, etc)
- [ ] Worn big-end bearings (regular heavy knocking, perhaps less under load)
- [ ] Worn main bearings (rumbling and knocking, perhaps worsening under load)
- [ ] Piston slap (most noticeable when cold)

Length (distance)

Inches (in)	x 25.4	= Millimetres (mm)	x 0.0394	=	Inches (in)
Feet (ft)	x 0.305	= Metres (m)	x 3.281	=	Feet (ft)
Miles	x 1.609	= Kilometres (km)	x 0.621	=	Miles

Volume (capacity)

Cubic inches (cu in; in³)	x 16.387	= Cubic centimetres (cc; cm³)	x 0.061	=	Cubic inches (cu in; in³)
Imperial pints (Imp pt)	x 0.568	= Litres (l)	x 1.76	=	Imperial pints (Imp pt)
Imperial quarts (Imp qt)	x 1.137	= Litres (l)	x 0.88	=	Imperial quarts (Imp qt)
Imperial quarts (Imp qt)	x 1.201	= US quarts (US qt)	x 0.833	=	Imperial quarts (Imp qt)
US quarts (US qt)	x 0.946	= Litres (l)	x 1.057	=	US quarts (US qt)
Imperial gallons (Imp gal)	x 4.546	= Litres (l)	x 0.22	=	Imperial gallons (Imp gal)
Imperial gallons (Imp gal)	x 1.201	= US gallons (US gal)	x 0.833	=	Imperial gallons (Imp gal)
US gallons (US gal)	x 3.785	= Litres (l)	x 0.264	=	US gallons (US gal)

Mass (weight)

Ounces (oz)	x 28.35	= Grams (g)	x 0.035	=	Ounces (oz)
Pounds (lb)	x 0.454	= Kilograms (kg)	x 2.205	=	Pounds (lb)

Force

Ounces-force (ozf; oz)	x 0.278	= Newtons (N)	x 3.6	=	Ounces-force (ozf; oz)
Pounds-force (lbf; lb)	x 4.448	= Newtons (N)	x 0.225	=	Pounds-force (lbf; lb)
Newtons (N)	x 0.1	= Kilograms-force (kgf; kg)	x 9.81	=	Newtons (N)

Pressure

Pounds-force per square inch (psi; lbf/in²; lb/in²)	x 0.070	= Kilograms-force per square centimetre (kgf/cm²; kg/cm²)	x 14.223	=	Pounds-force per square inch (psi; lbf/in²; lb/in²)
Pounds-force per square inch (psi; lbf/in²; lb/in²)	x 0.068	= Atmospheres (atm)	x 14.696	=	Pounds-force per square inch (psi; lbf/in²; lb/in²)
Pounds-force per square inch (psi; lbf/in²; lb/in²)	x 0.069	= Bars	x 14.5	=	Pounds-force per square inch (psi; lbf/in²; lb/in²)
Pounds-force per square inch (psi; lbf/in²; lb/in²)	x 6.895	= Kilopascals (kPa)	x 0.145	=	Pounds-force per square inch (psi; lbf/in²; lb/in²)
Kilopascals (kPa)	x 0.01	= Kilograms-force per square centimetre (kgf/cm²; kg/cm²)	x 98.1	=	Kilopascals (kPa)
Millibar (mbar)	x 100	= Pascals (Pa)	x 0.01	=	Millibar (mbar)
Millibar (mbar)	x 0.0145	= Pounds-force per square inch (psi; lbf/in²; lb/in²)	x 68.947	=	Millibar (mbar)
Millibar (mbar)	x 0.75	= Millimetres of mercury (mmHg)	x 1.333	=	Millibar (mbar)
Millibar (mbar)	x 0.401	= Inches of water (inH₂O)	x 2.491	=	Millibar (mbar)
Millimetres of mercury (mmHg)	x 0.535	= Inches of water (inH₂O)	x 1.868	=	Millimetres of mercury (mmHg)
Inches of water (inH₂O)	x 0.036	= Pounds-force per square inch (psi; lbf/in²; lb/in²)	x 27.68	=	Inches of water (inH₂O)

Torque (moment of force)

Pounds-force inches (lbf in; lb in)	x 1.152	= Kilograms-force centimetre (kgf cm; kg cm)	x 0.868	=	Pounds-force inches (lbf in; lb in)
Pounds-force inches (lbf in; lb in)	x 0.113	= Newton metres (Nm)	x 8.85	=	Pounds-force inches (lbf in; lb in)
Pounds-force inches (lbf in; lb in)	x 0.083	= Pounds-force feet (lbf ft; lb ft)	x 12	=	Pounds-force inches (lbf in; lb in)
Pounds-force feet (lbf ft; lb ft)	x 0.138	= Kilograms-force metres (kgf m; kg m)	x 7.233	=	Pounds-force feet (lbf ft; lb ft)
Pounds-force feet (lbf ft; lb ft)	x 1.356	= Newton metres (Nm)	x 0.738	=	Pounds-force feet (lbf ft; lb ft)
Newton metres (Nm)	x 0.102	= Kilograms-force metres (kgf m; kg m)	x 9.804	=	Newton metres (Nm)

Power

Horsepower (hp)	x 745.7	= Watts (W)	x 0.0013	=	Horsepower (hp)

Velocity (speed)

Miles per hour (miles/hr; mph)	x 1.609	= Kilometres per hour (km/hr; kph)	x 0.621	=	Miles per hour (miles/hr; mph)

Fuel consumption*

Miles per gallon (mpg)	x 0.354	= Kilometres per litre (km/l)	x 2.825	=	Miles per gallon (mpg)

Temperature

Degrees Fahrenheit = (°C x 1.8) + 32   Degrees Celsius (Degrees Centigrade; °C) = (°F - 32) x 0.56

It is common practice to convert from miles per gallon (mpg) to litres/100 kilometres (l/100km), where mpg x l/100 km = 282

A

ABS (Anti-lock brake system) A system, usually electronically controlled, that senses incipient wheel lockup during braking and relieves hydraulic pressure at wheels that are about to skid.

Air bag An inflatable bag hidden in the steering wheel (driver's side) or the dash or glovebox (passenger side). In a head-on collision, the bags inflate, preventing the driver and front passenger from being thrown forward into the steering wheel or windscreen.

Air cleaner A metal or plastic housing, containing a filter element, which removes dust and dirt from the air being drawn into the engine.

Air filter element The actual filter in an air cleaner system, usually manufactured from pleated paper and requiring renewal at regular intervals.

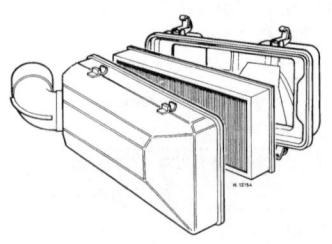

Air filter

Allen key A hexagonal wrench which fits into a recessed hexagonal hole.

Alligator clip A long-nosed spring-loaded metal clip with meshing teeth. Used to make temporary electrical connections.

Alternator A component in the electrical system which converts mechanical energy from a drivebelt into electrical energy to charge the battery and to operate the starting system, ignition system and electrical accessories.

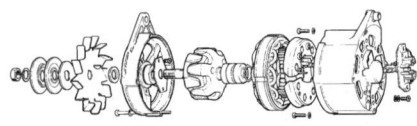

Alternator (exploded view)

Ampere (amp) A unit of measurement for the flow of electric current. One amp is the amount of current produced by one volt acting through a resistance of one ohm.

Anaerobic sealer A substance used to prevent bolts and screws from loosening. Anaerobic means that it does not require oxygen for activation. The Loctite brand is widely used.

Antifreeze A substance (usually ethylene glycol) mixed with water, and added to a vehicle's cooling system, to prevent freezing of the coolant in winter. Antifreeze also contains chemicals to inhibit corrosion and the formation of rust and other deposits that would tend to clog the radiator and coolant passages and reduce cooling efficiency.

Anti-seize compound A coating that reduces the risk of seizing on fasteners that are subjected to high temperatures, such as exhaust manifold bolts and nuts.

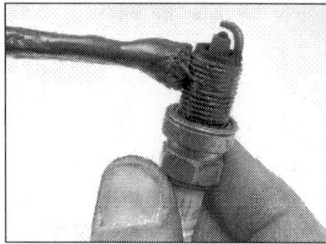

Anti-seize compound

Asbestos A natural fibrous mineral with great heat resistance, commonly used in the composition of brake friction materials. Asbestos is a health hazard and the dust created by brake systems should never be inhaled or ingested.

Axle A shaft on which a wheel revolves, or which revolves with a wheel. Also, a solid beam that connects the two wheels at one end of the vehicle. An axle which also transmits power to the wheels is known as a live axle.

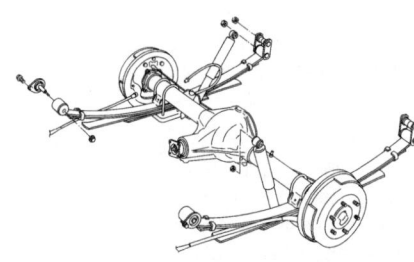

Axle assembly

Axleshaft A single rotating shaft, on either side of the differential, which delivers power from the final drive assembly to the drive wheels. Also called a driveshaft or a halfshaft.

B

Ball bearing An anti-friction bearing consisting of a hardened inner and outer race with hardened steel balls between two races.

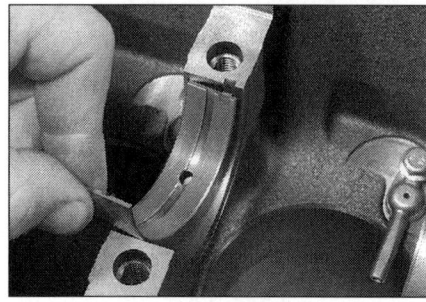

Bearing

Bearing The curved surface on a shaft or in a bore, or the part assembled into either, that permits relative motion between them with minimum wear and friction.

Big-end bearing The bearing in the end of the connecting rod that's attached to the crankshaft.

Bleed nipple A valve on a brake wheel cylinder, caliper or other hydraulic component that is opened to purge the hydraulic system of air. Also called a bleed screw.

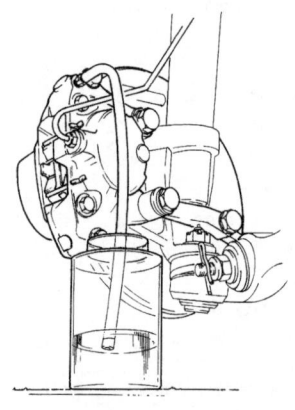

Brake bleeding

Brake bleeding Procedure for removing air from lines of a hydraulic brake system.

Brake disc The component of a disc brake that rotates with the wheels.

Brake drum The component of a drum brake that rotates with the wheels.

Brake linings The friction material which contacts the brake disc or drum to retard the vehicle's speed. The linings are bonded or riveted to the brake pads or shoes.

Brake pads The replaceable friction pads that pinch the brake disc when the brakes are applied. Brake pads consist of a friction material bonded or riveted to a rigid backing plate.

Brake shoe The crescent-shaped carrier to which the brake linings are mounted and which forces the lining against the rotating drum during braking.

Braking systems For more information on braking systems, consult the *Haynes Automotive Brake Manual*.

Breaker bar A long socket wrench handle providing greater leverage.

Bulkhead The insulated partition between the engine and the passenger compartment.

C

Caliper The non-rotating part of a disc-brake assembly that straddles the disc and carries the brake pads. The caliper also contains the hydraulic components that cause the pads to pinch the disc when the brakes are applied. A caliper is also a measuring tool that can be set to measure inside or outside dimensions of an object.

Camshaft A rotating shaft on which a series of cam lobes operate the valve mechanisms. The camshaft may be driven by gears, by sprockets and chain or by sprockets and a belt.

Canister A container in an evaporative emission control system; contains activated charcoal granules to trap vapours from the fuel system.

Canister

Carburettor A device which mixes fuel with air in the proper proportions to provide a desired power output from a spark ignition internal combustion engine.

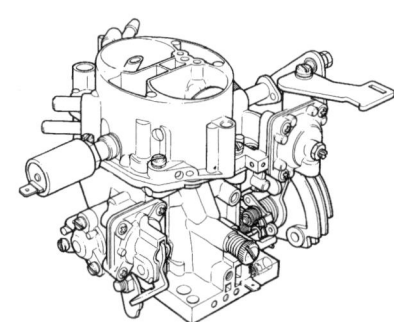

Carburettor

Castellated Resembling the parapets along the top of a castle wall. For example, a castellated balljoint stud nut.

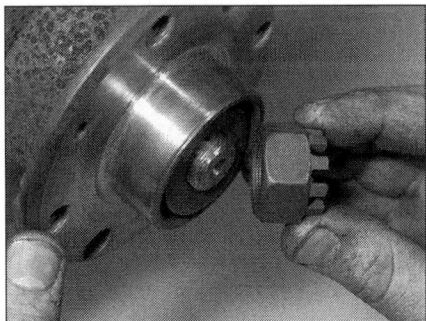

Castellated nut

Castor In wheel alignment, the backward or forward tilt of the steering axis. Castor is positive when the steering axis is inclined rearward at the top.

Catalytic converter A silencer-like device in the exhaust system which converts certain pollutants in the exhaust gases into less harmful substances.

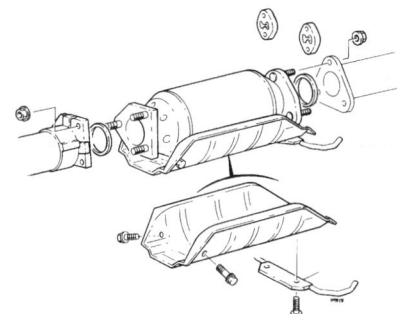

Catalytic converter

Circlip A ring-shaped clip used to prevent endwise movement of cylindrical parts and shafts. An internal circlip is installed in a groove in a housing; an external circlip fits into a groove on the outside of a cylindrical piece such as a shaft.

Clearance The amount of space between two parts. For example, between a piston and a cylinder, between a bearing and a journal, etc.

Coil spring A spiral of elastic steel found in various sizes throughout a vehicle, for example as a springing medium in the suspension and in the valve train.

Compression Reduction in volume, and increase in pressure and temperature, of a gas, caused by squeezing it into a smaller space.

Compression ratio The relationship between cylinder volume when the piston is at top dead centre and cylinder volume when the piston is at bottom dead centre.

Constant velocity (CV) joint A type of universal joint that cancels out vibrations caused by driving power being transmitted through an angle.

Core plug A disc or cup-shaped metal device inserted in a hole in a casting through which core was removed when the casting was formed. Also known as a freeze plug or expansion plug.

Crankcase The lower part of the engine block in which the crankshaft rotates.

Crankshaft The main rotating member, or shaft, running the length of the crankcase, with offset "throws" to which the connecting rods are attached.

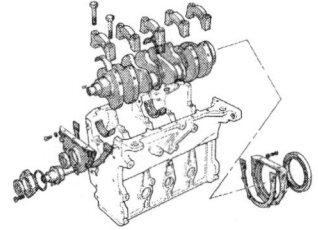

Crankshaft assembly

Crocodile clip See Alligator clip

D

Diagnostic code Code numbers obtained by accessing the diagnostic mode of an engine management computer. This code can be used to determine the area in the system where a malfunction may be located.

Disc brake A brake design incorporating a rotating disc onto which brake pads are squeezed. The resulting friction converts the energy of a moving vehicle into heat.

Double-overhead cam (DOHC) An engine that uses two overhead camshafts, usually one for the intake valves and one for the exhaust valves.

Drivebelt(s) The belt(s) used to drive accessories such as the alternator, water pump, power steering pump, air conditioning compressor, etc. off the crankshaft pulley.

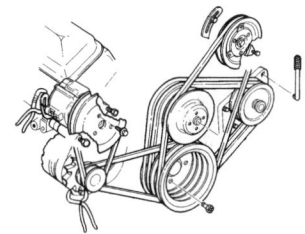

Accessory drivebelts

Driveshaft Any shaft used to transmit motion. Commonly used when referring to the axleshafts on a front wheel drive vehicle.

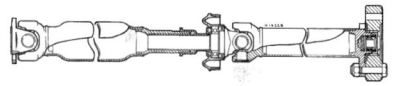

Driveshaft

Drum brake A type of brake using a drum-shaped metal cylinder attached to the inner surface of the wheel. When the brake pedal is pressed, curved brake shoes with friction linings press against the inside of the drum to slow or stop the vehicle.

Drum brake assembly

E

EGR valve A valve used to introduce exhaust gases into the intake air stream.

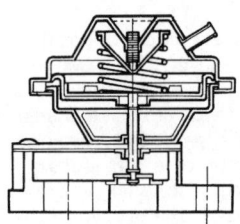

EGR valve

Electronic control unit (ECU) A computer which controls (for instance) ignition and fuel injection systems, or an anti-lock braking system. For more information refer to the *Haynes Automotive Electrical and Electronic Systems Manual.*

Electronic Fuel Injection (EFI) A computer controlled fuel system that distributes fuel through an injector located in each intake port of the engine.

Emergency brake A braking system, independent of the main hydraulic system, that can be used to slow or stop the vehicle if the primary brakes fail, or to hold the vehicle stationary even though the brake pedal isn't depressed. It usually consists of a hand lever that actuates either front or rear brakes mechanically through a series of cables and linkages. Also known as a handbrake or parking brake.

Endfloat The amount of lengthwise movement between two parts. As applied to a crankshaft, the distance that the crankshaft can move forward and back in the cylinder block.

Engine management system (EMS) A computer controlled system which manages the fuel injection and the ignition systems in an integrated fashion.

Exhaust manifold A part with several passages through which exhaust gases leave the engine combustion chambers and enter the exhaust pipe.

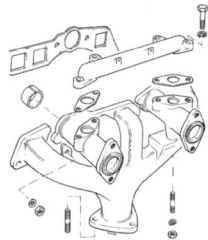

Exhaust manifold

F

Fan clutch A viscous (fluid) drive coupling device which permits variable engine fan speeds in relation to engine speeds.

Feeler blade A thin strip or blade of hardened steel, ground to an exact thickness, used to check or measure clearances between parts.

Feeler blade

Firing order The order in which the engine cylinders fire, or deliver their power strokes, beginning with the number one cylinder.

Flywheel A heavy spinning wheel in which energy is absorbed and stored by means of momentum. On cars, the flywheel is attached to the crankshaft to smooth out firing impulses.

Free play The amount of travel before any action takes place. The "looseness" in a linkage, or an assembly of parts, between the initial application of force and actual movement. For example, the distance the brake pedal moves before the pistons in the master cylinder are actuated.

Fuse An electrical device which protects a circuit against accidental overload. The typical fuse contains a soft piece of metal which is calibrated to melt at a predetermined current flow (expressed as amps) and break the circuit.

Fusible link A circuit protection device consisting of a conductor surrounded by heat-resistant insulation. The conductor is smaller than the wire it protects, so it acts as the weakest link in the circuit. Unlike a blown fuse, a failed fusible link must frequently be cut from the wire for replacement.

G

Gap The distance the spark must travel in jumping from the centre electrode to the side

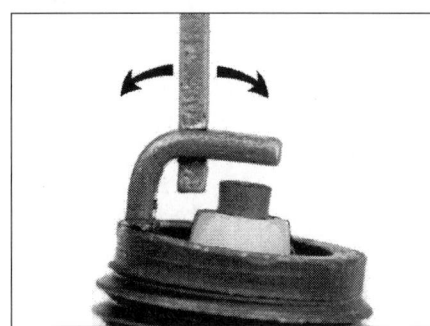

Adjusting spark plug gap

electrode in a spark plug. Also refers to the spacing between the points in a contact breaker assembly in a conventional points-type ignition, or to the distance between the reluctor or rotor and the pickup coil in an electronic ignition.

Gasket Any thin, soft material - usually cork, cardboard, asbestos or soft metal - installed between two metal surfaces to ensure a good seal. For instance, the cylinder head gasket seals the joint between the block and the cylinder head.

Gasket

Gauge An instrument panel display used to monitor engine conditions. A gauge with a movable pointer on a dial or a fixed scale is an analogue gauge. A gauge with a numerical readout is called a digital gauge.

H

Halfshaft A rotating shaft that transmits power from the final drive unit to a drive wheel, usually when referring to a live rear axle.

Harmonic balancer A device designed to reduce torsion or twisting vibration in the crankshaft. May be incorporated in the crankshaft pulley. Also known as a vibration damper.

Hone An abrasive tool for correcting small irregularities or differences in diameter in an engine cylinder, brake cylinder, etc.

Hydraulic tappet A tappet that utilises hydraulic pressure from the engine's lubrication system to maintain zero clearance (constant contact with both camshaft and valve stem). Automatically adjusts to variation in valve stem length. Hydraulic tappets also reduce valve noise.

I

Ignition timing The moment at which the spark plug fires, usually expressed in the number of crankshaft degrees before the piston reaches the top of its stroke.

Inlet manifold A tube or housing with passages through which flows the air-fuel mixture (carburettor vehicles and vehicles with throttle body injection) or air only (port fuel-injected vehicles) to the port openings in the cylinder head.

J

Jump start Starting the engine of a vehicle with a discharged or weak battery by attaching jump leads from the weak battery to a charged or helper battery.

L

Load Sensing Proportioning Valve (LSPV) A brake hydraulic system control valve that works like a proportioning valve, but also takes into consideration the amount of weight carried by the rear axle.

Locknut A nut used to lock an adjustment nut, or other threaded component, in place. For example, a locknut is employed to keep the adjusting nut on the rocker arm in position.

Lockwasher A form of washer designed to prevent an attaching nut from working loose.

M

MacPherson strut A type of front suspension system devised by Earle MacPherson at Ford of England. In its original form, a simple lateral link with the anti-roll bar creates the lower control arm. A long strut - an integral coil spring and shock absorber - is mounted between the body and the steering knuckle. Many modern so-called MacPherson strut systems use a conventional lower A-arm and don't rely on the anti-roll bar for location.

Multimeter An electrical test instrument with the capability to measure voltage, current and resistance.

N

NOx Oxides of Nitrogen. A common toxic pollutant emitted by petrol and diesel engines at higher temperatures.

O

Ohm The unit of electrical resistance. One volt applied to a resistance of one ohm will produce a current of one amp.

Ohmmeter An instrument for measuring electrical resistance.

O-ring A type of sealing ring made of a special rubber-like material; in use, the O-ring is compressed into a groove to provide the sealing action.

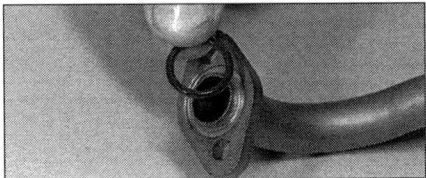

O-ring

Overhead cam (ohc) engine An engine with the camshaft(s) located on top of the cylinder head(s).

Overhead valve (ohv) engine An engine with the valves located in the cylinder head, but with the camshaft located in the engine block.

Oxygen sensor A device installed in the engine exhaust manifold, which senses the oxygen content in the exhaust and converts this information into an electric current. Also called a Lambda sensor.

P

Phillips screw A type of screw head having a cross instead of a slot for a corresponding type of screwdriver.

Plastigage A thin strip of plastic thread, available in different sizes, used for measuring clearances. For example, a strip of Plastigage is laid across a bearing journal. The parts are assembled and dismantled; the width of the crushed strip indicates the clearance between journal and bearing.

Plastigage

Propeller shaft The long hollow tube with universal joints at both ends that carries power from the transmission to the differential on front-engined rear wheel drive vehicles.

Proportioning valve A hydraulic control valve which limits the amount of pressure to the rear brakes during panic stops to prevent wheel lock-up.

R

Rack-and-pinion steering A steering system with a pinion gear on the end of the steering shaft that mates with a rack (think of a geared wheel opened up and laid flat). When the steering wheel is turned, the pinion turns, moving the rack to the left or right. This movement is transmitted through the track rods to the steering arms at the wheels.

Radiator A liquid-to-air heat transfer device designed to reduce the temperature of the coolant in an internal combustion engine cooling system.

Refrigerant Any substance used as a heat transfer agent in an air-conditioning system. R-12 has been the principle refrigerant for many years; recently, however, manufacturers have begun using R-134a, a non-CFC substance that is considered less harmful to the ozone in the upper atmosphere.

Rocker arm A lever arm that rocks on a shaft or pivots on a stud. In an overhead valve engine, the rocker arm converts the upward movement of the pushrod into a downward movement to open a valve.

Rotor In a distributor, the rotating device inside the cap that connects the centre electrode and the outer terminals as it turns, distributing the high voltage from the coil secondary winding to the proper spark plug. Also, that part of an alternator which rotates inside the stator. Also, the rotating assembly of a turbocharger, including the compressor wheel, shaft and turbine wheel.

Runout The amount of wobble (in-and-out movement) of a gear or wheel as it's rotated. The amount a shaft rotates "out-of-true." The out-of-round condition of a rotating part.

S

Sealant A liquid or paste used to prevent leakage at a joint. Sometimes used in conjunction with a gasket.

Sealed beam lamp An older headlight design which integrates the reflector, lens and filaments into a hermetically-sealed one-piece unit. When a filament burns out or the lens cracks, the entire unit is simply replaced.

Serpentine drivebelt A single, long, wide accessory drivebelt that's used on some newer vehicles to drive all the accessories, instead of a series of smaller, shorter belts. Serpentine drivebelts are usually tensioned by an automatic tensioner.

Serpentine drivebelt

Shim Thin spacer, commonly used to adjust the clearance or relative positions between two parts. For example, shims inserted into or under bucket tappets control valve clearances. Clearance is adjusted by changing the thickness of the shim.

Slide hammer A special puller that screws into or hooks onto a component such as a shaft or bearing; a heavy sliding handle on the shaft bottoms against the end of the shaft to knock the component free.

Sprocket A tooth or projection on the periphery of a wheel, shaped to engage with a chain or drivebelt. Commonly used to refer to the sprocket wheel itself.

Starter inhibitor switch On vehicles with an

automatic transmission, a switch that prevents starting if the vehicle is not in Neutral or Park.

Strut See MacPherson strut.

T

Tappet A cylindrical component which transmits motion from the cam to the valve stem, either directly or via a pushrod and rocker arm. Also called a cam follower.

Thermostat A heat-controlled valve that regulates the flow of coolant between the cylinder block and the radiator, so maintaining optimum engine operating temperature. A thermostat is also used in some air cleaners in which the temperature is regulated.

Thrust bearing The bearing in the clutch assembly that is moved in to the release levers by clutch pedal action to disengage the clutch. Also referred to as a release bearing.

Timing belt A toothed belt which drives the camshaft. Serious engine damage may result if it breaks in service.

Timing chain A chain which drives the camshaft.

Toe-in The amount the front wheels are closer together at the front than at the rear. On rear wheel drive vehicles, a slight amount of toe-in is usually specified to keep the front wheels running parallel on the road by offsetting other forces that tend to spread the wheels apart.

Toe-out The amount the front wheels are closer together at the rear than at the front. On front wheel drive vehicles, a slight amount of toe-out is usually specified.

Tools For full information on choosing and using tools, refer to the *Haynes Automotive Tools Manual*.

Tracer A stripe of a second colour applied to a wire insulator to distinguish that wire from another one with the same colour insulator.

Tune-up A process of accurate and careful adjustments and parts replacement to obtain the best possible engine performance.

Turbocharger A centrifugal device, driven by exhaust gases, that pressurises the intake air. Normally used to increase the power output from a given engine displacement, but can also be used primarily to reduce exhaust emissions (as on VW's "Umwelt" Diesel engine).

U

Universal joint or U-joint A double-pivoted connection for transmitting power from a driving to a driven shaft through an angle. A U-joint consists of two Y-shaped yokes and a cross-shaped member called the spider.

V

Valve A device through which the flow of liquid, gas, vacuum, or loose material in bulk may be started, stopped, or regulated by a movable part that opens, shuts, or partially obstructs one or more ports or passageways. A valve is also the movable part of such a device.

Valve clearance The clearance between the valve tip (the end of the valve stem) and the rocker arm or tappet. The valve clearance is measured when the valve is closed.

Vernier caliper A precision measuring instrument that measures inside and outside dimensions. Not quite as accurate as a micrometer, but more convenient.

Viscosity The thickness of a liquid or its resistance to flow.

Volt A unit for expressing electrical "pressure" in a circuit. One volt that will produce a current of one ampere through a resistance of one ohm.

W

Welding Various processes used to join metal items by heating the areas to be joined to a molten state and fusing them together. For more information refer to the *Haynes Automotive Welding Manual*.

Wiring diagram A drawing portraying the components and wires in a vehicle's electrical system, using standardised symbols. For more information refer to the *Haynes Automotive Electrical and Electronic Systems Manual*.

Note: *References throughout this index relate to Chapter•page number*

Preserving Our Motoring Heritage

< The Model J Duesenberg Derham Tourster. Only eight of these magnificent cars were ever built – this is the only example to be found outside the United States of America

Almost every car you've ever loved, loathed or desired is gathered under one roof at the Haynes Motor Museum. Over 300 immaculately presented cars and motorbikes represent every aspect of our motoring heritage, from elegant reminders of bygone days, such as the superb Model J Duesenberg to curiosities like the bug-eyed BMW Isetta. There are also many old friends and flames. Perhaps you remember the 1959 Ford Popular that you did your courting in? The magnificent 'Red Collection' is a spectacle of classic sports cars including AC, Alfa Romeo, Austin Healey, Ferrari, Lamborghini, Maserati, MG, Riley, Porsche and Triumph.

A Perfect Day Out

Each and every vehicle at the Haynes Motor Museum has played its part in the history and culture of Motoring. Today, they make a wonderful spectacle and a great day out for all the family. Bring the kids, bring Mum and Dad, but above all bring your camera to capture those golden memories for ever. You will also find an impressive array of motoring memorabilia, a comfortable 70 seat video cinema and one of the most extensive transport book shops in Britain. The Pit Stop Cafe serves everything from a cup of tea to wholesome, home-made meals or, if you prefer, you can enjoy the large picnic area nestled in the beautiful rural surroundings of Somerset.

> John Haynes O.B.E., Founder and Chairman of the museum at the wheel of a Haynes Light 12.

< Graham Hill's Lola Cosworth Formula 1 car next to a 1934 Riley Sports.

The Museum is situated on the A359 Yeovil to Frome road at Sparkford, just off the A303 in Somerset. It is about 40 miles south of Bristol, and 25 minutes drive from the M5 intersection at Taunton.
Open 9.30am - 5.30pm (10.00am - 4.00pm Winter) 7 days a week, *except Christmas Day, Boxing Day and New Years Day*
Special rates available for schools, coach parties and outings Charitable Trust No. 292048

FSC
www.fsc.org
MIX
Papier | Fördert
gute Waldnutzung
FSC® C083411

Zeitfracht Medien GmbH
Ferdinand-Jühlke-Straße 7
99095 Erfurt, Deutschland
produktsicherheit@kolibri360.de